COGNITION

COGNITION

TENTH
EDITION

Thomas A. Farmer
California State University, Fullerton

and

Margaret W. Matlin
SUNY Geneseo

WILEY

Editorial Director	Veronica Visentin
Assistant Editor	Ethan Lipson
Senior Editorial Manager	Leah Michael
Editorial Manager	Judy Howarth
Content Management Director	Lisa Wojcik
Content Manager	Nichole Urban
Senior Content Specialist	Nicole Repasky
Production Editor	Meghana Antony
Photo Researcher	Anindita Adiyal
Cover Photo Credit	© Lorna Roberts / Shutterstock

This book was set in 10/12 TimesLTStd-Roman by SPi Global and printed and bound by Quad Graphics.

Founded in 1807, John Wiley & Sons, Inc. has been a valued source of knowledge and understanding for more than 200 years, helping people around the world meet their needs and fulfill their aspirations. Our company is built on a foundation of principles that include responsibility to the communities we serve and where we live and work. In 2008, we launched a Corporate Citizenship Initiative, a global effort to address the environmental, social, economic, and ethical challenges we face in our business. Among the issues we are addressing are carbon impact, paper specifications and procurement, ethical conduct within our business and among our vendors, and community and charitable support. For more information, please visit our website: www.wiley.com/go/citizenship.

Library of Congress Cataloging-in-Publication Data

LCCN: 2018051254

V10010835_060519

CONTENTS

7 MENTAL IMAGERY AND COGNITIVE MAPS   134

10 LANGUAGE II: LANGUAGE PRODUCTION AND BILINGUALISM 215

PREFACE

The 1st edition of this textbook was published in 1983, and was followed by eight more editions published over the course of roughly three decades. Margaret W. Matlin was the sole author of the 1st through 8th editions. After 30 years of dedication to this and other textbooks, Margaret has retired from the textbook writing enterprise. In the wake of her retirement, Thomas A. Farmer, Lecturer in Psychology at California State University—Fullerton, was contracted by Wiley to carry out the revision and updating process starting with the 9th edition of the textbook (2015). Margaret Matlin and Thomas Farmer thus share authorship for this 10th edition of *Cognition*.

Message from Author Thomas Farmer

I took Cognitive Psychology during the Spring Semester, 1999, as an undergraduate Psychology major at James Madison University in Harrisonburg, Virginia. Margaret Matlin's *Cognition* was the assigned textbook, and at that point in time, it was in its 4th edition. I remember the textbook as engaging, thought provoking, and highly accessible. In hindsight, I think that *Cognition* helped ignite my interests in topics related to the mind–body–environment relationship, and certainly contributed to my decision to pursue research opportunities in the cognitive sciences. I am thus immensely grateful for the opportunity to carry this textbook into its 10th edition.

The revisions and updates that I instituted in this edition of *Cognition* are additive in nature. For the most part, I did not remove discussions of key concepts, debates, theoretical topics, or methodological considerations. Instead, I supplemented the existing text with additional explanation, examples, and up-to-date citations. I expanded more heavily in certain places, aiming to provide readers with an overview of both classical and more contemporary treatments of a concept or theoretical framework. Additionally, I have increased the number of experiments discussed, the amount of detail embedded in their discussion, and have made a concerted effort to highlight basic components of experimental design and behavioral testing methodologies. My hope is that these additions will facilitate a greater appreciation for the rigorous experimental research so characteristic of the field. I think that these additions will aid students in the development of their ability to critically assess links between experimental design and the conclusions drawn from their results.

In the preface to the 8th edition of *Cognition*, Margaret noted that the field of cognitive psychology has changed in many ways over the past decade. She then discussed three of these changes: (1) an increase in reliance on neuroscience and neuroscientific testing methods in the scientific study of human cognition, (2) an increase in the interdisciplinary nature of research on cognitive processes, and (3) a sharp increase in the application of research in the cognitive sciences to real-world problems. I strongly agree with her observations, and have continued her mission to integrate these recent advances into this textbook. Indeed, cognitive neuroscience, interdisciplinary collaboration, and real-world application were three of the factors that motivated my decisions about how to revise and update material in this edition of the book.

In her textbooks, Margaret repeatedly demonstrates a keen ability to provide comprehensive treatments of complex research topics while writing in a style that makes them understandable to a wide range of undergraduate audiences. Although I could never perfectly mirror Margaret's elegant writing style, I tried my best to imitate it. Thus, I strived to maintain the clarity and accessibility so characteristic of Margaret's work.

In the remainder of this preface, I (1) provide an overview of the more substantial content-based additions to this edition, (2) highlight the features and organization of the book, and (3) acknowledge the many individuals who have contributed to this and previous editions.

Content-Based Additions to the 10th Edition

As noted above, very few topics were eliminated in my updating and revision of this textbook. Instead, most content-based revisions and updates involve the addition of information detailing more recent conceptualizations of key concepts and principles. Some of the more substantial changes include the following:

Chapter 1 now includes a discussion of the magnetoencephalography (MEG) cognitive neuroscientific testing method, along with a more comprehensive historical overview of individuals who have contributed to the emergence of the field of experimental psychology.

Chapter 2 includes an enhanced explanation of the speech recognition process and an extended discussion of deficits in face recognition (prosopagnosia).

Chapter 3 includes an updated discussion of research involving the Stroop task.

Chapter 4 was modified to include a more in-depth overview of the manner in which individual differences in working-memory capacity map onto variability in performance on an array of cognitive tasks. Additionally, the section on working-memory abilities in clinical populations has been extended to include a discussion of the relationship between working memory and generalized anxiety disorder (GAD).

Chapter 5 now details recent research on the effects of different amnesias on cognitive processing, as well as an extended discussion of expertise effects.

Chapter 6 now includes a discussion of test anxiety.

Chapter 7 now discusses research on individual differences in cognitive style, and provides a corresponding overview of cognitive neuroscientific research supporting these style differences.

Chapter 8 contains an updated overview of research involving the implicit attitude test, along with a discussion of more recent methodological extensions of the paradigm.

Chapter 9 includes the reintroduction of "good enough processing," along with a more integrative discussion of the cognitive neuroscience of language.

Chapter 10 now provides an overview of research supporting a compelling role for gesture in learning, as well as a more up-to-date overview of controversy regarding the bilingual advantage.

Chapters 11 and 12 contain updated references to the classical problem solving and decision-making effects detailed in these chapters, along with a discussion of more recent research involving these effects.

Chapter 13 continues to provide an overview of research on lifespan developmental questions as they pertain to memory, language, and metacognitive abilities.

Features of This Textbook

I genuinely believe that cognitive psychology can have practical applications that stretch far beyond the classroom. Therefore, students must be able to understand and remember the material. Here are some of the ways in which I consider this textbook to be student-oriented:

1. The writing style is clear and interesting, with frequent examples to make the information more concrete. Indeed, over the years, Margaret has received letters and comments from hundreds of students and professors expressing enthusiasm for the accessibility and clarity of the writing. This edition of the textbook has been line-edited in order to ensure precision and clarity.

2. The text demonstrates how our cognitive processes are relevant in our everyday, real-world experiences.

3. The book frequently examines how cognition can be applied to other disciplines, such as clinical psychology, social psychology, consumer psychology, education, communication, business, medicine, and law.

4. The 1st chapter introduces five major themes that are repeatedly emphasized throughout the book. Because the current research in cognitive psychology is so extensive, students need a sense of continuity that helps them appreciate the connections among many diverse topics.

5. An outline appears before each chapter, providing a helpful framework for understanding the new material.

6. Each new term is presented in **boldface print**. Every term is also accompanied by a concise definition that appears in the same sentence. In addition, pronunciation guides are provided for new

terms with potentially ambiguous pronunciation. If students are hesitant about pronouncing terms such as *schema* and *saccadic,* they will be reluctant to use these words or ask questions about them.

7. Many easy-to-perform demonstrations illustrate important research in cognition, and they clarify central concepts in the discipline. These demonstrations were designed so that they would require equipment that undergraduate students typically have on hand.

8. Each chapter concludes with point-by-point summaries for each section of a chapter, followed by comprehensive review questions and a list of new terms. These features provide students with additional opportunities to review material and to identify knowledge gaps.

9. Each chapter concludes with a list of recommended readings, along with a brief description of each resource. This feature should be useful if students are searching for a topic for a literature-review paper. Furthermore, professors can consult these resources when they want to update a specific lecture.

10. A glossary at the end of the book provides a definition of every keyword. I tried to include additional contextual information wherever it might be useful, in order to clarify the terms as much as possible. For example, the word *antecedent* can be used in many contexts. Accordingly, my definition for *antecedent* begins with the phrase, "In conditional reasoning. ..."

11. The subject index is comprehensive and detailed. Students can quickly locate the keywords, because they appear in boldface.

The Textbook's Organization

A textbook needs to be interesting and helpful. It must also reflect current developments in the discipline, and it should allow instructors to adapt its structure to their own teaching plans. The following features should therefore be useful for professors:

1. The tenth edition of **Cognition** offers a comprehensive overview of the field, including chapters on perceptual processes, memory, imagery, general knowledge, language, problem solving and creativity, reasoning and decision making, and cognitive development.

2. Each chapter is a self-contained unit. For example, terms such as *heuristics, schema,* and *top-down processing* are defined in every chapter where they are used. This feature allows professors considerable flexibility in the sequence of chapter coverage. Some professors may wish to discuss the topic of imagery (Chapter 7) prior to the three chapters on memory. Others might want to assign the chapter on general knowledge (Chapter 8) during an earlier part of the academic term.

3. Each section within a chapter can stand as a discrete unit, especially because every section concludes with a section summary. Professors may choose to discuss the individual sections in a different order. For example, one professor may want students to read the section on schemas prior to the chapter on long-term memory. Another professor might prefer to subdivide Chapter 13, on cognitive development, so that the 1st section of this chapter (on memory) follows Chapter 5, the 2nd section (on metacognition) follows Chapter 6, and the 3rd section (on language) follows Chapter 10. In summary, these separate sections provide professors with additional flexibility.

4. In previous editions, Margaret went to great lengths to emphasize the importance of individual differences in the study of cognitive processes. I carry on this tradition by exploring individual differences in each cognitive process discussed in this book. I take great care to emphasize to the reader how an individual difference effect can further inform our understanding of a process as it relates to theories of cognition, as well as to other clinical and social issues.

5. In all, the bibliography contains over 2,000 references, over half of which have been published since the year 2005. As a result, the textbook provides a current overview of cognitive psychology.

6. **TEST BANK:** Professors who teach courses in cognitive psychology consistently emphasize the importance of a high-quality Test Bank. The multiple-choice questions must be clear and unambiguous, and they must not focus on relatively trivial details. Most of the questions should be conceptually rich, rather than requiring brief, obvious answers. Furthermore, each chapter in

the Test Bank should contain a large number of questions, so that professors can select a different sample every time they create an examination. The Test-Bank questions available here to instructors emphasize conceptual knowledge, as well as applications to real-world situations. Furthermore, I have rated each question as "easy," "moderate," and "difficult." These difficulty ratings can help professors to create a test that is appropriate for the students in their classes.

For more information, professors should contact their Wiley sales representative about the Test Bank for the tenth edition of *Cognition*. They can also visit the Wiley website for this book, www.wiley.com/college/matlin.

Acknowledgments

I offer my sincerest thanks to the many great minds who provided me with countless hours of academic guidance and support over the years, including: Morten Christiansen, Kenny Coventry, Melissa Ferguson, Fernanda Ferreira, Barbara Finlay, John Henderson, Florian Jaeger, Sheena Rogers, Michael Spivey, Michael Tanenhaus, Richard West, and Jason Zevin. I'm honored and truly lucky to have had the opportunity to learn from each one of you.

I would also like to thank the many individuals at John Wiley & Sons for their substantial contributions to the development and production of the 10th edition of *Cognition*, especially Veronica Visentin for her guidance in the updating and revision of this textbook (and to Chris Johnson for his support during the 9th edition revision process). Additionally, I thank all of the Wiley sales representatives for their excellent work and enthusiastic support, and especially Marti Mount for her years of service in Iowa City and its surrounding areas.

Many thanks are also in order for the graduate students who have served as Teaching Assistants for my Introduction to Cognitive Psychology course: Kimberly Halvorson, Valerie Beck, Francis Smith, Caglar Tas, and Sharong Yan. Your commitment to excellence in the classroom was always apparent. I also express an especially large amount of gratitude to Caitie Hilverman for her unwavering friendship and hours of fun and stimulating academic conversation.

In the preface to the 8th edition, Margaret offered thanks to a number of students who have provided useful input, feedback, and suggestions to various editions of *Cognition*. She also thanked a number of colleagues for making suggestions about references and for providing feedback on various passages over time. Given their valuable contributions to previous editions, I would also like to offer my thanks to these individuals:

Ned Abbott, Laura Aizpuru, Drew Appleby, Jennifer Balus, Alesya Borisyuk, Tim Bowersox, Mary Jane Brennan, Stacey Canavan, Angela Capria, Elizabeth Carey, A. Eleanor Chand, Lindsay Ciancetta, Kristina Condidorio, Melissa Conway, Amanda Crandall, Ganie DeHart, Lucinda DeWitt, Thomas Donnan, Miriam Dowd, Elizabeth Einemann, Connie Ellis, K. Anders Ericsson, Beverly Evans, Michelle Fischer, Hugh Foley, Sarah Gonnella, Moises Gonzales, Mark Graber, Katie Griffin, Laurie Guarino, Benjamin Griffin, Sven Halstenburg, Elliot D. Hammer, Heather Henderson, Douglas Herrmann, Eve Higby, Jessica Hosey, Don Hudson, Hideaki Imai, Ken Kallio, Peter Kang, Becky Keegan, Jay Kleinman, Kristen Kolb, Maria Korogodsky, Jessica Krager, Patricia Kramer, Mary Kroll, Leslie Lauer, Eun Jung Lim, Rodrigo Liong, Jean Lu, Colin M. MacLeod, Edwardo Martinez, Sally Matlin, Pamela Mead, Kristen Merkle, Pamela Mino, Kaveh Moghbeli, Jacquilyn Moran, Michelle Morante, Monica Morris, Lisbet Nielsen, Jennifer Niemczyk, Paul Norris, Danielle Palermo, Jill Papke, Dorin Parasca, Matt Pastizzo, Christopher Piersante, Heather Quayle, Alison Repel, Judith Rickey, Mary Riley, Margery Schemmel, Brooke Schurr, Bennett L. Schwartz, Laura Segovia, Richard Slocum, John Tanchak, Brenna Terry, Sherri Tkachuk, Nancy Tomassino, Laura Uribarri, Dan Vance, Lori Van Wallendael, Douglas Vipond, Sara Vonhold, Julia Wagner, Heather Wallach, Melissa Waterman, Alan Welsh, Lauren Whaley, Rachelle Yablin.

Many reviewers have provided invaluable feedback on one of multiple editions of the 1st nine editions of this textbook. Both Margaret and I would like to express our appreciation for these reviewer contributions. I list each reviewer's name and affiliation below, noting that affiliations were accurate at least until the publication of the 8th edition of *Cognition*: Lise Abrams, University of Florida; John Agnew, University of Colorado, Boulder; Tom Alley, Clemson University; Harriett Amster, University of Texas, Arlington; Mark Ashcraft, Cleveland State University; Kurt Baker, Emporia State University; Heather Bartfeld, Texas A&M University; James Bartlett, University of Texas at Dallas; Richard Block, Montana State University; Kyle Cave, University of Southampton (United Kingdom); Stephen Christman, University of Toledo; Tim Curran, University of Colorado; Lucinda DeWitt, University of Minnesota; Mike Dodd, University of

Nebraska, Lincoln; Francis T. Durso, University of Oklahoma; Susan E. Dutch, Westfield State College; Randolph Easton, Boston College; James Enns, University of British Columbia; Ira Fischler, University of Florida; Kathleen Flannery, Saint Anselm College; John Flowers, University of Nebraska; Nancy Franklin, SUNY Stony Brook; Joanne Gallivan, University College of Cape Breton; Linda Gerard, Michigan State University; Barbara Goldman, University of Michigan, Dearborn; Sallie Gordon, University of Utah; Richard Gottwald, University of Indiana, South Bend; Kenneth R. Graham, Muhlenberg College; Catherine Hale, University of Puget Sound; Mark Hale, Rowan University; Harold Hawkins, University of Oregon; Morton A. Heller, Winston-Salem State University; Joseph Hellige, University of Southern California; Richard High, Lehigh University; Philip Higham, University of Northern British Columbia; Robert J. Hines, University of Arkansas, Little Rock; Mark Hoyert, Indiana University Northwest; Matthew Hunsinger, Mary Baldwin College; Margaret Intons-Peterson, Indiana University; Timothy Jay, North Adams State College; Kathy E. Johnson, Indiana University-Purdue University Indianapolis; James Juola, University of Kansas; Gretchen Kambe, University of Nevada, Las Vegas; Richard Kasschau, University of Houston; and R. A. Kinchla, Princeton University; Joseph Lao, Teachers College, Columbia University; Susan Lima, University of Wisconsin, Milwaukee; Christine Lofgren, University of California, Irvine; Bill McKeachie, University of Michigan; Anita Meehan, Kutztown University of Pennsylvania; Eduardo Mercado, University at Buffalo, SUNY; Heather Mong, Laurentian University; Julien Musolino, Rutgers University; Janet Nicol, University of Arizona; Michael W. O'Boyle, Iowa State University; William Oliver, Florida State University; David G. Payne, SUNY Binghamton; W. Daniel Phillips, Trenton State College; Thomas Piccin, Loyola University Maryland; Joan Piroch, Coastal Carolina University; David Pittenger, Marietta College; Dana Plude, University of Maryland; Catherine Powright, University of Ottawa; Sara Ransdell, Nova Southeastern University; David Rapp, Northwestern University; Andrea Richards, University of California, Los Angeles; Tony Ro, Rice University; Michael Root, Ohio University; Jonathan Schooler, University of Pittsburgh; Mithell Serman, University of Wisconsin, Stout; Matthew Sharps, California State University, Fresno; Greg Simpson, University of Kansas; Louisa M. Slowiaczek, Loyola University, Chicago; Albert Smith, Cleveland State University; Donald A. Smith, Northern Illinois University; Patricia Snyder, Albright College; David Somers, Boston University; Garrett Strosser, Southern Utah University; Margaret Thompson, University of Central Florida; Jyotsna Vaid, Texas A & M University; James P. Van Overschelde, University of Maryland; Christian Vorstius, Florida State University; Richard K. Wagner, Florida State University; Thomas B. Ward, University of Alabama; Paul Zelhart, East Texas State University.

I conclude by expressing much gratitude to my loving, patient, and supportive husband Giuseppe Vezzoli. We've had a great run, and I look forward to the future. I also send my sincerest regards to the members of my family who have offered much love, guidance, and support over the years, including my parents Thomas and Catherine Farmer, my sister Amy Farmer, and grandparents Charlotte Estep, Patricia Farmer, Raymond Farmer, and H. B. Estep.

In the 8th edition of *Cognition*, Margaret concluded the preface with the following words of thanks to members of her family. I conclude by carrying them over to the preface of *Cognition*, 10th edition:

The final words of thanks belong to my family members. My husband, Arnie Matlin, encouraged me to write the first edition of this book during the early 1980s. His continuing enthusiasm, superb sense of humor, and loving support always bring joy to my writing, and certainly to my life! Our daughters and their husbands now live in other parts of the United States, but I always value their perspectives. I'd like to thank Sally Matlin and Jay Laefer, who now live in the San Francisco Bay area. Thanks also to Beth Matlin-Heiger, Neil Matlin-Heiger, and our grandchildren, Jacob and Joshua Matlin-Heiger), who live in the Boston area. Their continuing pride in my accomplishments makes it even more rewarding to be an author! Last, I would like to express my gratitude to four other important people who have shaped my life, my parents by birth and my parents by marriage: Helen and Donald White, and Clare and Harry Matlin.

THOMAS A. FARMER
Palm Springs, California

An Introduction to Cognitive Psychology

Chapter Introduction

Cognitive psychology is a subdiscipline of experimental psychology focused on investigating the mental processes that give rise to our perceptions and interpretations of the world around us.

In this chapter, we first explore a definition of cognition before walking through an example designed to provide clarity regarding the topics covered in the remainder of this textbook. We then examine a handful of historical developments that contributed to the emergence of cognitive psychology as a coherent subdiscipline of experimental psychology. Indeed, understanding the historical events that occurred prior to the emergence of cognitive psychology will help you appreciate how a cognitive approach differs from other approaches. In the third section of this chapter, we review contributions from multiple fields outside of psychology that have served as the basis for recent spikes in our current understanding of how the mind works. As you can imagine, recent advances in the field of neuroscience have had an immeasurable effect on our current understanding of how neural systems support mental processes.

We conclude this chapter with an overview of the general themes that you will encounter time and time again throughout this textbook. Additionally, we detail the large number of learning features that are built into this textbook. Their design is based on research in areas of cognitive psychology, such as human memory, and will help you to maximize the amount of information that you maintain as you read.

What Is Cognitive Psychology?

The term **cognition**, or mental activity, refers to the acquisition, storage, transformation, and use of knowledge. Although many have argued that nonhuman animals also have cognitive abilities, our focus here is on the inner workings of the human mind. You will likely have the opportunity to learn more about nonhuman animal cognition in other courses offered by the Psychology and Biology departments at your university.

Cognition is inescapable. At any point that you are awake, your cognitive processes are at work. They grant you the ability to recognize and interpret stimuli in your environment and to act (or react) strategically to environmental input. Cognitive processes afford you the ability to plan, to create, to interact with others, and to process all of the thoughts, sensations, and emotions that you experience on a daily basis. Your cognitive abilities operate together in intricate and highly coordinated ways to create your conscious experiences.

While reading this paragraph, for example, you are performing multiple cognitive tasks at the same time. In order to reach this paragraph, you used pattern recognition to create words from an assortment of squiggles and lines that form the letters on this page. You also consulted your memory and your knowledge about language to search for word meanings and to link together the ideas in this paragraph. Additionally, right now, as you think about these cognitive tasks, you are engaging in another cognitive task called *metacognition*—you were thinking about your own thought processes. Perhaps you made an inference such as, "This book may help me learn to study more effectively." You may have also used decision making by saying to yourself, for instance, "I'll finish this section of the book before I eat lunch."

If cognition operates every time you acquire some information, place it in storage, transform that information, and use it…then cognition includes a wide range of mental processes! This textbook will explore many of these mental processes, such as perception, memory, imagery, language, problem solving, reasoning, and decision making.

Cognitive psychology has two meanings: (1) Sometimes it is a synonym for the word *cognition*; (2) Sometimes it refers to a particular theoretical approach to psychology. Specifically, the **cognitive approach** is a theoretical orientation that emphasizes people's thought processes and their knowledge. For example, a cognitive explanation of ethnic stereotypes would emphasize topics such as the influence of these stereotypes on the judgments we make about people from different ethnic groups (Whitley & Kite, 2010).

I took Introduction to Cognitive Psychology during my junior year of college. I remember quite vividly that I had enrolled for the course because it was required, but I honestly had no idea what the term "cognitive psychology" meant. Even after our brief discussion of a definition of cognition, some of you may still not have a strong sense of what a cognitive psychologist really studies. Below, I offer a brief demonstration that should help you gain a stronger sense of what you're in store for over the course of the semester.

Open up a Web browser, pull up a recent episode of a television show or a random video clip, and do the following: 1) Watch one minute of the video; 2) Exit your Web browser; and 3) In only two minutes, write down (or type) everything that you experienced as you watched the TV or video clip. Go ahead…give it a shot. It will only take you a total of three minutes.

I just completed the demonstration myself. I went online and selected a random music video, and I watched one minute of it. Here's what I was able to type in two minutes after closing the Web browser:

- There was a strong bass line.

- I have never heard this song before.

- Approximately 20 people were standing close together. Music was playing but no one was moving.

- One person at the center of the group of people was female, and she was wearing a turquoise dress that looked kind of fancy.

- The camera moved from left to right but remained focused on the 20 or so people standing in a group.

- Somebody coughed in the next room (not in the video, but in the room next to where I'm sitting and watching this video).

- A female voice started to sing. She's singing in a language that I don't know. It sounds like it could be Swedish, but I don't know.

Most of you were probably able to generate a list of bullet points. Now focus on the list and think about everything that you had to do in order to produce it. Or, if you didn't really complete the exercise yourself, think about all of the types of processes that I had to complete in order to produce the list above.

Importantly, I had to create a rich internal interpretation of the video in order to have a meaningful, conscious *experience* of it. In order to do so, I had to process auditory information (the music), linguistic information (the lyrics, although I couldn't really understand them), and visual information (the visual images that accompanied the music in the video).

I also had to rely heavily on information that is stored in my memory as a guide for how to interpret the auditory and visual streams of information I encountered while watching the video. Many of you are likely to be in your early 20s. That means that you have had approximately 20 years of experience with the world around you. Based on that experience, you've come to possess *knowledge* about facts (such as, "Brooklyn is one of the five boroughs of New York City"), and about patterns that are embedded in environmental stimuli (for example, the word "the" rarely comes before a verb). Crucially, notice how important this stored knowledge is for your ability to interpret and understand the video you watched. In the case of my video, I had to know which features of a person are characteristic of males versus females. If I lacked this knowledge, I would not have been able to list the 4th bullet point above. I also wouldn't have been able to note that a female voice was singing (as per the 7th bullet point above). Linking the physical characteristics of the auditory and visual streams you processed to knowledge stored in your memory was thus necessary for you to create a meaningful interpretation of the video.

Attentional processes also contributed to my interpretation, and thus experience, of the video. Do you think that I remembered every detail of the video well enough to be able to precisely describe it? Probably not. I had to perceive and interpret information from the environment (the video) on a very fast timescale. Under such time pressure, I had to strategically allocate my attention to elements and events occurring in the video that seemed most relevant and important. I also noted that I heard someone in a room next to me cough. This cough had nothing to do with the video I was watching, and yet I still processed it (enough to report my perception of the cough after the video was complete . . . it was part of my experience watching the video).

And, in order to type the list of bullet points, I had to access my stored memories about the video, transform those memories into a linguistic code, and then move my fingers around a keyboard in order to type linguistic descriptions of my memories.

After thinking about your experience with this demonstration, do you have a stronger sense of what is meant by the term "cognition?" Information from the environment was taken in through sensory systems, and it was linked to knowledge that you possess. New memories (of your experiences while watching and interpreting the video) were created. And, they were accessed at a later point in time in order for you to write out descriptions of your interpretation of the video. In this sense, you acquired, stored, transformed, and used knowledge that you gleaned from experience.

Why should you and other students learn about cognition? One reason is that the cognitive approach has widespread influence on other areas of psychology, such as clinical psychology and psychotherapy (e.g., Erdelyi & Goldberg, 2014; Gu, Strauss, Bond, & Cavanagh, 2015; Snyder, Miyake, & Hankin, 2015), educational psychology (O'Donnell & King, 2014; Schonert-Reichl et al., 2015), and social psychology (e.g., Seyfarth & Cheney, 2015; Srull & Wyer, 2015; Todd, Thiem, & Neel, 2016). Let's consider an example from clinical psychology. One cognitive task asks people to recall a specific memory from their past. People who are depressed tend to provide a general summary, such as "visiting my grandmother." In contrast, people who are not depressed tend to describe an extended memory that lasts more than one day, such as "the summer I drove across the country" (Wenzel, 2005). Whether a person is depressed or not thus influences an individual's ability to access and report experiences from their memories. Relatedly, cognitive psychology also influences interdisciplinary areas. A journal called *Cognitive Neuropsychology*, for example, publishes research that examines specific neurological problems—such as an extreme difficulty in recognizing people's faces—when other cognitive skills are normal (e.g., Wilson et al., 2010).

Another reason to study cognitive psychology is that cognition occupies a major portion of human psychology as it relates to your daily life experiences. In fact, almost everything you have done in the past hour required you to perceive, remember, use language, or think. As you'll soon see, psychologists have discovered some impressive information about every topic in cognitive psychology. Even though cognitive psychology is extraordinarily central in every human's daily life, many college students cannot define this term accurately (Maynard, 2006; Maynard et al., 2004). For a demonstration of this point, try Demonstration 1.1.

Demonstration 1.1 | Awareness About Cognitive Psychology

Locate several friends at your university or college who have not enrolled in any psychology courses. Ask each person the following questions:

1. How would you define the term "cognitive psychology"?

2. Can you list some of the topics that would be included in a course in cognitive psychology?

When Amanda Maynard and her coauthors (2004) asked introductory psychologists to define "cognitive psychology," only 29% provided appropriate definitions. How adequate were the responses that your own friends provided?

The final reason for studying cognition is more personal. Your mind is an impressively sophisticated piece of equipment, and you use this equipment every minute of the day. If you purchase a new cellphone, you typically receive a brochure that describes its functions (or nowadays, at least a link to a website with this information). No one ever issued, however, a brochure for your mind when you were born. In a sense, this textbook is like a brochure or owner's manual, describing information about how your mind works. Understanding cognition = understanding the abilities that provide you with the experience of a rich internal mental life.

Historical Perspective on the Field

The cognitive approach to psychology traces its origins to the classical Greek philosophers and to developments that began in the 19th century. As we will also see in this section, however, the contemporary version of cognitive psychology emerged within the last 60–70 years. In this section, we first consider a set of historical developments that led to the emergence of the field of experimental psychology. We then focus briefly on a series of events that contributed to the emergence of cognitive psychology—a field that is widely viewed as a key subdiscipline of psychology. To conclude this section, we consider the nature of cognitive psychology as it exists in present times.

Origins of Cognitive Psychology

Philosophers and other theorists have speculated about human thought processes for more than 23 centuries. For example, the Greek philosopher Aristotle (384–322 BCE) examined topics such as perception, memory, and mental imagery. He also discussed how humans acquire knowledge through experience and observation (Barnes, 2004; Sternberg, 1999). Aristotle emphasized the importance of **empirical evidence**, or scientific evidence obtained by careful observation and experimentation. His emphasis on empirical evidence and many of the topics he studied are consistent with 21st-century cognitive psychology. In fact, Aristotle can reasonably be called the first cognitive psychologist (Leahey, 2003). Psychology as a discipline in and of itself did not emerge, however, until the late 1800s.

Wilhelm Wundt

Most scholars who study the history of psychology believe that Wilhelm Wundt (pronounced "Voont") should be considered the founder of experimental psychology (Benjamin, 2009; Pickren & Rutherford, 2010). Wundt lived in Leipzig, Germany, between 1832 and 1920. Students traveled from around the world to study with Wundt, who taught about 28,000 students during the course of his lifetime (Bechtel et al., 1998; Benjamin, 2009; Fuchs & Milar, 2003).

Wundt proposed that psychology should study mental processes, and advocated the use of a technique called introspection in order to do so. In this case, **introspection** meant that carefully trained observers would systematically analyze their own sensations and report them as objectively as possible, under standardized conditions (Blumenthal, 2009; Pickren & Rutherford, 2010; Zangwill, 2004b). For example, observers might be asked to objectively report their reactions to a specific musical chord, and to do so without relying on their previous knowledge about music.

Wundt's introspection technique sounds subjective, not objective, to most current cognitive psychologists. As you'll see throughout this textbook, our introspections are sometimes inaccurate (Wilson, 2009;

Zangwill, 2004b). For example, you may introspect that your eyes are moving smoothly across this page of your textbook. As we will discuss in Chapter 3, however, cognitive psychologists have determined that your eyes actually move in small jumps while you are reading.

Early Memory Researchers

One of the earliest (1850–1909) systematic investigations of a cognitive process came from the German psychologist Hermann Ebbinghaus (Baddeley et al., 2009; Schwartz, 2011). Ebbinghaus was interested in human memory. He examined a variety of factors that might influence performance on memory tasks, such as the amount of time between two presentations of a list of items. He frequently chose nonsense syllables (e.g., DAX), rather than actual words. This precaution reduced the potentially confounding effects of people's previous experience with language on their ability to recall information from their memories (Fuchs & Milar, 2003; Zangwill, 2004a).

Meanwhile, in the United States, similar research was being conducted by psychologists such as Mary Whiton Calkins (1863–1930). Calkins reported a memory phenomenon called the recency effect (Schwartz, 2011). The **recency effect** refers to the observation that our recall is especially accurate for the final items in a series of stimuli (such as a list of words or numbers). In addition, Calkins emphasized that psychologists should study how real people use their cognitive processes in the real world, as opposed to in artificial laboratory tasks (Samelson, 2009). Calkins was also the first woman to be president of the American Psychological Association. In connection with that role, she developed guidelines for teaching college courses in introductory psychology (Calkins, 1910; McGovern & Brewer, 2003). During her career, Calkins also published four books and more than 100 scholarly papers (Pickren & Rutherford, 2010).

William James

Another central figure in the history of cognitive psychology was an American named William James (1842–1910). James was not impressed with Wundt's introspection technique or Ebbinghaus's research with nonsense syllables. Instead, James preferred to theorize about our everyday psychological experiences (Benjamin, 2009; Hunter, 2004a; Pickren & Rutherford, 2010). He is best known for his textbook *Principles of Psychology*, published in 1890.

Principles of Psychology provides clear, detailed descriptions about people's everyday experiences (Benjamin, 2009). It also emphasizes that the human mind is active and inquiring. James's book foreshadows numerous topics that fascinate 21st-century cognitive psychologists, such as perception, attention, memory, understanding, reasoning, and the tip-of-the-tongue phenomenon (Leary, 2009; Pickren & Rutherford, 2010). Consider, for example, James's vivid description of the tip-of-the-tongue experience:

> *Suppose we try to recall a forgotten name. The state of our consciousness is peculiar. There is a gap therein but no mere gap. It is a gap that is intensely active. A sort of wraith of the name is in it, beckoning us in a given direction, making us at moments tingle with the sense of our closeness and then letting us sink back without the longed-for term.*
>
> **(James, 1890, p. 251)**

Behaviorism

The work of early memory researchers such as Ebbinghaus and Calkins appealed to the notion that information is somehow stored in the mind. Their work suggested that internally stored knowledge about words or objects was one important component of cognitive processing. During the first half of the 20th century, however, behaviorism became the most prominent theoretical perspective in the United States. According to the principles of **behaviorism**, psychology must focus on objective, observable reactions to stimuli in the environment, rather than on subjective processes such as introspection (Benjamin, 2009; O'Boyle, 2006).

The most prominent early behaviorist was the U.S. psychologist John B. Watson (1913), who lived from 1878 to 1958. Watson and other behaviorists emphasized observable behavior, and they typically studied nonhuman animals (Benjamin, 2009). Most behaviorists believed that it was inappropriate to theorize and speculate about unobservable components of mental life. As a result, the behaviorists did not study concepts such as a mental image, an idea, or a thought (Epstein, 2004; Skinner, 2004). Instead, the behaviorists focused heavily on learning. That is, they were particularly interested in quantifying the manner in which changes in an organism's environment produced changes in its behavior.

It is possible to objectively quantify how well an organism has learned about properties of its environment. For example, consider placing a rat in a complicated maze—the end of which contains a piece of cheese for the rat to enjoy as a reward for making it through the maze. Rewarding rats for successfully navigating to the end of a maze provides researchers with an opportunity to objectively measure learning. For example, researchers may choose to count the number of errors made by the rat (such as a turn down a dead-end path) while completing the maze on each of 30 consecutive days. A decrease in error rate over time, in this case, is interpretable as representing an increase in learning. Because researchers can quantify learning over time, they also have the ability to systematically manipulate properties of the learning task, such as maze complexity, in order to determine what factors influence the speed of learning. Note here, however, that in behaviorist experiments, clear and quantifiable manipulations of the learning environment were implemented in order to examine how they influenced a quantifiable metric of learning. The behaviorists never argued or otherwise appealed to the notion that a rat may be storing information about the spatial layout of the maze (and thus, *internally representing* visual and spatial components of the maze) as they learned about its layout over time.

The lack of a willingness to acknowledge that information about one's environment is stored and can be accessed at some later point in time led to a reaction against strong versions of behaviorist doctrine. In fact, examples of "pure behaviorism" are now difficult to locate. For instance, the Association of Behavioral Therapy is now known as the Association for Behavioral and Cognitive Therapies. Recent articles in their journal, *Cognitive and Behavioral Practice*, have focused on using cognitive behavioral therapy for a variety of clients, including people with eating disorders, elderly adults with posttraumatic stress disorder, and severely depressed adolescents.

Although the behaviorists did not conduct research in cognitive psychology, they did contribute significantly to contemporary research methods. For example, behaviorists emphasized the importance of the **operational definition**, a precise definition that specifies exactly how a concept is to be measured. Similarly, cognitive psychologists in the 21st century need to specify exactly how memory, perception, and other cognitive processes will be measured in an experiment. Behaviorists also valued carefully controlled research, a tradition that is maintained in current cognitive research (Fuchs & Milar, 2003). We must also acknowledge the important contribution of behaviorists to applied psychology. Their learning principles have been used extensively in psychotherapy, business, organizations, and education (Craske, 2010; O'Boyle, 2006; Rutherford, 2009).

Try Demonstration 1.2 before you read further.

The Gestalt Approach

Behaviorism thrived in the United States for several decades, although it had less influence on European psychology (G. Mandler, 2002). An important development in Europe at the beginning of the 20th century was gestalt (pronounced "geh-*shtahlt*") psychology. **Gestalt psychology** emphasizes that we humans have basic tendencies to actively organize what we see, and furthermore, that the whole is greater than the sum of its parts (Benjamin, 2009).

Demonstration 1.2	An Example of Gestalt Psychology

Quickly look at the figure below and describe what you see. Keep your answer in mind until the next page, when we will discuss this figure.

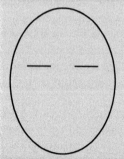

Consider, for example, the figure represented in Demonstration 1.2. You probably saw a human face, rather than simply an oval and two straight lines. This figure seems to have unity and organization. It has a **gestalt**, or overall quality that transcends the individual elements (Fuchs & Milar, 2003).

Gestalt psychologists valued the unity of psychological phenomena. As a result, they strongly objected to Wundt's introspective technique of analyzing experiences into separate components (Pickren & Rutherford, 2010). They also criticized the behaviorists' emphasis on breaking behavior into observable stimulus–response units and ignoring the context of behavior (Baddeley et al., 2009; Benjamin, 2009). Gestalt psychologists constructed a number of laws that explain why certain components of a pattern seem to belong together. In Chapter 2, we'll consider some of these laws, which help us to quickly recognize visual objects.

Gestalt psychologists also emphasized the importance of insight in problem solving (Fuchs & Milar, 2003; Viney & King, 2003). When you are trying to solve a problem, the parts of the problem may initially seem unrelated to each other. However, with a sudden flash of insight, the parts fit together into a solution. Gestalt psychologists conducted most of the early research in problem solving. In Chapter 11 of this textbook, we will examine their concept of insight, as well as more recent developments.

Frederic Bartlett

In the early 1900s, the behaviorists were dominant in the United States, and the gestalt psychologists were influential in continental Europe. Meanwhile in England, a British psychologist named Frederic Bartlett (1886–1969) conducted his research on human memory. His important book *Remembering: An Experimental and Social Study* (Bartlett, 1932) is considered one of the most influential books in the history of cognitive psychology (Benjamin, 2009). Bartlett rejected the carefully controlled research of Ebbinghaus (Pickford & Gregory, 2004). Instead, he used meaningful materials, such as lengthy stories.

Bartlett discovered that people made systematic errors when trying to recall these stories. He proposed that human memory is an active, constructive process, in which we interpret and transform the information we encounter. We search for meaning, trying to integrate this new information so that it is more consistent with our own personal experiences (Benjamin, 2009; Pickford & Gregory, 2004; Pickren & Rutherford, 2010).

Bartlett's work was largely ignored in the United States during the 1930s, because most U.S. research psychologists were committed to behaviorism. However, about half a century later, U.S. cognitive psychologists discovered Bartlett's work and admired his use of naturalistic material, in contrast to Ebbinghaus's artificial nonsense syllables. Bartlett's emphasis on a schema-based approach to memory foreshadowed some of the research we will explore in Chapters 5 and 8 (Benjamin, 2009; Pickford & Gregory, 2004).

Cognitive Revolution

By the late 1930s and throughout the 1940s, psychologists were becoming increasingly disappointed with the behaviorist outlook that had dominated U.S. psychology in previous decades. It was difficult to explain complex human behavior using only behaviorist concepts such as observable stimuli, responses, and reinforcement (G. Mandler, 2002; Neisser, 1967). Research in human memory began to blossom at the end of the 1950s, further increasing the disenchantment with behaviorism. Psychologists proposed models of human memory instead of focusing only on models of animal learning (Baddeley et al., 2009; Bower, 2008). The behaviorist approach tells us little about numerous psychologically interesting processes, such as the thoughts and strategies that people use when they try to solve a problem (Bechtel et al., 1998), or how people access their stored knowledge about language in order to produce a sentence.

Another influential force came from research on children's thought processes. Jean Piaget (pronounced "Pea-ah-*zhay*") was a Swiss theorist who lived from 1896 to 1980. Piaget's books began to attract the attention of U.S. psychologists and educators toward the end of the 1950s, and his perspectives continue to shape developmental psychology (Feist, 2006; Hopkins, 2011; Pickren & Rutherford, 2010). According to Piaget, children actively explore their world in order to understand important concepts (Gregory, 2004b). Children's cognitive strategies change as they mature, and adolescents often use sophisticated strategies in order to conduct their own personal experiments about how the world works.

Research and theory from other academic and intellectual fields also increased the emerging popularity of the study of human cognition (Bermudez, 2014). For example, new developments in linguistics increased psychologists' dissatisfaction with behaviorism (Bargh & Ferguson, 2000; Bower, 2008). The most important contributions came from the linguist Noam Chomsky (1957), who emphasized that the structure of language was too complex to be explained in behaviorist terms (Pickren & Rutherford, 2010; Pinker, 2002). Chomsky and other linguists argued that humans have an inborn ability to master all the complicated and varied aspects of language (Chomsky, 2004). This perspective clearly contradicted the behaviorist perspective that language acquisition can be entirely explained by the same kinds of learning principles that apply to laboratory animals.

The growing support for the cognitive approach is often referred to as the "cognitive revolution" (Bruner, 1997; Shiraev, 2011). This term refers to a strong shift away from behaviorist approaches to the study of human behavior. Instead, experimental psychologists began to focus on how organism-internal processes, such as memory, attention, and language, work together to give rise to the human ability to consciously perceive, interpret, and act in the world around them.

We have traced the historical roots of cognitive psychology and provided a brief overview of reasons that psychologists became disenchanted with the behaviorist worldview. But, when was the field of cognitive psychology actually "born"? Cognitive psychologists generally agree that the birth of cognitive psychology can be listed as 1956 (Eysenck & Keane, 2010; G. Mandler, 2002; Thagard, 2005). During this prolific year, researchers published numerous influential books and articles on attention, memory, language, concept formation, and problem solving. In 1967, an influential psychologist named Ulric Neisser (1928–2012) published a booked called *Cognitive Psychology*. The publication of this book served as one of the first comprehensive treatments of cognitive processing. It is seen as one of the most important factors contributing to the emergence of cognitive psychology as a field. In fact, because Neisser was the first person to use the term "Cognitive Psychology," he has often been called "the father of cognitive psychology" (e.g., American Psychological Science, n.d.).

Cognitive Psychology in Present Times

Since the cognitive revolution and the onset of cognitive psychology as a field, cognitive psychology has had an enormous influence on the discipline of psychology. For example, almost all psychologists now recognize the importance of mental representations, a term that behaviorists would have rejected in the 1950s. Indeed, all areas of psychology incorporate key principles from cognitive psychology in their models of human development and behavior. For instance, psychologists are also studying how cognitive processes operate in our everyday social interactions (e.g., Cacioppo & Berntson, 2005a; Cameron, Payne, & Doris, 2013; Critcher, Inbar, & Pizzaro, 2013; Easton & Emery, 2005; Neel, Neufeld, & Neuberg, 2013; Todd & Burgmer, 2013). Demonstration 1.3 illustrates the important influence of cognitive psychology in many other areas of psychological inquiry.

Cognitive psychology has its critics, however. One common complaint concerns the issue of ecological validity. Studies are high in **ecological validity** if the conditions in which the research is conducted are similar to the natural setting where the results will be applied.

In contrast, consider an experiment in which participants must memorize a list of unrelated English words, presented at 5-second intervals on a white screen in a barren laboratory room. Half of the people are instructed to create a vivid mental image of each word; the other half receive no instructions. The experiment is carefully controlled. The results of this experiment would tell us something about the way memory operates. However, this task is probably low in ecological validity because it cannot be applied to the way people learn in the real world (Sharps & Wertheimer, 2000). How often do you try to memorize a list of unrelated words in this fashion?

Demonstration 1.3	The Widespread Influence of Cognitive Psychology

Locate a psychology textbook used in some other class. An introductory textbook is ideal, but textbooks in developmental psychology, social psychology, abnormal psychology, etc., are all suitable. Glance through the subject index for terms beginning with *cognition* or *cognitive*, and locate the relevant pages. Depending on the nature of the textbook, you may also find entries under terms such as memory, language, and perception.

Most cognitive psychologists prior to the 1980s did indeed conduct research in artificial laboratory environments, often using tasks that differed from daily cognitive activities. However, current researchers frequently study real-life issues. For example, Chapter 3 describes how people are much more likely to make driving errors if they are talking on a handheld cell phone (Folk, 2010). Furthermore, Chapters 5 and 6 discuss numerous methods for improving your memory (e.g., Davies & Wright, 2010a). Chapter 12 provides many suggestions about how to improve your decision-making ability (Kahneman, 2011). In general, most cognitive psychologists acknowledge that the discipline must advance by conducting both ecologically valid and laboratory-based research.

Mind, Brain, and Behavior

By the mid-1970s, the cognitive approach had replaced the behaviorist approach as the dominant theory in psychological research (Robins et al., 1999). But, cognitive psychology as it exists today has become an increasingly interdisciplinary pursuit. The rigorous experimental approach to psychological research that is characteristic of cognitive psychology has become increasingly supplemented by theories and methodologies borrowed from other fields. In this section, we first consider the interdisciplinary field of cognitive science. Indeed, researchers from many different fields have interests in how the human mind works. As we will see, cross-disciplinary research can produce synthetic contributions to our understanding of the human mind that transcend the contributions from any individual discipline. Next, we touch on theoretical questions concerning how the concept of "the mind" relates to the human brain. To conclude, we will provide an overview of cognitive neuroscience methodologies. These methodologies allow us to gain insight into how our neural hardware supports different cognitive processes.

Cognitive Science

Cognitive psychology is part of a broad field known as cognitive science. **Cognitive science** is an interdisciplinary field that tries to answer questions about the mind. Cognitive science includes contributions from cognitive psychology, neuroscience, computer science, philosophy, and linguistics. In some cases, researchers in the fields of sociology, anthropology, and economics also make contributions to the field of cognitive science. This field emerged when researchers began to notice connections among a variety of disciplines, and thus began to collaborate with one another (Bermúdez, 2010; Sobel, 2001; Thagard, 2005).

According to cognitive scientists, thinking requires us to manipulate our internal representations of the external world. Cognitive scientists focus on these internal representations. Cognitive scientists value interdisciplinary studies, and they try to build bridges among the academic areas. Both the theory and the research in cognitive science are so extensive that no one person can possibly master everything (Bermúdez, 2010; Sobel, 2001; Thagard, 2005). However, if all these different fields remain separate, then cognitive scientists won't achieve important insights and identify relevant connections. Therefore, cognitive science tries to coordinate the information that researchers have gathered throughout each relevant discipline.

Below, we examine just one of many examples that highlight the value of interdisciplinary communication when trying to understand the inner workings of the human mind. More specifically, we look at how interactions between cognitive psychologists and computer scientists have produced deeper insight into cognition than would otherwise be possible.

Artificial Intelligence

Artificial intelligence (AI) is a branch of computer science. It seeks to explore human cognitive processes by creating computer models that show "intelligent behavior" and also accomplish the same tasks that humans do (Bermúdez, 2010; Boden, 2004; Chrisley, 2004). Researchers in artificial intelligence have tried to explain how humans recognize a face, create a mental image, and write a poem, as well as hundreds of additional cognitive accomplishments (Boden, 2004; Farah, 2004; Thagard, 2005).

We need to draw a distinction between "pure AI" and computer simulation. **Pure artificial intelligence** is an approach that designs a program to accomplish a cognitive task as efficiently as possible, even if the computer's processes are completely different from the processes used by humans. For example, the most high-powered computer programs for chess will evaluate as many potential moves as possible in as little time as possible (Michie, 2004). Chess is an extremely complex game, in which both players together can make about 10^{128} possible different moves. Consider a computer chess program named "Hydra." The top chess players in the world make a slight error about every 10 moves. Hydra can identify this error—even though chess experts cannot—and it therefore wins the game (Mueller, 2005). Researchers have designed **pure AI** systems that can play chess, speak English, or diagnose an illness. However, as one researcher points out, "I wouldn't want a chess-playing program speculating as to the cause of my chest pain" (Franklin, 1995, p. 11).

As we have seen, pure AI tries to achieve the best possible performance. In contrast, **computer simulation** or **computer modeling** attempts to take human limitations into account. The goal of computer simulation is to program a computer to perform a specific cognitive task in the same way that humans actually perform this task. A computer simulation must produce the same number of errors—as well as correct responses—that a human produces (Carpenter & Just, 1999; Thagard, 2005).

Computer simulation research has been most active in such areas as memory, language processing, problem solving, and logical reasoning (Bower, 2008; Eysenck & Keane, 2010; Thagard, 2005). For example, Carpenter and Just (1999) created a classic computer-simulation model for reading sentences. This model was based on the assumption that humans have a limited capacity to process information. As a result, humans will read a difficult section of a sentence more slowly. Consider the following sentence:

The reporter that the senator attacked admitted the error.

Carpenter and Just (1999) designed their computer simulation so that it took into account the relevant linguistic information contained in sentences like this one. The model predicted that processing speed should be fast for the words at the beginning and the end of the sentence. However, the processing should be slow for the awkward two-verb section, "attacked admitted." In fact, Carpenter and Just demonstrated that the human data matched the computer simulation quite accurately.

Surprisingly, people can accomplish some tasks quite easily, even though these tasks are beyond the capacity of computer simulations. For example, a 10-year-old girl can search a messy bedroom for her watch, find it in her sweatshirt pocket, read the pattern on the face of the watch, and then announce the time. However, no current computer can simulate this task. Computers also cannot match humans' sophistication in learning language, identifying objects in everyday scenes, or solving problems creatively (Jackendoff, 1997; Sobel, 2001).

Computer Metaphor of the Mind

During the 1970s–1990s (and even still today), the computer has been a popular metaphor for the human mind. According to the **computer metaphor**, our cognitive processes work like a computer. That is, computers and human minds are both examples of complex, multipurpose machinery (Clark, 2013). Researchers acknowledge the obvious differences in physical structure between the computer and the human brain. Both human brains and computers may operate, however, according to similar general principles. For example, both humans and computers can compare symbols and can make choices according to the results of the comparison. Furthermore, computers have a processing mechanism with a limited capacity. Humans also have limited attention and short-term memory capacities. Chapter 3 details research clearly demonstrating that humans cannot pay attention to numerous tasks at the same time.

Computer models need to describe both the structures and the processes that operate on these structures. Thagard (2005) suggests that a computer model resembles a recipe in cooking. A recipe has two parts: (1) the ingredients, which are somewhat like the *structures*; and (2) the cooking instructions for working with those ingredients, which are somewhat like the *processes*. Researchers who favor the computer approach try to design the appropriate "software." With the right computer program and sufficient mathematical detail, researchers hope to imitate the flexibility and the efficiency of human cognitive processes (Boden, 2004).

Beginning in the 1960s, psychologists began to create models of how information flows through cognitive systems. This **information-processing approach** argued that (a) our mental processes are similar to the operations of a computer, and (b) information progresses through our cognitive system in a series of stages, one step at a time (Gallistel & King, 2009; Leahey, 2003; MacKay, 2004). Information processing models of cognitive processes such as memory, visual object recognition, or language comprehension, share a series of general assumptions detailed below.

1. Stimuli (maybe a visual object such as a chair or a word from a sentence) occur or are present in one's environment. Information about those stimuli is transported to your sensory receptors (your eyes, your ears, etc.) through a physical medium (light, sound waves). Your sensory receptors process that information, and are responsible for making sure that it gets to your brain. Note that taking in information about your environment through your senses is similar to inputting information into a computer (e.g., by typing a word and pressing the "Enter" key).

2. The information that is provided to your brain via your senses is processed and decoded over the course of multiple processing stages. For example, upon seeing a chair, your visual system seems to first process different features of the chair such as its color, its edges, and its size. After those features are recognized, information progresses to other parts of the visual object recognition system in order for the features to get bound together. Eventually, the visual information reaches a stage at which it has been processed enough in order for you to match it to your stored knowledge about objects in the world. At this stage, you have recognized the object in your environment as a chair. Notice here that under these types of approaches, information is processed in incremental stages. This stage-like processing is similar to how older computers worked. Specific sub-systems process input based on rules (or algorithms). After the information gets processed in that subsystem, it is sent to another subsystem so that it can be further processed and interpreted.

3. Eventually, after a stimulus has been processed enough in order for it to be identified and interpreted, a decision must be made about how to respond to the stimulus.

4. If you decide to respond to the stimulus, a motor command is sent to the parts of the system that are responsible for telling your body how to move. You then initiate an action that allows you to respond as strategically as possible to the stimulus that you had just finished processing. This action component is akin to a computer responding to some input (e.g., by displaying a word that you had typed onto your monitor).

Many versions of this classical approach viewed processing as a series of separate operations; in other words, information processing was considered to be serial. During **serial processing**, the system must complete one step or processing stage before information can proceed to the next step in the flowchart (Fodor, 1983).

A great appreciation for the analogy between the human mind and the computer arose because computer programs must be detailed, precise, unambiguous, and logical (Boden, 2004). Researchers can represent the functions of a computer with a flowchart that shows the sequence of stages in processing information. Throughout the remainder of this book, you will see some examples of these flowcharts.

Every metaphor, however, has its limitations. The computer metaphor of the mind, and of information processing more generally, was never intended to be a model of how *the brain* processes information. Back in the 1960s and up until the early 1980s, the scientific community had a very limited sense of how the brain processed and interpreted complex stimuli in the environment. Most of the neuroimaging equipment that we discuss at the end of this section was still in the early phases of development. As a result, these models were designed to capture regularities in how people processed information about different classes of stimuli, such as linguistic, visual, and auditory information. Cognitive psychologists conducted many experiments that served to illuminate the types of environmental information that could be processed by the mind, what types of information seemed to be processed before other types of information, and what factors influenced the ease with which information could be processed. These data were used to create models of information flow through cognitive systems, although they were not intended to serve as models of how the physical brain actually processed information (see Marr, 1982, for an extended discussion of these distinctions).

The Connectionist Approach

Many of the classical information-processing models have a difficult time accounting for the kinds of cognitive tasks that humans do very quickly, accurately, and without conscious thought. For example, AI models cannot explain how you can instantly perceive a visual scene (Bermúdez, 2010; Leahey, 2003). Glance up from your book, and then immediately return to this paragraph. When you looked at this visual scene, your retina presented about one million signals to your cortex—all at the same time. If your visual system had used serial processing in order to interpret these one million signals, you would still be processing that visual scene, rather than reading this sentence!

In 1986, James McClelland, David Rumelhart, and their colleagues at the University of California, San Diego, published an influential two-volume book entitled *Parallel Distributed Processing* (McClelland & Rumelhart, 1986; Rumelhart et al., 1986). This approach contrasted sharply with the traditional information-processing approach. As previously noted, the classical computer metaphor approach was never intended to appeal to how the brain processed information. Classic information-processing models were only meant to serve as abstract flowcharts that captured what we knew at the time about people's performance on cognitive tasks.

In contrast, the **connectionist approach** argues that cognitive processes can be understood in terms of networks that link together neuron-like processing units; in addition, many operations can proceed simultaneously—rather than one step at a time. In other words, human cognition is often *parallel*, not strictly serial (Barrett, 2009; Gazzaniga et al., 2009). Two other names that are often used interchangeably with connectionism are the **parallel distributed processing (PDP) approach** and the **neural-network approach**.

During the 1970s, neuroscientists developed research techniques that could explore the structure of the cerebral cortex. The **cerebral cortex** is the outer layer of the brain that is essential for your cognitive processes. One important discovery in this research was the numerous connections among neurons, a pattern that resembles many elaborate networks (Bermúdez, 2014; Rolls, 2004; Thagard, 2005).

This network pattern suggests that an item stored in your brain cannot be localized in a specific pinpoint-sized location of your cortex (Barrett, 2009; Fuster, 2003; Woll, 2002). Instead, the neural activity for that item seems to be *distributed* throughout a section of the brain. For example, researchers cannot pinpoint one small portion of your brain that stores the name of your cognitive psychology professor. Instead, that information is probably distributed throughout numerous neurons in a region of your cerebral cortex. Notice that the term "parallel *distributed* processing" captures the distributed nature of the neurons in your brain.

The researchers who developed the connectionist approach proposed a model that simulates many important features of the brain (Bermúdez, 2010; Levine, 2002; Woll, 2002). Most importantly, these networks are designed based on the basic principles associated with how neurons pass electrical signals to each other. Naturally, the model captures only a fraction of the brain's complexity. However, like the brain, the model includes simplified neuron-like units, numerous interconnections, and neural activity distributed throughout the system.

Many psychologists welcomed the connectionist approach as a groundbreaking new framework. It was groundbreaking in that it provided a way to understand how populations of neurons worked together in order to represent knowledge. Thus, unlike the classic information-processing perspective, researchers who operate under a connectionist modeling approach create computational models of neural processing that do appeal to how the brain actually works. They have developed models in areas as unrelated to one another as college students' stereotypes about a group of people and children's mastery of irregular verbs (Bermúdez, 2014; Christiansen & Chater, 2001). Researchers continue to explore whether the PDP approach can adequately account for the broad range of skills demonstrated by our cognitive processes.

Keep in mind that the connectionist approach uses the human brain—rather than the serial-computer—as the basic model (Woll, 2002). This more sophisticated design allows the connectionist approach to achieve greater complexity, flexibility, and accuracy as it attempts to account for human cognitive processes.

Cognitive Neuroscience

The sophistication of neuroimaging technology has increased in recent times. Additionally, given advances in computer hardware, we have an ever-increasing ability to process large datasets more quickly than ever before. As a result, data collected from cognitive neuroscientific methodologies are becoming a substantially more valuable tool in understanding how multiple neural systems contribute to our processing and interpretation of the world around us. **Cognitive neuroscience** combines the research techniques of cognitive psychology with various methods for assessing the structure and function of the brain (Marshall, 2009).

In recent decades, researchers have examined which structures in the brain are activated when people perform a variety of cognitive tasks (Gazzaniga et al., 2009). Furthermore, psychologists now use neuroscience techniques to explore the kind of cognitive processes that we use in our interactions with other people; this new discipline is called **social cognitive neuroscience** (Cacioppo, 2007; Cacioppo & Berntson, 2005a; Easton & Emery, 2005). For example, researchers have identified a variety of brain structures that are active when people look at a photograph of a face and judge whether the person is trustworthy (Winston et al., 2005). However, neurological explanations for some cognitive processes are elusive. For example, take several seconds to stand up and walk around the room in which you are reading. As you walk, notice what you see in your environment. This visual activity is actually extremely complicated, requiring billions of neurons and more than 50 regions of the surface of your brain (Emery & Easton, 2005).

Because the brain is so complex, we need to be very cautious when we read summaries of cognitive neuroscience research in the popular media. For example, I discovered a newspaper article that claimed, "Scientists Find Humor Spot in the Brain." In reality, numerous parts of the brain work together to master the complicated task of appreciating humor. This observation is not unique to humor. Instead, just about all naturalistic cognitive processing tasks that we face on a daily basis are complex, such that multiple neural systems work together to provide us with the ability to process that information.

Let's examine several neuroscience techniques that provide particularly useful information for cognitive psychologists. We discuss these methodologies up front because they are used in many of the experiments detailed throughout the remainder of this book.

Brain Lesions

In humans, the term **brain lesions** refers to the destruction of an area in the brain, most often by strokes, tumors, blows to the head, and accidents. The formal research on lesions began in the 1860s, but major advances came after World War II, when researchers examined the relationship between damaged regions of the brain and cognitive deficits (Farah, 2004; Kolb & Whishaw, 2009). Tragically, neurologists continue to learn more about specific cognitive deficits from the thousands of U.S. soldiers with brain lesions from the Iraq and Afghanistan wars (e.g., Department of Veterans Affairs, 2010; Oakie, 2005).

The study of brain lesions has definitely helped us understand the organization of the brain. However, the results are often difficult to interpret. For example, a brain lesion is not limited to just one specific area. As a result, researchers typically cannot associate a cognitive deficit with a specific brain structure (Gazzaniga et al., 2009; Kalat, 2009). In this textbook, we will occasionally discuss research on people with brain lesions. However, other neuroscience techniques provide better-controlled information about the neural structures involved in cognitive processing (Hernandez-García et al., 2002).

Positron Emission Tomography (PET Scan)

When you perform a cognitive task, your brain needs chemicals such as oxygen to support neural activity. The brain does not store oxygen. Instead, blood flow increases in the activated part of the brain in order to carry oxygen to that site. Brain-imaging techniques measure brain activity indirectly. These techniques are based on the following logic: By measuring certain properties of the blood in different regions of the brain while people perform a cognitive task, we can determine which brain regions contribute to performance on that cognitive task (Coren et al., 2004; Szpunar, 2010).

In a **positron emission tomography (PET) scan**, researchers measure blood flow in the brain by injecting the participant with a low dose of a radioactive chemical just before this person works on a cognitive task. This chemical travels through the bloodstream to the parts of the brain that are activated during the tasks. While the person works on the task, a special camera makes an image of the accumulated radioactive chemical in various regions of the brain. For example, the participant might perform two slightly different cognitive tasks. By comparing the two brain images, researchers can determine which parts of the brain are activated when the participant works on each task (Kolb & Whishaw, 2011; Szpunar, 2010). PET scans can be used to study such cognitive processes as attention, memory, and language.

PET scans require several seconds to produce data, so this method does not provide useful information about the time course of processing a stimulus in the environment. If the activity in a specific brain region increases and then decreases within this brief period, the PET scan will record an average of this activity level (Hernandez-García et al., 2002). For example, you can scan an entire room in 2 or 3 seconds, so an average activity level for this entire scene would not be meaningful. Furthermore, in the current era, PET

[handwritten margin note: PET: will show region where activity was, but not good info about time course; expensive]

scans are used less often than some other imaging techniques because they are expensive and they expose people to radioactive chemicals (Kalat, 2009).

Functional Magnetic Resonance Imaging

Handwritten margin note: fMRI: measures activity pretty fast; provide info about location of activity; still does not show time course of activity

Functional magnetic resonance imaging (fMRI) is based on the principle that oxygen-rich blood is an index of brain activity (Cacioppo & Berntson, 2005b; Kalat, 2009; Szpunar, 2010). The research participant reclines with his or her head surrounded by a large, doughnut-shaped magnet. This magnetic field produces changes in the oxygen atoms. A scanning device takes a "photo" of these oxygen atoms while the participant performs a cognitive task.

The fMRI technique was developed during the 1990s, based on the magnetic resonance imaging (MRI), which is used in medical settings. In general, an fMRI is preferable to a PET scan because it is less invasive, with no injections and no radioactive material (Gazzaniga et al., 2009). In addition, an fMRI can measure brain activity that occurs fairly quickly—in about one second (Frith & Rees, 2004; Huettel et al., 2004; Kalat, 2009).

The fMRI technique is more precise than a PET scan in that it provides a more detailed image of an individual's brain. It also produces more robust illustrations of the parts of the brain that are involved in processing a stimulus. The fMRI technique can also detect subtle differences in the way that the brain processes language. For example, Gernsbacher and Robertson (2005) used this technique to discover a different pattern of brain activation when students read sentences like, "The young child played in a backyard," as opposed to "A young child played in a backyard." Notice the subtle difference in meaning between "A child" and "The child." Would you have thought that your brain responded differently to these almost identical phrases?

PET scans and functional magnetic resonance imaging provide information about location. That is, they provide information about which parts of the brain contribute to processing a certain type of stimuli. fMRIs are much more common today than PET scans because fMRIs do not use radioactive material, and because they provide better resolution (Bermúdez, 2010; Bernstein & Loftus, 2009). Neither of these techniques, however, provides insight into questions associated with *time* course, fMRI and PET are not able to provide information about when, or how quickly, certain processes occur. In addition, neither PET scans nor fMRIs can tell us precisely what a person is thinking. For instance, some news commentators have suggested using brain scans to identify terrorists. The current technology for this precise kind of identification is clearly inadequate.

Event-Related Potential Technique

Handwritten margin note: ERP: shows fluct. in brain activity; IDs electrical change over brief time; not really locat. info

As we've seen, PET scans and the fMRI technique are too slow to provide precise information about the timing of brain activity. In contrast, the **event-related potential (ERP) technique** records the very brief fluctuations in the brain's electrical activity, in response to a stimulus such as an auditory tone or a visual word (e.g., Bernstein & Loftus, 2009; DeLong, Urbach, & Kutas, 2005; Gazzaniga et al., 2009; Kolb & Whishaw, 2011; Molinaro, Barraza, & Carreiras, 2013).

To use the event-related potential technique, researchers place electrodes on a person's scalp (usually 32 or 64 electrodes, depending on the system). Each electrode records the electrical activity generated by populations of neurons located in the brain. The ERP technique cannot identify the response of a single neuron. However, it can identify electrical changes over a very brief period produced by populations of neurons in some region of the brain (Kutas & Federmeier, 2011).

For example, suppose that you are participating in a study that examines how humans respond to facial movement. Specifically, you have been instructed to watch a video that lasts one second. One video shows a woman opening her mouth; a second video shows her closing her mouth. The electrodes are fastened to your scalp, and you watch numerous presentations of both the mouth-opening and the mouth-closing videos. Later, the researchers will average the signal for each of the two conditions, to eliminate random activity in the brain waves (Puce & Perrett, 2005).

The ERP technique provides a reasonably precise picture of changes in the brain's electrical potential while people perform a cognitive task. Consider the research on mouth movement, for example. If you were to participate in this study, your brain would show a change in electrical potential about half of a second after you saw each mouth movement. However, your brain would respond more dramatically when you watch her mouth open than when you watch a mouth close (Puce & Perrett, 2005).

Why does this fine-grained ERP analysis show that your brain responds differently to these two situations? Puce and Perrett propose that a mouth-opening movement is more important, because it signals that a person is about to say something. You, therefore, need to be attentive, and this exaggerated ERP reflects this attentiveness. In contrast, it's less important to notice that someone has finished talking.

Magnetoencephalography (MEG)

PET scans and fMRI provide compelling information about the brain regions involved in the cognitive processing of some stimulus, although they do not provide clear information about the time course of processing. ERP, on the other hand, provides precise information about the time course underlying cognitive processing, but does not offer reliable information about the neural substrates that contribute to such processing. As a result of these complementary methodological strengths and limitations, cognitive neuroscientific researchers often examine effects of interest using different methodologies. This endeavor involves piecing together information about time course and (neural substrate) localization in order to develop models and theories of cognitive processing.

[margin note: PET & fMRI: info about brain regions involved; ERP: info about time course of cog. processing]

Newer methodological advances, however, may be able to provide more direct information about which parts of the brain contribute to the elicitation of some effect, while simultaneously illuminating the time course of processing events that contribute to it. Although a handful of recent methodological advances can simultaneously produce time course and localization information (see, most notably, information about the Optical Imaging technique, Gratton & Fabiani, 2010; Tse et al., 2007), we focus here on the magnetoencephalography (MEG) technique.

Whereas the ERP technique records fluctuations in neuronally produced electrical activity, the **magnetoencephalography (MEG) technique** records magnetic field fluctuations produced by neural activity during the processing of stimuli presented to participants (Hämäläinen, Hari, Ilmoniemi, Knuutila, & Lounasmaa, 1993). In this sense, it provides time-course information roughly identical to the ERP technique. Unlike the EEG/ERP technique, however, it also provides some coarse-grained information about the neural sources responsible for the observed fluctuations. MEG-based investigations into cognitive processing have become increasingly frequent over the past 15 years (although they have been hampered by the high costs associated with maintaining an MEG facility, thus limiting accessibility).

[margin note: MEG: magnetic field fluctuations; better spatial loc than ERP, but not as good as PET or fMRI]

During an MEG experiment, a participant is placed in an electromagnetically shielded room, and large numbers (up to 300) of magnetically sensitive sensors are placed on their scalp. As with the ERP technique, a stimulus is presented for some amount of time, and the physical properties of waveforms are continuously recorded from each sensor. Average time-locked fluctuations in the waveforms recorded by groups of sensors during stimulus processing provide researchers with information about when, after the onset of a stimulus, neural activity was engaged. The magnetic signals recorded during processing are more robust to distortion as they pass through the skull than are the electrical signals recorded by the ERP technique. This property of magnetic signals allows for substantially more reliable inferences about the neural sources of observed effects in MEG than can be made from ERP data. This spatial localization information is not as precise as the information provided by PET and fMRI techniques. It can, however, provide rough estimates of the spatial location of neural tissue that contributed to fluctuations in magnetic field activity at some point during stimulus processing.

A detailed investigation of cognitive neuroscience techniques is beyond the scope of this book. You can also obtain more information from other resources (e.g., Gazzaniga et al., 2009; Kalat, 2009; Kolb & Whishaw, 2011; Luck, 2014). It's important to point out, however, that neuroscientists have not developed a detailed explanation for any human cognitive process, despite the claims in the popular media (Gallistel & King, 2009). In any event, the increased ease and accessibility of these cognitive neuroscientific techniques means that more integrative and neurally grounded theories of mind and brain are on the horizon.

Textbook Overview

In this textbook, we examine many different kinds of mental processes. We'll begin with perception, attention, and memory—three processes that contribute to all other cognitive tasks. We'll then consider language, which is probably the most challenging cognitive task that humans need to master. Later chapters discuss "higher-order" processes. As the name suggests, these higher-order cognitive processes depend upon the more basic processes introduced in earlier chapters. The final chapter examines cognition across the life span, from infancy to old age. Let's preview Chapters 2 through 13. Then, we'll explore five themes that can help you appreciate some general characteristics of cognitive processes. Our final section provides hints on how you can use your book more effectively.

Chapter Preview

Chapter 2: *Visual and auditory recognition.* These perceptual processes require linking the stimuli that are registered by your senses to the stored knowledge that you have about the world. For example, visual recognition allows you to recognize each letter on this page, whereas auditory recognition allows you to recognize the words you hear when a friend is talking to you.

Chapter 3: *Attention.* Attention is a process that helps you determine which stimuli in the environment you choose to focus on at some point in time. The last time you tried to follow a friend's story while also reading your biology textbook, you probably noticed the limits of your attention. This chapter also examines a related topic called *consciousness*. **Consciousness** is your awareness of the external world, as well as your thoughts and emotions about your internal world.

Chapter 4: *Working memory.* **Memory** is the process of maintaining information over time. Memory is such an important part of cognition that it requires several chapters. Chapter 4 describes working memory (**short-term memory**). You're certainly aware of the limits of working memory when you forget someone's name that you heard less than a minute earlier.

Chapter 5: Long-term memory. The second of our memory chapters focuses on long-term memory. We'll explore the factors that influence your ability to recall information stored in your long-term memory. We'll also investigate the factors, such as mood, that can influence your ability to remember information. We'll then explore memory for everyday life events, as well as people's accuracy during eyewitness testimony.

Chapter 6: *Strategies for memory improvement.* The last of the general memory chapters provides suggestions for how to improve your memory. In particular, we focus on cognitive strategies that you can use in order to improve exam performance. This chapter also considers **metacognition**, which is your knowledge about your own cognitive processes. For instance, do you know whether you could remember the definition for *metacognition* if you were to be tested tomorrow?

Chapter 7: *Mental imagery.* Here, we focus on **imagery**, which is the mental representation of things that are not physically present. One important controversy in the research on imagery is whether your mental images truly resemble perceptual images. Another important topic concerns the mental images we have for physical settings. For example, the cognitive map you have developed for your college campus may show several buildings lined up in a straight row, even though their actual positions are much more random.

Chapter 8: *General Knowledge.* In this chapter, we focus on issues related to how we store and organize our general knowledge. One area of general knowledge is **semantic memory**, which includes factual knowledge about the world as well as knowledge about word meanings. General knowledge also includes schemas (pronounced "*skee*-mahz"). **Schemas** are generalized kinds of information about situations. For example, you have a schema for the typical sequence of events that happen when you enter a restaurant.

Chapter 9: *Language I. Introduction to language and language comprehension.* Research on language processes is vast, such that we cover it in two chapters. In this first chapter, we discuss the properties of human language before examining language *comprehension*. For example, you may hear someone that you have never met before mumble a sentence, and yet you can easily arrive at the intended message. Reading is the second topic covered in Chapter 9; you'll see that reading is much more complex than you might think! We'll also explore how people process **discourse**, which refers to a long passage of spoken or written language.

Chapter 10: *Language II: Language Production and Bilingualism.* In this second of the language chapters, we examine language *production*. One component of speaking is its social context. For example, when you describe an event to friends, you probably check to make certain that they possess the background knowledge necessary to understand the message you intend to convey. Writing requires some cognitive processes that are different from those necessary for speaking, but both of them require working memory and long-term memory. Our final language topic is bilingualism. Even though learning a single language is challenging, many people can speak two or more languages fluently.

Chapter 11: *Problem solving and creativity.* Here, we consider problem solving. Suppose that you want to solve a problem, such as how to complete a course assignment if you do not understand the instructions. You may solve the problem by using a strategy such as dividing the problem into several smaller problems. Chapter 11 also explores creativity. As you'll see, people are often less creative if they have been told that they will be rewarded for their creative efforts.

Chapter 12: *Deductive reasoning and decision making.* In this chapter, we address deductive reasoning and decision making. Reasoning tasks require you to draw conclusions from several known facts. In many cases, your background knowledge interferes with drawing accurate conclusions. In decision making, you make a judgment about uncertain events. For example, people often cancel an airplane trip after reading about a recent plane accident, even though statistics clearly show that driving is more dangerous.

Chapter 13: *Cognitive development throughout the lifespan.* This chapter examines cognitive processes in infants, children, and elderly adults. People in these three age groups are more competent than you might guess. For example, 6-month-old infants can recall an event that occurred two weeks earlier. Young children are also very accurate in remembering events from a medical procedure in a doctor's office. Furthermore, elderly people are competent on many memory tasks, and they actually perform better than younger adults on some tasks, such as crossword puzzles (Salthouse, 2012).

Themes in the Book

This book repeatedly emphasizes certain themes that are designed to guide you and to offer you a framework for understanding many of the complexities of our mental abilities. We introduce these themes below:

Theme 1: Cognitive processes are active, rather than passive.

Classical behaviorists viewed humans as passive organisms. Under such a theoretical worldview, humans were thought to wait for a stimulus to arrive from the environment before executing a response. In contrast, the cognitive approach proposes that people can willfully seek out information. Attentional and perceptual systems work together to facilitate your ability to strategically seek out and process information that is most relevant for your current goals. In addition, memory is a lively process that requires you to continually synthesize and transform information. When you read, you actively draw inferences that were never directly stated. In summary, your mind is not a sponge that passively absorbs information leaking out from the environment. Instead, you continually search, process, and synthesize.

Theme 2: Cognitive processes are remarkably efficient and accurate.

The amount of material in your memory is astonishing. Just think about all the facts, names, and phone numbers that you know. And consider language comprehension. Speech unfolds at an extremely fast rate determined by a speaker, and yet most of the time, your interpretation of the speech signal is highly accurate.

Furthermore, your cognitive systems are designed such that they can limit the amount of information to which you have access. Although at face value these limitations may sound like a bad thing, they may be helpful sometimes. Consider a situation in which you are eating lunch with friends at a busy restaurant. Your attentional abilities allow you to direct your attention to the speech of your friends. At the same time, they also provide you with the ability to filter out all of the background noise in the restaurant. Imagine how difficult life would be if you had to process every bit of information about every environmental stimulus at the same point in time. It would be overwhelming.

Before you read further, try Demonstration 1.4, which is based on a Demonstration by Hearst (1991).

Demonstration 1.4 ‖ Looking at Unusual Paragraphs

How fast can you spot what is unusual about this paragraph? It looks so ordinary that you might think nothing is wrong with it at all, and, in fact, nothing is. But it is atypical. Why? Study its various parts, think about its curious wording, and you may hit upon a solution. But you must do it without aid; my plan is not to allow any scandalous misconduct in this psychological study. No doubt, if you work hard on this possibly frustrating task, its abnormality will soon dawn upon you. You cannot know until you try. But it is commonly a hard nut to crack. So, good luck!

I trust a solution is conspicuous now. Was it dramatic and fair, although odd? Author's hint: I cannot add my autograph to this communication and maintain its basic harmony.

Theme 3: Cognitive processes handle positive information better than negative information.

We understand sentences better if they are worded in the affirmative—for example, "Mary is honest," rather than the negative wording, "Mary is not dishonest." In addition, we have trouble noticing when something is missing, as illustrated in Demonstration 1.4 (Hearst, 1991). (The answer to this demonstration appears at the end of this chapter, as does the credit for this quotation.) We also tend to perform better on a variety of different tasks if the information is emotionally positive (that is, pleasant), rather than emotionally negative (unpleasant). In short, our cognitive processes are designed to handle *what is*, rather than *what is not* (Hearst, 1991; Matlin, 2004).

Theme 4: Cognitive processes are interrelated with one another; they do not operate in isolation.

This textbook discusses each cognitive process in one or more separate chapters. However, this organizational plan does not imply that every process can function by itself, without interfacing with other processes. For example, decision making typically requires perception, memory, general knowledge, and language. In fact, all higher mental processes require careful integration of our more basic cognitive processes.

Theme 5: Many cognitive processes rely on both bottom-up and top-down processing.

Bottom-up processing emphasizes the importance of information from the stimuli registered on your sensory receptors. Bottom-up processing uses only a low-level sensory analysis of the stimulus. In contrast, **top-down processing** emphasizes how our concepts, expectations, and memory influence our cognitive processes. Top-down processing requires higher-level cognition, including the processes emphasized in Chapters 5 and 8 of this textbook. Both bottom-up processing and top-down processing work simultaneously to ensure that our cognitive processes are typically fast and accurate.

Consider pattern recognition. You recognize your aunt partly because of information available from the stimulus—information about your aunt's face, height, shape, and so forth. This bottom-up processing is important. At the same time, however, you must possess stored knowledge about the physical characteristics of your aunt, or if you saw her, she would seem like an ordinary person. The reliance on stored knowledge about her physical identity—knowledge necessary to recognize a person as your aunt and not as a stranger—is an example of the top-down knowledge-driven component of visual recognition. Furthermore, consider the role of context. There may be a higher likelihood of seeing your aunt in her own house than seeing your best friend from college in the same location. This top-down knowledge may speed up the visual recognition of your aunt in her house. As we'll see throughout this book, knowledge and context work together to shape the way that we access and process information in our physical environments.

How to Use Your Book Effectively

Your textbook includes several features that are specifically designed to help you understand and remember the material. As you read the list that follows, figure out how to use each feature most effectively.

Chapter Outline

Notice that each chapter begins with an outline. When you start to read a new chapter, first examine the outline so that you can appreciate the general structure of a topic. For example, notice that Chapter 1 has four main topics, each appearing in large boldface print, starting with **What Is Cognitive Psychology?** The second-level headings are smaller, such as **Origins of Cognitive Psychology** here in Chapter 1. The third-level headings are the smallest and appear in text at the beginning of relevant subsections in italics.

Chapter Introductions

Each chapter begins with an introductory section that encourages you to think about how your own cognitive experiences are related to the material in the chapter. They are designed to emphasize the central components of the cognitive process discussed in each chapter. By combining the material from the outline and the opening paragraph, you'll be better prepared for the specific information about the research and theories presented in each chapter. You may be tempted to skip the chapter outline and the chapter introductions. This organizational structure will, however, help you understand the major groupings of topics throughout the chapter before you begin to read.

Demonstrations

I designed the demonstrations in this book to make the research more meaningful. The informal experiments in these demonstrations require little or no equipment, and you can perform most of them by yourself. Students have told me that these demonstrations help make the material more memorable, especially when they try to picture themselves performing the tasks in a research setting. As you will see in our discussions of memory systems, we remember information more accurately when we try to relate the material to ourselves.

Individual Differences Focus

The term **individual differences** refers to variation in the way that groups of people perform on the same cognitive task. Prior to roughly 1995, cognitive psychologists rarely investigated how individual differences could influence people's thought processes. Instead, they focused strongly on measuring the behavior of multiple participants in an experiment, and then calculating the statistical mean (average) performance per each condition of an experiment. But, should you have taken a statistics course already, you likely learned that average estimates of performance do not provide information about variability in individual subject performance. Some participants may have performed really well on a task whereas others may have exhibited more difficulty. And, in many cases, understanding why certain individuals performed better or worse on a task can provide deeper insight into the cognitive process under investigation.

The exploration of individual differences in cognitive performance is consistent with a relatively new approach that makes connections among the various disciplines within psychology. John T. Cacioppo (2007) wrote about this important issue when he was the president of the Association for Psychological Science. APS is an organization that focuses on psychology research in areas such as cognitive psychology, social psychology, and biopsychology. Cacioppo emphasized that psychology can make major advances by combining each of these areas with one of three specific perspectives. These three perspectives are abnormal psychology, individual differences, and developmental psychology. For instance, a group of researchers could combine one area (e.g., cognitive psychology) with a perspective (e.g., abnormal psychology).

Consider individuals who have major depression. **Major depression** is a psychological disorder in which feelings of sadness, discouragement, and hopelessness interfere with the ability to perform daily mental and physical functions. In an earlier era, psychologists seldom studied whether depressed individuals might differ from other people when performing cognitive tasks. This situation is puzzling, because therapists—and the individuals themselves—frequently noticed these problems on cognitive tasks. Fortunately, many contemporary psychologists now conduct research on the relationship between psychological disorders and cognitive performance (e.g., Hertel & Matthews, 2011). Such a pursuit can provide novel insight, for example, into the ways in which cognitive processes may be impaired or otherwise influenced by the presence of psychopathology.

This kind of interdisciplinary research is important from both practical and theoretical standpoints. As you know, Theme 4 emphasizes that our cognitive processes are interrelated. Therefore, cognitive aspects of psychological problems—such as major depression—could certainly be related to attention, memory, and other cognitive processes. And, if depressed individuals underperform compared to nondepressed individuals on a memory task, the next most reasonable question to ask is "Why?" Perhaps individuals with depression do not encode information into memory in the same way as those without depression. Or, perhaps attentional differences between the two groups explain why they differed in memory performance. Notice here that pursuing either of these two potential explanations for the group difference will likely yield more information not only about cognitive processing in depressed individuals, but also about memory systems more generally.

Other researchers who investigate individual differences choose to compare groups of people who differ on a demographic characteristic. For example, you may have heard from someone at some point in your life that men and women differ in their language- or spatial abilities. In Chapter 7, however, we'll see that women and men are actually similar in most kinds of spatial abilities. Indeed, although gender differences may be an important area of inquiry in some other areas of psychology, men and women tend to demonstrate extremely similar patterns of performance in most cognitive psychology experiments.

In order to increase your awareness of the emerging focus on individual differences research in cognitive psychology, each chapter contains research that illuminates some type of individual differences effect. For example, Chapter 2 contains a discussion of how individuals with a schizophrenia diagnosis perform more slowly than a control group (without schizophrenia or other significant mental health problems) on facial recognition tasks. Chapter 5 contains a discussion of the manner in which the presence of an anxiety disorder can influence performance on different types of memory tasks.

Application

As you read each chapter, notice the numerous applications of cognitive psychology. Indeed, research in cognition has important applications to areas such as education, medicine, business, and clinical psychology. For example, understanding the factors that can increase the accurate retrieval of information from memory is not only interesting for theoretical reasons. People recall information better if it is concrete, rather than abstract, and if they try to determine whether the information applies to themselves (Paivio, 1995; Rogers et al., 1977; Symons & Johnson, 1997). Each time that you take an exam, you must access information that is stored in your memory. As a result, the scientific study of memory can provide valuable information that you can apply to your own study strategies and test-taking behaviors in order to increase your exam performance.

Section Summaries

As we will discuss in the chapters on memory, repeated exposures to information increases accurate memory for that information. In order to provide you with another opportunity to think about key concepts in each chapter, section summaries appear for each section at the end of the chapter. When you reach the end of the chapter, cover the summary points provided for each section and see which important points you remember. Then, read the section summary and notice which items you remembered incorrectly or incompletely. Take extra care to revisit the text associated with the points on which you experienced difficulty.

End of Chapter Review Questions

At the end of each chapter, you will find a set of essay-style review questions. These questions provide you with yet another opportunity to quiz yourself, in a different format, on the material contained in the chapter. Many review questions ask you to apply your knowledge to an everyday problem. Other review questions encourage you to integrate information from several parts of the chapter. Thinking about each question will provide you with another opportunity to identify the areas in which you may have difficulty with the material.

Keywords

Notice that each new term in this book appears in boldface type (for example, **cognition**) when it is first discussed. I have included the definition in the same sentence as the term, so you do not need to search an entire paragraph to discover the term's meaning. Also notice that phonetic pronunciation is provided for a small number of words that are often mispronounced. Students tell me that they feel more comfortable using a word during class discussion if they are confident that their pronunciation is correct. (I also included pronunciation guides for the names of several prominent theorists and researchers, such as Wundt and Piaget.)

Keywords List & Glossary

At the end of each chapter, a new term list shows these terms in order of their appearance in the chapter. Check each item to see whether you can supply a definition and an example. You can consult the chapter for a discussion of the term. Your textbook also includes a glossary at the end of the book. The glossary will be helpful when you need a precise definition for a technical term. It will also be useful when you want to check your accuracy while reviewing the list of new terms in each chapter.

Recommended Readings

Each chapter features a list of recommended readings. This list can supply you with resources if you want to write a paper on a particular topic or if an area is personally interesting. In general, I tried to locate books, chapters, and articles that provide more than an overview of the subject but are not overly technical.

SECTION SUMMARY POINTS

What Is Cognitive Psychology?

1. The term *cognition* refers to the acquisition, storage, transformation, and use of knowledge; *cognitive psychology* is sometimes used as a synonym for cognition, and sometimes it refers to a theoretical approach to psychology.

2. Multiple systems and processes contribute to your conscious interpretation of the world around you.

3. It's useful to study cognitive psychology because (a) cognitive activities are a major part of human psychology, (b) the cognitive approach influences other important areas of psychology, and (c) you can learn how to use your cognitive processes more effectively.

Historical Perspective on the Field

1. Many historians maintain that Wilhelm Wundt is responsible for creating the discipline of psychology; Wundt also developed the introspection technique.

2. Hermann Ebbinghaus and Mary Whiton Calkins conducted early research on human memory.

3. William James examined numerous everyday psychological processes, and he emphasized the active nature of the human mind.

4. Gestalt psychology emphasized that people use organization to perceive patterns, and they often solve problems by using insight.

5. Beginning in the early 20th century, behaviorists such as John B. Watson rejected the study of mental processes; the behaviorists helped to develop the research methods used by current cognitive psychologists.

6. Cognitive psychology began to emerge in the mid-1950s. This new approach was stimulated by disenchantment with behaviorism, as well as a growing interest in linguistics, human memory, and developmental psychology.

Mind, Brain, and Behavior

1. Cognitive science examines questions about the mind; it includes disciplines such as cognitive psychology, neuroscience, artificial intelligence, philosophy, linguistics, anthropology, sociology, and economics.

2. Theorists who are interested in artificial intelligence (AI) approaches to cognition typically try to design computer models that accomplish the same cognitive tasks that humans do.

3. The approach called "pure artificial intelligence" attempts to design programs that can accomplish cognitive tasks as efficiently as possible.

4. The approach called "computer simulation" attempts to design programs that accomplish cognitive tasks the way that humans do.

5. According to the computer metaphor, human cognitive processes work like a computer that can process information quickly and accurately.

6. According to the information-processing approach, mental processes operate like a computer, with information flowing through a series of storage areas.

7. Enthusiasm for the classic information-processing approach has declined, because cognitive psychologists now realize that human thinking requires more complex models.

8. Cognitive psychology has had a major influence on the field of psychology. In the current era, cognitive psychologists are more concerned about ecological validity than in previous decades.

9. According to the connectionist approach, cognitive processes can be represented in terms of networks of neurons; furthermore, many operations can proceed at the same time, in parallel, rather than one step at a time. → (NOT serial)

10. The area of cognitive neuroscience combines the research techniques of cognitive psychology with a variety of methods for assessing the brain's structure and function.

11. Brain lesions, PET scans, and the Functional magnetic resonance imaging (fMRI) are cognitive neuroscientific methodologies that provide information about which brain structures are involved in cognitive processing; fMRI is now more commonly used than PET scans.

12. The event-related potential technique uses electrodes to track the very brief changes in the brain's electrical activity, in response to specific stimuli. It does not provide information about where in the brain the processing occurred, but it gives very precise estimates of the time course of cognitive processing.

CHAPTER REVIEW QUESTIONS

1. Define the terms *cognition* and *cognitive psychology*. Now think about your ideal career, and suggest several ways in which the information from cognitive psychology would be relevant to this career.

2. Compare the following approaches to psychology, with respect to their specific emphasis on human thinking: (a) William James's approach, (b) behaviorism, (c) gestalt psychology, and (d) the cognitive approach.

3. This chapter addresses the trade-off between ecological validity and carefully controlled research. Define these two concepts. Then compare the following approaches in terms of their emphasis on each concept: (a) Ebbinghaus's approach to memory, (b) James's approach to psychological processes, (c) the behaviorist approach, (d) the cognitive psychology approach from several decades ago, and (e) current cognitive psychology research.

4. List several reasons for the increased interest in cognitive psychology and the decline of the behaviorist approach. In addition, describe the field of cognitive science, noting the disciplines that are included in this field.

5. The section on cognitive neuroscience described five different research techniques. Answer the following questions for each technique: (a) What are its strengths? (b) What are its weaknesses? (c) What kind of research questions can it answer?

6. What is artificial intelligence, and how is the information-processing approach relevant to this topic? Select three specific cognitive processes that might interest researchers in artificial intelligence. Then provide examples of how pure AI and the computer-simulation investigations of these cognitive processes would differ in their focus.

7. How does connectionism differ from the classical artificial-intelligence approach? List three characteristics of the PDP approach. In what way is this approach based on discoveries in cognitive neuroscience?

8. Theme 4 emphasizes that your cognitive processes are interrelated. Think about a problem you have solved recently, and point out how the solution to this problem depended upon perceptual processes, memory, and other cognitive activities.

9. As you'll see in Chapters 5 and 6, your long-term memory is more accurate if you carefully think about the material you are reading; it is especially accurate if you try to relate the material to your own life. Review the section called "How to Use Your Book" and describe how you can use each feature to increase your memory for the material in the remaining chapters of this book.

10. Review each of the five themes of this book. Which of them seem consistent with your own experiences, and which seem surprising? From your own life, think of an example of each theme.

KEYWORDS

cognition	short-term memory	imaging (fMRI)	parallel distributed	schemas
cognitive psychology	working memory	event-related potential	processing (PDP)	discourse
cognitive approach	long-term memory	(ERP)	approach	Theme 1
empirical evidence	ecological validity	technique	neural-network approach	Theme 2
introspection	cognitive neuroscience	magnetoencephalography	cerebral cortex	Theme 3
recency effect	social cognitive	(MEG) technique	serial processing	Theme 4
behaviorism	neuroscience	artificial intelligence	parallel processing	Theme 5
operational definition	brain lesions	(AI)	cognitive science	bottom-up processing
gestalt psychology	positron emission	computer metaphor	consciousness	top-down processing
gestalt	tomography	pure AI	memory	individual differences
information-processing	(PET scan)	computer simulation	metacognition	major depression
approach	functional magnetic	computer modeling	imagery	
sensory memory	resonance	connectionist approach	semantic memory	

RECOMMENDED READINGS

Bermúdez, J. L. (2014). *Cognitive science: An introduction to the science of the mind.* New York: Cambridge University Press. Cognitive science is an interdisciplinary area, and this textbook does a good job of explaining how multiple fields, including psychology, contributed to a more interdisciplinary understanding of how the mind works.

Clark, A. (2013). *Mindware: An introduction to the philosophy of cognitive science.* Oxford University Press, Inc. Written by a leading philosopher in the field of cognitive science, this book provides a very accessible overview of multiple approaches to modeling the complexities of the human mind.

Pickren, W. E., & Rutherford, A. (2010). *A history of modern psychology in context.* Hoboken, NJ: Wiley. I highly recommend this clearly written, well-organized overview of the history of psychology.

Spivey, M. (2007). *The continuity of mind.* Oxford University Press. Although this book is a bit advanced, it provides a clear and concise critique of the classical information processing approach to cognitive psychology. The author then argues for a newer, more interactive perspective on the relationship between perception, cognition, and action.

ANSWER TO DEMONSTRATION 1.4

The letter *e* is missing from this entire passage. The letter *e* is the most frequent letter in the English language. Therefore, a long passage—without any use of the letter *e*—is highly unusual. The exercise demonstrates the difficulty of searching for something that is not there (Theme 3).

Quotation on page 25 from: Hearst, E. (1991). Psychology and nothing. *American Scientist, 79,* 432–443.

Visual and Auditory Recognition

Chapter Introduction

Hold your hand directly in front of your eyes. It is likely that you perceive a solid object that includes distinctive characteristics. For example, you can easily identify its size, shape, and color. You also notice that your hand is a unified object, clearly located in front of a more distant and less clearly defined background. Shifting your gaze back to the text in this textbook, your eyes perceive a series of squiggles on this page. You can instantly, however, identify each squiggle as a letter of the alphabet. And, you can recognize combinations of letters as entire words. Your visual system perceives more than just one shape at a time. In fact, you can quickly and effortlessly identify hundreds of shapes in any natural scene (Geisler, 2008).

Your auditory abilities are equally impressive. You can, for example, recognize the words spoken by your friend, as well as music, squeaking chairs, and footsteps.

As you'll see in this chapter, our visual and auditory achievements are impressively efficient and accurate (Grill-Spector & Kanwisher, 2005; Lappin & Craft, 2000). Did you know, for example, that you can identify a complex scene—such as a baseball game or a wedding—within about one-tenth of a second (Gallistel & King, 2009)?

This chapter explores several aspects of perceptual processing. We begin with some background information on recognizing visual objects. We next examine two important topics in vision: top-down processing and specialized recognition processes. Finally, we shift to the perceptual world of audition as we consider speech perception. These perceptual processes are vitally important because they prepare the "raw" sensory information so that it can be used in the more complex mental processes—such as reading—which we discuss here and in later chapters of this book.

Overview of Visual Object Recognition

Perception uses previous knowledge to gather and interpret the stimuli registered by the senses. For example, you use perception to interpret each of the letters on this page. Consider how you managed to perceive the letter at the end of the word *perception*. You combined (1) information registered by your eyes, (2) your previous knowledge about the shape of the letters of the alphabet, and (3) your previous knowledge about what to expect when your visual system has already processed the fragment *percep-tio-*. Notice that perception combines aspects of both the outside world (the visual stimuli) and your own inner world (your previous knowledge). This observation provides a good example of Theme 5 of this book. In order to make sense of the world around you, perception combines bottom-up and top-down processing.

When someone speaks, they are creating a physical signal in the form of sound waves. Those sound waves travel to your ear, and portions of your auditory system are responsible for analyzing the physical properties (such as amplitude and frequency) of the sound waves. The analysis of the physical properties of input occurring early after it makes contact with your sensory receptors constitutes the "bottom-up" part of perception. After early sensory processing, additional higher-level processing of the input occurs. As an internal representation of the stimulus is constructed, it is matched to information stored in your long-term memory. An object (in this case, a linguistic sound received through the auditory modality) is recognized once bottom-up information has been processed enough for this matching process to occur. Any guiding role that your stored knowledge plays in facilitating your ability to recognize an object (either one intercepted in the visual or auditory modality) constitutes the "top-down" portion of the recognition process.

Many colleges offer an entire course on the topic of perception, so we cannot do justice to this discipline in just one chapter. Other resources can provide information about sensory processes such as the nature of the receptors in the eye and the ear, as well as more details about other areas of perception (Foley & Matlin, 2010; Goldstein, 2010a; Wolfe et al., 2009). These books examine how we perceive important characteristics of visual objects, such as shape, size, color, texture, and depth. These resources also investigate other perceptual systems—audition, touch, taste, and smell. Additionally, understanding how the stored knowledge that you possess interacts with, and fundamentally shapes, lower-level sensory processing is a current hot topic in many areas of the cognitive sciences (e.g., Bar et al., 2006; Chang et al., 2006; Clark, 2013a; Dikker et al., 2010; Noë, 2004; Pickering & Clark, 2014; Pickering & Garrod, 2013). Because perception contributes to just about every other cognitive process in some way or another, it's one of the most heavily researched topics in the cognitive sciences.

As a result of the limited room that we have to discuss perceptual processes, this chapter focuses most heavily on object recognition. During **object recognition** or **pattern recognition**, you identify a complex arrangement of sensory stimuli, and you perceive that this pattern is separate from its background. When you recognize an object, your sensory processes transform and organize the raw information provided by your sensory receptors. You also compare the sensory stimuli with information that you have stored in your memory.

In this first section of the chapter, we focus on visual processing. During visual processing, light bounces off surfaces in the environment, thus carrying information about the contents of your external visual world to your visual sensory receptors (your eyes). We consider three topics: (a) the visual system, (b) how organization operates in visual perception, and (c) three theories about object recognition.

The Visual System

Psychologists have developed two terms to refer to perceptual stimuli. The **distal stimulus** is the actual object that is "out there" in the environment—for example, the pen on your desk. The **proximal stimulus** is the information registered on your sensory receptors—for example, the image that your pen creates on

object recognition = pattern recog.

distal stimulus = the actual object

proximal stimulus = the info registered (ex: the image)

| **Demonstration 2.1** | The Immediate Recognition of Objects |

Turn on a television set and adjust the sound to "mute." Now change the channel with your eyes closed. Open your eyes and then immediately shut them. Repeat this exercise several times. Notice how you can instantly identify and interpret the image on the TV screen, even though you did not expect that image and have never previously seen it in that exact form. In less than a second—and without major effort—you can identify colors, textures, contours, objects, and people.

This demonstration was originally suggested by Irving Biederman (1995), who noted that people can usually interpret the meaning of a new scene in one-tenth of a second. Consistent with Theme 2, humans are impressively efficient in recognizing patterns.

your retina. Your **retina** covers the inside back portion of your eye; it contains millions of neurons that register and transmit visual information from the outside world.

When we recognize an object, we manage to figure out the identity of the distal stimulus, even when the information available in the proximal stimulus is far from perfect (Kersten et al., 2004; Palmer, 2003; Pasternak et al., 2003). For example, you recognized the human face in Demonstration 1.2 even though the face lacks a nose, mouth, and ears. Gazzaniga and his colleagues (2009) point out that object recognition depends primarily on shape, rather than on color or texture. You recognized this human face, even though it was blue.

Try Demonstration 2.1 to illustrate your skill in identifying the distal stimulus. As this demonstration emphasizes, you can recognize objects in a new scene that has been presented for about one-tenth of a second (Biederman, 1995). Does this mean that your visual system manages to take the proximal stimulus, representing perhaps a dozen objects, and recognize all of these objects within one-tenth of a second?

Fortunately, your visual system has some assistance from one of its other components—your sensory memory (Gregory, 2004a). **Sensory memory** is a large-capacity storage system that records information from each of the senses with reasonable accuracy. In relation to vision, **iconic memory**, or **visual sensory memory**, preserves an image of a visual stimulus for a brief period after the stimulus has disappeared (Hollingworth, 2006b; Parks, 2004; Sperling, 1960).

Visual information that is registered on the retina (the proximal stimulus) must make its way through the visual pathway, a set of neurons between the retina and the primary visual cortex. The **primary visual cortex** is located in the occipital lobe of the brain; it is the portion of your cerebral cortex that is concerned with basic processing of visual stimuli. (See Figure 2.1.) It is also the first place where information from

[handwritten note: info from both eyes combines here]

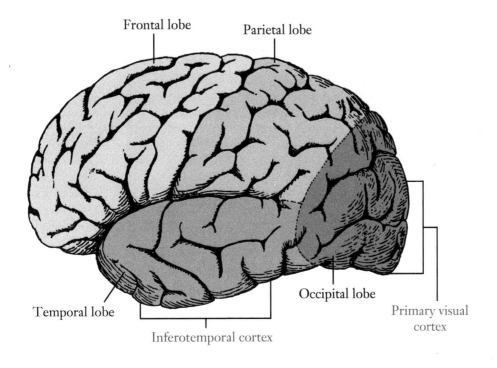

Frontal lobe   Parietal lobe

Temporal lobe

Inferotemporal cortex

Occipital lobe

Primary visual cortex

FIGURE 2.1

A schematic drawing of the cerebral cortex, as seen from the left side, showing the four lobes of the brain.

Notice the primary visual cortex (discussed in this section). The inferotemporal cortex plays an important role in recognizing complex objects such as faces.

your two eyes is combined (Briggs & Usrey, 2010). If you place your hand at the back of your head, just above your neck, the primary visual cortex lies just beneath your skull at that location.

  Visual information can travel from your retina to your primary visual cortex extremely quickly (~50–80 milliseconds; Nowak, Munk et al., 1995). The primary visual cortex is only the first stop within the cortex. For instance, researchers have identified at least 30 additional areas of the cortex that play a role in visual perception (Bruce et al., 2003; Felleman & Van Essen, 1991; Frishman, 2001; Sillito, 2004). These regions beyond the primary visual cortex are activated during object recognition. Researchers are currently studying the functions of these regions. For example, your ability to recognize a tool—such as a fork or scissors—depends partly on your parietal lobe (Almeida et al., 2010; Mahon et al., 2010). It is important to note, however, that researchers have not yet discovered which brain regions are paired with each component of the object recognition process (Pasternak et al., 2003; Purves & Lotto, 2003).

Organization in Visual Perception

Our visual system is designed to impose organization on the richly complicated visual world (Geisler & Super, 2000; Palmer, 2003).

  In Chapter 1, we introduced a historical approach to psychology called "gestalt psychology." One important principle in **gestalt psychology** is that humans have basic tendencies to organize what they see; without any effort, we see patterns rather than random arrangements (Gordon, 2004; Schirillo, 2010). For example, when two areas share a common boundary, the **figure** has a distinct shape with clearly defined edges. In contrast, the **ground** is the region that is "left over," forming the background. As gestalt psychologists pointed out, the figure has a definite shape, whereas the ground simply continues behind the figure. The figure also seems closer to us and more dominant than the ground (Kelly & Grossberg, 2000; Palmer, 2003; Rubin, 1915). Even young infants demonstrate some of the gestalt principles of organization (Quinn et al., 2002).

  In an **ambiguous figure–ground relationship**, the figure and the ground reverse from time to time, so that the figure becomes the ground and then becomes the figure again. Figure 2.2 illustrates the well-known vase–faces effect. At first, you see a white vase against a dark grey background, but a moment later, you see two dark grey faces against a white background. Even in this ambiguous situation, our perceptual system imposes organization on a stimulus, so that one portion stands out and the remainder recedes into the background. We are so accustomed to the certainty of the figure–ground relationship that we are surprised when we encounter a situation where the figure and the ground exchange places (Wolfe et al., 2009).

  The explanation for these figure–ground reversals seems to have two components: (1) The neurons in the visual cortex become adapted to one figure, such as the "faces" version of Figure 2.2, so you are more likely to see the alternative or "vase" version; and (2) furthermore, people try to solve the visual paradox by alternating between two reasonable solutions (Gregory, 2004a; Long & Toppino, 2004; Toppino & Long, 2005).

FIGURE 2.2
The vase–faces effect: An example of an ambiguous figure–ground relationship.

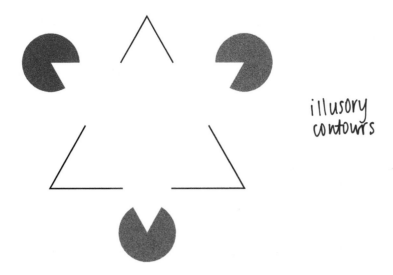

illusory contours

Surprisingly, we can even perceive a figure–ground relationship when a scene has no clear-cut boundary between the figure and the ground. One category of visual illusions is known as illusory contours. In **illusory contours** (also called **subjective contours**), we see edges even though they are not physically present in the stimulus. In the illusory contour in Figure 2.3, for example, people report that an inverted white triangle seems to loom in front of the outline of a second triangle and three small dark grey circles. Furthermore, the triangle appears to be brighter than any other part of the stimulus (Grossberg, 2000; Palmer, 2002).

In our everyday life, we typically perceive scenes more accurately if we "fill in the blanks." However, in the case of illusory contours, this rational strategy leads to a perceptual error (Mendola, 2003; Purves & Lotto, 2003). You can see why gestalt psychologists were especially intrigued by ambiguous figure–ground relationships and illusory contours (Foley & Matlin, 2010; Wolfe et al., 2009). Human perception is more than the sum of the information in the distal stimulus.

Theories of Visual Object Recognition

Researchers have proposed many different theories of object recognition. According to one early theory, your visual system compares a stimulus with a set of **templates** or, specific patterns that you have stored in memory. It then notes which template matches the stimulus.

example

Note, however, that every day, you manage to recognize letters that differ substantially from the classic version of a letter, especially in handwritten text. For instance, notice in Figure 2.4 that all of the letter Cs in the word *Cognitive* are somewhat different. You can see that the letter Ps in *Psychology* are also somewhat different. Still, you can recognize each of those letters, even if you view the letters from a different perspective (Palmer, 2003). The template approach fares even worse in recognizing the more complex objects that occupy your visual world. Perception requires a more flexible system than matching a pattern against a specific, stored template (Gordon, 2004; Jain & Duin, 2004; Wolfe et al., 2009).

The two other theories—feature analysis and recognition-by-components—are more sophisticated. As you read about these two current theories, keep in mind that we don't need to decide that one theory is correct and the other is wrong. Human perception is somewhat flexible, and we may use different approaches for different object recognition tasks (Mather, 2006). Another thing to keep in mind is that these theories differ mostly in terms of the format in which the information necessary for recognition is stored in memory.

theories differ in the way info for recognition is stored in memory

Feature-Analysis Theory

Several **feature-analysis theories** propose a relatively flexible approach in which a visual stimulus is composed of a small number of characteristics or components (Gordon, 2004). Each visual characteristic is called a **distinctive feature**. Consider, for example, how feature-analysis theorists might explain the way that we recognize letters of the alphabet. They argue that we store a list of distinctive features for each letter. For example, the distinctive features for the letter R include a curved component, a vertical line, and a diagonal line. When you look at a new letter, your visual system notes the presence or absence

distinctive feature = each indiv. feature/ characteristic/compon.

*ex. of distinct. feats. for R : | ⟩ *

Cognitive Psychology

Cognitive Psychology

Cognitive Psychology

Cognitive Psychology

COGNITIVE PSYCHOLOGY

Cognitive Psychology

Cognitive Psychology

FIGURE 2.4

An example of variability in the shape of letters.

Notice specifically the difference in the shape of the letter P in Cognitive Psychology.

[handwritten margin note: handwriting differs but each letter includes sp. components]

[handwritten margin note: Feature analysis = 20]

of the various features. It then compares this list with the features stored in memory for each letter of the alphabet. People's handwriting may differ, but each of their printed Rs will include these three features.

Try Demonstration 2.2, which is based on a chart developed by Eleanor Gibson (1969). The feature-analysis theories propose that the distinctive features for each of the alphabet letters remain constant, whether the letter is handwritten, printed, or typed. These models can also explain how we perceive a wide variety of two-dimensional patterns, such as figures in a painting, designs on fabric, and illustrations in books. However, most research on this topic focuses on our ability to recognize letters and numbers.

Feature-analysis theories are consistent with the psychological research. For example, the psychological research by Eleanor Gibson (1969) demonstrated that people require a relatively long time to decide whether one letter is different from a second letter when those two letters share a large number of critical features. According to the table in Demonstration 2.2, the letters P and R share many critical features, whereas the letters O and L do not share any critical features. Gibson's research participants were slower to signal a decision about whether P and R were different letters relative to whether O and L were different.

Other psychological research analyzes the letters and numbers in the addresses that people write on envelopes (Jain & Duin, 2004). For example, Larsen and Bundesen (1996) designed a model based on feature analysis that correctly recognized an impressive 95% of the numbers written in street addresses and zip codes.

The feature-analysis theories are also compatible with evidence from neuroscience (Gordon, 2004; Palmer, 2002). The research team of Hubel and Wiesel focused on the primary visual cortex of anesthetized animals (Hubel, 1982; Hubel & Wiesel, 1965, 1979, 2005). They presented a simple visual stimulus—such as a vertical bar of light—directly in front of each animal's eyes. Hubel and Wiesel then recorded how a particular neuron in the primary visual cortex responded to that visual stimulus. They continued to test how a variety of neurons in this region of the cortex responded to visual stimuli. Hubel and Wiesel's results showed that each neuron responded especially vigorously when the bar was presented to a specific retinal region and when the bar had a particular orientation. For example, suppose that a bar of light is presented to a particular location on the animal's retina. One specific neuron might respond strongly when the bar has a vertical orientation. Another neuron, just a hairbreadth away within the visual cortex, might respond most vigorously when the bar is rotated about 10 degrees from the vertical. The visual system contains feature detectors that are present when we are born (Gordon, 2004). These detectors help us recognize certain features of letters and simple patterns.

| Demonstration 2.2 | A Feature-Analysis Approach |

Eleanor Gibson proposed that letters differ from each other with respect to their distinctive features. The demonstration below includes an abbreviated version of a table she proposed. Notice that the table shows whether a letter of the alphabet contains any of the following features: four kinds of straight lines, a closed curve, an intersection of two lines, and symmetry. As you can see, P and R share many features. However, W and O share only one feature. Compare the following pairs of letters to determine which distinctive features they share: A and B; E and F; X and Y; I and L.

Features	A	E	F	H	I	L	V	W	X	Y	Z	B	C	D	G	J	O	P	R	Q
Straight																				
horizontal	+	+	+	+		+					+				+					
vertical		+	+	+	+	+						+		+		+		+	+	
diagonal/	+						+	+	+	+	+									
diagonal\	+						+	+	+	+								+	+	
Closed Curve												+		+			+	+	+	+
Intersection	+	+	+	+				+		+							+	+	+	
Symmetry	+	+		+	+		+	+	+	+		+	+	+			+			

Source: Gibson, E. J. (1969). *Principles of perceptual learning and development*. New York: Prentice Hall.

There are, however, several problems with the feature-analysis approach. For example, the feature-analysis theories were constructed to explain the relatively simple recognition of letters. In contrast, the shapes that occur in nature are much more complex (Kersten et al., 2004). How can you recognize a horse? Do you analyze the stimulus into features such as its mane, its head, and its hooves? Wouldn't any important perceptual features be distorted as soon as the horse moved—or as soon as you moved? Horses and other objects in our environment contain far too many lines and curved segments. Recognizing these objects is far more complex than recognizing letters (Palmer, 2003; Vecera, 1998).

The recognition-by-components approach we next discuss is especially important because it specifically addresses how people recognize the complex kinds of stimuli that we find in everyday life.

The Recognition-by-Components Theory

Irving Biederman and his colleagues developed a theory to explain how humans recognize three-dimensional shapes (Biederman, 1990, 1995; Hayworth & Biederman, 2006; Kayaert et al., 2003). The basic assumption of their **recognition-by-components theory** is that a specific view of an object can be represented as an arrangement of simple 3-D shapes called **geons**. Just as the letters of the alphabet can be combined into words, geons can be combined to form meaningful objects (Vuong, 2010).

You can see five of the proposed geons in Part A of Figure 2.5. Part B of this figure shows six of the objects that can be constructed from the geons. As you know, letters of the alphabet can be combined to form words with different meanings, depending upon the specific arrangements of the letters. For example, *no* has a different meaning from *on*. Similarly, geons 3 and 5 from Figure 2.5 can be combined to form different meaningful objects. A cup is different from a pail, and the recognition-by-components theory emphasizes the specific way in which these two geons are combined.

(A)   (B)

FIGURE 2.5

Five of the basic geons (A) and representative objects that can be constructed from the geons (B).

Source: Biederman, I. (1990). Higher-level vision. In E. N. Osherson, S. M. Kosslyn, & J. M. Hollerbach (Eds.), *An invitation to cognitive science* (Vol. 2, pp. 41–72). Cambridge, MA: MIT.

In general, an arrangement of three geons gives people enough information to classify an object. Notice, then, that Biederman's recognition-by-components theory is essentially a feature-analysis theory that explains how we recognize three-dimensional objects.

Biederman and his colleagues have conducted fMRI research with humans, and they also recorded neuronal responses in anesthetized monkeys. Their findings show that areas of the cortex beyond the primary visual cortex respond to geons like those in Figure 2.5A (Hayworth & Biederman, 2006; Kayaert et al., 2003). Furthermore, computer-modeling research suggests that young children may initially represent each object as an undifferentiated complete object. In contrast, older children and adults can represent an object as a collection of geons (Doumas & Hummel, 2010).

The recognition-by-components theory does, however, require an important modification, largely as a result of the observation that people recognize objects more quickly when those objects are seen from a standard viewpoint, rather than a much different viewpoint (Friedman et al., 2005; Graf et al., 2005). Notice, for instance, how your own hand would be somewhat difficult to recognize if you look at it from an unusual perspective. One modification of the recognition-by-components theory is called the **viewer-centered approach** this approach proposes that we store a small number of views of three-dimensional objects rather than just one view (Mather, 2006). Suppose that we see an object from an unusual angle, and this object does not match any object shape we have stored in memory. We must then mentally rotate the image of that object until it matches one of the views that are stored in memory (Tarr & Vuong, 2002; Wolfe et al., 2009). This mental rotation may require an additional second or two, and we may not even recognize the object.

At present, both the feature-analysis theory and the recognition-by-components theory (modified to include the viewer-centered approach) can explain some portion of our remarkable object recognition skills. However, researchers must explore whether these theories can account for our ability to recognize objects that are more complicated than isolated cups and pails. For example, how were you able to immediately identify numerous complex objects in the scene you viewed on your television screen in Demonstration 2.1? The theoretical explanations will become more detailed as researchers continue to explore how we recognize real-world objects and scenes using increasingly sophisticated research methods (e.g., Gordon, 2004; Henderson, 2005; Hollingworth, 2006a, 2006b; Wolfe et al., 2009).

Top-Down Processing and Visual Object Recognition

Our discussion so far has emphasized how people recognize isolated objects. We have not yet considered, however, how our knowledge and expectations can aid the recognition process. In real life, when you try to decipher a hastily written letter of the alphabet, the surrounding letters of the word might be helpful. Similarly, the context of a coffee shop is useful when you try to identify an object that consists of a narrow, curved geon that is attached to the side of a wider, cylindrical geon.

Here, we first consider in more detail the differences between bottom-up and top-down processing. We will then consider how these two processes work together in a complementary fashion to help us recognize words during the reading process. Finally, we'll see how we can sometimes make mistakes if our top-down processing is overly active.

Bottom-Up versus Top-Down Processing

So far, this chapter has focused on bottom-up processing. **Bottom-up processing** emphasizes that the stimulus characteristics are important when you recognize an object. Specifically, the physical stimuli from the environment are registered on the sensory receptors. This information is then passed on to higher, more sophisticated levels in the perceptual system (Carlson, 2010; Gordon, 2004).

For example, glance away from your textbook and focus on one specific object that is nearby. Notice its shape, size, color, and other important physical characteristics. When these characteristics are registered on your retina, the object recognition process begins. This information starts with the most basic (or bottom) level of perception, and it works its way up until it reaches the more "sophisticated" cognitive regions of the brain, beyond your primary visual cortex. The combination of simple, bottom-level features helps you recognize more complex, whole objects.

The very first part of visual processing may be bottom-up (Palmer, 2002). An instant later, however, the second process begins. This second process in object recognition is top-down processing. **Top-down processing** emphasizes how a person's concepts, expectations, and memory can influence object recognition.

In more detail, these higher-level mental processes all help in identifying objects. Based on many years of learning about how the world works, you expect certain shapes to be found in certain locations, and you expect to encounter these shapes because of your past experiences. These expectations help you recognize objects very rapidly. In other words, your expectations at the higher (or top) level of visual processing will work their way down and guide our early processing of the visual stimulus (Carlson, 2010; Dikker et al., 2009; Donderi, 2006; Gregory, 2004a).

Think how your top-down processing helped you to quickly recognize the specific nearby object that you selected a moment ago. Your top-down processing made use of your expectations and your memory about objects that are typically nearby. This top-down process then combined together with the specific physical information about the stimulus from bottom-up processing. As a result, you could quickly and seamlessly identify the object (Carlson, 2010). As we noted earlier, object recognition requires both bottom-up and top-down processing (Theme 5). Before you read further, try Demonstration 2.3.

Demonstration 2.3	Context and Pattern Recognition

Can you read the following sentence?

THE MAN RAN.

As you might imagine, top-down processing is strong when a stimulus is registered for just a fraction of a second. Top-down processing is also strong when stimuli are incomplete or ambiguous (Groome, 1999). How does top-down processing operate in vision? Researchers have proposed that specific structures along the route between the retina and the visual cortex may play a role. These structures may store information about the relative likelihood of seeing various visual stimuli in a specific context (Kersten et al., 2004).

Cognitive psychologists think that both bottom-up and top-down processing are necessary to explain the complexities of object recognition (Riddoch & Humphreys, 2001). For example, you recognize a coffee cup because of two almost simultaneous processes: (1) Bottom-up processing forces you to register the component features, such as the curve of the cup's handle; and (2) the context of a coffee shop encourages you to recognize the handle on the cup more quickly, because of top-down processing. Let's now consider how this top-down processing facilitates reading.

b/c you have to use your memory & prev. experience

Top-Down Processing and Reading

As Demonstration 2.3 shows, the same shape—an ambiguous letter—can sometimes be perceived as an H and sometimes as an A. In this demonstration, you began to identify the whole word "THE," and your tentative knowledge of that word helped to identify the second letter as an H. Similarly, your knowledge of the words "MAN" and "RAN" helped you identify that same ambiguous letter as an A in this different context.

Researchers have demonstrated that top-down processing can influence our ability to recognize a variety of objects (e.g., Carreiras et al., 2013; Farmer et al., 2015; Gregory, 2004a; Hollingworth & Henderson, 2004; Kersten et al., 2004; Kutas & Federmeier, 2011; Rahman & Sommer, 2008).

Psychologists who study reading have realized for decades that a theory of recognition must include factors other than the information in the stimulus. When you read, suppose that you do identify each letter by analyzing its features. In addition, suppose that each letter contains four distinctive features, a conservative guess. Taking into account the number of letters in an average word—and the average reading rate—this would mean that you would need to analyze about 5,000 features every minute. This estimate is ridiculously high; your perceptual processes couldn't handle that kind of workload (Dahan, 2010).

Furthermore, we can still manage to read a sentence, even if some of the middle letters in a word have been rearranged. For example, Rayner and his colleagues (2006) found that college students could read normal sentences at the rate of about 255 words per minute. They could still read jumbled sentences such as, "The boy cuold not slove the probelm so he aksed for help." However, their reading rate dropped to 227 words per minute.

One of the most widely demonstrated phenomena in the research on recognition is the word superiority effect. According to the **word superiority effect**, we can identify a single letter more accurately and more rapidly, when it appears in a meaningful word than when it appears alone or in a meaningless string of unrelated letters (Dahan, 2010; Palmer, 2002; Vecera & Lee, 2010). For instance, you can recognize the letter *p* more easily if it appears in a word such as *plan* than if it appears in a nonword such as *pnla*. In fact, dozens of studies have confirmed the importance of top-down processing in letter recognition (e.g., Grainger & Jacobs, 2005; Palmer, 1999; Reicher, 1969; Williams et al., 2006). For example, the letter *s* is quickly recognized in the word *island*, even though the *s* is not pronounced in this word (Krueger, 1992).

Researchers have also shown that the context of a sentence facilitates the recognition of a word in a sentence. For example, people quickly recognize the word *juice* in the sentence, "Mary drank her orange juice," relative to a word that is possible but not expected, such as *water* (Altarriba, et al., 1996; Ashby et al., 2005; Balota et al., 1985; Ehrlich & Rayner, 1981; Kliegl et al., 2004).

Let's discuss one classic study that explored the effects of sentence context on the processing of a word. Rueckl and Oden (1986) demonstrated that both the features of the stimulus and the nature of the context influence word recognition. In other words, both bottom-up and top-down processing operate in a coordinated fashion. These researchers used stimuli that were either letters or letter-like characters. For example, one set of stimuli consisted of a perfectly formed letter *n*, a perfectly formed letter *r*, and three symbols that were intermediate between those two letters. Notice these stimuli arranged along the bottom of Figure 2.6. In each case, this particular stimulus was embedded in the letter sequence "bea-s." As a result, the study included five stimuli that ranged between "beans" and "bears." (In other words, this variable tested the effects of bottom-up processing.)

The nature of the context was also varied by using the sentence frame, "The _____ raised (bears/beans) to supplement his income." The researchers constructed four sentences by filling the blank with a carefully selected term: "lion tamer," "zookeeper," "botanist," and "dairy farmer." You'll notice that a lion tamer and a zookeeper are more likely to raise bears, whereas the botanist and the dairy farmer are more likely to raise beans. Other similar ambiguous letters and sentence frames were also constructed, each using four different nouns or noun phrases. (In other words, this second variable tested the effects of top-down processing.)

Figure 2.6 shows the results of Rueckl and Oden's (1986) study. As you can see, people were definitely more likely to choose the "bears" response when the line segment on the right side of the letter was short, rather than long: The features of the stimulus are extremely important because word recognition operates partly in a bottom-up fashion.

You'll also notice, however, that people were somewhat more likely to choose the "bears" response in the lion tamer and zookeeper sentences than in the botanist and dairy farmer sentences: The context is important because word recognition also operates partly in a top-down fashion. Specifically, our knowledge

FIGURE 2.6
The influence of stimulus features and sentence context on word identification.
Source: Rueckl, J. G., & Oden, G. C. (1986). The integration of contextual and featural information during word identification. *Journal of Memory and Language, 25,* 445–460.

about the world leads us to expect that lion tamers and zookeepers would be more likely to raise bears than beans.

Think about how these context effects can influence your reading speed. The previous letters in a word help you identify the remaining letters more quickly. Furthermore, the other words in a sentence help you identify the individual words more quickly. Without context to help you read faster, you might still be reading the introduction to this chapter!

So far, we have considered only neatly printed text; top-down processing certainly operates in this situation. What happens when you read a note from someone with bad handwriting? A journal article by Anthony Barnhart and Stephen Goldinger (2010) is appropriately titled "Interpreting chicken-scratch: Lexical access for handwritten words." According to this article, when students in this study were reading a handwritten note with sloppy, ambiguous handwriting, they were even more likely to rely on top-down processing than when students were reading neatly printed text.

b/o it prob. wasn't clearly obvi what each letter was

"Smart Mistakes" in Object Recognition

According to Theme 2, our cognitive processes are remarkably efficient and accurate. However, when we occasionally do make a mistake, that error can often be traced to a "smart mistake," such as overusing the strategy of top-down processing. Because we overuse top-down processing, we sometimes demonstrate **change blindness**; we fail to detect a change in an object or a scene. *→ don't see/notice a change*

Overusing top-down processing can also lead us to demonstrate a second mistake, called **inattentional blindness**; when we are paying attention to some events in a scene, we may fail to notice when an unexpected but completely visible object suddenly appears (Most et al., 2005). Let's now consider these two kinds of visual-processing errors. *→ don't notice something that's unusual in a scene*

⌐ ex: bear costume at basketball practice

Change Blindness

Imagine that you are walking along a sidewalk near your college campus. During your stroll, a stranger then approaches you and asks for directions to a particular building. While this conversation is occurring, two people—who are carrying a wooden door sideways—walk between you and this stranger. When they have passed by, the original stranger has been replaced by one of the door-holding strangers. (The door was blocking your vision, so you could not directly see the strangers switching places.) Would you notice that you are no longer talking with the same individual? You may be tempted to reply, "Of course!"

When Daniel Simons and Daniel Levin (1997a, 1997b, 1998) tried this stranger-and-the-door study, only half of the bystanders reported that one stranger had been replaced by a different stranger. Many were still "clueless" when they were explicitly asked, "Did you notice that I'm not the same person who approached you to ask for directions?" (Simons & Levin, 1998, p. 646). Take a moment to try Demonstration 2.4,

| Demonstration 2.4 | Detecting the Difference Between Two Pictures |

Look carefully at the two scenes until you have detected which feature is different. The answer appears in the in-text discussion of this demonstration.

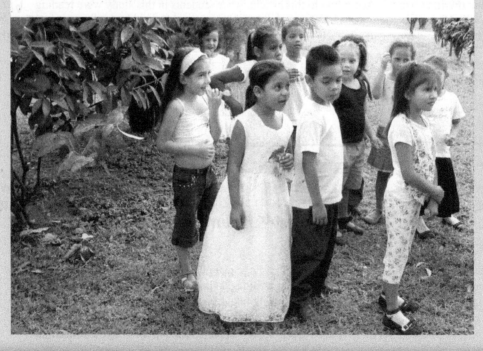

where you'll see two photos of children in a park. How quickly can you detect the difference between these two similar scenes?

To locate the feature that is different in these two photos, look at the little girl with the black top and shorts. In one version, you can see part of a white sock on her left ankle. In the other version, this part of the sock is black.

This chapter examines how we see objects. When perceiving an entire scene, our top-down processing encourages us to assume that the basic meaning of the scene will remain stable. This assumption is rational, and the mistaken perception makes sense (Carlson, 2010; Rensink, 2010; Saylor & Baldwin, 2004). In the real world, one person does not suddenly morph into a different individual!

Laboratory research provides other examples of change blindness. For instance, Rensink and his colleagues (1997) asked participants to look at a photo, which was briefly presented twice. Then a slightly different version of the photo was briefly presented twice. This sequence of alternations was repeated until the participants detected the change.

This result showed that people quickly identified the change when this change was important. For example, when a view of a pilot flying a plane showed a helicopter either nearby or far away, participants required only 4.0 alternations to report the change. In contrast, they required 16.2 alternations to report a change that was unimportant, such as the height of a railing behind two people seated at a table.

Again, these results make sense (Saylor & Baldwin, 2004). The basic meaning of the scene with the pilot is drastically different if the helicopter is nearby, rather than distant. In contrast, the height of the railing doesn't change the actual meaning of the scene at the table.

Additional studies confirm that people are surprisingly blind to fairly obvious changes in the objects that they are perceiving (e.g., Saylor & Baldwin, 2004; Scholl et al., 2004; Simons et al., 2002). In general, when we look at a scene with numerous objects, we typically do not store a detailed representation of every item in that scene (Gillam et al., 2007). Interestingly, this effect also extends to the auditory modality, in an effect termed "Change Deafness." Fenn et al. (2011) demonstrated, for example, that individuals overwhelmingly fail to notice when the voice of a speaker changes in the middle of a telephone conversation (Fenn et al., 2011).

Inattentional Blindness

In general, psychologists use the term *change blindness* when people fail to notice a change in some part of the stimulus. In contrast, they use the term *inattentional blindness* when people fail to notice that a new object has appeared. In both cases, however, people are using top-down processing as they concentrate on some objects in a scene. As a result, when an object appears that is not consistent with their concepts, expectations, and memory, people often fail to recognize this changed object (change blindness) or the introduction of a new object (inattentional blindness).

Let's now consider a dramatic study about inattentional blindness. Simons and Chabris (1999) asked participants to watch a videotape of people playing basketball. These participants were instructed to mentally tally the number of times that members of a specified group made either a bounce pass or an aerial pass. Shortly after the video began, a person dressed in a gorilla suit wandered into the scene and remained there for 5 seconds. Amazingly, 46% of the participants failed to notice the gorilla! Other research confirms that people often fail to notice a new object if they are paying close attention to something else (Chabris & Simons, 2010; Most et al., 2001; Most et al., 2005). Incidentally, Daniel Simons's website contains some interesting demonstrations of his research, including both the "door study," discussed above, as well as the "gorilla study": http://www.simonslab.com./videos.html

As you might imagine, people are more likely to experience inattentional blindness when the primary task is cognitively demanding (Simons & Jensen, 2009). If the primary task in this study had been to monitor moves in a leisurely chess game—rather than moves in basketball—wouldn't people be less likely to experience inattentional blindness?

We have just seen that people frequently make two similar perceptual errors, change blindness and inattentional blindness. Theme 2 of this textbook states that our cognitive processes are remarkably efficient and accurate. How can we reconcile the two kinds of errors with this theme? One important point is that many of the visual stimuli that people fail to see are not high in ecological validity (Rachlinski, 2004). Studies are high in **ecological validity** if the conditions in which the research is conducted are similar to the natural setting where the results will be applied. Frankly, I doubt if anyone reading this book has seen someone in a gorilla suit strolling through a basketball game!

change blindness : fail to notice change

inattentional blindness: fail to notice something new appear

→ esp. when the object is unusual / not expected

Still, you can probably recall a time when you were looking for something and failed to locate it when it was in an unexpected location. Both change blindness and inattentional blindness can also operate in our daily lives.

Simons and Levin (1997a) emphasized that we actually function very well in our normal visual environment. If you are walking along a busy city street, a variety of perceptual representations will rapidly change from one glance to the next. People move their legs, shift a bag to another arm, and disappear behind traffic signs. If you precisely tracked each detail, your visual system would be rapidly overwhelmed by the trivial changes. Instead, your visual system is fairly accurate in creating the "gist," or general interpretation of a scene. You focus only on the information that appears to be important, such as the proximity of an approaching bus as you cross the street, and you ignore unimportant details. Change blindness and inattentional blindness illustrate a point we made in connection with Theme 2: Our cognitive errors can often be traced to a rational strategy.

Specialized Visual Recognition Processes

Up to this point, our exploration of visual recognition has focused primarily on how we perceive letters of the alphabet or a variety of objects. It is interesting to note, however, that the processing of certain types of visual stimuli appears to be supported, at least in part, by neural and cognitive processes that are somewhat specialized. That is, certain parts of the brain are particularly active when presented with a specific class of stimuli. Specialized recognition processes have been proposed for the recognition of faces (e.g., Kanwisher et al., 1997; Sergent et al., 1992), particular locations and spatial layouts (e.g., Epstein & Kanwisher, 1998), and visual words (e.g., Dehaene et al., 2002). These types of stimuli are frequent and highly important for navigating and interpreting one's visual environment. It is thus possible that certain portions of neural tissue become highly specialized over the course of development to support the processing of them (McCandliss et al., 2003).

In this section, we focus on face recognition research. How do you manage to recognize a friend by simply looking at their face? The task ought to be challenging, because all faces have the same general shape. A further complication is that you can recognize the face of your friend Monica, even when you see her face from a different angle, in an unusual setting, and wearing an unexpected frowning expression. Impressively, you manage to overcome all these sources of variation (Esgate & Groome, 2005; McKone, 2004; Styles, 2005). Almost instantly, you perceive that this person is indeed Monica. Notice how important face recognition abilities are for your social life (and think about how strange life would be if you weren't able to recognize individual faces).

As discussed above, we recognize most objects by identifying the individualized features that combine together to create these objects. Researchers emphasize, however, that most people perceive faces in a different fashion from other stimuli. Tanaka and Farah (1993), for example, found that research participants were significantly more accurate in recognizing a facial feature when it appeared within the context of a whole face, rather than in isolation. For example, they recognized a nose in the context of a whole face much more accurately than an isolated nose. The same participants also judged parts of a house. In this "house condition," they were equally accurate in recognizing a house feature (such as a window) within the context of a complete house versus recognizing that window in isolation.

Other research has demonstrated that young infants track the movement of a photographed human face more than any other similar stimuli (Bruce et al., 2003; Johnson & Bolhuis, 2000).

Taken together, this research suggests that face perception is somehow "special" (Farah, 2004; McKone, 2004), in the sense that faces apparently have a special, privileged status in our perceptual system. We recognize faces on a **holistic (recognition) basis**—that is, in terms of their overall shape and structure (Richler et al., 2011). In other words, we perceive a face in terms of its **gestalt,** or overall quality that transcends its individual elements. It makes sense that face perception has a special status given the importance of faces in our social interactions (Fox, 2005; Macrae & Quadflieg, 2010; Styles, 2005).

Neuroscience Research on Face Recognition

Much of the research on face recognition comes from a disability known as prosopagnosia (pronounced "pros-o-pag-*no*-zhe-ah"). People with **prosopagnosia** cannot recognize human faces, though they perceive other objects relatively normally (Farah, 2004).

Consider the case of a woman with prosopagnosia who was in her early 30s, and she had recently completed her PhD. She described an experience when she went to pick up her infant son at his daycare center. "I went to the wrong baby at my son's daycare and only realized that he was not my son when the entire daycare staff looked at me in horrified disbelief" (Duchaine & Nakayama, 2006, p. 166).

Many neuroscience case studies show that individuals with prosopagnosia can easily recognize common objects. For example, a man with prosopagnosia may quickly identify a chair, a coffee cup, or a sweater. He may even look at a woman's smiling face and report that she looks happy. However, he may fail to recognize that this woman is his own wife! Furthermore, people with prosopagnosia often report that the various parts of a person's face—such as the nose, the mouth, and two eyes—seem independent of one another, instead of forming a unified, complete face (Farah, 2004; Gazzaniga et al., 2009).

Prosopagnosia is a difficult disorder to treat, which is particularly unfortunate because those with the disorder report high levels of social anxiety (Yardley et al., 2008). Research on the efficacy of multiple proposed remediation paradigms has produced mixed results, and when studies do report gains in face recognition, they are often modest (Bate et al., 2015; De Hann, Young, & Newcombe, 1991; Ellis & Young, 1988; Powell, Letson, Davidoff, Valentine, & Greenwood, 2008; Schamlzl, Palermo, Green, Brundson, & Coltheart, 2008). Nonetheless, the presence of this disorder is often taken as additional evidence that special mechanisms underlie face processing.

Earlier, we mentioned that the occipital lobe, at the back of your brain, is the location in the part of the cortex that is responsible for the initial, most basic visual processing. Information then travels from the occipital lobe to numerous other locations throughout the brain. The location most responsible for face recognition is the temporal cortex, at the side of your brain (Farah, 2004; Kanwisher et al., 2001; Sinha et al., 2010). The specific location that some think to be specialized for face recognition is known as the fusiform face area. It exists in the lower portion of the temporal cortex (Kanwisher et al., 1997). Researchers have also tested monkeys by using neuroscience recording techniques. They report that certain cells in the inferotemporal cortex respond especially vigorously to a photo of another monkey's face (Rolls & Tovee, 1995; Wang et al., 1996).

Chapter 1 described the **fMRI** technique, a technique for obtaining images of human brain activity. The fMRI studies have demonstrated that the fusiform face area is more activated when an individual is exposed to images of faces. They have shown that the brain responds more quickly to faces presented in the normal, upright position, in comparison to faces presented upside-down (D'Esposito et al., 1999). Similarly, behavioral research shows that people are much more accurate in identifying upright faces compared to upside-down faces, a phenomenon called the **face-inversion effect** (Macrae & Quadflieg, 2010; Wilford & Wells, 2010; Wolfe et al., 2009). This research is far from complete, but it may explain why face perception seems to follow different rules, emphasizing holistic processing rather than isolated components.

It is important to note, however, that there exists a great deal of controversy about how to interpret these and similar neuroscientific data. Although the behavioral data point to certain processing differences for specific classes of stimuli (such as faces), it is less clear that the processing of those stimuli are really supported by—or otherwise localized to—a specific area of cortex. For example, stimuli other than faces seem to produce patterns of activation in the fusiform face area that are similar to the patterns of activity produced by faces. Indeed, some have argued that the fusiform face area is really an area that is sensitive to the processing of stimuli with which individuals have a great deal of expertise (Gauthier et al., 2000). In fact, Gauthier and colleagues (2000) found that when car experts and bird experts were exposed to either cars or birds, respectively, the fusiform face area was activated. Thus, the fusiform face area may not be designed to process only information about faces. As with many topics is cognitive neuroscience, future research will be necessary in order to determine whether or not there are specific neural structures that are designed to process specific classes of visual stimuli.

Applied Research on Face Recognition

As we have noted earlier, many cognitive psychologists now emphasize the importance of ecological validity. The applied research on face recognition focuses on real-life situations that assess our ability to recognize people's faces.

Kemp and his coauthors (1997) studied the accuracy of supermarket cashiers who had been instructed to make judgments about ID photos. Specifically, undergraduate students were given credit cards that showed a 1″ × 1″ color photo of their faces. Each student was told to select some items at a supermarket and then present his or her credit card to the cashier. The cashier could then decide whether to accept or reject the credit card.

When the students carried a credit card that showed their own photo, the cashiers correctly accepted the card 93% of the time. However, when students carried a card that showed a photo of another person—who looked fairly similar—they correctly rejected the photo only 36% of the time. In other words, they let someone with an incorrect photo ID slip past them 64% of the time!

Another applied study on face recognition focused on security surveillance systems. Many banks, businesses, and institutions use a video security system, typically filming people who walk through a door. Burton and coauthors (1999) asked people to look at video clips of psychology professors walking through the entrance of the Department of Psychology at the University of Glasgow in Scotland.

First, all of the participants in the study saw a series of video clips of 10 professors. Next, they all saw a series of high-quality photos of 20 professors; 10 of these professors had appeared in a video, and 10 had not. The participants were instructed to rate each photo using a scale from 1 (indicating certainty that they *had not* seen this person in the video) to 7 (indicating certainty that they *had* seen this person in the video).

Burton and colleagues (1999) also tested three categories of participants. Twenty of the participants had been taught by all 10 professors in the video clips. Twenty were other students who had never been taught by any of these professors, and 10 were experienced police officers who were not familiar with any of the professors.

Figure 2.7 shows the ratings provided by the three categories of participants. As you can see, the students who were familiar with the professors had highly accurate recognition. These students were very confident in identifying the 10 professors who had actually appeared in the videos, and they were also very confident that the other 10 professors had not appeared in the videos.

However, when students were unfamiliar with the professors, they were only slightly more confident about the professors they had actually seen in the video compared to the professors whom they had not seen. Unfortunately, the experienced police officers were no more accurate than the second group of students. Additional research confirms that people are much more accurate in identifying familiar faces than unfamiliar faces (Bruce et al., 2001).

These two applied psychology studies have explored whether people can accurately match two images of a person's face. Other research examines whether people can make accurate judgments about a specific characteristic of a person's face. For example, Matthew Rhodes (2009) reviewed studies in which research participants had tried to guess an unfamiliar person's age. In general, people guessed quite accurately. Notice that this research has an important application when clerks are trying to decide whether a young person is old enough to purchase products such as alcohol or tobacco.

FIGURE 2.7
Participants' confidence about having seen a target person in an earlier video, as a function of kind of observer and whether or not the target person actually appeared in the video.

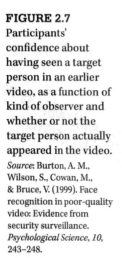

Source: Burton, A. M., Wilson, S., Cowan, M., & Bruce, V. (1999). Face recognition in poor-quality video: Evidence from security surveillance. *Psychological Science, 10*, 243–248.

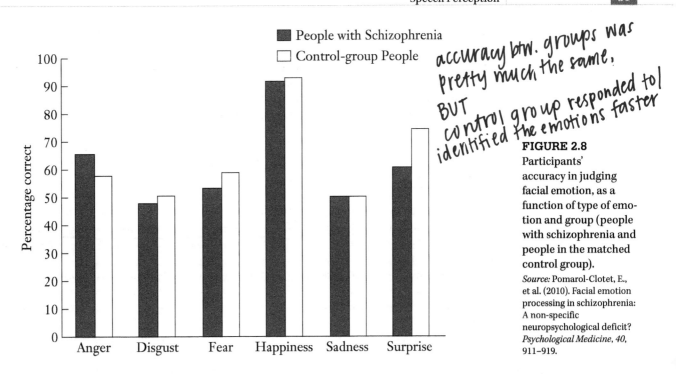

accuracy btw. groups was pretty much the same, BUT control group responded to/ identified the emotions faster

FIGURE 2.8
Participants' accuracy in judging facial emotion, as a function of type of emotion and group (people with schizophrenia and people in the matched control group).
Source: Pomarol-Clotet, E., et al. (2010). Facial emotion processing in schizophrenia: A non-specific neuropsychological deficit? *Psychological Medicine, 40,* 911–919.

Face recognition research can also shed light on how individuals with clinical diagnoses process visual information differently than those without similar diagnoses. A good example of this interdisciplinary research focuses on the relationship between schizophrenia and face identification.

Schizophrenia is one of the most serious psychological disorders. People with **schizophrenia** typically do not show intense emotions, and they may have hallucinations. For students studying cognitive psychology, an especially important facet is disordered *thinking*. Furthermore, individuals with schizophrenia tend to perform poorly on many cognitive tasks (Reichenberg & Harvey, 2007)

Researchers have also reported that people with schizophrenia seem to have difficulty in perceiving faces and facial expressions (Bediou et al., 2005; Hall et al., 2004; Martin et al., 2005). However, Edith Pomarol-Clotet and colleagues (2010) hypothesized that this poor performance in judging faces might be due to more general problems on cognitive tasks, rather than a specific difficulty with faces. These researchers therefore carefully matched their two samples, a group of 22 individuals with schizophrenia and 20 community members without schizophrenia. The two groups were matched with respect to their score on an intelligence test, as well as age and gender.

Each person judged a standardized set of 60 photographs of people's faces; these photos have been widely used in research on facial expression. There were 10 photographs for each of six emotions, and each photo showed a moderate amount of the specified emotion. As you can see in Figure 2.8, the two groups of people had similar accuracy rates. Further analyses showed no significant difference between the two groups on any of the six emotions. However, the individuals in the control group responded significantly *faster* than the individuals with schizophrenia, consistent with previous research (Pomarol-Clotet et al., 2010). It's not clear why the two groups had similar scores, but matching for intelligence may be an important factor.

Speech Perception

Speech perception seems perfectly easy and straightforward. . .until you begin to think about everything you must accomplish in order to perceive a spoken sentence. During **speech perception**, your auditory system must record the sound vibrations generated by someone talking. The system must then translate these vibrations into a sequence of sounds that you perceive to be speech. Adults who speak English produce about 15 sounds every second (Kuhl, 1994). Therefore, you must somehow perceive about 900 sounds each minute.

In order to perceive a word, you must distinguish the sound pattern of one word from the tens of thousands of irrelevant words that are stored in your memory. And—as if these tasks are not challenging enough—you must separate the voice of the speaker from the irrelevant background noises. This background typically includes other simultaneous conversations as well as a wide variety of nonspeech sounds (Brown & Sinnott, 2006; Mattys & Liss, 2008; Plack, 2005). In fact, it's astonishing that we ever manage to perceive spoken language!

Speech perception is extremely complex, and you can locate more details in other textbooks (Foley & Matlin, 2010; Goldstein, 2010b; Wolfe et al., 2009). We'll consider two aspects of speech perception in this section: (1) characteristics of speech perception and (2) theories of speech perception.

Characteristics of Speech Perception

The next time you listen to a radio announcer, pay attention to the sounds you are hearing rather than the meaning of the words. When describing these speech sounds, psychologists and linguists use the term *phoneme* (pronounced "*foe*-neem"). A phoneme is the basic unit of spoken language, such as the sounds *a*, *k*, and *th*. The English language uses between 40 and 45 phonemes, a number that includes both vowels and consonants (Dahan, 2010). When you listen to spoken English, you may think that you hear brief quiet periods throughout this string of sounds. However, most of the words are simply run together in a continuous series.

In the text that follows, we consider several important characteristics of speech perception.

Word Boundaries

Have you ever heard a conversation in an unfamiliar language? The words may seem to run together in a continuous stream, with no boundaries of silence to separate them. You may think that the boundaries between words seem much more distinct in English—almost as clear-cut as the white spaces that identify the boundaries between any two adjacent words in this textbook. In most cases, however, the actual acoustical stimulus of spoken language shows no clear-cut pauses to mark the boundaries. An actual physical event—such as a pause—marks a word boundary less than 40% of the time (Davis et al., 2002; McQueen, 2005; Sell & Kaschak, 2009).

Impressively, we are rarely conscious that it is difficult to resolve word boundaries. The research shows that our speech recognition system initially considers several different hypotheses about how to divide a phrase into words. This system immediately and effortlessly uses our knowledge about language in order to place the boundaries in appropriate locations (Grossberg et al., 2004; McQueen, 2005; Pitt, 2009; Samuel, 2011). Fortunately, this knowledge usually leads us to the correct conclusions.

Variability in Phoneme Pronunciation

Perceiving phonemes does not initially seem like a challenging task. After all, don't we simply hear a phoneme and instantly perceive it? Actually, phoneme perception is not that easy. For example, speakers vary tremendously in the pitch and tone of their voices, as well as their rate of producing phonemes (McQueen, 2005; Plack, 2005; Uchanski, 2005).

Inter-speaker variability is the term used to refer to the observation that different speakers of the same language produce the same sound differently. Factors such as the speaker's gender, age, and regional dialect all contribute to interspeaker variability in phoneme pronunciation (Bent & Holt, 2017). Imagine, for example, how different the *r* in *ran* would sound coming from a four-year-old female speaker relative to a 60-year-old male speaker (Magloughlin, 2016).

A second source of variability is that speakers often fail to produce phonemes in a precise fashion (Foley & Matlin, 2010; Pitt, 2009; Plack, 2005). Try Demonstration 2.5 to appreciate the problem of sloppy pronunciation that listeners must decode.

Demonstration 2.5	Variability in Phoneme Pronunciation

Turn on the radio and locate a station on which you hear someone talking. After hearing one or two sentences, turn the radio off, and write down the two sentences. Try to determine whether the speaker produced each phoneme in a precise fashion. For instance, did the speaker omit some portion of a word (e.g., *sposed* instead of *supposed*)? Did he or she pronounce consonants such as *k* or *p* precisely? Now try pronouncing the words in each sentence very carefully, so that every phoneme can be clearly identified.

A third source of variability is called **coarticulation**. When you are pronouncing a particular phoneme, your mouth remains in somewhat the same shape it was when you pronounced the previous phoneme; in addition, your mouth is preparing to pronounce the next phoneme. As a result, the phoneme you produce varies slightly from time to time, depending upon the surrounding phonemes (Conway et al., 2010; Diehl et al., 2004; McQueen, 2005). For example, notice that the *d* in *idle* sounds different from the *d* in *don't*.

Context and Speech Perception

People are active listeners, consistent with Theme 1. Instead of passively receiving speech sounds, we can use context as a cue to help us figure out a sound or a word (Cleary & Pisoni, 2001; Warren, 2006). We saw earlier in this chapter that context and other top-down factors influence visual perception. Top-down factors also influence speech perception (Theme 5), because we use our vast knowledge about language to help us perceive ambiguous words.

For example, when you are listening to your professors' lectures, extraneous noises will sometimes mask a phoneme. People knock books off desks, cough, turn pages, and whisper. Still, without much effort, you can usually reconstruct the missing sound. People tend to show **phonemic restoration**. They can fill in a missing phoneme, using contextual meaning as a cue (Conway et al., 2010).

In a classic study, Warren and Warren (1970) showed that people are skilled at using the meaning of a sentence to select the correct word from several options. They played tape recordings of several sentences for their research participants:

1. It was found that the *eel was on the axle.

2. It was found that the *eel was on the shoe.

3. It was found that the *eel was on the orange.

The researchers inserted a coughing sound in the location indicated by the asterisk. These spoken sentences were identical with one exception: A different word was spliced onto the end of each sentence. The results showed that people typically heard the "word" *eel as *wheel* in the first sentence, *heel* in the second sentence, and *peel* in the third. In this study, then, people were able to reconstruct the missing word on the basis of a context cue at the end of the sentence, which occurred four words later!

Notice that phonemic restoration is a kind of illusion. People think they hear a phoneme, even though the correct sound vibrations never reach their ears. Phonemic restoration is a well-documented phenomenon, and it has been demonstrated in numerous studies (Liederman et al., 2011; Samuel, 2011; Warren, 2006). Our ability to perceive a word on the basis of context also allows us to overcome a speaker's sloppy pronunciations, the problem we mentioned earlier.

One important explanation for the influence of context on perception is top-down processing, although researchers have offered additional explanations (Foley & Matlin, 2010; Grossberg et al., 2004; Plack, 2005). The top-down processing approach argues that we use our knowledge about language to facilitate recognition, whether we are looking at objects or listening to speech.

Perceiving language is not merely a passive process in which words flow into our ears, providing data for bottom-up processing. Instead, we actively use our knowledge about language to create expectations about what we might hear (Brown, Salverda, Dilley, & Tanenhaus, 2011; Dahan & Tanenhaus, 2004; Kleinschmidt & Jaeger, 2015; Magnuson et al., 2008).

Visual Cues as an Aid to Speech Perception

Try Demonstration 2.6 when you have the opportunity. This simple exercise illustrates how visual cues contribute to speech perception (Gazzaniga et al., 2009; Smyth et al., 1994). Information from the speaker's lips and face helps to resolve ambiguities from the speech signal. Similarly, you can hear conversation more accurately when you closely watch the speaker's lips, instead of listening to a conversation over the phone (Massaro & Stork, 1998). Even with a superb phone connection, you miss the lip cues that would inform you whether the speaker was discussing *Harry* or *Mary*.

Researchers have demonstrated that we integrate visual cues with auditory cues during speech perception—even if we don't recognize the usefulness of these visual cues (Nicholls et al., 2004). These results have been replicated for speakers of English, Spanish, Japanese, and Dutch (Massaro, 1998; Massaro et al., 1995).

Demonstration 2.6 ‖ Visual Cues and Speech Perception

The next time you are in a room with both a television and a radio, try this exercise. Switch the TV set to the news or some other program where someone is talking straight to the camera; keep the volume low. Now turn on your radio and tune it between two stations, so that it produces a hissing noise. Turn the radio's volume up until you have difficulty understanding what the person on television is saying. The radio's "white noise" should nearly mask the speaker's voice. Face the TV screen and close your eyes; try to understand the spoken words. Then open your eyes. Do you find that speech perception is now much easier?

Source: Based on Smyth et al., 1987.

Research by McGurk and MacDonald (1976) provides a classic illustration of the contribution of visual cues to speech perception. These researchers showed participants a video of a woman whose lips were producing simple syllables, such as "gag." Meanwhile, the researchers presented different auditory information (coming from the same machine), such as "bab."

When the observers were asked to report what they perceived, their responses usually reflected a compromise between these two discrepant sources of information. In this case, the listeners typically reported hearing the word "dad." The **McGurk effect** refers to the influence of visual information on speech perception, when individuals must integrate both visual and auditory information (Beauchamp et al., 2010; Rosenblum, 2005; Samuel, 2011).

[margin note: when sight and sound must be integrated ...]

Michael Beauchamp and colleagues (2010) have identified the location within the cerebral cortex that gives rise to the McGurk effect. This region is called the superior temporal sulcus. (In Figure 2.1, this region is located in the right side of the horizontal groove along the center of the temporal lobe of the cortex.) This discovery makes sense, because previous research shows that this region is responsible for other tasks where sight and sound must be integrated (Hein & Knight, 2008).

In summary, then, we manage to perceive speech by overcoming the problems of a less-than-ideal speech stimulus. We do so by ignoring the variability in phoneme pronunciation and by using context to resolve ambiguous phonemes. If we can watch the speaker who is producing the stream of speech, the visual information from the speaker's lips provides additional helpful clues.

Theories of Speech Perception

[margin note: 2 categories of speech perception theories: 1. we have a special mechanism for it 2. same gen. mechanisms handle both other cog. processes & speech perception]

Most current theoretical approaches to speech perception fall into one of two categories. Some theorists believe that we humans must have a special mechanism in our nervous system that explains our impressive skill in speech perception. Others admire humans' skill in speech perception, but they argue that the same general mechanisms that handle other cognitive processes also handle speech perception.

Earlier in this chapter, we examined two theories of visual pattern perception. Unfortunately, researchers have not developed such detailed theories for speech perception. One reason for this problem is that humans are the only species who can understand spoken language. As a result, cognitive neuroscientists have a limited choice of research techniques.

The Special Mechanism Approach

[margin note: suggests we process speech more quickly and accurately than other types of sound]

According to the **special mechanism approach** (also called the **speech-is-special approach**), humans are born with a specialized device that allows us to decode speech stimuli (Samuel, 2011). As a result, we process speech sounds more quickly and accurately than other auditory stimuli, such as instrumental music.

Supporters of the special mechanism approach argue that humans possess a **phonetic module** (or a **speech module**), a special-purpose neural mechanism that specifically processes all aspects of speech perception; it cannot handle other kinds of auditory perception. This phonetic module would presumably enable listeners to perceive ambiguous phonemes accurately. It would also help you to segment the blurred stream of auditory information that reaches your ears, so that you can perceive distinct phonemes and words (Liberman, 1996; Liberman & Mattingly, 1989; Todd et al., 2006).

The special mechanism approach to speech perception suggests that the brain is organized in an unusual way. Specifically, the module that handles speech perception would *not* rely on the general cognitive functions discussed throughout this book—functions such as recognizing objects, remembering events, and solving problems (Trout, 2001). One argument in favor of the phonetic module was thought to be categorical perception. Early researchers asked people to listen to a series of ambiguous sounds, such as a sound halfway between a *b* and a *p*. People who heard these sounds typically showed **categorical perception**; they heard either a clear-cut *b* or a clear-cut *p*, rather than a sound partway between a *b* and a *p* (Liberman & Mattingly, 1989).

When the special mechanism approach was originally proposed, supporters argued that people show categorical perception for speech sounds, but they hear nonspeech sounds as a smooth continuum. However, research shows that humans also exhibit categorical perception for some complex nonspeech sounds (Esgate & Groome, 2005).

The General Mechanism Approaches

Although some still favor the special mechanism approach (Trout, 2001), most theorists now favor one of the general mechanism approaches (e.g., Cleary & Pisoni, 2001; Conway et al., 2010; Holt & Lotto, 2008; Toscano et al., 2010; Wolfe et al., 2009). The **general mechanism approaches** argue that we can explain speech perception without proposing any special phonetic module. People who favor these approaches believe that humans use the same neural mechanisms to process both speech sounds and nonspeech sounds (Foley & Matlin, 2010). Speech perception is therefore a learned ability—indeed, a very impressive learned ability—but it is not really "special."

Current research seems to favor the general mechanism approach. As we just noted, humans exhibit categorical perception for complex nonspeech sounds. Other research supporting the general mechanism viewpoint uses event-related potentials (ERPs). This research demonstrates that adults show the same sequence of shifts in the brain's electrical potential, whether they are listening to speech or to music (Patel et al., 1998).

Other evidence against the phonetic module is that people's judgments about phonemes are definitely influenced by visual cues, as we saw in the discussion of the McGurk effect (Beauchamp et al., 2010; Rosenblum, 2005; Samuel, 2011). If speech perception can be influenced by visual information, then it becomes more difficult to argue that a special phonetic module handles all aspects of speech perception.

Researchers have developed several different general mechanism theories of speech perception (e.g., Fowler & Galantucci, 2005; McQueen, 2005; Todd et al., 2006). These theories tend to argue that speech perception proceeds in stages and that it depends upon familiar cognitive processes such as feature recognition, learning, and decision making.

In summary, our ability to perceive speech sounds is impressive. However, this ability can probably be explained by our general perceptual abilities—combined with our other cognitive abilities—rather than any special, inborn speech mechanism. We manage to distinguish speech sounds in the same way we manage a wide variety of complex cognitive skills.

SECTION SUMMARY POINTS

Overview of Visual Object Recognition

1. Perception uses previous knowledge to gather and interpret the stimuli registered by the senses; in object recognition, we identify a complex arrangement of sensory stimuli.

2. Visual information from the retina is transmitted to the primary visual cortex; other regions of the cortex are also active when we recognize objects.

3. According to gestalt principles, people tend to organize their perceptions, even when they encounter ambiguous figure–ground stimuli and even in illusory-contour stimuli, when no boundary actually separates the figure from the background.

4. Feature-analysis theory is one theory of object recognition; it is supported by research showing that people require more time to make a decision about two letters of the alphabet when those

letters share many critical features. This theory is also supported by neuroscience research.

5. The recognition-by-components theory argues that objects are represented in terms of an arrangement of simple 3-D shapes called "geons." Furthermore, according to the viewer-centered approach, we also store several alternative views of these 3-D shapes, as viewed from different angles.

Top-Down Processing and Visual Object Recognition

1. Bottom-up processing emphasizes the importance of the stimulus in object recognition; in contrast, top-down processing emphasizes how a person's concepts, expectations, and memory influence object recognition. Both processes work together to allow us to recognize objects.

2. When we read, context can facilitate recognition; for example, the word superiority effect shows that we can identify a single

letter more accurately and more rapidly when it appears in a meaningful word than when it appears by itself or in a meaningless string of letters.

3. During reading, the context of a sentence influences how we identify a word in that sentence.

4. Overactive top-down processing can also encourage us to make two kinds of errors: (a) change blindness, or errors in recognizing that an object has changed—for instance, a different man is now carrying a door; and (b) inattentional blindness, or failing to notice that a new object has appeared—for instance, a gorilla suddenly appears in a basketball game.

Specialized Visual Recognition Processes

1. People can quickly recognize the faces of people they know; we seem to process a face in terms of its gestalt, or its overall shape and structure.

2. A variety of neuroscience methods—including research with people who have prosopagnosia, research with monkeys, and the fMRI technique—have shown that cells in the inferotemporal cortex play a role in perceiving faces.

3. Applied research suggests that people are not very accurate in judging whether a photo matches the face of the cardholder. Furthermore, people are not very accurate in judging whether a photo of an unfamiliar person matches a person in a video that they saw earlier.

4. Individuals with schizophrenia can identify facial emotion as accurately as people in a control group, when the two groups are matched for age, gender, and intelligence, although individuals with schizophrenia typically take longer to make these decisions.

CHAPTER REVIEW QUESTIONS

1. Think of a person whom you know well, who has never had a course in cognitive psychology. How would you describe perception to this person? As part of your description, provide examples of two visual tasks and two auditory tasks that this person performs frequently. Provide relevant details, using terms from the key list for this chapter.

2. Imagine that you are trying to read a sloppily written number that appears in a friend's class notes. You conclude that it is an 8, rather than a 6 or a 3. Why would the feature-analysis approach explain this better than an approach that requires matching the number with a specific template?

3. Look up from your book and notice two nearby objects. Describe the characteristics of each "figure," in contrast to the "ground." How would Biederman's recognition-by-components theory describe how you recognize these objects?

4. Distinguish between bottom-up and top-down processing, with respect to vision. Explain how top-down processing can help you recognize the letters of the alphabet in the word "alphabet." How would the word superiority effect operate if you tried to identify one letter in the word "alphabet," if this printed word were presented very quickly on your computer? If you were trying to read a friend's barely legible handwriting, would your

Speech Perception

1. Speech perception is an extremely complicated process; it demonstrates that humans can quickly perform impressively complex cognitive tasks.

2. Even when the acoustical stimulus contains no clear-cut pauses, people are very accurate in determining the boundaries between adjacent words.

3. The pronunciation of a specific phoneme varies greatly, depending upon the vocal characteristics of the speaker, imprecise pronunciation, and the variability caused by coarticulation.

4. When a sound is missing from speech, listeners frequently demonstrate phonemic restoration, using context to help them perceive the missing sound.

5. People use visual cues to facilitate speech perception, as illustrated by the McGurk effect; the superior temporal sulcus is a part of the cortex that integrates sight and sound, and this integration also helps to account for the McGurk effect.

6. According to the special mechanism approach to speech perception, humans have a special brain device (or module) that allows us to perceive phonemes more quickly and accurately than nonspeech sounds.

7. The current evidence supports a general mechanism approach to speech perception, rather than a special mechanism; research suggests that humans perceive speech sounds in the same way we perceive nonspeech sounds.

top-down processing increase or decrease, relative to reading a printed word on your computer screen?

5. This chapter emphasizes visual and auditory object recognition, but it can also apply to the other senses. How would top-down processing (e.g., prior knowledge) operate when you smell a certain fragrance and try to identify it? Then answer this question for both taste and touch.

6. According to the material in this chapter, face recognition seems to be "special," and it probably differs from other visual recognition tasks. Discuss this statement, mentioning research about the comparison between faces and other visual stimuli. Be sure to describe material from neuroscience research on this topic.

7. We examined research comparing people with schizophrenia and without schizophrenia, with respect to identifying facial expressions. What did this study find? Why might the results of this study differ from the results of previous research about schizophrenia?

8. Our visual world and our auditory world are both richly complicated. Describe several ways in which the complexity of the proximal stimuli is challenging, when we try to determine

the "true" distal stimuli. How does the gestalt approach help to explain visual perception? What factors help us overcome the difficulties in recognizing everyday speech?

9. What kinds of evidence support the general mechanism approach to speech perception? Contrast this approach with the special mechanism approach. How could the special mechanism approach be applied to our skill in perceiving faces?

10. Throughout this book, we will emphasize that the research from cognitive psychology can be applied to numerous everyday situations. For example, you learned some practical applications of the research on face perception. Skim through this chapter and describe at least five other practical applications of the research on visual and auditory recognition.

KEYWORDS

perception
object recognition
pattern recognition
distal stimulus
proximal stimulus
retina
sensory memory
iconic memory
visual sensory memory
primary visual cortex
gestalt psychology

figure
ground
ambiguous figure–ground
    relationship
illusory contours
subjective contours
templates
feature-analysis theories
distinctive feature
recognition-by-
    components

theory
geons
viewer-centered approach
bottom-up processing
top-down processing
word superiority effect
change blindness
inattentional blindness
ecological validity
holistic (recognition)
gestalt

prosopagnosia
fMRI
face-inversion effect
schizophrenia
speech perception
phoneme
inter-speaker variability
coarticulation
phonemic restoration
McGurk effect

special mechanism
    approach
speech-is-special
    approach
phonetic module
speech module
categorical perception
general mechanism
    approaches

RECOMMENDED READINGS

Chabris, C. F., & Simons, D. J. (2010). *The invisible gorilla and other ways our intuitions deceive us.* New York: Crown. This book, written for a general audience, provides details on the counterintuitive findings discussed in the "Smart Mistakes" section of this chapter.

Gazzaniga, M. S., Ivry, R. B., & Mangun, G. R. (2009). *Cognitive neuroscience: The biology of the mind* (3rd ed.). New York: Norton. Here's an excellent book that provides many details on the neuroscience related to cognition. The book also includes topics beyond the scope of your textbook, such as emotion and developmental neuroanatomy.

Goldstein, E. B. (Ed.). (2010). *Encyclopedia of perception.* Thousand Oaks, CA: Sage. This two-volume resource examines a wide variety of topics, providing several pages on each entry. The topics include many described in this chapter, but also intriguing topics you might not have considered, such as auditory agnosia, body perception, and phantom-limb sensations.

Henderson, J. M. (Ed.). (2005). *Real-world scene perception.* Hove, UK: Psychology Press. Most of the chapters in your textbook focus on how we perceive isolated objects. This interesting book addresses more complicated questions about how we perceive scenes in the everyday world.

3 Attention and Consciousness

Chapter Introduction

Take a few minutes to pay attention to your attention. First, look around you and try to take in as many visual objects as possible. If you are reading this book in a room, for instance, try to notice all the objects that surround you. Be sure to notice their shape, size, location, and color. Assuming that you're reading in a typical room, there's a good chance that you find yourself surrounded by many objects. If you're reading this chapter at your university library, you might find that you are surrounded not only by a complex array of visual objects, but by other people as well. In either case, if you try to focus your attention on all objects and people in your environment, you'll soon feel that your attention is overworked. You might even get a headache.

Now continue this same exercise, but also try to notice every sound in your environment, such as the hum of a computer, the noise of a clock ticking, or the quiet chatter of two people who are whispering to one another. Next, try to maintain all these visual and auditory stimuli, but also notice your skin senses. Can you feel the pressure that your watch creates on your wrist, and can you sense a slight itch or a subtle pain? If you somehow manage to pay simultaneous attention to your vision, hearing, and skin senses, try expanding your attention to include smell and taste. You'll easily discover that you cannot attend to everything at once (Chun et al., 2011; Cowan, 2005). In other words, "We don't have the brains for it" (Wolfe et al., 2009, p. 189). Interestingly, though, we seldom give much thought to our attention. Instead, attention just "happens," and similar to visual processing, it seems as natural to us as breathing (LaBerge, 1995). Attention is involved in just about any cognitive task that you perform on a daily basis, such that we examine it early in this textbook.

We will begin our discussion by considering the distinction between divided and selective attention and will discuss experimental tasks that are often used to study each of these processes. After this basic overview of attention, we examine the influence of attention in the domain of reading. Reading is an effortful cognitive process that relies heavily on your attentional abilities. Examining the role of attention in reading will provide you with a concrete example of how attention intersects with other cognitive processes. Our third and fourth sections explore biological and theoretical explanations for attention. The final topic of the chapter, consciousness, focuses on our awareness about the external world and our cognitive processes.

Overview of Attention

Attention can be defined as a concentration of mental activity that allows you to take in a limited portion of the vast stream of information available from both your sensory world and your memory (Shomstein, 2010; Styles, 2006; Weierich & Barrett, 2010). Meanwhile, the unattended items lose out, and they are not processed in detail. Notice, then, that attention is a vitally important "gatekeeper." It allows you to direct your mental effort toward thoughts and environmental stimuli that are most important to you given your current goals. At the same time, your attentional systems allow you to filter out information that is not useful or important given your current goal state. Without attention, you would have to devote an equal amount of mental effort to every thought and environmental stimulus that could be available to you at some point in time. Certainly, you can appreciate how difficult it would be to complete any one task under such overwhelming circumstances.

As is the case for almost every topic covered in this textbook, attention tasks rely on both bottom-up and top-down processing. Specifically, we sometimes concentrate our mental activity because an interesting stimulus in the environment has captured our attention (*bottom-up processing*). For example, an object in your peripheral vision might suddenly move, and you turn your head to see it more clearly. Other times, we concentrate our mental activity because we want to pay attention to some specific stimulus (*top-down processing*). For example, you might be searching for a particular friend in a crowded cafeteria.

By the end of this chapter, you should come to have an appreciation for the fact that the word "attention" does not refer to one process or one system. Instead, it refers to multiple coordinated systems and processes that together provide you with the ability to strategically allocate your attention.

In this first section, we focus on the historical distinction between divided versus selective attention. Given the importance of selective attention for many cognitive tasks, we then examine three types of tasks that have been used to scientifically study selective attention. We also consider some key insights into the nature of selective attention that have been learned through research using these tasks.

Divided Attention

In a **divided-attention task**, you try to pay attention to two or more simultaneous messages, responding appropriately to each message. You may try to use *divided attention*, for example, when concentrating on both your professor's lecture and a nearby whispered conversation between two students.

When attempting to equally divide your attention between two or more messages, both your speed and your accuracy suffer. These problems are especially likely if the tasks are challenging—for instance, if two people are talking quickly to you at the same time (Chabris & Simons, 2010; Folk, 2010; Proctor & Vu, 2010), or if you are trying to attend to multiple locations at the same time (Ester et al., 2014).

When people **multitask**, they try to accomplish two or more tasks at the same time (Salvucci & Taatgen, 2008). When people are multitasking, they strain the limits of attention, as well as the limits of their working memory and their long-term memory (Logie et al., 2011). Recent research focuses on people who use their cell phones while they are also engaged in another cognitive task. For example, college students walk more slowly when they are talking on cell phones (Hyman, 2010). Furthermore, the research shows that college students read their textbooks significantly more slowly when they are responding to instant messages.

According to the research, students also earn lower grades when they are tested on the material they had been reading while multitasking (Bowman et al., 2010). They may *believe* that they can multitask, but the research does not support this illusion (Willingham, 2010). A general guideline is that you'll typically perform faster and more accurately if you work on one task at a time (Chabris & Simons, 2010).

This research on divided attention also has specific implications for people who use cell phones while driving. Many U.S. states and Canadian provinces have passed laws prohibiting the use of handheld cell phones and text messaging during driving. The studies show that people make significantly more driving errors when they are having a conversation on a handheld cell phone, compared to driving without conversation (Folk, 2010; Kubose et al., 2006; Strayer & Drews, 2007). In a representative study, Collet and his coauthors (2009) tested people while they were talking on a handheld cell phone and driving in a simulated-driving task. Their reaction times were about 20% slower than without the cell phone conversation. Unfortunately, even a hands-free cell phone causes problems with divided attention (Chabris & Simons, 2010; Folk, 2010). For instance, in heavy-traffic conditions, Strayer and his colleagues (2003) found that the people in the hands-free cell phone group took significantly longer to apply the brakes, compared to those in a control group.

In further testing, Strayer and his colleagues discovered that the participants who used cell phones showed a form of inattentional blindness (as discussed in Chapter 2). For example, their attention was reduced for information that appeared in the center of their visual field. Even if you use a hands-free cell phone, your attention may wander away from a dangerous situation right in front of you! Furthermore, if you are the driver, do not allow any passenger to carry on a cell phone conversation. This is even more distracting than a conversation between you and your passenger. Apparently, if you hear half of a conversation, it's less predictable. Therefore, drivers are distracted by trying to guess the content of the other half of the conversation (Emberson et al., 2010).

Task switching is closely related to multitasking. If you are deeply engrossed in writing a research paper and your roommate keeps interrupting, you are likely to work more slowly and make more errors during the transitions (Kiesel et al., 2010; Vandierendonck et al., 2010).

Selective Attention

As you've just read, a divided-attention task requires people to try to pay *equal* attention to two or more kinds of information. In contrast, a **selective-attention task** requires people to pay attention to certain kinds of information while ignoring other ongoing information (Gazzaniga et al., 2009; Wolfe et al., 2009). You might sometimes wish that you could follow two conversations simultaneously. However, imagine the chaos you would experience if you simultaneously paid attention to all the information registered by your senses. You would notice hundreds of simultaneous sights, sounds, tastes, smells, and touch sensations. You could not focus your mental activity enough to respond appropriately to just a few of these sensations. Fortunately, then, selective attention actually simplifies our lives. As Theme 2 suggests, our cognitive apparatus is impressively well designed. Features such as selective attention—which could at face value seem to be drawbacks—may actually be beneficial (Gazzaniga et al., 2009; Shomstein, 2010).

We will now consider three different kinds of selective-attention tasks: Dichotic listening, the Stroop Effect, and Visual Search.

Dichotic Listening

You've probably held a phone to one ear to hear an important message, while your other ear registers the words from a loud nearby conversation. This situation is known as *dichotic listening* (pronounced "die-*kot*-ick").

In the laboratory, **dichotic listening** is studied by asking people to wear earphones; one message is presented to the left ear, and a different message is presented to the right ear. Typically, the research participants are asked to **shadow** the message in one ear. That is, they listen to that message and repeat it after the speaker. If the listener makes mistakes in shadowing, then the researcher knows that the listener is not paying appropriate attention to that specified message (Styles, 2005).

In the classic research, people noticed very little about the unattended second message (Cherry, 1953; Gazzaniga et al., 2009; McAdams & Drake, 2002). For example, people didn't even notice that the second message was sometimes switched from English words to German words. People did notice, however, when the voice of the unattended message was switched from male to female.

In general, people can process only one message at a time (Cowan, 2005). However, people are more likely to process the unattended message when (1) both messages are presented slowly, (2) the main task is not challenging, and (3) the meaning of the unattended message is immediately relevant (e.g., Duncan, 1999; Harris & Pashler, 2004; Marsh et al., 2007). In addition, when people perform a dichotic listening task, they sometimes notice when their name is inserted in the unattended message (Clump, 2006; Gazzaniga et al., 2009; Wood & Cowan, 1995). Have you ever attended a social gathering when you are surrounded by many simultaneous conversations? Even if you are paying close attention to one conversation, you may notice if your name is mentioned in a nearby conversation; this phenomenon is sometimes called the **cocktail party effect**. ← *hear your name even though you're not actively listening for it*

In one study, for example, Wood and Cowan (1995) found that about one-third of the participants reported hearing their name in the message that they were supposed to ignore. But why did the participants *ignore* their own name about two-thirds of the time? One possible explanation is that the Wood and Cowan study was conducted in a laboratory, so this research may not have high ecological validity (Baker, 1999). In an unstructured social setting, your attention may easily wander to other intriguing conversations. Furthermore, the capacity of a person's working memory could help to explain why some people hear their name, but others do not. As we'll see in Chapter 4, **working memory** is the brief, immediate memory for material that we are currently processing. Conway and his coauthors (2001) found that students who had a high working-memory capacity noticed their name only 20% of the time. In contrast, students with a low working-memory capacity noticed their name 65% of the time on the same dichotic-listening task. Apparently, people with a relatively low capacity have difficulty blocking out the irrelevant information such as their name (Cowan, 2005). In other words, they are easily distracted from the task they are supposed to be completing.

In summary, when people's attention is divided, they can sometimes notice characteristics of unattended messages, such as the speaker's gender and whether their own name is mentioned. On the other hand, under more challenging conditions, they may not even notice whether the unattended message is in English or in a foreign language.

So far, we have emphasized a type of selective attention that focuses on hearing, using the dichotic-listening task. The remaining topics in this section focus on vision.

The Stroop Effect

Imagine a situation in which you are presented with a series of colored squares (red, green, blue, etc.) and are asked to name the color of each square. Now, imagine a different situation in which you are presented with a series of words for colors (the words "RED", "GREEN", "BLUE", etc.). In this situation, however, the color-based meanings of the words are incongruent with the ink colors in which the words are printed (for example, the word "RED" printed in yellow ink). In either condition, your task is to say out loud the names of the ink colors as quickly as possible. For example, in the colored-square condition, your task would be to say "blue" if the color of the square is indeed blue, whereas in the incongruent word condition discussed above, the correct response would be "yellow."

Do you think it would take you longer to name the ink color of the colored square or the ink color of the incongruent word?

The task described above is designed to illuminate what is now famously known as the Stroop effect, named after James R. Stroop (1935). According to the **Stroop effect**, people take a long time to name the ink color when that color is used in printing an incongruent word. In contrast, they can quickly name that same ink color when it appears as a solid patch of color. Before reading any further, open up your favorite Internet search engine and search "Stroop Effect Demonstration;" you will find many online demonstrations of this task. I strongly encourage you to complete a few. Doing so will provide you with a strong sense of the difficulty that arises in the incongruent condition.

In a typical study on the Stroop effect, people may require about 100 seconds to name the ink color of 100 words that are incongruent color names (for example, blue ink used in printing the word YELLOW). In contrast, they require only about 60 seconds to name the ink colors for 100 colored patches (C. M. MacLeod, 2005). Notice why the Stroop effect demonstrates selective attention: People take longer to pay attention to a color when they are distracted by another feature of the stimulus—namely, the meaning of the name itself (Styles, 2006).

STROOP: selective attention b/c you have to pay attention to color of the print but (and) while you ignore meaning of the word

One popular explanation for the Stroop effect is that adults have had much more practice in reading words than in naming colors (T. L. Brown et al., 2002; Cox et al., 2006; Luck & Vecera, 2002). The more automatic process (reading the word) interferes with the less automatic process (naming the color of the ink). As a result, we automatically—and involuntarily—read the printed words. In fact, it's difficult to prevent yourself from reading those words, even if you want to! For instance, right now, stop reading this paragraph! Were you successful?

Hundreds of researchers have examined variations of the Stroop effect. For instance, many clinical psychologists have used a related technique called the emotional Stroop task (C. MacLeod, 2005;

C. M. MacLeod, 2005). On the **emotional Stroop task**, people are instructed to name the ink color of words that could have strong emotional significance to them. These individuals often require more time to name the color of the stimuli, presumably because they have trouble ignoring their emotional reactions to the words themselves (Most, 2010).

For example, suppose that someone appears to have a **phobic disorder**, which is an excessive fear of a specific object. A person with a fear of spiders would be instructed to name the ink colors of printed words such as *hairy* and *crawl*. People with phobias are significantly slower on these anxiety-arousing words than on control words. In contrast, people without phobias show no difference between the two kinds of words (Williams et al., 1996). These results suggest that people who have a phobic disorder are hyper-alert to words related to their phobia, and they show an attentional bias to the meaning of these stimuli. An **attentional bias** describes a situation in which people pay extra attention to some stimuli or some features. In the emotional Stroop task, for example, the participants pay *less* attention to the ink color of the words. For example, adults who showed an attentional bias toward suicide-related words were more likely than other adults to make a suicide attempt within the following 6 months (Cha et al., 2010). Other research shows that people who are depressed take a long time to report the color of words related to sadness and despair (C. MacLeod, 2005).

The Stroop Task has also been used in research on eating disorders. Let's consider a study by Abbie Pringle and her coauthors (2010), at the University of Oxford in England. These researchers distributed an online screening questionnaire to female dieters who had responded to an earlier advertisement. A total of 82 women met the specified criterion of very frequent dieting. The researchers had created a set of emotionally relevant words that referred to topics such as body shape, body weight, and eating. Then they matched these words with a control group of neutral words, so that the two groups of stimuli were similar in both word length and word frequency.

The women then completed this diet-focused version of the Stroop task. They also completed the 26-item Eating Attitudes Test, a standardized test that assesses whether people are at risk for developing eating disorders. According to the results of this study, slow responses to body-shape words predicted women's attitudes about eating. Specifically, when women took much longer to read those words related to shape (as opposed to the control words), they were especially likely to have high scores on the Eating Attitudes Test.

Pringle and her colleagues (2010) point out that these results are consistent with the cognitive-behavioral approach (e.g., Beck, 2011). According to the **cognitive-behavioral approach**, psychological problems arise from inappropriate thinking (cognitive factors) and inappropriate learning (behavioral factors). This study therefore shows a relationship between these women's potential for eating disorders and their thought patterns about words related to body shape.

The emotional Stroop task has also been used in research on the effects of **posttraumatic stress disorder (PTSD)** in combat veterans. *PTSD* is an anxiety disorder characterized by repeated re-experiencing (through nightmares, flashbacks, etc.) of an extremely traumatic event (American Psychological Association, 2010). Although this disorder is not specific to individuals who have participated in combat, its prevalence in combat veterans is high, ranging from between 11 and 30% depending on the specific conflict in which a veteran was engaged (U. S. Department of Veteran Affairs, 2016).

Khanna and colleagues (2017), for example, administered an emotional Stroop task to combat veterans with and without a PTSD diagnosis. The emotional Stroop task contained combat related words ("bomb", "seize"), generally negative / threatening words ("tax", "witch"), or neutral words ("self", "flour"). For combat veterans with PTSD, the amount of time necessary for color naming was higher for combat-related words than for words on the other two lists. This effect was not present for the combat veterans without PTSD.

Of interest, magnetoencephalography (MEG) responses were recorded as the veterans named the ink colors of words in each condition. Recall from Chapter 1 that the **magnetoencephalography (MEG) technique** records magnetic field fluctuations produced by neural activity during the processing of stimuli. Additionally, researchers can make reasonable determinations about the source location of the neural activity responsible for stimulus-evoked magnetic field fluctuations due to the robust nature of the signal emitted from magnetic fields.

Khanna and colleagues found that combat veterans with PTSD exhibited reduced activity around the right ventral prefrontal cortex when processing combat-related words, relative to those without PTSD. This and other prefrontal areas of cortex have been implicated in the systems responsible for the allocation of attention and for emotion regulation. Thus, in response to stimuli that may trigger traumatic memories, PTSD-affected individuals appear to access associated emotions at least partially as a result of either a trigger-induced attentional impairment or a trigger-induced weakening of emotional regulation ability.

Visual Search

Let's now consider visual search, the third topic within our general area of selective attention. In **visual search**, the observer must find a target in a visual display that has numerous distractors. In some cases, our lives may depend on accurate visual searches. For instance, airport security officers search travelers' luggage for possible weapons, and radiologists search a mammogram to detect a tumor that could indicate breast cancer. In these examples, trained experts must visually inspect a complicated image in order to detect a very specific set of visual features that could be indicative of danger. But, visual search is something that everyone does on a daily basis. For example, my desk is currently very messy (it's the end of the semester), but I needed to find a pen. I had to create a mental image of the pen, and then allocate my attention to specific areas of my desk until I found the object that I was looking for.

Researchers have identified an impressive number of variables that influence visual searches. For example, Jeremy Wolfe and his colleagues (2005) found that people are much more accurate in identifying a target if it appears frequently. If the target appears—in a visually complex background—on 50% of the trials, participants missed the target 7% of the time. When the same target appeared in this same complex background on only 1% of the trials, participants missed the target 30% of the time.

Let's examine two stimulus variables in more detail: (1) whether we are searching for a single, isolated feature or a combined set of features; and (2) whether we are searching for a target in which a particular feature is present or a target in which this feature is absent. Before you read further, however, try Demonstration 3.1.

isolated or combined feature

feature present or absent

Demonstration 3.1	The Isolated-Feature/Combined-Feature Effect

First, look at the two figures marked "Part A." In each case, search for a black X. Notice whether you take about the same amount of time on these two tasks. After trying Part A, continue by reading the additional instructions.

Additional instructions: For the second part of this demonstration, return to Part B. Look for the black X in each of the two figures in Part B. Notice whether you take the same amount of time on these two tasks or whether one takes slightly longer.

Part A

A1

A2

Part B

B1

B2

1. **The isolated-feature/combined-feature effect.**   Demonstration 3.1 is based on classic research by Treisman and Gelade (1980). According to their research, if the target differed from the irrelevant items in the display with respect to a simple feature such as color, observers could quickly detect the target. In fact, people can detect this target just as fast when it is presented in an array of 24 items as when it is presented in an array of only 3 items (Horowitz, 2010; Styles, 2006; Treisman, 1993; Treisman & Gelade, 1980).

   When you tried Part A of Demonstration 3.1, you probably found that the black X seemed to "pop out," whether the display contains two or 23 irrelevant items. In contrast, Part B of Demonstration 3.1 required you to search for a target that is a combination (or conjunction) of two properties. When you searched for a black X among light gray X's, black O's, and light gray O's, you probably found that you had to pay attention to one item at a time, using serial processing. You were distracted by stimuli that resembled the target because they were either black or X-shaped (Serences et al., 2005).

   This second task is more complex, and the time taken to find the target increases dramatically as the number of distractors increases (Wolfe, 2000, 2001; Wolfe et al., 2009). As a result, Figure B2 required a more time-consuming search than Figure B1 did. This demonstration supports the **isolated-feature/combined-feature effect**: People can typically locate an isolated feature more quickly than a combined feature (Quinlan, 2010).

   locate an isolated feature faster than a combined feature

   Now try Demonstration 3.3 before you read further.

2. **The feature-present/feature-absent effect.**   Theme 3 of this book states that our cognitive processes handle positive information better than negative information. In this case, "positive" means that a feature is present, whereas "negative" means that a feature is missing. The research of Treisman and Souther (1985) provides additional support for this theme, as you can see from Demonstration 3.2. This research illustrates the **feature-present/feature-absent effect**: People can typically locate a feature that is present more quickly than a feature that is absent.

   locate a feature that's present faster than a feature that's absent

   Notice in Part A of this demonstration that the circle with the line seems to "pop out" from the display. The search is rapid when we are looking for a particular feature that is *present*. Treisman and Souther (1985) found that people performed rapid searches for a feature that was present (like the circle with the line in Part A), whether the display contained zero irrelevant items or numerous irrelevant items. When people are searching for a feature that is present, the target item in the display usually captures their attention automatically (Franconeri et al., 2005; Matsumoto, 2010; Wolfe, 2000, 2001). In fact, this "pop-out"

| *Demonstration 3.2* | Searching for Features That Are Present or Absent |

In Part A, search for the circle with the line. Then, in Part B, search for the circle without the line.

(A) (B)

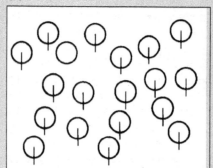

Source: Based on Treisman & Souther, 1985.

effect is automatic, and researchers emphasize that locating the target is strictly a bottom-up process (Boot et al., 2005).

In contrast, notice what happens when you are searching for a feature that is *absent* (like the circle without the line in Part B). Treisman and Souther (1985) found that the search time increased dramatically as the number of irrelevant items increased. When people search for a feature that is absent, they typically examine every item, one item at a time. They therefore must use a kind of attention that emphasizes both bottom-up processing and top-down processing. This task is substantially more challenging, as Wolfe has also found in his extensive research on the feature-present/feature-absent effect (Wolfe, 2000, 2001; Wolfe et al., 2009).

Another example of the feature-present/feature-absent effect was discovered by Royden and her coauthors (2001). According to their research, people can quickly locate one moving target when it appears in a group of stationary distractors. In contrast, they take much longer to locate one stationary target when it appears in a group of moving distractors. In other words, it's easier to spot a movement-present object than a movement-absent object.

As we have seen in this discussion of visual search, we search more quickly for an isolated feature, as opposed to a conjunction of two features. Furthermore, we search more quickly for a feature that is present as opposed to a feature that is absent.

Eye Movements in Reading

In this section, we focus more specifically on a selective attention task that most of you perform daily—namely, when you make decisions about when and where to move your eyes to a new region of text while you read.

Our eye movements provide important information about the way our minds operate when we perform a number of everyday cognitive tasks (Engbert et al., 2005; Radach et al., 2004b; Yang & McConkie, 2004). For example, researchers have studied how our eyes move when we are looking at a scene or searching for a visual target (e.g., Castelhano & Rayner, 2008; Henderson & Ferreira, 2004b; Irwin & Zelinsky, 2002) and when we are driving (Fisher & Pollatsek, 2007). Researchers have also discovered that our eyes move when we are speaking (Griffin, 2004; Meyer, 2004). One particularly compelling use of eye-movement data has been to examine which objects people look at in a visual scene as they hear spoken language (Cooper, 1974; Tanenhaus et al., 1995). When people look to objects in a visual display while hearing spoken language, their patterns of looking behavior provide invaluable data regarding the types of information people use to understand the spoken linguistic signal (see Tanenhaus, 2007, for an overview of this exciting research topic). We consider many experimental paradigms that involve eye movement data throughout this textbook. In this section, however, we focus on patterns of eye movements that people make when they read.

Overview of Eye Movements in Reading

For a moment, pay attention to the way your eyes are moving as you read this paragraph. When people are asked to describe how they move their eyes while they read, they often report that they move their eyes smoothly and continuously across a line of text. But in reality, your eyes actually make a series of little jumps as they move across the page (Rayner & Liversedge, 2004; Reichle & Laurent, 2006). This very rapid movement of the eyes from one spot to the next is known as saccadic (pronounced "suh-*cod*-dik") eye movement. The purpose of a **saccadic eye movement** during reading is to bring the center of your retina into position over the words you want to read. A very small region in the center of the retina, known as the fovea, has better acuity than other retinal regions. Therefore, the eye must be moved so that new words can be registered on the fovea (Castelhano & Rayner, 2008; Chun et al., 2011; Irwin, 2004). Saccadic eye movement is another example of Theme 1 (active cognitive processes): We actively search for new information, including the material we will be reading (Findlay & Gilchrist, 2001; Radach & Kennedy, 2004).

When you read a passage in English, each saccade moves your eye forward by about seven to nine letters (Rayner, 1998). Researchers have estimated that people make between 150,000 and 200,000 saccadic movements every day (Irwin, 2003; Rayner, 2009; Weierich & Barrett, 2010). You cannot process much visual information when your eyes are moving (Irwin, 2003; Radach & Kennedy, 2004; Weierich & Barrett, 2010).

However, a fixation occurs during the period between two saccadic movements. During each **fixation**, your visual system pauses briefly in order to acquire information that is useful for comprehending the written text (Rayner, 2009). The duration of a fixation in English typically ranges from 200 to 250 milliseconds, although many factors influence precisely how long an individual fixation will last (Juhasz & Rayner, 2003; Rayner, 1998).

The term perceptual span refers to the number of letters and spaces that we perceive during a fixation (Rayner & Liversedge, 2004). Researchers have found large individual differences in the size of the perceptual span (Irwin, 2004). When you read English, this perceptual span normally includes letters lying about four positions to the left of the letter you are directly looking at, as well as the letters up to about 15 positions to the right of that central letter (Rayner, 2009).

Notice that this perceptual span for English is definitely lopsided. After all, when we read English, we are looking for visual information in the text that lies to the right. In fact, given this perceptual span, when readers are fixating a current word, they can experience parafoveal preview benefits (e.g. Rayner, 1975; Inhoff, 1987; Ashby & Rayner, 2004). **Parafoveal preview** refers to the fact that readers can access information about upcoming words even though they are currently fixated on a word to the left (in English) of those words. Parafoveal preview can cause shorter fixation durations on a nearby word when information about the properties of the text is available parafoveally (see Schotter, Angele, & Rayner, 2012, for an overview). As one example of a parafoveal preview effect, the material in the extreme right side of the perceptual span is useful for noticing the white spaces between words, because these spaces provide information about word length. However, we usually cannot actually identify a word that lies more than eight spaces to the right of the fixation point (Rayner, 1998).

Other research has demonstrated that saccadic eye movements show several predictable patterns. For example, when the eye jumps forward in a saccadic movement, it usually moves toward the center of a word, rather than to a blank space between words or between sentences (Engbert & Krügel, 2010). The eye also jumps past short words, words that appear frequently in a language, and words that are highly predictable in a sentence (Drieghe et al., 2004; Kliegl et al., 2004; White & Liversedge, 2004). In contrast, the size of the saccadic movement is small if the next word in a sentence is misspelled or if it is unusual (Pynte et al., 2004; Rayner et al., 2004; White & Liversedge, 2004). All these strategies make sense, because a large saccadic movement would not be useful if the material is challenging.

Properties of the written language system can influence the general pattern of eye movements discussed above. For example, researchers have determined that Chinese readers move their eyes only two to three characters in a saccade. This makes sense because each character in the Chinese written language is more densely packed with information, compared to each letter in written English (Rayner, 2009; Shen et al., 2008; Tsang & Chen, 2008).

Selective Attention in Reading

Reading is one of the most complex behaviors that humans can perform. Reading involves the coordination of visual, linguistic, oculomotor, and attentional systems. All of these systems must work together so that a reader can generate a decision about whether to move the eyes to a new word, or to gather more information by continuing to fixate the same location. And, this decision must be made quickly, given that the average fixation on a word is only 200–250 milliseconds (see reviews by Clifton et al., 2007; Clifton & Staub, 2011 for a more detailed discussion of factors that influence patterns of eye movements during reading).

The selective attention component of the reading process should be evident to you after our discussion of eye movements during reading. You must fixate a word long enough to gather as much information as necessary before moving on. And, while you're currently gathering information from text on which you are currently fixated, you must also make a decision about where to move your eyes next. For example, consider the following sentence:

It was so windy today that Caitie left work early to go outside and fly a kite before going home for the day.

Based on the knowledge that you have about how the world works, and about how written English typically unfolds, you should be able to easily predict that the word *kite* will occur before your eyes actually make it to that word. A large amount of research demonstrates that when people are highly certain of the identity of an upcoming word, there is a much higher probability that they will skip it, relative to a context

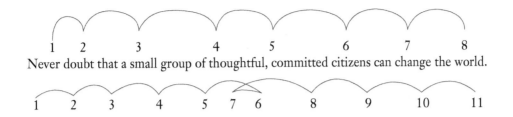

FIGURE 3.1
Eye movement patterns
and fixations for a good
reader (top numbers)
and a poor reader
(bottom numbers).

in which the word is not predictable (Rayner et al., 2011). And, if a highly predictable word is not skipped, it is usually fixated for only a short amount of time (Altarriba, Kroll, Sholl, & Rayner, 1996; Ashby et al., 2005; Balota, Pollatsek, & Rayner, 1985; Ehrlich & Rayner, 1981).

Good readers differ from poor readers with respect to their saccadic eye movements. Figure 3.1 shows how two such readers might differ when reading the same sentence. Good readers make larger jumps. They are also less likely to make **regressions**, by moving their eyes backward to earlier material in the sentence. People often make regressions when they realize that they have not understood the passage they are reading (White & Liversedge, 2004). The good reader also has shorter pauses before moving onward (Castelhano & Rayner, 2008). It is quite possible that differences in attentional abilities can provide one explanation for this and many other documented differences between good and poor readers.

In summary, the research shows that a wide variety of cognitive factors have an important influence on the pattern and speed of our saccadic eye movements (McDonald & Shillcock, 2003; Reichle et al., 1998). Saccadic eye movements clearly help us become more active, flexible readers (Rayner, 2009; Rayner et al., 2008).

Neuroscience of Attention

During recent decades, researchers have developed a variety of sophisticated techniques for examining the biological basis of behavior. Chapter 1 introduced many of these approaches. Research using these techniques has identified a network of areas throughout the brain that accomplish various attention tasks (Diamond & Amso, 2008; Posner & Rothbart, 2007b).

Several regions of the brain are responsible for attention. In this discussion, however, we'll focus on structures in the cerebral cortex, as shown in Figure 3.2. Take a moment to compare Figure 3.2 with Figure 2.1, which shows the regions of the cortex that are most relevant in object recognition.

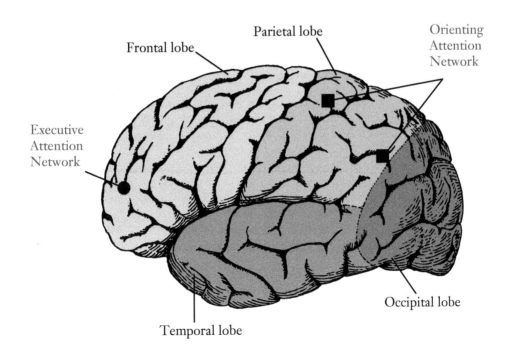

FIGURE 3.2
A schematic drawing of
the cerebral cortex, as
seen from the left side,
showing the four lobes
of the brain and the
regions that are most
important on attention
tasks.

According to Michael Posner and Mary Rothbart, several systems in the cortex process different aspects of attention (Posner & Rothbart, 2007a, 2007b; Rothbart et al., 2011; Tang & Posner, 2009). We will discuss two of them, the orienting attention network and the executive attention network.

The Orienting Attention Network

Imagine that you are searching the area around your bathroom sink for a lost contact lens. When you are selecting information from sensory input, your orienting attention network is activated. The **orienting attention network** is generally responsible for the kind of attention required for visual search, in which you must shift your attention around to various spatial locations (Chun & Wolfe, 2001; Posner & Rothbart, 2007b). Figure 3.2 shows that two important components of the orienting attention network are located in the region of the cortex known as the parietal lobe (pronounced "pah-*rie*-uh-tul").

How did researchers identify the parietal cortex as the region of the brain that we use in visual searches? Several decades ago, the only clue to the organization of the brain was provided by people with brain lesions (Posner, 2004). The term **brain lesion** refers to specific brain damage caused by strokes, accidents, or other traumas.

People who have brain damage in the parietal region of the right hemisphere of the brain have trouble noticing a visual stimulus that appears on the left side of their visual field. In contrast, people with damage in the left parietal region have trouble noticing a visual stimulus on the right side (Luck & Vecera, 2002; Posner & Rothbart, 2007a, 2007b; Styles, 2005). Neurologists use the term **unilateral spatial neglect** when a person ignores part of his or her visual field (Gazzaniga et al., 2009). These lesions produce unusual deficits. For instance, a woman with a lesion in the left parietal region may have trouble noticing the food on the right side of her plate. She may eat only the food on the left side of her plate, and she might even complain that she didn't receive enough food (Farah, 2000; Humphreys & Riddoch, 2001). Surprisingly, however, she may seem completely unaware of her deficit. In another study, researchers tested a man with a lesion in his right parietal lobe. They showed him a figure of an ordinary clock and asked him to draw it. His drawing showed only half of the clock, with the other half completely empty (Bloom & Lazerson, 1988).

Some of the more recent research on the orienting attention network has used PET scans. In studies using **positron emission tomography (PET scan)**, the researchers measure blood flow in the brain by injecting the participant with a radioactive chemical just before he or she performs a cognitive task. As discussed in Chapter 1, this chemical travels through the blood to the parts of the brain that are active during the cognitive task. A specialized camera makes an image of the accumulated chemical. According to PET-scan research, the parietal cortex shows increased blood flow when people perform visual searches and when they pay attention to spatial locations (Posner & Rothbart, 2007b).

The orienting network develops during the first year of life. For example, by about 4 months of age, infants can disengage their attention from an overstimulating situation, and they can shift this attention to an object such as a new toy (Posner & Rothbart, 2007a; Rothbart et al., 2011).

The Executive Attention Network

The Stroop task described above relies primarily on your executive attention network. The **executive attention network** is responsible for the kind of attention we use when a task focuses on conflict (Miller & Cohen, 2001; Posner & Rothbart, 2007a, 2007b). On the Stroop task, for example, you need to inhibit your automatic response of reading a word, so that you can name the color of the ink (Fan et al., 2002).

More generally, the executive attention network inhibits your automatic responses to stimuli (Stuss et al., 2002). As you can see in Figure 3.2, the prefrontal portion of the cortex is the region of your brain where the executive attention network is especially active. The executive attention network is primarily involved during top-down control of attention (Farah, 2000). This network begins to develop at about age 3, much later than the orienting attention network (Posner & Rothbart, 2007a; Rothbart et al., 2011). Posner and Rothbart (2007b) argue that the executive attention network is extremely important when you acquire academic skills in school, for example, when you learned to read. There is also some evidence that adults can enhance their executive attention network by learning meditation, adopted from traditional Chinese techniques (Tang & Posner, 2009).

Executive attention also helps you learn new ideas (Posner & Rothbart, 2007a). For example, as you are reading this passage, your executive attention network has been actively taking in new information. Ideally, you have also been comparing this executive attention network with the orienting attention network. This process of reading and understanding a college-level textbook can be challenging. Not surprisingly, the location of the executive attention network overlaps with the areas of your brain that are related to general intelligence (Duncan et al., 2000; Posner & Rothbart, 2007b).

In summary, PET scans and other neuroscience techniques have identified one brain region that is typically active when we are searching for objects (the orienting attention network). Neuroscience research also demonstrates that a different brain region is typically active when we must inhibit an automatic response and produce a less-obvious response (the executive attention network).

Theories of Attention

Let us first summarize an approach to attention that was proposed several decades ago, when cognitive psychology was in its infancy. Then we will discuss Anne Treisman's feature-integration theory, which is probably the most influential contemporary explanation of attention (Styles, 2005).

Early Theories of Attention

The first approaches to attention emphasized that people are extremely limited in the amount of information that they can process at any given time. A common metaphor in these theories was the concept of a bottleneck (Gazzaniga et al., 2009). This metaphor was especially appealing because it matches our introspections about attention. The narrow neck of a bottle restricts the flow into or out of the bottle. **Bottleneck theories** proposed a similar narrow passageway in human information processing. In other words, this bottleneck limits the quantity of information to which we can pay attention. So, when one message is currently flowing through a bottleneck, the other messages must be left behind. Researchers proposed many variations of this bottleneck theory (e.g., Broadbent, 1958; Treisman, 1964).

However, as you may recall from the discussion of the theories of object recognition (Chapter 2), researchers rejected the template theory because it was not flexible enough. Similarly, researchers rejected the bottleneck theories because those theories underestimate the flexibility of human attention (Luck & Vecera, 2002; Tsang, 2007). Neuroscience research demonstrates that information is not lost at just one phase of the attention process, as the bottleneck theories suggest. Instead, information is lost throughout many phases of attention, from the beginning through later processing (Kanwisher et al., 2001; Luck & Vecera, 2002).

[handwritten margin note: the things that get "filtered out" that you don't pay attention to don't immediately get lost]

Feature-Integration Theory

[handwritten note: Treisman = feature-integration]

Anne Treisman has developed an elaborate theory of attention and perceptual processing. Her original theory was elegantly simple (Treisman & Gelade, 1980). As you might expect, the current version is more complex (Holcombe, 2010; Quinlan, 2010). Let's consider (1) the basic elements of feature-integration theory, (2) research on the theory, and (3) the current status of the theory.

1. **The basic elements.**   According to Treisman's **feature-integration theory**, we sometimes look at a scene using distributed attention, and we process all parts of the scene at the same time. On other occasions, we use focused attention, and we process each item in the scene one at a time. Treisman also suggested that distributed attention and focused attention form a continuum, rather than two distinctive categories. As a result, you frequently use a kind of attention that is somewhere between those two extremes.

    Let's examine these two kinds of processing before considering other components of Treisman's theory (Treisman & Gelade, 1980; Treisman, 1993). One kind of processing uses distributed attention. **Distributed attention** allows you to register features automatically; you use parallel processing across the field, and you register all the features simultaneously. Distributed attention is a relatively low-level kind of processing. In fact, this kind of processing is so effortless that you are not even aware that you're using it.

    The second kind of processing in Treisman's theory is called focused attention. **Focused attention** requires slower serial processing, in which you identify one object at a time. This more demanding kind of processing is necessary when the objects are more complex. Focused

[handwritten margin note: Distributed attention - parallel - multiple things at once   Focused attention - serial - one thing at a time]

---

*In some of her research, Treisman uses the phrase "divided attention," rather than "distributed attention." However, I will use "distributed attention" in this textbook, in order to avoid confusing this concept with the research on divided attention discussed on earlier pages.

attention identifies which features belong together—for example, a square shape may go with a blue color.

2. **Research on the theory.**   Treisman and Gelade (1980) examined distributed attention and focused attention by studying two different stimulus situations. In this study, one situation used isolated features (and therefore it used distributed attention). In contrast, the other situation used combinations of features (and therefore it used focused attention).

Let's first consider the details of the research on *distributed attention*. According to Treisman and Gelade, if you process isolated features in distributed attention, then you should be able to rapidly locate a target among its neighboring, irrelevant items. That target should seem to "pop out" of the display automatically, no matter how many items are in the display.

To test their hypothesis about distributed attention, Treisman and Gelade conducted a series of studies. You already tried Demonstration 3.1A (p. 78), which illustrated part of their study. Remember the results of that demonstration: If the target differed from all the irrelevant items in the display with respect to one simple feature such as color, you could quickly detect this target. In fact, you could detect it just as fast when it appeared in an array of 23 items as when it appeared in an array of only 3 items (Treisman, 1986; Treisman & Gelade, 1980). Distributed attention can operate in a parallel fashion and relatively automatically; the target seemed to "pop out" in Demonstration 3.1A.

In contrast, consider the research on *focused attention*. In Demonstration 3.1B, you searched for a target that was a conjunction (or combination) of properties. When you searched for a black X buried among light gray X's, black O's, and light gray O's, you needed to use focused attention. In other words, you were forced to focus your attention on one item at a time, using serial processing. This task is more complex. Treisman and Gelade (1980) and other researchers have found that people need more time to find the target when there are a large number of distractors in a focused-attention task (Parasuraman & Greenwood, 2007).

Another effect related to feature-integration theory is called an *illusory conjunction*. Specifically, when we are overwhelmed with too many simultaneous visual tasks, we sometimes form an illusory conjunction (Botella et al., 2011; Treisman & Schmidt, 1982; Treisman & Souther, 1986). An **illusory conjunction** is an inappropriate combination of features, perhaps combining one object's shape with a nearby object's color. Many studies have demonstrated, for example, that a blue N and a green T can produce an illusory conjunction in which the viewer actually perceives either a blue T or a green N (e.g., Ashby et al., 1996; Hazeltine et al., 1997; Holcombe, 2010).

This research on illusory conjunctions confirms a conclusion demonstrated in other perception research. Contrary to our commonsense intuitions, the human visual system actually processes an object's features independently. For example, when you look at a red apple, you actually analyze its red color separately from its round shape. In other words, your visual system sometimes has a **binding problem** because it does not represent the important features of an object as a unified whole (Holcombe, 2010; Quinlan, 2010; Wheeler & Treisman, 2002).

When you use focused attention to look at the apple, you will accurately perceive an integrated figure—a red, round object. Focused attention allows the binding process to operate (Bouvier & Treisman, 2010; Quinlan, 2010; Vu & Rich, 2010). To use a metaphor, focused attention acts like a form of glue, so that an object's color and its shape can stick together.

In contrast, suppose that a researcher shows you two arbitrary figures, for example, a blue N and a green T. Suppose also that your attention is overloaded or distracted, so that you must use distributed attention. In this situation, the blue color from one figure may combine with the T shape from the other figure. As a result, you may perceive the illusory conjunction of a blue T.

Other research shows that our visual system can create an illusory conjunction from verbal material (Treisman, 1990; Wolfe, 2000). For example, suppose that your attention is distracted, and a researcher shows you two nonsense words, *dax* and *kay*. You might report seeing the English word *day*. When we cannot use focused attention, we sometimes form illusory conjunctions that are consistent with our expectations. As Chapter 2 emphasized, top-down processing helps us screen out inappropriate combinations. As a result, we are more likely to perceive familiar combinations (Treisman, 1990).

Demonstration 3.3 | Awareness About Automatic Motor Activities

Take a moment to see how aware you are about how you perform one or more of these motor activities. In each case, be as specific as possible about exactly how you perform each step of each activity.

1. Describe in detail how you pick up a pen and write your name.

2. Describe in detail how you stand up from a sitting position.

3. Describe in detail how you walk across the room.

4. Describe in detail how you open one of the doors in the place where you live.

---

3. **Current status of the theory.** The basic elements of feature-integration theory were proposed more than 25 years ago. Since that time, researchers have conducted dozens of additional studies, and the original, straightforward theory has been modified.

As we will see throughout this textbook, psychologists often propose a theory that initially draws a clear-cut distinction between two or more psychological processes. With extensive research, however, theorists frequently conclude that reality is much more complex. Rather than two clear-cut categories, we find that distributed attention can occasionally resemble focused attention (Bundesen & Habekost, 2005).

Furthermore, your visual system may use distributed attention to quickly gather information about the general gist of a scene. For example, suppose that you are standing near a lake, looking out at the beach. Obviously, you cannot use focused attention to register every pebble on the beach. Treisman and her coauthors suggest that your distributed attention can quickly gather information about the average size of these pebbles. In this fashion, you can form a fairly accurate overall impression of this natural scene (Chong et al., 2008; Emmanouil & Treisman, 2008; Treisman, 2006).

Many questions remain about how visual attention helps us gather relevant information from a real-world scene. However, the current version of feature-integration theory provides an important framework for understanding visual attention (Holcombe, 2010; Müller & Krummenacher, 2006; Quinlan, 2010). Before you read further, try Demonstration 3.3.

Consciousness

Our final topic in this chapter—consciousness—is a controversial subject. One reason for the controversy is the variety of different definitions for the term (Baumeister et al., 2011; Dehaene et al., 2006; Velmans, 2009). I prefer a broad definition. **Consciousness** means the awareness that people have about the outside world and about their perceptions, images, thoughts, memories, and feelings (Chalmers, 2007; Revonsuo, 2010; Zeman, 2004).

[handwritten margin note: awareness about the outside world & perceptions, thoughts, etc]

Notice that the contents of consciousness can include your perceptions of the world around you, your visual imagery, the comments you make silently to yourself, the memory of events in your life, your beliefs about the world, your plans for activities later today, and your attitudes toward other people (Coward & Sun, 2004; Dijksterhuis & Aarts, 2010). As David Barash (2006) writes,

> *Thus, consciousness is not only an unfolding story that we tell ourselves, moment by moment, about what we are doing, feeling, and thinking. It also includes our efforts to interpret what other individuals are doing, feeling, and thinking, as well as how those others are likely to perceive one's self. (p. B10)*

Consciousness is closely related to attention, but the processes are definitely not identical (Dijksterhuis & Aarts, 2010; Hoffman, 2010; Lavie, 2007). After all, we are frequently not aware or conscious of the tasks we are performing with the automatic, distributed form of attention. For example, when you are driving, you may automatically put your foot on the brake in response to a red light. However, you may not be at all conscious that you performed this motor action—or any of the other motor activities in Demonstration 3.3. In general, consciousness is associated with the kind of controlled, focused attention that is not automatic (Dehaene & Naccache, 2001; Dijksterhuis & Aarts, 2010; Weierich & Barrett, 2010).

[handwritten margin note: related to attention but NOT the same]

[handwritten margin note: consciousness = more controlled, focused. NOT automatic]

Demonstration 3.4	Thought Suppression

This demonstration requires you to take a break from your reading and just relax for 5 minutes. Take a sheet of paper and a pen or pencil to record your thoughts as you simply let your mind wander. Your thoughts can include cognitive psychology, but they do not need to. Just jot down a brief note about each topic you think about as your mind wanders. One final instruction:

During this exercise, do not think about a white bear!

As Chapter 1 noted, the behaviorists considered topics such as consciousness to be inappropriate for scientific study. However, consciousness edged back into favor when psychologists began to adopt cognitive approaches (Dehaene & Naccache, 2001). In the 21st century, consciousness has become a popular topic for numerous books (e.g., Baruss, 2003; Edelman, 2005; Hassin et al., 2005; Revonsuo, 2010; Velmans, 2009; Velmans & Schneider, 2007; Zeman, 2004).

In recent years, cognitive psychologists have been especially interested in three interrelated issues concerned with consciousness: (1) our inability to bring certain thoughts into consciousness; (2) our inability to let certain thoughts escape from consciousness; and (3) blindsight, which reveals that people with a specific visual disorder can perform quite accurately on a cognitive task, even when they are not conscious of their accuracy. Before you read further, however, try Demonstration 3.4.

To what extent do we have access to our higher mental processes? Consider this situation: You are reading a book, and your eyes are moving over the page. However, you are daydreaming . . . and you aren't actually aware that you are not reading. During mindless reading, your eyes may move forward, but you do not process the meaning of the material. In fact, your eyes were moving erratically, rather than using the kind of normal saccadic movements we discussed earlier in this chapter (Reichle et al., 2010). You had no conscious awareness of your higher mental processes, until suddenly you became conscious that you didn't remember any information from the text.

A more general phenomenon, called mind wandering, occurs when your thoughts shift from the external environment in favor of internal processing (Barron et al., 2011; McVay & Kane, 2010; Smilek et al., 2010). Again, you may not be conscious that your mind has wandered to another topic.

Here's another example that demonstrates our inability to bring certain thoughts into consciousness. Answer the following question: "What is your mother's maiden name?" Now answer this second question: "How did you arrive at the answer to the first question?" If you are like most people, the answer to the first question appeared swiftly in your consciousness, but you probably cannot explain your thought process. Instead, the name simply seemed to pop into your memory.

In a classic article, Richard Nisbett and Timothy Wilson (1977) argued that we often have little direct access to our thought processes. As they pointed out, you may be fully conscious of the *products* of your thought processes (such as your mother's maiden name). However, you are usually not conscious of the *processes* that created these products (such as the memory mechanisms that produced her maiden name). Similarly, people may solve a problem correctly; however, when asked to explain how they reached the solution, they may reply, "It just dawned on me" (Nisbett & Wilson, 1977).

Psychologists currently believe that our verbal reports are somewhat accurate reflections of our cognitive processes (Ericsson & Fox, 2011; Fox et al., 2011; Johansson et al., 2006; Wilson, 1997). As we'll see in Chapter 6, we do have relatively complete access to some thought processes. For example, you can judge—with reasonable accuracy—how well you performed on a simple memory task. However, we have only limited access to other thought processes, such as how well you understand the information in a psychology essay. As Demonstration 3.3 showed, we are not aware of the step-by-step procedures in the motor activities that have become automatic (Diana & Reder, 2004; Levin, 2004).

We need to emphasize this topic of consciousness about thought processes, because it shows that cognitive psychologists should not rely on people's introspections (Johansson et al., 2006; Nisbett & Wilson, 1977; Wegner, 2002). For example, when several people are talking to me at once, it genuinely feels like I am experiencing an "attention bottleneck." However, as we saw earlier in this chapter, humans actually have fairly flexible attention patterns; we really do not experience a rigid bottleneck.

Thought Suppression

I have a friend who decided to quit smoking, so he tried valiantly to get rid of every idea associated with cigarettes. As soon as he thought of anything remotely associated with smoking, he immediately tried to push that thought out of his consciousness. Ironically, however, this strategy backfired, and he was haunted by numerous thoughts related to cigarettes. Basically, he could not eliminate these undesirable thoughts. When people engage in **thought suppression**, they try to eliminate the thoughts, ideas, and images that are related to an undesirable stimulus.

The research on thought suppression supports my friend's experience (Erskine et al., 2010). How successful were you in suppressing your thoughts in Demonstration 3.4? Did you have any difficulty carrying out the instructions?

The original source for the white bear study is literary, rather than scientific. Apparently, when the Russian novelist Tolstoy was young, his older brother tormented him by instructing him to stand in a corner and not think about a white bear (Wegner, 1996; Wegner et al., 1987). Similarly, if you have ever tried to avoid thinking about food when on a diet, you know that it's difficult to chase these undesired thoughts out of consciousness.

Wegner (1997b, 2002) uses the phrase **ironic effects of mental control** to describe how our efforts can backfire when we attempt to control the contents of our consciousness. Suppose that you try valiantly to banish a particular thought. Ironically, that same thought is especially likely to creep back into consciousness. In other words, you have trouble suppressing certain thoughts.

Wegner and his coauthors (1987) decided to test Tolstoy's "white bear" task scientifically. They instructed one group of students not to think about a white bear during a 5-minute period, and then they were allowed to think about a white bear during a second 5-minute period. These students were very likely to think about a white bear during the second period. In fact, they thought about bears more often than students in a control group. Students in this control group had been instructed to *think freely* about a white bear—without any previous thought-suppression session. In other words, initial suppression of specific thoughts can produce a rebound effect.

Many studies have replicated the rebound effect following thought suppression (e.g., Purdon et al., 2005; Tolin et al., 2002; Wegner, 2002). Furthermore, this rebound effect is not limited to suppressing thoughts about white bears and other relatively trivial ideas. For example, when people are instructed not to notice a painful stimulus, they are likely to become even more aware of the pain. Similar ironic effects—which occur when we try to suppress our thoughts—have been documented when people try to concentrate, avoid movement, or fall asleep (Harvey, 2005; Wegner, 1994).

The topic of thought suppression is highly relevant for clinical psychologists (Clark, 2005; Wegner, 1997a). For example, suppose that a client has severe depression, and the therapist encourages this person to stop thinking about depressing topics. Ironically, this advice may produce an even greater number of depressing thoughts (Wenzlaff, 2005). Thought suppression is also relevant for individuals who experience problems such as posttraumatic stress disorder, generalized anxiety disorder, and obsessive-compulsive disorder (Falsetti et al., 2005; Morrison, 2005; Purdon et al., 2005; Wells, 2005).

Blindsight

According to the first topic related to consciousness, we often have difficulty bringing some thoughts about our cognitive processes into consciousness. According to the second topic, we often have difficulty suppressing some thoughts from consciousness.

The research on a visual condition called *blindsight* reveals a third topic related to consciousness: In some cases, people can perform a cognitive task quite accurately, with no conscious awareness that their performance is accurate (Rasmussen, 2006; Weiskrantz, 2007). Blindsight refers to an unusual kind of vision without awareness. In more detail, **blindsight** is a condition in which an individual with a damaged visual cortex claims not to see an object; however, he or she can accurately report some characteristics of that object, such as its location (Kolb & Whishaw, 2009; Robertson & Treisman, 2010; Weiskrantz, 2007; Zeman, 2004).

Individuals with blindsight believe that they are truly blind in part or all of their visual field. In other words, their consciousness contains the thought, "I cannot see." In a typical study, the researchers present a stimulus in a region of the visual field that had previously corresponded to the damaged cortex. For example, a spot of light might be flashed at a location 10 degrees to the right of center. People with blindsight are then asked to point to the light. Typically, these individuals report that they did not even see the light, so they could only make a guess about its location.

Surprisingly, however, researchers discovered that the participants' performance is significantly better than chance—and often nearly perfect (Robertson & Treisman, 2010; Weiskrantz, 1997, 2007). People with blindsight can report visual attributes such as color, shape, and motion (Zeman, 2004).

Here is one possible explanation for this phenomenon. Most of the information that is registered on the retina travels to the visual cortex. However, a small portion of this retinal information travels to other locations in the cerebral cortex that are located outside the visual cortex (Weiskrantz, 2007; Zeman, 2004). A person with blindsight can therefore identify some characteristics of the visual stimulus—even with a damaged primary visual cortex—based on information registered in those other cortical locations.

The research on blindsight is especially relevant to the topic of consciousness. In particular, it suggests that visual information must pass through the primary visual cortex in order to be registered in consciousness. However, suppose that some part of this information "takes a detour" and bypasses the primary visual cortex. Then it is possible that the individual will not be *conscious* of the visual experience. However, he or she may indeed *perceive* this stimulus (Farah, 2001; Zeman, 2004).

[handwritten margin note: blindsight: they are not conscious of the visual stimuli presented, but they still perceived it at some level]

In summary, this discussion has demonstrated that consciousness is a challenging topic. Our consciousness is not a perfect mirror of our cognitive processes; that is, we often cannot explain how these processes operate. It is also not a blackboard; we cannot simply erase unwanted thoughts from our consciousness. Consciousness is not even an accurate reporter, as the research on blindsight demonstrates. As Wegner (2002) concludes, we usually assume that "How things seem is how they are" (p. 243). However, this convergence between our consciousness and reality is often an illusion.

SECTION SUMMARY POINTS

Overview of Attention

1. Attention is a concentration of mental activity; it allows our cognitive processes to take in limited portions of our sensory environment and our memory.

2. Research on divided attention shows that performance often suffers when people must attend to several stimuli simultaneously. For example, we cannot talk on a hands-free cell phone and drive carefully at the same time. The remaining attention processes considered in this chapter require selective attention.

3. The dichotic-listening technique is the first of the selective-attention tasks discussed in this section. The research shows that we typically notice little about an irrelevant auditory message. Occasionally, however, we may notice the gender of the speaker or our own name.

4. A second kind of a selective-attention task is the Stroop effect. A variant called the "emotional Stroop task" demonstrates that people with certain disorders have difficulty identifying the ink color of words relevant to their disorder; for example, people with eating disorders take longer than other people to report the ink color of words related to body shape.

5. A third kind of selected-attention task is visual search. For example, we can locate a target faster if it appears frequently, if it differs from irrelevant objects on only one dimension (e.g., color), and if a specific feature of a stimulus (e.g., a line) is present rather than absent.

Eye Movements in Reading

1. People do not smoothly and continuously move their eyes across a line of text when they read. Instead, eye movements during reading are saccadic eye movements—or, extremely quick jumps from one location to another.

2. Fixations occur between saccades. The duration of a fixation is influenced by many physical and linguistic properties of the text.

3. During a fixation while reading in English, readers can access some visual information to the right of the current fixation—a phenomenon often referred to as parafoveal processing.

4. While fixated on a word, readers need to make decisions about how long to stay at the current location, and where to move next. These decisions are complex, but illustrate one selective attention component of the reading process.

5. Design features of the text influence patterns of eye movements during reading, as does the skill level of an individual reader.

Neuroscience of Attention

1. According to case studies, some people who have a lesion in the parietal region of the right hemisphere cannot notice visual objects in the left visual field. *[handwritten: unilateral spatial neglect]*

2. PET-scan research has also established that the orienting attention network is active when people perform visual searches or when they notice spatial locations.

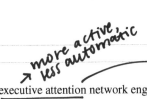
more active → less automatic

3. The executive attention network engages the prefrontal cortex.

4. This executive attention network is important in attention tasks that focus on conflict (e.g., the Stroop task), in the top-down control of attention, and in learning new information.

Theories of Attention

1. Early theories of attention emphasized a "bottleneck" that limits attention at a particular part of processing, but this perspective is now considered too simplistic.

2. Treisman proposed the feature-integration theory, which *parallel* contains two components: (a) distributed attention, which can be used to register single features automatically, and (b) focused *serial* attention, which requires slower serial processing in order to search for combinations of features.

3. In Treisman's theory, illusory conjunctions may arise when attention is overloaded.

4. With some modifications, Triesman's feature-integration theory is still able to account for many important aspects of visual attention.

CHAPTER REVIEW QUESTIONS

1. What is divided attention? Give several examples of divided-attention tasks you have performed within the past 24 hours. What does the research show about the effects of practice on divided attention? Describe some examples of your own experience with practice and divided-attention performance.

2. What is selective attention? Give several examples of selective-attention tasks—both auditory and visual—that you have performed within the past 24 hours. In what kind of circumstances were you able to pick up information about the message you were supposed to ignore? Does this pattern match the research?

3. This chapter discussed the Stroop effect in some detail. Can you think of any academic tasks you routinely perform, where you also need to suppress the most obvious answer in order to provide the correct response? What attentional system in your cortex is especially active during these tasks?

4. Imagine that you are trying to carry on a conversation with a friend at the same time you are reading an interesting article in a magazine. Describe how the bottleneck theories and automatic versus controlled processing would explain your performance. Then describe Treisman's feature-integration theory and think of an example of this theory, based on your previous experiences.

5. Imagine that you are searching the previous pages of this chapter for the term "dichotic listening." What part of your brain is activated during this task? Now suppose that you are trying to learn the meaning of the phrase "dichotic listening." What

Consciousness

1. Consciousness, or awareness, is different from attention, because we may not be conscious of the tasks we perform when using the automatic, distributed form of attention.

2. Research suggests that people are sometimes unaware of their higher mental processes. For example, they may not be aware when their mind is wandering. Furthermore, they may solve a problem but not be conscious of how they actually reached the solution.

3. Research on thought suppression illustrates the difficulty of eliminating some thoughts from consciousness; ironically, if you try to avoid thinking about an issue, you may actually think about it more frequently. People with psychological problems may have trouble suppressing intrusive thoughts or images that are relevant to their disorder.

4. Individuals with blindsight can identify characteristics of an object, even when their visual cortex is destroyed and they have no conscious awareness of that object.

part of your brain is activated during this task? Describe how research has clarified the biological basis of attention.

6. In what sense do saccadic eye movements represent a kind of attention process? Describe the difference between written English and written Chinese; how do readers differ in these two languages?

7. Define the word "consciousness." Based on the information in this chapter, do people have complete control over the information stored in consciousness? Does this information provide an accurate account of your cognitive processes? How is consciousness different from attention?

8. Cognitive psychology has many practical applications. Based on what you have read in this chapter, what applications can you suggest for driving and highway safety? Describe the research described in this chapter, and then list three or four ways that the material on attention can be applied to a job or a hobby that you have had.

9. Cognitive psychology can also be applied to clinical psychology. Discuss some applications of the Stroop effect and thought suppression to the area of psychological problems and their treatment.

10. Chapters 2 and 3 both examine perception. To help you synthesize part of this information, describe as completely as possible how you are able to perceive the letters in a word, using both bottom-up and top-down processing. Describe how your attention would operate in both a selective-attention situation and a divided-attention situation. How would saccadic eye movements be relevant?

KEYWORDS

attention	attentional bias	effect	brain lesion	focused attention
divided-attention task	posttraumatic stress	feature-present/	unilateral spatial neglect	illusory conjunction
multitask	disorder (PTSD)	feature-absent	positron emission	binding problem
selective-attention task	magnetoencephalo-	effect	tomography	consciousness
dichotic listening	graphy (MEG)	saccadic eye movement	(PET scan)	mindless reading
shadow	technique	fovea	executive attention	mind wandering
cocktail party effect	cognitive-behavioral	fixation	network	thought suppression
working memory	approach	perceptual span	bottleneck theories	ironic effects of mental
Stroop effect	visual search	parafoveal preview	feature-integration	control
emotional Stroop task	isolated-feature/	regressions	theory	blindsight
phobic disorder	combined-feature	orienting attention network	distributed attention	

RECOMMENDED READINGS

Dijksterhuis, A., & Aarts, H. (2010). Goals, attention and (un)consciousness. *Annual Review of Psychology, 61*, 467–490. This interesting article explores a surprising phenomenon that is beyond the scope of your textbook. Specifically, when we want to pursue a goal, we may unconsciously decide to do this before we are consciously aware we would like to do it.

Goldstein, E. B. (Ed.). (2010). *Encyclopedia of perception*. Thousand Oaks, CA: Sage. This excellent two-volume resource examines a wide variety of topics. Because the entries are in alphabetical order, the many entries under the topic of "Attention" provide a useful extension of this current chapter.

Posner, M. I., & Rothbart, M. K. (2007). Research on attention networks as a model for the integration of psychological science. *Annual Review of Psychology, 58*, 1–23. This chapter emphasizes the neuroscience research on attention, and it argues that attention plays a major role in cognitive development and in psychological disorders.

Rayner, K., Shen, D., Bai, X., & Yan, G. (Eds.). (2008). *Cognitive and cultural influences on eye movements*. Tianjin, China: Tianjin People's Publishing House. Here is a wonderful book that appropriately expands cognitive psychology beyond the traditional boundaries of English-speaking research. The book is based on papers presented at a conference in China, and the contributers also include psychologists from Spain, Germany, Finland, and Turkey.

Working Memory

4

Chapter Introduction

Imagine hearing the following sentence, *"The woman at the park next to the lake was at least 40."* As a listener, you must store earlier encountered information, such as *"The woman at the park next to the lake"* so that when you finally hear *"was at least 40,"* you can remember that *"The woman..."* was the person who was *"at least 40."* Thus, to understand spoken language, you must be able to keep recently encountered information active in memory while processing additional incoming linguistic information. The memory system supporting one's ability to store information while simultaneously processing other incoming information is called "working memory." Working memory plays a central role not just in language understanding, but also in many of the cognitive processing tasks that you perform on a daily basis.

The capacity to simultaneously process and store information is not infinite. Instead, it is limited, and these limitations place strong capacity demands on the amount of information that your cognitive systems can pass on to long-term memory. Consider reading this sentence: *"The woman at the table in the park next to the lake in the countryside was at least 40."* Do you get the sense that processing this sentence (which is indeed completely grammatical) was more difficult? There were so many intervening phrases (*"at the table," "in the park," "next to the lake,"* etc...) that by the time you encountered *"was at least 40,"* you may have had a difficult time remembering all of the details associated with *"The woman..."* The difficulty you likely experienced while reading this sentence suggests that the amount of information you can store on the short term while also processing additional information is limited. You may become aware of these limits when you try mental arithmetic, work on a reasoning task, or solve a complicated problem (Gathercole et al., 2006; Schwartz, 2011; Just & Carpenter, 1992; Waters & Caplan, 1999).

[handwritten margin note: working memory = updated view of short-term memory]

In this chapter, we start by inspecting some of the classic research on "short-term memory." Short-term memory is a term that many of you are likely to be more familiar with than "working memory." Indeed, short-term memory and working memory refer to the same cognitive process. The term "working memory" represents an updated view of the more traditional "short-term memory." We'll start this chapter with an overview of classic research on short-term memory, before switching to a discussion of working memory. We will cover the components of the working-memory system, and will address the empirical observations motivating a theoretical switch from short-term memory to working memory. We conclude by a discussion of the role that working-memory capacity limits play in multiple cognitive domains and in the applied cognitive sciences.

Classical Research on Short-Term Memory

Pretend you are in the following situation: It's the first day of your summer internship, and your new supervisor says, "OK, I want you to meet Sarah Anderson, because you'll be working mostly with her this week. She said she would be in the meeting room down the hall." Your new supervisor walks you down the hall to the meeting room, and you try to make pleasant conversation during the short stroll. As you approach the meeting room, however, you find yourself thinking, "Now what is the name of the important person I'm about to meet? How could I possibly forget it?!?"

Unfortunately, some memories are so fragile that they evaporate before you even begin to use them. As you'll soon see, research confirms that your memory is limited in both its duration and its capacity when you must remember new information. In fact, your memory is limited, even when the delay is less than 1 minute (Paas & Kester, 2006). Limits on your short-term memory capacity influence how much information can be passed on to other cognitive systems for additional processing.

Originally, these memory limits were conceptualized in terms of limits in the capacity of **short-term memory**. Short-term memory refers to the memory system that is responsible for holding onto a small amount of information that has been recently taken in from the environment. As we will see below, short-term memory has a limited capacity, both in terms of the amount of time that the short-term memory system can hold onto information and in the amount of information that it can hold. Short-term memory can be contrasted with **long-term memory**. Long-term memory has a large capacity and contains your memory for experiences and information that have accumulated throughout your lifetime. We will focus extensively on long-term memory in the chapters that follow.

[handwritten margin note: George Miller: STM chunking ~ 7 ± 2]

Regarding short-term memory, George Miller (1956) wrote a famous article entitled "The Magical Number Seven, Plus or Minus Two: Some Limits on Our Capacity for Processing Information." Miller proposed that we can hold only a limited number of items in short-term memory. Specifically, he suggested that people can remember about seven items (give or take two). In other words, we can usually remember between five and nine items. But, what counts as an "item?" Miller used the term *chunk* to describe the basic unit in short-term memory. A **chunk** is a memory unit that consists of several components that are strongly associated with one another (Schwartz, 2011). Miller suggested, therefore, that short-term memory holds approximately seven chunks.

For example, we could remember a random sequence of about seven numbers or else a random sequence of about seven letters. However, it is often the case that you can organize several adjacent numbers or letters so that they form a single chunk. For example, suppose that your telephone area code is 617, and all the office phone numbers at your college begin with the same digits, 346. If 617 forms one chunk and 346 forms another chunk, then the phone number 617-346-3421 really contains only six chunks (that is, 1+1+4). The entire number may be within your memory span. Miller's (1956) article received major attention, and the magical number 7±2 became a prominent concept known to almost all psychology students.[*]

Miller's article was unusual because it was written at a time when behaviorism was very popular. As you know, behaviorism emphasized observable external events. In contrast, Miller's article proposed that people engage in internal mental processes in order to convert stimuli into a manageable number of chunks. Miller's work also helped to inspire some of the classic research on short-term memory, some of which we review immediately below.

---

[*]In more recent research, Nelson Cowan (2005) argues that the magical number is really in the range of four, when we consider the "pure capacity" of short-term memory—without the possibility of chunking.

In the text that follows, we discuss early studies designed to measure short-term memory capacity limitations, followed by a discussion of how word meaning influences the number of items we can store in short-term memory. We conclude this first section by considering the Atkinson–Shiffrin model of information processing.

Short-Term Memory Capacity Limits

Between the late 1950s and the 1970s, researchers frequently used two methods to assess how much information our short-term memory could hold. One measure was the Brown/Peterson & Peterson technique, and the other measure was based on the serial-position effect. Let's consider these two methods, and then we will consider another factor called "semantic similarity," which can influence short-term-memory capacity.

The Brown/Peterson & Peterson Technique

Demonstration 4.1 shows a modified version of the Brown/Peterson & Peterson technique, a method that provided much of the original information about short-term memory. John Brown (1958, 2004), a British psychologist, and Lloyd Peterson and Margaret Peterson (1959), two U.S. psychologists, independently demonstrated that material held in memory for less than one minute is frequently forgotten. This technique therefore bears the names of all three researchers. In the standard setup, the **Brown/Peterson & Peterson technique** involves presenting participants with some items that they are instructed to remember. Participants then perform a distracting task. After spending some time on the distracting task, participants are subsequently asked to recall the original items.

Peterson and Peterson (1959) asked research participants to study three unrelated letters of the alphabet, such as CHJ. The participants then saw a three-digit number, and they counted backward by threes from this number for a short period. This counting activity prevented them from rehearsing the three-letter sequence during the delay. (**Rehearsal** means repeating the items silently.) Finally, the participants tried to recall the letters they had originally seen. On the first few trials, people recalled most of the letters. However, after several trials, the previous letters produced interference, and recall was poor. After a mere 5-second delay—as you can see from Figure 4.1—people forgot approximately half of the letters they had seen.

The early research using the Brown/Peterson & Peterson technique showed that our memory is fragile for material stored for just a few seconds. This technique also inspired hundreds of studies on short-term memory, and it played an important role in increasing the support for the cognitive approach (Bower, 2000; Kintsch et al., 1999).

Demonstration 4.1	A Modified Version of the Brown/Peterson & Peterson Technique

Take out six index cards. On one side of each card, write one of the following groups of three words, one underneath another. On the back of the card, write the three-digit number. Set the cards aside for a few minutes and practice counting backwards by threes from the number 792.

Next, show yourself the first card, with the side containing the words toward you, for about 2 seconds. Then immediately turn over the card and count backward by threes from the three-digit number shown. Go as fast as possible for 20 seconds. (Use a watch with a second hand to keep track of the time.) Then write down as many of the three words as you can remember. Continue this process with the remaining five cards.

1.	appeal		4.	flower	
	Simple	687		classic	573
	Burden			predict	
2.	sober		5.	silken	
	persuade	254		idle	433
	content			approve	
3.	descend		6.	begin	
	neglect	869		pillow	376
	elsewhere			carton	

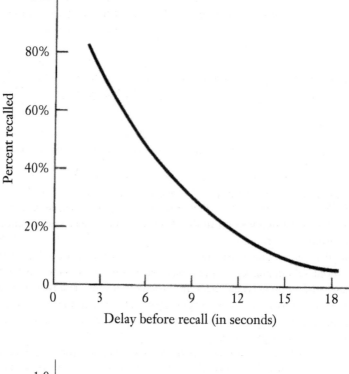

FIGURE 4.1

Typical results for the percentage recalled with the Brown/Peterson & Peterson technique, after numerous previous trials.

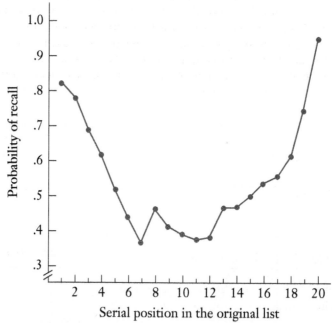

FIGURE 4.2

The relationship between an item's serial position and the probability that it will be recalled.

Source: Rundus, D. (1971). Analysis of rehearsal processes in free recall. *Journal of Experimental Psychology, 89,* 63–77.

serial-position effect curve – recency & primary effect

Serial Position Effect

Researchers have also used the serial-position effect to investigate properties of short-term memory, often by presenting participants with lists of words and then requiring participants to recall them once they have all been presented. The term **serial-position effect** refers to the U-shaped relationship between a word's position in a list and its probability of accurate recall. Figure 4.2 shows a classic illustration of the serial-position effect in research (Rundus, 1971). The U-shaped curve is very common, and it continues to be found in more recent research (e.g., Schwartz, 2011; Thompson & Madigan, 2005; Ward et al., 2005).

As you can see, the curve shows a strong **recency effect**, with better recall for items at the end of the list. Many researchers have argued that this relatively accurate memory for the final words in a list means that these items were still in short-term memory at the time of recall. In addition, the items did not move onward to a more permanent form of memory. Thus, one way of measuring the size of short-term memory is to count the number of accurately recalled items at the end of the list (Davelaar et al., 2005, Davelaar et al., 2006; R. G. Morrison, 2005). When researchers use this serial–position curve method, the size of short-term memory is estimated to be about three to seven items.

Incidentally, the serial–position curve in Figure 4.2 also shows a strong **primacy effect**, with enhanced recall accuracy for items at the beginning of the list. These early items are presumably easy to remember for two reasons: (1) They don't need to compete with any earlier items, and (2) People rehearse these early items more frequently. In general, then, people have better recall for items at the beginning and end of a list. They have less-accurate recall for the middle items.

Semantic Similarity of the Items in Short-Term Memory

Another factor that can influence short-term memory is **semantics**, or the meaning of words and sentences. Consider, for example, a classic study by Wickens and his colleagues (1976). Their technique uses an important concept from memory research called proactive interference. **Proactive interference (PI)** means that people have trouble learning new material because previously learned material keeps interfering with their new learning.

As an example of proactive interference, suppose that you had previously learned three items—XCJ, HBR, and TSV—in a Brown/Peterson & Peterson test of memory. You will then have trouble remembering a fourth item, KRN, because the three previous items keep interfering. However, if the experimenter shifts the category of the fourth item from letters to, say, simple geometric shapes, your memory will improve. You will experience a **release from proactive interference**. In fact, your performance on that new category of items will be almost as high as it had been on the first item, XCJ.

Many experiments have demonstrated release from PI when the category of items is shifted, for example, from letters to numbers. However, Wickens and his coauthors (1976) demonstrated that release from PI could also be obtained when the researchers shifted the *semantic category* of the items. Their study employed five semantic categories, which you can see in Figure 4.3. Wickens and his colleagues initially gave people three trials on the Brown/Peterson & Peterson test. In other words, on each trial they saw a list of three words, followed by a three-digit number. After counting backward from this number for 18 seconds, they tried to recall the three words.

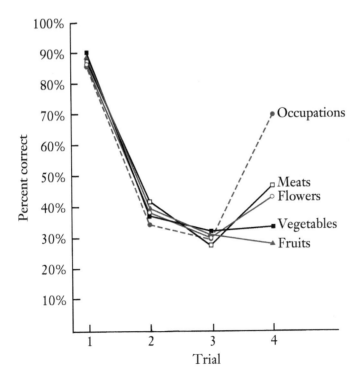

FIGURE 4.3
Release from proactive interference, as a function of semantic similarity.
On Trials 1, 2, and 3, each group saw words belonging to the specified category (e.g., occupations). On Trial 4, everyone saw the same list of three fruits.
Source: Wickens, D. D., Dalezman, R. E., & Eggemeier, F. T. (1976). Multiple encoding of word attributes in memory. *Memory & Cognition, 4,* 307–310.

On each trial in this study, participants saw three related words. For example, participants in the Occupations condition might begin with "lawyer, firefighter, teacher" on Trial 1. On Trials 2 and 3, they saw lists of additional occupations. Then on Trial 4, they saw a list of three fruits—such as "orange, cherry, pineapple"—as did the people in the other four conditions.

Look through the five conditions shown at the right side of Figure 4.3. Wouldn't you expect the buildup of proactive interference on Trial 4 to be the greatest for those in the fruits (control) condition? After all, people's short-term memory should be filled with the names of other fruits that would interfere with the three new fruits.

recall will be more difficult when categories are semantically similar

How should the people in the other four conditions perform? If meaning really is important in short-term memory, then their recall in these conditions should depend upon the semantic similarity between these items and fruit. For example, people who had seen vegetables on Trials 1 through 3 should do rather poorly on the fruit items, because vegetables and fruit are similar—they are edible and they are produced by plants. People who had seen either flowers or meats should do somewhat better, because flowers and meats each share only one attribute with fruits. However, people who had seen occupations should do the best of all, because occupations are not edible and they are not produced by plants. As per Figure 4.3, the results match these predictions perfectly. In general, then, semantic factors influence the number of items that we can store in short-term memory. Specifically, words that we have previously stored can interfere with the recall of new words that are similar in meaning. Furthermore, the degree of semantic similarity is related to the amount of interference. The importance of semantic factors in working memory has also been confirmed by other researchers (Cain, 2006; Potter, 1999; Lewis, 1996; Van Dyke, 2007; Van Dyke, Johns, & Kukona, 2014; Walker & Hulme, 1999). We know, then, that the number of items stored in short-term memory depends on both chunking strategies and word meaning.

Atkinson & Shiffrin's Model of Information Processing

During the 1950s and 1960s, many psychologists conducted research on topics related to short-term memory. Around the same time, Richard Atkinson and Richard Shiffrin (1968) proposed one classic information-processing model. Put generally, the **information-processing approach** is one approach to cognition, arguing that (a) our mental processes are similar to the operations of a computer, and (b) information progresses through our cognitive system in a series of stages, one step at a time (Gallistel & King, 2009; Leahey, 2003; MacKay, 2004).

The **Atkinson–Shiffrin model** proposed that memory involves a sequence of separate steps. In each step, information is transferred from one storage area to another.

Figure 4.4 provides a graphic example of the information-processing approach to memory, with arrows indicating the transfer of information. According to the model, external stimuli from the environment first enter sensory memory. **Sensory memory** is a storage system that records information from each of the senses with reasonable accuracy (Schwartz, 2011). During the 1960s and 1970s, psychologists frequently studied both visual sensory memory and auditory sensory memory (e.g., Darwin et al., 1972; Parks, 2004; Sperling, 1960). The model proposed that information is stored in sensory memory for 2 seconds or less, and then most of it is forgotten. For example, your auditory memory briefly stores the last words of a sentence spoken by your professor, but this memory disappears within about 2 seconds.

Atkinson and Shiffrin's model proposed that some material from sensory memory then passes on to short-term memory. Memories in short-term memory are fragile—though not as fragile as those in sensory memory (J. Brown, 2004). Atkinson and Shiffrin noted that information in short-term memory can be lost within about 30 seconds, unless it is somehow repeated (through rehearsal, for example).

According to the model, only a fraction of the information in short-term memory passes on to long-term memory (Leahey, 2003). As previously noted, long-term memory has an enormous capacity because it contains memories that are decades old, in addition to memories of events that occurred several minutes ago. Atkinson and Shiffrin's model proposed that information stored in long-term memory is relatively permanent, compared to the information stored in short-term memory.

In addition, Atkinson and Shiffrin proposed **control processes**, which are intentional strategies—such as rehearsal—that people may use to improve their memory (Hassin, 2005; Raaijmakers & Shiffrin, 2002). The original form of this model focused on the role of short-term memory in learning and memory. This model did not explore how short-term memory plays an important role when we perform other cognitive tasks (Roediger et al., 2002).

FIGURE 4.4
Atkinson and Shiffrin's
model of memory.
Source: Atkinson, R. C.,
& Shiffrin, R. M. (1968).
Human memory: A
processed system and its
control process. In K. W.
Spence & J. T. Spence (Eds.),
*The psychology of learning
and motivation: Advances in
research and theory* (Vol. 2,
pp. 89–105). New York:
Academic Press.

Let's see how the Atkinson–Shiffrin model could account for the task you are working on right now. For instance, the sentences in the previous paragraph served as "external input," and they entered into your sensory memory. Only a fraction of that material passed into your short-term memory, and then only a fraction passed from short-term memory to long-term memory. In fact, without glancing back, can you recall the exact words of any sentence in that previous paragraph?

Atkinson and Shiffrin's (1968) information-processing model dominated memory research for many years. However, its influence is now diminished. For instance, most cognitive psychologists now consider sensory memory to be the very brief storage process that is part of perception, rather than an actual memory (Baddeley et al., 2009). Many researchers also question Atkinson and Shiffrin's (1968) clear-cut distinction between short-term memory and long-term memory (Baddeley et al., 2009; J. Brown, 2004).

Although the Atkinson–Shiffrin model is no longer a viable information processing model of memory, it contributed to the growing appeal of cognitive psychology for decades after it was initially proposed. For instance, researchers conducted numerous studies to determine whether short-term memory really is distinctly different from long-term memory, what properties of items make them easier to store in short-term memory, and how short-term processes influenced what information was able to progress on to long-term memory for more long-lasting storage.

The Turn to Working Memory

During the early 1970s, Alan Baddeley and Graham Hitch were examining the wealth of research on short-term memory. They soon realized that researchers had ignored one very important question: What does short-term memory actually accomplish for our cognitive processes? Eventually, they agreed that its major function is to hold several interrelated bits of information in our mind, all at the same time, so that a person can work with this information and then use it appropriately (Baddeley et al., 2009; Baddeley & Hitch, 1974). This observation served as the foundation for a radical shift in the study of capacity limitations on cognitive processes—namely, the shift away from short-term memory in its traditional sense, and toward the notion of working memory.

Working memory is the brief, immediate memory for the limited amount of material that you are currently processing; part of working memory also actively coordinates your ongoing mental activities. In other words, working memory lets you keep a handful of items active and accessible, so that you can use them for a wide variety of cognitive tasks, and so that they can be integrated with additional incoming

---

Demonstration 4.2 ‖ The Limits of Short-Term Memory

A. Try each of the following mental multiplication tasks. Be sure not to write down any of your calculations. Do them entirely "in your head."

1. $7 \times 9 =$

2. $74 \times 9 =$

3. $74 \times 96 =$

B. Now read each of the following sentences, and construct a mental image of the action that is being described. (Note: Sentence 3 is technically correct, though it is confusing.)

1. The repairman departed.

2. The librarian that the secretary met departed.

3. The salesperson that the doctor that the nurse despised met departed.

---

information (Baddeley, 2007; Baddeley et al., 2009; Hassin, 2005; Pickering, 2006b). That is, working memory doesn't simply *store* information. Consistent with its name, it actively *works* with that information (Levin et al., 2010; Schmeichel & Hofmann, 2011).

Demonstration 4.2 illustrates the limits of our working memory. Try each task before reading further.

In Demonstration 4.2, you probably had no difficulty with the first mathematics task and the first reading task. The second math and reading tasks were more challenging, but you could still manage. The third tasks probably seemed beyond the limits of your working memory. Notice that as each task got more difficult, you had to store more information and keep it active while also working with (or, processing) the information at the same time. For example, if you are trying to comprehend the sentence that you are reading right now, you need to keep the beginning words in mind until you know how the sentence is going to end. (Think about it: Did you in fact keep those initial words in your memory until you reached the word *end*?) People also use this kind of working memory for a wide range of cognitive tasks, such as language comprehension, mental arithmetic, reasoning, and problem solving (Baddeley & Hitch, 1974; Logie, 2011).

According to the **working-memory approach** proposed by Baddeley, our immediate memory is a multipart system that temporarily holds and manipulates information while we perform cognitive tasks. Baddeley's model of working memory is different from earlier models because he proposed multiple components for our working memory (Schwartz, 2011). Figure 4.5 illustrates the current design of the model, featuring the phonological loop, the visuospatial sketchpad, the central executive, and the episodic buffer, (Baddeley, 2000a, 2000b, 2001; Baddeley et al., 2009).

Furthermore, this "workbench" holds both new material and old material that you have retrieved from storage (long-term memory). In Figure 4.5, notice that three components of working memory have direct connections with long-term memory.

Before continuing with our discussion of working memory, I want to explicitly state three important points about our limited working-memory capacity:

1. Working memory IS short-term memory. The term "short-term memory" is now considered outdated in modern day Cognitive Psychology. "Short-term memory" implies a **passive** process. It was historically conceptualized as an information storehouse with a number of shelves to hold partially processed information until it moves on to another location (presumably long-term memory). Instead, Baddeley emphasizes that we manipulate information. As a result, your working memory is an **active process**. It is like a workbench where material is constantly being handled, combined, and transformed. Working memory is thus a more popular reconceptualization of short-term memory that places an emphasis on *simultaneous* processing and storage of information (Eysenck & Keane, 2010; Schwartz, 2011; Surprenant & Neath, 2009).

2. All of the information learned through classical research on "short-term memory" also applies to working memory. Thus, working-memory capacity is limited (although not strictly to 7 +/− 2 chunks of information, as we discuss below), and is still time-limited (information typically lasts in working memory for no more than 30 seconds). The working-memory model we discuss in the rest of this chapter can account for most of the properties of short-term memory that were discussed in the previous section.

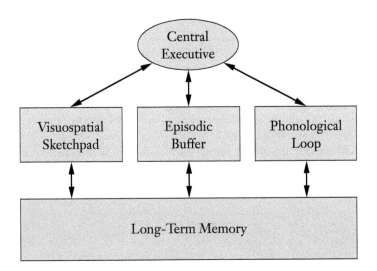

FIGURE 4.5 The working-memory approach: A simplified version of Alan Baddeley's (2000b) model of working memory.

Note: This diagram shows the phonological loop, the visuospatial sketchpad, the central executive, and the episodic buffer—as well as their interactions with long-term memory.
Source: Baddeley, A. D. (2000b). The episodic buffer: A new component of working memory? *Trends in Cognitive Sciences, 4,* 417–423.

3. According to some psychologists, the research suggests that working memory and long-term memory are basically the same (e.g., Eysenck & Keane, 2010; Jonides et al., 2008; MacDonald & Christiansen, 2002; Öztekin et al., 2010). Indeed, there is a great deal of controversy about how to divide our memory systems, and about whether or not they should be divided in the first place. For our purposes here, however, we will consider working memory as a limited-capacity processing buffer that allows for the temporary processing and storage of recently encountered information. You'll learn more about debates regarding how memory systems should be divided and conceptualized in an upper-level course on learning and memory.

[handwritten: → working memory]

Let's begin our analysis of the working-memory system by first considering why Baddeley felt compelled to conclude that working memory includes several components. Indeed, short-term memory, as in the Atkinson–Shiffrin model, was considered to be one unified process (thus occupying one box in the Atkinson–Shiffrin model). Working memory, on the other hand, involves multiple components that work together in order to provide us with the ability to simultaneously process and store information on a short-term basis. The remaining portions of this section will be dedicated to providing an overview of each of the four components of the working-memory system as proposed by Baddeley and colleagues (Baddeley, 2000a, 2000b, 2001, 2006; Baddeley et al., 2009; Gathercole & Baddeley, 1993; Logie, 1995): the phonological loop, the visuospatial sketchpad, the central executive, and the episodic buffer.

[handwritten: 4 components of W-M system]

Evidence for Components with Independent Capacities

An important study by Baddeley and Hitch (1974) provided convincing evidence that working memory is not unitary. They presented a string of random numbers to participants, who rehearsed the numbers in order. The string of numbers varied in length from zero to eight items. In other words, the longer list approached the upper limit of short-term memory, according to Miller's (1956) 7 ± 2 proposal. At the same time, the participants also performed a spatial reasoning task. This reasoning task required them to judge whether certain statements about letter order were correct or incorrect. For example, suppose that the participants see the two letters BA. If they also see the statement, "A follows B," they should respond by pressing a "yes" button. In contrast, suppose that they see the two letters BA, accompanied by the statement, "B follows A." In this case, the participants should press the "no" button.

Imagine yourself performing this task. Wouldn't you think you would take much longer and make many more errors on the reasoning task if you had to keep rehearsing eight numerals, instead of only one? To the surprise of everyone—including the participants in the study—people performed remarkably quickly and accurately on both of these two simultaneous tasks. For example, Baddeley and Hitch (1974) discovered that these participants required less than a second longer on the reasoning task when instructed

*[handwritten: 4 components of WM:
- phonological loop
- visuospatial sketchpad
- central executive
- episodic buffer]*

to rehearse all eight numerals, in contrast to a task that required no rehearsal. Even more impressive, the error rate remained at about 5%, no matter how many numerals the participants rehearsed (Baddeley, 2012; Baddeley et al., 2009).

The data from Baddeley and Hitch's (1974) study clearly contradicted the view that our temporary storage has only about seven slots, as Miller (1956) had proposed. Specifically, this study suggested that people can indeed perform two tasks simultaneously—for instance, one task that requires verbal rehearsal and another task that requires visual or spatial judgments. Incidentally, some other studies actually do suggest that verbal and visual tasks can interfere with each other (Morey & Cowan, 2004, 2005). However, most memory theorists believe that working memory seems to have several components, which can operate somewhat independently of each other (Baddeley et al., 2009; Davelaar et al., 2005; Miyake & Shah, 1999). Below, we examine each of the four components of Baddeley's working-memory system.

Phonological Loop

According to the working-memory model, the **phonological loop** can process a limited number of sounds for a short period of time. The phonological loop processes language and other sounds that you hear, as well as the sounds that you make. It is also active during **subvocalization**, for example, when you silently pronounce the words that you are reading.

Given that the phonological loop stores information in terms of sounds, we would expect to find that people's memory errors can often be traced to **acoustic confusions**; that is, people are likely to confuse similar-sounding stimuli (Baddeley, 2003, 2012; Wickelgren, 1965). When participants are shown a series of letters and asked to remember them, their accuracy at recall is lower when the letters have similar sounding names (Conrad and Hull, 1964; Jones, Macken, & Nicholls, 2004). For example, consider having to remember the letters C, T, D, G, V, and B as opposed to the letters C, W, Q, K, R, and X. People make fewer errors when the letters do not sound similar, relative to when they do.

Notice an important point: In many studies on acoustic confusions, the letters were presented visually. However, people must have been "translating" these visual stimuli into a format based on the sound properties of the letters. That is, they converted visually presented letters in the external visual world to a sound-based (phonological) code inside their minds. Importantly, they used those sound-based codes in order to rehearse the letter names in the phonological loop. People confuse acoustically similar sounds with one another when they are rehearsing the items in the phonological loop. When the letter names stored in the phonological loop are similar, and you must rehearse them in order to remember them, you may stumble and silently pronounce the wrong sound. This phenomenon is akin to stumbling on a rhyming tongue twister such as "She sells seashells." Research on acoustic confusions is but one example of how we use our phonological loops to simultaneously process and store sound-based information.

The phonological loop plays a crucial role in our daily lives beyond its obvious role in working memory (Baddeley, 2006; R. G. Morrison, 2005; Schwartz, 2011). For example, we use the phonological loop on simple counting tasks. Try counting the number of words in the previous sentence, for example. Can you hear your "inner voice" saying the numbers silently? Now try counting the number of words in that same sentence, but rapidly say the word "the" subvocally while you are counting. When our phonological loop is preoccupied with saying "the," we can't even perform a simple counting task! Theme 4 of this textbook states that our cognitive processes are interrelated with one another; they do not operate in isolation. Why does it get difficult to count while repeating the word "the" to yourself? The capacity of the phonological loop is limited. By repeating the word "the," you have taken up some of the capacity of the phonological loop, thus limiting your ability to store more sounds.

Let's consider some representative examples of how the phonological loop plays a central role in other cognitive processes:

1. Working memory is the "gateway" to long-term memory. For example, think about your experience while reading this section. All of the information that you have encountered while reading passed into your phonological loop. Notice that you probably can't recall every word that you read. But, you can recall specific facts, the details of experiments that were discussed, and so forth. The information that you can currently recall left your phonological loop and ended up in long-term memory.

(handwritten margin notes:)

so we may be able to perform two tasks (like visual or verbal tasks) simultaneously

PHONOLOGICAL LOOP
- *subvocalization*
- *acoustic confusion*
- *inner-voice*
- *self-instruction*
- *activate frontal lobe & temporal lobe in left hemisphere*
- *TMS*
- *limited capacity*
- *process lang. & sounds*
- *pronounce words you read*
- *learning new words*
- *producing language*
- *learning new language*

2. You use your phonological loop during **self-instruction** when you silently remind yourself about something you need to do in the future or how to use some complicated equipment. In fact, talking to yourself—in moderation!—is a useful cognitive strategy (Gathercole et al., 2006).

3. You use your phonological loop when you learn new words in your first language (Baddeley et al., 2009; de Jong, 2006; Knott & Marslen-Wilson, 2001). You also use it when you are reading. Be honest: The first time you see a long word, such as *phonological*, can you read that word without silently pronouncing it?

4. The phonological loop plays an important role when you produce language, for example, when you tell a friend about a trip you made last summer (Acheson & MacDonald, 2009) and also when you are learning a new language (Masoura & Gathercole, 2005).

5. Mathematical calculations and problem-solving tasks require the phonological loop, so that you can keep track of numbers and other information (Bull & Espy, 2006).

Neuroscience Research on the Phonological Loop

Researchers have sometimes used neuroscience techniques to explore the phonological loop. In general, these studies have shown that phonological-loop tasks activate part of the frontal lobe and part of the temporal lobe in the left hemisphere of the brain (Baddeley, 2006; Thompson & Madigan, 2005). This finding makes sense. Compared to the right hemisphere of the brain, the left hemisphere is more likely to process information related to language.

Let's consider a neuroscience study by Leonor Romero Lauro and her colleagues (2010), which provides more specific details. **Transcranial Magnetic Stimulation (TMS)** is a neuroscience technique that uses a magnetic field to briefly stimulate a specific location on the cortex. (No surgery or other invasive procedures are involved.) This stimulation interferes—very briefly—with information processing, but it does not harm the brain. Romero Lauro and her colleagues administered TMS for two parts of the brain, so that they could confirm how the phonological loop processes language.

Figure 2.1 in Chapter 2 shows a diagram of the cortex. One location that Romero Lauro and her colleagues studied was in the left frontal lobe, the part of the brain that might be activated when you *rehearse* verbal material. The other location they studied was in the left parietal lobe, the part of the brain that might be activated when you *store* auditory information. These researchers also included a sham procedure, which resembled each TMS procedure, but without any actual stimulation.

Immediately after either the TMS stimulation or the sham procedure, the participants saw a sentence, accompanied by a sketch. The sentence either matched or did not match the sketch. For example, a short, simple sentence might be, "The boy is giving the cat to the woman." An *incorrect* match would show the woman giving the cat to the boy. As it happened, this task was so simple that the participants almost always provided the right answer, even with the TMS procedure. In other words, neither the left frontal lobe nor the left parietal lobe is highly engaged in the processing of short, simple sentences.

A second group contained sentences that were long, but had simple syntax. A long but simple sentence might be, "The girl is eating cake and the boy is drinking milk." Participants in this condition made the most errors if the TMS had been administered to the left parietal lobe. Apparently, the stimulation in this area reduced the participants' ability to store all the words in this long sentence, and so they made errors. In other words, it appears that the left parietal lobe is engaged while processing long but simple sentences.

A third group of sentences were long, and they also had complex grammar. A long, complex sentence might be, "The cat that the boy is watching is drinking milk." Participants in this condition made many errors if the TMS had been administered to *either* the left parietal lobe or the left frontal lobe. Apparently, the *left frontal lobe* could not effectively rehearse these grammatically complex sentences. Furthermore, the *left parietal lobe* could not effectively store these long sentences immediately following TMS. In other words, both the left frontal lobe and the left parietal lobe are engaged when rehearsing and storing complex, lengthy sentences.

Notice, then, that the research on the phonological loop suggests that our working memory is much more sophisticated than just a storehouse of 7 ± 2 items. Even if we focus just on the phonological loop, the findings are complex.

Visuospatial Sketchpad

A second component of Baddeley's model of working memory is the **visuospatial sketchpad**, which processes both visual and spatial information. This kind of working memory allows you to look at a complex scene and gather visual information about objects and landmarks. It also allows you to navigate from one location to another (Logie, 2011; Logie & Della Sala, 2005; Vandierendonck & Szmalec, 2011a). Incidentally, the visuospatial sketchpad has been known by a variety of different names, such as *visuospatial working memory*, and *short-term visual memory*. You may encounter these alternate terms in other discussions of working memory.

As you begin reading about the visuospatial sketchpad, keep in mind the classic research by Baddeley and Hitch (1974), which we discussed earlier. People can work simultaneously on one phonological task (rehearsing an eight-digit number) and one visuospatial task (making judgments about the spatial location of the letters A and B) without much alteration in their performance. These and similar results provide evidence that working memory contains different components, and that these components—such as the phonological loop and the visuospatial sketchpad—are responsible for working-memory operations on different types of input (sound-based or visual).

The visuospatial sketchpad allows you to store a coherent picture of both the visual appearance of the objects and their relative positions in a scene (Hollingworth, 2004, 2006a; Logie, 2011; Vandierendonck & Szmalec, 2011b). The visuospatial sketchpad also stores visual information that you encode from a verbal description (Baddeley, 2006; Pickering, 2006a). For example, when a friend tells a story, you may find yourself visualizing the scene.

Earlier, we saw that the phonological loop has a limited capacity. The visuospatial sketchpad also has a limited capacity (Alvarez & Cavanaugh, 2004; Baddeley, 2006; Hollingworth, 2004). I remember tutoring a high school student in geometry. When working on her own, she often tried to solve her geometry problems on a small scrap of paper. As you might imagine, the limited space caused her to make many errors. Similarly, when too many items enter your visuospatial sketchpad, you cannot represent them accurately enough to recover them successfully.

Alan Baddeley describes a personal experience that made him appreciate how one visuospatial task can interfere with another (Baddeley, 2006; Baddeley et al., 2009). As a British citizen, he became very intrigued with U.S. football while spending a year in the United States. On one occasion, he decided to listen to a football game while driving along a California freeway. In order to understand the game, he tried to form clear, detailed images of the scene and the action. While creating these images, however, he discovered that his car began drifting out of its lane!

Apparently, Baddeley found it impossible to perform one task requiring a mental image—with both visual and spatial components—at the same time that he performed a visuospatial task that required him to keep his car within specified boundaries. In fact, Baddeley found that he actually had to switch the radio to music in order to drive safely.

Research on the Visuospatial Sketchpad

Baddeley's dual-task experience during driving inspired him to conduct some laboratory studies. This research confirmed that people have trouble performing two visuospatial tasks at the same time (Baddeley, 1999, 2006; Baddeley et al., 1973). In general, however, psychologists have conducted less research on the visuospatial sketchpad than on the phonological loop (Baddeley et al., 2009). One problem is that we do not have a standardized set of visual stimuli that would be comparable to the words that we process using the phonological loop. Another problem is that research participants (at least in Western cultures) tend to provide names for stimuli presented in a visual form. Beginning at about age 8, people look at a shape and provide a name, such as "It's a circle inside a square" (Pickering, 2006a). If you use a verbal coding for this form, you'll probably use your phonological loop for further processing, rather than your visuospatial sketchpad.

How can researchers encourage participants to use the visuospatial sketchpad, instead of the phonological loop? Maria Brandimonte and her colleagues (1992) instructed participants to repeat an irrelevant syllable ("la-la-la") while looking at a complex visual stimulus. When the phonological loop was occupied with this repetition task, the participants usually did not provide names for the stimuli. Instead, they were more likely to use visuospatial coding.

Students in psychology and other social sciences probably use their phonological loop more often than their visuospatial sketchpad. In contrast, students in disciplines such as engineering, art, and architecture frequently use visual coding and the visuospatial sketchpad in their academic studies.

However, we all use our visuospatial sketchpad in everyday life. For example, look at one specific object that is within your reach. Now close your eyes and try to touch this object. Your visuospatial sketchpad presumably allowed you to retain a brief image of that scene while your eyes were closed (Logie, 2003). In addition, your visuospatial sketchpad is activated when you try to find your way from one location to another or when you track a moving object (Coluccia, 2008; Logie, 2003; Wood, 2011). This kind of working memory is also useful in many leisure activities, such as videogames, jigsaw puzzles, and games involving a maze (Pickering, 2006a).

Neuroscience Research on the Visuospatial Sketchpad

In general, the neuroscience research suggests that visual and spatial tasks typically activate several regions in the right hemisphere of the cortex, rather than the left hemisphere (Gazzaniga et al., 2009; Logie, 2003; Thompson & Madigan, 2005). Furthermore, working-memory tasks with a strong visual component typically activate the occipital region, a part of the brain that is responsible for visual perception (Baddeley, 2001). (Refer again to Figure 2.1). However, the specific location of brain activity depends on task difficulty and other characteristics of the task (Logie & Della Sala, 2005). In addition, various regions of the frontal cortex are active when people work on visual and spatial tasks (Logie & Della Sala, 2005; E. E. Smith, 2000). Research on spatial working memory also suggests that people mentally rehearse this material by shifting their selective attention from one location to another in their mental image (Awh et al., 1999). As a result, this kind of mental rehearsal typically activates areas in the frontal and parietal lobes (Olesen et al., 2004; Posner & Rothbart, 2007b). These are the same areas of the cortex that are associated with attention, as we discussed in Chapter 3.

Central Executive

According to the working-memory model, the **central executive** integrates information from the phonological loop, the visuospatial sketchpad, the episodic buffer (discussed below), and long-term memory. The central executive also plays a major role in focusing attention, selecting strategies, transforming information, and coordinating behavior (Baddeley et al., 2009; Reuter-Lorenz & Jonides, 2007). In addition, Baddeley (2012) argues that the central executive has a wide variety of different functions, such as focusing attention and switching between tasks. The central executive is therefore extremely important and complex. However, it is also the least understood component of working memory (Baddeley, 2006; Bull & Espy, 2006).

In addition, the central executive is responsible for suppressing irrelevant information (Alloway, 2011; Baddeley, 2006, 2012; Hasher et al., 2007). In your everyday activities, your central executive helps you decide what to do next. It also helps you decide what *not* to do, so that you don't become sidetracked from your primary goal.

Characteristics of the Central Executive

Most researchers emphasize that the central executive plans and coordinates, but it does not store information (Baddeley, 2000b, 2006; Logie, 2003). As you know, both the phonological loop and the visuospatial sketchpad have specialized storage systems.

Compared to the two systems we've discussed, the central executive is more difficult to study using controlled research techniques. However, the central executive plays a critical role in the overall functions of working memory. Baddeley (1986) provides a literary analogy. Suppose that we were to concentrate on, say, the phonological loop in our analysis of working memory. Then the situation would resemble a critical analysis of Shakespeare's play *Hamlet* that focuses on Polonius—certainly a minor character—and completely ignores the Prince of Denmark!

Baddeley (1999, 2006) proposes that the central executive works like an executive supervisor in an organization. According to this metaphor, an executive decides which topics deserve attention and which should be ignored. An executive also selects strategies and decides how to tackle a problem. Similarly, your own brain's central executive plays an important role when you try to solve mathematical problems (Bull & Espy, 2006). A good executive also knows not to continue using an ineffective strategy (Baddeley, 2001). Furthermore, like any executive in an organization, the central executive has a limited ability to perform simultaneous tasks. Our cognitive executive cannot make numerous decisions at the same time, and it cannot work effectively on two challenging projects at the same time. Be sure to try Demonstration 4.3, which examines the familiar activity of daydreaming.

Demonstration 4.3 ‖ A Task That Requires Central-Executive Resources

Your assignment for this demonstration is to generate a sequence of random numbers. In particular, make sure that your list contains a roughly equal proportion of the numbers 1 through 10. Also, be sure that your list does not show any systematic repetition in the sequence. For example, the number 4 should be followed equally often by each of the numbers 1 through 10.

As quickly as you can, write a series of digits on a piece of paper (at the rate of approximately one digit per second). Keep performing this task for about 5 minutes. If you find yourself daydreaming, check back at the numbers you have generated. During these periods, you'll probably find that your numbers do *not* form a truly random sequence.

The Central Executive and Daydreaming

Let's look at a representative study about the central executive. At this very moment, you may be engaged in the slightly embarrassing activity we typically call "daydreaming." For example, right now you might be thinking about a TV show you saw last night or what you will be doing next weekend, rather than the words that your sensory receptors are currently registering. Interestingly, daydreaming requires the active participation of your central executive. Consider part of a study by Teasdale and his colleagues (1995), which you tried in Demonstration 4.3. These researchers selected a task that would require a major part of your central executive's limited resources. This task, called the *random-number generation task*, requires the research participants to supply one digit every second, creating the random sequence described in this demonstration. As the demonstration illustrates, the task is challenging. Approximately every 2 minutes, the researcher interrupted the task and asked the participants to write down any thoughts.

The researchers then inspected the trials on which the participants reported that they had been thinking about the numbers. On these trials, the results showed that the participants had been able to successfully generate a random sequence of numbers. In contrast, when the participants reported daydreaming, their number sequences were far from random. Apparently, their daydreaming occupied such a large portion of the resources of the central executive that they could not create a genuinely random sequence of numbers.

Neuroscience Research on the Central Executive

In general, researchers know less about the biological characteristics of the central executive than they know about the phonological loop or the visuospatial sketchpad. However, neuroscientists have gathered data from people with frontal-lobe lesions, as well as from neuroimaging research.

This neuroscience research clearly shows that the frontal region of the cortex is the most active portion of the brain when people work on a wide variety of central-executive tasks (Baddeley, 2006; Derakshan & Eysenck, 2010b; Jonides et al., 2008). Furthermore, both sides of the frontal region play a role in most central-executive activities (Kolb & Whishaw, 2009). For example, suppose that you are writing a paper for your cognitive psychology course. While you are working on the paper, your central executive may inhibit you from paying attention to some research articles, thus distracting you from your specific topic. The central executive is also active when you plan the order of topics in your outline. In addition, it guides you as you make decisions about your time frame for writing the paper.

Recent Views of the Central Executive

In Chapter 3, we discussed the *executive attention network*. This network, which involves the prefrontal portions of cortex, is strongly implicated in the top-down control of attention. It is involved in goal-directed behavior, and is especially important in allowing someone to maintain conscious awareness of goals that have already been established. For example, when someone wants to reach for their glass of diet coke on a table full of many glasses, the executive attention network assists in keeping that goal active while the glass is identified and arm-movement toward the glass is initiated. It is also important for helping an individual inhibit actions. Consider, for example, the decisions you need to make while crossing the street. You need to look both ways and decide whether or not a threat would be present (in the form of a moving vehicle that could hit you) before crossing. The executive attention network assists you in inhibiting action (and thus, to not cross a street when it may be dangerous). These are but only a handful of the many tasks to which the executive attention network contributes (Carlson, 2005; Balota, Law, & Zevin, 2000; Diamond 2006).

[handwritten marginalia: possibly the same thing or at least very similar — central executive & executive attention network]

Notice that this description of the *executive attention network*, as discussed in Chapter 3, seems to have a lot in common with our discussion of the central executive, above. McCabe and colleagues (2010) highlight an interesting trend in cognitive science. Whereas cognitive psychologists typically talk about a central executive component of working memory, researchers in the cognitive neurosciences have, over the past 2 decades or so, spent a lot of time working on the executive attention network. Both terms refer to very similar functions—namely, to organize and coordinate the results of multiple processing systems or subsystems. McCabe et al. administered a series of working-memory tasks, similar in nature to those in Demonstration 4.2, along with a series of tasks used by cognitive neuroscientists to study the prefrontal executive attention network (such as the Stroop task, discussed in Chapter 3). They found a very strong correlation between the different types of tasks. One possible interpretation of this strong correlation is that the executive attention network is, in many respects, the same thing as the central executive component of the working-memory system.

Future research will certainly be necessary in order to determine how executive attention relates to the central executive, and more generally to the working-memory system discussed here. No matter how one prefers to interpret the relationship between executive attention and the central executive tasks, however, there is little debate about the necessity of a "coordinator" or "organizer" process. Such a process helps us integrate information from multiple senses and systems, thus allowing us to interpret the world and decide how to react to stimuli in our environment.

Episodic Buffer

Approximately 25 years after Alan Baddeley proposed his original model of working memory, he added a fourth component of working memory called the *episodic buffer* (Baddeley, 2000a, 2000b, 2006, 2012; Baddeley et al., 2009; Baddeley et al., 2011). You can locate this component in Figure 4.5. The **episodic buffer** serves as a temporary storehouse that can hold and combine information from your phonological loop, your visuospatial sketchpad, and long-term memory.

Why did Baddeley feel compelled to propose this episodic buffer? As Baddeley explains, his original theory had proposed that the central executive plans and coordinates various cognitive activities (Baddeley, 2006; Baddeley et al., 2009). However, the theory had also stated that the central executive did not actually *store* any information. Baddeley therefore proposed the episodic buffer as the component of working memory where auditory, visual, and spatial information could all be combined with the information from long-term memory. This arrangement helps to solve the theoretical problem of how working memory integrates information from different modalities (Baddeley et al., 2009, Baddeley et al., 2011; Ketelsen & Welsh, 2010; R. G. Morrison, 2005).

[handwritten marginalia: —stores, since Baddeley said CE doesn't store info]

The episodic buffer actively manipulates information so that you can interpret an earlier experience, solve new problems, and plan future activities. For instance, suppose that you are thinking about an unfortunate experience that occurred yesterday, when you unintentionally said something rude to a friend. You might review this event and try to figure out whether your friend seemed offended. For example, you may attempt to recall this person's facial expression, as well as her or his verbal response. Naturally, you'll also need to access some information from your long-term memory about your friend's customary behavior.

The episodic buffer also allows you to bind together some concepts that had not been previously connected (Baddeley et al., 2009). For instance, you might suddenly recall a time when a person had made a rude comment to you. You can then link your friend's reaction with your own personal experiences. The episodic buffer also binds words into meaningful "chunks" or phrases, which you can remember much more accurately than words in random order (Baddeley et al., 2011). Because the episodic buffer is relatively new, very few journal articles examine the neuroscience research (e.g., Baddeley et al., 2010). However, Baddeley and his colleagues emphasize that the episodic buffer has a limited capacity—just as the capacities of the phonological loop and the visuospatial sketchpad are limited (Baddeley, 2000a, 2006; Baddeley et al., 2011). Furthermore, this episodic buffer is just a temporary memory system, unlike the relatively permanent long-term memory system. This episodic buffer allows us to create a richer, more complex representation of an event. This complex representation can then be stored in our long-term memory.

[handwritten marginalia: EPISODIC BUFFER — temp. storehouse; hold & combine info from PL, VS, and LTM; actively manipulates info; helps interpret prev-experiences, solve new probs, plan future activities; bind together concepts not previously connected; bind words into meaningful chunks of phrases; limited capacity; temp. mem. system; helps create richer, more complex representation of an event]

We have now examined four components of the working-memory model, as proposed by Alan Baddeley and his colleagues. This model is widely supported. However, other psychologists have devised somewhat different theories about working memory (e.g., Conway et al., 2007; Cowan, 2005, 2010; Ketelsen & Welsh, 2010; Logie & van der Meulen, 2009). Still, all of these theories consistently argue that working memory is complex, flexible, and strategic.

The current perspective on working memory is certainly different from the view held during the 1950s and 1960s that short-term memory is relatively rigid and had a fixed capacity. As our understanding of how different parts of the brain are connected increases, we will likely come to understand more about how the components of the working-memory system interact to produce our ability to simultaneously process and store information.

Applications of Working Memory

Working memory allows us to keep some information active in our memory while simultaneously working with that information, and while taking in additional relevant information. Individual differences in working memory predict performance on a startlingly diverse set of lab-based and real-world tasks, including attention tasks (Bleckly, Durso, Crutchfield, Engle, & Khanna, 2003; Conway, Cowan, & Bunting, 2001), visual processing tasks (Sobel, Gerrie, Poole, & Kane, 2007; see Luck & Vogel, 2013, for a review), writing ability in children (Swanson & Berninger, 1996), mathematics achievement (De Smedt, Janssen, Bouwens, Verschaffel, Boets, & Ghesquière, 2009), one's ability to self-regulate emotional expression (Schmeichel, Volokhov, & Demaree, 2008), and tasks designed to gauge the accuracy of eye witness testimony (Jaschinski & Wentura, 2002). Working memory is clearly a cognitive construct that carries with it a great deal of explanatory force. In this section, we examine the role of working memory in two applied domains. First, we provide a brief summary of the extensive body of work that demonstrates strong links between working memory capacity and academic performance. Then, we look at the role of working memory in three different clinical populations.

Working Memory and Academic Performance

Over the past 2-3 decades, psychologists have begun to focus on individual differences in working memory. In many of these studies, working-memory span tasks (very similar in nature to the tasks contained in Demonstration 4.2) were used to assess an individual's working-memory capacity. Variability in the size of an individual's working-memory capacity is strongly predictive of an individual's academic performance. Let's consider several of these areas of research:

1. Scores on working-memory tasks are positively correlated with overall intelligence and grades in school (Baddeley et al., 2009; Cowan et al., 2007; Levin et al., 2010; Oberauer et al., 2007).

2. Scores on tests of working memory—especially the phonological loop—are usually positively correlated with reading ability (Bayliss et al., 2005; Daneman & Carpenter, 1980; Swanson, 2005; Waters & Caplan, 1996).

3. Scores on central-executive tasks are correlated with verbal fluency, reading comprehension, reasoning ability, and note-taking skills (Jarrold & Bayliss, 2007; Levin et al., 2010; Novick, Trueswell, & Thompson-Schill, 2005; Oberauer et al., 2007).

These and similar data highlight the importance of working memory for academic achievement. Below, we examine the relationship between working-memory skills in individuals with either depression or Attention-Deficit/Hyperactivity Disorder (ADHD), as compared to individuals without these clinical diagnoses.

Working Memory Abilities in Clinical Populations

Here, we focus on the role of working memory in individuals with clinical depression, Attention Deficit Hyperactivity Disorder (ADHD), and Generalized Anxiety Disorder (GAD).

Working Memory and Major Depression

An individual who experiences **major depression** feels sad, discouraged, and hopeless; he or she typically reports feeling fatigued, with little interest in leisure activities (American Psychiatric Association, 2000). Between 10% and 15% of U.S. adults will experience major depression at some point during their lifetime (American Psychiatric Association, 2000). Because major depression is relatively common, it's important to consider how this disorder is related to working memory.

Let's look at a representative study by Gary Christopher and John MacDonald (2005), which compared the working-memory performance of individuals who were either depressed or nondepressed. These researchers tested 35 hospitalized inpatients who met the criteria for major depression, as well as 29 hospital assistants who worked at the same hospital but did not experience depression. The average ages were comparable, 38 for the individuals with depression and 37 for the individuals without depression. The two groups were also comparable in terms of vocabulary skills.

Christopher and MacDonald examined the three major components of Baddeley's model of working memory. For instance, they administered two tests that assessed phonological loop functioning. One task, for example, asked people to look at a series of similar-sounding letters (such as CDP), while simultaneously repeating the word "the." Then they were instructed to remember the letters in the correct order. The individuals with depression correctly repeated 3.4 letters in a row, in contrast to 5.3 letters for individuals without depression. This difference was statistically significant.

The researchers also administered one test that assessed the visuospatial sketchpad. First, the participants saw a series of visual patterns. Each pattern was arranged in a 3×3 display of black and white squares. Each pattern was then presented for 1 second, beginning with two of these patterns and working up to a longer series. Then the participants saw a "probe pattern," and they reported whether this specific pattern matched one of the original patterns in the series. The individuals with depression had an average span of 6.7, in contrast to 7.8 for individuals without depression. Although the difference between the two groups was not as large as on the phonological task, the difference was still statistically significant.

Christopher and MacDonald also administered four tests that assessed the central executive. Large differences emerged between the two groups on two tests of central-executive functioning. Specifically, one task required participants to listen to a series of letters and then report them in the reverse order. The individuals with depression had an average span of 2.8, in contrast to an average span of 4.9 for individuals without depression. A final central-executive task required participants to recall the last four letters of a string of letters that varied in length from four to eight letters. The individuals with depression had an average span of 3.2, in contrast to an average span of 7.4 for individuals without depression.

At this point, it's not clear why people with major depression have difficulty with some working-memory tasks, but not others. Still, the general results are consistent with clinical reports: People with depression often comment that they have trouble concentrating. They also tend to have a **ruminative style**; they may worry about all the things that are wrong in their life (De Lissnyder et al., 2010; Nolen-Hoeksema, 2006). These tendencies probably contribute to problems with working memory.

As Christopher and MacDonald (2005) conclude, "These findings emphasize the profound impact that depression has on the day-to-day cognitive activity of people suffering from depression" (p. 397). Poor performance on these daily activities could increase the level of depression even further. Clearly, clinical psychologists and other mental-health professionals need to know about these potential deficits in working memory for people who are clinically depressed.

Working Memory and ADHD

Working memory deficits have also been identified in individuals with ADHD. According to estimates, about 3% to 7% of the U.S. population have ADHD. **Attention-Deficit/Hyperactivity Disorder (ADHD)** is a psychological disorder characterized by inattention, hyperactivity, and impulsivity (American Psychiatric Association, 2000).

Research indicates that individuals with ADHD exhibit lower performance on both visual and verbal working memory tasks than individuals without an ADHD diagnosis. The interesting question, however, is associated with why these deficits exist. Think about possible explanations based on our discussion of the multicomponent working-memory model discussed in this chapter. Perhaps individuals with ADHD have less robust phonological loops or visuospatial sketchpads, such that their brains are not able to encode visual and sound-based material as well as individuals without the diagnosis. Indeed, some evidence suggests that there are subtle verbal working memory impairments and larger visuospatial working-memory impairments in individuals with ADHD (Nigg, 2006). Crucially, however, individuals with ADHD have deficits in the central-executive components of the working-memory system. Indeed, people with ADHD often have more difficulty than others on central-executive tasks, especially when they must inhibit a response, plan a project, or work on two tasks at the same time (Alloway, 2011; Baddeley et al., 2009; Barkley, 2006, 2010; Martinussen et al., 2005; Nikolas & Nigg, 2013; Willcutt et al., 2005). As a result, these individuals have difficulty paying close attention at school, at work, and in other activities (American Psychiatric Association, 2000).

Working Memory and Generalized Anxiety Disorder

Generalized Anxiety Disorder (GAD) is a debilitating disorder characterized by chronic, persistent, excessive worry (American Psychiatric Association, 2010). The chronic worrying experienced by affected individuals causes severe impediments to one's social, occupational, and personal life, and may cause symptoms such as muscle tension, irritability, and fatigue.

One reasonable hypothesis regarding the relationship between working memory and GAD involves the degree to which excessive worry interferes with one's working memory ability. As discussed throughout this chapter, working memory resources are limited in capacity. Excessive worrying may very well tax this resource pool, thus reducing the amount of working-memory resources left over to support other cognitive processes.

Hayes, Hirsch, and Mathews (2008) tested this hypothesis by asking high and low worriers to press a series of keys on a computer keyboard in a random order. Producing random sequences is taxing on one's working memory resources because it requires an individual to suppress the tendency to produce structured patterns. Thus, in their paradigm, less random sequences of button presses reflect a depletion of working memory resources. High- and low-worriers were asked to complete this random sequence generation task twice—one time while thinking about a worry-invoking circumstance in the individual's current life, and one time while thinking about a current positive circumstance.

High-worry individuals produced significantly less-random sequences in the worry-related relative to positive thought condition whereas no corresponding effect was detected for low-worry individuals. The authors interpreted this result as evidence that individuals prone to worry use up so much of their limited-capacity working-memory resources while worrying that fewer resources are left over to support the random sequence generation task. The excessive worrying so indicative of GAD may very well cause reductions in working memory resources, thus reducing one's ability to perform other cognitive and perceptual tasks. This effect may have particularly widespread negative consequences for daily functioning as a result of the large number of cognitive processes supported or otherwise influenced by working memory (as discussed at the beginning of this section).

Summary

The working-memory system is complex. It is a multicomponent system that requires coordination from an executive controller. In light of these properties, it is difficult to identify precisely which components of the working-memory system are atypical in clinical populations. Some of the most exciting work in cognitive psychology today is focused squarely on understanding what aspects of working memory break down in individuals with clinical diagnoses, and why. Keep our discussion of working memory in mind when you take other psychology courses. It's likely that your understanding of working memory may grant you deeper insight into how it contributes to information processing in other domains of psychology and in atypical populations.

SECTION SUMMARY POINTS

Classical Research on Short-Term Memory

1. In 1956, George Miller proposed that we can hold about seven chunks of information in short-term memory.

2. The Brown/Peterson & Peterson technique, which prevents rehearsal, shows that people have only limited recall for items after a brief delay. The recency effect in a serial-position curve is also used in measuring the limited capacity of short-term memory.

3. Word meaning can also influence the number of items we store in short-term memory; when the semantic category changes between adjacent trials, our recall for the new material increases.

4. According to the Atkinson–Shiffrin (1968) model, the items that we store in short-term memory can be lost within about 30 seconds unless they are repeated; people can use rehearsal and other control processes to improve their short-term memory.

5. Information from short-term memory that is not lost from short-term memory is passed on to long-term memory.

The Turn to Working Memory

1. Alan Baddeley and his colleagues proposed a working-memory approach in which immediate memory is not a passive storehouse;

instead, it resembles a workbench where material is continuously being combined and transformed.

2. In a classic study, Baddeley and Hitch (1974) demonstrated that people could perform a verbal task and a spatial task simultaneously, with minimal reduction in speed and accuracy on either task.

3. In the working-memory approach, the phonological loop briefly stores a limited number of sounds; additional research shows that items stored in the loop can be confused with other similar-sounding items.

4. The phonological loop is also used for long-term memory, self-instruction, learning new words, producing language, and solving problems.

5. Neuroscience research reveals that phonological tasks typically activate the left hemisphere, including the frontal lobe (for rehearsal), and the parietal lobe (for storage).

6. A second component of the working-memory approach is the visuospatial sketchpad, which stores visual and spatial information. The capacity of this feature is also limited; two visuospatial tasks will interfere with each other if they are performed simultaneously.

7. Activation of the visuospatial sketchpad is typically associated with the right hemisphere, especially the occipital region (for visual tasks), the frontal region, and the parietal region.

8. The central executive integrates information from the phonological loop, the visuospatial sketchpad, and the episodic buffer—as well as from long-term memory. The central executive is important in such tasks as focusing attention, selecting strategies, and suppressing irrelevant information. However, it does not store information.

9. The central executive cannot perform two complex tasks simultaneously; for example, daydreaming interferes with generating a random-number sequence.

10. According to neuroscience research, the central executive primarily activates various regions within the frontal lobe.

11. A relatively new component in Baddeley's working-memory approach is called the "episodic buffer"; this component temporarily stores material from the phonological loop, the visuospatial sketchpad, and long-term memory. It also binds together stimuli that were not previously connected.

Applications of Working Memory

1. Research shows that high scores on working-memory tasks are correlated with intelligence, grades in school, reading ability, and verbal fluency.

2. Adults who experience major depression frequently have difficulty with a variety of tasks involving the phonological loop, the visuospatial sketchpad, and the central executive.

3. Individuals with ADHD show working memory deficits in both visual and verbal working memory tasks, relative to control groups. This difference is most likely due to deficits in central executive functioning.

CHAPTER REVIEW QUESTIONS

1. Describe Miller's classic concept about the magical number 7 ± 2. Why are chunks relevant to this concept? Why was Miller's emphasis different from the behaviorist approach? How did the Atkinson–Shiffrin model incorporate the idea of limited memory?

2. What is the serial-position effect? Why is this effect related to short-term memory? Also discuss another classic method of measuring short-term memory.

3. This chapter described an important study by Conrad and Hull (1964), which showed that people recall more letters from the sequence "C, W, Q, K, R, X" than from the sequence "C, T, D, G, V, B." What does this study tell us about working memory? If you rehearsed these letters, what part of your brain would be most active?

4. Suppose that you have just been introduced to five students from another college. Using the information about semantic similarity, why would you find it difficult to remember their names immediately after they have been introduced? How could you increase the likelihood that you would remember their names?

5. According to the discussion of Baddeley's approach, working memory is not just a passive storehouse. Instead, it is like a workbench where material is continually being handled, combined, and transformed. Why is the workbench metaphor more relevant for Baddeley's model than for the Atkinson–Shiffrin model?

6. This chapter describes Baddeley and Hitch's (1974) research on remembering numbers while performing a spatial reasoning task (the "A follows B" task). Why does this research suggest that a model of working memory must have at least two separate stores?

7. Name some tasks that you have performed today that required the use of your phonological loop, the visuospatial sketchpad, the central executive, and the episodic buffer. Can you think of a specific task that uses all four of these working-memory components, as well as long-term memory?

8. What does the central executive do? With respect to its role in working memory, which tasks are similar to those of a business executive?

9. Turn to Figure 2.1. Using the descriptions that you have read in the current chapter, point out which parts of the brain are active for tasks that require (a) the phonological loop, (b) the visuospatial sketchpad, and (c) the central executive.

10. For many decades, researchers in the area of human memory primarily studied college students who are enrolled in introductory psychology courses. Why would the research on working memory not be applicable for a group of people who are currently experiencing major depression?

KEYWORDS

working memory
short-term memory
long-term memory
chunk
Brown/Peterson &
　Peterson
technique

rehearsal
serial-position effect
recency effect
primacy effect
semantics
proactive interference (PI)
release from proactive

interference
control processes
working-memory
　approach
phonological loop
subvocalization
acoustic confusions

self-instruction
Transcranial Magnetic
Stimulation (TMS)
visuospatial sketchpad
central executive
episodic buffer
major depression

ruminative style
Attention-Deficit/
　Hyperactivity
Disorder (ADHD
Generalized Anxiety
　Disorder (GAD)

RECOMMENDED READINGS

Baddeley, A., Eysenck, M. W., & Anderson, M. C. (2009). *Memory*. New York: Psychology Press. This textbook would be especially useful for students who want more details on Baddeley's approach to working memory.

Derakshan, N., & Eysenck, M. (Eds.). (2010). *Emotional states, attention, and working memory*. New York: Psychology Press. This book includes chapters on how working memory can be influenced by depression, anxiety, and stress, but it also explores how positive emotions can enhance cognitive performance.

Nigg, J. T. (2006). *What causes ADHD?: Understanding what goes wrong and why*. Guilford Press. A comprehensive overview of how cognitive processing differs between those with and without ADHD.

Schwartz, B. L. (2011). *Memory: Foundations and applications*. Thousand Oaks, CA: Sage. Here is an excellent, well-balanced book for students who would like additional information about memory. The chapters on memory and the brain and on memory disorders are especially helpful.

Vandierendonck, A., & Szmalec, A. (Eds.). (2011). *Spatial working memory*. New York: Psychology Press. As the title emphasizes, this book focuses on the *spatial* components of the visuospatial sketchpad. The editors argue that this component of the working-memory model has received relatively little attention. The nine chapters in the book explore topics such as memory for spatial sequences and developmental disorders in spatial memory.

Long-Term Memory

5

Chapter Introduction

Over the course of human development, and based on many years of experience with the world, you have come to possess a strikingly large amount of knowledge. This knowledge takes many forms. You know the names of your high school science teachers, of your friends and family, and of movie and TV stars. You know the physical characteristics of your best friend's face, what your cognitive psychology professor looks like, and you could probably easily identify a picture of your current living room from a collection of pictures of hundreds of other living rooms. You also have stored knowledge about events in which you have participated over time. For example, there's a good chance that many of you can recall many specific details about the day that you graduated from high school. You also know lots of basic facts about the world, such as the fact that the first President of the United States was George Washington, and that 2 + 5 = 7. Additionally, you probably know how to ride a bike, drive a car, or play an instrument. All of the information that is currently stored in your mind constitutes your "memory."

This chapter represents the first of four chapters that explore key concepts and principles associated with long-term memory. We begin with a brief overview of long-term memory, before turning to a discussion of key principles related to long-term memory—namely, how you get information into long-term memory, and how you access and retrieve it. We then discuss autobiographical memory—or, memory for events that you have experienced in your life. We conclude by examining how the principles that govern long-term memory can be applied to increase our understanding of real-world issues.

Overview of Long-Term Memory

As noted in earlier chapters, psychologists often divide memory into two basic categories: **working memory** (the brief, immediate memory for material we are currently processing) and long-term memory. Working memory is fragile—the information that you want to retain can disappear from memory after less than a minute. Additionally, the capacity of working memory is limited—you can only simultaneously process and store so much information at one point in time.

In contrast, your long-term memory is very high capacity and can retain material for many decades. **Long-term memory** refers to the high-capacity storage system that contains your memories for experiences and information that you have accumulated throughout your lifetime. Information in long-term memory can last for a few minutes to many decades. For example, Bahrick and colleagues (1975) found that people were 90% correct at recognizing their high school classmates' pictures and names, taken from their high school yearbooks, even 15 years after graduating! Information is said to be stored in your long-term memory if it is not lost or otherwise discarded by your working memory systems. Like many psychologists, however, I'm not firmly convinced that working memory and long-term memory are two distinctly different kinds of memory. I do think, however, that the division is a convenient way to partition the enormous amount of existing research and scientific knowledge about our memory processes.

Psychologists often subdivide long-term memory into more specific categories. Once again, this subdivision reflects convenience, rather than a conviction that the subdivisions represent distinctly different kinds of memory or are supported by completely different neural systems. Classically, long-term memory has been subdivided into three subtypes: episodic memory, semantic memory, and procedural memory (Herrmann, Yoder, et al., 2006). Let's briefly consider these three components.

Episodic memory focuses on your memories for events that happened to you personally; it allows you to travel backward in subjective time to reminisce about earlier episodes in your life (Gallistel & King, 2009; Surprenant & Neath, 2009). Episodic memory includes your memory for an event that occurred 10 years ago, as well as a conversation you had 10 minutes ago. Episodic memory is the major focus of this current chapter.

In contrast, **semantic memory** describes your organized knowledge about the world, including your knowledge about words and other factual information. For example, you know that the word *semantic* is related to the word *meaning*, and you know that Ottawa is the capital of Canada. Chapter 8 of this textbook focuses on semantic memory and your general knowledge about the world.

The episodic and semantic components of our long-term memory store information based on meaning. For example, you are probably not able to remember every single word contained in the opening paragraph of this chapter. You are probably able to remember, however, the basic points that were made in the opening paragraph. This observation suggests that information that gets encoded in your long-term memory is coded largely in terms of its meaning.

Finally, **procedural memory** refers to your knowledge about how to do something. For instance, you know how to ride a bicycle, and you know how to send an e-mail message to a friend. It's unclear that procedural memory is highly meaning based. Instead, it is often conceptualized in terms of sequences of motor-based information that are necessary in order to complete action components of a task.

In the two sections that follow, we discuss two aspects of long-term memory. Our first topic is encoding. During **encoding**, you process information and represent it in your memory (Einstein & McDaniel, 2004). The second topic is retrieval. During **retrieval**, you locate information in storage, and you access that information. Note, however, that these two processes cannot be separated (Hintzman, 2011). For instance, psychologists need to test how accurately you can retrieve information in order to examine how effectively you encoded the information. Research on long-term memory almost always involves both an encoding and retrieval component. Acknowledging the inseparability of these processes, we first discuss topics that highlight factors influencing encoding, although issues associated with retrieval will arise. We then place the spotlight on the retrieval process. In fact, many memory errors can be traced to inadequate retrieval strategies (Einstein & McDaniel, 2004). This observation suggests that information was sufficiently encoded and maintained. At a point in time when it had to be recalled, however, properties of the retrieval task were the root cause of your inability to recall the information.

Encoding in Long-Term Memory

The term **encoding** refers to how you process information and represent it in your memory. We focus on three important questions about encoding in long-term memory:

1. Are you more likely to remember items that you processed in a deep, meaningful fashion, rather than items processed in a shallow, superficial fashion?

2. Are you more likely to remember items if the context at the time of encoding matches the context at the time of retrieval?

3. How do emotional factors influence memory accuracy?

Before you read further though, complete Demonstration 5.1. It is an important demonstration that we will reference many times in this and subsequent chapters. So, be sure to spend some time with it.

Levels of Processing

CRAIK & LOCKHART / levels of processing / depth of processing

In 1972, Fergus Craik and Robert Lockhart wrote an extremely influential article about how we encode information. This **levels-of-processing approach** argues that deep, meaningful processing of information leads to more accurate recall than shallow, sensory kinds of processing. (This theory is also called the **depth-of-processing approach**.)

In Demonstration 5.1, you used deep processing when you considered a word's meaning (e.g., whether that word would fit in a sentence). The levels-of-processing approach predicts that your recall will be more accurate when you use a deep level of processing, in terms of meaning. In contrast, you will be less likely to recall a word when you consider its physical appearance (e.g., whether it is typed in capital letters) or its sound (e.g., whether it rhymes with another word).

In general, then, people achieve a deeper level of processing when they extract more meaning from a stimulus. When you analyze for meaning, you may think of other associations, images, and past experiences related to the stimulus. In general, you are more likely to remember a stimulus that you analyzed at a very deep level (Healy et al., 2011; Roediger, Gallo, & Geraci, 2002). As you'll see in Chapter 6, most memory-improvement strategies emphasize deep, meaningful processing.

Demonstration 5.1 | **Levels of Processing**

Read each of the following questions and answer "yes" or "no" with respect to the word that follows.

1.	Is the word in capital letters?	BOOK
2.	Would the word fit this sentence:	
	"I saw a _____ in a pond"?	duck
3.	Does the word rhyme with BLUE?	safe
4.	Would the word fit this sentence:	
	"The girl walked down the _____"?	house
5.	Does the word rhyme with FREIGHT?	WEIGHT
6.	Is the word in small letters?	snow
7.	Would the word fit this sentence:	
	"The _____ was reading a book"?	STUDENT
8.	Does the word rhyme with TYPE?	color

9.	Is the word in capital letters?	flower
10.	Would the word fit this sentence:	
	"Last spring we saw a _____ "?	robin
11.	Does the word rhyme with BALL?	HALL
12.	Is the word in small letters?	TREE
13.	Would the word fit this sentence:	
	"My _____ is 6 feet tall"?	TEXTBOOK
14.	Does the word rhyme with SAY?	DAY
15.	Is the word in capital letters?	FOX

Now, without looking back over the words, try to remember as many of them as you can. Calculate the percentage of items you recalled correctly for each of the three kinds of tasks: physical appearance, rhyming, and meaning.

Let's examine some of the research on the levels-of-processing approach. We'll first consider general material, and then we'll consider an especially deep level of processing called *self-reference*.

Levels of Processing and Memory for General Material

The major hypothesis emerging from Craik and Lockhart's (1972) paper was that deeper levels of processing during encoding should produce better recall. For example, in an experiment similar to Demonstration 5.1, Craik and Tulving (1975) found that people were about three times as likely to recall a word if they had originally answered questions about its meaning rather than if they had originally answered questions about the word's physical appearance. Numerous reviews of the research conclude that deep processing of verbal material generally produces better recall than shallow processing (Craik, 1999, 2006; Lockhart, 2001; Roediger & Gallo, 2001).

Deep levels of processing encourage recall because of two factors: distinctiveness and elaboration. **Distinctiveness** means that a stimulus is different from other memory traces. For example, suppose that you are interviewing for a job. You've just learned that one woman is especially important in deciding whether you will be hired, and you want to be sure to remember her name. You'll need to use deep processing and spend extra time processing her name. You'll try to figure out something unusual about her name that makes it different from other similar names you've heard during this interview (Worthen & Hunt, 2011). When you provide a distinctive encoding for a person's name, irrelevant names will be less likely to interfere (Craik, 2006; Schacter & Wiseman, 2006; Surprenant & Neath, 2009). As a result, the memory you have for the name will increase given that you've conducted mental operations that cause the memory to be different in some way from other potentially similar entries in long-term memory.

The second factor that operates with deep levels of processing is **elaboration**, which requires rich processing in terms of meaning and interconnected concepts (Craik, 2006; R. E. Smith, 2006; Worthen & Hunt, 2011). For example, if you want to understand the term *levels of processing*, you'll need to appreciate how this concept is related to both distinctiveness and elaboration. Think about the way you processed the word *duck* in Demonstration 5.1. Perhaps you recalled that you had recently seen ducks on a pond and that a restaurant menu had listed roast duck. This kind of semantic encoding encouraged rich processing. In contrast, suppose that the instructions for this item had simply asked whether the word *duck* was printed in capital letters. You would have simply answered "yes" or "no," without spending time on extensive elaboration.

Let's consider research on the importance of elaboration. Craik and Tulving (1975) asked participants to read sentences and decide whether the words that followed were appropriate to the sentences. Some of the sentence frames were simple, such as "She cooked the _____." Other sentence frames were elaborate, such as "The great bird swooped down and carried off the struggling _____." The word that followed these sentences was either appropriate (for example, rabbit) or inappropriate (for example, rock). You'll notice that both kinds of sentences required deep or semantic processing. However, the more elaborate, more detailed sentence frame produced far more accurate recall.

Levels of Processing and the Self-Reference Effect

According to the **self-reference effect**, you will remember more information if you try to relate that information to yourself (Burns, 2006; Gillihan & Farah, 2005; Schmidt, 2006). Self-reference tasks tend to encourage especially deep processing. Let's look at some representative research on the self-reference effect and discuss several factors that help to explain the self-reference effect. We conclude this section by examining the manner in which properties of the experimental task used to study the self-reference task can influence the results of the experiment.

1. **Representative research.** In the classic demonstration of the self-reference effect, T. B. Rogers and his coauthors (1977) asked participants to process each English word according to the specified instruction. They processed words according to (a) their visual characteristics, (b) their acoustic (sound) characteristics, or (c) their semantic (meaning) characteristics. They processed a fourth category of words according to (d) self-reference instructions; the participants were told to decide whether a particular word could be applied to themselves.

   The results showed that recall was poor for the two tasks that used shallow processing—that is, processing in terms of visual characteristics or acoustic characteristics. Recall was much better when people had processed in terms of semantic characteristics. Recall was highest, however, in the self-reference condition. Apparently, when we think about a word in connection with ourselves, we develop a particularly memorable coding for that word. For example, suppose that you are trying to decide whether the word *generous* applies to yourself. You might remember how you loaned your notes to a friend who had missed class, and you shared a box of candy with your friends—yes, *generous* does apply.

The research on the self-reference effect also supports Theme 3 of this textbook. Specifically, our cognitive system handles positive instances more effectively than negative instances. In the self-reference studies, people are more likely to recall a word that *does* apply to themselves, rather than a word that *does not* apply (Ganellen & Carver, 1985; Roediger & Gallo, 2001).

Research shows that the self-reference effect is quite powerful (e.g., Howard & Klein, 2011; Kesibir & Oishi, 2010; Rathbone & Moulin, 2010). Symons and Johnson (1997) gathered the results of 129 different studies that had tested the self-reference effect in the research prior to their own article. Then they performed a **meta-analysis**, which is a statistical method for synthesizing numerous studies on a single topic. A meta-analysis computes a statistical index that tells us whether a particular variable has a statistically significant effect, when combining all the studies. Symons and Johnson's meta-analysis confirmed the pattern we have described: People recall significantly more items when they use the self-reference technique, rather than semantic processing or any other processing method.

2. **Factors responsible for the self-reference effect.**   Let's now consider another issue: Why should we recall information especially well when we apply it to ourselves? As Tulving and Rosenbaum (2006) emphasize, a cognitive phenomenon typically requires more than just one explanation. Let's consider three cognitive factors that contribute to the self-reference effect.

One factor is that the "self" produces an especially rich set of cues. You can easily link these cues with new information that you are trying to learn. These cues are also distinctive. For example, your trait of honesty seems different from your trait of intelligence (Bellezza, 1984; Bellezza & Hoyt, 1992).

A second factor is that self-reference instructions encourage people to consider how their personal traits are connected with one another. The research shows that this kind of elaboration leads to more accurate retrieval (Burns, 2006; Klein & Kihlstrom, 1986; Thompson et al., 1996).

A third factor is that you rehearse material more frequently if it is associated with yourself. You're also more likely to use rich, complex rehearsal when you associate material with yourself (Thompson et al., 1996). These rehearsal strategies facilitate later recall. In short, several major factors work together to increase your ability to remember material related to yourself.

3. **Participants' failure to follow instructions.**   The self-reference effect is an experimentally robust effect. Mary Ann Foley and her coauthors (1999) have demonstrated, however, that the research may actually *underestimate* the power of self-reference. Specifically, these investigators speculated that research participants might sometimes "cheat" when they have been instructed to use relatively shallow processing for stimuli. In fact, the participants might actually use the self-reference technique instead.

In one of their studies, Foley and her coauthors (1999) instructed students to listen to a list of familiar, concrete nouns. However, before hearing each word, they were told about the kind of mental image they should form. Let's consider two of the conditions, in which the students were instructed (1) to "visualize the object," or (2) to "imagine yourself using the object."

For the first analysis of the data, Foley and her colleagues classified the results according to the instructions supplied by the experimenter, prior to each word. Notice in Table 5.1 that this first analysis produced identical recall for the two conditions. That is, students recalled 42% of the words, whether they had been instructed to use relatively shallow processing or deep, self-reference processing.

Table 5.1   Percentage of Items Recalled, as a Function of Imagery Condition and Analysis Condition

	Visualize the Object	Imagine Yourself Using the Object
First analysis of data	42%	42%
Second analysis of data	23%	75%

Source: Based on Foley et al., 1999.

Fortunately, however, Foley and her coauthors had also asked the students to describe their visual image for each word during the learning task. As these researchers had suspected, people in the "visualize the object" condition often inserted themselves into the mental image, so that they had actually used self-reference processing. In a second analysis, the researchers sorted the words according to the processing methods that the students had actually used, rather than the instructions they had received. As you can see, the second analysis revealed that the recall was more than three times as high when the students had used self-reference, rather than visualizing the object.

The research by Foley and her colleagues (1999) has important implications beyond this particular study. This research shows that our cognitive processes are active (Theme 1). People do not just passively follow instructions and obey the researcher precisely. Researchers need to keep in mind that participants are likely to transform the instructions, and this transformation can influence the results of the study.

Encoding-Specificity Principle

[handwritten margin note: encoding-specificity: better recall if context of retrieval is similar to context during encoding]

Consider the following scenario. You are in the bedroom and realize that you need something from the kitchen. Once you arrive in the kitchen, however, you have no idea why you made the trip. Without the context in which you encoded the item you wanted, you cannot retrieve this memory. You return to the bedroom, which is rich with contextual cues, and you immediately remember what you wanted. Similarly, an isolated question on an exam may look completely unfamiliar, although you might remember the answer in the appropriate context.

These examples illustrate the **encoding-specificity principle**, which states that recall is better if the context during *retrieval* is similar to the context during *encoding* (Baddeley et al., 2009; Surprenant & Neath, 2009; Tulving & Rosenbaum, 2006). When the two contexts do not match, you are more likely to forget the items. Three other similar terms for the encoding-specificity principle are context-dependent memory, transfer-appropriate processing, and reinstatement of context (Craik, 2006; Roediger & Guynn, 1996). Let's now consider this topic of encoding specificity in more detail. We'll begin with some representative research, and then we'll see how the research forces us to modify our earlier conclusions about levels of processing.

Research on Encoding Specificity

In a representative study, Viorica Marian and Caitlin Fausey (2006) tested people living in Chile who were fluent in both English and Spanish. The participants listened to four stories about topics such as chemistry and history. They heard two stories in English and two in Spanish. After a short delay, the participants listened to questions about each story. Half of the questions were asked in the language that matched the language of the original story (e.g., Spanish–Spanish), and half had a mismatch between the language of the story and the language of the questions (e.g., Spanish–English). The participants were instructed to answer in the same language that was used for the questions.

Figure 5.1 illustrates encoding specificity. In other words, people were relatively accurate if they had heard the story and answered the questions in the same language. However, they were less accurate if they heard the story in one language and answered the questions in a different language.

How do these context effects help us to function more competently in our daily lives? Basically, we often forget material that is associated with contexts other than our present context (Bjork, 2011). After all, we don't need to remember numerous details that might have been important in a previous setting but are no longer relevant at the present time (Bjork & Bjork, 1988). For instance, as a college student, you don't want your memory to be cluttered with details about the math textbook you used in fifth grade or the senior trip you took in high school.

Encoding specificity is relatively easy to demonstrate in real life. However, context effects are often inconsistent in the laboratory (e.g., Baddeley, 2004; Nairne, 2005; Roediger & Guynn, 1996). Let's consider two potential explanations.

1. **Different kinds of memory tasks.** One explanation for the discrepancy between real life and the laboratory is that the two situations typically test different kinds of memory (Roediger & Guynn, 1996). To explore this point, we need to introduce two important terms: recall and recognition. On a **recall task**, the participants must reproduce the items they learned earlier. (For example, can

FIGURE 5.1
Percentage of items correctly recalled, as a function of language used during encoding and language used during retrieval.

Source: Marian, V., & Fausey, C. M. (2006). Language-dependent memory in bilingual learning. *Applied Cognitive Psychology, 20,* 1025–1047.

[handwritten note:] recall = can you reproduce the item?
recognition = did you see the sp. item earlier?

you recall the definition for *elaboration*?) In contrast, on a **recognition task**, the participants must judge whether they saw a particular item at an earlier time. (For example, did the word *morphology* appear earlier in this chapter?)

[handwritten note:] real-life examples = usually recall
lab = usually focus on recognition

Let's return to encoding specificity. Our real-life examples of encoding specificity typically describe a situation in which we *recall* an earlier experience, and that experience occurred many years earlier (Roediger & Guynn, 1996). Encoding specificity is typically strong in these real-life, long-delay situations. For example, when I smell a particular flower called verbena, I am instantly transported back to a childhood scene in my grandmother's garden. I specifically recall walking through the garden with my cousins, an experience that happened decades ago. In contrast, the laboratory research usually focuses on *recognition*, rather than *recall*: "Did this word appear in the material you saw earlier?" Furthermore, that list was typically presented less than an hour earlier. Encoding specificity is typically weak in these laboratory, short-delay situations.

To summarize, the encoding-specificity effect is most likely to occur in memory tasks that (a) assess your recall, (b) use real-life incidents, and (c) examine events that happened long ago.

2. **Physical versus mental context.**   In the studies on encoding specificity, researchers often manipulate the physical context in which material is encoded and retrieved. However, *physical* context may not be as important as *mental* context. It is possible that physical details—such as the characteristics of the room—are relatively trivial in determining whether the encoding context matches the retrieval context. Instead, the encoding-specificity principle may depend on how similar the two environments *feel*, rather than on how similar they *look* (Eich, 1995).

Levels of Processing and Encoding Specificity

Craik and Lockhart's (1972) original description of the levels-of-processing approach emphasized *encoding*, or how items are placed into memory. It did not mention details about *retrieval*, or how items are recovered from memory. However, according to the encoding-specificity principle, people recall more material if the retrieval conditions match the encoding conditions (Moscovitch & Craik, 1976). Thus, encoding specificity can override level of processing. In fact, shallow processing can actually be more effective than deep processing when the retrieval task emphasizes superficial information. Notice that this point is not consistent with the original formulation of the levels-of-processing approach.

Let's consider a study that demonstrates the importance of the similarity between encoding and retrieval conditions (Bransford et al., 1979). Suppose that you performed the various encoding tasks in Demonstration 5.1. Imagine, however, that you were then tested in terms of rhyming patterns, rather than in terms of recalling the words on that list. For example, you might be asked, "Was there a word on the list that rhymed with *toy*?" People usually perform better on this rhyming test if they had originally performed the shallow-encoding task (rhyming), rather than the deep-encoding task (meaning).

This area of research demonstrates that deep, semantic processing is effective only if the retrieval conditions also emphasize these deeper, more meaningful features (Roediger & Guynn, 1996). Henry Roediger (2008) wrote an important article, in which he emphasized that the classic laws of memory have vanished. Consider the levels of processing effect and the encoding-specificity effect. Both of these effects work most of the time. However, when an important variable is changed, then the effect may disappear.

Retrieval in Long-Term Memory

Retrieval (marginal note: *Retrieval = locate info from/in LTM & have access to the info*) refers to the processes that allow you to locate information that is stored in long-term memory and to have access to that information. In our discussion of encoding, retrieval was necessary in order to determine what information had been encoded. We did not, however, specifically address processes that contribute to retrieval ability. Here, we move retrieval to the center stage. Let's first consider the distinction between two kinds of retrieval tasks—explicit and implicit memory tasks. We then explore the related topic of amnesia as it relates to retrieval.

Sometimes we retrieve material from memory in an effortless fashion. You may see a friend and her name seems to spontaneously appear in your memory. Other times, however, retrieval requires hard work! For example, you might try to recover someone's name by strategically recreating the context in which you last encountered this person (Koriat, 2000; Roediger, 2000). Who else was present, how long ago was it, and where did this event take place? Before reading any further, try Demonstration 5.2.

Explicit Versus Implicit Memory Tasks

On an **explicit memory task**, a researcher directly asks you to remember some information; you realize that your memory is being tested, and the test requires you to intentionally retrieve some information that you previously learned (Roediger & Amir, 2005; Schwartz, 2011).

(marginal note: *recall & recognition = explicit mem. task; explicit → direct; implicit → indirect*)

Almost all the studies we have discussed in Chapter 4 and the first section of Chapter 5 have used explicit memory tests. The most common explicit memory test is recall. Both recall and recognition tasks (discussed above) are examples of explicit memory tasks. In contrast, an implicit memory task assesses your memory indirectly. On an **implicit memory task**, you see the material (usually a series of words or pictures); later, during the test phase, you are instructed to complete a cognitive task that does not directly ask you for either recall or recognition (Roediger & Amir, 2005; B. L. Schwartz, 2011; Whitten, 2011).

Demonstration 5.2 | **Explicit and Implicit Memory Tasks**

Take out a piece of paper. Then read the following list of words:

picture	commerce	motion	village	vessel
window	number	horse	custom	amount
fellow	advice	dozen	flower	kitchen bookstore

Now cover up that list for the remainder of the demonstration. Take a break for a few minutes and then try the following tasks:

A. Explicit Memory Tasks

1. Recall: On the piece of paper, write down as many of those words as you can recall.
2. Recognition: From the list below, circle the words that appeared on the original list:

woodpile	fellow	leaflet	fitness	number	butter
motion	table	people	dozen	napkin	
picture	kitchen	bookstore	horse	advice	

B. Implicit Memory Tasks

1. Word completion: From the word fragments below, provide an appropriate, complete word. You may choose any word you wish.

   v_s_e_   l_t_e_   v_l_a_e   p_a_t_c   m_t_o_   m_n_a_
   n_t_b_o_   c_m_e_c_   a_v_c_   t_b_e_   f_o_e_   c_r_o_
   h_m_w_r_   b_o_s_o_e

2. Repetition priming: Perform the following tasks:
   - Name three rooms in a typical house.
   - Name three different kinds of animals.
   - Name three different kinds of stores.

For example, in Part B1 of Demonstration 5.2, you filled in the blanks in several words. Previous experience with the material—in this case, the words at the beginning of this demonstration—probably facilitated your performance on the task (Roediger & Amir, 2005).

On an implicit memory task, the researchers avoid using words such as *remember* or *recall*. For example, consider this following scenario:

> *A young woman is walking aimlessly down the street, and she is eventually picked up by the police. She seems to be suffering from an extreme form of amnesia, because she has lost all memory of who she is. She cannot even remember her name, and she is carrying no identification. Then the police have a breakthrough idea: They ask her to begin dialing phone numbers. As it turns out, she dials her mother's number, even though she is not aware whose number she is dialing.*

Daniel Schacter tells this story to illustrate the difference between explicit and implicit measures of memory (as cited in Adler, 1991). Here, dialing a phone number was a test of implicit memory. Implicit memory shows the effects of previous experience that creep out automatically—during your normal behavior—when you are not making any conscious effort to remember the past (De Houwer et al., 2009; Kihlstrom et al., 2007; Roediger & Amir, 2005).

Psychologists initially developed implicit measures so that they could measure attitudes and beliefs in social psychology. However, these techniques soon spread to cognitive psychology, as well as clinical psychology, health psychology, and other applied areas (De Houwer et al., 2009; Lane, Kang, & Banaji, 2007). Researchers have devised many techniques to assess implicit memory (Amir & Selvig, 2005; Roediger & Amir, 2005; Wiers & Stacy, 2006). You tried two of these in Demonstration 5.2. Look back at Task B1. If you stored the words from the original list in your memory, you would be able to complete those words (for example, *commerce* and *village*) faster than the words in Task B1 that had not been on the list (for example, *letter* and *plastic*).

Task B2 illustrates a second measure of implicit memory, called a *repetition priming task*. In a **repetition priming task**, recent exposure to a word increases the likelihood that you'll think of this particular word when you are subsequently presented with a cue that could evoke many different words. For example, in Task B2, you were likely to supply the words *kitchen, horse*, and *bookstore*—words that you had seen at the beginning of the demonstration. In contrast, you were less likely to supply words that you had not seen, such as *dining room, cow*, and *drugstore*.

During the last 30 years, implicit memory has become a popular topic in psychology (Roediger & Amir, 2005), although some researchers argue that implicit memory is not entirely different from explicit memory (Reder et al., 2009; Roediger, 2008).

A variety of studies demonstrate that adults often cannot remember stimuli when they are tested on an explicit memory task. However, they may remember the stimuli when tested on an implicit memory task. Some of the studies on explicit and implicit memory illustrate a pattern that researchers call a *dissociation*. A **dissociation** occurs when a variable has large effects on Test A, but little or no effects on Test B; a dissociation also occurs when a variable has one kind of effect if measured by Test A, and the opposite effect if measured by Test B. The term *dissociation* is similar to the concept of a statistical interaction, a term that might sound familiar if you have completed a course in statistics.

Let's consider an illustration of a dissociation based on the research about the level-of-processing effect. As you know from the first section of this chapter, people typically recall more words if they have used deep levels of processing to encode them. For example, participants recall more words on an *explicit memory test* if they had originally used semantic encoding, rather than encoding physical appearance.

However, on an *implicit memory test*, semantic and perceptual encoding may produce similar memory scores, or people may even score lower if they had used semantic encoding (e.g., Jones, 1999; Richardson-Klavehn & Gardiner, 1998). Notice that these results fit the definition of a dissociation because depth of processing has a large positive effect on memory scores on Test A (an explicit memory task), but depth of processing has no effect or even a negative effect on memory scores on Test B (an implicit memory task).

Anxiety Disorders and Explicit and Implicit Memory Tasks

It turns out that the presence of psychological disorders represents one type of factor that can modulate performance on retrieval tasks. For example, Kristin Mitte (2008) was interested in memory patterns of people who have anxiety disorders. The broad category called **anxiety disorders** includes psychological problems such as (1) **generalized anxiety disorder**, in which a person experiences at least six months of intense, long-lasting anxiety and worry; (2) **posttraumatic stress disorder**, in which a person keeps re-experiencing an extremely traumatic event; and (3) **social phobia**, in which a person becomes extremely anxious in social situations (American Psychiatric Association, 2000).

According to Mitte, some of the studies have shown that people with anxiety disorders remember threatening words very accurately, compared to people without these disorders. However, other studies have shown no differences. Mitte speculated that the results might depend on the nature of the memory task. Therefore, she specifically examined the research about implicit memory tasks, as well as two categories of explicit memory tasks (recognition and recall). She located 165 different research studies that had tested a total of 9,046 participants, most of whom were between the ages of 18 and 60. Then she conducted several meta-analyses—a statistical method for synthesizing numerous studies on a single topic. No matter how Mitte analyzed the data for implicit memory tasks, high-anxious and low-anxious people performed similarly.

How about the results for recognition tasks, one of the two categories that assess explicit memory? Once again, high-anxious and low-anxious people performed similarly on recognition tests. The meta-analysis for the recall tasks, however, showed statistically significant differences between high- and low-anxiety individuals. Specifically, high-anxious participants were *more likely* than low-anxious participants to recall the negative, anxiety-arousing words. In contrast, high-anxious participants were *less likely* than low-anxious participants to recall both the neutral words and the pleasant words. The high-anxious participants apparently remembered so many of these anxiety-arousing words that they were less likely to remember the other, less-disturbing words.

Mitte (2008) points out that this meta-analysis cannot tell us why high-anxious people and low-anxious people differ in their patterns of recall. It may be that anxious individuals pay more attention to the threatening words, and so these words are easier to remember. Alternatively, the recall bias may be linked to a well-developed network of concepts related to the threatening words. When an anxious person recalls a small number of these threatening words, other related words may be easily accessible.

Individuals with Amnesia

People with **amnesia** have severe deficits in their episodic memory (Buckner, 2010). Amnesia can occur for many reasons, although the most common source of amnesia stems from brain damage (trauma to the head, stroke, neurological disease, etc.). One form of amnesia is **retrograde amnesia**, or loss of memory for events that occurred prior to brain damage. This deficit is especially severe for events that occurred during the years just before the damage (Gazzaniga et al., 2009; Meeter et al., 2006; Meeter & Murre, 2004). For example, one woman known by the initials L.T. could not recall events in her life that happened prior to an accident that injured her brain. However, her memory was normal for events after the injury (Conway & Fthenaki, 2000; Riccio et al., 2003).

Retrograde amnesia is often characterized as a disorder in which individuals suffer autobiographical memory impairment (memories for past experiences and information related to oneself—defined above, and discussed at length below). More recent research suggests, however, that at least some affected individuals also experience deficits in their semantic memory (or, your long-term memory including your knowledge about words and other factual information).

Gregory, McCloskey, and Landau (2014), for example, studied the memory abilities of a patient with retrograde amnesia. The patient had been a professional artist prior to experiencing amnesia-inducing brain damage caused by encephalitis. The patient, however, lost the ability to recall the names of painters who had created famous works of art. This observation suggests that some individuals with retrograde amnesia may lose not only their memory for previous events and life experiences, but also some of the fact-based knowledge stored in long-term memory. Results such as the one discussed above are suggestive of the idea that retrograde amnesia affects more than one memory system.

The other form of amnesia is **anterograde amnesia,** or loss of the ability to form memories for events that have occurred after brain damage (Kalat, 2009). For several decades, researchers had studied a man with anterograde amnesia who was known by his initials, H.M. (James & MacKay, 2001; Milner, 1966). H.M. had such serious epilepsy that neurosurgeons operated on his brain in 1953. Specifically, they removed a portion of his temporal lobe region, as well as his **hippocampus**, a structure underneath the cortex that is important in many learning and memory tasks (Kalat, 2009).

The operation successfully cured H.M.'s epilepsy, but it left him with a severe kind of memory loss. The studies showed that H.M. had normal semantic memory, and he could accurately recall events that occurred before his surgery. However, he could not learn or retain new information. For example, he could not remember meeting certain people, even when he had spoken to them, and they had left the room for just a few minutes (Gazzaniga et al., 2009).

The research demonstrates that people with anterograde amnesia often recall almost nothing on tests of explicit memory, such as recall or recognition. That is, they perform poorly when asked to consciously remember an event that happened after they developed amnesia. They also have trouble imagining events that will occur in the future (Buckner, 2010). After all, you need information about previous events to figure out what you might do in the future!

Let's consider the pioneering work conducted by Elizabeth Warrington and Lawrence Weiskrantz (1970). These researchers presented a list of English words to individuals with anterograde amnesia. Then the researchers administered several recall and recognition tasks. Compared to control-group participants, the individuals with amnesia performed much more poorly on both kinds of explicit memory tasks. So far, then, the results are not surprising.

However, the researchers also administered implicit memory tasks. The tasks were presented as word-guessing games, though they actually assessed people's implicit memory for the words shown earlier. For example, the researchers showed the previously presented English words in a mutilated form that was difficult to read. The participants were told to guess which word was represented. Surprisingly, both the participants with amnesia and the control-group participants were correct 45% of the time. These results have been replicated many times since the original research, using both visual and auditory tasks (e.g., Roediger & Amir, 2005; Schacter et al., 1994), although some researchers have reported exceptions (Reder et al., 2009).

Notice that the research by Warrington and Weiskrantz (1970) is a good example of a dissociation. In this case, the dissociation was evident because the memory-status variable (amnesic versus control) had a major effect when measured by explicit memory tests, but had no effect when measured by implicit memory tests.

Autobiographical Memory

In essence, all memory is false to some degree. Memory is inherently a reconstructive process, whereby we piece together the past to form a coherent narrative that becomes our autobiography. In the process of reconstructing the past, we color and shape our life's experiences based on what we know about the world. (p. 373)
Source: Bernstein, D. M., & Loftus, E. F. How to tell if a particular memory is true or false.
Perspectives on Psychological Science, 4, 370–374. On page 373. Copyright © 2009.
Reprinted by permission of Sage Publications.

As we noted at the beginning of the chapter, **autobiographical memory** is your memory for events and issues related to yourself. Autobiographical memory usually includes a verbal narrative. It may also include imagery about these events, emotional reactions, and procedural information (Kihlstrom, 2009). In general, the research in this area examines recall for naturally occurring events that happen outside the laboratory. In fact, your autobiographical memory is a vital part of your identity because it shapes your personal history and your self-concept (Lampinen et al., 2004; Lieberman, 2007; McAdams, 2004).

The previous two sections in this chapter focused on encoding and retrieval in long-term memory, and they primarily examined laboratory research. In general, the dependent variable in those studies is the *number of items* correctly recalled—a *quantity*-oriented approach to memory (Koriat et al., 2000). In contrast, in autobiographical memory, the dependent variable is usually memory *accuracy*; does your recall match the actual events that happened, or does it distort the events?

The studies of autobiographical memory are typically high in ecological validity (Bahrick, 2005; Esgate & Groome, 2005; Lampinen et al., 2004). A study has **ecological validity** if the conditions in which the research is conducted are similar to the natural setting to which the results will be applied.

Our discussion of autobiographical memory first looks at schemas. Schemas can shape your memory for a previous event, so that this memory becomes more consistent with your current viewpoint. Next, we'll examine source monitoring, which shows that you can make mistakes when you try to remember where and when you learned certain information. We then discuss "flashbulb memory," a topic that focuses on especially vivid memories for important events. Our final topic is eyewitness testimony, an area of research that has obvious applications in the courtroom.

This discussion of autobiographical memory illustrates several important characteristics of our memory for life events:

1. Although we sometimes make errors, our memory is often accurate for a variety of information (Theme 2). For example, adults can recall the names of streets near their childhood home and material from their elementary school textbooks (Read & Connolly, 2007).

2. When people do make mistakes, these mistakes generally concern peripheral details and specific information about commonplace events, rather than central information about important events (Goldsmith et al., 2005; Tuckey & Brewer, 2003). In fact, it's usually helpful *not* to remember numerous small details that would interfere with memory for more important information (Bjork et al., 2005).

3. Our memories often blend together information from a variety of sources; we actively construct a unified memory at the time of retrieval (Davis & Loftus, 2007; Koriat, 2000).

Schemas and Autobiographical Memory

This discussion of schemas emphasizes how you remember common, ordinary events. A **schema** consists of your general knowledge or expectation, which is distilled from your past experiences with someone or something (Davis & Loftus, 2007; Koriat et al., 2000). For example, you have probably developed a schema for "eating lunch." You tend to sit in a particular area with the same group of people. Your conversation topics may also be reasonably standardized. You have also developed a schema for the events that occur during the first day of a class at your university. Because of your personal memories, you have even developed a schema for yourself (Ross & Wang, 2010).

We use schemas to guide our recall. As time passes, we still remember the gist of an event, although we may forget the information that is irrelevant for a particular schema (Davis & Loftus, 2007; Goldsmith et al., 2005). For example, during recall, we often show a **consistency bias**; that is, we tend to exaggerate the consistency between our past feelings and beliefs and our current viewpoint (Davis & Loftus, 2007; Schacter, 2001). For example, suppose that a researcher asks you today to recall how you felt about feminism when you were a high school student. You would tend to construct your previous emotions and values so that they would be consistent with your current emotions and values. As Schacter (2001) summarizes the consistency bias, "The way we were depends on the way we are" (p. 139). As a result, we underestimate how much we have changed throughout our lives.

The consistency bias suggests that we tell our life stories so that they are consistent with our current schemas about ourselves (Ceballo, 1999). For example, a historian named Emily Honig (1997) interviewed Chicana garment workers who had participated in a strike at a garment manufacturing company in El Paso, Texas. Shortly after the strike, these women viewed the strike as a life-transforming experience that had changed them from timid factory workers into fearless, self-confident activists.

Honig returned to interview these same women several years later. The women recalled that they had always been assertive and nonconforming, even prior to the strike. It's possible that they selectively recalled assertive episodes from their prestrike lives—episodes that were consistent with their current self-schemas. As Honig argues, these Chicana garment workers are "not inventing nonexistent past experiences, but they are retelling them with the language, perceptions, and mandates of their present" (p. 154).

We have seen that schemas can influence our memories of the past, such that they seem more similar to our present feelings, beliefs, and actions. Now we will consider source monitoring and reality monitoring. Both of these topics examine whether our memory is consistent with the actual events in our lives.

Source Monitoring and Reality Monitoring

Something like this situation has certainly happened to you. You are trying to recall where you learned some background information about a movie you saw recently. Did a friend tell you this information, or did you learn it from a review of the movie? This process of trying to identify the origin of a particular memory is called **source monitoring** (Johnson, 1997, 2002; Pansky et al., 2005). Unfortunately, we do not spontaneously monitor the source of our memories, although our memory performance would be more accurate if we did so (Higham et al., 2011).

In a typical study, Marsh and his colleagues (1997) asked college students to discuss an open-ended question on a topic such as methods for improving their university. One week later, the participants returned for a source-monitoring test. Specifically, the participants were told to identify whether each item on a list had been their own idea or someone else's idea. Interestingly, they seldom made source-monitoring mistakes; that is, they seldom claimed that an idea generated by another person had really been their own idea.

Some source-monitoring errors can be puzzling. For example, people may plagiarize inadvertently. In some legal cases, for example, a songwriter believes that he or she has composed a truly new song. However, the melody of the song may actually be based on a melody that another songwriter had composed at an earlier date (Defeldre, 2005; Dunlosky & Metcalfe, 2009).

In some cases, the mistakes in source monitoring can have very serious consequences. Marcia Johnson (1996, 1998, 2002) has emphasized that source-monitoring errors can occur at a societal level, not just at the individual level. The results can be devastating. An important source-monitoring failure occurred in 2003, when President George W. Bush was trying to provide justifications for starting the Iraq War. In his State of the Union address in early 2003, Bush discussed one important reason to justify invading Iraq. Specifically, he announced that Iraq was negotiating with an African country to buy uranium (an ingredient used in making nuclear weapons). Six months later, the public learned that this claim was based on clearly falsified documents from Niger, a country in west-central Africa. Also, the Central Intelligence Agency claimed that their agents had tried to warn the President that the information from Niger was false. Furthermore, President Bush claimed that this State of the Union address had been cleared by the CIA (Isikoff & Lipper, 2003). Unfortunately, several different errors in source monitoring on "the uranium question" apparently helped to push the United States into an expensive, destructive war that has killed thousands of U.S. troupes and hundreds of thousands of Iraqi individuals.

Marcia Johnson (2002) emphasizes that government agencies, the media, and corporation executives need to be meticulous about checking the accuracy of their information. Their goal should be to limit both the frequency and the size of source-monitoring errors.

So far, we have examined a problem called *source-monitoring errors*, in which you make a mistake by thinking that Source A provided some information, when Source B actually provided this information. A related kind of problem is called "reality monitoring." In **reality monitoring**, you try to identify whether an event really occurred, or whether you actually imagined this event (Dunlosky & Metcalfe, 2009; Reed, 2010; Schwartz, 1991). For example, you might *think* that you told a friend that an upcoming event had been cancelled. However, in reality, you had debated whether to call her or send a message . . . and you never actually conveyed that message.

In a representative study about reality monitoring, college students saw a series of familiar objects, such as a pencil (Henkel, 2011). For half of the objects, the students performed a specified action, such as breaking a pencil. For the remaining half of the objects, the students were instructed to *imagine* themselves performing a specific action, without actually doing anything to the object. One week later, the students saw photos of some of the completed actions, such as a broken pencil. One more week after that, the students were instructed to indicate whether they had actually performed each action. When they had not seen a photo of the completed action, fewer than 10% were confident that they had completed the action. In contrast, when they had seen the relevant photo three times, 25% were confident that they had actually completed this action.

Flashbulb Memories

At some point in the near future, try Demonstration 5.3. This demonstration illustrates the so-called flashbulb-memory effect. The term **flashbulb memory** refers to your memory for the circumstances in which you first learned about a very surprising and emotionally arousing event. Many people believe that they can accurately recall all the minor details about what they were doing at the time of this event (Brown & Kulik, 1977; Esgate & Groome, 2005).

For example, President John F. Kennedy was shot in 1963, yet many older adults believe that they have accurate recall for the trivial details of that news report (Neisser & Libby, 2000).

Roger Brown and James Kulik (1977) were the first researchers to study whether various important political events triggered contextually rich memories. In fact, Brown and Kulik (1977) introduced the

---

Demonstration 5.3 ‖ Flashbulb Memory

Ask several acquaintances whether they can identify any memories of a very surprising event. Tell them, for example, that many people believe that they can recall—in vivid detail—the circumstances in which they learned about the death of President Kennedy, or the September 11, 2001, terrorist attacks.

Also tell them that other vivid memories focus on more personal important events. Ask them to tell you about one or more memories, particularly noting any small details that they recall.

---

term "flashbulb memory." They reported that people tended to describe details such as their location when they heard the news and the person who gave them the news. Notice whether your friends included this information in their responses to Demonstration 5.3.

Brown and Kulik (1977) suggested that people's flashbulb memories are more accurate than memories of less surprising events. However, many later studies suggested that people make numerous errors in recalling details of national events, even though they claimed that their memories for these events were very vivid (Roediger, Marsh, & Lee, 2002; Schooler & Eich, 2000; Schwartz, 1991). Furthermore, people's memory for an expected event are just as accurate as their memory for a surprising event (Coluccia et al., 2010; Curci & Luminet, 2009).

Several researchers have studied people's ability to recall details about a tragedy that was especially vivid for many U.S. residents—the terrorist attacks of September 11, 2001. Let's look at an important study by Jennifer Talarico and David Rubin (2003), and then we'll discuss additional observations about people's memory for that particular event.

On September 12, the day after the attacks, Talarico and Rubin asked students at a North Carolina university to report specific details about how they had learned about the attacks. The students also provided similar information for an ordinary event that had occurred at about the same time. This memory about an ordinary event served as a control condition that could be contrasted with the "flashbulb memory" of the attack.

After the initial session, the students were randomly assigned to one of three recall-testing sessions. Some returned to be tested 1 week later, others returned 6 weeks later, and still others returned 32 weeks later. At these recall-testing sessions, Talarico and Rubin asked the students a variety of questions, including the details of their memory for the attack, as well as for the everyday event. These details were checked against the details that the students had supplied on September 12. Then the researchers counted the number of consistent and inconsistent details.

Figure 5.2 shows the results. The number of details provided on September 12 provides the baseline for the number of consistent details. As you can see, the consistency drops over time for each of the three testing sessions. However, notice that the size of the drop was similar for the terrorist-attack memory and for the everyday memory. As the figure shows, the number of inconsistent details increases slightly over time for both kinds of memories. Interestingly, however, the students in all conditions reported that they were highly confident that their recall of the terrorist attacks had been accurate.

Other research about memory for 9/11 shows that students at a college in New York City recalled significantly more factual details about the tragedy, compared to students at colleges in California and Hawaii (Pezdek, 2003). This finding makes sense because the New York City students lived much closer to the World Trade Center at the time they learned about the attack. They were also much more likely than the other students to know people whose lives were impacted by the event. Another study showed that people's memory accuracy for the September 11 tragedy was not related to demographic variables such as gender, age, or education (Conway et al., 2009).

So, what can we conclude from this information about flashbulb memories? It's likely that we do not need to invent any special mechanism to explain them. Yes, these memories can sometimes be more accurate than our memories for ordinary events. However, these enhanced memories can usually be explained by several standard mechanisms, such as rehearsal frequency, distinctiveness, and elaboration (Neisser, 2003; Read & Connolly, 2007). Furthermore, both flashbulb memories and "ordinary memories" grow less accurate with the passage of time (Kvavilashvili et al., 2003; Read & Connolly, 2007).

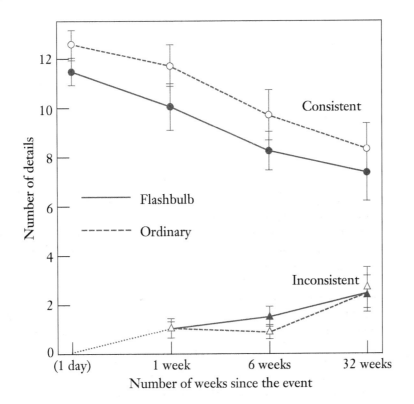

FIGURE 5.2
Average number of consistent and inconsistent details reported for a flash-bulb event (September 11, 2001, Attacks) and an ordinary event, as a function of the passage of time.
Source: Talarico, J. M., & Rubin, D. C. (2003). Confidence, not consistency, characterizes flashbulb memories. *Psychological Science, 14,* 455–461.

Eyewitness Testimony

We have seen throughout this chapter that people's long-term memory is reasonably accurate, especially if we consider memory for the gist of a message. However, eyewitness testimony requires people to remember specific details about people and events. In these cases, mistakes are more likely (Castelli et al., 2006; Wells & Olson, 2003). When eyewitness testimony is inappropriate, the wrong person may go to jail or—in the worst cases—be put to death (Kovera & Borgida, 2010).

Example of Inappropriate Eyewitness Testimony

Consider the case of Gary Graham, who was a suspect in the murder of Bobby Lambert. In truth, there was no convincing evidence for Graham's guilt—nothing like DNA or fingerprint evidence. When Graham came to trial, jury members were informed that Graham had a pistol similar to one that had shot Lambert. They were not told that the Houston police had concluded that it was not the same pistol. Furthermore, eight eyewitnesses had seen the killer near the store, but only one of them identified Graham as the killer. Graham's fate—the death penalty—was sealed by the eyewitness testimony of one woman. This woman testified that she had seen his face at night for about 3 seconds, from a distance of about 30 feet. Graham's case was never reviewed. Was Gary Graham genuinely guilty? We'll never know, because he was executed on June 22, 2000 (Alter, 2000). Reports like this one have led psychologists to question the validity of eyewitness testimony (Kovera & Borgida, 2010).

Let's examine some psychological research on eyewitness testimony. We will first consider how inaccuracies can arise when people are given misleading information after the event that they had witnessed. Next, we'll discuss several factors that can influence the accuracy of eyewitness testimony. We'll then see whether witnesses who are confident about their eyewitness testimony are also more accurate about their judgments.

The Post-Event Misinformation Effect

Many errors in eyewitness testimony can be traced to incorrect information. In the **post-event misinformation effect**, people first view an event and are then given misleading information about it. Later on, they mistakenly recall the misleading information, rather than the event they actually saw (Davis & Loftus, 2007; Pansky et al., 2005; Pickrell et al., 2004).

In Chapter 4, we discussed **proactive interference**, which means that people have trouble recalling new material because previously learned, old material keeps interfering with new memories. The misinformation effect resembles a second kind of interference called *retroactive interference*. In **retroactive interference**, people have trouble recalling old material because some recently learned, new material keeps interfering with old memories. For example, suppose that an eyewitness saw a crime, and then a lawyer supplied some misinformation while asking a question. Later on, the eyewitness may have trouble remembering the events that actually occurred at the scene of the crime because the new misinformation creates retroactive interference.

In the classic experiment on the misinformation effect, Elizabeth Loftus and her coauthors (1978) showed participants a series of slides. In this sequence, a sports car stopped at an intersection, and then it turned and hit a pedestrian. Half the participants saw a slide with a yield sign at the intersection; the other half saw a stop sign. Twenty minutes to one week after the participants had seen the slides, they answered a questionnaire about the details of the accident.

A critical question on this questionnaire contained information that was either consistent with a detail in the original slide series, inconsistent with that detail, or neutral (because it did not mention the detail). For example, the first group of people who had seen the yield sign were asked, "Did another car pass the red Datsun while it was stopped at the yield sign?" (consistent). A second group of people were asked, "Did another car pass the red Datsun while it was stopped at the stop sign?" (inconsistent). For the third group of people, the type of sign was not mentioned (neutral). To answer this question, all participants saw two slides, one with a stop sign and one with a yield sign. They were asked to select which slide they had previously seen.

As Figure 5.3 shows, people who had seen the inconsistent information were much less accurate than people in the other two conditions. They often selected a sign on the basis of the information in the questionnaire, rather than the original slide. Many studies have replicated the detrimental effects of misleading post-event information (e.g., Pickrell et al., 2004; Schacter, 2001; Wade et al., 2002).

The misinformation effect can be at least partly traced to faulty source monitoring (Davis & Loftus, 2007; Schacter et al., 1998; Zhu et al., 2010). For instance, in the study by Loftus and her colleagues (1978), the post-event information in the inconsistent-information condition encouraged people to create a mental image of a stop sign. During testing, they had trouble deciding which of the two images—the stop sign or the yield sign—they had actually seen in the original slide series.

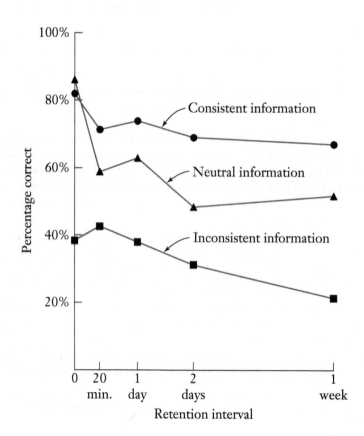

FIGURE 5.3
The effect of type of information and delay on proportion of correct answers.

Source: Loftus, E. F., Miller, D. G., & Burns, H. J. (1978). Semantic integration of verbal information into visual memory. *Journal of Experimental Psychology: Human Learning and Memory, 4,* 19–31.

The research on the misinformation effect emphasizes the active, constructive nature of memory. As Theme 1 points out, cognitive processes are active, rather than passive. The **constructivist approach** to memory emphasizes that we construct knowledge by integrating new information with what we know. As a result, our understanding of an event or a topic is coherent, and it makes sense (Davis & Loftus, 2007; Mayer, 2003; Pansky et al., 2005). In the case of the study by Loftus and her colleagues (1978), many people in the inconsistent condition made sense of the event by concluding that the car had probably paused at the stop sign.

Notice, then, that the consistency bias is one component of the constructivist approach. In short, memory does not consist of a list of facts, all stored in intact form and ready to be replayed like a DVD. Instead, we construct a memory by blending information from a variety of sources (Davis & Loftus, 2007; Hyman & Kleinknecht, 1999).

Factors Affecting the Accuracy of Eyewitness Testimony

As you can imagine, a variety of factors influence whether eyewitness testimony is accurate. We have already mentioned three potential problems in eyewitness testimony: (1) People may create memories that are consistent with their schemas; (2) people may make errors in source monitoring; and (3) post-event misinformation may distort people's recall. Here are several other important variables:

1. Eyewitnesses make more errors if they saw a crime committed during a stressful circumstance, for instance, when someone was carrying a weapon (Kovera & Borgida, 2010). A survey of U.S. law enforcement officers showed that about 85% of the officers were aware of this issue (Wise et al., 2011).

2. Eyewitnesses make more errors when there is a long delay between the original event and the time of the testimony. As time passes, recall accuracy decreases for most of our ordinary memories. A long delay in eyewitness testimony also allows additional opportunities for "contamination" from post-event misinformation (Dysart & Lindsay, 2007; Kovera & Borgida, 2010; Read & Connolly, 2007).

3. Eyewitnesses make more errors if the misinformation is plausible. For instance, in the classic study by Loftus and her colleagues (1978), a stop sign is just as plausible as a yield sign, so the participants in that study frequently made errors. People are also likely to say that an event occurred in their own life (when it really did not) if the event seems consistent with other similar experiences (Castelli et al., 2006; Davis & Loftus, 2007; Hyman & Loftus, 2002).

4. Eyewitnesses make more errors if there is social pressure (Roebers & Schneider, 2000; Roediger & McDermott, 2000; Smith et al., 2003). People make many errors in eyewitness testimony when someone pressured them to provide a specific answer (for example, "Exactly when did you first see the suspect?"). In contrast, the testimony is more accurate when people are allowed to report an event in their own words, when they are given sufficient time, and when they are allowed to respond, "I don't know" (Koriat et al., 2000; Wells et al., 2000).

5. Eyewitnesses make more errors if someone has provided positive feedback. For instance, they are much more certain about the accuracy of their decision if they had previously been given positive feedback—even a simple "Okay" (Douglass & Steblay, 2006; Semmler & Brewer, 2006). Unfortunately, in real-life lineups, the eyewitnesses often hear this kind of encouragement (Wells & Olson, 2003).

The Relationship Between Memory Confidence and Memory Accuracy

In some studies, researchers ask participants to judge how confident they are about the accuracy of their eyewitness testimony. Interestingly, in many situations, participants are almost as confident about their misinformation-based memories as they are about their genuinely correct memories (Kovera & Borgida, 2010; Wells & Olson, 2003). In other words, people's confidence about their eyewitness testimony is not strongly correlated with the accuracy of their testimony. In fact, the correlations are typically between +.30 and +.50[*] (Leippe & Eisenstadt, 2007).

This research has practical applications for the legal system. For example, a survey of U.S. law enforcement officers showed that only about 21% of the officers were aware that memory confidence is not

---

[*]A correlation is a statistical measure of the relationship between two variables, in which .00 represents no relationship and +1.00 represents the strongest positive relationship.

strongly correlated with memory accuracy (Wise et al., 2011). Unfortunately, jury members are also much more likely to believe a confident eyewitness than an uncertain one (Brewer et al., 2005; Koriat et al., 2000). However, as you now know, the research shows that a confident eyewitness is not necessarily an accurate eyewitness.

Special Topics in Long-Term Memory

If you've read the previous sections of this chapter, you should have a strong sense of how research on long-term memory intersects with other fields of psychology, and more generally, with how we understand the world in which we live. The purpose of this section is to foster your appreciation for the strong amount of continuity that exists between the core topics of cognitive psychology and your daily life. First, we examine research on expertise, with a particular emphasis on social information processing biases introduced by our own expertise. We next examine how the emotional content of information can influence its encoding, before concluding with a discussion of the false versus recovered memories debate.

Expertise

We've seen that people with amnesia experience severe memory deficits. In contrast, people with **expertise** demonstrate impressive memory abilities, as well as consistently exceptional performance on representative tasks in a particular area (Ericsson, 2003a, 2003b, 2006). K. Anders Ericsson is the psychologist who currently has the greatest "expertise" in the area of expertise. As Ericsson and his coauthors emphasize, a key to acquiring expertise is deliberate, intensive practice—on a daily basis (Duckworth et al., 2011; Ericsson, 2003a; Ericsson et al., 2004; Ericsson, Nandagopal, & Roring, 2009).

Our first topic in this discussion illustrates that people's expertise is context specific. Next, we'll examine some of the ways in which memory experts and novices differ. Our final topic—indirectly related to expertise—explores how people can identify individuals from their own ethnic background more accurately than individuals from another ethnic group.

The Context-Specific Nature of Expertise

Researchers have studied memory experts in numerous areas, such as chess, spelling competitions, sports, ballet, maps, musical notation, and memorizing extremely long sequences of numbers. In general, researchers have found a strong positive correlation between knowledge about an area and memory performance in that area (Duckworth et al., 2011; Schraw, 2005). Surprisingly, however, people who are experts in one area may not display outstanding general memory skills (Kimball & Holyoak, 2000; Wilding & Valentine, 1997). Consider Chao Lu, a 23-year-old graduate student at a Chinese university (Hu et al., 2009). In 2005, he set a new Guinness World Record by correctly reciting the first 67,890 digits of pi. However, his average digit span was 9.3, compared to the digit spans of control students, which ranged between 6.8 and 11.5. His success cannot be traced to innate ability. Instead, Chao Lu was intensely motivated; in fact, he practiced for *7 years* and developed an elaborate system of encoding and retrieving the numbers.

Other research shows that memory experts typically do not receive exceptional scores on tests of intelligence (Wilding & Valentine, 1997). For example, men who are experts in remembering information at the horse races do not score especially high on standard IQ tests. In fact, one horse race expert had an eighth-grade education and an IQ of 92 (Ceci & Liker, 1986). Again, their expertise tends to be focused on a specific area.

How Do Experts and Novices Differ?

From the information we've discussed—as well as from other resources—we know that memory experts have several advantages over nonexperts (Ericsson & Kintsch, 1995; Ericsson & Lehmann, 1996; Herrmann, Gruneberg, et al., 2006; Herrmann, Yoder, et al., 2006; Kimball & Holyoak, 2000; McCormick, 2003; Noice & Noice, 1997; Roediger, Marsh, & Lee, 2002; Schraw, 2005; Simon & Gobet, 2000; Van Overschelde et al., 2005; Wilding & Valentine, 1997). Let's consider several ways in which experts tend to have better memory strategies than novices:

1. Experts possess a well-organized, carefully learned knowledge structure, which assists them during both encoding and retrieval. For instance, chess players store a large number of common patterns that they can quickly access.

2. Experts are more likely to reorganize the new material that they must recall, forming meaningful chunks in which related material is grouped together.

3. Experts typically have more vivid visual images for the items they must recall.

4. Experts work hard to emphasize the distinctiveness of each stimulus during encoding.

5. Experts rehearse in a more strategic fashion. For example, an actor may rehearse her or his lines by focusing on words that are likely to trigger recall.

6. Experts are better at reconstructing missing portions of information from material that they partially remember.

7. Experts are more skilled at predicting the difficulty of a task and at monitoring their progress on this task.

As discussed at the beginning of this chapter, and in Chapter 4, the working memory and long-term memory systems are not completely separable and thus independent from one another—instead, they interface. Information stored in long-term memory can be brought into the working memory system in order to inform or otherwise facilitate the early portions of stimulus processing. This observation is highly apparent in the domain-specific information processing skills of experts versus novices.

In a functional magnetic resonance imaging (fMRI) study, Hruska and colleagues (2016) had expert (senior gastroenterologists) and novice (2nd year medical student) doctors read clinical cases and reason about the course of action one should take in treating the individuals described in these cases. Remember from Chapter 1 that **Functional magnetic resonance imaging (fMRI)** is a neuroimaging technique that provides precise information about how activated different brain regions are during cognitive processing in some domain. In this study, the doctors' brains were scanned in an fMRI machine as they reasoned about the facts associated with different clinical cases.

Hruska and colleagues found that areas of the prefrontal cortex implicated in working-memory processes were more activated in the novice relative to the expert doctors. They interpreted this result as evidence that expert doctors possessed more sophisticated long-term memory knowledge. Moreover, this more robust knowledge base was recruited by the working-memory system during case reasoning, thus reducing the burden on the working-memory system, as evident in the expert-doctor reductions in prefrontal cortical activation. Consistent with bullet points (1) and (2) directly above, the more knowledge you possess about a domain can ease the burden of processing experienced when encountering relevant information, and this expertise-related reduction can affect multiple cognitive systems.

Own-Ethnicity Bias

The information on expertise has interesting implications for face recognition. Specifically, you are generally more accurate in identifying members of your own ethnic group than members of another ethnic group, a phenomenon called **own-ethnicity bias** (Brigham et al., 2007; Chiroro et al., 2008; Kovera & Borgida, 2010; Pauker et al., 2010; Walker & Hewstone, 2006). This effect is also known as the *other-ethnicity effect* or the *cross-ethnicity effect.**

Hugenberg and his colleagues (2010) point out that the own-ethnicity bias has stronger research-based support, compared to studies on most other variables related to face recognition. The own-ethnicity bias is related to expertise, because people typically have more opportunities to interact with individuals from their own ethnic group, rather than other ethnic groups (Hugenberg et al., 2010). Expertise can develop with frequent experiences and interactions.

In fact, research in the United States typically shows that Black, East Asian, European American, and Latina/o individuals are more accurate in recognizing faces of people from their own ethnic group (Brigham et al., 2007; Gross, 2009; MacLin & Malpass, 2001; Meissner et al., 2005; Ng & Lindsay, 1994; Wright et al., 2003).

Faces representing your own ethnic group acquire distinctiveness. As you know from previous discussions in this chapter, your memory is most accurate when the stimuli are distinctive. Consistent with this research, Van Wallendael and Kuhn (1997) found that Black students rated Black faces as more distinctive than European American faces. In contrast, European American students rated European American faces as more distinctive than Black faces.

* The original phrases used the term *race*; I will substitute the more contemporary term *ethnicity*.

In the United States, Blacks represent about 13% of the population, and LatinX individuals represent about 16% of the population (U.S. Census Bureau, 2012b). In many European countries, White residents form the largest ethnic group. However, the second-largest group is not likely to be Black or LatinX residents. In Germany, for example, many of the residents are from a Turkish background. A study conducted with White and Turkish individuals demonstrated the own-ethnicity bias with each of these groups (Sporer & Horry, 2011).

The largest non-White population in Great Britain is South Asian, a group with origins in countries such as India, Pakistan, and Bangladesh. South Asians represent only about 4% of the British population (Walker & Hewstone, 2006). As a result, White people would have relatively little experience in interacting with South Asian people. In contrast, South Asian people would have relatively extensive experience interacting with White people.

Pamela Walker and Miles Hewstone (2006) studied facial recognition in British high school students who were either White or South Asian. Each student looked at photographs of faces that had been altered. Within each gender category, the faces differed along a continuum. On one end of the continuum, the faces looked clearly South Asian; at the other end, the faces looked clearly White. Other faces represented intermediate combinations of the two sets of facial features. In each case, the student saw photos of two faces—one after the other—and then judged whether the two faces were the same or different.

As you can see in Figure 5.4, the British White students made more accurate judgments for White faces than for South Asian faces. In contrast, the British South Asian students were equally accurate for both kinds of faces. It would be interesting to see whether British White students also demonstrate more of the own-ethnicity bias in long-term memory for faces, compared to South Asian students.

We would expect to find that the own-ethnicity bias would decrease when people have greater contact with members of other ethnic groups. The research generally shows some support for the contact hypothesis, although the evidence is not strong (Brigham et al., 2007; Meissner & Brigham, 2001; Wright et al., 2003).

How can people work to overcome the other-ethnicity effect? Hugenberg and his coauthors (2010) suggest that people first need to know that they are likely to show the other-ethnicity effect. However, they can become more accurate in identifying people from other ethnic groups if they make a genuine effort to learn facial distinctions that are relevant for other ethnic groups.

Some researchers have explored expertise in social categories other than ethnicity. For example, Anastasi and Rhodes (2003) studied younger-adult and older-adult participants. They found that participants from these two age groups were more accurate in identifying people in their own group.

Emotions and Memory

In our discussion of retrieval-related phenomena above, we noted that encoding specificity can modify the levels-of-processing effect. In some cases, the match between encoding and retrieval is even more

FIGURE 5.4
Percentage of accurate responses in a discrimination task, as a function of the ethnic group of the student and the ethnic group of the faces.

Source: Walker, P. M., & Hewstone, M. (2006). A perceptual discrimination investigation of the own-race effect and intergroup experience. *Applied Cognitive Psychology, 20,* 461–475.

Demonstration 5.4 ‖ Remembering English Words

1_____2_____3_____4_____5_____6_____7

Very Pleasant   Very Unpleasant

On a sheet of paper, write each of the words below. Then rate each word, using the above scale.

1. Hope	9. Loss	17. Insult
2. Fool	10. Trust	18. Praise
3. Style	11. Theft	19. Panic
4. Interest	12. Liberty	20. Praise
5. Quarrel	13. Decay	21. Travel
6. Hunger	14. Comfort	22. Fraud
7. Cure	15. Benefit	23. Wisdom
8. Beauty	16. Trouble	24. Rumble

Now cover up this list for the remainder of the demonstration. Take a break for a few minutes. Then write down as many words as you can recall.

Later, count how many of the following words you remembered correctly: Hope, Style, Interest, Cure, Beauty, Trust, Liberty, Comfort, Benefit, Praise, Travel, Wisdom.

Then count how many of the following words you remembered correctly: Fool, Quarrel, Hunger, Loss, Theft, Decay, Trouble, Insult, Panic, Grudge, Fraud, Rumble.

Did you recall more from the first category or the second category?

Source: Balch, W. R. (2006). Introducing psychology students to research methodology: A word-pleasantness experiment. *Teaching of Psychology, 33*, 132–134.

---

important than deep processing. But, the notion of context, and what counts as context during encoding, can be pretty broad, extending to the emotional content of information that you encounter. Before you read further, try Demonstration 5.4.

In everyday speech, we often use the terms *emotion* and *mood* interchangeably, and the terms are somewhat similar. However, psychologists define **emotion** as a reaction to a specific stimulus. In contrast, **mood** refers to a more general, long-lasting experience (Bower & Forgas, 2000). For example, you may have a negative emotional reaction to the unpleasant fragrance you just smelled in a locker room, even though you may be in a relatively positive mood today.

In 1978, I proposed that the people's enhanced recall of pleasant items is part of a more general Pollyanna Principle (Matlin & Stang, 1978). The **Pollyanna Principle** states that pleasant items are usually processed more efficiently and more accurately than less-pleasant items. This principle holds true for a wide variety of phenomena in perception, language, and decision making (Matlin, 2004). Let's consider several ways in which the emotional nature of the stimuli can influence long-term memory.

1. **More accurate recall for pleasant items.** For more than a century, psychologists have been interested in the way that emotional tone can influence memory (e.g., Balch, 2006; Hollingworth, 1910; Thompson et al., 1996; Waring & Kensinger, 2011). In a typical study, people learn lists of words that are pleasant, neutral, or unpleasant. Then their recall is tested after a delay of several minutes to several months. In a review of existing research on the topic, we found that in 39 of the 52 studies that we located on long-term memory, pleasant items were recalled significantly more accurately than unpleasant items (Matlin, 2004; Matlin & Stang, 1978). Incidentally, neutral items are usually recalled least accurately of all, suggesting that the intensity of an item's emotional tone is also important (Bohanek et al., 2005; Talarico et al., 2004). In sum, we typically recall pleasant stimuli better than terrifying stimuli, which are—in turn—recalled better than blandly boring stimuli.

   In Demonstration 5.4—a simplified version of a study conducted by William Balch (2006)—count how many pleasant words you recalled, compared to the number of unpleasant words. Was your recall more accurate for the pleasant words than for the unpleasant words? When Balch tested introductory psychology students, he found that they recalled significantly more pleasant words.

   Now focus on the neutral stimuli. Waring and Kensinger (2011) explored people's recognition for photos of stimuli that had previously been judged to be (1) very positive, such as candy; (2) very negative, such as a snake; or (3) neutral, such as a postage stamp. Each item was shown with a neutral background, such as a river. About 10 minutes later, participants completed a surprise

Table 5.2 Correct Recognition of Positive, Negative, and Neutral Stimuli, as Well as the Background Setting

	Correct Recognition of the Stimulus	Correct Recognition of the Background
Positive Stimuli	70%	44%
Negative Stimuli	71%	37%
Neutral Stimuli	56%	48%

Source: Based on Waring & Kensinger (2011).

recognition test. They looked at each of the previous photos (both the stimuli and the backgrounds), as well as some photos that had not been previously presented. In each case, they judged whether they had in fact seen the item. Table 5.2 shows that people recalled positive stimuli and negative stimuli equally well, perhaps because the delay was short. In contrast, their recall for neutral stimuli was substantially lower. Now look at their recognition of the background setting. Table 5.2 shows that this score was highest for the neutral stimuli. In other words, there is a trade-off. When the central stimulus is boring, people explore (and remember) the background more accurately than in other conditions. Notice an additional point: When the stimuli are negative, people do not remember the background very accurately.

How about our memory for real-life events? People generally recall pleasant events more accurately than unpleasant events (Mather, 2006; Matlin, 2004; Walker et al., 1997). A related finding is that drivers quickly forget their near-accidents. In fact, one study showed that they remember only 20% of these accidents just two weeks later (Chapman & Underwood, 2000).

2. **More accurate recall for neutral stimuli associated with pleasant stimuli.** Media violence is an important issue in North American culture. Surveys suggest that about 60% of television programs depict some form of violence. Furthermore, numerous studies have concluded that media violence can have an impact on both children's and college students' aggression (Bushman & Gibson, 2011; Bushman & Huesmann, 2010; Kirsh, 2011). However, let's consider a different aspect of media violence: Do people remember commercials less accurately when they are associated with violent media? To answer this question, Brad Bushman (1998) recorded 15-minute segments of two videos. One video, *Karate Kid III*, showed violent fighting and destruction of property. The other video, *Gorillas in the Mist*, was judged equally exciting by undergraduate students, but it contained no violence. Bushman then inserted two 30-second advertisements for neutral items into each of the two video clips.

College students watched either the violent or the nonviolent film clip. Then they were asked to recall the two brand names that had been featured in the commercials and to list everything they could recall about the commercials. The results showed significantly better recall—on both measures—for commercials that had appeared in the nonviolent film. Additional research confirms that anger and violence typically reduce memory accuracy (Bushman, 2005; Gunter et al., 2005).

3. **Over time, unpleasant memories fade more than pleasant memories.** W. Richard Walker and his coauthors (1997) asked undergraduate students to record one personal event each day for about 14 weeks and to rate both the pleasantness and the intensity of the event. Three months later, the participants returned, one at a time, for a second session. A researcher then read each event from the previous list, and the student was instructed to rate the current pleasantness of that event. In an analysis of the results, the rating did not change for those events that were originally considered to be neutral. However, the events originally considered to be pleasant were now considered to be *slightly* less pleasant. In contrast, the events originally considered to be unpleasant were now considered to be *much* less unpleasant (that is, closer to neutral). This last observation is consistent with the Pollyanna Principle: People tend to rate unpleasant past events more positively with the passage of time, a phenomenon called the **positivity effect**.

In a related study, Walker and his colleagues (2003) tested two groups of students. One group consisted of students who did not have tendencies toward depression, and the other group had depressive tendencies. Those who did not have depressive tendencies showed the usual positivity effect. In contrast, the students with depressive tendencies showed the same amount of fading for unpleasant and pleasant events. In other words, when people at risk for depression look back on their lives, the unpleasant events still remain unpleasant. As you can imagine, this research has important implications for clinical psychologists (Hertel & Matthews, 2011). Therapists must address a depressed client's interpretation of past events, as well as the client's current situation.

In relation to research on the role of emotional status of a stimulus and memory, then, we see repeated demonstrations of situations in which pleasant stimuli usually fare better than less-pleasant ones: (1) We often remember them more accurately; (2) we tend to forget information when it is associated with violent, unpleasant stimuli; and (3) over time, pleasant memories become slightly less pleasant, whereas unpleasant memories become much less unpleasant.

The Recovered-Memory/False-Memory Controversy

In our discussion of autobiographical memory (above)—a special type of episodic memory—we noted that it is not always accurate and is susceptible to bias from multiple internal and external sources. If you scan popular magazines, you seldom come across articles about working memory, the encoding-specificity principle, or source monitoring. However, in recent years, one topic from cognitive psychology was especially popular in both the media and professional journals: the controversy about recovered memory versus false memory (e.g., Gallo, 2006; Goodman et al., 2007). For instance, Smith and Gleaves (2007) reported that cognitive psychologists, therapists, and lawyers had published more than 800 books and articles about this topic. These so-called "memory wars" have not been resolved, though most professionals now seem to favor a compromise position. We will summarize several important components of this issue. Before you read further, however, be sure that you have tried Demonstration 5.5.

The Two Contrasting Positions in the Controversy

Most of the discussion about false memory focuses on childhood sexual abuse. One group of researchers argues that these memories can be forgotten for many years and then recovered during adolescence or adulthood. According to this **recovered-memory perspective**, some individuals who experienced sexual abuse during childhood managed to forget that memory for many years. A child would be especially likely to forget these traumatic events if the abuser was a close relative or a trusted adult. At a later time, this presumably forgotten memory may come flooding back into consciousness (Brewin, 2011; Cromer & Freyd, 2007; Freyd et al., 2005; Freyd et al., 2010; Pezdek & Freyd, 2009; Rubin et al., 2008; Smith & Gleaves, 2007).

A second group of researchers has a different interpretation of phenomena like these. We must emphasize that this second group agrees that childhood sexual abuse is a genuine problem that needs to be

---

| *Demonstration 5.5* | Remembering Lists of Words |

For this demonstration, you must learn and recall two lists of words. Before beginning, take out two pieces of paper. Next, read List 1, then close the book and try to write down as many of the words as possible. Then do the same for List 2. After you have recalled both sets of words, check your accuracy. How many items did you correctly recall?

List 1	List 2
bed	water
rest	stream
awake	lake
tired	Mississippi
dream	boat

List 1	List 2
wake	tide
snooze	swim
blanket	flow
doze	run
slumber	barge
snore	creek
nap	brook
peace	fish
yawn	bridge
drowsy	winding

addressed. However, these people don't trust the accuracy of many reports about the sudden recovery of early memories. Specifically, the **false-memory perspective** proposes that most of these recovered memories are actually incorrect memories. In other words, they are constructed stories about events that never occurred (Bernstein & Loftus, 2009; Davis & Loftus, 2007; Reyna et al., 2007).

The Potential for Memory Errors

Our discussion throughout this section on autobiographical memory should convince you that memory is less than perfect. For example, people are often guided by schemas, rather than their actual recall of an event. Also, the research on source monitoring shows that people cannot recall with absolute accuracy whether they performed an action or merely imagined performing it. In addition, we noted that flashbulb memories are not as accurate as many people believe. Furthermore, we saw that eyewitness testimony can be flawed, especially when witnesses receive misinformation.

Similar problems arise in recalling memories from childhood. For instance, during therapy, some psychotherapists may repeatedly suggest to clients that they might have been sexually abused during childhood. This suggestion could be blended with reality to create a false memory. These statements encourage clients to invent a false memory, especially because as we previously discussed, people make more errors when they experience social pressure (Bernstein & Loftus, 2009; Schwartz, 1991; Smith et al., 2003).

We cannot easily determine whether a memory of childhood abuse is correct. After all, the situation is far from controlled, and other independent witnesses are rarely available. Furthermore, the current cognitive neuroscience techniques cannot reliably distinguish between accurate and inaccurate recall of abuse (Bernstein & Loftus, 2009).

However, psychologists have conducted research and created theories that are designed to address the recovered-memory/false-memory issue. Let's first consider laboratory research that demonstrates false memory. Then we'll discuss why sexual abuse during childhood may sometimes require a different kind of explanation, compared to false memory for emotionally neutral material.

Arguments for False Memory

Research in the psychology laboratory clearly demonstrates that people often "recall" seeing a word that was never actually presented. In contrast to the real-life recall of sexual abuse, the laboratory research is very straightforward and unemotional. Researchers simply ask participants to remember a list of words they had seen earlier, and their accuracy can be objectively measured. For example, Demonstration 5.5 asked you to memorize and recall two lists of words, and then you checked your accuracy. Take a moment now to check two other items. On List 1, did you write down the word *sleep*? Did you write *river* on List 2?

If you check the original lists in Demonstration 5.5, you'll discover that neither *sleep* nor *river* was listed. In research with lists of words like these, Roediger and McDermott (1995) found a false-recall rate of 55%. People made intrusion errors by listing words that did not appear on the lists. Intrusions are common on this task, because each word that does appear on a list is commonly associated with a missing word, in this case *sleep* on the first list and *river* on the second list.

This study has been replicated numerous times, using different stimuli and different testing conditions (e.g., Gallo, 2010; Hintzman, 2011; Neuschatz et al., 2007). Many researchers argue that similar intrusions could occur with respect to childhood memories of abuse. People may "recall" events that are related to their actual experiences, but these events never actually occurred.

Other studies have demonstrated that laboratory-research participants can construct false memories for events during childhood that never actually happened. In laboratory research, these false memories include being attacked by a small dog, being lost in a shopping mall, seeing someone possessed by demons, having a skin sample removed by a school nurse, and becoming ill after eating hard-boiled eggs (e.g., Bernstein et al., 2005; Geraerts et al., 2010; Gerrie et al., 2005; Hyman & Kleinknecht, 1999; Mazzoni & Memon, 2003; Pickrell et al., 2004).

However, we need to emphasize that only a relatively small percentage of people actually claim to remember an event that did not occur. For example, researchers tried to implant a false memory that the research participant had attended a wedding at the age of 6. According to this fake story, the 6-year-old had accidentally bumped into a table containing a punch bowl, spilling punch on a parent of the bride. Interestingly, 25% of the participants eventually recalled this false memory—an entire event that did not actually occur (Hyman et al., 1995; Hyman & Loftus, 2002). Notice, however, that 75% of the students refused to "remember" the specific event.

Arguments for Recovered Memory

One problem is that these laboratory studies have little ecological validity with respect to memory for childhood sexual abuse (Freyd & Quina, 2000; Geraerts et al., 2010). Consider the studies on recalling word lists. There's not much similarity between "remembering" a word that never appeared on a list, compared to a false memory of childhood sexual abuse (Bernstein & Loftus, 2009). Events such as spilling the contents of a punch bowl can be embarrassing. However, these events have no sexual content, and they could be discussed in public. In contrast, the research shows that people cannot be convinced to create false memories for more embarrassing events, such as having had an enema as a child (Pezdek et al., 1997).

Some individuals have been sexually abused as children, and they continually remember the incidents, even decades later. Others, however, may genuinely not recall the abuse. For example, researchers have studied individuals whose sexual abuse had been documented by medical professionals or the legal system. Still, some of these individuals fail to recall the episode when interviewed as adults (Goodman et al., 2003; Pezdek & Taylor, 2002). Indeed, some people can forget about the sexual abuse for many years, but they suddenly recall it decades later.

Jennifer Freyd and her colleagues have proposed an explanation for these cases of recovered memory (DePrince & Freyd, 2004; Freyd et al., 2005; Freyd et al., 2010; Pezdek & Freyd, 2009). These researchers emphasize that childhood sexual abuse is genuinely different from relatively innocent episodes such as spilled wedding punch. In particular, they propose the term **betrayal trauma** to describe how a child may respond adaptively when a trusted parent or caretaker betrays him or her by sexual abuse. The child depends on this adult and must actively inhibit memories of abuse in order to maintain an attachment to this person.

Both Perspectives Are At Least Partially Correct

In reality, both the recovered-memory perspective and the false-memory perspective are at least partially correct. Indeed, some people have truly experienced childhood sexual abuse, and they may forget about the abuse for many decades until a critical event triggers their recall. In contrast, other people have never experienced childhood sexual abuse. However, a suggestion about abuse may create a false memory of childhood experiences that never really occurred. In still other cases, people can provide quite accurate testimony—even years afterward—about how they have been abused (Brainerd & Reyna, 2005; Castelli et al., 2006; Goodman & Paz-Alonso, 2006).

We have seen throughout this chapter that human memory is both flexible and complex. These memory processes can account for temporarily forgetting events, they can account for the construction of events that never actually happened, and they can also account for relatively accurate memory, even when the events are terrifying.

SECTION SUMMARY POINTS

Overview of Long-Term Memory

1. In contrast to short-term memory, long-term memory is high capacity and quite durable, lasting from minutes to decades.

2. Long-term memory can be subdivided into three categories: episodic memory, semantic memory, and procedural memory; this current chapter focuses on episodic memory.

3. Encoding and retrieval are tightly linked to one another, although it is possible that in some cases, a person may know something but fail to recall the information when prompted.

Encoding in Long-Term Memory

1. The research on levels of processing shows that people typically remember stimuli more accurately with deep, meaningful processing, rather than with shallow, sensory processing.

2. Deep processing encourages more accurate recall because of distinctiveness and elaboration.

3. Research on the self-reference effect demonstrates that your memory is typically more accurate if you relate the stimuli to your own personal experience.

4. To obtain a valid assessment of the self-reference effect, the stimuli must be classified in terms of the participant's *actual* mental activities, rather than in terms of the experimenter's instructions.

5. The self-reference effect is effective for several reasons: (a) because the self is a rich source of memory cues, (b) because self-reference instructions encourage people to think about how their own characteristics are interrelated, and (c) because self-reference increases people's rich, complex rehearsal.

6. According to the encoding-specificity effect, our recall is more accurate if the context during retrieval is similar to the context during encoding.

7. The encoding-specificity effect is most likely to operate in certain situations: (a) when memory is tested by recall instead of

recognition, (b) when real-life events are studied, (c) when the original event happened long ago, and (d) when mental context is emphasized.

8. Encoding specificity can modify the levels-of-processing principle.

Retrieval in Long-Term Memory

1. Explicit-memory tasks instruct participants to recall or recognize information. In contrast, implicit-memory tasks require participants to perform a cognitive task, such as completing a word that has missing letters.

2. People who have anxiety disorders are similar to other people in their memory for high-anxiety words on implicit memory tasks and on explicit recognition tasks; however, they actually *recall* more anxiety-arousing words than other people.

3. Individuals with retrograde amnesia have difficulty recalling events that occurred prior to brain damage.

4. Individuals with anterograde amnesia have difficulty recalling events that occurred after brain damage. They may recall almost nothing on tests of explicit memory; however, on tests of implicit memory, they typically perform as accurately as people without brain damage.

Autobiographical Memory

1. Research on autobiographical memory shows that our memories are usually accurate, although we may make errors on some details, and we may blend together information from different events.

2. Memory schemas encourage us to make some errors in recalling events; in addition, we may reveal a consistency bias by exaggerating the similarity between our current self-schema and our previous characteristics.

3. The research on source monitoring shows that we may have difficulty deciding where we learned some information.

4. The research on reality monitoring shows that we may have difficulty deciding whether something really happened, instead of imagining it.

5. Flashbulb memories are rich with information, and we are often confident that they are accurate; however, even our memories for national tragedies are not especially accurate.

6. In eyewitness testimony, the post-event misinformation effect can occur if misleading information is introduced after a witness has seen an event. The research is consistent with the constructivist approach to memory.

7. Errors in eyewitness memory are more likely if the crime occurred during stressful circumstances, if the witness observed an event long ago, if the misinformation is plausible, if social pressure was applied, or if positive feedback was supplied to the eyewitness.

8. An eyewitness's self-confidence is not strongly correlated with his or her memory accuracy.

Special Topics in Long-Term Memory

1. Expertise has an important effect on long-term memory, although expertise is context-specific. Compared to novices, experts have cognitive advantages such as well-organized knowledge structures and vivid visual images.

2. According to the research on the own-ethnicity bias, people are more accurate in recognizing faces from their own ethnic group, in part because their expertise makes these faces more distinctive.

3. Research on the influence of emotions on memory shows that (a) people generally recall pleasant stimuli more accurately than unpleasant stimuli, and (b) people recall more information if they see the material during a pleasant media presentation, rather than a violent media presentation

4. Both sides of the recovered-memory/false-memory controversy are at least partially correct. Some people may indeed forget about a painful childhood memory, recalling it years later. Other people apparently construct a memory of abuse that never really occurred, and still other people continue to have accurate memory for abuse, many years afterward.

CHAPTER REVIEW QUESTIONS

1. Suppose that you are in charge of creating a public service announcement for television. Choose an issue that is important to you, and describe at least five tips from this chapter that would help you make an especially memorable advertisement. Be sure to include depth of processing as one of the tips.

2. What is encoding specificity? Think of a recent example in which encoding specificity could explain why you temporarily forgot something. How strong are the effects of encoding specificity, in real life and in the laboratory?

3. In this chapter, we examined how emotions and mood can influence your long-term memory. Explain how these two factors might be relevant in your everyday life.

4. Give several examples of explicit and implicit memory tasks you have performed in the past few days. What is dissociation, and

how is it relevant in the research that has been conducted with both normal adults and people with amnesia?

5. Although this textbook focuses on cognitive psychology, several topics discussed in this chapter are relevant to other areas, such as social psychology, personality psychology, and abnormal psychology. Summarize this research, discussing topics such as the self-reference effect, emotions and memory, and the consistency bias.

6. Define the term "autobiographical memory," and describe several topics that have been studied in this area. How does research in this area differ from more traditional laboratory research? List the advantages and disadvantages of each approach.

7. Describe how schemas could lead to a distortion in the recall of a flashbulb memory. How might misleading post-event information

also influence this recall? In answering the two parts of this question, use the terms *proactive interference* and *retroactive interference.*

8. The constructivist approach to memory emphasizes that we actively revise our memories in light of new concerns and new information. How would this approach be relevant if a woman were to develop a false memory about her childhood, and she also shows a strong consistency bias? How would this approach be relevant for other topics in the section about autobiographical memory?

9. Chapter 6 emphasizes methods for improving your memory. However, the present chapter also contains some relevant

information and hints about memory improvement. Review Chapter 5, and make a list of suggestions about memory improvement that you could use when you study for the next examination in cognitive psychology.

10. Researcher Daniel Schacter (2001) wrote a book describing several kinds of memory errors. He argues, however, that these errors are actually by-products of a memory system that usually functions quite well. What textbook theme is related to his argument? Review this chapter and list some of the memory errors people may commit. Explain why each error is a by-product of a memory system that works well in most everyday experiences.

KEYWORDS

working memory
long-term memory
episodic memory
semantic memory
procedural memory
encoding
retrieval
levels-of-processing
    approach
depth-of-processing
    approach
distinctiveness

elaboration
self-reference effect
meta-analysis
encoding-specificity
    principle
recall task
recognition task
emotion
mood
Pollyanna Principle
positivity effect
explicit memory task

implicit memory task
repetition priming task
dissociation
anxiety disorders
generalized anxiety
    disorder
post-traumatic stress
    disorder
social phobia
amnesia
retrograde amnesia
anterograde amnesia

hippocampus
expertise
Functional magnetic
    resonance imaging
    (fMRI)
own-ethnicity bias
autobiographical memory
ecological validity
schema
consistency bias
source monitoring
reality monitoring

flashbulb memory
post-event misinformation
    effect
proactive interference
retroactive
    interference
constructivist approach
recovered-memory
    perspective
false-memory
    perspective
betrayal trauma

RECOMMENDED READINGS

Applied Cognitive Psychology. If you are interested in the topics discussed in Chapter 5, you will enjoy browsing through this journal. Some examples of the research include children's responses to cross-examination, police officers' beliefs about how to interview crime suspects, and adults' memory for children's faces.

Handbook of eyewitness psychology. Memory for people (Vol. **1**, Toglia, M. P., et al., Eds.), *Memory for events* (Vol. 2, Lindsay, R. C. L., et al., Eds.) (2007). Mahwah, NJ: Erlbaum. I strongly recommend this two-volume handbook for college libraries, as well as anyone interested in the psychological or legal components of eyewitness testimony. The chapters are clearly written, with numerous references to psychological research and legal cases.

Kovera, K. B., & Borgida, E. (2010). Social psychology and law. In S. T. Fiske, D. T. Gilbert, & G. Lindzey (Eds.), *The handbook of social psychology* (5th ed., Vol. **2**, pp. 1343–1385). Hoboken, NJ: Wiley. This excellent chapter provides information about the own-ethnicity bias and eyewitness testimony, and it also includes many additional topics of interest to cognitive psychologists, social psychologists, and people interested in legal issues.

Schwartz, B. L. (2011). *Memory: Foundations and applications.* Thousand Oaks, CA: Sage. Several chapters of this excellent textbook are relevant for Chapter 5, including chapters on memory and the brain, episodic memory, autobiographical memory, and false memory.

6 Memory Strategies and Metacognition

Chapter Introduction

When college students ask the question "*How much time should I spend studying for a class?*" the typical answer provided by many professors and academic advisors tends to be "*Roughly 2 hours for every hour that you spend in class.*" Data suggest, however, that the average college student spends only half of this recommended amount of time actually studying (see McCormick, 2011, for an overview of recent data on the study habits of college students). These data are not surprising, given that there are only 24 hours in a day, eight of which should be spent sleeping, and college students face many demands on their limited time. Naturally, more study time tends to result in better classroom performance (although as we'll discuss below, this relationship isn't quite as straightforward as one would expect). But realistically, one person can complete only so many tasks during a typical day while also maintaining their health and their sanity! In this chapter, we discuss strategies aimed at increasing memory, many of which can be applied to study habits in order to make one's time spent studying more efficient.

We'll start this chapter by reviewing some tips for memory improvement based on the chapters that you've already read. Then we'll look at several other useful memory strategies that you can apply to enhance your memory for course material and for everyday memory tasks. Additionally, your choice of memory strategies will typically be guided by your metacognition, which is your knowledge about your cognitive processes, as well as your control of these cognitive processes. The second half of this chapter will encourage you to explore how metacognition can help you use your cognitive processes more effectively. Keeping in mind the time pressure faced by many extremely busy college students, integrating some of the information provided in this chapter with your current study habits may help you to become more efficient in using the limited study time that is available to you.

Memory Strategies I: Memory Strategies Informed by Memory Concepts

Take a moment to consider the hundreds to thousands of hours that you have already spent studying during your high school and college careers. Now think about the amount of time that your college professors have spent teaching you strategies for improving your memory for course material. Perhaps a history teacher urged the class to begin studying early for an upcoming exam, rather than trying to master everything the night before the exam. Maybe a math teacher taught you how to remember the abbreviations for the three basic trigonometry formulas. Possibly a French language teacher mentioned that you could remember vocabulary more effectively if you used **mental imagery**. When my cognitive psychology class begins the chapter on memory strategies and metacognition, we try the exercise I've just described. In contrast to the thousands of hours my students have spent learning in class and studying for exams, most report that their professors or high schools teachers spend very little time providing guidance on how to increase your memory for course material. The main goal of this chapter is to provide you with this guidance.

When you use a **memory strategy**, you perform mental activities that can help to improve your encoding and retrieval. Most memory strategies help you remember something that you learned in the past. For example, when you take an exam in Art History, your professor may ask you to write an essay about the stylistic differences between Renaissance and Baroque paintings. To answer this question, you'll need to remember information from the professor's lectures during the last month and from the Art History chapters that you finished reading last night.

Let's begin the advice about memory improvement by considering information that you learned about in previous chapters.

Divided Attention

In Chapter 3, you learned that people are generally not successful at tasks that require divided attention. Although people may think that they are great at multitasking, people typically perform better when focusing all of their mental efforts on one task at a time. This guideline is important when you listen to lectures and read your textbooks (Chabris & Simons, 2010; deWinstanley & Bjork, 2002). If you type notes on your laptop during lecture, avoid the urge to check your e-mail, message a friend on Facebook, or shop online (and indeed, data suggest that students with Internet access in lecture rooms do spend a lot of time "multitasking," Fried, 2008). Even though you think that you're able to listen to lecture while performing other tasks, there's a good chance that these distractions reduce the amount of lecture information to which you are able to attend.

Working Memory

Chapter 4 pointed out the limits of working memory. These limits would be relevant when professors speak too quickly or display their detailed PowerPoint slides too briefly. In such cases, components of the working memory system such as the phonological loop and the visuospatial sketchpad may become overly taxed as a result of too much input arriving via the auditory or visual input modalities. The result is likely to be that less information has a chance of making it into long-term memory. If you encounter these situations during lecture, figure out how to respond strategically. You may want to complete the reading assignments before class in order to familiarize yourself with the concepts. If the professor makes the slides available before class, study them in advance.

As an aside, I note here that research on the effects of having access to lecture slides before and during a lecture on exam performance is quite mixed. Some evidence suggests that no significant differences in exam performance are observed when students have access to the slides before lecture versus when they don't (Babb & Ross, 2009). Other research indicates that when students can use the information from the slides—incorporating additional notes from the lecture—they tend to perform better on examinations (Marsh & Sink, 2010). So, if the slides are available, make sure to take detailed notes and spend some time revisiting the notes that you have taken in relation to the material on the slides.

Levels of Processing

One of the most useful general principles for memory improvement comes from the discussion about levels of processing in Chapter 5. Specifically, the research on **levels of processing** shows that you will generally recall information more accurately if you process it at a deep level, rather than a shallow level (Craik & Lockhart, 1972; Esgate & Groome, 2005; Roediger, 2008).

We noted that deep levels of processing facilitate learning because they require elaboration and distinctiveness. We first examine elaboration, followed by a focus on distinctiveness.

Elaboration

If you want to emphasize **elaboration**, you will concentrate on the specific meaning of a particular concept; you'll also try to relate this concept to your prior knowledge and to interconnected concepts that you have already mastered. You should emphasize rich, elaborate encoding, for instance, by explaining a concept to yourself (De Koning et al., 2011; Esgate & Groome, 2005; Herrmann et al., 2002). In contrast, if you use simple **rehearsal**, or repeating the information you want to learn, you aren't likely to benefit much in terms of accurate recall at some later point in time.

Here's a specific application of elaboration that you can use when you need to master a complex topic. Einstein and McDaniel (2004) propose that you can learn and remember complex material more easily if you create and answer "why questions." To answer these questions, you must use deep processing to think about the meaning of the material and connect this new material with the information you already know. For example, suppose that your American History professor requires you to learn the Ten Amendments in the U.S. Bill of Rights. Many people have trouble remembering the Third Amendment. According to this Amendment, when citizens are asked to provide housing and food for soldiers, these citizens must be paid appropriately. Think about why this amendment is difficult to remember. It is more or less meaningless to most U.S. residents in the 21st century. We need to consider why this issue was important enough in American history to deserve one of the Ten Amendments. Einstein and McDaniel (2004) suggest that we should think about the citizens of that era. They had little money, and yet they had been forced to house and feed soldiers during the Revolutionary War. Now we can understand why this amendment was so necessary! When material seems difficult to remember, asking "why" questions—or identifying even more generally why it is difficult to remember—promotes deep processing, and thus promotes better memory.

As another example of memory benefits experienced through deep processing of material, students learned more in a psychology course on personality theories if they had maintained a journal in which they applied various theories to personal friends, political figures, and characters from television programs (Connor-Greene, 2000). In this case, students elaborated on the material and analyzed it in a complex, meaningful fashion, rather than simply rehearsing it.

Distinctiveness

In addition to elaboration, we highlighted in Chapter 5 that deep processing also increases **distinctiveness**, which means that one memory trace should be different from all other memory traces. People tend to forget information if it is not distinctly different from the other memory traces in their long-term memory.

Distinctiveness is an especially important factor when we try to learn names. For example, I often need to recall someone's name. Let's say that I have just met a young woman named Kate. I've often made the mistake of telling myself, "That's easy. I'll just remember that she looks like the student in my Cognitive Psychology class named Kate." Later on, I'll realize that I actually have three students in that class named Kate. My encoding had not been sufficiently distinctive. As a result, the face I was trying to recall was extremely vulnerable to interference from other students' faces. With interference from other items, we easily forget the target name (Schacter & Wiseman, 2006; Tulving & Rosenbaum, 2006).

As we emphasized in Chapter 5, one especially deep level of processing takes advantage of the **self-reference effect**, in which you enhance long-term memory by relating the material to your own experiences. For example, one of the reasons that I include demonstrations in this textbook is to provide you with personal experiences that focus on some of the important principles of cognitive

Demonstration 6.1	Instructions and Memory

Learn the following list of pairs by repeating the members of each pair several times. For example, if the pair were CAT–WINDOW, you would say over and over to yourself, "CAT–WINDOW, CAT–WINDOW, CAT–WINDOW." Just repeat the words, and do not use any other study method. Allow yourself one minute to learn this list.

CUSTARD–LUMBER	IVY–MOTHER
JAIL–CLOWN	LIZARD–PAPER
ENVELOPE–SLIPPER	SCISSORS–BEAR
SHEEPSKIN–CANDLE	CANDY–MOUNTAIN
FRECKLES–APPLE	BOOK–PAINT
HAMMER–STAR	TREE–OCEAN

Now, cover up the pairs. Try to recall as many responses as possible:

ENVELOPE	_____	JAIL	_____
FRECKLES	_____	IVY	_____
TREE	_____	SHEEPSKIN	_____
CANDY	_____	BOOK	_____
SCISSORS	_____	LIZARD	_____
CUSTARD	_____	HAMMER	_____

Next, learn the list of pairs below by visualizing a mental picture in which the two objects in each pair are in some kind of vivid interaction. For example, if the pair were CAT–WINDOW, you might make up a picture of a cat jumping through a closed window, with the glass shattering all around. Just make up a mental image and do not use any other study method. Allow yourself one minute to learn this list.

SOAP–MERMAID	MIRROR–RABBIT
FOOTBALL–LAKE	HOUSE–DIAMOND
PENCIL–LETTUCE	LAMB–MOON
CAR–HONEY	BREAD–GLASS
CANDLE–DANCER	LIPS–MONKEY
DANDELION–FLEA	DOLLAR–ELEPHANT

Now, cover up the pairs above. Try to recall as many responses as possible:

CANDLE	_____	DOLLAR	_____
DANDELION	_____	CAR	_____
BREAD	_____	LIPS	_____
MIRROR	_____	PENCIL	_____
LAMB	_____	SOAP	_____
FOOTBALL	_____	HOUSE	_____

Finally, count the number of correct responses on each list. Did you recall a greater number of words with the imagery instructions? Incidentally, you may have found it very difficult to avoid using imagery on the first list, because you are reading a section about memory improvement. In that case, your recall scores were probably similar for the two lists. You may wish to test a friend instead.

psychology. If you read your textbook in a reflective fashion, you'll try to think about how to apply major concepts to your own life. I'm hopeful, for instance, that this chapter will encourage you to see how memory strategies and metacognition can be helpful in many other college courses. Now try Demonstration 6.1.

Encoding Specificity

Chapter 5 also discussed the **encoding-specificity principle**, which states that recall is often better if the context at the time of encoding matches the context at the time when your retrieval will be tested. As we noted in Chapter 5, context effects are often inconsistent (e.g., Baddeley, 2004; Nairne, 2005; Wong & Read, 2011). For example, you probably will *not* improve your grade if you decide to study for an upcoming exam by reviewing the material in the specific classroom where you'll be taking this exam.

However, the research on encoding specificity does provide some other more general strategies. For instance, when you are trying to devise study strategies, consider how you will be tested on your next examination (Herrmann et al., 2006; Koriat, 2000). Let's suppose that your exam will contain essays. This format requires you to *recall* information—not simply to *recognize* it. When you are learning the material, make an effort to quiz yourself periodically by closing your notebook and trying to recall the material on the pages you've just read. During studying, try answering the Chapter Review Questions. You can also create some essay questions and then answer them, a strategy that would also increase your deep processing of the material.

Memory Strategies II: Practice and Mnemonics

Here, we turn to some additional suggestions about memory strategies. We begin with suggestions that focus on issues related to practice.

Memory Strategies Emphasizing Practice

Everyone has heard the old saying "Practice Makes Perfect." According to the **total-time hypothesis**, the amount of information that you learn depends on the total time you devote to learning. This hypothesis is generally true (Baddeley, 1997; Roediger, 2008), although the relationship between study time and later recall ability isn't completely straightforward. For instance, researchers have found that measuring "the number of hours spent studying" is not a predictor of a student's grade-point average. Instead, study time predicts grade-point average only when the researchers also assess the *quality* of study strategies (Plant et al., 2005). For instance, one hour spent actively learning the material—using deep levels of processing—will usually be more helpful than two hours spent reading information that you do not exert a great deal of effort to process. In sum, although overall time spent studying does not significantly correlate with overall Grade Point Average, research indicates that college students' study habits, study skills, and study attitudes are strong predictors of students' grades in college (Hartwig & Dunlosky, 2012).

Acknowledging the imperfect relationship between the time spent studying and both recall and recognition accuracy, let's explore two practice-related effects that provide insight into the best ways to use your limited study time.

Distributed-Practice Effect

According to the **distributed-practice effect**, you will remember more material if you spread your learning trials over time (**spaced learning**). You'll remember less if you try "cramming," by learning the material all at once (**massed learning**). The studies generally support this principle for both recall tasks and recognition tasks (Koriat & Helstrup, 2007; Landauer, 2011; Metcalfe, 2011). Research also confirms the spacing effect with real-life material that can be difficult to master, such as English vocabulary, math knowledge, and people's names (Carpenter & DeLosh, 2005; Kornell, 2009; Pashler et al., 2007; Rohrer & Taylor, 2006).

In one classic example, Bahrick and Phelps (1987) had participants learn Spanish–English word pairs (e.g. *smile—sorinsa*, much like in Deomnstration 6.1). The total amount of study time was held constant for all participants, although study episodes were spaced such that some participants studied again one day later whereas others had a second study session 30 days later. After even eight years, participants in the 30-day condition retained significantly more English–Spanish word pairs than did the other participants. The spacing of practice or study sessions clearly confers advantages for memory retention relative to unspaced (or crammed) study sessions.

One reason that distributed practice is helpful for long-term recall is that it introduces **desirable difficulties**, in other words, a learning situation that is somewhat challenging, but not too difficult (Bjork et al., 2011; Koriat & Helstrup, 2007; McDaniel & Einstein, 2005). Suppose that you need to learn some key concepts for a biology class. If you test yourself on one concept several times in a row, the concept will seem easy by your third or fourth repetition. In contrast, if you allow several minutes to pass before the second repetition, you'll pay more attention to that concept. In addition, the task will be slightly more difficult because you will have begun to forget the concept (Bjork et al., 2011; Einstein & McDaniel, 2004). As a result, you'll make some mistakes, and you will not be overconfident that you have mastered the concepts. According to the current research, a delay of at least one day between practice sessions is especially effective in boosting long-term retention (Bahrick & Hall, 2005; Cepeda et al., 2006).

Testing Effect

Professors administer tests in an academic course so that they can assess how much you have learned. Tests don't only serve, however, as a means by which to evaluate the amount of knowledge that a student has acquired. It turns out that being tested on material also increases memory for the material. This phenomenon is referred to as the **testing effect**.

Taking a test is an excellent way to boost your long-term recall for academic material (e.g., Campbell & Mayer, 2009; Roediger et al., 2010; Vojdanoska et al., 2010). For example, Roediger and Karpicke (2006b)

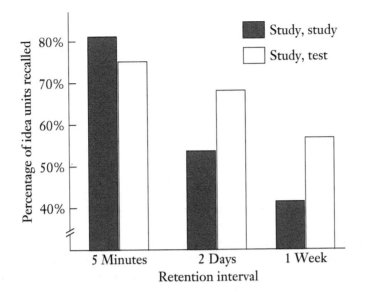

FIGURE 6.1
The effects of learning condition (Repeated study versus Testing) and retention interval on percentage of idea units correctly recalled.
Source: Roediger, H. L., III, & Karpicke, J. D. (2006b). Test enhanced learning: Taking memory tests improves long-term retention. *Psychological Science, 17,* 249–255.

asked students to read short essays on a science-related topic. Then, half of the students studied the same essays again. The other half took a test on the contents of the essay. They received a blank sheet of paper and wrote down as much as they could recall from the essay. They did not, however, receive feedback about the accuracy of their recall.

During the last step of the study, everyone received a final test in which they wrote down their recall from the essay. Some students received this final test just five minutes after the last activity (either studying or taking the first test). Others were tested after a delay of either two days or one week.

As evident in Figure 6.1, when students took the test only five minutes after the last activity, those who had restudied the material performed slightly better than those who had completed a test on the material. However, after a delay of two days or one week, students earned much higher scores if their last activity had been taking a test—even though they had received no feedback about their accuracy on that test.

Apparently, when you take a test, this testing provides practice in retrieving the relevant material. Furthermore, that test produces desirable difficulties. When you try to recall the material you had read, you'll see that the task is somewhat challenging, and you will not be overconfident (Pashler et al., 2007; Roediger & Karpicke, 2006a, 2006b; Whitten, 2011). Amazingly, the increased memory benefits associated with testing are substantially long-lasting, stretching from just a few weeks up until at least nine months (Carpenter et al., 2009; Carpenter et al., 2008). In addition, when students complete a second test, their recall shows greater organization, compared to students who only received additional study time (Zaromb & Roediger, 2010).

The beneficial effects of testing stretch far beyond increased memory for the same information in the same testing formats. For example, Carpenter et al. (2006) originally tested memory for learned information in a short essay format, and then tested participants again using a multiple-choice format. Participants whose last activity had been taking a test outperformed participants in a study-only control group, even when the format of the second test was different from the format of the first. Thus, testing increases memory at a later point in time that is transferable across different types of tests and test questions. When a textbook for your course comes with online supplementary material, go online and look at the material. Many times, you'll find that the supplementary material contains mock quizzes. Research on the testing effect indicates that completing those will not only increase your memory for that material in the future but will also help you identify the material on which you need to spend more time studying.

Test Anxiety

According to numerous studies, people who are high in test anxiety often perform poorly on examinations (Cassady, 2004). Psychologists have usually attributed this poor performance to high levels of worry. The traditional explanation is that worry intrudes on people's consciousness, blocking them from retrieving the correct answers on a test. However, Cassady (2004) proposes that test anxiety also decreases students' skills in understanding the information in their textbooks.

Cassady examined, specifically, the link between anxiety and reading comprehension by instructing 277 undergraduate students to read several paragraphs from a textbook, and then to read it a second time. Next, everyone completed a measure called the Cognitive Test Anxiety Scale, followed by a multiple-choice test on the earlier textbook material. The students then repeated this procedure with a comparable passage from a different textbook. Then, they completed a study-skills survey prior to the multiple-choice test.

Cassady found that scores on the Cognitive Test Anxiety Scale were strongly correlated with performance on the multiple-choice tests. In other words, people who are highly anxious tend to perform poorly on a reading-comprehension test. Scores on the Cognitive Test Anxiety Scale were also strongly correlated with scores on the study-skills survey. In other words, people who are highly anxious tend to report poorer study skills. Surprisingly, however, study skills were not strongly correlated with recall on the multiple-choice test.

In a second, similar study, Cassady (2004) found that people with high scores on the Cognitive Test Anxiety Scale also made more errors in summarizing the textbook material. These people also made more errors on a test that assessed their ability to make correct inferences, based on the textbook material. In summary, when people are highly anxious about taking tests, they may experience interference from high levels of worry. In addition, they perform poorly on a variety of tasks related to reading comprehension. Test anxiety is a very real phenomenon, with the potential to exert negative effects on academic success. If you personally suffer from this form of anxiety, it may be wise to see a trained professional in order to learn to cope with and ultimately overcome it.

Mnemonics Using Imagery and Organization

The preceding discussion focused on the benefits of practice-related memory strategies. Here, we focus on the memory benefits associated with mnemonics (pronounced "ni-*mon*-icks," with a silent initial *m*). **Mnemonics** are mental strategies designed to improve your memory (Dunlosky & Bjork, 2008b; Worthen & Hunt, 2011). We discuss two types of mnemonics: (1) mnemonics using mental imagery and (2) mnemonics using organization.

Imagery

Examine your results for Demonstration 6.1. This demonstration is a simplified version of a study by Bower and Winzenz (1970), who asked one group of participants to simply repeat pairs of words silently. Other participants tried to construct a mental image of the two words in vivid interaction with each other. Later, the participants saw the first word of each pair, and they were asked to supply the second word. The results showed that people in the imagery condition recalled more than twice as many items when compared to the people in the repetition condition.

Visual imagery can be a powerful strategy for enhancing memory (Davies & Wright, 2010b; Reed, 2010). The research demonstrates that imagery is especially effective when the items that must be recalled are shown interacting with each other (Carney & Levin, 2001; McKelvie et al., 1994). For example, if you want to remember the pair *piano-toast*, try to visualize a piano chewing a large piece of toast. In general, an interacting visual image is especially helpful if the image is bizarre (Davidson, 2006; Worthen, 2006). One reason that visualization mnemonics are effective is that they are motivating and interesting (Herrmann et al., 2002).

As one example, if you need to remember unfamiliar vocabulary items, the keyword method is especially helpful. In the **keyword method**, you identify an English word (the keyword) that sounds similar to the new word you want to learn. Then, you create an image that links the keyword with the meaning of this new word. The research on the keyword method shows that it can help students who are trying to learn new English vocabulary words, vocabulary in another language, or people's names (Carney & Levin, 2001, 2011; Herrmann et al., 2002; Worthen & Hunt, 2011).

One Thanksgiving, our Spanish-speaking guests were from Nicaragua, where the word for *turkey* is *chompipe* (pronounced, "chom-*pea*-pay"). I had trouble remembering this word until I created an image of a turkey chomping down on an enormous pipe, as in Figure 6.2.

FIGURE 6.2 The keyword representation for the pair of words *Turkey-Chompipe.*

Another imagery technique is based on establishing a series of familiar locations, such as the driveway, garage, and front door in a family home. Next, you create a mental image of each item that you want to remember. Then you place a mental image of each item in one of those locations. This method is especially useful if you want to remember the items in a specified order (Einstein & McDaniel, 2004; Groninger, 1971; Hunter, 2004b). Incidentally, try Demonstration 6.2 before you read further.

Organization

The other main class of mnemonic strategies involves the key principles of **organization**. When people use mnemonics that involve organization, they try to bring systematic order to the material they want to learn. This class of mnemonics necessitates the use deep processing to sort items into categories (Esgate & Groome, 2005). Indeed, research suggests that when you have constructed a well-organized framework, retrieval efficiency increases (Wolfe et al., 2005; Worthen & Hunt, 2011).

We examine four widely acknowledged mnemonic strategies that emphasize organization. You will likely find that some of these may be more helpful than others (Schwartz, 2011). For example, you may find that chunking works well when you try one memory task, but the hierarchy technique might be more effective for a different memory task.

Chunking. We already discussed one mnemonic that involves organization in Chapter 4. **Chunking**, in which we combine several small units into larger units, is a basic organizational principle that eases the processing demands on working memory. For instance, Demonstration 6.2 is a modified version of a study by Bower and Springston (1970). These researchers found that people recalled much more material when

---

Demonstration 6.2 | Remembering Lists of Letters

Read the following list of letters and then cover up the list. Try to recall them as accurately as possible.

YMC AJF KFB ISA TNB CTV

Now read the following list of letters and then cover them up. Try to recall them as accurately as possible.

AMA PHD GPS VCR CIA CBS

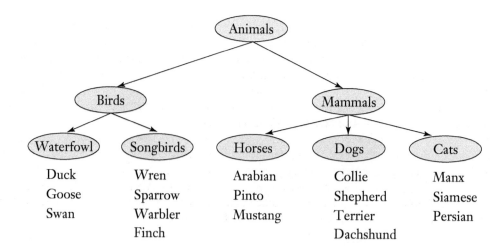

FIGURE 6.3
An example of a
hierarchy.

a string of letters was grouped according to meaningful, familiar units, rather than in arbitrary groups of three. In Demonstration 6.2, did you recall a larger number of items on the second list, which was organized according to familiar chunks?

Hierarchy Technique. A second effective way to organize material is to construct a hierarchy. A **hierarchy** is a system in which items are arranged in a series of classes, from the most general classes to the most specific. For example, Figure 6.3 shows part of a hierarchy for animals.

Gordon Bower and his colleagues (1969) asked people to learn words that belonged to four hierarchies similar to the one in Figure 6.3. Some people learned the words in an organized fashion, in the format of the upside-down trees you see in Figure 6.3. Others saw the same words, but the words were randomly scattered throughout the different positions in each tree. The group who had learned the organized structure recalled more than three times as many words as the group who learned the random structure. Structure and organization clearly enhance your recall (Baddeley, 1999; Herrmann et al., 2002; Worthen & Hunt, 2011).

An outline is one example of a hierarchy, because an outline is divided into general categories, and each general category is further subdivided. An outline is valuable because it provides organization and structure for concepts that you learn in a particular discipline. For example, look at the chapter outline. The outline features three general sections: memory strategies as they are related to memory concepts, memory strategies related to practice and mnemonics, and metacognition. When you have finished reading this chapter, see if you can construct—from memory—a hierarchy similar to Figure 6.3. Begin with the three general categories, and then subdivide each category into more specific topics. Then, recheck the chapter outline to see whether you omitted anything. If you study the outline of each chapter, you will have an organized structure that can enhance your recall on an examination.

In fact, according to a study by Gurung (2003), students in introductory psychology classes report that they seldom use chapter outlines when studying for exams. However, it's possible that students in more advanced courses (such as cognitive psychology!) know that they can learn more effectively if they understand how a topic is organized.

First-Letter Technique. Another popular mnemonic that makes use of organization is the **first-letter technique**; you take the first letter of each word you want to remember, and then you compose a word or a sentence from those letters. Maybe you learned the order of the colors of the rainbow by using the letters ROY G. BIV to recall Red, Orange, Yellow, Green, Blue, Indigo, and Violet. As you may have learned in a statistics class, the nominal, ordinal, interval, and ratio scales conveniently spell *noir*, the French word for "black."

Students frequently use first-letter mnemonics. Unfortunately, however, the laboratory research does not consistently show that this technique is effective (Herrmann et al., 2002). Still, in those cases where it does work, its effectiveness can probably be traced to the fact that these first letters frequently enhance retrieval. For instance, suppose that you are experiencing a memory block for a certain term. If you know the first letter of that term, you'll be more likely to retrieve the item (Herrmann et al., 2002).

Narrative Technique. A fourth organizational method, called the **narrative technique**, instructs people to make up stories that link a series of words together.

In a classic study, Bower and Clark (1969) told a group of people to make up narrative stories that incorporated a set of English words. People in a control group received no special instructions. In all, each group learned 12 lists of words. The results showed that participants in the narrative-technique group recalled about six times as many words as those in the control group. The narrative technique is clearly an effective strategy for enhancing memory, and it has also been used successfully with people who have impaired memory (Wilson, 1995). However, techniques such as this are effective only if you can generate the narrative easily and reliably, during both learning and recall.

We have reviewed several categories of memory strategies that can help you study more effectively. These strategies cannot improve your performance on exams, however, unless you actually use them. Students often resist using resources that could help them. For instance, students enrolled in a Web-based introductory psychology course seldom used any of the online study material until just two days before their exam (Maki & Maki, 2000). The online practice quizzes, chapter summaries, and outlines that often come with the supplementary textbook material are there for a reason.

Prospective Memory

The memory-related concepts we have focused on up until this point involve **retrospective memory**, or remembering information that you acquired in the past. In contrast, we will now focus on **prospective memory**, or remembering that you need to do something in the future. Some typical prospective memory tasks include remembering to bring your research-methods book to class today, to pick up a friend at work this afternoon, and to submit your cognitive psychology homework assignment by noon next Wednesday.

Prospective-memory errors are quite frequent in a number of clinical populations. For example, long-term opiate users and individuals with schizophrenia experience a higher degree of prospective-memory errors relative to control participants (Raskin et al., 2014; Terrett et al., 2014). Older adult populations also demonstrate a higher number of prospective-memory errors relative to younger adults (Rendell et al., 2011). Don't worry though. Prospective-memory errors are not usually indicative of an underlying psychiatric disorder or of old age. Instead, it is well documented that everyone experiences prospective-memory errors. These errors are ranked among the most common types of memory lapses (Cook et al., 2005; Einstein & McDaniel, 2004; McDaniel & Einstein, 2007), and are a frequent source of embarrassment.

Tasks involving prospective-memory actually include two components. First, you must establish that you intend to accomplish a particular task at some future time. Second, at that future time, you must fulfill your original intention (Einstein & McDaniel, 2004; McDaniel & Einstein, 2007). Occasionally, the primary challenge is to remember the actual content of the action. You've probably experienced the feeling that you know you are supposed to do something, but you cannot remember what it is. However, most of the time, the primary challenge is simply to remember to perform an action in the future (McDaniel & Einstein, 2007).

Let's first compare prospective-memory tasks with more standard retrospective-memory tasks, and then we'll consider the related topic of absentmindedness. With this background in mind, we'll consider several specific suggestions about how to improve prospective memory.

Comparing Prospective and Retrospective Memory

Prospective memory is typically focused on action. In contrast, retrospective memory is most likely to focus on remembering information and ideas (Einstein & McDaniel, 2004). Furthermore, the research on prospective memory is more likely to emphasize **ecological validity**. As discussed in previous chapters, a study has ecological validity if the conditions in which the research is conducted are similar to the natural setting to which the results will be applied. In other words, researchers try to design tasks that resemble the kind of prospective-memory tasks we face in our daily lives.

Despite their differences, prospective memory and retrospective memory are governed by some of the same variables. For example, your memory is more accurate for both kinds of memory tasks if you use both distinctive encoding and effective retrieval cues. In addition, both kinds of memory are more accurate when you have only a short delay prior to retrieval (Einstein & McDaniel, 2004). Also, prospective memory and retrospective memory show similar rates of forgetting, with the passage of time (Tobias, 2009). Finally, prospective memory relies on regions of the frontal lobe that also play a role in retrospective memory (Einstein & McDaniel, 2004).

Absentmindedness and Prospective Memory Failures

One intriguing component of prospective memory is absentmindedness. Most people do not publicly reveal their absentminded mistakes. You may therefore think that you are the only person who forgets to pick up a quart of milk on your way home from class, who dials Chris's phone number when you wanted to speak to Alex, or who fails to include an important attachment when sending an e-mail. In fact, I recall attending a session at a psychology conference, which focused on the current research about prospective memory. One researcher asked the audience to guess the most frequent kind of prospective-memory error. The clear winner was the "missing attachment mistake."

One problem is that the typical prospective-memory task represents a divided-attention situation. You must focus on your ongoing activity, as well as on the task you need to remember in the future (Marsh et al., 2000). Absentminded behavior is especially likely when the prospective-memory task requires you to disrupt a customary activity. Suppose that this customary activity is driving from your college to your home. Now suppose that you have a prospective-memory task that you must perform today, for example, buying milk at the grocery store on your way home. In cases like this, your long-standing habit dominates the more fragile prospective memory, and you fall victim to absentminded behavior (Cohen et al., 2012).

Prospective-memory errors are more likely in highly familiar surroundings when you are performing a task automatically. For instance, consider people who want to stop smoking. They typically acknowledge that they automatically light up a cigarette in the kitchen, right after breakfast (Tobias, 2009). They will probably need to move directly to a different room, in order to break the smoking habit.

Absentminded behavior is also more likely if you are preoccupied or distracted, you are feeling time pressure, or find yourself otherwise under a lot of stress. In most cases, absentmindedness is simply irritating. However, sometimes these slips can produce airplane collisions, industrial accidents, and other disasters that influence the lives of hundreds of individuals (Finstad et al., 2006). For example, Dismukes and Nowinski (2007) studied the records of 75 airplane crashes that could be attributed to the crew members' memory failures. Out of 75 crashes, 74 could be traced to prospective-memory errors, and only one could be traced to a retrospective-memory error.

Suggestions for Improving Prospective Memory

Earlier in the chapter, we discussed numerous suggestions that you could use to aid your retrospective memory. You can use some of these internal strategies to aid your prospective memory as well. For example, if you create a vivid, interactive mental image of a quart of milk, you might avoid driving past the grocery store in an absentminded fashion (Einstein & McDaniel, 2004).

One of the best ways to avoid prospective-memory errors is to provide yourself with reminders to complete a task at a certain point of time in the future. These reminders, however, must be distinctive if you want to perform a prospective-memory task (Engelkamp, 1998; Guynn et al., 1998). For example, suppose that you want to remember to give Tonya a message tomorrow. It won't be helpful just to rehearse her name or just to remind yourself that you have to convey a message. Instead, you must form a strong connection between these two components, linking both Tonya's name and the fact that you must give her a message.

External memory aids are especially helpful on prospective-memory tasks (McDaniel & Einstein, 2007). An **external memory aid** is defined as any device, external to yourself, that facilitates your memory in some way (Herrmann et al., 2002; Worthen & Hunt, 2011). Some examples of external memory aids include a shopping list, a rubber band around your wrist, and the ringing of an alarm clock, to remind you to make an important phone call at a specified time. Even using the calendar function on your cell phone to list things to be done and the times at which they are to be done constitutes an example of an external memory aid.

The placement of your external memory aid is also important. For example, my nephew sometimes drove to his mother's home for dinner, and she typically told him about some items in the refrigerator that he must remember to take home when he left. After several prospective-memory lapses, he thought of an ideal external memory aid: When he arrives for dinner, he places his car keys in a conspicuous location in the refrigerator (White, 2003). Notice his strategic application of this memory aid. He is highly unlikely to drive home without the refrigerated items.

My students report that they often use informal external mnemonics to aid their prospective memory. When they want to remember to bring a book to class, they place it in a location where they will confront the book on the way to class. They also write reminders on the back of their hands. Other students describe ry | | **123** |

Table 6.1 Memory-Improvement Strategies

1. Suggestions from Previous Chapters

  a. Do not divide your attention between several simultaneous tasks.

  b. Keep in mind that your working memory is limited; figure out strategies to overcome this problem.

  c. Process information in terms of its meaning, rather than at a shallow level; emphasize elaborative encodings, distinctiveness, and self-reference.

  d. When you study, apply the encoding-specificity principle by creating questions for yourself that have the same format as the questions on your exam.

  e. Don't be overconfident about the accuracy of your memory for events in your life.

2. Techniques Related to Practice

  a. The amount you learn depends on the total time that you spend practicing.

  b. You'll learn more effectively if you spread your learning trials over time (the distributed-practice effect).

  c. You'll enhance your memory simply by taking tests on the material.

3. Mnemonics Using Imagery

  a. Use imagery, especially imagery that shows an interaction between the items that need to be recalled.

  b. Use the keyword method; for example, if you are learning vocabulary in another language, identify an English word that sounds like the target word, and link the English word with the meaning of that target word.

4. Mnemonics Using Organization

  a. Use chunking by combining isolated items into meaningful units.

  b. Construct a hierarchy by arranging items in a series of categories (e.g., Figure 6.3).

  c. Take the first letter of each item you want to remember and compose a word or sentence from these letters (first-letter technique).

  d. Create a narrative, or a story that links a series of words together.

5. Improving Prospective Memory

  a. Create a vivid, interactive mental image to prompt future recall.

  b. Create a specific reminder or an external memory aid.

the sea of colored sticky notes that decorate their dormitory rooms. These external memory aids are only helpful, however, if you can use them easily and if they successfully remind you of what you are supposed to remember. Now that you are familiar with the challenges of prospective memory, review the memory-improvement techniques listed in Table 6.1 and complete Demonstration 6.3.

Demonstration 6.3 ‖ Prospective Memory

Make a list of five prospective-memory tasks that you need to accomplish within the next day or two. These should be tasks that you must remember to complete on your own, without anyone else providing a reminder.

For each item, first describe the method you would customarily use to remember to do the task. Also note whether this method is typically successful. Then, for each task where you usually make a prospective-memory error, try to figure out a more effective reminder. (Incidentally, one prospective-memory task that you may forget to do is to complete this demonstration!)

Metamemory

Metacognition refers to your knowledge and control of your cognitive processes. One important function of metacognition is to supervise the way you select and use your memory strategies. If you have carefully studied the information in this textbook and in your cognitive psychology class, then you already know more than most people about the general factors that can influence your memory (Magnussen et al., 2006). We discuss metacognition in this chapter on memory strategies for the following reason: Your knowledge about your cognitive processes can guide you in selecting strategies to improve your future cognitive performance. That is, because you understand the different types of memory (what they are, how they work, factors that influence encoding and retrieval, and so forth), you have the knowledge necessary to make conscious decisions about how to control or regulate your study strategies.

Metacognition is also important because a general goal in college should be to learn how to think and how to become a reflective person. As a reflective person, you can consider what you have done and what you plan to do in the future (Dominowski, 2002). Consistent with Theme 1, metacognition is an extremely active process. As you'll see, metacognition requires focused thinking and self-assessment (Koriat & Helstrup, 2007). The topic of metacognition belongs to a larger issue in psychology, called **self-knowledge**, or what people believe about themselves (Wilson, 2009). Self-knowledge includes the topics in this chapter, as well as your knowledge about your social behavior and your personality. Furthermore, social psychologists are beginning to study people's metacognition about their attitudes (Rucker et al., 2011). For example, you might wonder to yourself, "Maybe I like Pat and Devon because they look attractive, rather than because they are nice people."

Before we consider the details about metacognition, let's briefly review topics related to metacognition that were described in three previous chapters of this book. For instance, in Chapter 3, you saw that people often have limited consciousness about their higher mental processes. As a result, they may not be able to identify which factors actually helped them solve a problem. Chapter 4 explored Alan Baddeley's (2007) theory of working memory. According to Baddeley's approach, the central executive plays an important role in planning your cognitive behavior. For example, your central executive is essential in the metacognitive task of planning which topics you'll spend the most time studying when you are preparing for an exam. Chapter 5 discussed how people may have difficulty on source-monitoring tasks. For instance, you may not be able to recall whether you actually gave a book to a friend—or whether you merely imagined you had done so.

In the remainder of this chapter, we will examine several important kinds of metacognition. Our first topic is **metamemory**, a topic that refers to people's knowledge, monitoring, and control of their memory (Dunlosky & Bjork, 2008a). Metamemory is extremely important when you want to improve your memory. We will therefore explore several components of metamemory. Second, we will consider an additional kind of metacognition, which is called *metacomprehension*.

Accuracy of Metamemory

Have you ever completed an exam, handed it in, and felt pretty good about your performance on the exam, only to find out a week later that you scored a low C? If this sounds familiar, you already know that your metamemory is not always accurate in predicting your memory performance.

When does your metamemory accurately predict your actual memory performance? The answer to this question depends on several important characteristics of the task. Let's start by focusing on people's estimates about their *total score* for a memory test compared to their estimates for *individual items* on a memory test.

Metamemory: Estimating the Accuracy for Total Score Versus the Accuracy for Individual Items

In general, people tend to be overconfident if you ask them to predict their *total score* on a memory test. In contrast, people tend to be accurate if you ask them to predict which *individual* items they will remember and which ones they will forget.

In some of the metamemory studies, students begin by studying a list of paired associates, such as *coat-sandwich*. That is, when they see the word *coat*, they know that they must respond *sandwich*. Then the students are asked to predict the total number of correct responses they will supply on a later test (Koriat, 2007; Koriat & Bjork, 2006a, 2006b). In this situation, they are likely to commit the **foresight bias**, or, the tendency, when studying for a future exam, to be overconfident about performance on that exam. In this case, individuals overestimate the number of answers they will correctly supply on a future test (Koriat et al., 2008).

Another problem here is that the participants are studying those word pairs while the correct responses are visible, so their prediction will probably be overly optimistic. Similarly, students who are reading a chapter in a textbook are often overconfident that they can remember a concept when they are looking directly at a description of the concept (Gurung & McCann, 2011). Keep this issue in mind if you are

FIGURE 6.4
Estimated total
score versus Actual
total score, as a
function of actual test
performance.
Source: Dunning, D.,
Johnson, K., Ehrlinger, J., &
Kruger, J. (2003). Why people
fail to recognize their own
incompetence. *Current
Directions in Psychological
Science, 12,* 83–87. Copyright
© 2003. Reprinted by
permission of SAGE
Publications.

learning technical terminology or you are studying vocabulary words in another language. You would be more likely to provide an accurate estimate if you conscientiously used flashcards to assess your learning (Hartwig & Dunlosky, 2012). For example, you might write the English word on one side and the French word on the other side. Similarly, suppose that you have a psychology exam that will be based on a textbook. A good plan would be to read the material on a page, close the book, and summarize the information on that page. You may have a general idea about the material. However, when your book is closed, you may discover that you cannot provide specific information. In any case, check to see if your answer is correct.

In other studies, students estimate their total scores *after* finishing an exam. For example, Dunning and his coauthors (2003) asked students in a sophomore-level psychology course to estimate the total score that they thought they had earned on an examination they had just completed. Then, these researchers graded the test and divided the students into four groups, based on their actual test score. Figure 6.4 shows the performance for the four groups: the bottom quartile, second quartile, third quartile, and top quartile. Notice that the students in the top quartile estimated their total actual scores very accurately. The students in the third quartile were almost as accurate. However, the less-competent students clearly overestimated their performance. Notice, for instance, that the students in the bottom quarter of the class overestimated their performance by about eight items. Ironically, less-competent students are often not aware of their limitations (Dunlosky & Metcalfe, 2009). In other words, they do not know that they do not know the material!

So far, we have seen that people tend to be overconfident when they estimate the *total* number of correct items. However, the situation is more hopeful when we measure metamemory in a different fashion. In fact, the research shows that people's metamemory can be highly accurate when they predict which *individual* items they'll remember and which ones they'll forget (Koriat & Helstrup, 2007; Lovelace, 1984).

Metamemory: Estimating the Score Immediately Versus After a Delay

People do not tend to provide accurate memory estimates for individual items if they make these estimates immediately after learning the items. In contrast—if they delay their judgments—they are reasonably accurate in predicting which items they will recall (Koriat & Helstrup, 2007; Narens et al., 2008; Roediger et al., 2010; Weaver et al., 2008). These delayed judgments are especially likely to provide accurate assessments of your memory performance because they assess long-term memory (Rhodes & Tauber, 2011). When you actually take the test, you will need to draw the answers from your long-term memory. In contrast, the immediate judgments would assess your working memory, which is less relevant for predicting your actual recall on an examination.

These particular findings suggest an important practical application. Suppose that you are studying your notes for an exam, and you are trying to determine which of the topics need more work. Be sure to wait a few minutes before assessing your memory, because your metamemory is more likely to be accurate.

Metamemory About Factors Affecting Memory Accuracy

Above, we reviewed evidence that students' estimates about their memory are generally more accurate under the following conditions: (1) when they predict their accuracy on individual test items, rather than total scores, and (2) when they predict their accuracy after a delay, rather than immediately after seeing the items.

But, are college students sufficiently aware of some strategic factors that can influence their memory performance? In many cases, the answer seems to be "no" (Diaz & Benjamin, 2011; Gurung, 2003, 2004; McCabe, 2011). Moreover, students who earn low scores on exams are likely to use no specific memory strategies in learning material for an exam (McDougall & Gruneberg, 2002). In addition, students' awareness of their memory should help them identify which memory strategies work best for them and which ones are ineffective. However, students tend to believe that "all memory strategies are created equal" (Suzuki-Slakter, 1988). For example, students typically believe that simple repetition is just as effective as the keyword method, which was illustrated in Figure 6.2 (Pressley et al., 1984, 1988). However, you already know that repetition is not effective.

Put this research to good practice. Try using various study strategies that seem appropriate for you. Then on your next test, identify which methods were indeed most effective. You'll be much more likely to revise your strategies if you can demonstrate that they improve your own performance.

As we've just seen, students may believe that some factors have no effect on memory, although these factors actually *do* have an effect. In contrast, let's consider some research that shows the reverse pattern: Students may believe that some factors do have an effect on memory, although these factors actually *do not* have an effect. For example, students believe that they are more likely to remember a word if it is printed in a large font size, rather than a small font size (Kornell et al., 2011; Rhodes & Castel, 2009). Students also tend to believe that they are more likely to remember a word if it is spoken at a loud volume, rather than a quiet volume (Rhodes & Castel, 2009).

Metamemory and the Regulation of Study Strategies

It's possible that you have already developed your metamemory well enough that you can easily identify which memory strategies work best for you. But, even if that's the case, your exam performance may still be poor unless you effectively regulate your study strategies. One key way to do so is by spending more time studying the difficult topics. Indeed, memory tasks require a substantial amount of decision making as you plan how to master the material (Koriat & Helstrup, 2007; Metcalfe, 2000). Consistent with Theme 4, you must often coordinate at least two cognitive processes—in this case, memory and decision making.

Here, we examine the way that students make decisions about how they will allocate their study time in preparing for a memory test. In some circumstances, students may spend more time on the difficult items than on the easy items. But, when the material is more challenging and the time is limited, students will spend the most time learning the items that are just within their grasp (Kornell & Metcalfe, 2006).

Allocating Time When the Task Is Easy

Nelson and Leonesio (1988) examined how students distribute their study time when they can study at their own pace. In their study, students were allowed a reasonable amount of time to study the material. The results were clear. Students allocated somewhat more study time for the items that they believed would be difficult to master. The correlations here averaged about +.30. (A correlation of .00 would indicate no relationship, and a correlation of +1.00 would be a perfect correlation between each item's judged difficulty and its study time.) In other words, the students did not passively review all the materials equally. This research on metamemory reveals that people often take an active, strategic approach to this cognitive task, a finding that is consistent with Theme 1 about active processing.

One of my professors in graduate school suggested an interesting strategy for examining research data (Martin, 1967). As he pointed out, whenever you see a number, you should ask yourself, "Why is it so high, and why is it so low?" In this case, the correlation is as *high* as +.30 because students do realize that the difficult items require more time. This general relationship has been replicated in later research (Nelson et al., 1994; Son & Kornell, 2008; Son & Schwartz, 2002). In contrast, why is this crucial correlation as *low* as +.30? Unfortunately, students are less than ideal in regulating their study strategies. They spend longer than necessary studying items they already know, and not enough time studying the items they have not yet mastered. One possible explanation for these results is that students are not very accurate in judging whether their mastery of material has actually improved when they have spent more time studying it (Townsend & Heit, 2011).

Allocating Time When the Task Is Difficult

Think about the exams you've taken so far this term. In psychology courses, for instance, your exams require you to remember conceptual information about psychology, rather than a simple list of paired words. In addition, students in real-life settings have only a limited time to study for their exams (Kornell & Metcalfe, 2006). Son and Metcalfe (2000) addressed this discrepancy by designing a situation that more closely resembles the challenging learning situation that college students often face. Their test material was a series of eight encyclopedia-style biographies. A good reader would need about 60 minutes to read them all completely. However, the researchers increased the time pressure for this task by allowing the students only 30 minutes to read all the material. The students began the study by reading a single paragraph from each biography; they ranked these paragraphs in terms of their perceived difficulty. Then the researchers informed them that they would have 30 minutes to read the material, and they could choose how to spend their time.

The results of this study demonstrated that students spent the majority of their study time on the biographies that they considered easy, rather than those they considered difficult. Notice that this strategy is wise, because they can master more material within the limited time frame. The take-home message from this and other studies is that when students are facing time pressure, they choose to study material that seems relatively easy to master (Kornell & Metcalfe, 2006; Metcalfe, 2002). Furthermore, Metcalfe (2002) tested students who had expertise in a given area. Compared to novices, these "expert" students chose to concentrate their time on more challenging material.

Conclusions About the Regulation of Study Strategies

As you can see from this discussion, students often regulate their study strategies in a sophisticated fashion. When they have time to master a relatively easy task, they allocate the most time to the difficult items. On a more challenging task—with time pressure—they realistically adjust their study strategies so that they focus on the items they are likely to master in the limited time frame (Kornell & Metcalfe, 2006).

We have seen that students regulate their study strategies. Furthermore, they can also *regulate the regulation* of their study strategies! That is, they choose one style for easy tasks and a different style for difficult tasks. As Metcalfe (2000) concludes, "Rather than simply being passive repositories for knowledge and memories, humans can use their knowledge of what they know to exert control over what they know [and] what they will know" (p. 207).

Tip-of-the-Tongue and Feeling-of-Knowing Effects

At some point during the last week, it's likely that you've had one (or both) of the following memory experiences:

1. The **tip-of-the-tongue effect** describes your subjective experience of knowing the target word for which you are searching, yet you cannot recall it right now (Bacon, 2010; Brown, 2012; Schwartz & Metcalfe, 2011).

2. The **feeling-of-knowing effect** describes the subjective experience of knowing some information, but you cannot recall it right now (Hertzog et al., 2010; Norman et al., 2010).

What's similar about both of these effects? They both involve situations in which you know that you know something. Having knowledge that you know something is another example of metamemory. But, what factors influence the likelihood that you'll be able to recall something you know that you know?

Tip-of-the-Tongue Effect

The tip-of-the-tongue experience is generally an involuntary effect. In contrast, the feeling of knowing is more conscious. You carefully assess whether you could recognize the answer if you were given several options, as in a multiple-choice question (Brown, 2012; Koriat & Helstrup, 2007). Both of these effects activate the frontal lobe of the brain, which is also important in other metacognitive tasks (Maril et al., 2005). Both of these effects are clearly related to metacognition because you make judgments about whether you know some information.

Demonstration 6.4 ‖ The Tip-of-the-Tongue Phenomenon

Look at each of the definitions below. For each definition, supply the appropriate word if you know it. Indicate "don't know" for those that you are certain you don't know. Mark "TOT" next to those for which you are reasonably certain you know the word, though you can't recall it now. For these TOT words, supply at least one word that sounds similar to the target word. The answers appear at the end of the chapter. Check to see whether your similar-sounding words actually do resemble the target words.

1. An absolute ruler, a tyrant.

2. A stone having a cavity lined with crystals.

3. A great circle of the earth passing through the geographic poles and any given point on the earth's surface.

4. Worthy of respect or reverence by reason of age and dignity.

5. Shedding leaves each year, as opposed to evergreen.

6. A person appointed to act as a substitute for another.

7. Five offspring born at a single birth.

8. A special quality of leadership that captures the popular imagination and inspires unswerving allegiance.

9. The red coloring matter of the red blood corpuscles.

10. A flying reptile that was extinct at the end of the Mesozoic Era.

11. A spring from which hot water, steam, or mud gushes out at intervals, found in Yellowstone National Park.

12. The second stomach of a bird, which has thick, muscular walls.

Now try Demonstration 6.4 to see whether any of the definitions encourages a tip-of-the-tongue experience. In our discussion of this topic, we will first consider the classic study by Brown and McNeill (1966). Then we'll examine some of the later research, as well as a related topic, called the "feeling of knowing."

Brown and McNeill (1966) conducted the first formal investigation in this area. Their description of a man "seized" by a tip-of-the-tongue state may capture the excruciating frustration that you sometimes feel when you fail to retrieve a word from the tip of your tongue:

> *The signs of it were unmistakable; he would appear to be in mild torment, something like the brink of a sneeze, and if he found the word his relief was considerable. (p. 326)*

In their research, Brown and McNeill produced the tip-of-the-tongue state by giving people the definition for an uncommon English word—such as *sampan, ambergris,* or *nepotism*—and asking them to identify the word. Sometimes people supplied the appropriate word immediately, and other times they were confident that they did not know the word. However, in still other cases, the definition produced a tip-of-the-tongue state. In these cases, the researchers asked people to provide words that resembled the target word in terms of sound, but not meaning. For example, when the target word was *sampan,* people provided these similar-sounding responses: *Saipan, Siam, Cheyenne, sarong, sanching,* and *symphoon.*

Think about why the tip-of-the-tongue phenomenon is one kind of metacognition. People are familiar enough with their memory for the target word to say, "This word is on the tip of my tongue." Their knowledge is indeed fairly accurate, because they are likely to identify the first letter and other attributes of the target word. They are also likely to provide similar-sounding words that really do resemble the target word (Brown & McNeill, 1966).

In the decades following the publication of Brown and McNeill's study, researchers have identified more information about the tip-of-the-tongue effect. The studies show, for instance, that young adults report having approximately one tip-of-the-tongue experience each week (Schwartz & Metcalfe, 2011). However, bilingual individuals experience the tip-of-the-tongue effect more frequently than monolinguals. One reason for this difference is that bilinguals have a greater total number of separate words in their semantic memory, compared to monolinguals (Gollan & Acenas, 2004; Gollan et al., 2005).

Researchers have also documented the tip-of-the-tongue phenomenon in non-English languages such as Polish, Japanese, and Italian (Brown, 2012; Schwartz, 1999, 2002). Research in these other languages demonstrates that people can retrieve other characteristics of the target word, in addition to its first letter and number of syllables. For example, Italian speakers can often retrieve the grammatical gender of the target word that they are seeking (Caramazza & Miozzo, 1997; Miozzo & Caramazza, 1997). Interestingly, the deaf community has a similar term, the **tip-of-the-finger effect**, which refers to the subjective experience of knowing the target sign, but that sign is temporarily inaccessible (Brown, 2012; Schwartz & Metcalfe, 2011).

Feeling of Knowing

The feeling of knowing is the subjective experience that you know some information, but you cannot recall it right now. So, you contemplate the question, and you judge that you could recognize the answer, for example, if you saw this item on a multiple-choice exam (Brown, 2012; Hertzog et al., 2010; Koriat & Helstrup, 2007).

People typically have a strong feeling of knowing if they can retrieve a large amount of partial information (Koriat & Helstrup, 2007; Schwartz et al., 1997; Schwartz & Smith, 1997). For example, I was recently thinking about how people can become captivated by reading fiction, and I recalled a wonderful essay that I had read in the *New Yorker* magazine. The author was an Indian woman, and she wrote that she didn't have many books during her early childhood in the United States. This essay described how she became enchanted with books once she started school.

I knew that I had read one of this author's novels and some of her short stories. But what was her name? This name was not on the tip of my tongue, but I definitely had a "feeling of knowing"; I knew that I could recognize her name, if I had several choices. Fortunately, Google came to the rescue: I entered "Indian American women authors," and a website provided a list of 10 possible candidates. Aha! The seventh person on that list was Jhumpa Lahiri!

In reality, the tip-of-the-tongue effect and the feeling-of-knowing effect are fairly similar, though your tip-of-the-tongue experiences may be more extreme and more irritating (Brown, 2012). The current neuroimaging data suggest that these two effects are associated with somewhat different brain patterns. For example, the right prefrontal region of the cortex is more likely to be associated with the tip-of-the-tongue effect. In contrast, the left prefrontal region is more likely to be associated with the feeling-of-knowing effect (Brown, 2012; Maril et al., 2005).

Metacomprehension

Did you understand the material on the tip-of-the-tongue phenomenon? Are you aware that you've started reading a new subtopic, which is part of the general discussion of metacognition? How much longer can you read today before you feel that you can't absorb any more? As you think about these issues, you are engaging in metacomprehension.

Metacomprehension refers to your thoughts about language comprehension. Most research on metacomprehension focuses on reading comprehension, rather than on the comprehension of spoken speech (Maki & McGuire, 2002). In this sense, the concept of metacomprehension refers to whether or not an individual can assess the degree to which that individual understands information to which they have been exposed. Why is this important? Consider a situation in which you are in the process of starting to study for an upcoming exam. You decide to reread the assigned reading. Having the ability to precisely identify which information you understand in the reading and which information you find confusing should provide you with the information you need in order to regulate your studying behavior. Naturally, if you have this sensitivity, you can focus your efforts more strongly on the information you don't understand. And hopefully, those focused efforts will lead to a higher degree of understanding, and thus to higher exam grades.

Here we consider two topics related to metacomprehension: (1) how accurate is the typical college student's metacomprehension? and (2) how can you improve your metacomprehension skills?

Metacomprehension Accuracy

In general, college students are not very accurate in their metacomprehension skills. For example, they may not notice that a paragraph contains inconsistencies or missing information. Instead, they think they understand it (Dunlosky & Lipko, 2007; Dunlosky & Metcalfe, 2009; Griffin et al., 2008; McNamara, 2011). Additionally, students often believe that they have understood something they have read because they are familiar with its general topic. However, they often fail to retain specific information, and they may overestimate how they will perform when they are tested on the material (Dunlosky & Lipko, 2007; Maki & McGuire, 2002; McNamara, 2011).

Let's consider a classic study about metacomprehension in more detail. Pressley and Ghatala (1988) tested introductory psychology students by assessing their metacomprehension, as well as their performance on tests of reading ability. Specifically, these researchers selected reading-comprehension tests from the Scholastic Aptitude Test, an earlier form of the current SAT. If you took the SAT, you'll recall that the questions about reading comprehension typically contain between one and three paragraphs, in essay form. The essay remains visible while you answer several multiple-choice questions, so you do not need to rely on your memory. Each question has five possible answers. Therefore, a person who simply guesses on an answer would be correct 20% of the time.

Next, the students in Pressley and Ghatala's study answered the multiple-choice questions, and then they rated how certain they were that they had answered each question correctly. If they were absolutely certain that their answer had been correct, they were told to answer 100%. If they were just guessing, they were told to report 20%. They were also instructed to provide an appropriate intermediate percentage for intermediate levels of confidence. These certainty rating served as the measure of metacomprehension.

Incidentally, you should notice that this task focuses on metacomprehension. The test would have assessed *metamemory*, rather than metacomprehension, if (1) There had been a delay between the reading task and the presentation of the multiple-choice questions and (2) If the essay was no longer present.

Let's examine the results. When a student had answered a reading comprehension question *correctly*, he or she supplied an average certainty rating of 73%. In other words, the students were fairly confident about these items, which is appropriate. However, when a student answered a question *incorrectly*, he or she supplied an average certainty rating of about 64%. Unfortunately, this is about the same level of confidence that the students showed for the items they answered correctly! Furthermore, these data suggest that students are often highly overconfident. In general, the research shows that readers are not very accurate in estimating whether they have understood the material that they have just read (McDaniel & Butler, 2011).

Other research shows that irrelevant features may lead students to overestimate their understanding of a textbook passage. For example, Serra and Dunlosky (2010) asked students to read a description about lightning storms. Some students read the passage with a photo of lightning accompanying each of six paragraphs. Other students read the same passage without any photos. Students in the six-photos group judged that their comprehension was higher, compared to students in the no-photos group. However, the two groups actually earned similar scores on a short-answer quiz.

When people *are* skilled at metacomprehension, they typically receive high scores on tests of reading comprehension (Maki & McGuire, 2002; Maki et al., 2005). According to research by Maki and her coauthors (1994), for example, readers who were accurate at assessing which sections of a text they had understood were also likely to receive higher scores on a reading-comprehension test. In fact, metacomprehension accuracy and reading-comprehension scores were significantly correlated $(r = +.43)$.

One particularly interesting finding on metacomprehension is that an individual's perception of her or his reading skill is a strong predictor of metacomprehension accuracy during reading-related tasks. Kwon and Linderholm (2014) found that individuals who believed that they were skilled readers were more accurate assessors of whether or not they understood text passages. The authors also found that this data pattern remained true even after controlling for an individual's actual reading ability. One possibility for this relationship is that skilled readers had more accurate assessments of their own reading ability, and thus were better able to regulate their reading when comprehension decreased. Indeed, metacomprehension requires you to *regulate* your reading, so that you know how to read more effectively (Dunlosky & Metcalfe, 2009). For example, good and poor readers differ in their awareness that certain reading strategies are useful. Good readers are more likely to report that they try to make connections among the ideas they have read. They also try to create visual images, based on descriptions in the text (Kaufman et al., 1985; Pressley, 1996). Additionally, good readers outline and summarize material in their own words when they are reading textbooks (McDaniel et al., 1996).

Students also become somewhat more accurate in assessing their performance after they gain experience in reading the text and after they receive feedback (Ariel & Dunlosky, 2011; Maki & Serra, 1992; Schooler et al., 2004). However, the improvement is not dramatic. College students clearly need some hints on how to increase their metacomprehension abilities and how to take advantage of their reading experiences.

Improving Metacomprehension

Ideally, students should be accurate in assessing whether they understand what they have read. In other words, their subjective assessments should match their performance on an objective test. One effective method for improving metacomprehension is to read a passage, wait a few minutes, and then try to explain the passage to yourself, *without* looking at the written passage (Chiang et al., 2010; Dunlosky & Metcalfe, 2009; McDaniel & Butler, 2011). This procedure not only improves your judgment about how well you know the passage, but it should also increase your score on a test about this material (Baker & Dunlosky,

Demonstration 6.5 | Assessing Your Metacomprehension Skills

Answer each of the following questions about your own metacomprehension. If you answer "no" to any question, devise a plan for improving metacomprehension, and apply this plan when you read the next assigned chapter in this textbook.

1. Before beginning to read an assignment, do you try to assess how carefully you should read the material?

2. In general, are you accurate in predicting your performance on the exam questions that focus on the reading assignments?

3. After you read a short section (roughly a page in length), do you make yourself summarize what you have just read—using your own words?

4. After reading a chapter in this textbook, do you test yourself on the list of new terms and on the review questions?

5. Do you reread a portion of your textbook when it doesn't make sense or when you realize that you haven't been paying attention?

6. Do you try to draw connections among the ideas in your textbook?

7. Do you try to draw connections between the ideas in your textbook and the information you have learned in class?

8. When you read a term you do not know, do you try to determine its meaning by looking it up in a dictionary or in the glossary of your textbook?

9. When you review your textbook prior to a test, do you spend more time reviewing the topics that you consider difficult, compared to the topics that you have already mastered?

10. When reading through several journal articles to see whether they might be relevant for a paper you are writing, do you first try to assess—without reading every word—the general scope or findings of each article?

2006; Dunlosky et al., 2005; Thiede et al., 2005). Furthermore, when you use this kind of active reading, you are less likely to "zone out" and fail to notice that you are no longer paying attention to your reading (Schooler et al., 2004).

Researchers have pointed out that students may have difficulty applying the more sophisticated metamemory strategies, especially if they have limited working-memory capacity. However, these students can substantially improve their reading comprehension by reading the same material a second time (Chiang et al., 2010; Griffin et al., 2008). Demonstration 6.5 will help you consider your own metacomprehension skills and think about some strategies for self-management. As researchers emphasize, metacomprehension and strategy use are essential components of skilled reading (McCormick, 2003; Schooler et al., 2004).

SECTION SUMMARY POINTS

Memory Strategies I: Memory Strategies Informed by Memory Concepts

1. Divided attention and limited working memory are two aspects of cognition that can cause problems for memory accuracy.

2. Using deep levels of processing (including elaboration, distinctiveness, and the self-reference method) can increase memory accuracy. Encoding specificity is also sometimes helpful. However, it is important to avoid the dangers of overconfidence.

3. Three general memory-improvement strategies were discussed that focus on aspects of practice: the total-time hypothesis, the distributed-practice effect, and the testing effect.

Memory Strategies II: Practice and Mnemonics

1. Some useful mnemonics focus on imagery; these include visualizing the items in vivid interaction and the keyword method.

2. Other useful mnemonics focus on organization; these include chunking, the hierarchy technique, the first-letter technique, and the narrative technique.

3. Prospective memory refers to remembering to do something in the future. Although prospective and retrospective memories have somewhat different focuses, they share some important similarities.

4. People make more errors on prospective-memory tasks when they are in a divided-attention situation, when they need to disrupt a habitual activity to perform the prospective-memory task, and when they are preoccupied or otherwise under stress.

5. In general, prospective memory is more accurate if people use the same memory strategies they use in retrospective-memory tasks and if they use external memory aids.

Metamemory

1. Metacognition is your knowledge and control of your cognitive processes; three important components of metacognition are metamemory, the tip-of-the-tongue phenomenon, and metacomprehension.

2. A variety of factors influence people's metamemory accuracy. Specifically, people are more accurate when they are judging

individual items, when their judgment is delayed, and when they judge their performance on multiple-choice questions, rather than performance on essays.

3. In general, students are not sufficiently aware that some memory strategies are more effective than others.

4. When the task is easy, students spend somewhat more time studying difficult material, rather than easy material. When the task is difficult and time is limited, students typically study the material that they are most likely to master.

5. The research on the tip-of-the-tongue phenomenon shows that— even when people cannot remember the word for which they are

searching—they can often identify important attributes such as the sound of the word.

6. The phrase "feeling of knowing" refers to situations in which you think you could select the correct answer from several choices, even though the target isn't actually on the tip of your tongue.

7. Studies on metacomprehension suggest that students are often overconfident in judging whether they understand the material they have read, especially if they have low reading ability or if they perceive their reading ability to be low.

8. Students' metacomprehension can be improved if they wait a few minutes and then try to summarize the material. Good readers also use a variety of strategies to regulate their reading.

CHAPTER REVIEW QUESTIONS

1. One trend throughout this chapter is that deep levels of processing can enhance your memory. Review the material in the section on memory strategies and identify which studies use some form of deep processing. Also explain why deep processing would be important in metacognition.

2. In general, your memory is more accurate when you have a small amount of information that you need to remember. Point out why the elaboration strategy doesn't follow this trend. Then choose at least two topics from this chapter and use elaboration to make the material easier to remember.

3. Review the list of memory-improvement strategies in Table 6.1. Which of these did you already use before you graduated from high school? Which did you discover while studying for exams, after you entered college?

4. Without looking at Table 6.1, describe as many of the memory-improvement techniques from this chapter as you can remember. Which techniques focus on strategies and which focus on metacognition? In each case, describe how you can use each one to remember some information from this chapter for your next exam in cognitive psychology.

5. How is prospective memory different from retrospective memory? What factors make prospective memory more difficult? Think of a specific person you know who complains about his or her memory. What hints could you provide to this person to encourage better prospective-memory performance?

6. Prior to reading this chapter, did you ever think about the topic of metamemory—even if you didn't know this term? Recall this

chapter's discussion about factors that can influence people's metamemory accuracy. Which factors are consistent with your own experiences?

7. What evidence suggests that people can supply information about a target, when they report that a word is on the tip of their tongue? Why is this topic related to metacognition? What other components of the tip-of-the-tongue effect and the feeling-of-knowing effect would be interesting topics for future research?

8. Several parts of this chapter emphasize that people tend to be overconfident about their ability to remember material and to understand written material. Summarize this information. Then describe how you can apply this information when you are reading and studying for your next exam in your course on cognitive psychology.

9. Some parts of the section on metacognition emphasize how people can control and modify their study strategies and reading strategies, in addition to simply knowing about their own cognitive processes. Describe the research on strategy regulation. In what ways has your own strategy regulation changed since you began college? Suppose that you have not changed: What strategies and study techniques would be most useful to modify?

10. What kind of metacomprehension tasks are relevant when you are reading this textbook? List as many different tasks as possible. Why do you suppose that metacomprehension for reading passages of text would be less accurate than people's metamemory for learning pairs of words (e.g., the task described in Demonstration 6.1)?

KEYWORDS

memory strategy	foresight bias	mnemonics	retrospective memory	feeling-of-knowing
levels of processing	total-time hypothesis	mental imagery	prospective memory	effect
elaboration	distributed-practice	keyword method	ecological validity	tip-of-the-finger effect
rehearsal	effect	organization	external memory aid	metacomprehension
distinctiveness	spaced learning	chunking	metacognition	
self-reference effect	massed learning	hierarchy	self-knowledge	
encoding-specificity	desirable difficulties	first-letter technique	metamemory	
principle	testing effect	narrative technique	tip-of-the-tongue effect	

RECOMMENDED READINGS

Benjamin, A. S. (Ed.). (2011). *Successful remembering and successful forgetting: A festschrift in honor of Robert A. Bjork*. New York: Psychology Press. Although some of the chapters in this book are aimed at graduate students and faculty, the majority of them provide some practical information about academic achievement.

Brandimonte, M. A., Einstein, G. O., & McDaniel, M. A. (Eds.). (2014). *Prospective memory: Theory and applications*. Psychology Press.

Brown, A. S. (2012). *The tip of the tongue state*. New York: Psychology Press. Here is the definitive book about both the tip-of-the-tongue effect and the feeling-of-knowing effect. In addition to the topics discussed in your text-book, Brown's book examines issues such as the cause of these phenomena and individual differences.

Davies, G. M., & Wright, D. B. (Eds.). (2010). *Current issues in applied memory research*. New York: Psychology Press. Several chapters in Davies and Wright's book examine how research on memory can be applied to education. Other themes in their book focus on applications to law and to neuroscience.

Dunlosky, J., & Bjork, R. A. (Eds.). (2008). *Handbook of metamemory and memory*. New York: Psychology Press. The chapters in this book are based on research, and most of them would be interesting to motivated undergraduates.

Dunlosky, J., & Metcalfe, J. (2009). *Metacognition*. Los Angeles: Sage. Here is an excellent, well-written summary of information about metamemory, the tip-of-the-tongue effect, and related topics.

ANSWER TO DEMONSTRATION 6.4

1. despot
2. geode
3. meridian
4. venerable
5. deciduous
6. surrogate
7. quintuplets
8. charisma
9. hemoglobin
10. pterodactyl
11. geyser
12. gizzard

7 | Mental Imagery and Cognitive Maps

Chapter Introduction

During perception, you rely on knowledge stored in memory to interpret the environmental stimuli registered by your senses. In other words, **perception** requires both bottom-up and top-down processing (Kosslyn et al., 2001). But, it is possible to have sensory-related experiences without bottom-up input being registered by your sensory receptors. For example, take a moment to close your eyes and create a clear mental image of the cover of this textbook. Be sure to include details such as its size, shape, and color, as well as the photo of the nautilus shell. Now try to create an auditory image. Can you hear the voice of a close friend saying your name? Finally, close your eyes again and create a "mental map" of the most direct route between your current location and the nearest store where you can buy a quart of milk. In each of these example exercises, you were able to create a mental image of something without seeing or hearing it. Thus, the processes that give rise to your ability to create mental images are exclusively top-down in nature (Kosslyn & Thompson, 2000). In other words, mental imagery is knowledge-driven—it involves utilizing the information stored in long-term memory to create internal images of sounds and objects that you have previously experienced.

This chapter explores three important aspects of imagery that have intrigued contemporary researchers. First, we examine the nature of visual images, with an emphasis on the way that we can transform these images. We then consider the nature of auditory images, a relatively new topic in cognitive psychology. Our third topic focuses on cognitive maps, which are mental representations of geographic information, including the environment that surrounds us.

Classical Research on Visual Imagery

Mental imagery (also called **imagery**) refers to the mental representation of stimuli when those stimuli are not physically present in the environment (Kosslyn et al., 2010). You can have a mental image for any sensory experience. Most of the psychological research on mental images, however, has focused on **visual imagery**, or the mental representation of visual stimuli. Fortunately, during the past decade, the research has increased for **auditory imagery**, which is the mental representation of auditory stimuli.

In this section, we first examine some key topics and questions related to research on mental imagery before discussing mental rotation, a form of visual imagery. We then consider a controversial debate in the field of mental imagery—namely, a debate about the format of the stored knowledge that we access when creating mental images.

Overview of Mental Imagery

use mental imagery everyday

We use mental imagery for a wide variety of everyday cognitive activities (Denis et al., 2004; Tversky, 2005a). For example, consider a situation in which you can't find your car keys, although you know that they must be somewhere on your messy desk. You must create and maintain a mental image of your keys while you visually inspect your messy desk to find your keys. If you didn't maintain some type of mental image while you were searching, then how would you know that the coffee mug sitting on your desk isn't the thing you're looking for?

Additionally, some professions emphasize mental imagery as a crucial component of performance on the job (Reed, 2010). Would you want to fly on an airplane if your pilot had weak spatial imagery? Imagery is also important in clinical psychology. Therapists often work with clients who have psychological problems such as post-traumatic stress disorder, depression, or eating disorders. With each of these disorders, individuals sometimes report that they experience intrusive, distressing mental images (Dargan et al., 2015; Mazhari et al., 2015; Moran et al., 2015). Therapists have successfully worked with clients by encouraging them to create alternative, more positive images (Bisby et al., 2010; Brewin et al., 2010; Liu & Chan, 2015).

Spatial ability is extremely important in the **STEM disciplines**, that is, science, technology, engineering, and mathematics (Ganis et al., 2009). For instance, Albert Einstein is well known as one of the geniuses of the last 100 years. Einstein reported that his own thinking processes typically used spatial images, instead of verbal descriptions (Newcombe, 2010). Unfortunately, elementary school teachers in the United States rarely teach children about spatial skills. In fact, the curriculum may not emphasize spatial skills until students enroll in a geometry class. Psychologist Nora Newcombe (2010) describes some interesting methods for enhancing young children's spatial skills. A typical task might require students to mentally rotate a picture until it resembles one of five options. Many high school and college students believe that they cannot possibly improve their spatial skills. However, training in spatial skills improves spatial performance for students of any age (Ganis et al., 2009; Reed, 2010; Twyman & Newcombe, 2010).

Although imagery and perception share many characteristics, they are not identical. During the act of perceiving an object in the visual world, for example, sensory information is registered by your sensory systems. Early after information has been registered by your senses, features of the sensory stimulus are detected (edges, lines, color, and so forth). This bottom-up information about the properties of an environmental stimulus is then processed in progressively more complex ways until an internal representation of the stimulus arises. As this representation is constructed, it is matched to information stored in your long-term memory. An object is recognized once bottom-up information has been processed enough for this matching process to occur.

Just about every topic in this book relies on both bottom-up and top-down processes, working together in concert to provide you with the ability to successfully perform some type of cognitive task. Mental imagery, however, is a rare exception. Indeed, by definition, mental imagery is knowledge-driven. You rely on what you know—and thus, information stored in your long-term memory—to create internal mental images. For example, when you create a mental image of the shape of Colorado, no one would suggest that the rods and cones in your retina are registering a Colorado-shaped pattern of stimulation. The subjective experiences for visual imagery and visual perception are obviously different, and it takes about one-tenth of a second longer to create a visual image (Reddy et al., 2010). Sometimes, these internal mental images are created while you are laying in bed trying to fall asleep, or when you're daydreaming. In these cases, mental images arise as a result of general thought processes. In fact, the ability to create and manipulate mental images has often been considered a hallmark of creativity and imagination (Brann, 1991; Thomas, 1999). Note, however, that internal mental images are often necessary to perform some cognitive task. In the visual search example above, in which someone must find their keys on a messy desk, a mental image of the keys is necessary in order to successfully search. In this sense, mental imagery is not a form of perception, per se, but is a close relative of perception.

Chapter 1 of this textbook provided an overview of the history of psychology. You may recall that Wilhelm Wundt is often described as the founder of psychology. Wundt and other early psychologists considered imagery to be an important part of the discipline (Palmer, 1999). In contrast, behaviorists such as John Watson strongly opposed research on mental imagery because it could not be connected to observable behavior. In fact, Watson even argued that imagery did not exist (Kosslyn et al., 2010). As a result, North American psychologists seldom studied imagery during the behaviorist period between 1920 and 1960 (Ganis et al., 2009; Kosslyn et al., 2010). For example, I used PsycINFO to search for the term "mental imagery" in any part of every journal article published during the decade from 1950 through 1959. The search identified only 34 articles. As cognitive psychology gained popularity, however, researchers rediscovered imagery. The topic continues to be important in contemporary cognitive psychology, especially with the development of more sophisticated techniques in cognitive neuroscience (Ganis et al., 2009; Reed, 2010).

Mental imagery is a challenging topic to study. Compared with a topic such as verbal memory, the topic of mental imagery is elusive and inaccessible. Researchers have attacked this problem by using the following logic: Suppose that a mental image really *does* resemble a physical object. Then people should be able to make judgments about this mental image in the same way that they make judgments about the corresponding physical object (Hubbard, 2010). For example, we should be able to rotate a mental image in the same way that we can rotate a physical object. Judgments about distance in a mental image should also be similar, as well as judgments about shape. In addition, a mental image should create interference when we try to perceive a physical object. Furthermore, we should be able to discover two interpretations of a mental image of an ambiguous figure, and we should be able to produce other vision-like effects when we construct a mental image.

Mental Rotation

As you might expect, research on mental imagery is difficult to conduct, especially because researchers cannot directly observe mental images and because they fade so quickly (Kosslyn et al., 2006). However, psychologists have modified some research techniques that were originally developed for studying visual perception so that they can now be applied to the study of mental images (Allen, 2004). As a result, the investigation of imagery has made impressive advances. Try Demonstration 7.1, which illustrates an important research technique that we'll examine shortly.

Suppose that you are a researcher who wants to study whether people rotate a mental image in the same way that they rotate a physical object. It's tempting to think that you could simply ask people to analyze their mental images and use these reports as a basis for describing mental imagery. However, consider why these introspective reports could be inaccurate and biased. We may not always have conscious access to the processes associated with our mental imagery (Anderson, 1998; Pylyshyn, 2006).

Demonstration 7.1 illustrates a classic experiment by Roger Shepard and his coauthor Jacqueline Metzler (1971). Researchers have explored the mental-rotation issue more than any other topic connected with imagery. Here was their reasoning. Suppose that you are holding a physical, geometric object in your hands, and you decide to rotate it. It will take you longer to rotate this physical object by 180 degrees than to rotate it only 90 degrees.

Now suppose that our mental images operate the same way that physical objects operate. It will take you longer to rotate this mental image 180 degrees, instead of 90 degrees. Again, remember that this entire

Demonstration 7.1 | Mental Rotation

For the top pair of objects, labeled *A*, look at the object on the left. Try rotating it in any direction you wish. Can you rotate it so that it matches the object on the right? Which of these three pairs of objects are the same, and which are different? Record your answers; we'll discuss this study shortly.

Source: Shepard, R. N., & Metzler, J. (1971). Mental rotation of three-dimensional objects. *Science, 171,* 701–703. Copyright 1971 American Association for the Advancement of Science.

question was quite daring during this era. No genuine behaviorist would ever consider research about mental images!

In Demonstration 7.1, notice that, in the top pair of designs (Part A), the left-hand figure can be changed into the right-hand figure by keeping it flat on the page and rotating it clockwise. Suddenly, the two figures match up, and you conclude "same." You can match these two figures by using a two-dimensional rotation. In contrast, the middle pair (Part B) requires a rotation in a third dimension. You may, for example, take the two-block "arm" that is jutting out toward you and push it over to the left and away from you. Suddenly, the figures match up, and you conclude "same." However, in the case of the bottom pair (Part C), you cannot rotate the figure on the left so that it matches the figure on the right. Therefore, you must conclude "different."

Shepard and Metzler (1971) asked eight extremely dedicated participants to judge 1,600 pairs of line drawings like these. They were instructed to pull a lever with their right hand if they judged the figures to be the same, and to pull a different lever with their left hand if they judged the figures to be different. In

FIGURE 7.1

Reaction time for deciding that pairs of figures are the same, as a function of the angle of rotation and the nature of rotation.

Note: The centers of the circles indicate the means, and the bars on either side provide an index of the variability of those means. *Source:* Shepard, R. N., & Metzler, J. (1971). Mental rotation of three-dimensional objects. *Science, 171,* 701–703. Copyright © 1971. American Association for the Advancement of Science.

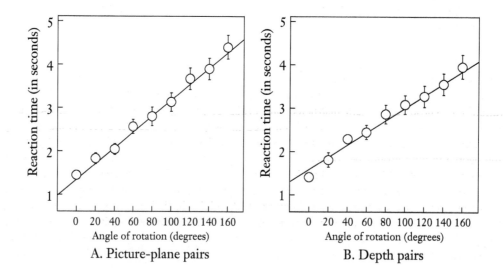

A. Picture-plane pairs   B. Depth pairs

each case, the experimenters measured the amount of time required for a decision. Notice, then, that the dependent variable is *reaction time*, in contrast to the dependent variable of *accuracy* used in most of the research we have examined in previous chapters.

Now look at Figure 7.1A, which shows the results for figures like Pair A from Demonstration 7.1. These figures require only a two-dimensional rotation, similar to rotating a flat picture. In contrast, Figure 7.1B shows the results for figures like Pair B in Demonstration 7.1. These figures require a three-dimensional rotation, similar to rotating an object in depth.

As both graphs show, people's decision time was strongly influenced by the amount of mental rotation required to match a figure with its mate. For example, rotating a figure 160 degrees requires much more time than rotating it a mere 20 degrees. Furthermore, notice the similarity between Figures 7.1A and 7.1B. In other words, the participants in this study performed a three-dimensional rotation almost as quickly as a two-dimensional rotation. (Pairs of figures like the two in Pair C in Demonstration 7.1 are based on different shapes, so these data are not included in either Figure 7.1A or 7.1B.)

As you can see, both figures show that the relationship between rotation and reaction time is a straight line.

Subsequent Research on Mental Rotation

The basic findings about mental rotation have been replicated many times. Using a variety of other stimuli, such as letters of the alphabet, researchers have found a clear relationship between angle of rotation and reaction time (e.g., Bauer & Jolicoeur, 1996; Cooper & Lang, 1996; Dahlstrom-Hakki et al., 2008; Kosslyn et al., 2006; Newcombe, 2002). That is, people make judgments more quickly if they need to rotate a mental image just a short distance.

If you are left-handed, you may wonder if handedness can influence the mental-rotation process. Kotaro Takeda and his coauthors (2010) asked the participants in their study to look at pictures of a human hand and to identify whether they were viewing a left hand or a right hand. Right-handers recognized a right hand faster than a left hand. In contrast, left-handers recognized right and left hands equally quickly. However, both groups recognized upright pictures faster—and more accurately—than upside-down pictures. This particular finding is consistent with the earlier research. After all, people take less time to rotate an image 0 degrees, rather than 180 degrees.

We also know that elderly people perform more slowly than younger people on a mental-rotation task. In contrast, age is not consistently correlated with other imagery skills, such as sense of direction or the ability to scan mental images (Beni et al., 2006; Dror & Kosslyn, 1994).

Other research shows that deaf individuals who are fluent in American Sign Language (ASL) are especially skilled in looking at an arrangement of objects in a scene and mentally rotating that scene by 180 degrees (Emmorey et al., 1998). Why should deaf people perform so well on these mental rotation tasks? They have an advantage because they have had extensive experience in watching a narrator produce a sign. Then, they must mentally rotate this sign 180 degrees. They need to perform this rotation frequently, so that they can match the perspective that they would use when producing this sign. (If you are not fluent in ASL, stand in front of a mirror and notice how you and a viewer would have very different perspectives for your hand movements.)

Cognitive Neuroscience Research on Mental Rotation Tasks

In one of the early neuroscience studies on mental rotation, Kosslyn et al. (2001) examined whether people use their motor cortex when they imagine themselves rotating one of the geometric figures in Demonstration 7.1. These researchers instructed one group of participants to rotate—with their own hands—one of the geometric figures that had been used in Shepard and Metzler's (1971) study. They instructed a second group of participants to simply watch as an electric motor rotated this same figure.

Next, the people in both groups performed the matching task that you tried in Demonstration 7.1, by rotating the figures mentally. Meanwhile, the researchers conducted PET scans to see which areas of the brain the participants were using during the mental-rotation task. Participants who had originally rotated the original geometric figure with their hands now showed activity in their primary motor cortex—the same part of the brain that had been active when they had rotated the figure with their hands. In contrast, consider the participants who had originally watched the electric motor as it rotated the figure. On the mental-rotation task, these people now showed no activity in the primary motor cortex. Without the "hands on" experience, their primary motor cortex was not active.

The nature of the instructions during the actual mental rotation can also influence the pattern of activation in the cortex. Specifically, when people received the standard instructions to rotate the figure, their right frontal lobes and their parietal lobes were strongly activated (Wraga et al., 2005; Zacks et al., 2003). However, this pattern of activation was different when researchers modified the instructions. In a second condition, the participants were instructed to imagine rotating themselves so that they could "see" the figure from a different perspective (Kosslyn et al., 2001). These instructions produced increased activity in the left temporal lobe, as well as in a part of the motor cortex (Wraga et al., 2005; Zacks et al., 2003). Notice, then, that a relatively subtle change in wording can make a dramatic change in the way that the brain responds to a mental-imagery task.

The research on mental rotation has practical implications for people who are recovering from a stroke. By watching the rotation of virtual-reality figures, these individuals can provide stimulation to their motor cortex. This form of "exercise" can shorten the time required before they make actual motor movements by themselves (Dijkerman et al., 2010; Ganis et al., 2009).

The Imagery Debate

Now that you have read about the research on visual imagery, let's consider the famous imagery debate. For several decades, cognitive psychologists have debated the potential explanations for mental imagery.

Stephen Kosslyn and his colleagues (2006) use the term **imagery debate** to refer to an important controversy: Do our mental images resemble perception (using an analog code), or do they resemble language (using a propositional code)?

The majority of theorists believe that information about a mental image is stored in an analog code (Howes, 2007; Kosslyn et al., 2006; Reisberg et al., 2003). An **analog code** is a representation that closely resembles the physical object. Notice that the word *analog* suggests the word *analogy*, such as the analogy between the real object and the mental image.

According to the analog-code approach, mental imagery is a close relative of perception (Tversky, 2005a). When you look at a sketch of a triangle, the physical features of that triangle are registered in your brain in a form that preserves the physical relationship among the three lines. Those who support analog coding propose that your mental image of a triangle is registered in a somewhat similar fashion, preserving the same relationship among the lines. Under this framework, when you are engaged in mental imagery, you create a mental image of an object that closely resembles the actual perceptual image on your retina (Ganis et al., 2009; Kosslyn et al., 2006). Note that supporters of the analog approach do not suggest that people literally have a picture in their head (Ganis et al., 2009; Kosslyn et al., 2006). They also point out that people often fail to notice precise visual details when they look at an object. These details will also be missing from their mental image of this object (Howes, 2007; Kosslyn et al., 2006).

In contrast to the analog-code position, other theorists argue that we store images in terms of a propositional code (Pylyshyn, 2003, 2006). A **propositional code** is an abstract, language-like representation;

storage is neither visual nor spatial, and it does not physically resemble the original stimulus (Ganis et al., 2009; Reed, 2010). According to the propositional-code approach, mental imagery is a close relative of language, not perception. For example, when you store a mental image of a triangle, your brain will register a language-like description of the lines and angles. Theorists have not specified the precise nature of the verbal description. However, it is abstract, and it does not resemble English or any other natural language. Your brain can then use this verbal description to generate a visual image (Kosslyn et al., 2006; Reed, 2010).

According to the propositional perspective, mental images are stored in an abstract, language-like form that does not physically resemble the original stimulus. Zenon Pylyshyn (2003, 2004, 2006) has been the strongest supporter of this perspective. Pylyshyn agrees that people do experience mental images. Pylyshyn notes, however, that these images are not a necessary, central component of imagery. He argues that it would be awkward—and perhaps even unworkable—to store information in terms of mental images. For instance, people would need a huge space to store all the images that they claim to have. Pylyshyn (2004, 2006) also emphasizes the differences between perceptual experiences and mental images. For example, you can re-examine and reinterpret a real photograph. Mental images are less likely to be so stable and easy to re-reference over time.

Teasing apart these two perspectives on the representational format of mental imagery is quite difficult. Shepard and Metzler's ground-breaking work on mental rotation, discussed above, supports an analog perspective. In general, the research on rotating geometric figures provides some of the strongest support for the analog-coding approach. We seem to treat mental images the same way we treat physical objects when we rotate them through space. In both cases, it takes longer to perform a large mental rotation than a small one, suggesting that you were considering, and thus activating, visual properties of the objects. In contrast, a propositional code would predict similar reaction times for these two conditions; the language-like description for the figure would not vary with the amount of rotation (Howes, 2007).

Neuroimaging research also provides a great deal of evidence in favor of the analog perspective. For example, the primary visual cortex is activated when people work on tasks that require detailed visual imagery (Ganis et al., 2009). This is the same part of the cortex that is active when we perceive actual visual objects. Furthermore, researchers have studied people who have prosopagnosia. People with **prosopagnosia** cannot recognize human faces visually, though they perceive other objects relatively normally (Farah, 2004). These individuals also have comparable problems in creating visual imagery for faces (Ganis et al., 2009).

Surveying a large number of studies, Kosslyn and his colleagues (2010) conclude that visual imagery activates between about 70% and 90% of the same brain regions that are activated during visual perception. For instance, when people have brain damage in the most basic region of the visual cortex, they have parallel problems in both their visual perception and their visual imagery. Furthermore, some individuals with brain damage cannot distinguish between (1) the colors registered during visual perception and (2) the visual imagery created in a mental image.

Additionally, as previously noted, people who have prosopagnosia cannot recognize human faces visually, though they perceive other objects relatively normally. The research shows that these individuals also cannot use mental imagery to distinguish between faces (Kosslyn et al., 2010).

Thus, behavioral and cognitive neuroscientific data support the notion that mental imagery is represented in an analog format. There is at least one phenomenon, however, that is difficult for the analog account to accommodate—the effect of ambiguous visual images. We discuss this effect below, and provide an explanation for why a propositional account may be more applicable under certain circumstances.

Visual Imagery and Ambiguous Figures

Before you read further, try Demonstration 7.2, and note whether you were able to reinterpret the figure. Most people have difficulty with tasks like this.

In the 1970s, Stephen Reed was concerned that mental imagery might have some limitations (Reed, 1974, 2010). Perhaps language helps us to store visual stimuli on some occasions. Reed's 1974 study tested people's ability to decide whether a specific visual pattern was a portion of a design that they had seen earlier. Specifically, Reed presented a series of paired figures. For example, people might first see a pattern like the Star of David in Demonstration 7.2, and then this figure disappeared. Next, after a brief delay, people saw a second pattern, such as a parallelogram with slanted right and left sides. In half of the

Look at the figure below, and form a clear mental image of the figure. Then turn to the paragraph labeled "Further instructions for Demonstration 7.2" at the bottom of Demonstration 7.3.

trials, the second pattern was truly part of the first one (for example, a parallelogram). In the other half, it was not (for example, a rectangle).

Suppose that people actually do store mental images in their head that correspond to the physical objects they have seen. Then they should be able to draw forth that mental image of the star and quickly discover the parallelogram shape hidden within it. However, the participants in Reed's (1974) study were correct only 14% of the time on the star/parallelogram example. Across all stimuli, they were correct only 55% of the time, hardly better than chance.

Reed (1974) argued that people could not have stored a visual image for figures like the Star of David, given the high error rate on items like this one. Instead, Reed proposed that people sometimes store pictures as descriptions, using the kind of propositional code discussed above. For example, suppose that you stored the description in Demonstration 7.2 as a verbal code, "two triangles, one pointing up and the other pointing down, placed on top of each other." When the instructions asked you whether the figure contained a parallelogram, you may have searched through your verbal description. Your search would locate only triangles, not parallelograms. Notice that Reed's (1974) research supports the verbal propositional-code approach, rather than the analog-code approach.

Similar research explored whether people could provide reinterpretations for a mental image of an ambiguous figure. For example, you can interpret the ambiguous stimulus in Figure 7.2 in two ways: a rabbit facing to the right or a duck facing to the left. Chambers and Reisberg (1985) asked participants to create a clear mental image of this figure. Next, the researchers removed the figure. The participants were then asked to give a second, different interpretation of that particular figure. None of the 15 people could do so. In other words, they apparently could not consult a stored mental image.

Next, the participants were asked to draw the figure from memory. Could they reinterpret this physical stimulus? All of them looked at the figure they had just drawn, and all 15 were able to supply a second interpretation. Chambers and Reisberg's research suggests that a strong verbal propositional code—such as "a duck that is facing left"—can overshadow a relatively weak analog code. Other similar research has replicated these findings. It's often easy to reverse a visual stimulus while you are looking at a physical picture that is ambiguous. In contrast, it's usually more difficult to reverse a *mental* image (Reisberg & Heuer, 2005). Now try Demonstration 7.3 before you read further.

FIGURE 7.2
An example of an ambiguous figure from chambers and reisberg's study.

Demonstration 7.3 || Reinterpreting Ambiguous Stimuli

Imagine the capital letter **H**. Now imagine the capital letter **X** superimposed directly on top of the **H**, so that the four corners of each letter match up exactly. From this mental image, what new shapes and objects do you see in your mind's eye?

(Further instructions for Demonstration 7.2: Without glancing back at the figure in Demonstration 7.2, consult your mental image. Does that mental image contain a parallelogram?)

It seems likely that people often use an analog code when they are thinking about fairly simple figures (like the two hands of a clock). In contrast, people may use a propositional code when the figures are more complex, as in the case of the research by Reed (1974) and Chambers and Reisberg (1985). As Kosslyn and his coauthors (2006) point out, our memory has a limited capacity for visual imagery. We may therefore have difficulty storing complex visual information in an analog code and then making accurate judgments about these mental images.

Verbal labels (and a propositional code) may be especially helpful if the visual stimulus is complex. For example, when I work on a jigsaw puzzle, I often find that I've attached a verbal label—such as "angel with outstretched wings"—to aid my search for a missing piece. In the case of these complex shapes, storage may be mostly propositional.

In other research, Finke and his colleagues (1989) asked people to combine two mental images, as in Demonstration 7.3. The participants in this study could indeed create new interpretations for these ambiguous stimuli. In addition to a combined **X** and **H** figure, they reported some new geometric shapes (such as a right triangle), some new letters (such as **M**), and some objects (such as a bow tie). Other research confirms that observers can locate similar, unanticipated shapes in their mental images (Brandimonte & Gerbino, 1996; Kosslyn et al., 2006; Rouw et al., 1997).

Individual differences in mental imagery

There has long existed a recognition that individuals may differ in the degree to which they rely on mental imagery or verbal descriptions during cognitive processing. Individuals who report the experience of constructing strong mental images are referred to as *visualizers*. Other individuals, often referred to as *verbalizers*, rely less on mental images and more on verbal descriptions (Paivio & Harshman, 1983; Riding & Douglas, 1993). These different cognitive styles do not represent discrete categories of individuals who only process information one way or the other. Instead, they represent biases that individuals have regarding the types of representations that tend to be activated during cognitive processing.

Individuals can self-report the experience of mental imagery, although self-report measures do not provide reliable insight into the types of processes that are engaged as the individual thinks. Cognitive neuroscientific techniques, on the other hand, may be able to shed light on whether individuals that self-report larger amounts of mental imagery are indeed more likely to activate portions of visual cortex than their verbalizing counterparts.

Nishimura and colleagues (2016) utilized the **magnetoencephalography (MEG)** *technique* in order to investigate this question. As discussed in Chapter 1, MEG is a cognitive neuroscientific testing method in which stimulus-evoked neuronal activity is recorded via sensors placed on the scalp. The sensors pick up on fluctuations in the magnetic fields produced by neural activity. Moreover, the robust nature of the magnetic field signal allows researchers to make reasonable inferences about where in the brain a sensor-detected signal was generated.

In their experiment, Nishimura and colleagues administered a scale designed to determine whether an individual has a more *visualizer* or *verbalizer* cognitive style. Neural responses were recorded as participants were asked to visualize objects, such as a famous landmark in the Japanese city of Kyoto, where this experiment was conducted. As hypothesized, *visualizers* produced more activity in occipital regions of cortex, regions that are strongly implicated in processing visual information. *Verbalizers,* on the other hand, produced more activation in areas often associated with linguistic processing, such as frontal cortical areas. This observation is consistent with the notion that different types of representations can be engaged by different individuals during imagery tasks.

Summary

In summary, the controversy about analog versus propositional coding is difficult to resolve. As with any big debate in cognitive psychology, there are currently no clear-cut winners (if there were, there wouldn't be any debate in the first place). The analog code apparently explains most stimuli and most tasks. And, generally speaking, the majority of people who conduct research on visual imagery support the analog position, perhaps partly because they personally experience vivid, picture-like images (Reisberg et al., 2003). Like most controversies in psychology, both the analog and the propositional approaches are probably at least partially correct, depending on the specific task. The research on ambiguous figures shows that people can create mental images using both propositional and analog codes. That is, we often use analog codes to provide picture-like representations that capture our mental images. However, when the stimuli or situations make it difficult to use analog codes, we may create a verbal representation, using a propositional code. Furthermore, some evidence exists that individual differences in cognitive style may partially determine the types of representations active during imagery. People who report greater degrees of visual imagery appear to activate visual cortex more so than do individuals who report reliance on verbal descriptions while thinking.

Factors That Influence Visual Imagery

As we have seen, the first systematic research on imagery demonstrated the similarity between rotating mental images and rotating physical objects. Researchers soon began to examine other attributes of mental images, such as the distance between two points and the shape of the mental image. In this section, we focus on a number of factors that have been shown to influence speed and accuracy on mental rotation and other visual imagery tasks. We conclude this section by addressing a controversial topic in cognitive psychology—namely, whether or not males and females differ in their spatial reasoning and other cognitive abilities.

Distance and Shape Effects on Visual Imagery

A classic study by Kosslyn and his colleagues (1978) showed that people took a long time to scan the distance between two widely separated points on a mental image of a map that they had created. In contrast, they quickly scanned the distance between two nearby points on a mental image of that map. Later research confirms that there is a linear relationship between the distance to be scanned in a mental image and the amount of time required to scan this distance (Borst & Kosslyn, 2008; Denis & Kosslyn, 1999; Kosslyn et al., 2006).

Consider, for example, another classic study on visual imagery. Allan Paivio (1978) asked participants to make judgments about the angle formed by the two hands on an imaginary clock. For instance, try to visualize the two hands on a standard, nondigital clock. Next, create a visual image of the angle formed by the two hands if the time were 3:20. Now create a visual image of the angle between the two hands if the time were 7:25. Which of these two "mental clocks" has the smaller angle between the two hands?

Paivio also gave the participants several standardized tests to assess their visual-imagery ability (similar to the one discussed above in relation to individual differences in cognitive style). As you can see in Figure 7.3, the high-imagery participants made decisions much more quickly than the low-imagery participants. As Figure 7.3 also shows, participants in both groups made decisions very slowly when they compared the angle formed by the hands at 3:20 with the angle of the hands at 7:25. After all, these two angles are quite similar. In contrast, their decisions were relatively fast if the two angles were very different in size, perhaps 3:20 and 7:05.

Think about the implications of this study. With real objects, people take a long time to make decisions when two angles are very similar to each other. When the two angles are very different, people respond quickly. The research demonstrates that people show the same pattern with their visual images. According to Paivio (1978), this study demonstrates strong support for the proposal that people use analog codes, rather than propositional codes.

Additional support for analog codes comes from research with visual images that represent more complex shapes. Shepard and Chipman (1970) asked participants to construct mental images of the shapes of various U.S. states, such as Colorado and Oregon. Then the participants judged the similarity between the

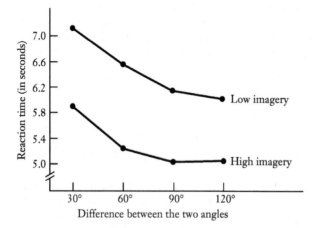

FIGURE 7.3 The influence of angle difference on reaction time for high-imagery and low-imagery people.

Source: Paivio, A. (1978). Comparison of mental clocks. *Journal of Experimental Psychology: Human Perception and Performance, 4,* 61–71.

two mental images, with respect to their shapes. For example—without looking at a map—do you think that Colorado and Oregon have similar shapes? How about Colorado and West Virginia?

These same participants also made shape-similarity judgments about pairs of states while they looked at an actual *physical* sketch of each state (rather than only its name). The results showed that the participants' judgments were highly similar in the two conditions. Once again, people's judgments about the shape of *mental* images are similar to their judgments about the shape of physical stimuli.

Let's review our conclusions about the characteristics of visual images, based on the research we have discussed so far:

1. When people rotate a visual image, a large rotation takes them longer, just as they take longer when making a large rotation with a physical stimulus.

2. People make distance judgments in a similar fashion for visual images and for physical stimuli.

3. People make decisions about shape in a similar fashion for visual images and for physical stimuli. This conclusion holds true for both simple shapes (angles formed by hands on a clock) and complex shapes (geographic regions, like Colorado or West Virginia).

Visual Imagery and Interference

Many studies show that your mental image can interfere with an actual physical image (e.g., Baddeley & Andrade, 1998; Craver-Lemley & Reeves, 1992; Kosslyn et al., 2006; Richardson, 1999). Let's examine the research related to interference, specifically focusing on visual imagery.

Think about a friend whom you have seen in the last day or two. Next, create a clear mental image of this friend's face. Keep this mental image in mind, and simultaneously let your eyes wander over this page. You will probably find that the task is difficult, because you are trying to "look" at your friend (in a visual image) at the same time that you are trying to look at the words on this page (a physical stimulus). Research has confirmed that visual imagery can interfere with your visual perception.

Consider a classic study about interference, conducted by Segal and Fusella (1970). In part of this study, they asked participants to create a visual image, for example, a visual image of a tree. As soon as the participant had formed the requested image, the researchers presented a real physical stimulus, for example a small blue arrow. The researchers then measured the participants' ability to detect the physical stimulus.

Segal and Fusella's (1970) results showed that people had more problems detecting the physical stimulus when the mental image was in the same sensory mode. For example, when the participants had been imagining the shape of a tree, they had trouble detecting the small blue arrow. The mental image interfered with the real visual stimulus. In contrast, when they had been imagining the sound of an oboe, they had no trouble reporting that they saw the arrow. After all, the imagined sound and the arrow—a visual stimulus—represented two different sensory modes.

In another study on visual interference, Mast and his colleagues (1999) told participants to create a visual image of a set of narrow parallel lines. Next, they were instructed to rotate their mental image of this set of lines, so that the lines were in a diagonal orientation. Meanwhile, the researchers presented a physical stimulus, a small segment of a line. The participants were told to judge whether this line segment had an exactly vertical orientation. The results showed that the imagined set of lines and the real set of lines produced similar distortions in the participants' judgments about the orientation of that line segment.

Visual Imagery and Other Vision-Like Processes

So far, we have examined a variety of characteristics related to visual imagery. Let's briefly consider another less-obvious characteristic of visual perception. We'll see that a relatively unknown visual characteristic has a mental-imagery counterpart.

Research in visual perception shows that people can see a visual target more accurately if the target is presented with vertical lines on each side of this target. Research by Ishai and Sagi (1995) shows that mental imagery produces the same masking effect. That is, people can see a visual target more accurately if they create mental images of vertical lines on each side of the target.

This study on the masking effect is especially important because of a research-methods issue called "demand characteristics." **Demand characteristics** are all the cues that might convey the experimenter's hypothesis to the participant. Some critics of the analog approach have proposed that the experimental results in imagery experiments might be traceable to one or more of these demand characteristics (Pylyshyn, 2003, 2006). For example, participants may be able to guess the results that the experimenter wants. Perhaps they might guess that a visual mental image is supposed to interfere with visual perception.

The masking effect, however, is virtually unknown to people who have not completed a psychology course in perception. The participants in the study by Ishai and Sagi (1995) would not know that visual targets are especially easy to see if they are surrounded by masking stimuli. Therefore, demand characteristics cannot account for the masking effect with mental images. As a result, we can be more confident that *visual imagery* really can produce the masking effect, just as *visual perception* can produce the masking effect. Visual imagery can indeed resemble visual perception.

Researchers have also examined whether mental imagery resembles visual perception in other respects. For example, people have especially good acuity for mental images that are visualized in the center of the retina, rather than in the periphery; visual perception operates the same way (Kosslyn, 1983). Other studies demonstrate additional parallels between mental images and visual perception (Kosslyn, 2001; Kosslyn & Thompson, 2000; Kosslyn et al., 2006).

Gender Comparisons in Spatial Ability

When psychologists conduct research about individual differences in cognition, one of the most popular topics is gender comparisons. Talk-show hosts, politicians—and even university presidents—feel free to speculate about gender differences. However, they rarely consult the extensive psychology research about gender comparisons. As a result, they rarely learn that most gender differences in cognitive abilities are small (Hyde, 2005; Matlin, 2012; Yoder, 2007). Researchers have conducted literally hundreds of studies on gender comparisons in cognitive abilities. If we want to understand gender comparisons in spatial ability, for example, we cannot focus on just one study.

When the research on a topic is abundant, psychologists often use a statistical technique called a meta-analysis. **Meta-analysis** is a statistical method for combining numerous studies on a single topic. Researchers begin by locating all appropriate studies on a topic such as gender comparisons in verbal ability. Then they perform a meta-analysis that combines the results of all these studies.

A meta-analysis yields a number called effect size, or d. For example, suppose that researchers conduct a meta-analysis of 18 studies about gender comparisons in reading comprehension scores. Furthermore, suppose that—on each of the 18 studies—females and males receive very similar scores. In this case, the d would be close to zero.

Psychologists have conducted numerous meta-analyses on cognitive gender comparisons. Janet Hyde (2005) wrote an important article that summarized all of these previous meta-analyses. Table 7.1 shows a tally of the effect sizes for the meta-analyses that have been conducted in three major areas of cognitive ability.

Table 7.1   The Distribution of Effect Sizes (d) Reported in Meta-Analyses for Three Kinds of Cognitive Skills

	Magnitude of Effect Size			
	Close to Zero	Small	Moderate	Large
	($d < 0.10$)	($d = 0.11$ to 0.35)	($d = 0.36$ to 0.65)	($d = 0.66$ to 1.00)
Verbal Ability	4	1	0	0
Mathematics	4	0	0	0
Spatial Ability	0	4	3	1

Source: Based on Hyde (2005).

As you can see in Table 7.1, four meta-analyses on verbal ability showed extremely small gender differences, with d values close to zero. One additional meta-analysis produced a d value considered to be "small," and no meta-analyses yielded a d value considered to be either moderate or large. In other words, these studies show *gender similarities* in verbal ability.

You can also see that all four meta-analyses on mathematics ability produced d values that are close to zero, once more showing *gender similarities*. These gender similarities in math ability are extremely important, especially because the headlines in the media usually claim that males are much better than females in their math skills (Hyde, 2005; Matlin, 2012). These math comparisons are consistent with an international study that focused on eighth-grade students in 34 different countries. Interestingly, the boys' average was higher than the girls' average in 16 countries, the girls' average was higher than boys' average in 16 countries, and girls and boys had the same averages in two countries (National Center for Education Statistics, 2004).

Let's now consider spatial ability, the topic related to our current discussion. Here, the gender differences are more substantial. Notice, however, that only one meta-analysis yielded a d value in the "large" category.

An important point is that spatial ability represents several different skills; it is not unitary (Caplan & Caplan, 2009; Chipman, 2004; Tversky, 2005b). One skill is spatial visualization. A typical task would be to ask people to look at a sketch of a busy street to find hidden drawings of human faces. Gender differences in spatial visualization are small, according to Hyde's (2005) summary of meta-analyses.

The second component of spatial ability is spatial perception. A typical task would be sitting in a dark room and adjusting an illuminated rod so that it is in an exactly vertical position. The two meta-analyses that specifically focused on spatial perception both produced d values of 0.44, a moderate gender difference (Hyde, 2005).

The third component of spatial ability is mental rotation. As you know from Demonstration 7.1, a typical task would be to look at two geometric figures and then decide whether they would be identical if you rotated one of the figures. Males are more likely than females to respond quickly on this task. The two meta-analyses that specifically focused on mental rotation produced d values of 0.56 and 0.73 (Hyde, 2005). For the sake of comparison, however, consider the gender differences in people's height. For height, the d is a substantial 2.0.

In other words, mental rotation is the only cognitive skill where a group of males is likely to earn higher scores than a group of females. However, we must emphasize that some studies report no gender differences in mental rotation. Furthermore, some studies report that the gender differences disappear when the task instructions are changed and when people receive training on spatial skills (Matlin, 2012; Newcombe, 2006; Terlecki et al., 2008).

In addition, a large portion of the gender differences in spatial rotation can be traced to the fact that boys typically have more experience with toys and sports (and perhaps even video games) that emphasize spatial skills (Voyer et al., 2000). In other words, this one area of cognitive gender differences can be reduced by providing girls with experience and training in spatial activities.

Auditory Imagery

Most research on the topic of mental imagery has tended to focus heavily on visual imagery, and it turns out that people tend to report more visual imagery than other types of mental imagery. Stephen Kosslyn and his coauthors (1990), for example, asked students to keep diaries about their mental imagery. They reported that about two-thirds of their images were visual. In contrast, images for hearing, touch, taste, and smell were much less common. Psychologists show a similar lopsidedness in their research preferences. Most of the research focuses on visual imagery, though the research on auditory imagery has increased during the last decade. In contrast, psychologists rarely investigate smell, taste, or touch imagery.

As we noted at the beginning of this chapter, auditory imagery is our mental representation of sounds when these sounds are not physically present. For example, can you create a vivid auditory image of a close friend's laughter? Can you create a vivid auditory image for the first few bars of a favorite song? What other categories of auditory images can you create in your "mind's ear"?

We can typically identify a variety of "environmental sounds," even though we might not use that particular term. For example, can you create an auditory image of the whining sound made by an almost-dead car battery? In addition, we typically have auditory imagery for the distinctive noises made by a variety of animals (Wu et al., 2006). This section on auditory imagery provides an introduction to the topic.

Psychologists have lamented the relative lack of research on auditory imagery (e.g., Kosslyn et al., 2010; Vuvan & Schmuckler, 2011). For example, Timothy Hubbard (2010) reviewed the research on the topic. The first paragraph of Hubbard's article begins, "Despite the resurgence in imagery research beginning in the late 1960s and early 1970s, auditory forms of imagery have received relatively little interest" (p. 302). Hubbard also discovered that some previous articles had claimed that they had found evidence of auditory imagery, but the evidence was not convincing. As you know from the studies on visual imagery, the research methods need to be carefully designed to demonstrate clear-cut evidence of mental imagery.

Is auditory imagery less vivid than visual imagery? Rubin and Berentsen (2009) asked people in the United States and Denmark to recall an event from their life and rate its vividness. In both countries, people reported higher imagery ratings for visual imagery than for auditory imagery. Even so, the relative lack of research on auditory imagery is puzzling.

Researchers have explored some characteristics of auditory imagery such as loudness (e.g., Hubbard, 2010; Vuvan & Schmuckler, 2011). In this section, we will briefly consider two topics that have clear implications for mental imagery: (1) auditory imagery and pitch and (2) auditory imagery and timbre.

Auditory Imagery and Pitch

One prominent feature of auditory imagery is pitch. **Pitch** is a characteristic of a sound stimulus that can be arranged on a scale from low to high (Foley & Matlin, 2010; Plack & Oxenham, 2005). One of the classic studies on pitch was conducted by Margaret J. Intons-Peterson, who was one of the creators of the important Brown/Peterson & Peterson technique for assessing short-term memory. (See Chapter 4.) Intons-Peterson and her coauthors (1992) examined how quickly people could "travel" the distance between two auditory stimuli that differ in pitch.

For example, Intons-Peterson and her colleagues asked students to create an auditory image of a cat purring. Then they asked the students to "travel" from the cat-purring image to an image with a slightly higher pitch, such as a slamming door. The participants pressed a button when they reached this slightly higher pitch. The results showed that the students needed about 4 seconds to travel that relatively short auditory distance.

The researchers also asked students to "travel" longer auditory distances, for example, from a cat purring to the sound of a police siren. The participants needed about 6 seconds to travel this relatively long distance. In the case of pitch, the distance between the two actual tones is indeed correlated with the distance between the two imagined tones.

Auditory Imagery and Timbre

Another important characteristic of a sound is called "timbre" (pronounced "*tam*-ber"). **Timbre** describes the sound quality of a tone. For example, imagine a familiar tune—such as *Happy Birthday*—played on the flute. Now contrast that sound quality with the same song played on a trumpet. Even when the two versions of this song have the same pitch, the flute tune seems relatively pure.

Consider a study by Andrea Halpern and her coauthors (2004), which focused on people's auditory imagery for the timbre of musical instruments. These researchers studied young adults who had completed at least 5 years of formal training in music. This requirement was necessary so that the participants would be familiar with the timbre of eight musical instruments, such as the basoon, flute, trumpet, and violin. Each participant first listened to the sound of every instrument, until he or she could name them all easily.

To assess auditory imagery for timbre, Halpern and her colleagues asked each participant to rate the similarity of timbres in two conditions. In the *perception condition*, the participants listened to a 1.5-second segment of one musical instrument, followed by a 1.5-second segment of another instrument. They heard all possible pairings of the eight different instruments. For every pair, the participants rated the similarity of the two perceptual stimuli. In the *imagined condition*, the participants heard the names of the instruments, rather than their sounds. They heard all possible pairings of the eight names for the different instruments.

The results showed that the ratings for timbre perception and for timbre imagery were highly correlated with each other $(r = .84)$. In other words, the participants showed that their cognitive representation for the timbre of an *actual* musical instrument is quite similar to the cognitive representation for the timbre of an *imagined* musical instrument. Clearly, researchers with an interest in imagery can explore many new topics that compare the relationship between auditory perception and auditory imagery.

Cognitive Maps

Have you had an experience like this? You've just arrived in a new environment, perhaps for your first year of college. You ask for directions, let's say, to the library. You hear the reply, "OK, it's simple. You go up the hill, staying to the right of the Northumbria Building. Then you take a left, and Meliora Hall will be on your right. The library will be over on your left." You struggle to recall some landmarks from the orientation tour. Was Seashore Hall next to Uris Hall, or was it over near Johnson Hall? Valiantly, you try to incorporate this new information into your discouragingly hazy mental map.

So far, this chapter has examined the general characteristics of mental images. This discussion primarily focused on a theoretical issue that has intrigued cognitive psychologists: Do our visual and auditory mental images resemble our perception of actual visual and auditory stimuli?

Now we consider cognitive maps, a topic that is clearly related to mental imagery. However, the research on cognitive maps focuses on the way we represent geographic space. More specifically, a **cognitive map** is a mental representation of geographic information, including the environment that surrounds us (Shelton & Yamamoto, 2009; Wagner, 2006). Notice, then, that the first two sections of this chapter emphasize our mental representations of sights and sounds. In contrast, this third section emphasizes our mental images of the *relationships* among objects, such as buildings on your college campus.

Let's discuss some background about cognitive maps, and then we'll see how distance, shape, and relative position are represented in these cognitive maps. We'll conclude this chapter by examining how we create mental maps from verbal descriptions.

Try to picture a home that you know quite well. Now picture yourself walking through this home. Does your cognitive map seem fairly accurate, or is this map somewhat fuzzy about the specific size and location of a room? A cognitive map can also represent larger geographic areas, such as a neighborhood, a city, or a country. In general, our cognitive maps represent areas that are too large to be seen in a single glance (Bower, 2008; Poirel et al., 2010; Wagner, 2006). As a result, we create a cognitive map by integrating the information that we have acquired from many successive views (Shelton, 2004; Spence & Feng, 2010). In general, the research on cognitive maps emphasizes real-world settings, as well as high ecological validity.

Research on cognitive maps is part of a larger topic called *spatial cognition*. **Spatial cognition** primarily refers to three cognitive activities: (1) our thoughts about cognitive maps; (2) how we remember the world we navigate; and (3) how we keep track of objects in a spatial array (Shelton, 2004; Spence & Feng, 2010).

Furthermore, spatial cognition is interdisciplinary in its scope. For example, computer scientists create models of spatial knowledge. Linguists analyze how people talk about spatial arrangements. Anthropologists study how different cultures use different frameworks to describe locations. Geographers examine all of these dimensions, with the goal of creating efficient maps. The topic is also relevant when architects design buildings and when urban planners construct new communities (Devlin, 2001; Tversky, 1999, 2000b).

In addition to theoretical issues related to spatial cognition, psychologists study applied topics. These include topics related to entertainment, such as video games (Spence & Feng, 2010). They also study life-and-death topics such as the communication of spatial information between air traffic controllers and airplane flight crews (Barshi & Healy, 2011; Schneider et al., 2011).

As you might expect, individual differences in spatial-cognition skills are quite large (Shelton & McNamara, 2004; Smith & Cohen, 2008; Wagner, 2006). However, people tend to be accurate in judging their ability to find their way to unfamiliar locations (Kitchin & Blades, 2002). In other words, your metacognition about your spatial ability may be reasonably correct.

Furthermore, these individual differences in spatial cognition are correlated with people's scores on tests of the visuospatial sketchpad (Gyselinck & Meneghetti, 2011). Spatial-cognition scores are also correlated with performance on the spatial tasks that we discussed in the first section of this chapter (Newcombe, 2010; Sholl et al., 2006). For example, people who are good at mental rotation are more skilled than others in using maps to find a particular location (Fields & Shelton, 2006; Shelton & Gabrieli, 2004).

Fortunately, people with poor spatial skills can improve their performance. Suppose that you are visiting an unfamiliar college campus (Smith & Cohen, 2008). You park your car, and you set out to find a specific building. You'll increase your chances of finding your way back to your car if you periodically turn around and study the scene you'll see on your return trip (Heth et al., 2002; Montello, 2005). As you might expect, it's also important to notice specific landmarks along this route (Ruddle et al., 2011). These strategies should improve the accuracy of your cognitive maps.

Try Demonstration 7.4 before you read further. This demonstration is based on research by Roskos-Ewoldsen and her colleagues (1998), which we will discuss shortly.

Our cognitive maps typically include survey knowledge, which is the relationship among locations that we acquire by directly learning a map or by repeatedly exploring an environment. Now look back at Demonstration 7.4. Which of the two tasks was easier? Your cognitive map will be easier to judge and more accurate if you acquire spatial information from a physical map that is oriented in the same direction that you are facing in your cognitive map.

In Question 1 of this demonstration, your mental map and the physical map have the same orientation, so this task should be relatively easy. In contrast, you need to perform a mental rotation in order to answer Question 2, so this task is more difficult. Research confirms that judgments are easier when your mental map and the physical map have matching orientations (Devlin, 2001; Montello, 2005; Montello et al., 2004).

Now we will consider how our cognitive maps represent three geographic attributes: distance, shape, and relative position. Theme 2 of this book states that our cognitive processes are generally accurate. This generalization also applies to cognitive maps. In fact, our mental representations of the environment usually reflect reality with reasonable accuracy, whether these cognitive maps depict college campuses or larger geographic regions.

According to Theme 2, however, when people *do* make cognitive mistakes, these mistakes can often be traced to a rational strategy. The mistakes that people display in their cognitive maps usually "make sense" because they are systematic distortions of reality (Devlin, 2001; Koriat 2000; Tversky, 2000b). These mistakes reflect a tendency to base our judgments on variables that are *usually* relevant. They also reflect a tendency to judge our environment as being more well organized and orderly than it really is.

At this point, we need to introduce a useful term in cognitive psychology, called a "heuristic." A **heuristic** (pronounced "hyoo-*riss*-tick") is a general problem-solving strategy that usually produces a correct solution . . . but not always. As you will see, people often use heuristics in making judgments about cognitive maps. As a result, they tend to show systematic distortions in distance, shape, and relative position.

Demonstration 7.4 || Learning from a Map

Study the diagram at the bottom of this demonstration for about 30 seconds, and then cover it completely. Now answer the following questions:

1. Imagine that you are standing at Position 3, facing Position 4. Point to Position 1.

2. Now, glance quickly at the diagram and then cover it completely. Imagine that you are now standing at Position 1, facing Position 2. Point to Position 4.

Distance and Shape Effects on Cognitive Maps

How far is it from your college library to the classroom in which your cognitive psychology course is taught? How many miles separate the place where you were born from the college or university where you are now studying? People's distance estimates are often distorted by factors such as (1) the number of intervening cities, (2) category membership, and (3) whether their destination is a landmark.

Distance Estimates and Number of Intervening Cities

In one of the first systematic studies about distance in cognitive maps, Thorndyke (1981) constructed a map of a hypothetical geographic region with cities distributed throughout the map. Between any two cities on the map, there were 0, 1, 2, or 3 other cities along the route. Participants studied the map until they could accurately reconstruct it. Then they estimated the distance between specified pairs of cities.

The number of intervening cities had a clear-cut influence on their estimates. For example, when the cities were really 300 miles apart on this map, people estimated that they were only 280 miles apart when there were no intervening cities. In contrast, these target cities were estimated to be 350 miles apart with three intervening cities. Notice that this error is consistent with the concept of heuristics. If cities are randomly distributed throughout a region, two cities are usually closer together when there are no intervening cities between them. In contrast, two cities are likely to be further apart when there are three intervening cities.

Distance Estimates and Category Membership

Research shows that the categories we create can have a large influence on our distance estimates. For example, Hirtle and Mascolo (1986) showed participants a hypothetical map of a town, and they learned the locations on the map. Then the map was removed, and people estimated the distance between pairs of locations. The results showed that people tended to shift each location closer to other sites that belonged to the same category. For example, people typically remembered the courthouse as being close to the police station and other government buildings. However, these shifts did not occur for members of different categories. For instance, people did not move the courthouse closer to the golf course.

People show a similar distortion when they estimate large-scale distances (Tversky, 2009). For instance, Friedman and her colleagues asked college students to estimate the distance between various North American cities (Friedman et al., 2005; Friedman & Montello, 2006). Students from Canada, the United States, and Mexico judged that distances were greater when they were separated by an international border. Specifically, they judged two cities to be an average of only 1,225 miles from each other if the cities were located in the same country. In contrast, they judged two cities to be an average of 1,579 miles from each other if they were located in different countries.

In other words, the estimated difference was 354 miles when the cities were separated by an international border. In reality, however, the actual difference was only 63 miles (Friedman & Montello, 2006). Students make a similar error when they estimate distances on their own college campus, and there is an invisible border between two parts of the campus (Uttal et al., 2010; Wagner, 2006). They are reluctant to say that two buildings could be near each other if they are on different sides of that invisible border.

According to a phenomenon called **border bias**, people estimate that the distance between two specific locations is larger if they are on *different* sides of a geographic border, compared to two locations on the *same* side of that border. Border bias can have far-reaching consequences. For example, Arul Mishra and Himanshu Mishra (2010) asked participants to imagine that they were thinking about buying a vacation home in the mountains, and their final choices were currently in either Oregon or Washington. While they were deciding, one group was told that an earthquake had hit Wells, Oregon, in a location 200 miles from both of these vacation homes. Another group received identical instructions, except that the earthquake had hit Wells, Washington. A third group (the control group) received the same initial instructions, but no earthquake was mentioned.

Figure 7.4 shows the results. Even though the epicenter of the earthquake was the same distance from both vacation homes, the participants in the "Oregon earthquake group" were 20% more likely than the control group to choose a Washington home. Similarly, the participants in the "Washington earthquake group" were 25% more likely than the control group to choose an Oregon home.

Notice that this study demonstrates a "same-category heuristic." It's generally a good strategy to guess that two cities are closer together if they are in the same state, rather than in adjacent states.

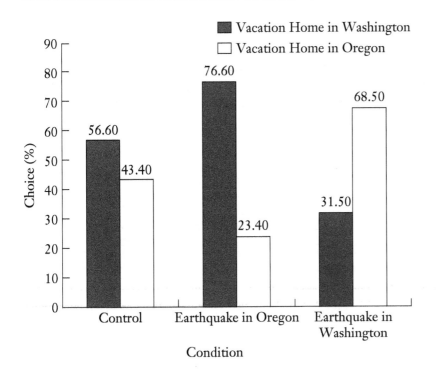

FIGURE 7.4 An example of border bias: percentage of participants choosing each vacation home, as a function of which state had experienced an earthquake.

When people hear about an earthquake, they prefer to select a home in a different state, rather than a home that is equally close, but in the same state (Mishra & Mishra, 2010). *Source:* Mishra, A., & Mishra, H. (2010). Border bias: The belief that state borders can protect against disasters. *Psychological Science, 21,* 1582–1586. Copyright © 2010. Reprinted by permission of SAGE Publications.

Distance Estimates and Landmarks

We have some friends who live in Rochester, the major city in our region of upstate New York. We sometimes invite them to come down for a meeting in Geneseo, about 45 minutes away from Rochester. "But it's so far away," they complain. "Why don't you come up here instead?" They are embarrassed when we point out that the distance from Geneseo to Rochester is exactly the same as the distance from Rochester to Geneseo!

The research confirms the **landmark effect**, which is the general tendency to provide shorter estimates when traveling to a landmark—an important geographical location—rather than a nonlandmark (Shelton & Yamamoto, 2009; Tversky, 2005b, 2009; Wagner, 2006). For example, McNamara and Diwadkar (1997) asked students to memorize a map that displayed various pictures of objects. The map included some objects that were described as landmarks, and some objects that were not landmarks. After learning the locations, the students estimated the distance on the map (in inches) between various pairs of objects.

Consistent with the landmark effect, these students showed an asymmetry in their distance estimates. In one study, for instance, students judged distances on an informal map (McNamara & Diwadkar, 1997). They estimated that the distance was an average of 1.7 inches when traveling from the landmark to the nonlandmark. However, the estimated distance was an average of only 1.4 inches when traveling from the nonlandmark to the landmark. Prominent destinations apparently seem closer than less-important destinations. This research also demonstrates the importance of context when we make decisions about distances and other features of our cognitive maps.

Cognitive Maps and Shape

Our cognitive maps represent not only distances but also shapes. These shapes are evident in map features such as the angles formed by intersecting streets. Once again, the research shows a systematic distortion. In this case, we tend to construct cognitive maps in which the shapes are more regular than they are in reality.

Consider the classic research by Moar and Bower (1983), who studied people's cognitive maps of Cambridge, England. All the participants in the study had lived in Cambridge for at least five years. Moar and Bower asked people to estimate the angles formed by the intersection of two streets, without using a map.

The participants showed a clear tendency to "regularize" the angles so that they were more like 90-degree angles. For example, three intersections in Cambridge had "real" angles of 67, 63, and 50 degrees. However, people *estimated* these same angles to be an average of 84, 78, and 88 degrees. As you may recall, the sum of the angles in a triangle should be 180 degrees, but in this study, the sum of the estimated angles was 250 degrees. Furthermore, this study showed that seven of the nine angles were significantly biased in the direction of a 90-degree angle.

What explains this systematic distortion? Moar and Bower (1983) suggest that we employ a heuristic. When two roads meet in most urban areas, they generally form a 90-degree angle. When people use the **90-degree-angle heuristic**, they represent angles in a mental map as being closer to 90 degrees than they really are.

You may recall a similar concept in the discussion of memory schemas in Chapter 5. It is easier to store a schematic version of an event, rather than a precise version of the event that includes all the trivial details. This 90-degree-angle heuristic has also been replicated in other settings (Montello et al., 2004; Tversky, 2005b; Wagner, 2006).

Relative Position Effects on Cognitive Maps

Which city is farther west—San Diego, California, or Reno, Nevada? If you are like most people—and the participants in a classic study by Stevens and Coupe (1978)—the question seems ludicrously easy. Of course, San Diego would be farther west, because California is west of Nevada. However, if you consult a map, you'll discover that Reno is in fact *west* of San Diego. Which city is farther north—Detroit or its "twin city" across the river, Windsor, in Ontario, Canada? Again, the answer seems obvious; any Canadian city must be north of a U.S. city!

Barbara Tversky (1981, 1998) points out that we use heuristics when we represent relative positions in our mental maps—just as we use heuristics to represent the angles of intersecting streets as being close to 90-degree angles, and just as we represent curves as being symmetrical. Tversky points out that these heuristics encourage two kinds of errors:

1. We remember a slightly tilted geographic structure as being either more vertical or more horizontal than it really is (the rotation heuristic).

2. We remember a series of geographic structures as being arranged in a straighter line than they really are (the alignment heuristic).

The Rotation Heuristic

According to the **rotation heuristic**, a figure that is slightly tilted will be remembered as being either more vertical or more horizontal than it really is (Taylor, 2005; Tversky, 2000b, 2009; Wagner, 2006). For example, Figure 7.5 shows that the coastline of California is obviously slanted. When we use the rotation heuristic for our cognitive map of California, we make the orientation more vertical by rotating the coastline in a clockwise fashion. Therefore, if your cognitive map reflects the distorting effects of the rotation heuristic, you will conclude (erroneously) that San Diego is west of Reno.

Similarly, the rotation heuristic encourages you to create a horizontal border between the United States and Canada. Therefore, you'll make the wrong decision about Detroit and Windsor. In reality, Windsor, in Canada, is south of Detroit.

Let's look at some research on the rotation heuristic. Barbara Tversky (1981) studied people's mental maps for the geographic region of the San Francisco Bay Area. She found that 69% of the students at a

FIGURE 7.5 The correct locations of San Diego and Reno.

This figure shows that Reno is farther west than San Diego. According to the rotation heuristic, however, we tend to rotate the coastline of California into a more nearly vertical orientation. As a result, we ineorrectly conclude that San Diego is farther west than Reno.

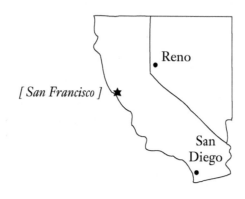

Bay Area university showed evidence of the rotation heuristic. When the students constructed their mental maps, they rotated the California coastline in a more north-south direction than is true on a geographically correct map. However, keep in mind that some students—in fact, 31% of them—were not influenced by this heuristic.

We also have evidence for the rotation heuristic in other cultures. People living in Israel, Japan, and Italy also tend to mentally rotate geographic structures. As a result, these structures appear to have either a more vertical or a more horizontal orientation in a mental map than in reality (Glicksohn, 1994; Tversky et al., 1999).

The Alignment Heuristic

According to the **alignment heuristic**, a series of separate geographic structures will be remembered as being more lined up than they really are (Taylor, 2005; Tversky, 1981, 2000b; 2009). To test the alignment heuristic, Tversky (1981) presented pairs of cities to students, who were asked to select which member of each pair was north (or, in some cases, east).

For example, one pair was Rome and Philadelphia. As Figure 7.6 shows, Rome is actually north of Philadelphia. However, because of the alignment heuristic, people tend to line up the United States and Europe so that they are along the same latitude. We know that Rome is in the southern part of Europe. We also know that Philadelphia is in the northern part of the United States. Therefore, we conclude—incorrectly—that Philadelphia is north of Rome.

Tversky's results indicated that many students showed a consistent tendency to use the alignment heuristic. For example, 78% judged Philadelphia to be north of Rome, and 12% judged that they were at the same latitude. Only 10% correctly answered that Rome is north of Philadelphia. On all eight pairs of items tested by Tversky, an average of 66% of participants supplied the incorrect answer. Other researchers have confirmed that people's cognitive maps are especially likely to be biased when northern cities in North America are compared with southern cities in Europe (Friedman et al., 2002).

The rotation heuristic and the alignment heuristic may initially sound similar. However, the rotation heuristic requires rotating a *single* coastline, country, building, or other figure in a clockwise or counterclockwise fashion so that its border is oriented in a nearly vertical or a nearly horizontal direction. In contrast, the alignment heuristic requires lining up *several separate* countries, buildings, or other figures in a straight row. Both heuristics are similar, however, because they encourage us to construct cognitive maps that are more orderly and schematic than geographic reality.

The heuristics we have examined in this chapter make sense. For example, our city streets tend to have right-angle intersections. Furthermore, a picture is generally hung on a wall in a vertical orientation, rather than at a slant. In addition, a series of houses is typically lined up so that they are equally far from the street.

However, when our mental maps rely too strongly on these heuristics, we miss the important details that make each stimulus unique. When our top-down cognitive processes are too active, we fail to pay enough attention to bottom-up information. In fact, the angle at an intersection may really be 70 degrees. Furthermore, that coastline may not run exactly north-south. In addition, those two continents are not really arranged in a neat horizontal line.

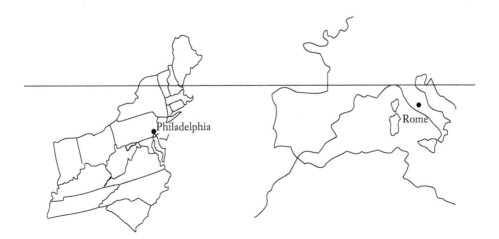

FIGURE 7.6 The correct locations of Philadelphia and Rome.

This figure shows that Philadelphia is farther south than Rome. According to the alignment heuristic, however, we tend to line up Europe and the United States. As a result, we incorrectly conclude that Philadelphia is north of Rome.

Creating a Cognitive Map

In everyday life, we often read or hear a description of a particular environment. For instance, a friend calls to give you directions to her house. You have never traveled there before, yet you create a cognitive map as you hear her describing the route. A cognitive map is a mental representation of geographic information, including the environment that surrounds us.

Similarly, a neighbor describes the setting in which his car was hit by a truck, or you may read a mystery novel explaining where the dead body was found in relation to the broken vase and the butler's fingerprints. In each case, you typically create a cognitive map.

It's important to emphasize that our cognitive maps are not perfect "map-in-the-head" replicas of geographic reality (Shelton & Yamamoto, 2009). However, they do help us represent the spatial aspects of our environment. When we encounter a description of a spatial setting, we do not simply store these isolated statements in a passive fashion. Instead—consistent with Theme 1—we actively create a cognitive map that represents the relevant features of a scene (Carr & Roskos-Ewoldsen, 1999; Tversky, 2005a, 2005b). Furthermore, people combine information from separate statements and combine them to form one integrated cognitive map (Newcombe & Huttenlocher, 2000).

Let's examine how people create these cognitive maps, typically based on verbal descriptions. We will begin by considering the classic research on this topic. Then we'll examine the spatial framework model, as well as information about the characteristics of cognitive maps.

In a classic study, Nancy Franklin and Barbara Tversky (1990) presented verbal descriptions of 10 different scenes, such as a barn or a hotel lobby, for example, "You are at the Jefferson Plaza Hotel. . .." Each description mentioned five objects located in plausible positions in relation to the observer (above, below, in front, in back, to the left side, or to the right side). The description mentioned only five objects, so that the memory load would not be overwhelming.

After the participants had read each description, they were instructed to imagine that they were turning around to face a different object. They were then asked to specify which object was located in each of several directions. (For example, which object is "above your head"?) In all cases, the researchers measured how long the participant took to respond to the question.

Franklin and Tversky were especially interested in discovering whether response time depended upon the location of the object that was being tested. Do we make all those decisions equally quickly?

These researchers found that people could rapidly answer which objects were above or below; their reaction times were short for these judgments. People required somewhat longer to decide which objects were ahead or behind. Furthermore, they took even longer to decide which objects were to the right or to the left. This research has been replicated in additional research (e.g., Bryant & Tversky, 1999). In all these studies, people judged the vertical dimension more quickly than ahead-behind or left-right dimensions. Do these results match your intuitions?

Franklin and Tversky (1990) also asked the participants to describe how they thought they had performed the task. All participants reported that they had constructed images of the environment as they were reading. Most of them also reported that they had constructed imagery that represented their own point of view as an observer of the scene.

The Spatial Framework Model

To explain their results, Franklin and Tversky proposed the spatial framework model (Franklin & Tversky, 1990; Tversky, 1991, 1997, 2005a, 2005b). The **spatial framework model** emphasizes that the above-below spatial dimension is especially important in our thinking, the front-back dimension is moderately important, and the right-left dimension is least important.

When we are in a typical upright position, the vertical (above-below) dimension is especially important for two reasons:

1. The vertical dimension is correlated with gravity, neither of the other two dimensions has this advantage. Gravity has an important asymmetric effect on the world we perceive; objects fall downward, not upward. Because of its association with gravity, the above-below dimension should be particularly important and thus particularly accessible. (Notice, then, that this asymmetry is "good," because we make decisions more quickly.)

2. The vertical dimension on an upright human's body is physically asymmetric. That is, the top (head) and the bottom (feet) are very easy to tell apart, and so we do not confuse them with each other.

These two factors combine to help us make judgments about the above-below dimension very rapidly.

The next most prominent dimension is the front-back dimension. When we are upright, the front-back dimension is not correlated with gravity. However, we usually interact with objects in front of us more easily than with objects in back of us, introducing an asymmetry. Also, a human's front half is not symmetric with the back half, again making it easy to distinguish between front and back. These two characteristics lead to judgment times for the front-back dimension that are fairly fast, although not as fast as for the above-below dimension.

The least-prominent dimension is right-left. This dimension is not correlated with gravity, and we usually perceive objects equally well, whether they are on the right or the left. Most of us show minor preferences for our right or left hand when we manipulate objects. However, this dimension does not have the degree of asymmetry we find for the front-back dimension. Finally, your right half is roughly symmetrical with your left half. You can probably remember occasions when you confused your right hand with your left hand, or when you told someone to turn left when you meant right. Apparently, we need additional processing time to ensure that we do not make this error. Therefore, right-left decisions take longer than either above-below or front-back decisions, consistent with other research (Bower, 2008).

In related studies, researchers have examined how people process directions on a physical map. The results demonstrate that people can make north-south (above-below) decisions significantly faster than east-west (right-left) decisions (Newcombe, 2002; Wagner, 2006).

In summary, then, Franklin and Tversky's spatial framework model proposes that the vertical or above-below dimension is most prominent for an upright observer (Franklin & Tversky, 1990; Tversky, 2005a, 2005b). The front-back dimension is next most prominent, and the right-left dimension is least prominent. Our cognitive maps, therefore, reveal certain biases. These biases are based on our long-term interactions with our bodies and with the physical properties of the external world (Tversky, 2005a, 2005b).

All the research on cognitive maps provides strong testimony for the active nature of human cognitive processes (Theme 1). We take in information, synthesize it, and go beyond the information we have received, so that we create a model to represent our knowledge (Tversky, 2005a, 2005b). As you will see throughout the rest of this textbook, an important general characteristic of our cognitive processes is our tendency to make inferences, so that we can draw conclusions beyond the information that we currently possess.

The Situated Cognition Approach

We have just seen how people make decisions about spatial locations, based on the human body and the world that we inhabit (Tversky, 2009). For example, the context of our bodies helps us make up-down decisions more quickly than front-back decisions, which are easier than right-left decisions.

Some cognitive psychologists point out that the situated cognition approach helps us understand many cognitive tasks. For example, situated cognition is important when we create mental maps (this chapter), form concepts (Chapter 8), and solve problems (Chapter 11). According to the **situated cognition approach**, we make use of helpful information in the immediate environment or situation. Therefore, our knowledge depends on the context that surrounds us (Robbins & Aydede, 2009; Tversky, 2009). As a result, what we know depends on the situation that we are in.

As Barbara Tversky (2009) points out, spatial thinking is vitally important for humans. You need to know where to go to find food, water, and shelter, and you need to find your way back home. One index of the central importance of spatial thinking is the phrases we use. For instance, we say, "Things are looking up," "That was an emotional high," "His spirits are down today," and "I seem to be going around in circles." We also make spatial diagrams to represent relationships. For example, you might create a diagram of your family tree, the roles of people in an organization, and the classification of various world languages.

SECTION SUMMARY POINTS

Classical Research on Visual Imagery

1. Spatial ability is important in the STEM disciplines; teachers can provide helpful training in spatial skills.

2. The amount of time that people take to rotate a mental image depends on the extent of the rotation, just as when we rotate a real

physical object. Deaf people use mental rotation during signing; they also perform well on mental-rotation tasks. The nature of the mental-rotation instructions has an influence on the region of the brain that is activated.

3. A controversy in cognitive psychology has focused on mental imagery, specifically, whether information is stored in picture-like

analog codes or language-like propositional codes. Research on the characteristics of mental images addresses this issue.

4. In several studies, the participants are instructed to create a mental image for an ambiguous figure; they may have difficulty reinterpreting this mental image so that they see a different figure.

5. According to neuroscience research, visual imagery activates about 70% to 90% of the same brain regions that are activated during visual perception. Furthermore, people with prosopagnosia cannot recognize human faces visually, and they also cannot create a mental image of a face.

6. The majority of research supports the analog viewpoint, as described by Stephen Kosslyn and his colleagues, but some people—on some tasks—apparently use a propositional code, as described by Zenon Pylyshyn.

Factors That Influence Visual Imagery

1. People take longer to "travel" a long mental distance, in contrast to a short mental distance.

2. When judging the shapes of mental images or visual images, people take longer to make decisions when the two stimuli have very similar physical shapes. This conclusion applies to simple shapes (e.g., the hands on a clock), as well as complex shapes (e.g., the shapes of U.S. states).

3. Visual images can interfere with visual perception; this conclusion applies to the perception of figures such as trees, as well as line segments.

4. Another vision-like property of mental images is enhanced acuity when a target is flanked by imaginary masks; this type of research is important because demand characteristics would be minimal.

5. Meta-analyses on spatial ability show small to moderate gender differences in spatial visualization and spatial perception; gender differences are somewhat larger in mental rotation, but these differences can be reduced by experience in spatial activities.

Auditory Imagery

1. Researchers have commented on the lack of research on auditory imagery, especially because auditory processes are an important part of human cognition; furthermore, some previous studies did not provide clear-cut evidence for auditory imagery.

2. Research on pitch shows that people can quickly travel the mental distance between two imagined musical tones that are similar in pitch; the "travel time" is longer when the two tones are different in pitch.

3. The word "timbre" refers to the sound quality of a tone. People listened to pairs of tones produced by a variety of musical instruments, and then they rated the perceived similarity of each pair. They also imagined the pairs of tones produced by the same musical instruments, and then they rated their similarity. Timbre perception and timbre imagery were highly correlated.

Cognitive Maps

1. A cognitive map is a mental representation of the surrounding environment; the research on this topic often emphasizes real-world settings, and it is interdisciplinary in scope.

2. Individual differences in spatial cognition are large, and they are correlated with mental-rotation ability.

3. You can make judgments about spatial cognition more easily if your cognitive map matches the orientation of a physical map.

4. Our cognitive maps usually represent reality with reasonable accuracy. However, we make systematic errors in these maps, usually reflecting the tendency to base our judgments on heuristics. We make judgments based on variables that are typically relevant, and we represent our environment as being more regular than it really is.

5. Estimates of distance on cognitive maps can be distorted by the number of intervening cities and by the category membership of the buildings on the cognitive maps. In addition, we estimate that landmarks are closer than a location that is not a landmark.

6. Shapes on cognitive maps can be distorted so that the angles formed by two intersecting streets are closer to 90 degrees than they are in reality.

7. The relative positions of geographic structures on cognitive maps can be distorted so that a slightly tilted structure will be remembered as being more vertical or more horizontal than it really is (rotation heuristic). Furthermore, a series of geographic structures will be remembered as being more lined up than they really are (alignment heuristic).

8. We often create cognitive maps of an environment that are based on a verbal description. In these maps, the up-down dimension has special prominence, and we make these judgments quickly. We make front-back judgments more slowly. The right-left dimension is most difficult, and we make these decisions very slowly. Franklin and Tversky (1990) explain these data in terms of the spatial framework model. We also make north-south decisions more quickly than east-west decisions.

9. The situated cognition approach emphasizes that we make use of helpful information in the immediate environment and the context of the situation.

CHAPTER REVIEW QUESTIONS

1. Summarize the two theoretical approaches that focus on the characteristics of mental images: the analog code and the propositional code. Describe the findings about mental rotation, size, shape, reinterpreting ambiguous figures, and any other topics you recall. In each case, note which theory the results support.

2. Most of this chapter deals with visual imagery, with a brief description of auditory imagery. We have little information about imagery in the other senses. How could you design a study on taste imagery that would be conceptually similar to one of the studies mentioned in the sections on visual imagery and auditory imagery?

3. According to the research in cognitive neuroscience, what evidence do we have that visual imagery resembles perception? Why does this research avoid the problem of demand characteristics, which might be relevant in other imagery research?

4. How do the studies on imagery and interference support the viewpoint that visual imagery operates like actual perceptions? Describe how the research on interference supports the analog storage of information about objects.

5. Suppose that you see a newspaper headline, "Males Have Better Spatial Ability, Study Shows." When reading this article, what cautions should you keep in mind, based on the discussion about gender comparisons in spatial ability?

6. One section of this chapter summarized some of the research on auditory imagery. Discuss this research, and describe why it is more difficult to study than visual imagery. How could researchers study auditory imagery and interference?

7. Cognitive maps sometimes correspond to reality, but sometimes they show systematic deviations. Discuss the factors that seem to produce systematic distortions when people estimate distance on mental maps.

8. What heuristics cause systematic distortions in geographic shape and in relative position represented on cognitive maps? How are these related to two concepts we discussed in earlier chapters—namely, top-down processing (Chapter 2) and schemas (Chapter 5)?

9. According to Franklin and Tversky's spatial framework model, the three dimensions represented in our cognitive maps are not equally important. Which dimension has special prominence? How does the spatial framework model explain these differences?

10. Cognitive psychologists often ignore individual differences. However, this chapter examined several ways in which individuals differ with respect to mental imagery and spatial cognition. Describe this information, and suggest other areas in which researchers could examine individual differences.

KEYWORDS

perception, mental imagery, imagery, visual imagery, auditory imagery, STEM disciplines, imagery debate, analog code, propositional code, prosopagnosia, magnetoencephalography (MEG), demand characteristics, meta-analysis, pitch, timbre, spatial cognition, heuristic, border bias, landmark effect, 90-degree-angle heuristic, rotation heuristic, alignment heuristic, cognitive map, spatial framework model, situated cognition approach

RECOMMENDED READINGS

Brockmole, J. R. (Ed.). (2009). *The visual world in memory*. New York: Psychology Press. Two chapters in Brockmole's book are especially relevant to the discussion of mental imagery, one on visual mental imagery and another on visual memory and navigation. Other chapters focus on memory for faces and real-world scenes.

Hubbard, T. L. (2010). Auditory imagery: Empirical findings. *Psychological Bulletin, 136*, 302–329. This clearly written article discusses many intriguing topics related to imagery for sounds, including harmony, sounds during dreaming, and auditory hallucinations.

Kosslyn, S. M. (2007). *Clear and to the point: 8 psychological principles for compelling PowerPoint® presentations*. New York: Oxford University Press. You have probably watched some PowerPoint® presentations that were difficult to follow. Stephen Kosslyn's expertise in visual imagery makes him the perfect guide for creating clear presentations!

Reed, S. K. (2010). *Thinking visually*. New York: Psychology Press. Psychologists have written numerous books about language and concepts, but remarkably few about visual imagery. Stephen Reed's book compares images with words, and it also discusses topics such as the production of images and spatial metaphors.

8 General Knowledge

Chapter Introduction

The world knowledge that you possess provides you with an exquisite ability to process and interpret information in the environment. For example, a bee may buzz past you as you are standing at a bus stop. Although its physical form, path of movement, and its buzzing sound are registered by your senses, you must have knowledge of a bee—and the typical physical properties of bees—in order to recognize it for what it is (and, to realize that there's a chance that you might get stung). Your semantic memory is your memory for general facts about the world around you. The first half of this textbook emphasizes how your cognitive systems register and process information from the outside world. We did not discuss, however, any details about how world knowledge is organized in your mind.

In this chapter, we first consider some background information about the world knowledge that you possess. We then explore three different frameworks that have been developed in order to explain how this knowledge is stored and organized. We conclude by examining scripts and schemes. These are knowledge-related principles that facilitate the integration of incoming information from the environment with the vast amount of knowledge stored in your long-term memory.

Background and Approaches to Semantic Memory

Consider the following sentence:

When Lisa was on her way back from the store with the balloon, she fell and the balloon floated away.

Think about all the information that you assume when you are reading this sentence. Now think about all of the inferences that you make. An **inference** refers to the logical interpretations and conclusions that were never part of the original stimulus material. For instance, consider just the word *balloon*. You know that balloons can be made of several lightweight substances, that they can be filled with air or a lightweight gas, and that their shape can resemble an animal or a cartoon character. However, a balloon is unlikely to be created from a hiking boot, it is unlikely to be filled with raspberry yogurt, and it is unlikely to be shaped like the Eiffel Tower.

Now cover all the rest of this page, beginning with the line of asterisks, and reread that entire sentence about the balloon. Think of five or more additional inferences that you are likely to make.

*   *   *   *   *   *   *

Here are some of the inferences that students in my classes have reported: Lisa is probably a female child, not a 40-year-old man, and she probably bought the balloon in the store. Furthermore, the balloon was attached to a string, but the other end of the string was not firmly attached to Lisa. When Lisa fell, she probably let go of the string. She may have scraped her knee, and it may have bled. As you can see, a sentence that initially seemed simple is immediately enriched by an astonishing amount of general knowledge about objects and events in the world. General knowledge allows you to go beyond a verbatim interpretation of the stimulus (such as the sentence above) by making inferences, or by making predictions about other similar stimuli (Landauer & Dumais, 1997; Papadopoulos et al., 2011).

Semantic memory refers to our organized knowledge about the world (Schwartz, 2011; Wheeler, 2000). If you are a typical English-speaking adult, you know the meaning of about 20,000 to 100,000 words (Baddeley et al., 2009; Saffran & Schwartz, 2003). You also know a tremendous amount of information about each word (Schmitt, 2014). For example, you know that a cat has fur and that an apple has seeds. You also know that a car is a good example of a vehicle. . .but an elevator is *not* a good example.

Semantic memory is often contrasted with **episodic memory**, which contains information about events that happen to us. Chapters 5 and 6 emphasized different aspects of episodic memory. The distinction between semantic and episodic memory is not clear-cut (McNamara & Holbrook, 2003). However, the term *semantic memory* usually refers to knowledge or information; it does not specify how we acquired that information (Barsalou, 2009). An example of semantic memory would be: "Tegucigalpa is the capital of Honduras." In contrast, episodic memory implies a personal experience, because episodic memory emphasizes when, where, or how this event happened to you (Corballis & Suddendorf, 2010; McNamara & Holbrook, 2003). An example of episodic memory would be: "This morning in my Political Science course, I learned that Tegucigalpa is the capital of Honduras."

Background Information

In normal conversation, the term *semantics* refers to the meaning of individual words. Psychologists, however, use the term *semantic memory* in a much broader sense (McNamara & Holbrook, 2003). For example, semantic memory includes general knowledge (e.g., "Martin Luther King, Jr., was born in Atlanta, Georgia"). It also includes lexical or language knowledge (e.g., "The word *justice* is related to the word *equality*"). In addition, semantic memory includes conceptual knowledge (e.g., "A square has four sides"). Semantic memory influences most of our cognitive activities. For instance, semantic memory helps us determine locations, read sentences, solve problems, and make decisions. Categories and concepts are essential components of semantic memory. In fact, you need to divide up the world into categories in order to make sense of your knowledge (Davis & Love, 2010).

A **category** is a set of objects that belong together. Your cognitive system considers these objects to be at least partly equivalent (Barsalou, 2009; Chin-Parker & Ross, 2004; Markman & Ross, 2003). For example, the category called "fruit" represents a certain category of food items. A category tells us something useful about their members (Close et al., 2010; Murphy, 2010; Ross & Tidwell, 2010). For example, suppose that you hear someone say, "Rambutan is a fruit." You conclude that you should probably eat it in a salad or a dessert, instead of frying it with onions and freshly ground pepper.

Psychologists use the term **concept** to refer to your mental representations of a category (Murphy, 2010; Rips et al., 2012; Wisniewski, 2002). In other words, the physical category called "fruit" is stored as a mental representation distributed throughout your cerebral cortex. For instance, you have a concept of "fruit," which refers to your mental representation of the objects in that category. Incidentally, I will follow the tradition in cognitive psychology of using italics for the actual word names (e.g., *justice*) and quotation marks for categories and concepts (e.g., "fruit").

Each of your academic courses requires you to form concepts (Barsalou, 2009; Goldstone & Kersten, 2003; Hannon et al., 2010). In an art history course, you may need to create a concept called "15th-century Flemish painting," and in a Spanish course, you learn a concept called "people whom you greet with the 'usted' form of a verb."

In previous chapters, we discussed the situated cognition approach to cognitive psychology. According to the **situated cognition approach**, we make use of information in the immediate environment or situation. As a result, our knowledge often depends on the context that surrounds us (Robbins & Aydede, 2009; Tversky, 2009). With respect to our general knowledge, we tend to code a concept in terms of the context in which we learned this information (Barsalou, 2009; Perry, Samuelson, & Burdinie, 2014). Without these rich resources, it's often difficult to transfer a concept from the classroom to the context of a real-life situation, as you may discover when you enter an art museum or when you try to use your Spanish if you travel to Latin America.

Your semantic memory allows you to organize the objects you encounter. Even though the objects are not identical, you can combine together a wide variety of similar objects by using a single, one-word concept (Milton & Wills, 2004; Wisniewski, 2004; Yamauchi, 2005). This coding process greatly reduces the space required for storage, because many objects can all be stored with the same label.

Your concepts also allow you to make numerous inferences when you encounter new examples from a category (Barsalou, 2009; Davis & Love, 2010; Jones & Ross, 2011). For example, even a young child knows that a member of the category "fruit" has the attribute "you can eat it." When she encounters a new kind of fruit, she makes the inference (usually correctly) that you can eat it. As we noted earlier, these inferences allow you to go beyond the given information, greatly expanding your knowledge. Otherwise—if you had no concepts—you would need to examine each new chair you encountered in order to figure out how to use it (Murphy, 2002).

But, how do we decide which objects are similar? In the following discussion, we'll examine two current approaches to semantic memory. Each approach provides a somewhat different perspective on the nature of similarity. These approaches include (1) the prototype approach and (2) the exemplar approach[*]

According to researchers who study semantic memory, each model can account for some aspect of it (Markman, 2002). In fact, it's unlikely that the wide variety of concepts could all be represented in semantic memory in the same fashion (Haberlandt, 1999; Hampton, 1997a). Therefore, as you read about these two approaches, you do not need to pick a favorite—each approach may more successfully capture experimental data under different sets of circumstances. We'll discuss this issue again at the end of this section.

Before continuing any further, however, I want to make one very important point. As an adult, you possess knowledge about many properties of the world: how events typically unfold, what different objects tend to look like, names of objects and people, and so forth. But, this knowledge exists for a reason. You come to possess this vast amount of knowledge as a result of learning about the world through experience with it. Thus, in order to truly appreciate the nature of semantic memory, one must focus not only on the knowledge possessed by an individual, but also on how one comes to possess that knowledge over the course of development. Indeed, knowledge states possessed by a four-year-old are quite different than those possessed by an 18 year old, which are in turn quite different than those possessed by a 60 year old. This observation suggests that the way that we process, interpret, and interact with our external world changes as a function of changes in our current understanding of it (e.g. Lupyan, 2010; 2012). You'll likely address many of these issues in a developmental psychology or cognitive development course. Indeed, one of the hottest topics in very recent cognitive psychology is aimed squarely at understanding how knowledge and learning processes interact with one another to continuously shape the knowledge that you possess about the world.

---

[*]An earlier approach, called the *feature comparison model*, proposed that we store concepts in memory according to a list of necessary characteristics (features). Most cognitive psychologists now believe that this model is not flexible enough to account for the way we create and use real-world categories and concepts.

The Prototype Approach

According to a theory proposed by Eleanor Rosch, we organize each category on the basis of a prototype. A **prototype** is the item that is the best, most typical example of a category; a prototype therefore is the ideal representative of this category (Fehr & Sprecher, 2009; Murphy, 2002; Rosch, 1973). According to this **prototype approach**, you decide whether a particular item belongs to a category by comparing this item with a prototype. If the item is similar to the prototype, you include that item within this category (Jäkel et al., 2008; Sternberg & Ben-Zeev, 2001; Wisniewski, 2002).

For example, you would conclude that a robin is a bird because it matches your ideal prototype for a bird. Suppose, however, that the item you are judging is quite different from the prototype, for example, a bee. In this case, you place the item in another category (the category "insect"), where it more closely resembles that category's prototype.

Rosch (1973) also emphasizes that members of a category differ in their **prototypicality**, or the degree to which they are representative of their category. A robin and a sparrow are very prototypical birds, whereas an ostrich and a penguin are typically nonprototypes. However, the situated cognition approach emphasizes the importance of context and specific situations. In the context of a zoo, for example, you might consider an ostrich and a penguin to be prototypical (Schwartz, 2011).

To help clarify the concept of prototypes, think of a prototype, or most typical member, for a particular group of students on your campus, perhaps students with a particular academic major. Also think of a nonprototype ("You mean he's an art major? He doesn't seem at all like one!"). Then try Demonstration 8.1 before you read further.

| *Demonstration 8.1* | Guessing Prototype Ratings |

Take a sheet of paper and write the numbers 1 through 12 in a column, beginning at the top left side of the page. Now look at the list of 12 items listed below. Think about which item is the *best* example of the category, "clothing." Write that object's name next to the number 1. Write the name of the second-best example of clothing next to the number 2, and so forth.

Bathing suit; Coat; Dress; Jacket; Pajamas; Pants; Shirt; Shoes; Skirt; Socks; Sweater; Underwear.

When you have completed the ranking, look at Table 8.1. As you can see, this table lists the "average prototypicality rating" that students supplied for each of these 12 types of clothing (Rosch & Mervis, 1975). Transfer each prototypicality rating from Table 8.1 to the appropriate item in your own list. For example, a bathing suit has a prototype rating of 11. As an informal method of assessing your responses, calculate a total for the ranks that you supplied for items 1 through 4, then for items 5 through 8, and finally for items 9 through 12.

Table 8.1   Prototype Ratings for Words in Three Categories

Item	Clothing	Vehicle	Vegetable
1	Pants	Car	Peas
2	Shirt	Truck	Carrots
3	Dress	Bus	String beans
4	Skirt	Motorcycle	Spinach
5	Jacket	Train	Broccoli
6	Coat	Trolley car	Asparagus
7	Sweater	Bicycle	Corn
8	Underwear	Airplane	Cauliflower
9	Socks	Boat	Brussels sprouts
10	Pajamas	Tractor	Lettuce
11	Bathing suit	Cart	Beets
12	Shoes	Wheelchair	Tomato

Source: Rosch, E. H., & Mervis, C. B. (1975). Family resemblances: Studies in the internal structure of categories. *Cognitive Psychology, 7*, 573–605.

Does your idea about prototypes match the pattern in Table 8.1? You may find that a few of your rankings differ greatly from those based on the participants in the norms gathered by Rosch and Mervis (1975). If so, can you suggest an explanation?

Some classic earlier theories had proposed that an item could belong to a category as long as it possessed the appropriate necessary and sufficient features (Markman, 1999; Minda & Smith, 2011). In those theories, category membership is very clear-cut. For example, for the category "bachelor," two defining features would be *male* and *unmarried*.

However, don't you think that your 32-year-old unmarried male cousin would be a much better example of a bachelor than either your 2-year-old nephew or an elderly Catholic priest? All three individuals are indeed male and unmarried. Therefore, a "necessary and sufficient" model would need to conclude that all three deserve to be categorized as "bachelors." That conclusion doesn't seem reasonable. In contrast, the prototype approach would argue that not all members of the category "bachelor" are created equal. Instead, your cousin is a more prototypical bachelor than your nephew or the priest (Lakoff, 1987).

Eleanor Rosch and her coauthors, as well as other researchers, have conducted numerous studies about the characteristics of prototypes. Their research demonstrates that all members of a category are not really equal (Medin & Rips, 2005; Murphy, 2010; Rogers & McClelland, 2004). Instead, a category tends to have a graded structure. A **graded structure** begins with the most representative or prototypical members, and it continues on through the category's nonprototypical members.

Let us examine several important characteristics of prototypes. Then we will discuss another important component of the prototype approach, which focuses on several different levels of categorization.

Characteristics of Prototypes

Prototypes differ from the nonprototypical members of categories in three major respects. As you will see, prototypes have a special, privileged status within a category.

1. *Prototypes are supplied as examples of a category*   Several studies have shown that people judge some items to be better examples of a concept than other items. In a classic study, for example, Mervis and her colleagues (1976) examined some norms. These norms are based on examples that people had provided for categories such as "birds," "fruit," and "sports." Mervis and her coauthors then asked a different group of people to supply prototype ratings for each of these examples.

    According to a statistical analysis, the items that were rated most prototypical were the same items that people had supplied most frequently in the category norms. For instance, for the category "bird," people judged a robin to be very prototypical, and *robin* was very frequently listed as an example of the category "bird." In contrast, people rated a penguin as low on the prototype scale, and *penguin* was only rarely listed as an example of the category "bird." In other words, if someone asks you to name a member of a category, you will probably name a prototype.

    Furthermore, the prototype approach accounts well for the typicality effect (Murphy, 2002; Rogers & McClelland, 2004). In this procedure, participants are asked whether an item belongs to a particular category. The **typicality effect** occurs when people judge typical items (prototypes) faster than items that are not typical (nonprototypes). For instance, when judging whether items belong to the category "bird," people judge *robin* more quickly than *penguin* (Dale et al., 2007; Farmer et al., 2006; Hampton, 1997b; Heit & Barsalou, 1996). Theorists point out that the typicality effect operates with everyday items, so the results are more useful than research conducted only with artificial concepts (Rips et al., 2012).

2. *Prototypes are judged more quickly than nonprototypes, after semantic priming*   The **semantic priming effect** means that people respond faster to an item if it was preceded by an item with similar meaning. The semantic priming effect helps cognitive psychologists understand important information about how we retrieve information from memory (McNamara, 2005; McNamara & Holbrook, 2003).

    The research shows that semantic priming facilitates people's responses to prototypes significantly more than it facilitates their responses to nonprototypes. Imagine, for example, that you are participating in a study on priming. Your task is to judge pairs of similar colors and to answer whether they are the same. On some occasions, you see the name of the color before you must judge the pair of colors; these are the primed trials. On other occasions, you do not see a color name as a "warning"; these are the unprimed trials. Rosch (1975) tried this priming setup for both prototype colors (for example, a true, bright red) and nonprototype colors (for example, a muddy red).

Rosch's results showed that priming was very helpful when people made judgments about prototypical colors. Specifically, they responded more quickly after primed trials than after nonprimed trials. However, priming actually inhibited the judgments for nonprototypical colors. In other words, if you see the word *red*, you expect to see a true, bright red color. However, if the color is a dark, muddy red, the priming offers no advantage. Instead, you actually need extra time in order to reconcile your image of a bright, vivid color with the muddy color you actually see on the screen.

3. *Prototypes share attributes in a family resemblance category*   Before we examine this issue, let's introduce a new term called family resemblance. **Family resemblance** means that no single attribute is shared by all examples of a concept; however, each example has at least one attribute in common with some other example of the concept (Love & Tomlinson, 2010; Milton & Wills, 2004; Rosch & Mervis, 1975).

Rosch and Mervis (1975) examined the role of prototypes in family resemblance categories. They asked a group of students to make prototypicality judgments about members of several categories. As you can see in Table 8.1, for example, the students rated a car as being the most prototypical vehicle and a wheelchair as being the least prototypical vehicle on this list. Then, Rosch and Mervis asked a different group of people to list the attributes possessed by each item. The results showed that the most prototypical item also had the largest number of attributes in common with the other items in the category. For example, a car (the most prototypical vehicle) has wheels, moves horizontally, and uses fuel. In contrast, an elevator has relatively few attributes in common with other items.

Check the categories "vegetable" and "clothing" in Table 8.1. Do the most prototypical items share more attributes with other items, compared to the nonprototypical items? Furthermore, is there any attribute you can identify that is both necessary and sufficient for either of these categories? Alternatively, would you conclude that the items on each list share only a "family resemblance" to one another?

Levels of Categorization

We have just examined three characteristics of prototypes that differentiate them from nonprototypes. The second major portion of prototype theory examines the way that our semantic categories are structured in terms of different levels of categorization.

Consider these examples: Suppose that you are sitting on a wooden structure that faces your desk. You can call that structure by several different names: *furniture, chair*, or *desk chair*. You can also refer to your pet as a *dog*, a *spaniel*, or a *cocker spaniel*. You can tighten the mirror on your car with a *tool*, a *screwdriver*, or a *Phillips screwdriver*.

In other words, an object can be categorized at several different levels. Some category levels are called **superordinate-level categories**, which means that they are higher-level or more general categories. "Furniture," "animal," and "tool" are all examples of superordinate-level categories. **Basic-level categories** are moderately specific. "Chair," "dog," and "screwdriver" are examples of basic-level categories. Finally, **subordinate-level categories** refer to lower-level or more specific categories. "Desk chair," "collie," and "Phillips screwdriver" are examples of subordinate categories.

As you continue to read the rest of this description of prototype theory, keep in mind that a prototype is *not* the same as a basic-level category. A prototype is the best example of a category. In contrast, a basic-level category refers to a category that is neither too general nor too specific.

Basic-level categories seem to have special status (Rogers & McClelland, 2004; Rosch et al., 1976; Wisniewski, 2002). In general, they are more useful than either superordinate-level categories or subordinate-level categories. Let's examine how these basic-level categories seem to have special privileges, in contrast to the more general or the more specific category levels.

1. *Basic-level names are used to identify objects*   Try naming some of the objects that you can see around you. You are likely to use basic-level names for these objects. You will mention *pen*, for example, rather than the superordinate term *writing instrument* or the subordinate term *Paper Mate Flair pen*.

Eleanor Rosch and her colleagues (1976) asked people to look at a series of pictures and identify each object. They found that people typically preferred to use basic-level names. Apparently, the basic-level name gives enough information without being overly detailed (Medin et al., 2000; Murphy, 2010; Rogers & McClelland, 2004). In addition, people produce the basic-level names faster than either the superordinate or the subordinate names (Kosslyn et al., 1995; Rogers & McClelland, 2004). Furthermore, when people see superordinate or subordinate terms, they frequently remember the basic-level version of these terms when they are later tested for recall (Pansky & Koriat, 2004). In other words, the basic level does have special, privileged status.

2. *Basic-level names are more likely to produce the semantic priming effect*   Eleanor Rosch and her colleagues (1976) used a variant of the semantic priming task. In this version, the researchers present the name of an object followed by two pictures. The participant must decide whether these two pictures are the same as one another. For example, you might hear the word *apple* and see pictures of two identical apples. The priming is effective because the presentation of this word allows you to create a mental representation of this word. This mental representation helps when you make the decision quickly.

   Rosch and her coworkers showed that priming with basic-level names was indeed helpful. The participants made faster judgments if they saw a basic-level term like *apple* before judging the apples. However, priming with superordinate names (such as *fruit*) was not helpful. Apparently, when you hear the word *fruit*, you create a general representation of fruit, rather than a specific representation that helps you make a judgment about apples.

3. *Different levels of categorization activate different regions of the brain*   Neuroscience research using PET scans has examined whether different regions of the brain tend to process different category levels (Kosslyn et al., 1995; Rips et al., 2012). On a typical trial, a participant might be asked to judge whether a word (e.g., *toy*, *doll*, or *rag doll*) matched a particular picture. This research showed that a superordinate term (e.g., *toy*) is more likely than a basic-level term (e.g., *doll*) to activate part of the prefrontal cortex. This finding makes sense, because this part of the cortex processes language and associative memory. If you need to decide whether the picture of the doll qualifies as a toy, you must consult your memory about category membership.

   In contrast, the research showed that subordinate terms (e.g., *rag doll*) are more likely than basic-level terms (e.g., *doll*) to activate part of the parietal region of the brain. The parietal lobe is active when you perform a visual search. Again, this finding makes sense. To answer the question about a rag doll, you must shift your attention away from the general shape of the object. For example, you need to conduct a visual search, so that you can determine if the fabric and the style of the doll indeed permit it to be categorized as a "rag doll."

Conclusions About the Prototype Approach

The prototype approach can account for our ability to form concepts about groups that are loosely structured. For example, we can create a concept for stimuli that merely share a family resemblance, when the members of a category have no single characteristic in common.

   An ideal model of semantic memory must, however, acknowledge that concepts can be unstable and variable. For example, our notions about the ideal prototype can shift as time passes and the context changes. In Demonstration 8.1, did you notice that the study, published in 1975, listed *dress* as a very prototypical example of clothing? Consider a related study by Laura Novick (2003) about prototypical vehicles. She found that U.S. college students rated *airplane* as being a prototypical vehicle during the period immediately following the terrorist attack of September 11, 2001. In contrast, *airplane* had been considered a nonprototypical vehicle in studies during the five years prior to this date. Furthermore, when the media coverage decreased after the attack, *airplane* decreased in prototypicality. In fact, 4.5 months after the attack, *airplane* was no longer a prototypical vehicle.

   Another problem with the prototype approach is that we often do store specific information about individual examples of a category. An ideal model of semantic memory would therefore need to include a mechanism for storing this specific information, as well as prototypes (Barsalou, 1990, 1992).

The Exemplar Approach and Semantic Memory

The prototype theory accounts for a number of important phenomena. Let's now examine a second approach to semantic memory, which emphasizes that your concept of a vehicle or an animal or a vegetable also includes information about some of the less-obvious members of the category, rather than just the most prototypical member.

The **exemplar approach** argues that we first learn information about some specific examples of a concept; we then classify each new stimulus by deciding how closely it resembles all of those specific examples (Benjamin & Ross, 2011; Love & Tomlinson, 2002; Schwartz, 2011). Each of those examples stored in memory is called an **exemplar**. The exemplar approach emphasizes that your concept of "dog" would include information about numerous examples of dogs you have known (Benjamin & Ross, 2011; Murphy, 2002). In contrast, the prototype approach would argue that your prototype of a dog would be an *idealized* representation of a dog, with average size for a dog and average other features—but not necessarily like any particular dog you've ever seen.

Consider another example. Suppose that you are taking a course in psychological disorders. Suppose also that you have just read four case studies in your textbook, and each case study described a depressed individual. You then read an article that describes a woman's psychological problems, but the article does not specify her disorder. You decide that she fits into the category "depressed person" because this description closely resembles the characteristics of those four earlier exemplars. Furthermore, this woman's problems do not resemble any exemplars in a set of case studies that you read last week, when you were learning about anxiety disorders.

The exemplar approach has successfully predicted people's performance on artificial categories, such as cartoon faces that can be shown with or without glasses, smiling or frowning, and so on (Medin & Rips, 2005; Rehder & Hoffman, 2005). How does this approach work with categories we use in our everyday lives? Before you read further, try Demonstration 8.2, which is based on a study by Evan Heit and Lawrence Barsalou (1996).

Heit and Barsalou (1996) wanted to determine whether the exemplar approach could explain the structure of several superordinate categories, such as "animal." When people make judgments about animals, do they base these judgments on specific exemplars or general prototypes? These researchers asked a group of undergraduates to supply the first example that came to mind for each of the seven basic-level categories in Part A of Demonstration 8.2. Then a second group of undergraduates rated the typicality of each of those examples, with respect to the superordinate category "animal." For instance, this second group would rate each example—such as *frog* or *salamander*—in terms of whether it was typical of the concept "animal." That second group also rated the seven basic-level categories. (I made this demonstration simpler, though not as well controlled; it includes all three tasks.)

Heit and Barsalou (1996) then assembled all the data. They wanted to see whether they could create an equation that would accurately predict—for the category "animal"—the typicality of the rating of the seven categories ("amphibian," "bird," "fish," and so on), based on the exemplars generated in a task like Task A of Demonstration 8.2. Specifically, they took into account the frequency of each of those exemplars. For example, the basic-level category "insect" frequently produced the exemplar *bee* but rarely produced the exemplar *Japanese beetle*. They also took into account the typicality ratings, similar to those you provided in Task B of the demonstration.

| *Demonstration 8.2* | Exemplars and Typicality |

A. For the first part of this demonstration, take out a sheet of paper and write the numbers 1 through 7 in a column. Then, next to the appropriate number, write the first example that comes to mind for each of the following categories:

1. amphibian

2. bird

3. fish

4. insect

5. mammal

6. microorganism

7. reptile

B. For the second part of the demonstration, look at each of the items you wrote on the sheet of paper. Rate how typical each item is for the category "animal." Use a scale where 1 = not at all typical, and 10 = very typical. For example, if you wrote *barracuda* on the list, supply a number between 1 and 10 to indicate the extent to which a barracuda is typical of an animal.

C. For the final part of this demonstration, rate each of the seven categories in Part A in terms of how typical each category is for the superordinate category "animal." Use the same rating scale as in Part B.

Source: Partly based on a study by Heit & Barsalou, 1996.

The information about exemplar frequency and exemplar typicality did accurately predict which of the seven categories were most typical for the superordinate category "animal" (Task C). In fact, the correlation between the predicted typicality and the actual typicality was statistically significant $(r = +.92)$, indicating an extremely strong relationship. For example, mammals were considered the most typical animals, and microorganisms were the least typical.

The prototype approach suggests that our categories consider only the most typical items (Wisniewski, 2002). If this proposal is correct, then we can forget about the less-typical items, and our categories would not be substantially changed. In another part of their study, Heit and Barsalou (1996) tried eliminating the less typical exemplars from the equation. The correlation between predicted typicality and actual typicality decreased significantly.

Notice the implications of this study: Suppose that you are asked a question such as, "How typical is an insect, with respect to the category 'animal'?" To make that judgment, you certainly think about a very prototypical insect—perhaps a combination of a bee and a fly. However, you also include some information about a caterpillar, a grasshopper, and maybe even a Japanese beetle.

Comparing the Prototype and Exemplar Approaches

Both of these approaches propose that you make decisions about category membership by comparing a new item against some stored representation of the category (Markman, 1999; Murphy, 2002). If the similarity is strong enough, you conclude that this new item does indeed belong to the category. In many situations, these two approaches make similar predictions about semantic memory (Rips et al., 2010).

However, the prototype approach proposes that your stored representation is *a typical member of the category*. In contrast, the exemplar approach proposes that your stored representation is *a collection of numerous specific members of the category* (Medin & Rips, 2005; Jäkel et al., 2008; Yang & Lewandowsky, 2004).

Furthermore, the exemplar approach emphasizes that people do not need to perform any kind of abstraction process (Barsalou, 2003; Heit & Barsalou, 1996; Knowlton, 1997). For example, suppose that you had read four case studies about depressed people. You would not need to devise a prototype—an ideal, typical person with depression. The exemplar approach argues that creating a prototypical person would force you to discard useful, specific data about individual cases.

One problem with the exemplar approach, however, is that our semantic memory would quickly become overpopulated with numerous exemplars for numerous categories (Love & Tomlinson, 2010; Nosofsky & Palmeri, 1998; Sternberg & Ben-Zeev, 2001). The exemplar approach may therefore be more suitable when you think about a category that has relatively few members (Knowlton, 1997). For instance, the exemplar approach might operate well for the category "tropical fruit," unless you happen to live in a tropical region of the world.

In contrast, the prototype approach may be more suitable when considering a category that has numerous members. For example, a prototype may be the most efficient approach for a large category such as "fruit" or "animal." Despite the encouraging results from Heit and Barsalou's (1996) study, the exemplar approach may be simply too bulky for some purposes. In many situations, it is not effective to use a classification strategy based purely on exemplars (Erickson & Kruschke, 1998, 2002).

Additionally, individual differences may be substantial in the way people represent categories. Perhaps some people store information about specific exemplars, especially for categories in which they have expertise. Other people may construct categories that do not include information about specific exemplars (Thomas, 1998). Instead, these individuals may construct categories based on more generic prototypes.

In reality, your semantic memory seems to be quite flexible. The prototype approach and the exemplar approach may both operate, and a concept could include information about both prototypes and specific exemplars (Love & Tomlinson, 2010; Minda & Smith, 2011; Wisniewski, 2002). In fact, one possibility is that the left hemisphere of your brain tends to store prototypes, and the right hemisphere tends to store exemplars (Bruno et al., 2003; Gazzaniga et al., 2009; Laeng et al., 2003). People may in fact use a combination of prototype strategies and exemplar strategies when they form categories in everyday life.

Network Models of Semantic Memory

The prototype and exemplar approaches both focus on categorization—that is, whether an item belongs to a category. In contrast, network approaches are more concerned about the interconnections among related items. Think for a moment about the large number of associations you have to the word *apple*. How can we find an effective way to represent the different aspects of meaning for *apple* that are stored in memory? A number of theorists favor network models. These **network models** of semantic memory propose a network-style organization of concepts in memory, with numerous interconnections.

The meaning of a particular concept, such as "apple" or "psychology," depends on the other concepts to which it is connected. The network models typically represent each concept as a **node**, or one unit located within the network. When you see or hear the name of a concept, the node representing that concept is activated. The activation expands or spreads from that node to other connected nodes, a process called **spreading activation**. The classic network theory of semantic memory was developed by Allan Collins and Elizabeth Loftus (1975). In this chapter, we will consider two more recent network approaches—Anderson's ACT-R Theory and the Parallel Distributed Processing (PDP) approach.

Anderson's ACT-R Approach

John Anderson of Carnegie Mellon University and his colleagues have constructed a series of network models, which they now call *ACT-R* (Anderson, 2000, 2009; Anderson & Schooler, 2000; Anderson & Schunn, 2000; Anderson et al., 2004). **ACT-R** is an acronym for "Adaptive Control of Thought-Rational"; this approach attempts to account for human performance on a wide variety of tasks (Anderson, 2009; Anderson et al., 2005).

The models that we've considered so far have a limited goal: to explain how we organize our cognitive concepts. In contrast, Anderson created ACT-R and its variants to explain every topic in your textbook. For example, these topics would include memory, learning, spatial cognition, language, reasoning, problem solving, and decision making (Anderson et al., 2004; Morrison & Knowlton, 2012).

Obviously, a theory that attempts to explain all of cognition is extremely complex. However, we will focus on the model's more specific view of **declarative knowledge**, or knowledge about facts and things. As you can see, declarative knowledge is the essence of this current chapter. Important earlier network models focused on networks for individual words (e.g., Collins & Loftus, 1975). Anderson, in contrast, designed a model based on larger units of meaning. According to Anderson (1990, 2009), the meaning of a sentence can be represented by a **propositional network**, which is a pattern of interconnected propositions.

Anderson and his coauthors define a **proposition** as the smallest unit of knowledge that people can judge to be either true or false. For instance, the phrase *white cat* does not qualify as a proposition because we cannot determine whether it is true or false. According to Anderson's model, each of the following three statements qualifies as a proposition:

1. Susan gave a cat to Maria.

2. The cat was white.

3. Maria is the president of the club.

These three propositions can appear by themselves, but they can also be combined into a sentence, such as the following:

Susan gave a white cat to Maria, who is the president of the club.

Figure 8.1 shows how this sentence could be represented by a propositional network. As you can see, each of the three propositions in the sentence is represented by a node, and the links are represented by arrows. Notice, too, that the network represents the important relationships in these three propositions. However, Figure 8.1 does not represent the exact wording of that key sentence. Propositions are abstract; they do not represent a specific set of words.

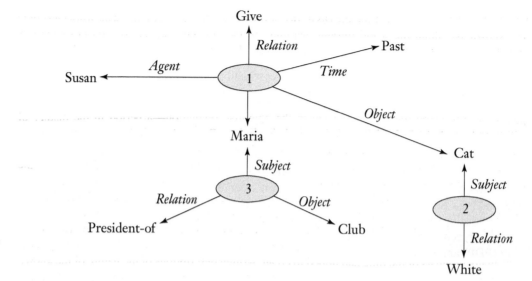

FIGURE 8.1

A propositional network representing the sentence "Susan gave a white cat to Maria, who is the president of the club."

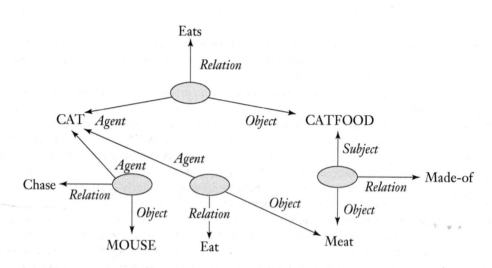

FIGURE 8.2 A Partial representation of the word *cat* in memory.

Furthermore, Anderson suggests that each of the concepts in a proposition can be represented by its own individual network. Figure 8.2 illustrates just a small part of the representation of the word *cat* in memory. Imagine what the propositional network in Figure 8.2 would look like if we could replace each of the concepts in that network with an expanded network representing the richness of meanings you have acquired. (For example, consider just the meaning of the concept *catfood*.) These networks need to be complicated in order to accurately represent the dozens of associations that we have for each item in semantic memory.

Anderson's model of semantic memory makes some additional proposals. For example, the links between nodes become stronger as they are used more often (Anderson, 2000; Anderson & Schunn, 2000; Sternberg & Ben-Zeev, 2001). Practice is vitally important in developing more extensive semantic memory (Anderson & Schooler, 2000).

Anderson's model has been highly praised for its skill in integrating cognitive processes and for its scholarship. Anderson and his colleagues have also conducted research using functional magnetic resonance imaging (fMRI). For instance, they examined how the changes in learning are reflected in selected regions of the cortex and the subcortex (Anderson et al., 2004; Anderson et al., 2005). For example, one task required people to access information that would be essential for performing other tasks. Anderson and his colleagues (2008) discovered that a specific region of the frontal lobe is activated in this situation.

ACT-R exhibits broad coverage. Its design affords it the ability to produce output that maps strongly onto human performance in many cognitive tasks. The design of the model, however, makes no appeal to neurobiological plausibility. That is, the model is not intended to make contact with the principles of neural processing or representation. It is a model that provides a way to explore assumptions and predictions about optimal human behavior. The parallel distributed processing approach—which we discuss next—incorporates neuroscientific principles as a way of providing an account of how a network can come to possess knowledge about the world through learning. In fact, the creators specifically designed this approach in terms of the neural networks found in the cerebral cortex.

The Parallel Distributed Processing Approach

In Chapter 1, we discussed the events that led to the cognitive revolution—a period in the history of the cognitive and psychological sciences following behaviorism. Researchers during this period shifted their focus away from the principles of learning (as dictated by behaviorist doctrine), and instead became heavily interested in how internal mental operations were carried out (setting the stage for many of the theoretical and empirical observations about mental life discussed so far in this textbook). During this time period in the history of cognitive science, many researchers were also interested in describing and otherwise characterizing the knowledge that adults possess. For example, Chomsky—a highly influential linguist and a key contributor to the onset of the cognitive revolution—hoped to formulate descriptions of grammatical rules that captured regularities observed in language. By studying and documenting these regularities, many linguists of the time had hoped to create written descriptions of the nature of the knowledge (about language) that must be stored in the mind. It is important to note, however, that in the pursuit of theories of knowledge—theories that relate heavily to the field of semantic memory—the principles of learning were deemphasized.

But, starting in the mid-1980-s, researchers in cognitive psychology experienced reinvigorated interest in learning, and in how information is processed by populations of neurons. These interests led to the advent of the parallel distributed processing approach to understanding the relationship between learning, neural processing, and cognition. The **parallel distributed processing (PDP) approach** proposes that cognitive processes can be represented by a model in which activation flows through networks that link together a large number of simple, neuron-like units (Bermúdez, 2010; Elman, 1990; Elman et al., 1996; Rogers & McClelland, 2004, 2011; Rumelhart & McClelland, 1986a; 1986b). The PDP approach emphasizes that we should represent concepts in terms of networks, rather than specific locations in the brain (Barrett, 2009). The word *distributed* tells us that these activations occur in several different locations. The word *parallel* tells us that these activations take place simultaneously, rather than one after another.

Crucially, these networks come to represent knowledge through training. That is, they are designed to loosely mimic connectivity among populations of neurons in the brain. Based on the principle that *neurons that fire together also tend to wire together*, the network learns to strengthen connections among relevant units in order to represent concepts and categories. Thus, through general computational and design principles coupled with exposure to structured input, the network learns—as a function of training—how to structure itself to optimally represent structure in the input to which it is exposed. This focus on learning, and the tight interrelationship of learning and stored knowledge, represents a relatively recent attempt in the cognitive sciences to capture the intimate relationship that exists between learning processes and the progressively more adult-like representation of knowledge.

Theorists often use two other names—**connectionism** and **neural networks**—in addition to "the PDP approach." The researchers who designed this approach tried to construct their model by taking into account the physiological and structural properties of populations of human neurons (Doumas & Hummel, 2012; Rogers & McClelland, 2011), and especially of how neurons send signals to each other. Before you read further, however, try Demonstration 8.3.

Demonstration 8.3 ‖ Parallel Distributed Processing

For each of the two tasks below, read the set of clues and then guess as quickly as possible what thing is being described.

Task A

1. It is orange.

2. It grows below the ground.

3. It is a vegetable.

4. Rabbits characteristically like this item.

Task B

1. Its name starts with the letter *p*.

2. It inhabits barnyards.

3. It is typically yellow in color.

4. It says, "Oink."

The designers of the PDP approach believe that the earlier models of categorization were too restrictive. Timothy Rogers and James McClelland (2011) point out a representative problem. Suppose that our categories are responsible for guiding how we store knowledge and how we generalize knowledge. How would the various categories manage to interact with one another?

Consider this example: A chicken belongs to the categories of "bird," "animal," and "a food that many people eat." We wouldn't be able to genuinely understand the concept of "chicken" unless those categories could somehow work together. The prototype approach is useful in many situations. However, the PDP approach provides a more flexible account for the richness, flexibility, and subtlety of our knowledge about the world.

Let's now consider four general characteristics of the PDP approach.

1. As suggested by the name *parallel distributed processing*, cognitive processes are based on parallel operations, rather than serial operations. Therefore, many patterns of activation may be proceeding simultaneously. One process does not need to be completely finished before another process begins its operations.

2. A network contains basic neuron-like units or nodes, which are connected together so that a specific node has many links to other nodes. (Notice that this concept is captured in the alternate name for the theory: *connectionism*.) PDP theorists argue that most cognitive processes can be explained by the activation of these networks (McNamara & Holbrook, 2003; Rogers & McClelland, 2011).

3. The process of spreading information from one node to other nodes is called *spreading activation*. As the name "parallel distributed processing" also suggests, a concept is represented by the pattern of activity distributed throughout a set of nodes (McClelland, 2000; Rogers & McClelland, 2011). Notice that this view is very different from the commonsense idea that all the information you know about a particular person or object is stored in one specific location in your brain.

4. Consistent with the concept of *situated cognition*, the current context often activates only certain components of a concept's meaning (Rogers & McClelland, 2011). If you stroll past the meat department at your grocery store, you won't necessarily connect those plastic-wrapped items with the animal that clucks, pecks for food, and lays eggs.

Each of the clues in Task A of Demonstration 8.3 probably reminded you of several possible candidates. Perhaps you thought of the correct answer after just a few clues, even though the description was not complete. Notice, however, that you did not use a serial search, conducting a complete search of all orange objects before beginning a second search of all below-ground objects, then all vegetables, then all rabbit-endorsed items. As we just noted, you used a parallel search, in which you considered all attributes simultaneously (Rogers & McClelland, 2004, 2011; Sternberg & Ben-Zeev, 2001).

Furthermore, your memory can cope quite well, even if one of the clues is incorrect. For instance, in Task B you searched for a barnyard-dwelling, oink-producing creature whose name starts with the letter *p*. The word *pig* emerged, despite the misleading clue about the yellow color. Similarly, if someone describes a student from Albany who is a tall male in your child development course, you can identify the appropriate student, even if he is actually from Syracuse.

The PDP approach argues that our knowledge about a group of individuals might be stored by connections that link these people with their personal characteristics. James McClelland's (1981) original example portrayed members of two gangs of small-time criminals, the Jets and the Sharks (McClelland, 1981). We'll use a simpler and presumably more familiar example that features five college students. Table 8.2 lists these students, together with their college majors, years in school, and political orientations.

Table 8.2   Attributes of Representative Individuals Whom a College Student Might Know

Name	Major	Year	Political Orientation
1. Joe	Art	Junior	Liberal
2. Marti	Psychology	Sophomore	Liberal
3. Sam	Engineering	Senior	Conservative
4. Liz	Engineering	Sophomore	Conservative
5. Roberto	Psychology	Senior	Liberal

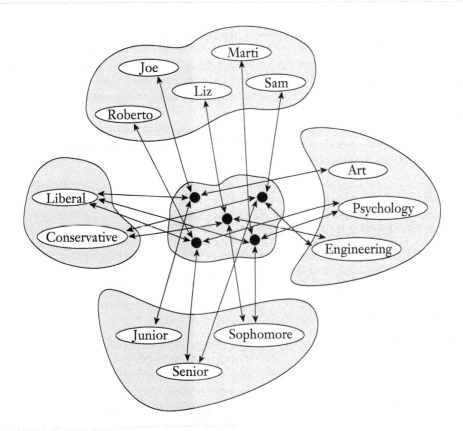

FIGURE 8.3
A sample of the units and connections that represent the individuals in Table 8.2.

Figure 8.3 shows how this information could be represented in network form. Notice that this figure represents only a fraction of the number of people whom a college student is likely to know and also just a fraction of the characteristics associated with each person. Take a minute to imagine how large a piece of paper you would need in order to represent all the people you know, together with their personal characteristics that you consider relevant.

According to the PDP approach, each individual's characteristics are connected in a mutually stimulating network. If the connections among the characteristics are well established through extensive practice, then an appropriate clue allows you to locate the characteristics of a specified individual (McClelland, 1995; McClelland et al., 1986; Rumelhart et al., 1986).

One advantage of the PDP model is that it allows us to explain how human memory can help us when some information is missing. Specifically, people can make a **spontaneous generalization** by using individual cases to draw inferences about general information (Rogers & McClelland, 2004, 2011). For example, suppose that your memory stores the information in Figure 8.3 and similar information about other college students. Suppose, also, that someone asks you whether engineering students tend to be politically conservative. PDP theory suggests that the clue *engineering student* would activate information about the engineering students you know, including information about their political orientation. You would reply that they do tend to be politically conservative, even though you did not directly store this statement in your memory.

Spontaneous generalization can also help to explain stereotyping (Bodenhausen et al., 2003), a complex cognitive process discussed later in this chapter and also in Chapter 12, on decision making. The PDP model emphasizes that we do not simply retrieve a memory in the same fashion that we might retrieve a book from a library. Instead, we reconstruct a memory, and this memory sometimes includes inappropriate information (McClelland, 1999).

PDP models also allow us to fill in missing information about a particular person or a particular object by making a best guess; we can make a **default assignment** based on information from other similar people or objects (Rogers & McClelland, 2004). Suppose, for example, that you meet Christina, who happens to be an engineering student. Someone asks you about Christina's political preferences, but you have never discussed politics with her. This question will activate information in the network about the political leanings of other engineers. Based on a default assignment, you would reply that she is probably conservative.

Incidentally, students sometimes confuse the terms *spontaneous generalization* and *default assignment*. Remember that spontaneous generalization means that we draw a conclusion about a general category (e.g., the category "engineering students"). In contrast, default assignment means that we draw a conclusion about a specific member of a category (e.g., a particular engineering student).

Notice, however, that both spontaneous generalization and default assignment can produce errors. For example, Christina may really be the president of your university's Anti-War Coalition.

So far, our discussion of parallel distributed processing has been concrete and straightforward. In reality, the theory is extremely complex, sophisticated, and abstract (e.g., Gluck & Myers, 2001; Rogers & McClelland, 2011). Let's now consider four theoretical features that are important in the PDP approach:

1. The connections between these neuron-like units are weighted, and these **connection weights** determine how much activation one unit can pass on to another unit (McClelland, 1999). As you learn more information, the values of these weights will change.

2. When a unit reaches a critical level of activation, it may affect another unit, either by exciting it (if the connection weight is positive) or by inhibiting it (if the connection weight is negative). Notice that this design resembles the excitation and inhibition of neurons in the human brain. Incidentally, Figure 8.3 shows only the excitatory connections, but you can imagine additional, inhibitory connections. For example, the characteristic *polite* might have a negative connection weight associated with some of the less civilized students in this figure.

3. Each new experience with a particular item will change the strength of connections among relevant units by adjusting the connection weights (Barsalou, 2003; McNamara & Holbrook, 2003; Rogers & McClelland, 2004, 2011). For example, while you have been reading about the PDP approach, you have been changing the strength of connections between the name *PDP approach* and related terms such as *network* and *spontaneous generalization*. The next time you encounter the term *PDP approach*, all these related terms are likely to be activated.

4. Sometimes we have only partial memory for some information, rather than complete, perfect memory. The brain's ability to provide partial memory is called **graceful degradation**. For example, Chapter 6 discussed the **tip-of-the-tongue phenomenon**, which occurs when you know which target you are seeking, but you cannot retrieve the actual target. Consistent with graceful degradation, you may know the target's first letter and the general sound of the word—even though the word itself refuses to leap into memory. Graceful degradation also explains why the brain continues to work somewhat accurately, even when an accident, stroke, or dementia has destroyed portions of the cortex (Rogers & McClelland, 2004).

We've examined some of the most important characteristics of the PDP approach. Clearly, the PDP approach offers an important perspective in cognitive psychology (Levine, 2002; McNamara & Holbrook, 2003). Some supporters are enthusiastic that the PDP approach seems generally consistent with the neurological design of neurons and the brain (Barrett, 2009; Rogers & McClelland, 2011). Many are therefore hopeful that PDP research may provide important links between psychology and neuroscience. In fact, the neural-process inspired models have been highly influential in accounting for the manner in which populations of neurons work together to learn, process, and represent information about structured regularities inherent to the environment (e.g., Bharucha, 1987; Chang et al., 2006; Christiansen & Chater, 1999; 2001; Dell et al., 1999; Gupta & MacWhinney, 1997; Harm & Seidenberg, 1999; McClelland & Elman, 1986; Seidenberg & Zevin, 2006; Valentin et al., 1994). Theorists emphasize that the PDP approach is most appropriate for tasks in which several processes operate simultaneously, and in which networks—just like brains—must learn about patterned input in one's environment that is highly structured. Indeed, pattern recognition, language, music, face recognition, and categorization, all involve input with a great deal of structure (such as, *in English, the word "the" precedes nouns*).

Schemas and Scripts

So far, our discussion of general knowledge has focused on words, concepts, and—occasionally—sentences. However, our cognitive processes also depend on world knowledge that is much more complex (Bicknell et al., 2010; Traxler, 2012; 2014). For example, our knowledge includes information about

Read the following paragraph, which is based on a description from Trafimow and Wyer (1993, p. 368):

After doing this, he found the article. He then walked through the doorway and took a piece of candy out of his pocket. Next, he got some change and saw a person he knew. Subsequently, Joe found a machine. He realized he had developed a slight headache. After he aligned the original, Joe put in the coin and pushed the button. Thus, Joe had copied the piece of paper.

Now turn to the list of new terms for Chapter 8 at the end of this chapter. Look at the first two columns of terms and write out the definition for as many of these terms as you know. Take about five minutes on the task. Then look at the paragraph labeled "Further instructions for Demonstration 8.4," which appears at the bottom of Demonstration 8.5.

familiar situations, behavior, and other "packages" of things we know. This generalized, well-integrated knowledge about a situation, an event, or a person is called a **schema** (Baddeley et al., 2009). Schemas often influence the way we understand a situation or an event, and we can think of them as the basic building blocks for representing our thoughts about people (Landau et al., 2010).

Consider, for example, the schema you have for the interior of a hardware store. It should have wrenches, cans of paint, garden hoses, and light bulbs. The store certainly should not have psychology textbooks, DVDs of Verdi operas, or birthday cakes.

Schema theories are especially helpful when psychologists try to explain how people process complex situations and events (Davis & Loftus, 2008). In this section of the chapter, we'll consider some background information on schemas and a subcategory called scripts. Then, we'll discuss how schemas can influence various components of cognition. First, however, try Demonstration 8.4.

Background on Schemas and Scripts

Schema theories propose that our memories encode "generic" information about a situation (Chi & Ohlsson, 2005; Davis & Loftus, 2008). We then use this information to understand and remember new examples of the schema. Specifically, schemas guide your recognition and understanding of new examples because you say to yourself, "This is just like what happened when . . ." (Endsley, 2006). Thus, schemas allow us to use stored knowledge to predict what will happen in a new situation. Schemas are one kind of **heuristic**, which is a general rule that is typically accurate. The predictions that we make from reliance upon schemas are usually correct, although they can sometimes lead us astray and thus cause us to make errors (Baddeley et al., 2009; Davis & Loftus, 2008). Still, these errors usually make sense within the framework of that schema. Consistent with Theme 2, our cognitive processes are generally accurate, and our mistakes are typically rational. For example, an event happens, and we immediately try to think of how the event is related to an established schema. If the event is not consistent with a schema, and this event is important to us, we usually feel obligated to reconcile the inconsistency.

Schemas and Scripts

One common kind of schema is called a script. A **script** is a simple, well-structured sequence of events that usually occur in a specified order; this script is associated with a highly familiar activity (Baddeley et al., 2009; Markman, 2002). A script is an abstraction, in other words, a prototype of a series of events that share an underlying similarity. The terms *schema* and *script* are often used interchangeably. However, *script* is actually a narrower term, referring to a sequence of events that unfold in a specified order (Woll, 2002; Zacks et al., 2001).

Consider a typical script, describing the standard sequence of events that a customer might expect in a traditional restaurant (Shank & Abelson, 1977). The "restaurant script" includes events such as sitting down, looking at the menu, eating the food, and paying the bill. We could also have scripts for visiting a dentist's office, for a trip to the grocery store, and for the first day of class in a college course. In fact, much of our education consists of learning the scripts that we are expected to follow in our culture (Schank & Abelson, 1995).

Several researchers have studied people's life scripts. A **life script** is a list of events that a person believes would be most important throughout his or her lifetime. Steve Janssen and David Rubin (2011), for example, discovered that people within a culture often share similar life scripts. They administered a life script questionnaire on the Internet to 595 Dutch participants, 90% of whom were female. The participants were asked to imagine a representative infant growing up in the Netherlands. Then they should list the seven most important events that would take place during this child's life. Interestingly, the participants' age did not have a significant effect on the listed events. Specifically, participants between the ages of 16–35, 36–55, and 56–75 were all especially likely to create a list that included having children, beginning school, marriage, falling in love, their parents' death, and first full-time job. A related study in Denmark also reported similar life scripts for younger and older individuals (Bohn, 2010).

Identifying the Script in Advance

In general, research demonstrates that people recall a script significantly more accurately if the script has been clearly identified in advance. For example, Trafimow and Wyer (1993) developed four different scripts, each describing a familiar sequence of actions: photocopying a piece of paper, cashing a check, making tea, and taking the subway. The researchers also added some details that were irrelevant to the script, such as taking a piece of candy out of a pocket. In some cases, the script-identifying event was presented first. In other cases, the script-identifying event was presented last. For instance, in Demonstration 8.4, you saw the information about copying the piece of paper *after* you had read the script.

Five minutes after reading all four descriptions, the participants were asked to recall the events from the four original descriptions. When the script-identifying event had been presented first, participants recalled 23% of those events. In contrast, they recalled only 10% when the script-identifying event had been presented last. As you might expect, the events in a sequence are much more memorable if you understand—from the very beginning—that these events are all part of a standard script (Davis & Friedman, 2007).

In the text that follows, we examine four ways in which schemas and scripts can operate during cognitive processing.

Schemas and Memory Selection

The research on schemas and memory selection has produced some complex findings. Let's look at several studies, and then we will identify some general trends related to this topic.

Be sure to try Demonstration 8.5, based on a classic study by Brewer and Treyens (1981). These authors asked participants in their study to wait, one at a time, in the room pictured in this demonstration. Each time, the experimenter explained that this was his office, and he needed to check the laboratory to see if the previous participant had completed the experiment. After 35 seconds, the experimenter asked the participant to move to a nearby room. Then, the experimenter asked each participant to remember everything in the room in which he or she had waited.

The results showed that people were highly likely to recall objects consistent with the "office schema." Nearly everyone remembered the desk, the chair next to the desk, and the wall. However, only a few recalled the wine bottle and the picnic basket. These items were not consistent with the office schema. When time is very limited—in this case, 35 seconds in that room—people may not have time to process these schema-irrelevant items.

In addition, some people in Brewer and Treyens's (1981) study "remembered" schema-consistent items that were not in the room. For example, several participants said they had remembered books, though none had been visible. Other research has shown that the number of schema-consistent errors is even greater after a two-day delay (Lampinen et al., 2001). This tendency to supply schema-consistent items represents an interesting reconstruction error (Davis & Loftus, 2008; Neuschatz et al., 2007).

Similarly, Neuschatz and his coauthors (2002) instructed students to watch a video of a man giving a lecture. The students were likely to make schema-consistent errors that were consistent with the "lecture schema," such as the lecturer referring to a concept from the previous lecture. The students were not likely to falsely remember events inconsistent with the "lecture schema," such as the lecturer dancing across the floor.

Demonstration 8.5 ‖ Schemas and Memory

After reading these instructions, cover them and the rest of the text in this demonstration so that only the picture shows. Present the picture to a friend, with the instructions, "Look at this picture of a psychology professor's office for a brief time." Half a minute later, close the book and ask your friend to list everything that was in the room.

(Further instructions for Demonstration 8.4: Now without looking back at Demonstration 8.4, write down the story from that demonstration, being as accurate as possible.)
Source: Reprinted from Brewer, W. F., & Treyens, J. C., Role of schemata in memory for places. *Cognitive Pscychology*, *13*, Fig. 1., © 1981, with permission from Elsevier.

However, we sometimes show *better* recall for material that violates our expectations (e.g., Davis & Loftus, 2008; Lampinen et al., 2000; Neuschatz et al., 2002). Specifically, people are more likely to recall schema-inconsistent material when that material is especially vivid and surprising (Brewer, 2000). For instance, Davidson (1994) asked participants to read a variety of stories that described well-known schemas such as "going to the movies." The results demonstrated that people were especially likely to recall schema-inconsistent events when those events interrupted the normal, expected story. For example, one story described a woman named Sarah who was going to the movies. The participants were very likely to remember a schema-inconsistent sentence about a child who ran through the movie theater and smashed into Sarah. In contrast, they were less likely to remember a schema-consistent sentence about an usher tearing the movie tickets in half and giving Sarah the stubs. Incidentally, before you read further, try Demonstrations 8.6 and 8.7.

Demonstration 8.6 ‖ Memory for Objects

Look at the objects below for about 15 seconds. Then turn to the bottom of demonstration 8.7, where you will find further instructions for this demonstration.

Source: From Intraub, H., and Richardson, M. (1989). Wide-angle memories of close-up scenes. *Journal of Experimental Psychology: Learning, Memory and Cognition, 15*, 179–187, Figure 1. © 1989 by the American Psychological Association. Reproduced with permission.

These results about schemas and memory may seem inconsistent. However, the outcome may depend on factors such as the details of the study and the length of the specific episode (Davis & Loftus, 2007, 2008; Lampinen et al., 2000). In general, the results show the following trends:

1. If the information describes a minor event—and time is limited—people tend to remember information accurately when it is consistent with a schema (e.g., the desk and the chair in the "office").

2. If the information describes a minor event—and time is limited—people do not remember information that is inconsistent with the schema (e.g., the wine bottle and the picnic basket).

3. People seldom create a completely false memory for a lengthy event that did not occur (e.g., the lecturer did not dance across the room).

4. When the information describes a major event that is inconsistent with the standard schema, people *are* likely to remember that event (e.g., the child who crashes into Sarah).

Schemas and Boundary Extension

Now take a moment to examine the objects you drew for Demonstration 8.6, and compare your sketch with the original photo. Does your sketch include the bottom edge of the garbage-can lid, which was not present in the original photo? Compared to the original photo, does your sketch show more background surrounding each garbage can, including the top of the picket fence? If so, you've demonstrated boundary extension.

Boundary extension refers to our tendency to remember having viewed a greater portion of a scene than was actually shown (Munger et al., 2005). We have a schema for a scene like the one depicted in Demonstration 8.6, which we could call "a photo of someone's garbage area," and our cognitive processes fill in the incomplete objects.

Notice that the earlier topics in this discussion of schemas were verbal; in boundary extension, however, the material is visual. Still, our schemas for complete objects help us fill in missing material during a memory task.

Demonstration 8.7 | Constructive Memory

Part 1

Read each sentence, count to five, answer the question, and go on to the next sentence.

Sentence	Question
The girl broke the window on the porch.	Broke what?
The tree in the front yard shaded the man who was smoking his pipe.	Where?
The cat, running from the barking dog, jumped on the table.	From what?
The tree was tall.	Was what?
The cat running from the dog jumped on the table.	Where?
The girl who lives next door broke the window on the porch.	Lives where?
The scared cat was running from the barking dog.	What was?
The girl lives next door.	Who does?
The tree shaded the man who was smoking his pipe.	What did?
The scared cat jumped on the table.	What did?
The girl who lives next door broke the large window.	Broke what?
The man was smoking his pipe.	Who was?
The large window was on the porch.	Where?
The tall tree was in the front yard.	What was?
The cat jumped on the table.	Where?
The tall tree in the front yard shaded the man.	Did what?
The dog was barking.	Was what?
The window was large.	What was?

Part 2

Cover the preceding sentences. Now read each of the following sentences and decide whether it is a sentence from the list in Part 1.

1.	The girl who lives next door broke the window.	(old _____, new _____)
2.	The tree was in the front yard.	(old _____, new _____)
3.	The scared cat, running from the barking dog, jumped on the table.	(old _____, new _____)
4.	The window was on the porch.	(old _____, new _____)
5.	The tree in the front yard shaded the man.	(old _____, new _____)
6.	The cat was running from the dog.	(old _____, new _____)
7.	The tall tree shaded the man who was smoking his pipe.	(old _____, new _____)
8.	The cat was scared.	(old _____, new _____)
9.	The girl who lives next door broke the large window on the porch.	(old _____, new _____)
10.	The tall tree shaded the girl who broke the window.	(old _____, new _____)
11.	The cat was running from the barking dog.	(old _____, new _____)
12.	The girl broke the large window.	(old _____, new _____)
13.	The scared cat ran from the barking dog that jumped on the table.	(old _____, new _____)
14.	The girl broke the large window on the porch.	(old _____, new _____)
15.	The scared cat which broke the window on the porch climbed the tree.	(old _____, new _____)
16.	The tall tree in the front yard shaded the man who was smoking his pipe.	(old _____, new _____)

Source: Bransford, J. D., & Franks, J. J. (1971). Abstraction of linguistic ideas. *Cognitive Psychology*, 2, 331–350.

(Further instructions for Demonstration 8.6: Draw from memory the scene you saw in Demonstration 8.6. Do not look back at that photo!)

Helene Intraub and her colleagues were the first researchers to document the boundary-extension phenomenon (e.g., Intraub, 1997; Intraub & Berkowits, 1996; Intraub et al., 1998). For example, Intraub and Berkowits (1996) showed college students a series of photos like the garbage scene in Demonstration 8.6. Each photo was shown briefly, for 15 seconds or less. Immediately afterward, the students were instructed to draw an exact replica of the original photo. The participants consistently produced a sketch that extended the boundaries beyond the view presented in the original photo. As a result, they drew more of the background that surrounded the central figure, and they also depicted a complete figure, rather than a partial one.

According to Intraub and her coauthors (1998), we comprehend a photograph by activating a perceptual schema. This schema features a complete central figure in the photo, but it also includes a mental representation of visual information that is just outside the boundaries of the photo. We also use perceptual schemas when we look at real-life scenes. Notice why schemas are relevant in boundary extension: Based on our expectations, we create perceptual schemas that extend beyond the edges of the photograph and beyond the scope of our retinas (Munger et al., 2005).

The boundary-extension phenomenon also has important implications for eyewitness testimony, a topic we discussed in Chapter 5. Eyewitnesses may recall having seen some features of a suspect's face, even though these features were not actually visible at the scene of the crime (Foley & Foley, 1998). In addition, after people search for a target in a crowded scene, they recall having viewed a complete target, even if it had been partially blocked by other figures (Foley et al., 2002). Apparently, the incomplete figure activates our imagery processes, so that we "fill in the blanks." Our memory tends to store these idealized, schema-consistent images, rather than partial figures.

Schemas and Memory Abstraction

Abstraction is a memory process that stores the meaning of a message, rather than the exact words. For example, you can probably remember much of the information about the concept "family resemblance" discussed earlier even though you cannot recall any specific sentence in its exact, original form.

Research demonstrates that people usually have poor word-for-word recall, or **verbatim memory**, even a few minutes after a passage has been presented (e.g., Koriat et al., 2000; Sachs, 1967). However, some professions require accurate verbatim memory. For instance, professional actors must remember the exact words from a Shakespeare play. But do the rest of us need verbatim memory in our everyday lives? Let's consider two approaches to the abstraction issue: the constructive approach and the pragmatic approach.

The Constructive Approach

Be sure that you tried Demonstration 8.7 before you read further. This is a simpler version of a classic study by Bransford and Franks (1971). How many sentences in Part 2 of the demonstration had you seen before? The answer is at the end of the chapter.

Bransford and Franks (1971) asked participants to listen to sentences from several different stories. Participants were then given a recognition test that also included some new items, many of which were combinations of the earlier sentences. Nonetheless, people were convinced that they had seen these new items before. This kind of error is called a *false alarm*. In memory research, a **false alarm** occurs when people "remember" an item that was not originally presented. Bransford and Franks found that people were especially likely to make false alarms when a complex sentence was consistent with the original schema. For instance, they frequently made false alarms for sentences such as, "The tall tree in the front yard shaded the man who was smoking his pipe." In contrast, participants seldom made false alarms for sentences that violated the meaning of the earlier sentences. For example, they seldom said that they had heard the sentence, "The scared cat that broke the window on the porch climbed the tree." Subsequent research shows similar findings (Chan & McDermott, 2006; Holmes et al., 1998; Jenkins, 1974).

Bransford and Franks (1971) proposed a constructive model of memory for prose material. According to the **constructive model of memory**, people integrate information from individual sentences in order to construct larger ideas. Later, they believe that they have already seen those complex sentences because they have combined the various facts in memory. Once sentences are fused in memory, we cannot untangle them into their original components and recall those components verbatim.

Notice that the constructive view of memory emphasizes that our cognitive processes are generally accurate, consistent with Theme 1 of this book. Sentences do not passively enter memory, where each is stored separately. Instead, we combine the sentences into a coherent story, fitting the related pieces together. We typically store an *abstract* of the information, rather than a word-for-word representation.

Constructive memory also illustrates Theme 2. Your memory is typically accurate. However, the errors in cognitive processing can often be traced to strategies that are generally useful. In real life, a useful heuristic is to fuse sentences together. However, this heuristic can lead us astray if we apply it inappropriately. As it turns out, the participants in Bransford and Franks's (1971) study used a constructive memory strategy that is useful in real life. However, it is typically inappropriate in a study that tests verbatim memory.

The Pragmatic Approach

Murphy and Shapiro (1994) developed a different view of memory for sentences, which they call the pragmatic view of text memory. The **pragmatic view of memory** proposes that people pay attention to the aspect of a message that is most relevant to their current goals. In other words:

1. People know that they usually need to accurately recall the gist of a sentence.

2. They also know that they usually do not need to remember the specific wording of the sentences.

3. However, in those cases where they *do* need to pay attention to the specific wording, then they know that their verbatim memory needs to be highly accurate.

Murphy and Shapiro (1994) speculated that people are particularly likely to pay attention to the exact wording of a sentence if the words are part of a criticism or an insult. After all, from the pragmatic viewpoint, the exact words *do* matter if someone is insulting you! In this study, participants read letters that presumably had been written by a young woman named Samantha. One group read a letter, supposedly written to her cousin Paul. In the letter, the hypothetical Samantha chatted about her new infant in a bland fashion. The letter included a number of neutral sentences such as, "It never occurred to me that I would be a mother so young" (p. 91).

A second group read a letter that was supposedly written by Samantha to her boyfriend, Arthur. Ten of the sentences that had been neutral in the bland letter to cousin Paul now appeared in a sarcastic context, though the exact words were identical. For example, the sentence, "It never occurred to me that I would be a mother so young" now referred to Arthur's infantile behavior.

Murphy and Shapiro then gave both groups a 14-item recognition test that included (a) five of the original sentences, (b) five paraphrased versions of those sentences with a slightly different form, such as, "I never thought I would be a mother at such a young age," and (c) four irrelevant sentences. People rarely made the mistake of falsely "recognizing" the irrelevant sentences. However, correct recognition was higher for the sentences from the sarcastic condition than for the sentences in the bland condition. Furthermore, people made more false alarms for the paraphrases of the bland sentences than for the paraphrases of the sarcastic sentences.

More generally, the researchers found that people were much more accurate in their verbatim memory for the sarcastic version (43%) than for the bland version (17%). Similar results have been reported by Schönpflug (2008). Perhaps, we are especially sensitive about emotionally threatening material, so we make an effort to recall the exact words of the sentences.

The Current Status of Schemas and Memory Abstraction

In reality, the constructive approach and the pragmatic approach to memory abstraction are actually compatible. Specifically, in many cases, we do integrate information from individual sentences so that we can construct a schema, especially when we don't need to remember the exact words. However, in some cases, we know that the specific words do matter, and so we pay close attention to the precise wording. If you are rehearsing for a play, or you are quarreling with a friend, you will need to remember more than the overall gist of a verbal message.

Notice that this conclusion about remembering both general descriptions and specific information is similar to our previous conclusions about semantic memory. As discussed earlier, your semantic memory can store both general prototypes and specific exemplar-based information.

Schemas and Memory Integration

Another important process in memory formation is integration. In **memory integration**, our background knowledge encourages us to take in new information in a schema-consistent fashion (Hamilton, 2005; Hirt et al., 1998; Koriat et al., 2000). As a result, people may remember this schema-consistent information, even though it was not part of the original stimulus material.

Once again, however, schemas do not always operate. For example, suppose that you are tested soon after you learned some new information. Your background knowledge may not alter that new information. In contrast, schema-consistent integration is more likely when there is a delay of a day or two before you are asked to recall the new material (Harris et al., 1989).

The research also suggests that our schemas may not influence memory if we are working on one relatively simple memory task. However, when people work on two simultaneous memory tasks, Sherman and Bessenoff (1999) found that they committed many schema-consistent errors. Specifically, the participants in this study incorrectly remembered that pleasant words had been used to describe a priest, whereas unpleasant words had been used to describe a dangerous person. Let's now examine Bartlett's studies on the integration of culture-consistent information, and then we will consider the more recent work on gender stereotypes.

The Classic Research on Memory Integration

Sir Frederick Bartlett (1932) was an important British researcher who studied people's memory for natural language material. Bartlett's theories and techniques foreshadowed the theories of contemporary cognitive psychologists. He also pioneered the research on applied cognition. For example, his laboratory research could be generalized to our everyday patterns of remembering and forgetting (Davies & Wright, 2010b). Bartlett believed that the most interesting aspect of memory was the complex interaction between the participants' prior knowledge and the material presented during the experiment. In particular, he argued that an individual's unique interests and personal background often shape the contents of memory.

In Bartlett's (1932) best-known series of studies, he asked British students to read a Native American story called "The War of the Ghosts." They were then asked to recall the story 15 minutes later. Bartlett found that the participants tended to omit material that did not make sense from the viewpoint of British students. For example, they often omitted a portion of the story in which a ghost had attacked someone, and this person did not feel the wound. These students also tended to shape the story into a more familiar framework so that it made sense from a British perspective. In many cases, the students' version was more similar to British fairy tales (Brewer, 2000).

Bartlett also asked his participants to recall the story again, after a delay of several days. As time passed after hearing the original story, the participants borrowed more heavily from their previous knowledge and included less information from the original story.

Subsequent research confirms that schemas can influence our memory when we are reading ambiguous or unclear material (Jahn, 2004; Schacter, 2001). As Brewer (2000) emphasizes, the research on schemas demonstrates how our cognitive processes actively work to make sense out of puzzling information (Theme 1). Specifically, our top-down processes often shape our memory for complex material (Theme 5).

The research also shows that schemas can mislead us, so that we make systematic errors and "remember" information that was not actually stated. In our daily lives, however, these schemas are usually helpful, rather than counterproductive. For instance, our background knowledge can help us recall stories from our own culture. Simple stories have definite, regular structures (Schank & Abelson, 1995). We become familiar with the basic structure of stories from experiences in our culture. Then we use this structure to interpret the new stories that we hear. In general, then, this background information helps us draw correct conclusions.

Research About Memory Integration Based on Gender Stereotypes

The research about gender stereotypes provides further information about how schemas can influence our conclusions. **Gender stereotypes** are the beliefs and opinions that we associate with females and males (Jackson, 2011; Whitley & Kite, 2010). Even when a gender stereotype is partially accurate, it cannot be applied to every individual of the specified gender (Eagly & Carli, 2007).

When people know someone's gender, they often draw conclusions about that individual's personal characteristics. For example, people usually rate men as being more competitive than women, and they usually rate women as being more nurturant than men. Some gender stereotypes may be partly true (Matlin, 2012). However, these stereotypes might prevent a corporation from hiring a competitive woman as a senior executive. These stereotypes might also prevent a school from hiring a nurturant man to teach first grade.

In this section, we will examine how the research methods from cognitive psychology can be used to examine people's gender stereotypes. Let's first examine research that employs explicit measures. Then, we'll see how implicit measures provide additional information about gender stereotypes.

Dunning and Sherman (1997) assessed gender stereotypes by using a recognition-memory task. They instructed students to read sentences such as, "The women at the office liked to talk around the water cooler." Later, the participants were tested for recognition memory. Specifically, participants saw a series of sentences. They were told to respond "old" if they had previously seen that same exact sentence, earlier in the session. Otherwise, they should respond "new."

Let's look at the results for new sentences that were *consistent* with a widely held gender stereotype about women's conversations: "The women at the office liked to gossip around the water cooler." The participants responded "old" to 29% of these sentences. Other new sentences were *inconsistent* with another widely held stereotype: "The women at the office liked to talk sports around the water cooler." The participants responded "old" to only 18% of these sentences. Apparently, when people saw the original sentence, they sometimes made the stereotype-consistent inference that the women must have been gossiping. They were less likely to make the gender-inconsistent inference that the women were discussing sports. Oakhill and her colleagues (2005) found similar results.

Dunning and Sherman's (1997) recognition test is an example of an explicit memory task. As discussed in Chapter 5, an **explicit memory task** directly instructs participants to remember information. For example, the participants in this study knew that their memory was being tested when they judged whether the sentences were old or new. People might guess that the researchers could be measuring their gender stereotypes, and they may be aware that it's not appropriate to hold rigid stereotypes (Matlin, 2012; Rudman, 2005). To reduce this "awareness problem," researchers have designed a variety of implicit memory tasks. The goal of these implicit memory measures is to assess people's gender stereotypes without asking them directly. Implicit memory measures are supposed to discourage people from providing socially desirable answers.

As Chapter 5 described, an **implicit memory task** asks people to perform a cognitive task that does not directly ask for recall or recognition. When researchers use implicit memory tasks to measure gender stereotypes, they assess people's general knowledge about gender in their culture. These implicit memory tasks also measure people's tendency to draw gender-consistent conclusions. Let's consider two different implicit memory tasks that show how gender stereotypes can influence people's implicit memory.

1. *Using neuroscience techniques to assess gender stereotypes*   Osterhout and his coauthors (1997) assessed gender stereotypes by using a neuroscience technique. The **event-related potential (ERP) technique** records tiny fluctuations in the brain's electrical activity, in response to a stimulus. Previous researchers had tested people who were instructed to read sentences such as, "I like my coffee with cream and dog." As you would expect, the ERPs quickly changed in response to the surprising word *dog*, relative to the onset of the highly expected word (*cream*).

   To examine gender stereotypes, Osterhout and his colleagues (1997) presented some sentences that would be consistent with gender stereotypes, such as, "The nurse prepared herself for the operation." These stereotype-consistent sentences did not elicit a change in the ERPs.

   In contrast, the ERPs changed significantly for stereotype-inconsistent sentences such as, "The nurse prepared himself for the operation." In reading the word *nurse*, people had made the gender-stereotyped inference that the nurse must be female. Consequently, the unexpected, stereotype-inconsistent word *himself* produced changes in the ERPs. In a related study, White and her colleagues (2009) found similar results, with greater ERP changes for stereotype-inconsistent pairs of words.

2. *Using the Implicit Association Test to assess gender stereotypes*   Brian Nosek, Mahzarin Banaji, and Anthony Greenwald (2002) used a very different method to assess implicit gender stereotypes. Specifically, they examined the gender stereotypes that mathematics is associated with males and that the arts are associated with females. Suppose that they had asked their research participants (college students at Yale University) an explicit question, such as: "Is math more strongly associated with males than with females?" When research is conducted with college students like these, the students are most likely to answer "No." After all, when students are asked an explicit question like this, they have time to be analytical and to recall that a "Yes" answer would not be socially appropriate. Now try Demonstration 8.8.

Demonstration 8.8	Using the Implicit Association Test to Assess Implicit Attitudes Toward Social Groups

Log onto the World Wide Web and visit a site sponsored by Harvard University: <https://implicit.harvard.edu/implicit/>

You can examine your own attitudes about gender, ethnicity, sexual orientation, people with disabilities, and elderly people. Be certain to follow the caution to make your responses as quickly as possible. More leisurely responses might assess explicit attitudes, rather than implicit attitudes.

Instead of an explicit measure, Nosek and his colleagues used the Implicit Association Test (e.g., Greenwald & Nosek, 2001; Greenwald et al., 1998; Nosek et al., 2007), such as the one you tried in Demonstration 8.8. An implicit task asks people to perform a task, but the participants do not know what the task is supposed to measure. The **Implicit Association Test (IAT)** is based on the principle that people can mentally pair two related words together much more easily than they can pair two unrelated words.

Specifically, when participants worked on the IAT, they sat in front of a computer screen that presented a series of words. On a typical trial—where the pairings were consistent with gender stereotypes—the participant would be told to press the key on the left if the word was related to math (e.g., *calculus* or *numbers*) and also if the word was related to males (e.g., *uncle* or *son*). This same participant would be told to press the key on the right if the word was related to the arts (e.g., *poetry* or *dance*) and also if the word was related to females (e.g., *aunt* or *daughter*).

Throughout the study, participants were urged to respond as quickly as possible, so that they would not consciously consider their responses. When completing the IAT, people with strong gender stereotypes would think that math and males fit in the same category, whereas the arts and females would fit in a different category. Therefore, their responses should be quick for this first portion of the task.

Then the instructions shifted so that the pairings were now *inconsistent* with gender stereotypes. Now, on a typical trial, the participant would press the left key if the word was related to math and also if the word was related to females. Also, the participant would press the right key if the word was related to the arts and also if the word was related to males. People with strong gender stereotypes should have difficulty associating math-related terms with women and arts-related terms with men. Their responses should therefore be much slower for this second part of the task.

Nosek and his coauthors (2002) found that the students responded significantly faster to the stereotype-consistent pairings (the first task), compared to the stereotype-inconsistent pairings (the second task). In other words, most of these Yale students believed that math and males seem to go together, whereas the arts and females seem to go together. Nosek et al. also analyzed the scores for women who strongly considered themselves to be feminine and strongly associated math with being masculine. These women specifically did *not* associate themselves with mathematics. In other words, gender stereotypes are not innocent cognitive tendencies. Instead, these stereotypes can have the power to influence people's self-images and their sense of academic competence.

Psychologists have designed other implicit measures to examine gender stereotypes and other categories such as ethnicity (Ito et al., 2006; Lane, Banaji, & Greenwald, 2007; Reynolds et al., 2006). Furthermore, if you are interested in the connection between social psychology and cognitive psychology, you can find additional information in several useful books (Jackson, 2011; Whitley & Kite, 2010).

An updated version of the Implicit Association Test (IAT) involves tracking the streaming *x, y* coordinates of computer-mouse trajectories as participants move the mouse to click on one of two response options on a computer display—a technique often referred to as "mouse-tracking" (Spivey, 2007; Spivey, Grosjean, & Knoblich, 2005; Freeman & Ambady, 2010). In their mouse-tracking experiment on gender stereotypes, Smeding and colleagues (2016) presented participants with displays containing two response boxes. For example, on the top-left of the display, participants might have seen a box containing the words "Science" and "Female". On the top right of the display, participants would then see the corresponding "Humanities" and "Male." Notice that these two response options contain stereotype-inconsistent labels. In another condition, participants would see these same two response boxes with the gender labels switched ("Science" appearing with "Male").

At the beginning of a trial, participants clicked a "Start" button at the bottom center of the display. Next, a male- or female-specifying noun, such as "Uncle" would appear at the center of the screen. Participants had to move the mouse to the response box containing the gender label consistent with the noun (in this case, to the box containing the word "Male"). The streaming *x, y* coordinates produced by the computer-mouse movement were sampled at a high rate, thus illuminating the trajectory of movement.

Participants almost always clicked on the correct response box. The dependent measure of interest, however, was how much the trajectory veered toward the incorrect response as participants moved to the box containing the correct response. The greater the curvature toward the ultimately nonselected (incorrect) response, the greater the amount of consideration participants gave to it before arriving at the box containing the correct response. Participants were not told that the trajectories of their mouse movements were being recorded. In this sense, computer-mouse trajectories reflect an implicit measure of the degree to which participants held gender-stereotyped beliefs.

The participants in the experiment were either female engineering students or female humanities students (data from male respondents were also collected, although we do not discuss them here due to space constraints). Thus, the participants were themselves students in either gender-stereotypical ("Humanities") or gender-nonstereotypical ("Science") fields.

The results were striking. Female engineering majors produced relatively straight trajectories when responding on stereotype incongruent trials, relative to stereotype-congruent trials. On stereotype-incongruent trials, however, female humanities majors produced trajectories that curved significantly more toward the box containing the incorrect gender label before arriving at the box with the correct gender label (relative to stereotype-congruent trials). Thus, women in stereotype-congruent fields of study (female humanities majors) were more sensitive to the presence of a mismatch between gender and stereotypical career, and this sensitivity was reflected by a more difficult and protracted decision process on stereotype inconsistent trials.

Smeding and colleagues interpreted these results as evidence that when women do not view themselves as part of or otherwise conforming to a gender stereotype, they are less likely to ascribe to or implicitly activate the stereotype.

The IAT is extremely popular, but most of the research has been conducted in the United States. You may wonder if the same gender stereotypes are likely to operate in other countries. Fortunately, an impressive cross-cultural study has examined this question. Brian Nosek and his colleagues (2009) worked with researchers in 34 different countries to gather the relevant information.

Specifically, these researchers wanted to determine whether national differences in gender stereotypes would be correlated with national differences in female and male students' scores on a cognitive test. This widely used test is called the "2003 Trends in International Mathematics and Science Study" (TIMS). Fortunately, the average scores on this test were available for eighth grade females and males in 34 different countries. Nosek and his coauthors (2009) used these data to calculate the "male advantage" for each country, specifically, the males' average score on the TIMS test minus the females' average on the TIMS test.

Furthermore, these researchers also recorded the average scores on the IAT for each country, because the test is available online in 17 different languages. (In fact, Demonstration 8.8 features the online version of the IAT.) About 300,000 people in those 34 countries had completed this test by the time these researchers gathered their data.

The results showed that the countries with the highest scores on the IAT measure of gender stereotyping were also likely to have the highest "male advantage" scores on both the math and science test (TIMS). Specifically, the correlation was +.34 for math scores and +.39 for science scores. In other words, the countries with the highest measures of gender stereotyping were also more likely to be the countries where males performed better than females in both math and science. Incidentally, the United States and Canada had average scores on both the IAT and the male-advantage measure.

You know from your psychology courses that correlational data can be difficult to interpret. However, Nosek and his coauthors (2009) write that a "likely explanation for the relation is that both the 8th grade test takers and the diverse IAT participants of a given country are influenced by the same socio-cultural context" (p. 10596). The title of this current chapter is "General Knowledge." In this case, people's semantic memory and schemas include information about gender differences, and the strength of this knowledge varies from country to country.

SECTION SUMMARY POINTS

Background and Approaches to Semantic Memory

1. Semantic memory includes both general knowledge and knowledge about language.

2. According to prototype theory, people compare new stimuli with prototypes (most typical examples) in order to categorize them.

3. People frequently supply prototypes as examples of a category, and they judge prototypes more quickly after semantic priming. Prototypes also share a large number of attributes with other items in the same family-resemblance category.

4. According to prototype theory, when people discuss a particular item, they use basic-level categories more often than subordinate-level or superordinate-level categories when identifying objects.

5. Basic-level names are more likely to produce the semantic priming effect, and different levels of categorization activate different regions of the brain.

6. The exemplar approach proposes that we classify a new stimulus by deciding how closely it resembles specific examples (i.e., exemplars) that we have already learned. The research suggests that our concepts may indeed include information about less typical exemplars.

7. It's possible that people may use both prototypes and exemplars to represent concepts.

Network Models of Semantic Memory

1. Network models emphasize the relationships that exist among information stored in semantic memory.

2. Anderson's ACT-R model attempts to explain a wide variety of cognitive processes. His model of declarative knowledge represents both sentences and concepts with a propositional-network structure.

3. Another network model is called the parallel distributed processing (PDP) or connectionist approach.

4. The PDP approach proposes that (a) cognitive processes are based on parallel operations, (b) networks link numerous neuron-like nodes, and (3) a concept is represented by a pattern of activity throughout that set of nodes.

5. The PDP approach also proposes features to explain cognitive phenomena such as spontaneous generalization, default assignment, the strengthening of connections, and graceful degradation.

Schemas and Scripts

1. A schema is generalized knowledge about a situation, an event, or a person; schemas are a kind of heuristic, in other words, a general rule that is typically accurate; schemas are important in many areas of psychology.

2. A script is a kind of schema that describes a simple, well-structured sequence of events, for example, a life script about the important events in a person's life; research shows that we can recall the elements in a script more accurately if the script is identified at the outset.

3. Schemas may operate during memory selection; for example, people recall items consistent with an office schema. However, we often recall schema-*inconsistent* information, for example, when a major event is surprising and inconsistent with the standard schema.

4. When we remember a scene, we often "remember" seeing complete objects, even though we really saw only parts of those objects (boundary extension).

5. According to the constructive model of memory, schemas encourage memory abstraction, so that people tend to remember the general meaning of a message, even if they forget the detail. According to the pragmatic view of memory, people often remember the exact words in a message when the specific words really matter. Both perspectives seem to operate, depending on the circumstances.

6. Schemas also influence memory integration; in Bartlett's classic research, people "recalled" information that never actually appeared in the original material. The tendency is stronger if recall is delayed and if people are performing another memory task at the same time.

7. The research on gender stereotypes shows that people frequently make schema-consistent inferences in explicit memory (e.g., a recognition test) and in implicit memory, for instance, with the ERP technique and the IAT task. Cross-cultural research shows that countries with the highest scores on the IAT are also the countries where boys earn higher scores than girls on a test that measures performance in science and mathematics.

CHAPTER REVIEW QUESTIONS

1. Think of a prototype for the category "household pet," and contrast it with a nonprototypical household pet. Compare these two animals with respect to (a) whether they would be supplied as examples of the category; (b) how quickly they could be judged after priming; and (c) the attributes that each would share with most other household pets.

2. Consider the basic-level category "dime," in contrast to the superordinate-level category "money" and the subordinate-level category "2005 dime." Describe these three levels, and then explain how the basic level has special status when we want to identify objects. Describe a person who would be most likely to use (a) the superordinate-level name and (b) the subordinate-level name. Think of an area in which you have more knowledge than the average student; when would you be most likely to use subordinate-level descriptions?

3. Describe the prototype approach and the exemplar approach to semantic memory. How are they similar, and how are they different? Based on the discussion in this chapter, when would

you be more likely to use a prototype approach in trying to categorize an object? When would you be more likely to use the exemplar approach? In each case, give an example from your daily experience.

4. Suppose that you read the following question on a true-false examination: "A script is a kind of schema." Describe how you would process that question in terms of the exemplar approach and network models.

5. Think of some kind of information that could be represented in a diagram similar to the one in Figure 8.3 (e.g., popular singers or famous novelists). Then provide examples of how the following terms could apply to this particular diagram: spontaneous generalization, default assignment, and graceful degradation.

6. If you were instructed to describe the characteristics of the PDP approach in a 5-minute overview, what would you say? Include examples, and also be sure to describe why the approach is called "parallel distributed processing." Chapter 5 discussed the topic of expertise. Think about a specific area in which you have more expertise than a friend who is a novice. How might the two of you differ with respect to the kind of network you have developed?

7. Describe three scripts with which you are very familiar. How would these scripts be considered heuristics, rather than exact predictors of what will happen the next time you find yourself in one of the situations described in the script?

8. You probably have a fairly clear schema of the concept "dentist's office." Focus on the discussion titled "Schemas and Memory Selection" and point out the circumstances in which you would be likely to remember (a) schema-consistent material and (b) schema-inconsistent material. How might boundary extension operate when you try to reconstruct the scene that you see from the dentist's chair?

9. What evidence do we have from explicit memory tasks that gender stereotypes encourage us to draw inferences that are consistent with those stereotypes? How would the demand characteristics mentioned in Chapter 7 be relevant to explicit memory tasks? Then discuss the two implicit memory tasks described in the discussion about inferences, and explain why they may be more effective than explicit tasks in assessing people's stereotypes.

10. Think of a schema or a script that occurs frequently in your life. Explain how that schema or script might influence your memory during four different processes: memory selection, boundary extension, memory abstraction, and memory integration. Be sure to consider how memory sometimes favors schema-consistent information and sometimes favors schema-inconsistent information, as well as the cases when memory accurately reflects bottom-up processing.

KEYWORDS

inference	family resemblance	declarative knowledge	graceful degradation	constructive model of
semantic memory	superordinate-level	propositional network	tip-of-the-tongue	memory
episodic memory	categories	proposition	phenomenon	pragmatic view of
category	basic-level categories	parallel distributed	schema	memory
concept	subordinate-level	processing (PDP)	heuristic	memory integration
situated cognition approach	categories	approach	script	gender stereotypes
prototype	exemplar approach	connectionism	life script	explicit memory task
prototype approach	exemplar	neural networks	boundary	implicit memory task
prototypicality	network models	spontaneous	extension	event-related potential
graded structure	node	generalization	abstraction	(ERP) technique
typicality effectz	spreading activation	default assignment	verbatim memory	Implicit Association
semantic priming effect	ACT-R	connection weights	false alarm	Test (IAT)

RECOMMENDED READINGS

Davis, D., & Loftus, E. F. (2008). Expectancies, emotion, and memory reports for visual events. In J. R. Brockmole (Ed.), *The visual world in memory* (pp. 178–214). New York: Psychology Press. Here is a clear and interesting chapter that describes how schemas can influence eyewitness testimony for visual events. An especially important focus is the research about how ethnicity can create biases in eyewitness testimony.

Elman, J. L. (Ed.). (1996). *Rethinking innateness: A connectionist perspective on development* (Vol. 10). MIT press. This highly influential volume provides a well-structured and highly readable introduction to the connectionist approach. Additionally, it focuses on how connectionist models can be used to understand learning and development. It also addresses the manner in which connectionist models have been used to resolve key controversies in nature versus nurture debates in the area of cognitive development.

Mareschal, D., Quinn, P. C. & Lea, S. E. G. (Eds.). (2010). *The making of human concepts*. New York: Oxford University Press. Much of the research on concepts is abstract and difficult to apply to everyday life. This book is well written, especially because the editors include an introduction at the beginning of each chapter. The content focuses on concepts in adults, children, and animals

Murphy, G. L. (2002). *The big book of concepts*. Cambridge, MA: MIT Press. Topics in this book include theories of concepts, the development of conceptual knowledge, and word meaning. The tongue-in-cheek title of this book is consistent with the author's sense of humor throughout the chapters.

Whitley, B. E., Jr., & Kite, M. E. (2010). *The psychology of prejudice and discrimination* (2nd ed.). Belmont, CA: Wadsworth Cengage. Bernard Whitley and Mary Kite are well known for their research about biases based on gender, age, and sexual orientation. Two chapters in their book specifically focus on stereotypes.

ANSWER TO DEMONSTRATION 8.7

Every sentence in Part 2 is new.

Language I: Introduction to Language and Language Comprehension

9

Chapter Introduction

Try to imagine a world without language. In fact, think about how your life would change if you woke up tomorrow and language were forbidden. Even nonverbal gestures and sign language would be prohibited, because they are alternate forms of language. Phones, televisions, radios, newspapers, books, and electronic communication would be virtually useless. Almost all college courses would disappear. You couldn't even talk to yourself, so it would be impossible to reminisce, remind yourself about a task you must complete, or make plans for the future. Your interactions with other people would be minimal, because language is such an important part of these interactions (Fiedler et al., 2011; Heine, 2010).

In fact, society could not function without language. As Steffensen (2011) remarks, "Language functions as airborne synapses; it contributes to inter-human coordination, thus allowing us to be smarter, more creative and more flexible, just like the brain is smarter and more flexible than a pile of neurons" (p. 205).

In Chapters 9 and 10, we will discuss the psychology of language (a field often referred to as psycholinguistics). We use language in thousands of different settings, from courtrooms to cartoons. Furthermore, language provides an excellent example of Theme 4 of this textbook, the interrelatedness of the cognitive processes. In fact, virtually every topic we have discussed so far in this book makes some contribution to language processing. The two chapters on language should also convince you that humans are active information processors (Theme 1). Rather than passively listening to language, we actively consult our previous knowledge, use various strategies, create expectations, and draw conclusions. When we speak, we can easily convey complex messages. Language is not only our most remarkable cognitive achievement, but it is also the most social of our cognitive processes (Fiedler et al., 2011).

The first of our two chapters on language focuses on language comprehension. After an introductory discussion about the nature of language, we will examine many factors that influence the ease with which people are able to accurately interpret an unfolding linguistic signal. The final two sections of this chapter focus on reading and on the comprehension of discourse. In Chapter 10, we will switch our focus from language understanding to the production of language, with a specific focus on both speaking and writing.

Overview of Psycholinguistics

Language use occurs on an impressively fast timescale. For example, when someone speaks in English, they produce about three words per second, assuming that they are an adult and lack significant cognitive impairment (Vigliocco & Hartsuiker, 2002). And, speech unfolds continuously. There are no pauses between the last sound of one word and the initial sound of the next (imagine how slow we would have to speak if there were). Moreover, when speakers speak, they get to do so on their own terms. They have the luxury of choosing the words they want to use, how fast they want to speak, the volume at which they prefer to speak, and the grammatical complexity of the utterances they produce.

Language comprehension involves arriving at an ultimately correct interpretation of a linguistic signal produced by a speaker. A listener must (1) encode the continuous stream of sounds produced by a speaker, (2) use information in the physical properties of a producer's message to identify words and to access their meaning, (3) apply your knowledge of the rules that govern permissible word order, in order to (4) create a global interpretation of the message that a speaker intended to convey.

As you can see, the task facing a listener is quite daunting. Recognizing this complexity, then, isn't it striking just how easily you can understand someone as they speak?

Questions about the psychological and underlying neurological processes that drive our ability to communicate so quickly and effortlessly are at the heart of the field of psycholinguistics. **Psycholinguistics**, is an interdisciplinary field that examines how people use language to communicate ideas. Psycholinguists focus not only on the processes that allow us to produce or comprehend language, but also on the key principles that govern the social norms of naturalistic conversation.

In this chapter, we focus on language comprehension. Language production and related topics are covered in Chapter 10. In the first section of this chapter, we cover some basic facts about language, and review some general terminological definitions that will be used throughout Chapters 9 and 10. We then consider some historical events that shaped the field of psycholinguistics as it exists today.

Relevant Terminology and Background on Language

Psycholinguists have developed a specialized vocabulary for language terms. We define these terms now because they will be used frequently throughout the remaining portion of this chapter.

A **phoneme** (pronounced "*foe*-neem") is the basic unit of spoken language, such as the sounds *a*, *k*, and *th*. The English language has about 40 phonemes (Mayer, 2004; Traxler, 2012). If you change just one phoneme in a word, you change the meaning of that word (Harley, 2008). For example, *kiss* has a very different meaning from *hiss*.

In contrast, a **morpheme** (pronounced "*more*-feem") is the basic unit of meaning. For example, the word *reactivated* actually contains four morphemes: *re-*, *active*, *-ate*, and *-ed*. Each of those segments conveys meaning. Many morphemes can stand on their own (like *giraffe*). In contrast, some morphemes must be attached to other morphemes in order to convey their meaning. For instance, *re-* indicates a repeated action. As you might guess, the term **morphology** refers to the study of morphemes; morphology therefore examines how we create words by combining morphemes.

Another major component of psycholinguistics is syntax. **Syntax** refers to the grammatical rules that govern how we organize words into sentences (Owens, 2001; Harley, 2008). A more inclusive and familiar term, **grammar**, encompasses both morphology and syntax; it therefore examines both word structure and sentence structure (Evans & Green, 2006).

Semantics is the area of psycholinguistics that examines the meanings of words and sentences (Carroll, 2004). A related term, **semantic memory**, refers to our organized knowledge about the world. We have discussed semantic memory throughout earlier chapters of this book, but especially in Chapter 8. Language allows us to access information stored in our semantic memories. Indeed, this stored knowledge is a driving force in our ability to use language.

Pragmatics—another important term—refers to our knowledge of the social rules that underlie language use; pragmatics takes into account the listener's perspective (Bardovi-Harlig, 2010; Harley, 2008). For example, think about how you would define the word *syntax* to a 12-year-old child, as opposed to a college classmate. Pragmatics is the discipline within linguistics that focuses most on social interactions (Holtgraves, 2010). Pragmatics is an especially important topic when we consider the production of language (Chapter 10), but pragmatic factors also influence comprehension.

Basic Facts About Human Language

The productivity of language is unlimited. For example, consider the number of 20-word sentences that you could potentially generate in the English language. You would need about 10,000,000,000,000 years—or 2,000 times the age of the earth—to say them all (Miller, 1967; Pinker, 1993). And, your ability to speak and comprehend language is based on many large pools of knowledge about language. For example, the ~40 phonemes in English can be combined to form roughly 200,000 words. And, as we discussed in Chapter 8, the average North American vocabulary size spans somewhere between 20,000 to 100,000 words (Baddeley et al., 2009; Saffran & Schwartz, 2003).

The ability to communicate using language represents one of the most complex cognitive processes in which humans engage. To illustrate this point, be sure that you have tried Demonstration 9.1.

Through completing Demonstration 9.1, you will realize that your ability to understand language is dependent upon every cognitive process that was discussed in Chapters 2–8.

The scientific study of language use and understanding is even more complex once one appreciates the amount of linguistic diversity expressed by the world's languages. Linguists estimate that about 7,000 languages are currently spoken throughout the world. If your own first language is English, your ideas about language are probably English-centered. In fact, many people don't realize that languages can work in many different ways until they have studied a foreign language.

Different languages do things differently. In English, word meaning does not depend on the relative pitch of the syllables in a word. However, in Mandarin Chinese, *ma* means "mother" when the word is

Demonstration 9.1 | How Other Cognitive Processes Contribute to Language

Look below at the list of chapters you have read so far. For each chapter, list at least one topic that is connected to language. The answers appear at the end of this chapter.

Chapter 2: Visual and Auditory Recognition

Chapter 3: Attention and Consciousness

Chapter 4: Working Memory

Chapter 5: Long-Term Memory

Chapter 6: Memory Strategies and Metacognition

Chapter 7: Mental Imagery and Cognitive Maps

Chapter 8: General Knowledge

spoken at a single pitch. In contrast, *ma* means "horse" when spoken in a tone that initially falls and then rises (Field, 2004). A child can create a yes–no question in English by using a rising intonation, such as "I going outside?" However, young children in Finland cannot use this option, because Finnish does not use this method for asking a question (Harley, 2008).

As another example of cross-linguistic differences, Sesotho—a language spoken in southern Africa—uses the passive voice more than English does (Bornkessel & Schlesewsky, 2006). Also, you probably know at least one European language in which the nouns have a grammatical gender, even though English nouns do not.

In summary, languages differ widely from one another on numerous dimensions (Share, 2008; Tomasello, 2003). Thus, the challenge facing a psycholinguist is to derive theories of language comprehension and production that can account for patterns of language processing in any of the world's languages.

A Brief History of Psycholinguistics

Let's consider some highlights in the history of psycholinguistics. Early philosophers in Greece and India debated the nature of language (Chomsky, 2000). Centuries later, both Wilhelm Wundt and William James also speculated about our impressive abilities in this area (Carroll, 2004; Levelt, 1998).

However, the current discipline of psycholinguistics can be traced to the 1960s, when psycholinguists began to test whether psychological research could support the theories of a linguist named Noam Chomsky (Harley, 2008; McKoon & Ratcliff, 1998). Chomsky is arguably the most influential theorist in 20th-century linguistics (N. Smith, 2000). We'll briefly consider Chomsky's theory, the reactions to his theory, and a more recent approach to psycholinguistics that emphasizes meaning.

Chomsky's Approach

People usually think of a sentence as an orderly sequence of words that are lined up in a row on a sheet of paper. Noam Chomsky (1957) created great enthusiasm among psychologists and linguists, because he proposed that there is more to a sentence than meets the eye (or the ear). Although Chomsky addressed many key components of language, his most influential work was on syntax. In fact, Chomsky's approach to syntax contributed to the decline of behaviorism. The behaviorists emphasized the *observable* aspects of linguistic behavior. They also argued that basic behaviorist theories of learning could explain how people communicate in the linguistic modality. But, as Chomsky pointed out, consider the sentence:

> Colorless green ideas sleep furiously.

What does this sentence mean? Unless you're being highly metaphorical, your answer is likely to be "That sentence doesn't make any sense." But, is this sentence grammatical? If you are a native English speaker, you are likely to answer "yes." Unless you have taken a linguistics class before, it's highly unlikely that you have ever seen this sentence. But, somehow, you still know it has grammatical properties that adhere to the grammatical rules of English. This demonstration, Chomsky argued, is evidence that knowledge of grammar can exist independently of semantic knowledge. It also demonstrates that grammatical rules can be applied to the analysis of a sentence that has never been seen, and thus, which a person has had no chance to learn. Indeed, Chomsky argued that instead of learning about grammatical rules, knowledge of grammar is something that people are born with. That is, he argued that we have an inborn understanding of the abstract principles that govern linguistic structure. As a result, children do not need to learn the basic, generalizable concepts that are universal to all languages (Chomsky, 2006; Field, 2004). This observation gained a great amount of traction. Indeed, it contributed to the shift away from behaviorist doctrine and toward a focus on the role of stored knowledge and internal processes in the study of human thought and behavior.

Of course, Chomsky argued, children need to learn many superficial characteristics of the language spoken in their community. For instance, children in Spanish-speaking communities will need to learn the difference between *ser* and *estar*. Spanish linguistic space is carved up somewhat differently from that of English, where children learn only one form of the verb *to be*. Still, Chomsky argues that all children have an inborn language ability. This ability allows them to produce and understand sentences they have never heard before (Chomsky, 2006).

In addition, Chomsky (1957, 2006) pointed out the difference between the deep structure and the surface structure of a sentence. The **surface structure** is represented by the words that are actually spoken or written. In contrast, the **deep structure** is the underlying, more abstract meaning of a sentence (Garnham, 2005; Harley, 2008). People use **transformational rules** to convert deep structure into a surface structure that they can speak or write.

Two sentences may have very different surface structures, but very similar deep structures. For example, consider these two sentences: (1) "Sara threw the ball" and (2) "The ball was thrown by Sara."

Notice how these two surface structures differ. None of the words occupy the same position in both sentences. In addition, three of the words in the second sentence do not even appear in the first sentence. However, "deep down," speakers of English feel that the sentences have identical core meanings (Harley, 2008). In fact, 40 minutes after seeing a sentence such as, "The ball was thrown by Sara," people are likely to report that they had seen a semantically similar sentence, such as "Sara threw the ball" (Radvansky, 2008).

Chomsky (1957, 2006) also pointed out that two sentences may have identical surface structures but very different deep structures; these are called **ambiguous sentences**. For example, I live near the small town of York in rural upstate New York. One day I drove past the announcement board outside the York Town Hall, and the message said: "POP CAN DRIVE." I was puzzled: Whose father is now allowed to drive, and why had he previously been prohibited from driving? To be honest, the alternate meaning (focusing on a community fundraiser) did not occur to me until the next day.

We will discuss ambiguity in more detail later in the chapter. However, context usually helps us resolve these ambiguities. Here are three additional ambiguous sentences, each of which has two meanings:

The shooting of the hunters was terrible.

They are cooking apples.

The lamb is too hot to eat.

See if you can determine the two or more meanings embedded in each sentence.

Reactions to Chomsky's Theory

Initially, psychologists responded enthusiastically to Chomsky's ideas about grammar (Bock et al., 1992; Williams, 2005). However, some of the research did not support his theories. For example, the research failed to support Chomsky's prediction that people would take longer to process sentences that required numerous transformations (Carroll, 2004). Furthermore, Chomsky's theories argue that all languages share the same universal patterns of grammar (Juffs, 2010). However, research has demonstrated that many non-European languages do not show these patterns (Everett, 2005, 2007; Tomasello, 2008).

Chomsky's more recent theories have provided more sophisticated linguistic analyses. For example, Chomsky later proposed that young language learners make only a limited number of hypotheses about the structure of their language (Chomsky, 1981, 2000; Harley, 2001). Chomsky's newer approach also emphasizes the information contained in the individual words of a sentence. For example, the word *discuss* conveys information about the word's meaning. However, *discuss* also specifies the requirement that *discuss* must include a noun later in the phrase (Ratner & Gleason, 1993). Consider a sentence that begins, "Rita discussed. . . ." The remainder of the sentence must include a noun phrase such as ". . . the novel."

Psycholinguistic Theories that Emphasize Meaning

Beginning in the 1970s, many psychologists became discouraged with Chomsky's emphasis on the grammatical aspects of language (Herriot, 2004). These psychologists began to develop theories that emphasized the human mind and semantics, rather than the structure of language (Tanenhaus, 2004; Treiman et al., 2003). In contrast to Chomsky's theory, the cognitive approaches argue that grammar and other aspects in language are interconnected with other cognitive processes such as attention, working memory, and world knowledge stored in our long-term memory. Proponents of cognitive approaches argue that we are skilled at language because our powerful brains can master many cognitive tasks. Language is just one

---

Demonstration 9.2 | **The Cognitive-Functional Approach to Language**

Imagine that you recently saw an event in which a man named Fred broke a window, using a rock. A person who was not present at the time asks you for information about the event. For each of the sentences below, construct a question that this person might have asked that would prompt you to reply with that specific wording for the sentence. For example, the brief response, "Fred broke the window" might have been prompted by the question, "What did Fred do?"

1. Fred broke the window with a rock.
2. The rock broke the window.
3. The window got broken.
4. It was Fred who broke the window.
5. It was the window that Fred broke.
6. What Fred did was to break the window.

Source: Based on Tomasello, 1998a, p. 483.

---

of those tasks, and it has the same status as tasks such as memory and problem solving (Carroll, 2004; Christiansen & Chater, 2008; Tomasello, 2003).

There are many types (and flavors) of cognitive approaches to language, each with their own foundations and emphases. No one theory is right or wrong. Instead, they each attempt to account for different components of language as they relate to cognition more generally.

Several psychologists have developed theories that emphasize meaning (e.g., Kintsch, 1998; Newmeyer, 1998; Tomasello, 2003). Here, we will briefly describe one representative theory, the cognitive-functional approach to language. The **cognitive-functional approach** emphasizes that the function of human language in everyday life is to communicate meaning to other individuals. As this name suggests, the cognitive-functional approach also emphasizes that our cognitive processes—such as attention and memory—are intertwined with our language comprehension and language production.

Michael Tomasello (2003, 2008) points out that young children have extremely powerful cognitive and social-learning skills. During the years when they are mastering language, they will hear several million adult sentences. As we'll see in Chapter 13, children analyze these sentences, and they use flexible strategies to create increasingly complex language (Kuhl, 2006).

Tomasello (1998a, 1998b) also emphasizes that adults use language strategically. Specifically, we structure our language in order to focus our listeners' attention on the information we want to emphasize. Be sure to try Demonstration 9.2, which illustrates a concrete example of the cognitive-functional approach (Tomasello, 1998a).

Notice how each of the sentences in this demonstration emphasizes a somewhat different perspective on the same event. Therefore, each of your questions will focus on a slightly different point of view. In short, the cognitive-functional approach argues that people can use language creatively, in order to communicate subtle shades of meaning.

On-line Sentence Comprehension

In the previous section, we discussed the complexities associated with accurately interpreting an incoming linguistic signal. In this section, we discuss factors that influence the degree of difficulty you may experience while comprehending a sentence. As we discuss this topic, we also consider different methodologies used by psycholinguists to examine how people comprehend language.

Negation and the passive voice

Consider a sentence in a newspaper column that reads: "Georgia rejected a challenge to a referendum that had barred same-sex unions." This sentence requires several readings to understand the basic message: Will the state of Georgia prohibit same-sex unions? The research on negatives is clear-cut. If a sentence contains a negative word, such as *no* or *not*, or an implied negative (such as rejected), the sentence almost always requires more processing time than a similar, affirmative sentence (Williams, 2005).

In a classic study, Clark and Chase (1972) showed a picture of a star above a plus sign. Then, they asked people to verify statements, such as the following:

Star is above plus.[+][*]

The participants responded quickly in this case, when the sentence was affirmative. They responded more slowly if the sentence contained the negative form isn't (e.g., "Plus isn't above star"). The participants also made fewer errors with affirmative sentences than with negative sentences. Notice that these results are consistent with Theme 3 of this textbook: Our cognitive processes handle positive information better than negative information.

As you can imagine, readers' understanding decreases as the number of negative terms increases. For example, people perform only slightly better than chance when they judge sentences such as, "Few people strongly deny that the world is not flat" (Sherman, 1976, p. 145). These findings have clear-cut practical applications in numerous areas, such as education, advertisements, and surveys (Kifner, 1994; Lenzner et al., 2010).

Many grammatical components of a sentence also influence the ease with which a sentence is processed. As we discussed earlier, Chomsky (1957, 1965) pointed out that the active and passive forms of a sentence may differ in their surface structure, even though they have similar deep structures. However, the active form is more basic. For example, we need to add extra words if we want to create the passive form of a sentence. As you might guess, the English language uses the active voice much more often than the passive voice (Fiedler et al., 2011).

The active form is also easier to understand (Christianson et al., 2010; Garnham, 2005; Williams, 2005). For example, Ferreira and her coauthors (2002) asked participants to determine whether each sentence in a series was plausible. The participants were highly accurate in responding "No" to sentences in the active voice, such as, "The man bit the dog." In contrast, their accuracy dropped to about 75% when the same sentences were converted to the passive voice, for example, "The dog was bitten by the man" (p. 13). Factors such as education level and whether or not an individual is a native English speaker influence the rate of accuracy on passive sentences. Both native English speakers and individuals with higher levels of education tend to have more accurate interpretations of sentences in the passive voice (Dąbrowska, 2012; Street & Dąbrowska, 2010).

Syntactic Complexity

When you're faced with the task of interpreting language as it unfolds in real-time—say, during a typical conversation—you do not have the luxury of taking time out to stop and think about the meaning of a sentence. Instead, a great deal of research indicates that language comprehension occurs incrementally. **Incremental interpretation** refers to the observation that when processing language, we do not wait until an entire sentence is spoken (or read) before making judgments about what it means. Language unfolds bit-by-bit over time. Thus, the systems responsible for language comprehension provide you with the ability to continuously update your interpretation of an incoming message as you encounter new bits of information.

As discussed above, sentences with negatives and sentences worded in the passive voice cause processing difficulty. Sentences in the passive voice are indeed more grammatically complex than those in the active voice. In fact, syntactic complexity is a strong determinant of the amount of processing difficulty an individual will experience during language processing.

Consider sentences (A) and (B) below.

A. The reporter that attacked the senator admitted the error.

B. The reporter that the senator attacked admitted the error.

The sentences contain the exact same words and are both grammatical. But, the words are ordered differently, and thus the sentences have different grammatical structures. Do you get the sense that the second sentence is more difficult than the first sentence?

Most sentences in English follow a specific pattern. The subject of the sentence usually comes first, followed by the verb, which is in turn often followed by an object. In (A), for example, *The reporter* is the subject of the sentence, *that attacked the senator* provides the reader with more information about the subject (such that, in reality, the subject of the sentence is *The reporter that attacked the senator*). The main verb of the sentence is *admitted*, and *the error* is the object of the verb. In other words, the grammar of sentence A is consistent with the grammar of most sentences in English.

In sentence (B), however, notice that *the senator* comes after the reporter. But, when you read the first part of the sentence (before the main verb *admitted*) it should be clear that the senator is the one performing the action—it serves as the subject of the sentence. The words *The reporter* that appear at the beginning of the sentence signal the object of the verb *attacked*. Thus, in the phrase *The reporter that the senator attacked*, an object comes before a subject. And, all of this happens before you even encounter the main verb (*admitted*). Sentence (B) is indeed more grammatically complex than sentence (A).

How does one determine where in a sentence people experience processing difficulty? Many researchers in linguistics and psycholinguistics use **on-line language processing measures**. On-line measures of sentence processing are designed to gauge the amount of difficulty one experiences as the linguistic signal unfolds unit-by-unit over time. Thus, researchers can assess which components of a sentence are more difficult to process than others.

One example of an on-line language processing measure is the **self-paced reading task** (Just et al., 1982). In this task, participants see a series of dashes on a screen that mask each word of the sentence, as in (1) below. The sentence unfolds word by word as participants press the spacebar on a keyboard (as in 2–10 below).

1. --- -------- ---- -------- --- ------- -------- --- -----

2. The -------- ---- -------- --- ------- -------- --- -----

3. --- reporter ---- -------- --- ------- -------- --- -----

4. --- -------- that -------- --- ------- -------- --- -----

5. --- -------- ---- attacked --- ------- -------- --- -----

6. --- -------- ---- -------- the ------- -------- --- -----

7. --- -------- ---- -------- --- senator -------- --- -----

8. --- -------- ---- -------- --- ------- admitted --- -----

9. --- -------- ---- -------- --- ------- -------- the -----

10. --- -------- ---- -------- --- ------- -------- --- error.

The amount of time that the participant looks at each word is measured in milliseconds. Thus, researchers have the ability to graph average Reaction Times (often abbreviated as RTs) elicited by each word or region of a sentence. These RTs provide an index of processing difficulty—or, the amount of effort required to process a newly encountered word given the previous words in a sentence. Higher RTs on a word or region of a sentence indicate higher processing difficulty.

Many self-paced reading experiments indicate that participants exhibit particular difficulty when processing sentences like (B) relative to sentences like (A). More specifically, RTs are higher on the main verb of the sentence (*admitted*) in sentences like (B) relative to (A) (Just & Carpenter, 1992; King & Just, 1991). This increase in RTs reflects the difficulty that readers experienced with the complex syntactic construction inherent to sentences like (B).

Multiple explanations exist for this observation. Some have argued, for example, that many complex grammatical structures are more difficult to process because they are more demanding on an individual's memory resources (Caplan & Waters, 1999; Gibson, 1998; Gordon et al., 2004; Just & Carpenter, 1992; King & Just, 1991; Lewis, Vasishth, & VanDyke, 2006; Swets et al., 2008). The object-before-subject ordering of the phrase before the main verb requires that an individual hold the object in memory while processing the subject. By the time that the participant encounters the main verb, their memory resources are taxed, and they thus experience processing difficulty when trying to interpret the sentence.

An alternative explanation for grammatical complexity effects is based not on memory, per se, but instead on practice. It turns out the sentences that are very grammatically complex—such as sentence (B)—are also very infrequent in language. As you read or during daily conversations, you rarely encounter them. Thus, you have less practice with them.

In fact, research shows that when people are given lots of practice with sentences that contain complex grammar, they get much better at processing them (MacDonald & Christiansen, 2002; Reali & Christiansen, 2007; Wells et al., 2009).

Currently, psycholinguists are conducting research to determine how memory demands and practice through language experience work together to explain why sentences with complex grammar are particularly difficult to understand.

Lexical and Syntactic Ambiguity

Suppose that you saw the following headline in your local newspaper: "Swedish Queen Silvia hurt evading New York photographer." You might initially wonder why the queen of a relatively peaceful nation would try to harm a photographer. Later, you realize that Queen Silvia was actually the person who was hurt. As you might imagine, sentences are often more difficult to understand if they contain an ambiguous word or an ambiguous sentence structure (Harley, 2010; Lenzner et al., 2010).

Lexical Ambiguity

Let's first consider how people deal with **lexical ambiguity**. Lexical ambiguity refers to the fact that a single word can have multiple meanings. Indeed, many words in English qualify as lexically ambiguous. For example, think about the word *bank*. It has at least two meanings: a financial institution or the area of land that runs along rivers. People typically pause longer when they are processing an ambiguous word in cases where the word appears alone—for example, when a lexical ambiguity is encountered while completing a questionnaire (Lenzner et al., 2010).

But, what happens when an ambiguous word appears in a sentence? For example, consider this sentence:

> *Pat took the money to the bank.*

Although *bank* has multiple meanings, you're probably not too likely to consider the "river bank" interpretation of it.

Psychologists have proposed many theories to explain how listeners process an ambiguous word (Traxler, 2012; Van Orden & Kloos, 2005). Current research supports the following explanation. People are likely to more strongly consider one particular meaning of a lexically ambiguous word (1) if that meaning is more common than the alternate meaning, and (2) if it appears in a sentence, and the rest of the sentence is consistent with that meaning (Hurley, 2011; Morris & Binder, 2001; Sereno et al., 2003).

In the example sentence, the "financial institution" interpretation of *bank* would receive the most activation. After all, this is the most common interpretation of *bank*, and the context of money also suggests this meaning. Some minimal activation may also build up for other meanings of *bank* (as in *riverbank* and *blood bank*). However, just a fraction of a second later, these alternative meanings are suppressed, and they are no longer active (Fetzer & Oishi, 2011; Traxler, 2012).

Syntactic Ambiguity

So far, we have considered ambiguous words. However, sometimes a sentence structure is ambiguous, especially if it contains no punctuation, a phenomenon often referred to as a **syntactic ambiguity** (Rayner et al., 2003). Try reading this sentence:

1. "After the Martians invaded the town that the city bordered was evacuated." (Tabor & Hutchins, 2004, p. 432).

Did you find yourself reading along quickly, and then you were suddenly lost? You had wandered down the wrong path. An ambiguous sentence is especially difficult if you read a long string of words that seem consistent with your initial interpretation. In contrast, you can correct your initial mistake more quickly with a shorter string of words. If Sentence 1 is still unclear, see if you can understand this shorter sentence:

2. "After the Martians invaded the town was evacuated." (Tabor & Hutchins, 2004, p. 432).

Now that you are familiar with the concept of ambiguity, try Demonstration 9.3.

As Rueckl (1995) observes, "Ambiguity is a fact of life. Happily, the human cognitive system is well-equipped to deal with it" (p. 501). But, one question that psycholinguists have pondered for many decades involves how our cognitive systems cope so readily with the processing of syntactically ambiguous sentences.

Part of the answer to this question involves the use of context. Indeed, readers and listeners rely heavily on context when making decisions about the intended meaning of a sentence containing a syntactic ambiguity. For example, imagine hearing the following sentence:

Put the apple on the towel . . .

When you hear *on the towel*, a syntactic ambiguity arises. The phrase *on the towel* could signal the destination for a putting action. Under this interpretation, one would pick up an apple and place it on a towel.

Demonstration 9.3 | ## Searching for Ambiguous Language

Ambiguity occurs quite often in the English language (Rodd et al., 2002). Perhaps the best source of ambiguous words and phrases is newspaper headlines. After all, these headlines must be very brief, so they often omit the auxiliary words that could resolve the ambiguity. Here are some actual newspaper headlines that colleagues, students, and I have seen:

1. "Eye drops off shelf"
2. "Squad helps dog bite victims"
3. "British left waffles on Falkland Islands"
4. "Bombing Rocks Hope for Peace"
5. "Clinton wins budget; more lies ahead"
6. "Miners refuse to work after death"
7. "Kids make nutritious snacks"
8. "Local high school dropouts cut in half"
9. "Iraqi head seeks arms"
10. "Oklahoma is among places where tongues are disappearing"

For the next few weeks, search the newspapers you normally read, looking for ambiguous headlines. Try to notice whether your first interpretation of the ambiguous portion was a correct or incorrect understanding of the phrase. If you find any particularly intriguing ambiguities, please send them to me! My (Thomas Farmer) address is: California State University—Fullerton, Department of Psychology, P.O. Box 6846, Fullerton, CA 92834.

But, *on the towel* could also serve as a modifier, thus providing more information about *the apple*. Under this interpretation, the use of *on the towel* could serve the grammatical purpose of signaling to a listener which of multiple apples to pick up. This interpretation would be akin to the sentence *Put the apple that's on the towel* . . . The inclusion of the "that" eliminates the ambiguity. In English, however, words such as *that* are optional, and often dropped.

Thus, as someone encounters *on the towel*, an ambiguity arises. In other words, two possible grammatical interpretations of the sentence become possible. Now, consider the following sentence:

Put the apple <u>on the towel</u> in the box.

Upon encountering *in the box*, the ambiguity goes away. This extra information signals to the listener that the modifier interpretation is the correct interpretation. Without any context, listeners may have a hard time deciding which interpretation is correct, at least until they hear the final phrase *in the box*. But, do listeners always experience difficulty when encountering a syntactic ambiguity? Or, could contextual information reduce this potential difficulty.

Michael Tanenhaus and colleagues (Tanenhaus, Spivey-Knowlton, Eberhard, & Sedivy, 1995) developed an innovative way to answer this question. Examine Figure 9.1, below.

Tanenhaus and colleagues asked participants to listen to sentences containing syntactic ambiguities, such as *Put the apple on the towel in the box*. Participants heard these ambiguous sentences, however, while viewing visual scenes, such as those on the left- or right-hand panels of Figure 9.1. Interestingly, these researchers used a piece of equipment called an **eye-tracker**. An eye-tracker is a special camera that allows one to determine precisely where in a visual display someone is looking. Thus, the researchers were able to measure patterns of eye movements around the visual displays as participants heard ambiguous sentences.

FIGURE 9.1
The one-apple (left) and two-apple (right) visual contexts utilized by Tanenhaus et al. (1995).

Notice that the visual display on the left-hand side of Figure 9.1 contains an apple, an empty towel, a box, and a flower. The flower served as a distractor object and was not important for the goals of the experiment.

When participants heard *Put the apple on the towel in the box* while viewing this display, they looked at the apple first. Upon hearing *on the towel*, they exhibited a strong tendency to look at the empty towel. Upon hearing *in the box*, however, they looked at the apple again before picking it up and placing it in the box. Thus, looks to the empty towel signaled that participants were initially entertaining the "putting destination" interpretation of the ambiguous phrase *on the towel*.

The pattern of eye movements was much different, however, when participants heard *Put the apple on the towel in the box* while viewing visual scenes such as the one depicted on the right side of Figure 9.1. Notice that in this image, there are two apples. One apple is already on a towel and the other is on a napkin. When participants heard *Put the apple*, they looked back and forth between the two apples. In this condition, however, they almost never looked at the empty towel at all. And, when they finally heard *in the box*, they still picked up the apple that was already on the towel and placed it in the box. In this condition, the lack of looks to the empty towel means that participants did not consider the "putting destination" interpretation of *on the towel* given this two-apple context. Instead, they preferred the modifier interpretation.

To summarize the results:

1. Upon hearing *on the towel* in the one-apple condition, participants looked at the empty towel in the display. This means that they were considering *on the towel* as the destination for the putting action.

2. In the two-apple condition, upon hearing *The apple*, participants looked back and forth between the two apples. Upon hearing *on the towel*, however, they almost never looked at the empty towel. Instead, they looked at the apple that was already sitting on the towel before picking it up and moving it. This pattern of looks indicates that participants did not really consider the same interpretation of *on the towel* as they did in the one-apple condition. Instead, they interpreted the phrase as providing more information about the apple, as if to provide an answer to the question of which apple they were going to have to move.

The differences in patterns of looking across the two different visual contexts constituted a fascinating discovery. This experiment demonstrated that context could exert an early influence on how one interpreted the grammar of a sentence. More importantly, however, these results demonstrated that context effects during language comprehension were not limited to linguistic context. Instead, nonlinguistic context—such as the properties of one's external visual world—could fundamentally change the way that one interprets language. Think for a moment about what this observation really means. The same linguistic signal may be interpreted in vastly different ways based on the environment in which it is heard.

Context is a driving force in the way that we interpret language as we encounter it in the real world. Indeed, this experiment helped usher in a new wave of research that sought to uncover which types of information people utilize when comprehending language.

Good-Enough Processing

Psychologists have written literally thousands of articles about language comprehension. In general, these articles show that people typically manage to read quite rapidly. For example, read the following sentence:

The authorities needed to decide where to bury the survivors.

When most people read this sentence quickly, they initially think that it sounds perfectly fine. If you read the sentence more carefully, you will notice the problem. Fernanda Ferreira and her colleagues suggest that we process language by using the "good-enough approach" (e.g., Christianson et al., 2010; Ferreira et al., 2002; Swets et al., 2008). According to **the good-enough approach** to language comprehension, we frequently process only part of a sentence. Consistent with Theme 2, this strategy usually works well for us. For instance, when I first saw this sentence about the burial, it seemed perfectly correct. However, I had not paid sufficient attention to bottom-up processing, so I missed the meaning of the specific word "survivors."

Ferreira and her coauthors emphasize that people usually do not work hard to create the most accurate, detailed interpretation of every sentence they read or hear. As Chapter 2 pointed out, college students can read normal sentences at the rate of about 255 words per minute (Rayner et al., 2006). If you paused to think about the true meaning of every word in every sentence, you would never complete any reading assignment! In Chapters 7 and 8, we discussed the term **heuristic**, which is a general rule that is typically accurate. Notice that the good-enough approach to language comprehension is another example of a heuristic (Ferreira & Patson, 2007). In many cases, we read quickly, and we try to grasp the general meaning of a sentence. Our knowledge of language typically leads us to an accurate interpretation. However, this strategy can sometimes lead to errors in language comprehension (Harley, 2008).

Brain and Language

The self-paced reading and eye-tracking methodologies discussed in the previous section produce indices of behavior that provide valuable insight into how people process language as they intercept it. Many psycholinguists, however, also rely on cognitive neuroscientific testing methods to examine the neural systems that contribute to language processing. **Neurolinguistics** is the discipline that examines the underlying neurological structures and systems that support language and language-related processes. Research in this area has become increasingly active in recent years, and it demonstrates that the neurological basis of language is very complicated. In this section, we first consider reasons for this complexity. We then review some early evidence that implicated specific parts of cortex in language production and comprehension, followed by more recent work on the topic. Next, we investigate the validity of the claim that language engages only one hemisphere of the brain. We conclude this section with a discussion of an exciting recent discovery regarding the neural underpinnings of language processing.

General Considerations

For many decades, researchers have speculated about the specific brain locations associated with language (Kanwisher, 2010). As you saw in Chapter 2, researchers have identified a specific region that many argue is responsible for face recognition. This region is the inferotemporal cortex, located in the lower portion of the temporal cortex (often referred to as the "fusiform face area").

Neurolinguists have been less successful in identifying specific areas responsible for a variety of language comprehension tasks. This difficulty makes sense, however, once one considers the scope of language use. As we noted earlier, the ability to successfully comprehend or produce language involves multiple cognitive processes, such as attention, working memory, long-term memory, motor systems, and perceptual systems. All of these systems must work together in intricate ways as one produces or comprehends language. Thus, linguistic knowledge (i.e., knowledge about grammar, words, and sounds of language) and linguistic processing abilities are vastly distributed throughout the brain. The distributed nature of language is a key contributor to the difficulties associated with specifying the neural underpinnings of language.

During the past decade, researchers have increasingly used the fMRI technique to investigate language in humans. As we noted in Chapter 1, **functional magnetic resonance imaging (fMRI)** is based on the principle that oxygen-rich blood is an index of brain activity in a particular region (Cacioppo & Berntson, 2005b; Kalat, 2009; Mason & Just, 2006).

As we will see later in this section, fMRI research has substantially increased our understanding of language in the brain. But, even this technique has its limitations. Kanwisher (2010) notes, for example, that there are large individual differences in the anatomical structure of the language-related regions of the brain. Suppose that researchers give 40 participants a very specific language task, and these researchers gather fMRI data while the participants perform this task. The researchers then combine these data, across all participants. Unfortunately, the individual differences are so strong that the fMRIs would not be able to identify one specific region of the brain that performs a specific language task.

Additionally, the processes that give rise to our language comprehension and production abilities occur on a very fast timescale. The fMRI technique cannot scan fast enough to provide us with fine-grained time-based information about when a particular brain region responds to some property of a linguistic signal. And yet, this time-based information is crucial to a complete understanding of how the brain processes language.

To address issues related to the time-course of language processing, researchers have instead relied on cognitive neuroscientific testing methods such as the **event-related potential (ERP) technique** (Delong et al., 2005; Federmeier & Kutas, 2001; Federmeier, 2007; Molinaro et al., 2013; Penolazzi et al., 2007; van Berkum et al., 2005). This and related techniques record very brief fluctuations in the brain's electrical activity elicited by the presentation of a linguistic stimulus.

Although the ERP technique provides precise information about the time-course of linguistic processing events, it does not provide reliable information about where in the brain a process occurs. Thus, no one methodology can provide all of the information necessary to form a complete understanding of the cognitive neuroscience of language. Instead, those who conduct research on the topic are charged with the daunting task of trying to piece together evidence from multiple methodologies in their pursuit of a neurally-grounded theory of on-line language processing. Keep these complexities in mind as you read the remainder of this section.

Aphasia

Before the advent of fancy neuroimaging equipment, researchers interested in the relationship between neural systems and cognitive processes relied on evidence gathered by examining the effects of brain damage. Indeed, neurolinguistic investigations began in the 1800s, when early researchers studied individuals who had language disorders. In fact, before the early 1970s, almost all the scientific information about neurolinguistics was based on people with aphasia. A person with **aphasia** has difficulty communicating, typically as a result of damage to the brain caused by a stroke or a tumor (Gazzaniga et al., 2009; Saffran & Schwartz, 2003).

Damage to two areas of the brain—identified in Figure 9.2—seem to be especially important for language-related processes.

Broca's area is located toward the front of the brain, and usually in the left hemisphere (in an area called the left inferior frontal gyrus, or LIFG). Damage to **Broca's area** typically leads to hesitant speech that primarily uses isolated words and short phrases (Dick et al., 2001; Gazzaniga et al., 2009). For example, one person with Broca's aphasia tried to describe the circumstances of his stroke:

Alright. . .Uh. . .stroke and uh. . .I. . .huh tawanna guy. . .h. . .h. . .hot tub and. . .And the. . .two days when uh. . .Hos. . .uh. . .huh hospital and uh. . .amet. . .am. . .ambulance. (Dick et al., 2001, p. 760)

Broca's aphasia is primarily characterized by an expressive-language deficit—or trouble producing language. These symptoms make sense. Broca's area is located in the vicinity of brain areas known to contribute to motor movement. To produce speech, you must move your lips and tongue. Therefore, it makes sense that these individuals have trouble with speech production.

However, people with Broca's aphasia may also have some trouble with language comprehension (Dick et al., 2001; Martin & Wu, 2005). For example, they may be unable understand the difference between "He showed her baby the pictures" and "He showed her the baby pictures" (Jackendoff, 1994, p. 149).

A second area involved in language processing is known as Wernicke's area. Wernicke's area is located toward the middle side of the brain. ("Wernicke" is pronounced either "*Ver*-nih-kee" or "*Wer*-nih-kee.")

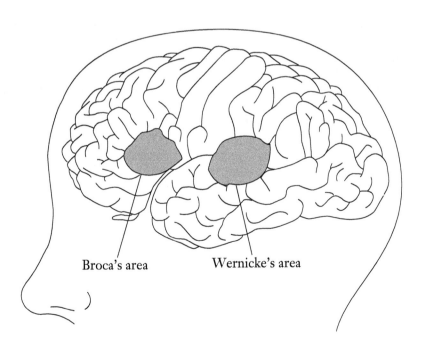

Broca's area   Wernicke's area

FIGURE 9.2 Broca's area and Wernicke's area: Two regions of the brain that are commonly associated with aphasia.

Damage to **Wernicke's area** typically produces serious difficulties understanding language (Gazzaniga et al., 2009; Harley, 2001). In fact, people with **Wernicke's aphasia** often have such severe problems with language comprehension that they cannot understand basic instructions such as, "Point to the telephone" or "Show me the picture of the watch."

However, many people with Wernicke's aphasia also have problems with language production. Specifically, their spoken language is often wordy and confused. They usually have relatively few pauses, compared to someone with Broca's aphasia (Gazzaniga et al., 2009; Harley, 2001). Here's how a person with Wernicke's aphasia tried to describe the circumstances of his stroke:

> *It just suddenly had a feffert and all the feffort had gone with it. It even stepped my horn. They took them from earth you know. They make my favorite nine to severed and now I'm a been habed by the uh stam of fortment of my annulment which is now forever. (Dick et al., 2001, p. 761)*

Revisiting Broca's Area

The basic information about Broca's aphasia and Wernicke's aphasia has been known for over a century. Originally, researchers argued that damage to Broca's area resulted in language production deficits. Damage to Wernicke's area, on the other hand, resulted to comprehension deficits. However, as we discussed above, this distinction turned out to be too simplistic. Both groups of aphasiacs tend to demonstrate difficulties in both comprehension and production-related processes. In fact, researchers have now shown that these two kinds of aphasia are much more similar than people had once believed (Gazzaniga et al., 2009; Harley, 2008). Additionally, it is important to keep in mind that studies involving brain-damaged patients are complicated by the fact that disorder-producing brain damage rarely occurs in exactly the same location across multiple individuals—even if they present with similar symptoms or are diagnosed with the same disorder. This reality makes it particularly difficult to reliably match symptom profiles to specific neural substrates using the brain lesion methodology.

The role of Broca's area in language processing, however, continues to be the focus of much debate. Indeed, clinicians note that individuals with Broca's aphasia often omit grammatical function words (such as, "the", "a", "an"), and often fail to produce words with the correct morphology. For example, they often omit the *+ing* from words like *running* that is necessary to signal the present progressive tense in English. (The present progressive tense is used to convey that an event is ongoing, as in the *The dogs are running through the streets*). These and similar observations led to the hypothesis that Broca's area is important for grammatical processing, grammatical operations, and the learning of grammar (Friederici, 2002; Musso et al., 2003). Thus, perhaps one of the reasons that individuals with Broca's aphasia exhibit production and some comprehension difficulties is that they have deficiencies in syntactic knowledge or in syntactic processing abilities.

It turns out, however, that Broca's area also appears to be involved in the processing of many types of stimuli, such as music (Koelsch, 2000), gestures that are associated with speech (Skipper et al., 2007), and some types of imagery (Binkofski et al., 2000; Just et al., 2004). Additionally, damage to Broca's area does not always lead to grammatical problems (Dick et al., 2001). These observations, taken together, suggest that Broca's area may not be responsible for language-specific processes, but instead may be involved in more general cognitive processes.

Novick, Trueswell, & Thompson-Schill (2005), for example, acknowledged that in fMRI experiments, Broca's area is often activated in many language-related tasks. They also noted, however, one very important general point about language. Whenever someone comprehends language, representational conflict always exists, and it exists at every level of the linguistic signal. For example, upon hearing the word *bank*, multiple meanings become possible. Or, in relation to syntax, there are often multiple possible syntactic interpretations of an unfolding linguistic signal, as we discussed in the previous section. Even when someone hears the sound *p*, it may, under some circumstances, sound more like a *b*.

This observation suggests that when someone uses language, there are always multiple possible representations that receive consideration (and thus, are activated). In order to arrive at the successful interpretation of an incoming signal or to produce the correct words and sounds when speaking, it is thus necessary to reduce activation associated with the incorrect possibility. Doing so allows the correct possibility to be the one that the system ultimately entertains.

Thus, these authors argue that the part of cortex historically referred to as Broca's area is not an area specific to language or grammar. Instead, it is part of an attention network (the Executive Attention Network, as discussed in Chapter 3). In relation to language, they argue that this network is responsible for helping the brain inhibit incorrect productions or interpretations of linguistic input. This inhibition process allows the language system to more quickly access the correct information.

If you read Chapter 3, this attention-based account of Broca's area may remind you of the Stroop effect. In the **Stroop effect**, people take a long time to name the ink color of a word when that color is used in printing an incongruent word. For example, if the printed word BLUE appears in red ink, people often need more time to say "red" than when the word BLUE appears in blue ink. Thus, on the incongruent trials, conflict is introduced (between the word for the ink color and the printed word). Broca's area, Novick et al. argue, helps you inhibit the incorrect word (the printed word), thus increasing the ease and likelihood that you will say the correct word.

In related work, January, Trueswell, and Thompson-Schill (2009) demonstrated that Broca's area was active both when participants completed the Stroop task and when individuals had to process sentences containing syntactic ambiguities. This result provides further support for the role of Broca's area in resolving conflict when it is present (see also Novick et al., 2010).

The research by Novick and colleagues thus suggests that Broca's area is not an area of cortex that is responsible for grammatical- or otherwise language-specific processes. Instead, it is part of a general attentional system that engages when representational conflict arises, and thus, when one must choose a correct interpretation or response.

But, the manner in which one chooses to interpret the results of fMRI experiments depends upon both the task that participants performed in the fMRI machine, and on how one chooses to analyze the large amount of data produced by the fMRI technique.

For example, several researchers at Massachusetts Institute of Technology have devised a new technique, called the **language-localizer task**, which compensates for the problem of individual differences in brain size that we discussed at the beginning of this section. Fedorenko, Behr, and Kanwisher (2012) placed participants in an fMRI scanner and asked them to perform several relatively complex language tasks that lasted 10 to 15 minutes. The researchers then gathered fMRI data during this period, and this information allowed them to create a "linguistic map" that applied only to this specific person.

Later, the researchers tested each person on a variety of language and nonlanguage tests. Then, they tried to figure out whether certain parts of each person's brain might respond only to language tasks. Using this technique, Fedorenko, Behr, and Kanwisher (2012) were able to identify specific regions of the left frontal lobe that responded only to language tasks, but not to other kinds of cognitive tasks such as performing mathematical problems or using spatial working memory. In further research using this approach, Fedorenko, Nieto-Castañón, and Kanwisher (2012) were able to locate portions of the left hemisphere (including portions of Broca's area) that appear to process specific linguistic information. For example, one location responded more vigorously to sentences than to "nonwords" consisting of jumbled letters.

Thus, some evidence exists that Broca's area may contribute to processes and operations that are specific to language. Indeed, the debate about whether or not all (or even a portion) of Broca's area is responsible for general cognitive processes (such as attention) or language-specific processes is very much an open debate. A recent paper by both Fedorenko and Thompson-Schill (2014), authors from opposing sides of the debate, highlights the complexities associated with resolving this and related issues. Clearly, further research will be necessary to resolve debates about the role of Broca's area in language processing.

Hemispheric Specialization

Earlier in this section, we noted that the early researchers examined people with aphasia. These scientists also noticed that individuals with speech disorders typically had more severe damage in the left hemisphere of the brain, rather than the right hemisphere. During the mid-1900s, researchers began a more systematic study of lateralization. **Lateralization** means that each hemisphere of the brain has somewhat different functions.

If you've read about lateralization in a popular magazine or website—rather than an academic resource—you may have seen a statement such as, "Language is localized in the left hemisphere of the brain." However, this statement is too strong. Yes, most neurolinguistic studies find greater activation in the left hemisphere than in the right (Borst et al., 2011; Gazzaniga et al., 2009; Traxler, 2012). Still, for about 5% of right-handers and about 50% of left-handers, language is either localized in the right hemisphere or is processed equally by both hemispheres (Kinsbourne, 1998).

The left hemisphere does indeed perform most of the work in language processing, for the majority of people. The left hemisphere is especially active during speech perception; it quickly selects the most likely interpretation of a sound (Gernsbacher & Kaschak, 2003; Scott, 2005). It is also very active when you are reading or trying to understand the meaning of a statement (Gernsbacher & Kaschak, 2003). In addition, high-imagery sentences activate the left hemisphere (Just et al., 2004).

For many years, people thought that the right hemisphere did not play a major role in language processing. However, we now know that this hemisphere does perform some tasks. For example, the right hemisphere is active when you are paying attention to the emotional tone of a message (Gernsbacher & Kaschak, 2003; Vingerhoets et al., 2003). It also plays a role in appreciating humor (Harley, 2010). In general, then, the right hemisphere is responsible for more abstract language tasks (Gernsbacher & Kaschak, 2003).

The left and right hemispheres often work together on tasks such as interpreting subtle word meanings, resolving ambiguities, and combining the meaning of several sentences (Beeman et al., 2000; Grodzinsky, 2006). For example, suppose that you are one of the majority of individuals for whom the left hemisphere is dominant for language. Imagine that you see the following ambiguous message, which I once spotted on a bumper sticker:

SOMETIMES I WAKE UP GRUMPY.

OTHER TIMES I LET HIM SLEEP IN.

On seeing the phrase, "SOMETIMES I WAKE UP GRUMPY," your left hemisphere is more active in constructing a meaning in which GRUMPY refers to "I" (i.e., the owner of the car). After reading the next sentence, "OTHER TIMES I LET HIM SLEEP IN," your right hemisphere appears to be more engaged when you search for a less obvious interpretation, in which GRUMPY refers to another person. Fortunately, for people who have normal brain functions, both hemispheres work together in a complementary fashion (Gazzaniga et al., 2009). Now, try Demonstration 9.4 before you read further.

Our discussion of hemispheric specialization has emphasized that the right hemisphere plays an important role in language comprehension, even though the left hemisphere receives most of the publicity. Morton Ann Gernsbacher and David Robertson (2005) provide a good example of the subtlety of right-hemisphere processing. Specifically, they created several sets of sentences, such as those shown in Demonstration 9.4.

As Gernsbacher and Robertson emphasize, when a series of sentences uses the word "The," these sentences seem to create a cohesive story in which the grandmother, the child, and other family members are

---

| *Demonstration 9.4* | Reading Two Sets of Sentences |

A. Read the following set of sentences:

A grandmother sat at a table.

A young child played in a backyard.

A mother talked on a telephone.

A husband drove a tractor.

A grandchild walked up to a door.

A little boy pouted and acted bored.

A grandmother promised to bake cookies.

A wife looked out at a field.

A family was worried about some crops.

B. Now read the following set of sentences:

The grandmother sat at a table.

The young child played in a backyard.

The mother talked on a telephone.

The husband drove a tractor.

The grandchild walked up to a door.

The little boy pouted and acted bored.

The grandmother promised to bake cookies.

The wife looked out at a field.

The family was worried about some crops.

Now answer this question: The first set and the second set differ only with respect to the first word in each sentence. However, did you have a general feeling that the two sets differed in the overall meaning that they conveyed?

Source: Gernsbacher, M. A., & Robertson, D. A. (2005). Watching the brain comprehend discourse. In A. F. Healy (Ed.), *Experimental cognitive psychology and its applications* (pp. 157–167). Washington, DC: American Psychological Association.

connected with each other. In contrast, the string of sentences with the word "A" seems disconnected; the characters don't seem like a cohesive unit. Impressively, the right hemisphere manages to respond differently to connected language than to disconnected language.

The Mirror System

A relatively recent topic in neurolinguistics focuses on the *mirror system*. The **mirror system** is a network involving the brain's motor cortex. Many argue that neurons in motor-related areas of the brain display special properties. These *mirror neurons* are activated both when you watch someone perform an action and when you perform the action yourself (Gallese et al., 2011; Gazzaniga et al., 2009; Glenberg, 2011a). This concept was initially reported by Giacomo Rizzolatti and his colleagues (Rizzolatti & Craighero, 2009; Rizzolatti et al., 1996). These researchers recorded the responses of single neurons in the motor cortex of several monkeys, as they watched a researcher breaking open a peanut; this was an action that the monkeys had frequently done. Surprisingly, each monkey's neurons responded vigorously to this particular action. In fact, these responses were very similar to the response pattern when the monkeys *themselves* broke open a peanut!

Additional research focuses on the mirror system in humans. For example, Calvo-Merino and her colleagues (2005) gathered fMRI data for individuals who were experts in classical ballet, while they watched (a) videos of classical ballet and (b) videos of a Brazilian form of martial arts, called *capoeira*. Their fMRIs showed significantly greater activation in the motor-cortex areas relevant to ballet movements, and relatively little activation in the areas relevant to capoeira. In contrast, individuals who were experts in capoeira showed the reverse activation pattern. In other words, experts can grasp meaning by *watching* another person, when they have fully developed the appropriate motor "vocabulary."

Rizzolatti and Craighero (2009) discuss another important point. Language is not limited to spoken and written messages; physical actions are also important. Specifically, these authors emphasize that sound-based language is *not* the only way that people can communicate with one another. They emphasize that sign language, based on gestures, represents a fully structured system of communication.

At this point, you might wonder how the topic of mirror neurons might be relevant to your own language. Neurolinguists do not agree about the details of this process (Gallese et al., 2011; Glenberg, 2011b). However, it appears that communication goes beyond hearing auditory stimuli and reading written material, because mirror neurons also play a role in language comprehension (Glenberg, 2011a, 2011b). Mirror neurons may be especially active when we try to listen to someone talking in a noisy setting—a setting where we really need assistance (Glenberg, 2011b). Apparently, we can also comprehend messages from the actions of other people.

In summary, due to the complexity of the problem and to methodological limitations, neurolinguists still have a long distance to travel. But, we are slowly starting to understand basic facts about the coordinated brain regions that allow us to produce and understand language.

Reading

Reading seems so simple to most adults that we forget how challenging the task is for most children, as well as for some adults (Traxler, 2012). Take a minute to think about the impressive variety of cognitive tasks you perform when reading a paragraph like this one. Reading requires you to use many cognitive processes that we have discussed in previous chapters (think back to Demonstration 9.1 and see how your responses may change when considering reading).

Despite the complexity of the reading process, however, adults typically don't think about the cognitive effort that is required when we read (Gorrell, 1999). For example, we can silently identify an isolated word in about 200 milliseconds, which is 1/5 of a second. In addition, we manage to read quickly, typically at the rate of about 255 words per minute (Rayner et al., 2006). Consistent with Theme 2, reading is remarkably efficient and accurate.

Here's an additional reason to admire your reading skills: In English, we do not have a one-to-one correspondence between letters of the alphabet and speech sounds. These irregular pronunciations make English more challenging than languages with consistent pronunciations, such as Spanish or Russian (Rayner et al., 2003; Traxler, 2012). In fact, try Demonstration 9.5 to illustrate this point. As we noted at the beginning of this chapter, most of the psycholinguistic research examines people whose language is

| Demonstration 9.5 | Noticing that Letters of the Alphabet Do Not Have a One-to-One Correspondence with Speech Sounds |

Each of the words below has a somewhat different pronunciation for the two-letter sequence "ea." Read each word aloud and notice the variety of phonemes that can be produced with those two letters.

beauty	deal	react
bread	great	séance
clear	heard	bear
create	knowledgeable	dealt

As you have demonstrated, this two-letter sequence can be pronounced in 12 different ways. Furthermore, each phoneme in the English language can be spelled in a variety of ways. Go back over this list of words and try to think of another word that has a different spelling for that particular sound. For example, the *eau* sound in *beauty* is like the *iew* sound in *view*.

Source: Based on Underwood & Batt, 1996.

English. Furthermore, we cannot generalize this research to Chinese readers, because their language uses symbols to represent complete words (Qu et al., 2011; Rayner et al., 2008; Traxler, 2012).

Let's begin section by comparing written language with spoken language. We will then consider the two pathways we can use when recognizing words. This second section provides you with a background for the final section in this chapter, which examines how we understand larger units of language—such as stories—in both written and spoken language.

Comparing Written and Spoken Language

In Chapter 2, we explored several components of spoken language comprehension. In this section on written language comprehension, we encounter a somewhat different set of challenges. Reading differs in many important ways from the comprehension of spoken language (Ainsworth & Greenberg, 2006; Dahan & Magnuson, 2006; Gaskell, 2009b; Nelson et al., 2005; Saffran & Schwartz, 2003; Traxler, 2012; Treiman & Kessler, 2009):

1. Reading is visual and is spread out across space, whereas speech is auditory and is spread out across time.

2. Readers can control the rate of input, whereas listeners usually cannot.

3. Readers can rescan the written input, whereas listeners must rely much more heavily on their working memory.

4. Readers usually encounter standardized, error-free input, whereas listeners often need to cope with variability, grammatical errors, sloppy pronunciation, and interfering stimuli.

5. Readers can see discrete boundaries between words, whereas listeners often encounter unclear boundaries in spoken language.

6. Readers encounter only the stimuli on a page, whereas listeners encounter both nonverbal cues and auditory cues, such as emphasized words and variations in pace. Researchers are just beginning to appreciate the importance of these additional cues (Glenberg, 2011a, 2011b).

7. Children require elaborate teaching to master some written languages—such as written English—but they learn spoken languages much more easily.

8. Adult readers typically learn new words more quickly when they appear in a written form, rather than a spoken form.

As you can imagine, these eight characteristics of written language have important implications for our cognitive processes. For example, we can consult the words on a page when we want to make sense out of a passage in a book; in contrast, we seldom have this luxury with spoken language.

Despite the differences between written and spoken language, however, both processes require us to understand words and appreciate the meaning of sentences. In fact, the research on individual differences highlights the similarity between the two comprehension processes. For adults, scores on reading comprehension tests are strongly correlated with scores on oral comprehension tests; typically, the correlation is about +.90 (Rayner et al., 2001).

Reading Words: Theoretical Approaches

So far, our examination of reading in this textbook has emphasized how we identify alphabetical letters (Chapter 2), how our saccadic eye movements scan a line of text (Chapter 3), and how working memory plays a role in reading (Chapter 4). Now we'll address an important question about reading: How do we look at a pattern of letters and actually recognize that word? For example, how do you manage to look at the 11 letters in the fourth word in this paragraph and realize that it says *examination*? How about a word with an unusual spelling, such as *choir* or *aisle*?

Researchers have debated whether readers actually "sound out" words while reading a passage. Some researchers conclude that readers always sound out the words, and other researchers conclude that they never sound them out. In the current era, the debate is mostly resolved (Coltheart, 2005). You have probably completed enough psychology courses to guess the answer: Sometimes readers sound out the words, and sometimes they do not. In fact, the **dual-route approach to reading** specifies that skilled readers employ both (1) a direct-access route and (2) an indirect-access route (Coltheart, 2005; Harley, 2008; Treiman & Kessler, 2009).

1. Sometimes you read a word by a **direct-access route**; you recognize this word *directly* through vision, without "sounding out" the words. For example, you look at the word *choir* and the visual pattern is sufficient to access the word and its meaning. You are especially likely to use direct access if the word has an irregular spelling and cannot be "sounded out"—for example, the words *one* or *through*.

2. Other times, you read a word by an **indirect-access route**; as soon as you see a word, you translate the ink marks on the page into some form of sound, before you can access a word and its meaning (Harley, 2010; Treiman et al., 2003). You are especially likely to use indirect access if the word has a regular spelling and can be sounded out—for example, the words *ten* and *cabinet*.

Notice why this second kind of process is indirect. According to this explanation, you must go through the intermediate step of converting the visual stimulus into a phonological (sound) stimulus. Think about whether you seem to use this intermediate step when you read. As you read this sentence, for example, do you have a speech-like representation of the words? You probably don't actually move your lips or say the words out loud when you read. But do you seem to have an auditory image for some of the words that you are reading? Let's now discuss the research.

The Direct-Access Route

A classic study demonstrates that people can recognize a word visually, without paying attention to the sound of that word. Bradshaw and Nettleton (1974) showed people pairs of words that were similar in spelling, but different in sound, such as *mown–down*, *horse–worse*, and *quart–part*. In one condition, the participants were instructed to read the first word silently and then pronounce the second word out loud. Now, if they had been translating the first member of a pair into sound, the sound of *mown* would interfere with pronouncing *down* out loud.

However, the results showed that the participants experienced no hesitation in pronouncing the second word. This finding—and other similar studies—suggests that we can go directly to the word; we do not silently pronounce every word during normal reading (Coltheart, 2005).

The Indirect-Access Route

Now let's shift to some research that supports the indirect-access approach. Many studies suggest that we often translate visual stimuli into sound during reading (Coltheart, 2005). Furthermore, the sound coding may enhance working memory, providing an auditory image to assist the visual image during reading (Harley, 2008; Rayner et al., 2003).

A study by Luo and his coauthors (1998) provides evidence for the indirect-access approach in college students. These researchers instructed the students to read a series of pairs of words and decide whether the two words were related or unrelated in meaning. A typical pair in the experimental condition was

| *Demonstration 9.6* | Reading Tongue Twisters |

Read each of the following tongue twisters silently to yourself:

1. The seasick sailor staggered as he zigzagged sideways.
2. Peter Piper picked a peck of pickled peppers. A peck of pickled peppers Peter Piper picked.
3. She sells seashells down by the seashore.
4. Congressional caucus questions controversial CIA-Contra-Crack connection.
5. Sheila and Celia slyly shave the cedar shingle splinter.

Now be honest. Could you "hear" yourself pronouncing these words as you were reading? Did you have to read them more slowly than other sentences in this book?

LION–BARE. As you know, the word BARE sounds the same as the word BEAR, which is indeed semantically related to LION.

The students frequently made errors on these pairs, because they incorrectly judged the two words as being semantically related. This error pattern suggests that they were silently pronouncing the word pairs when they made the judgments. In contrast, they made relatively few errors on control-condition word pairs, such as LION–BEAN. In this word pair, the second word looked like the word BEAR, although it did not sound the same.

Word sounds may be especially important when children begin to read. Numerous studies demonstrate that children with high phonological awareness have superior reading skills. That is, the children who are able to identify sound patterns in a word also receive higher scores on reading achievement tests (Levy, 1999; Share, 2008; Wagner & Stanovich, 1996; Ziegler et al., 2010).

Perhaps, you're thinking that children may need to translate the printed word into sound. After all, children even move their lips when they read, but adults usually do not. Try Demonstration 9.6 and see whether you change your mind. Adults read "tongue twisters" very slowly, which indicates that—at least in some circumstances—they are indeed translating the printed words into sounds (Harley, 2008; Keller et al., 2003).

As we noted earlier, the dual-route approach has the definite advantage of flexibility. This approach argues that the characteristics of the reading material determine whether access is indirect or direct. For instance, you may use indirect access the first time you see a long, uncommon word; you may use direct access for a common word (Bernstein & Carr, 1996; Harley, 2008).

The dual-route approach also argues that people's reading skills can determine whether they use indirect or direct access. Beginning readers would be especially likely to sound out the words, using indirect access. More advanced young readers would be especially likely to recognize the words directly from print. Adults also vary in their reading styles. People who are relatively poor readers primarily use indirect access, although better readers may be more likely to rely on direct access (Harley, 2008; Jared et al., 1999).

At present, the dual-route approach seems like a useful compromise. The dual-route approach is also consistent with brain-imaging research (Harley, 2008; Jobard et al., 2003). Readers can identify words either directly or indirectly, depending on their own reading skills and the characteristics of the text.

Implications for Teaching Reading to Children

We noted earlier that English is an "outlier language," because of the numerous irregular pronunciations for English words. Unfortunately, irregular pronunciation has important implications for teaching children to read in English.

Consider, for example, a study that measured children's reading skills in 14 different European countries; this standardized test was administered at the end of first grade. Languages such as Spanish and German have extremely predictable pronunciation, and children learning to read these languages had close to 100% reading-accuracy scores on a standardized test. Languages such as French and Portuguese are less predictable, and these children achieved reading-accuracy scores of about 80%. English was the least predictable of the languages, and these children achieved reading-accuracy scores of only 34% (Seymour et al., 2003; Ziegler et al., 2010).

So, how should children be taught to read English? For many years, reading teachers and reading researchers debated about the most effective way to teach reading. In general, those who favored the direct-access approach also favored the whole-word approach. The **whole-word approach** argues that readers can directly connect the written word—as an entire unit—with the meaning that this word represents (Rayner et al., 2001).

The whole-word approach emphasizes that the correspondence between the written and spoken codes in English is notoriously complex, as we saw in Demonstration 9.5. Supporters therefore argue that children should not learn to emphasize the way a word sounds. Instead, the whole-word approach encourages children to identify a word in terms of its context within a sentence. One problem, however, is that even skilled adult readers achieve only about 25% accuracy when they look at an incomplete sentence and guess which word is missing (Perfetti, 2003; Snow & Juel, 2005).

In contrast, people who favor the indirect-access hypothesis typically support the phonics approach. The **phonics approach** states that readers recognize words by trying to pronounce the individual letters in the word. If your grade school teachers told you to "sound it out" when you stumbled on a new word, they championed the phonics approach.

The phonics approach argues that speech sound is a necessary intermediate step in reading. It also emphasizes developing young children's awareness of phonemes. According to the research, it's clear that phonics training helps children who have reading problems (Harley, 2008; Perfetti, 2011; Traxler, 2012). For example, a meta-analysis of 34 studies showed that phonological training programs had a major impact on children's reading skills (Bus & van IJzendoorn, 1999).

For many years, the debate between the whole-word supporters and the phonics supporters was feverish (McGuinness, 2004; Traxler, 2012). In the current decade, however, most educators and researchers support some form of a compromise: Children should be taught to use phonics to access the pronunciation of a word; they should also use context as a backup to confirm their initial hypothesis.

Furthermore, educators typically favor some components of an approach called the whole-language approach (as opposed to the whole-*word* approach). According to the **whole-language approach**, reading instruction should emphasize meaning, and it should be enjoyable, to increase children's enthusiasm about learning to read. Children should read interesting stories and experiment with writing before they are expert spellers. They also need to use reading throughout their classroom experiences (Luria, 2006; McGuinness, 2004; Snow & Juel, 2005). A wealth of research demonstrates that the more experience an individual possesses with written language (especially in their earlier years), the better their reading and other language processes are likely to be later in life (Harm, McCandliss, & Seidenberg, 2003; Montag & MacDonald, 2015; Stanovich, 1986; 1988). An additional benefit of increased practice—and thus, of increased reading ability—is this: When children improve their reading skills, they also improve their ability in mathematics (Glenberg et al., 2011).

In addition, children need to have books that they can read outside of school, because even children with limited reading skills can benefit from leisure reading (Mol & Bus, 2011). There's even a social benefit when children have early experiences with reading. Specifically, preschool children become more socially aware, when their parents read to them. According to research by Raymond Mar and his colleagues, children whose parents frequently read to them are especially aware of other people's thoughts and feelings (Mar, 2011; Mar et al., 2010). This effect held true, even after the researchers eliminated several other potential explanations.

Before we leave this section on basic reading, however, we need to emphasize an important point. Our discussion assumes that children and adults have had the opportunity to learn how to read. In Canada and the United States, about 98% of adults achieve basic literacy (Luria, 2006). However, the reality is that more than 800 million adults throughout the world are illiterate. Approximately two-thirds of these individuals are women. Clearly, a person who cannot read will face tremendous disadvantages with respect to employment, health care, and everyday communication. Thus, there exists a critical need for increases in government funding on topics related to reading processes, literacy, and language learning.

Discourse Comprehension

We began this chapter with an overview of the nature of language; that overview considered both linguistic theory and the biological basis of language. Then, we explored basic reading processes. You'll notice that all these topics focus on the way we process small units of language, such as a phoneme, a letter, a word, or an isolated sentence. In your daily life, however, you are continually processing **discourse**, that is, interrelated units of language that are larger than a sentence (Traxler, 2012; Treiman et al., 2003). You listen to the news on the radio, you hear a friend telling a story, you follow the instructions for assembling a bookcase. . .and you read your cognitive psychology textbook.

In Chapter 8, we considered Frederic Bartlett's (1932) research, which focused on these larger linguistic units. Specifically, Bartlett demonstrated that people's recall of stories becomes more consistent with their schemas after a long delay. However, for the next four decades, psychologists and linguists primarily studied words and isolated sentences. In fact, the topic of discourse processing was not revived until the mid-1970s (Butcher & Kintsch, 2003; Graesser et al., 2003). Fortunately, research on discourse comprehension is now an active topic in psycholinguistics (Lynch, 2010; Traxler, 2012).

So far in this chapter, we've emphasized how context can help us understand sounds, letters, and words. Now we'll see that context also helps us comprehend larger linguistic units. As Chapter 8 pointed out, general background knowledge and expertise help to facilitate our conceptual understanding. Research on discourse comprehension also emphasizes the importance of scripts, schemas, and expertise (e.g., Harley, 2008; Mayer, 2004; Zwaan & Rapp, 2006).

At all levels of language comprehension, we see additional evidence of Theme 5. That is, the processing of the physical stimuli (bottom-up processing) interacts with the context provided by our expectations and previous knowledge (top-down processing). This interaction is especially prominent when we form an integrated, cohesive representation of the text and when we draw **inferences**, which are conclusions that go beyond the isolated phrase or sentence (Harley, 2010).

Our exploration of discourse comprehension in this section focuses on the following selected topics: (1) forming an integrated representation of the text, (2) drawing inferences during reading, and (3) teaching metacomprehension skills.

Forming an Integrated Representation of the Text

Reading comprehension is much more complicated than simply combining words and phrases. Readers must also gather information together and remember the various concepts, so that this information is both cohesive and memorable (Traxler, 2012; Zwaan & Rapp, 2006). In everyday life, we try to figure out the mental state of other people in our lives, a concept called **theory of mind** (Mar, 2011). For example, we might say, "Judith is usually very kind, but she really was mean to Kathy. Maybe she is worried about her final exams." Similarly, readers often try to figure out the mental states of the people they read about in a story or a book.

Listeners—as well as readers—form integrated representations when they hear spoken language. They also remember information and draw inferences when they are listening (e.g., Butcher & Kintsch, 2003; Lynch, 2010; Marslen-Wilson et al., 1993; Poole & Samraj, 2010). However, almost all the research examines discourse processing during reading, rather than during listening.

The research on reading shows that skilled readers frequently organize and integrate information into a cohesive story (Zwaan & Rapp, 2006). For example, look back at Demonstration 9.4 and the description of Gernsbacher and Robertson's (2005) study. These researchers demonstrated that readers are attuned to subtle linguistic evidence. Specifically, readers realize that a series of sentences forms a cohesive story if all the sentences begin with the word *the*, but not when the sentences begin with *a*.

Furthermore, when we form a cohesive representation, we often construct a mental model of the material we are reading (Long et al., 2006; Traxler, 2012; Zwaan & Rapp, 2006). In Chapter 7, for example, we saw that readers create cognitive maps, based on a written description of various locations.

Readers also construct internal representations that include descriptions of the characters in a story. This descriptive information may include the characters' occupations, relationships, emotional states, personal traits, goals, and actions (Carpenter et al., 1995; Trabasso et al., 1995). In fact, by middle school, some children can monitor events in the stories they are reading, noting twists in a story's plot or a character's unusual behaviors (Bohn-Gettler et al., 2011). However, some novelists can strain even an adult reader's working memory and long-term memory. For example, one of the sentences in James Joyce's *Ullyses* is 12,931 words long (Harley, 2010).

Readers often need to maintain these internal representations in long-term memory for many pages of a novel (Butcher & Kintsch, 2003; Gerrig & McKoon, 2001). In addition, readers often make inferences that go beyond the information supplied by the writer. Let's consider this topic in more detail.

| *Demonstration 9.7* | Reading a Passage of Text |

Read the following passage, and notice whether it seems to flow smoothly and logically:

1. Dick had a week's vacation due
2. and he wanted to go to a place
3. where he could swim and sunbathe.
4. He bought a book on travel.
5. Then he looked at the ads
6. in the travel section of the Sunday newspaper.
7. He went to his local travel agent
8. and asked for a plane ticket to Alaska.
9. He paid for it with his charge card.

Source: Huitema, J. S., Dopkins, S., Klin, C. M., & Myers, J. L. (1993). Connecting goals and actions during reading. *Journal of Experimental Psychology: Learning, Memory, and Cognition*, **19**, 1054.

Drawing Inferences During Reading

One of my favorite novels is called *The Kite Runner*. The novel follows two young boys growing up in Kabul, Afghanistan. Amir, the protagonist, is the son of a wealthy, influential man named Baba. Amir's friend, Hassan, lives nearby in the home of Baba's servant. Readers do not need to have a sophisticated knowledge about either social class in Afghanistan or the series of tragic political wars in this country. Even before we finish the first chapter, we know that the friendship between Amir and Hassan must have an unhappy ending. Whenever we read, we activate important mental processes by making inferences that go beyond the information presented on the printed page.

When we make an inference during reading, we use our world knowledge in order to access information that is not explicitly stated in a written passage (Harley, 2008; Lea et al., 2005; Traxler, 2012). We discussed inferences in Chapter 8 in connection with the influence of schemas on memory. Inferences are also important in reading. People combine the information they are reading, together with the information presented in a passage. Then, they draw a reasonable conclusion based on that combination. Consistent with Theme 1, people are active information processors.

Let's explore several issues that researchers have explored, in connection with inferences during reading. First, we'll consider the constructionist view of inferences. Then, we'll discuss factors that encourage inferences. Our final topic is higher-level inferences. Before you read further, try Demonstration 9.7.

The Constructionist View of Inferences

According to the **constructionist view of inferences**, readers usually draw inferences about the causes of events and the relationships between events. When you read a novel, for instance, you construct inferences about a character's motivations, personality, and emotions. You develop expectations about new plot developments, about the writer's point of view, and so forth (Sternberg & Ben-Zeev, 2001; Zwaan & Rapp, 2006).

This perspective is called a "constructionist view" because readers actively construct cohesive explanations when they integrate the current information with all the relevant information from the previous parts of the text, as well as their background knowledge (Harley, 2008; Traxler, 2012; Zwaan & Singer, 2003). The constructionist view argues that people typically draw inferences, even when the related topics are separated by several irrelevant paragraphs.

Let's consider a classic study by John Huitema and his coauthors (1993), who studied brief stories like the one you read in Demonstration 9.7. The introductory material in this demonstration led you to believe that Dick will soon be lounging on a sunny beach. You drew this inference on line 3, and this inference is contradicted five lines later, rather than in the very next sentence. The dependent variable here was the amount of time that participants had taken to read the crucial line about Dick's travel destination (line 8).

Huitema and his colleagues (1993) tested four conditions. You saw the far/inconsistent version of the story in Demonstration 9.7. In this version, several lines of text came between the first sentence, which stated the goal, and the inconsistent statement about Alaska. In the near/inconsistent version, the goal and the inconsistent statement were in adjacent sentences. In the far/consistent version, several lines of text

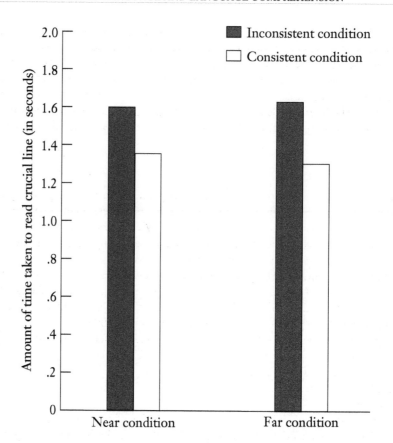

FIGURE 9.3

Amount of time taken to read the crucial line in the study by Huitema and his colleagues (1993), as a function of the amount of separation between the goal and the crucial line and the compatibility between the goal and the crucial line (consistent vs. inconsistent).

Source: Huitema, J. S., Dopkins, S., Klin, C. M., & Myers, J. L. (1993). Connecting goals and actions during reading. *Journal of Experimental Psychology: Learning, Memory, and Cognition, 19,* 1053–1060.

separated the goal and a consistent statement (in which Dick asked for a plane ticket to Florida—a place consistent with swimming). In the near/consistent version, the goal and the consistent statement were in adjacent sentences.

As you can see from Figure 9.3, participants in the *near* condition read the consistent version significantly more quickly than the inconsistent version. This finding is not surprising. However, you'll notice that participants in the *far* condition also read the consistent version significantly more quickly than the inconsistent version in the far condition . . . even though the relevant portions of the task were separated by four intervening lines.

The data from Huitema and his colleagues (1993) support the constructionist view. Readers clearly try to connect material within a text passage, and they consult information stored in long-term memory, in this case, the enthusiasm and sunbathing. During discourse processing, we try to construct a representation of the text that is internally consistent, even when irrelevant material intervenes (Klin et al., 1999; Rayner & Clifton, 2002; Underwood & Batt, 1996).

In other research, readers talked out loud about the text passages that they were reading (Suh & Trabasso, 1993; Trabasso & Suh, 1993). In some of these stories, the main character had an initial goal that was blocked but later fulfilled. About 90% of the participants specifically mentioned the initial goal during their comments about the last line. Suh and Trabasso emphasized that readers create causal inferences in order to integrate discourse and construct a well-organized story.

Factors That Encourage Inferences

Naturally, we do not always draw inferences when we read a passage. For instance, some readers fail to activate information that appeared much earlier in the passage (Harley, 2008; Zwaan & Rapp, 2006). As you might expect, people are more likely to draw inferences if they have a large working-memory capacity (Butcher & Kintsch, 2003; Long et al., 2006). They are also likely to draw inferences if they have excellent metacomprehension skills. These individuals are aware that they need to search for connections between two seemingly unrelated sentences (Ehrlich, 1998; Mayer, 2004).

People are also likely to draw inferences if they have expertise about the topic described in the text (Long et al., 2006). In fact, expertise in an area can compensate for a relatively small working-memory capacity (Butcher & Kintsch, 2003). Other research shows that people are not likely to construct inferences when they are reading scientific texts (Mayer, 2004; Millis & Graesser, 1994).

This part of our discussion has focused on factors that affect inferences, and we have seen that some inferences are more probable than others. In explaining these factors, however, let's recall an important point from Chapter 8: In some cases, we remember our inferences as often as the statements that actually occurred in the text. Our inferences blend with the text, forming a cohesive story. We often retain the gist or general meaning of a passage, forgetting that we constructed some elements that did not actually appear in the story.

Higher-Level Inferences

Researchers are now exploring higher-level inferences, beyond the level of the paragraph (Harley, 2008; Leavitt & Christenfeld, 2011). For example, some genres of books are especially likely to activate different expectations. Fans of the Harry Potter series—and other magical stories—know that they must suspend their everyday schemas. Of course, Hermione can arrange to be in two locations at the exact same time, and of course, Harry can understand conversations between snakes.

One kind of higher-level inference is based on our own preferences about the way we want a story to turn out. Perhaps you've turned the pages of a fast-paced spy novel and mentally shouted to your favorite character, "Watch out!" In fact, the research shows that readers who are involved in a story do develop strong mental preferences for a particular outcome (Rapp & Gerrig, 2006).

These mental preferences can be so strong that they can actually interfere with readers' ability to judge how the story turned out, making us pause as we try to decide whether that unhappy ending really did occur (Gerrig, 1998; Zwaan & Rapp, 2006). You may even find yourself so hopeful about a happy ending you've constructed that you need to read the final sentences several times, trying to convince yourself that the hero or heroine didn't die!

In summary, people often draw inferences when they read. They integrate material into a cohesive unit, and they are puzzled if they encounter something that contradicts the inferences they drew. People are especially likely to draw inferences if they have a large working-memory capacity or expertise. Inferences may be relatively rare in scientific texts and relatively common in novels. In novels, our own preferences may interfere with text comprehension.

Teaching Metacomprehension Skills

Our earlier discussion of reading examined how educators can teach basic reading skills to young children. Let's now briefly consider how educators can teach older students some important metacomprehension skills.

Chapter 6 focused on the general topic of **metacognition**, which is your knowledge about your cognitive processes, as well as your control of these cognitive processes. An important part of metacognition is **metacomprehension**, a term that refers to your thoughts about comprehension.

Most young children do not have the appropriate cognitive skills for metacomprehension; it's challenging enough to read individual words and sentences (Baker, 2005; Griffith & Ruan, 2005). Furthermore, some aspects of children's reading are counterintuitive. For example, doesn't it seem logical that reading skills would improve if children tried to relate the text to nearby photos? Surprisingly, however, pictures actually *reduce* reading skills (Torcasio & Sweller, 2010).

However, older children, teenagers, and adults can think about their reading and listening strategies (Lynch, 2010). For instance, when you read a book, you know that you should think about your relevant background knowledge. In addition, you consider whether you should read every sentence or else skim through the details. You also know that you should monitor whether you understand the material you have just read (Griffith & Ruan, 2005; Perfetti et al., 2005). Furthermore, you sometimes become aware that your mind has wandered away from the material you are reading (Smallwood & Schooler, 2006).

In the past, educators seldom trained students to develop their metacomprehension skills (Randi et al., 2005). However, educators are currently developing some helpful strategies. For instance, teachers can instruct students in middle school to think out loud, so that they can summarize passages, make predictions about possible outcomes, and describe puzzling sections (Israel & Massey, 2005; Schreiber, 2005; Wolfe & Goldman, 2005).

SECTION SUMMARY POINTS

Overview of Psycholinguistics

1. Psycholinguistics is the study of the cognitive processes involved in language production, language comprehension, and naturalistic communication; it is a large and interdisciplinary field.

2. Some of the central concepts in psycholinguistics are the phoneme, the morpheme, morphology, syntax, grammar, semantics, semantic memory, and pragmatics.

3. Many cognitive processes operate simultaneously and in tight-knit coordination during language use; visual and auditory processes, attention, working memory, long-term memory, and mental imagery are all necessary components of language processing.

4. According to Noam Chomsky, (a) language skills are innate in humans, (b) language is separate from other cognitive processes, and (c) the deep structure of a sentence captures its core meaning.

5. Many current psychologists emphasize the meaning of language, rather than linguistic structure. For example, the cognitive-functional approach to language emphasizes that we design our language so that listeners will pay attention to the information we want to emphasize.

On-line Sentence Comprehension

1. Sentences are more difficult to understand if they contain negatives or use the passive voice.

2. Syntactic complexity also influences the ease with which someone can understand a sentence. Sentences with more complex grammar are more difficult to understand.

3. The effects of syntactic complexity may arise as a result of increased memory demands. They may also arise, however, as a result of the fact that grammatically complex sentences are less frequent in language—thus, individuals have less experience with them.

4. Lexical ambiguity arises when one word has multiple possible meanings; in isolation, these words sometimes take longer to process. Sentence context, however, can reduce this effect.

5. Many times, an unfolding sentence may have multiple possible grammatical interpretations; in other words, they are syntactically ambiguous.

6. Context often provides readers and listeners with the ability to arrive at the correct interpretation of an ambiguity. Context does not only have to be linguistic in nature. Instead, even properties of the visual world can influence how one interprets sentences.

Brain and Language

1. Neurolinguistic research on adults with aphasia suggests that damage in Broca's area usually leads to difficulty in producing language, whereas damage in Wernicke's area usually leads to difficulty in understanding language; however, the distinction is not clear-cut.

2. In more recent research, Broca's area has also been shown to be involved in the processing of many different types of stimuli, such as music, and is also active during mental imagery.

3. Very recent research suggests that Broca's area is involved in the executive attention network. It contributes to one's ability to resolve conflict, either in responses or in representations. Work from other groups suggests, however, that a least part of Broca's area is involved in language-specific processes.

4. In general, the left hemisphere performs most components of language processing, such as speech perception and understanding meaning. However, the right hemisphere performs abstract language tasks such as creating a cohesive story.

5. Recent research using fMRIs highlights some specific brain regions in the left hemisphere that are responsible for well-defined language tasks such as distinguishing between sentences and non-words. Also, fMRI research confirms that the right hemisphere processes subtle distinctions in meaning.

6. Recent research on mirror neurons—in the brain's motor cortex—provides information about some nonverbal aspects of communication.

Reading

1. Reading is a challenging cognitive task that differs from understanding spoken language in many respects. For example, readers can control the rate of input and they can rescan the text; furthermore, there are clear-cut boundaries between words.

2. The dual-route approach to reading argues that readers sometimes recognize a word directly from the printed letters (by direct access), and sometimes they convert the printed letters into a phonological code to access the word and its meaning (by indirect access).

3. Skilled adult readers are more likely to use direct access. In contrast, beginning readers and less skilled adult readers are likely to sound out the words and understand meaning by indirect access.

4. According to research conducted in 14 European countries, when children learn to read languages like Spanish and German, they achieve almost perfect reading accuracy on a standardized test by the end of first grade, in contrast to only 34% of children learning to read English.

5. In teaching young students to read, the whole-word approach emphasizes visual recognition of words, whereas the phonics approach emphasizes sounding out the word. Most educators and researchers favor a combination of these approaches.

6. The whole-language approach emphasizes language meaning, as well as integrating reading throughout the curriculum and reading books at home.

7. Children with poor reading skills can benefit from early exposure to reading; another benefit is that preschoolers are more aware of other people's feelings if their parents read to them. Unfortunately, close to one billion adults throughout the world are illiterate.

Discourse Comprehension

1. Psycholinguists are increasingly focusing on discourse processing, or language units that are larger than a sentence.

2. Readers try to form integrated representations of discourse by using subtle cues, mental models, long-term memory, and inferences.

3. According to the constructionist view, people actively draw inferences that connect parts of the text, even though the parts may be widely separated.

4. Inferences are especially likely when people have large working-memory capacity, excellent metacomprehension skills, and expertise in the area. People also draw higher-level inferences, beyond the level of the paragraph.

5. Educators are beginning to emphasize teaching metacomprehension skills to older children and teenagers.

CHAPTER REVIEW QUESTIONS

1. Why is language one of the most impressive human accomplishments? Describe at least six cognitive processes that you are using while you are reading this sentence.

2. According to the discussion of factors affecting comprehension, we have more difficulty understanding a sentence if it is in the passive voice, instead of the active voice. Referring to the cognitive-functional approach, why would we occasionally choose to create a sentence such as, "The window was broken by Fred"?

3. Suppose that you are reading a story in which Sam is described as a "left-brain person." Suggest at least two reasons why this phrase is not consistent with the research.

4. Context is an important concept throughout this chapter. Explain how context is important in (a) processing an ambiguous word, (b) processing a syntactic ambiguity, and (c) background knowledge in understanding discourse.

5. This chapter emphasizes that memory contributes to language comprehension. Using the chapter outline as your guide, specify how both working memory and long-term memory are essential when you try to understand language.

6. Describe the constructionist view of inferences discussed in the last section of this chapter. Think about several kinds of reading tasks you have performed in the last two days. Be sure to include examples other than reading your textbook. Point out how the constructionist perspective would be relevant during each discourse-processing task.

7. Describe the research on metacomprehension skills. How could you apply these strategies to improve your own reading skills for a course other than cognitive psychology?

8. Summarize the parts of this chapter that describe individual differences. How might individual differences also be relevant in other aspects of language comprehension?

9. This chapter discussed both listening and reading. Which processes are similar, and which are different? In preparation for Chapter 10, compare speech production and writing in a similar fashion.

KEYWORDS

psycholinguistics	deep structure	lexical ambiguity	functional magnetic	phonics approach
phoneme	transformational rules	syntactic ambiguity	resonance	whole-language approach
morpheme	ambiguous sentences	eye-tracker	imaging (fMRI)	discourse
morphology	cognitive-functional	neurolinguistics	language-localizer task	inferences
syntax	approach	aphasia	mirror system	theory of mind
grammar	incremental	Broca's area	dual-route approach to	constructionist view of
semantics	interpretation	Broca's aphasia	reading	inferences
semantic memory	on-line language	Wernicke's area	direct-access route	metacognition
pragmatics	processing measures	Wernicke's aphasia	indirect-access route	metacomprehension
surface structure	self-paced reading task	lateralization	whole-word approach	

RECOMMENDED READINGS

Altmann, G. T. (1997). *The ascent of Babel: an exploration of language, mind, and understanding.* Oxford University Press. This book provides a compelling overview of human language, and of psycholinguistics. It is clearly written, highly accessible, and offers an ideal introduction to the cognitive science of language for those who find the topic intriguing. Be on the lookout for an updated second edition that is currently in the works.

Christiansen, M. H. & Chater, N. (2016). *Creating language: Integrating evolution, acquisition, and processing.* Cambridge, MA: MIT Press. This book, to be published at the beginning of 2016, provides a synthetic overview of multiple language-related topics. It focuses on language development across multiple timescales. It addresses theories of language evolution, and highlights the way that progress in the field of language evolution has informed theories of language learning and on-line language processing.

Harley, T. A. (2010). *Talking the talk: Language, psychology and science*. New York: Psychology Press. Trevor Harley wrote this book for a general audience, and it includes wonderful examples of language comprehension, as well as a chapter on animal communication.

Traxler, M. J. (2012). *Introduction to psycholinguistics: Understanding language science*. Chichester, England: John Wiley & Sons. Traxler's

textbook provides an excellent, current background on a variety of topics, including reading, sign language, and cognitive neuroscience. This textbook is ideal for those who possess serious interests in the field of psycholinguistics.

Trueswell, J.C. & Tanenhaus, M.K., (Eds.) (2005). *Processing world-situated language: Bridging the language-as-action and language-as-product traditions*. Cambridge, Mass: MIT Press. This volume is dedicated to psycholinguistic research that has utilized the visual world paradigm, as discussed in the second section of the chapter. It covers cutting-edge research from many subfields of psycholinguistics.

ANSWER TO DEMONSTRATION 9.1

Chapter 2: Visual recognition allows you to see letters and words, and auditory recognition allows you to hear phonemes and words. Chapter 3: Divided attention can permit you to take in information about two simultaneous verbal messages, whereas selective attention encourages you to pay attention to one message and ignore the other; saccadic eye movements are important in reading. Chapter 4: Working memory helps you store the stimuli (either visual or auditory) long enough to process and interpret them. Chapter 5: Long-term memory allows you to retrieve information you processed long ago. Chapter 6:

The tip-of-the-tongue phenomenon means that you will sometimes be unable to access certain words, whereas metacomprehension allows you to determine whether you understand a verbal message. Chapter 7: You create mental models when you process a description about a spatial layout. Chapter 8: Semantic memory stores the meaning of words and the relationships between concepts, whereas schemas and scripts provide background knowledge for processing language. Note: Additional answers are also possible for many of these chapters.

Language II: Language Production and Bilingualism

10

Chapter Introduction

The average North American produces ~16,000 words on a typical day (Mehl et al., 2007), and most of the time, those words are spoken under the assumption that someone else will hear them. Writing is also an act of language production, although instead of moving the mouth, writers convey a message by moving their hands (or, by vigorously moving their thumbs around their smartphone screens as they type a text message). Even when you type a paper for class, your goal is to convey your thoughts and ideas to someone else. Notice that both speaking and writing involve planning a message to convey, correctly ordering the parts of the message, and executing a response. They differ, however, in that speech usually occurs under time pressure. A speaker must keep up with the pace of a fast-moving conversation in order to avoid violating the social norms of communication. Writers on the other hand are usually granted the luxury of having more time to plan and revise before they send a message (either by submitting a paper or hitting the "Send" button on their cell phone).

Here's another feature of language production: Every sentence that you *comprehend* is a sentence that somebody *produced*. Historically, psycholinguists have studied language comprehension more heavily than language production (Costa et al., 2009; Garrett, 2009; Harley, 2008). It's difficult to experimentally manipulate the ideas that an individual wishes to say or write. In contrast, researchers can easily manipulate the text that a person hears or reads (Carroll, 2004). More recently, the fact that humans create the language that other humans must comprehend has motivated psycholinguistic research programs that address the symbiotic relationship between comprehension and production (Chang, Bock, & Dell, 2006; Dell & Chang, 2014; MacDonald, 2013; Pickering & Garrod, 2013).

We begin by examining spoken language, and then we consider written language. Our final topic, bilingualism, employs all four of these skills, thus serving as the ideal topic with which to wrap up our two-chapter overview of psycholinguistics.

Speaking I: Overview of Production Processes

Most of the 16,000 words that we speak on an average day are not spoken in isolation. Instead, they are spoken as we tell stories, chat, quarrel, and talk on the phone, just to name a few examples. Even when we listen to a friend, we produce supportive comments such as "yeah" and "mm hm." Indeed, speaking is one of our most complex cognitive and motor skills (Bock & Griffin, 2000; Dell, 2005).

We begin this first section of the chapter by discussing how we produce an individual word. Then we consider some common speech errors, focusing next on how we produce sentences. We conclude this section by briefly considering how language production proceeds when a speaker attempts to plan and convey a message involving multiple sentences.

Producing a Word

At first glance, word production may not seem particularly remarkable. After all, you simply open your mouth and a word emerges effortlessly. Word production becomes impressive, however, once we analyze the dimensions of the task (Traxler, 2012). As noted in Chapter 9, you can produce about three words each second (Vigliocco & Hartsuiker, 2002). Furthermore, the average college-educated North American has a speaking vocabulary of at least 75,000 words (Wingfield, 1993). We know many words and speak quickly. How are we able to search through the 75,000 words that we know, select the correct one, and articulate it clearly enough for someone else to understand?

Selecting the correct word involves activating the correct grammatical, semantic, and phonological information associated with the word (Meyer & Belke, 2009; Rapp & Goldrick, 2000). As Bock and Griffin (2000) point out, many factors "complicate the journey from mind to mouth" (p. 39). For example, consider the visual world example in Chapter 9 (Figure 9.1). When people are asked to look at a visual scene and describe it, they take roughly 900 milliseconds after fixating an object to initiate the production of the name for the object. Object naming requires precise and tight-knit coordination among visual, linguistic, and motor systems. In less than a second, a person can look at a visual object, recognize it, retrieve the name for it, plan how to say the object's name, and initiate the articulation of it. That's a short amount of time to do a whole lot of processing, an observation that emphasizes the truly impressive nature of our cognitive systems (Themes 2 and 4 of this textbook).

Some researchers argue that speakers retrieve grammatical, semantic, and phonological information of a word at the same time (Damian & Martin, 1999; Saffran & Schwartz, 2003). According to this approach, for example, you look at an apple and simultaneously access the grammatical properties of *apple*, the meaning of *apple*, and the phonemes in the word *apple*. Other researchers argue that we access each kind of information independently, with little interaction among these three components (Ferreira & Slevc, 2009; Meyer & Belke, 2009; Roelofs & Baayen, 2002).

Evidence for the "independent access" perspective comes from Miranda van Turennout and colleagues (1998), who conducted research with Dutch-speaking individuals. Dutch resembles languages such as Spanish, French, and German, in that Dutch nouns have a grammatical gender. These researchers presented pictures of objects and animals, and the participants tried to name the object as quickly as possible.

Using the event-related potential technique, these researchers demonstrated that speakers access the grammatical gender of the word about 40 milliseconds before they access the word's phonological properties. These results suggest that we do not acquire all the different kinds of information at exactly the same moment. Instead, we literally use split-second timing. Given the complexity associated with scientifically investigating language production, however, no clear answers to these types of debates currently exist.

Speech Errors

The content of the speech that most people produce is generally accurate and well formed, an essential ingredient for successful communication. In spontaneous language samples, people make an error less than once every 500 sentences (Dell, Burger, & Svec, 1997; Vigliocco & Hartsuiker, 2002). However, some high-status speakers—including former U.S. presidents—often make speech errors.

Researchers have been particularly interested in the kind of speech errors called slips-of-the-tongue. **Slips-of-the-tongue** are errors in which sounds or entire words are rearranged between two or more different words. These slips of the tongue have historically served as the key piece of evidence used to inform theories of language production (Levelt, 1992). They are informative because they reveal our extensive knowledge about the sounds, structure, and meaning of the language we are speaking (Dell et al., 2008; Traxler, 2012).

Types of Slip-of-the-Tongue Errors

Gary Dell and his coauthors propose that three kinds of slips-of-the-tongue are especially common in English (Dell, 1995; Dell et al., 2008):

1. Sound errors, which occur when sounds in nearby words are exchanged—for example, *snow flurries → flow snurries*.

2. Morpheme errors, which occur when **morphemes** (the smallest meaningful units in language, such as *-ly* or *in-*) are exchanged in nearby words—for example, *self-destruct instruction → self-instruct destruction*.

3. Word errors, which occur when words are exchanged—for example, *writing a letter to my mother → writing a mother to my letter*.

Furthermore, we are likely to create a word (e.g., *leading*), rather than a nonword (e.g., *londing*) when we make a slip-of-the-tongue error (Griffin & Ferreira, 2006; Rapp & Goldrick, 2000). Finally, we seldom create a word that begins with an unlikely letter sequence. For example, English speakers rarely create a slip-of-the-tongue such as *dlorm* when trying to say *dorm* (Dell et al., 2000). These two principles reflect the importance of our knowledge about the English language and Theme 5's emphasis on top-down processing (Dell et al., 2008).

In almost all cases, the errors occur across items from the same category (Clark & Van Der Wege, 2002; Fowler, 2003; Traxler, 2012). For instance, in sound errors, initial consonants interchange with other initial consonants (as in the *flow snurries* example). The pattern of these errors suggests that the words we are currently pronouncing are influenced by both the words we have already spoken and the words we are planning to speak (Dell, Burger, & Svec, 1997).

Explanations for Speech Errors

Dell and his colleagues propose a comprehensive theory for speech errors that is based on the connectionist approach (discussed in Chapter 8) and includes the concept of spreading activation (Dell, 1986, 1995, 2005; Dell, Burger, & Svec, 1997; Dell et al., 1997; Dell et al., 2008). Let us consider a brief overview of how you might produce a sound error. When you are about to speak, each element of the word you are planning to say will activate the sound elements to which it is linked. For example, Figure 10.1 shows how the words in the tongue twister "She sells seashells" might activate each of the six sounds in the last word, *seashells*.

Usually, we utter the sounds that are most highly activated, and usually these sounds are the appropriate ones. However, each sound can be activated by several different words. Notice, for example, that the *sh* sound in the sound-level representation of *seashells* (i.e., *seshelz*) is highly "charged" because it receives activation from the first word in the sentence, *she*, as well as the *sh* in *seashells*.

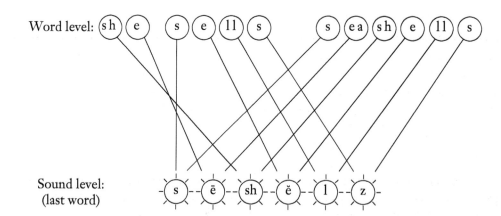

FIGURE 10.1 An example of Dell's model of sound processing in sentence production (simplified). See text for explanation.

Slips-of-the-Tongue

Keep a record of all the slips-of-the-tongue that you either hear or make yourself in the next two days. Classify each slip as a sound error, morpheme error, or word error. Does this slip-of-the-tongue produce an actual word? Also note whether the mistake occurs across items from the same category. Finally, see if you can determine why the mistake occurred, using an analysis similar to Dell's.

As Dell (1995) emphasizes, incorrect items sometimes have activation levels that are just as high as (or higher than) the correct items. For example, in Figure 10.1, the activation level for *sh* is just as high as the level for *s*. By mistake, a speaker may select an incorrect sound in a sentence, such as "She sells sheashells." Try Demonstration 10.1 to determine the form and function of the slips-of-the-tongue that you typically make or hear from other speakers.

Producing a Sentence

Sometimes we produce a word in isolation (such as yelling a profane word when you realize that you've overslept for an exam). Most of the time, however, and especially when you're producing language during naturalistic conversation, words must be combined together to form sentences. Every time you speak a sentence, you must overcome the limits of your memory and attention in order to plan and deliver that sentence (Griffin, 2004; Harley, 2008). Sentence production requires a series of stages (Levelt, 1993). During the first stage, often referred to as message planning, we mentally plan the **gist**, or the overall meaning of the message we intend to generate. In other words, we begin by producing speech in a top-down fashion (Clark & Van Der Wege, 2002; Griffin & Ferreira, 2006). Grammatical encoding happens next (Stage 2). During grammatical encoding, the words necessary to convey the planned message are selected, and the correct morphology is added to the words (such as adding +ing to the end of a verb to convey that an action is ongoing). Additionally, each word must be ordered, one after another, in a way that is consistent with the grammatical rules of the language being spoken. In the third stage, often referred to as *phonological encoding*, we convert the units of the planned utterance into a sound code, and this information is used in order to generate the correct movements of the mouth and vocal tract during the speaking act (Carroll, 2004; Treiman et al., 2003).

There is a great deal of controversy about which aspects of grammatical encoding come first (do we retrieve words first and then order them correctly, or vice versa?). If you continue on to an upper-level course in psycholinguistics, you will likely spend a lot of time addressing these debates. One general observation about sentence production, however, is that the stages typically overlap in time. We often begin to plan the final part of a sentence before we have pronounced the first part of that sentence (Fowler, 2003; Treiman et al., 2003). Under ideal circumstances, a speaker moves rapidly through these stages. For instance, Griffin and Bock (2000) showed college students a simple cartoon. In less than two seconds, the students began to produce a description such as, "The turtle is squirting the mouse with water."

The speech-production process is more complex than most people imagine. For example, you must also plan the **prosody** of an utterance, or the "melody" of its intonation, rhythm, and emphasis (Keating, 2006;

Demonstration 10.2 ‖ The Structure of Narratives

During the next few weeks, try to notice your daily conversations. What happens when someone you know begins to tell a story? First, how does the storyteller announce that she or he is about to begin the narrative? Does the structure of the narrative match the six-part sequence we discussed? Does the storyteller attempt to check whether the listeners have the appropriate background knowledge? What other characteristics do you notice that distinguish this kind of discourse from a normal conversation in which people take turns speaking?

Plack, 2005; Speer & Blodgett, 2006; Watson & Gibson, 2004). A speaker can use prosody to clarify an ambiguous message. For example, read the following two sentences out loud: (a) "What's that ahead in the road?" and (b) "What's that, a head in the road?" (Speer & Blodgett, 2006, p. 505).

Producing Discourse

When we speak, we typically produce **discourse**, or language units that are larger than a sentence (Harley, 2008). Unfortunately, most of the research on language production focuses on isolated words and sentences (Griffin & Ferreira, 2006).

One category of discourse is the **narrative**, the type of discourse in which someone describes a series of actual or fictional events (Griffin & Ferreira, 2006). The events in a narrative are conveyed in a time-related sequence, and they are often emotionally involving (Guerin, 2003; Strömqvist & Verhoeven, 2004).

Storytellers usually have a specific goal that they want to convey. However, they do not completely pre-plan the organization at the beginning of the story (H. H. Clark, 1994). Storytellers typically choose their words carefully, presenting their own actions in a favorable light (Berger, 1997; Edwards, 1997). They also try to make the story more entertaining (Dudukovic et al., 2004; Dudukovic, Marsh & Tversky, 2004).

The format of a narrative is unusual because it allows the speaker to "hold the floor" for an extended period. During that time, the speaker usually conveys six parts of the narrative: (1) a brief overview of the story, (2) a summary of the characters and setting, (3) an action that made the situation complicated, (4) the point of the story, (5) the resolution of the story, and (6) the final signal that the narrative is complete (e.g., ". . . and so thats why I decided that I had to learn Japanese"). These features tend to make the story cohesive and well organized (H. H. Clark, 1994). Now that you know something about the function and structure of narratives, try Demonstration 10.2.

Speaking II: Language Production and Naturalistic Communication

Producing language while speaking is inherently social. Language production researchers must focus not only on the linguistic information contained in the message, but also on many nonlinguistic properties of a communicative act. We next examine the contributions of gestures to the production process, followed by a discussion of the social context in which speech occurs.

Using Gestures: Embodied Cognition

While we speak, we execute elaborate motor movements of the mouth, the tongue, and other parts of the vocal system. But, these aren't the only movements that we make. We often accompany our speech with gestures. **Gestures** are visible movements of any part of your body, which you use to communicate (Hostetter & Alibali, 2008; Jacobs & Garnham, 2007; McNeill, 2005). As Geneviéve Calbris (2011) writes, a gesture is "the mental image's witness" (p. 293).

The same intentional gestures may convey different meanings in different cultures (Ambady & Weisbuch, 2010; Calbris, 2011). For example, suppose that you make a circle with your thumb and your first finger. This gesture signifies "money" in Japan, and "perfect!" in France. However, in Malta—an island off the coast of Italy—this same gesture is an obscene insult.

Many different types of gestures occur alongside speech. **Iconic gestures** are gestures with a form that represents the concept about which a speaker is talking. For example, a speaker telling her friend about a car crash that she witnessed on the way to work might vigorously push her left and right fists together as she explains the impact. In this sense, she has manually simulated the concept of two objects crashing into one another. **Deictic gestures** involve pointing to some object or location while speaking, and are often accompanied by words such as "This" or "That." Notice that both iconic and deictic gestures convey information that may help a conversational partner understand the message that a speaker wishes to convey. **Beat gestures**, on the other hand, are gestures that occur in a rhythm that matches the speech rate and prosodic content of speech. These gestures do not convey specific information to a listener, but may be made by a speaker to help that speaker maintain a current speech pattern.

Gestures can influence how you think (Goldin-Meadow, 2003; Goldin-Meadow & Beilock, 2010). For example, the spontaneous motor movements of your hands can sometimes help you remember the word you want to produce (Carroll, 2004; Griffin, 2004). In a representative study, Frick-Horbury and Guttentag (1998) read the definitions for 50 low-frequency, concrete English nouns. The researchers then asked each participant to identify the target word. For example, the definition "a pendulum-like instrument designed to mark exact time by regular ticking" (p. 59) was supposed to suggest the noun *metronome*. Notice, then, that this technique resembles the tip-of-the-tongue research described in Chapter 6.

In Frick-Horbury and Guttentag's (1998) study, however, half of the participants were instructed to hold a rod with both hands; therefore, their hand movements were restricted. The average score for these individuals was 19 words out of 50. In contrast, the participants with unrestricted hand movements earned an average score of 24 words out of 50. Other research has confirmed this finding. According to these researchers, when our verbal system cannot retrieve a word, a gesture can sometimes help activate the relevant information (Brown, 2012).

Gestures can also facilitate learning. Cook and colleagues (2017), for example, had children view videos of a computer avatar providing lessons about mathematical computations. In one condition, the avatar gestured during the mathematics lesson, and in another condition, the avatar did not gesture. Children who learned from the version of the video with gestures solved related math problems more quickly than children in the other condition. The use of computer avatars here is cleaver. The avatar was able to provide the exact same verbal (nongesture-related) information in both conditions, thus ruling out the possibility that subtle verbal differences across condition could serve as an experimental confound.

We frequently produce gestures when we speak, especially when we want to discuss a concept that is easier to describe with body movements than with words (Ambady & Weisbuch, 2010). Try Demonstration 10.3 to illustrate this point. We are also more likely to produce a gesture when we have had previous experience with the relevant physical activity (Hostetter & Alibali, 2010).

The gestures that speakers make during a conversation with another person also contain information that helps listeners better interpret a speaker's intended meaning. For example, imagine a conversation between two people in a kitchen. Two red apples are visible on the kitchen counter, one that sits on a folded napkin and one that sits on a kitchen towel (think back to Figure 9.1 in Chapter 9). A hungry speaker who wants to eat an apple could say, "Hand me the red apple on the napkin." That same speaker could also say, "Please hand me the apple?" while pointing to the one on the napkin. Notice that in this example, gesture makes communication easier for both the speaker and the listener. The speaker can use fewer words, and the listener must process fewer words. Indeed, in a meta-analysis of 63 gesture experiments, Hostetter (2011)

Demonstration 10.3 ‖ **Using Gestures to Communicate Information**

Answer each of the following questions, using only words and no body movements. Hold this book in both hands while you try this exercise.

1. Define the word "spiral."

2. Give directions on how to walk from your current location to another location about 10 minutes away.

3. Describe the shape of the steps in a staircase.

4. Describe how you peel a carrot.

5. If you have recent experience in driving a car, give instructions for how to insert the key into the door of a locked car, and then open the door.

6. If you have recent experience in riding a bicycle, give instructions about how you get on a bike and begin to ride.

Which of these items was the most difficult to describe without using any gestures?

Visual Depiction of the Tower of Hanoi Problem

FIGURE 10.2 Visual depiction of the Tower of Hanoi problem.

found that gestures do increase the listener's understanding. This observation was especially true when they are made as a speaker is describing concrete actions.

Perhaps even more impressively, gestures can convey information that is not explicitly stated in speech, and that a speaker didn't even knowingly intend to convey. Consider the famous Tower of Hanoi puzzle as depicted in Figure 10.2. To solve the puzzle, one must get the three discs that appear on the left-most peg over to the right-most peg. But, there are three rules: (1) the ordering of the discs (smallest of top, largest on bottom) must be the same at the end of the task, (2) only one disc may be moved at a time, and (3) a larger disc can never be placed on top of a smaller disc at any point in time. See if you can solve it.

Cook and Tanenhaus (2009) asked participants to solve the Tower of Hanoi puzzle by themselves. Participants in one condition were asked to learn how to solve the puzzle while working with a "real-life" version of it. Crucially, the discs in this "real-life" version of the task were relatively heavy given their size, such that participants had to use some arm muscle in order to lift and move the discs. In a second condition, a separate set of participants taught themselves how to solve the puzzle by working with it on a computer display. In this condition, however, participants were able to slide the discs across the display using the computer mouse without doing any heavy lifting.

After learning the puzzle, participants in both conditions became teachers. They were asked to teach new participants (the new learners) how to solve the puzzle. During the teaching session, the new learners were seated in front of a computer screen displaying the Tower of Hanoi puzzle, and the teachers explained to the new learners how to solve it. The computer mouse-movements made by the new learners were recorded during the process.

Three aspects of the results reported by Cook and Tanenhaus highlight the powerful role that gesture plays during communication.

1. The teachers made gestures as they explained the puzzle to the new learners that contained information about how they themselves had originally learned the task. Those who had to lift heavy discs produced higher gestures while explaining the puzzle to the new learners than those who just had to slide a cursor across the screen.

2. New learners who received instructions from the teachers in the real-life condition made significantly higher and more arched movements while moving the discs around the computer display than did the learners who were taught by teachers in the computer condition.

3. The content of the speech made by teachers in either condition did not differ in any respect. Thus, no information in the speech produced by any of the teachers explicitly mentioned things such as "slide" or "lift." This observation means that the movements produced by the new learners did not occur due to speech differences. Instead, differences in the height and shape of the gestures made by teachers in each condition were the cause of different movements produced by the new learners.

Think about these results for a minute. When speakers gesture, they may be transmitting information that they didn't know they were transmitting! And, the information transmitted through gesture even influenced someone else's behavior during learning.

In recent years, cognitive psychologists have become increasingly interested in a concept called embodied cognition. **Embodied cognition** emphasizes that people use their bodies to express their knowledge (Hostetter & Alibali, 2008; Richardson et al., 2003; Zwaan et al., 2002). In other words, there is an ongoing connection between your motor system and the way we process spoken language, for example, when you make gestures or indicate some kind of motion (Glenberg & Kaschak, 2002; Hostetter & Alibali, 2008; Richardson et al., 2003; Tomasello, 2008; Zwaan et al., 2002). Notice that the embodied cognition approach focuses on concrete physical actions, rather than the abstract meaning of language (Holtgraves, 2010).

During the behaviorist era, psychologists emphasized visible motor activity. As the cognitive psychology approach grew in popularity, psychologists could read entire issues of a relevant journal, without any mention of motor actions. However, the recent attention to embodied cognition has convinced many psychologists that we frequently think nonverbally (Ambady & Weisbuch, 2010), and that much of our cognitive processing involves using our perceptual and motor systems in order to mentally simulate events. Given the emphasis on action, research on gesture is often discussed in relation to theories of embodied cognition. Think for a minute about what aspects of the embodied cognition framework are illustrated by the discussion of the Tower of Hanoi experiment above.

During naturalistic communication, speakers make gestures and listeners have the ability to access information contained in those gestures. This observation is but one example of how information not contained in a verbal linguistic signal contributes to communication. Next, we zoom-in further on the role of social context in language production.

The Social Context of Language Production

Language is definitely a social instrument (Fiedler et al., 2011; Holtgraves, 2010; Segalowitz, 2010). In fact, conversation is like a complicated dance (Clark, 1985, 1994). Speakers cannot simply utter words aloud and expect to be understood. Instead, these speakers must consider their conversation partners, make numerous assumptions about those partners, and design appropriate utterances (Tomasello, 2008).

This complicated dance requires precise coordination. When two people enter a doorway simultaneously, they need to coordinate their motor actions. Similarly, two speakers must coordinate turn-taking, they must agree on the meaning of ambiguous terms, and they must understand each other's intentions (Clark & Van Der Wege, 2002; Harley, 2008; Holtgraves, 2010; Pickering & Garrod, 2004). When Helen tells Sam, "The Smithsons are on their way," both participants in the conversation need to understand that this is an indirect invitation for Sam to start dinner, rather than to call the police for protection (Clark, 1985).

This example of language use is called *pragmatics*. **Pragmatics** focuses on the social rules and world knowledge that allow speakers to successfully communicate messages to other people (De Groot, 2011; Degen & Tanenhaus, 2014; Flores Salgado, 2011; Goldenberg & Coleman, 2010; Holtgraves, 2010). Two important topics in the research on pragmatics are common ground and an understanding of directives. We also consider a concept called *framing*, which examines why we sometimes have trouble communicating with people who have different perspectives.

Common Ground

Suppose that a young man named Andy asks his friend Lisa, "How was your weekend?" and Lisa answers, "It was like being in Conshohocken again." Andy will understand this reply only if they share a similar understanding about the characteristics or events that took place in Conshohocken. In fact, we would expect Lisa to make this remark only if she is certain that she and Andy share the appropriate common ground (Clark & Van Der Wege, 2002; Stone, 2005).

Common ground occurs when conversationalists share the similar background knowledge, schemas, and perspectives that are necessary for mutual understanding (Brown-Schmidt et al., 2008; Harley, 2008; Holtgraves, 2010; Traxler, 2012). In fact, the speakers need to collaborate to make certain that they share common ground with their conversational partners (Tomasello, 2008). For example, speakers should make certain that their listeners are paying attention and they have the appropriate background knowledge. If their listeners look puzzled, speakers need to clarify any misunderstandings (Haywood et al., 2005; Holtgraves, 2010). Unfortunately, however, speakers often think that they are communicating effectively, even when their listeners cannot understand their message (Fay et al., 2008).

Have you ever had difficulty explaining some object or procedure to another person, in a phone conversation? Clark and Wilkes-Gibbs (1986) conducted a classic study on the collaboration process that we use when trying to establish common ground. Try Demonstration 10.4, which is a modification of this study.

The participants in Clark and Wilkes-Gibbs's (1986) study played this game for six trials; each trial consisted of arranging all 12 figures in order. On the first trial, Person 1 required an average of nearly four turns to describe each figure and make certain that Person 2 understood the reference. (A typical "turn" consisted of a statement from Person 1, followed by a question or a guess from Person 2.)

As Figure 10.3 shows, however, the director and the matcher soon developed a mutual shorthand, and the number of required turns decreased rapidly over trials. Just as two dancers become more skilled as

Demonstration 10.4 | Collaborating to Establish Common Ground

For this demonstration, you need to make two photocopies of the figures below. Then, cut the figures apart, keeping each sheet's figures in a separate pile and making certain the dot is at the top of each figure. Now locate two volunteers and a watch that can measure time in seconds. Your volunteers should sit across from each other or at separate tables, with their figures in front of them. Neither person should be able to see the other's figures.

Appoint one person to be the "director" and the other the "matcher." The director should arrange the figures in random order, in two rows of six figures each. This person's task is to describe the first figure in enough detail so that the "matcher" is able to identify that figure and

place it in Position 1 in front of him or her. The goal is for the matcher to place all 12 figures in the same order as the director's figures. They may use any kind of verbal descriptions they choose, but no gestures or imitation of body position. Record how long it takes them to reach their goal, and then make sure that the figures do match.

Ask them to try the game two more times, with the same person serving as director. Record the times again, and note whether the time decreases on the second and third trials; are these volunteers increasingly efficient in establishing common ground? Do they tend to develop a standard vocabulary (e.g., "the ice skater") to refer to a given figure?

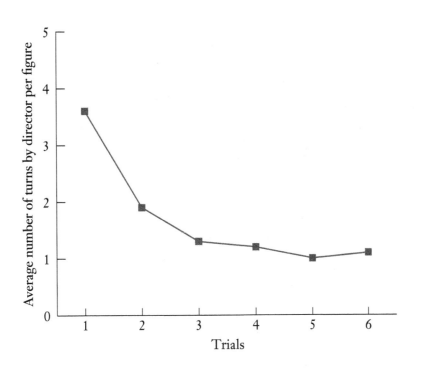

FIGURE 10.3
Average number of turns that directors in Clark and Wilkes-Gibb's study required for each figure, as a function of trial number.
Source: Clark, H. H., & Wilkes-Gibbs, D. (1986). Referring as a collaborative process. *Cognition, 22*, 1–39.

they practice together at coordinating their movements, conversational partners become more skilled in communicating efficiently (Barr & Keysar, 2006).

Additional research confirms that people who work together collaboratively can quickly and efficiently develop common ground (Barr & Keysar, 2006; Schober & Brennan, 2003). For example, physicians often adjust their conversations according to the medical sophistication of each patient. If a patient with diabetes initially uses the term "blood sugar level," the physician is less likely to use the technical term, "blood glucose concentration" (Bromme et al., 2005).

We have been discussing how people can establish common ground, even with strangers. However, this process is far from perfect. For example, speakers often overestimate their listeners' ability to understand a message (Barr & Keysar, 2006; Holtgraves, 2010; Schober & Brennan, 2003). Now let's consider how people make requests.

Directives

A **directive** is a sentence that asks someone to do something. For example, suppose that a man named Bob is driving. A police officer stops him, and Bob clearly knows that he has been speeding. Of course, most of us would automatically accept the speeding ticket.

However, let's suppose that Bob is considering giving a bribe to the officer. One possibility is that Bob might make a direct request. As the name suggests, a **direct request** resolves the interpersonal problem in a very obvious fashion. In this situation, an example of a direct request would be, "How much money should I pay you to *not* get a ticket?" Basically, if Bob is considering a bribe like this one, he needs to figure out the consequences of a bribe. Does this officer seem to be honest? If so, a direct bribe would probably lead to Bob being arrested for bribing an officer—the worst possible outcome.

In contrast, an **indirect request** uses subtle suggestions to resolve an interpersonal problem, rather than stating the request in a straightforward manner. In this situation, some people might say, "Well, officer, maybe it would be easier if we can take care of the ticket right now, without going through all that paperwork." Linguists have argued that we typically state a request in a relatively brief but clear manner (Grice, 1989; Traxler, 2012). So why should we use all these extra words to make an indirect request?

According to a group of researchers at Harvard, people need to be strategic decision makers in their social interactions (Lee & Pinker, 2010; Pinker et al., 2008). In this case, if the officer is *dishonest*, Bob's indirect request will lead to Bob not getting a ticket. If the officer is *honest*, Bob's indirect request will lead to Bob getting a ticket—not a great outcome, but certainly better than being arrested for bribing a police officer. Notice how this study about requests is an example of Theme 4 of this textbook. In this case, the language we choose (Chapter 10) is related to our decision-making strategies (Chapter 12).

So far, we've seen that speakers are typically attuned to the social context of speech. They usually work to achieve common ground, and they can be strategic in selecting appropriate directives. Now let's look at framing, a topic that has important political implications.

Framing

When psychologists study the social aspects of speech, they typically look at conversations between two people or conversations in small groups. However, linguists and sociologists typically study how large groups use language.

For example, George Lakoff is a cognitive scientist in the Linguistics Department at University of California Berkeley. Lakoff examines how language can structure our thinking. Specifically, he uses the term **frame** to describe our mental structures that simplify reality (Lakoff, 2007, 2009, 2011). Our frames tend to structure what "counts" as facts.

For example, consider the word *responsibility*. Some people frame this word in terms of *individual responsibility*: You are responsible for making money for yourself and your family; your authority is based on wealth and power. Other people frame this word in terms of *social responsibility*. You have empathy for other people, and you are responsible for helping people who have less money and less power than you do. You need to care for people beyond your family and community.

Notice a problem, however. When people have different frames, it may be difficult to talk with others about many important contemporary issues. This problem will be especially dramatic when they do not share common ground.

Language Production and Writing

Students spend a major portion of their daily life taking notes on lectures and reading assignments, writing papers, and writing essays on exams. Think about the last major writing project that you finished, perhaps a review of the research on a particular topic. In addition to language comprehension and production processes, this project probably required letter recognition, attention, memory, imagery, background knowledge, metacognition, reading, problem solving, creativity, reasoning, and decision making.

Researchers seldom study writing in college students, though they have conducted studies on children's writing (e.g., Martins et al., 2010; Robins & Treiman, 2009; Treiman & Kessler, 2009). For example, reading is a topic that inspires hundreds of books and research articles each year, whereas writing inspires only several dozen (Harley, 2008).

Most adults write fairly often. For example, a large-scale study asked adults in three regions of the United States to keep a diary for two days, recording how frequently they wrote (Cohen et al., 2011). The participants reported writing an average of two hours each day. Several factors—gender, ethnicity, education, and age—were not related to time spent writing. However, employed people spent more time writing than nonemployed people.

You are more likely to write in isolation. This observation does not mean, however, that there isn't a social component to writing. Many times, you write with the goal of communicating a message, thought, or idea to someone else, and you are likely to tailor the form and content of a written message to your intended audience (or, the person who will be reading what you wrote). Writing also takes more time, especially because writing uses more complex syntax. In addition, people revise their writing far more often than their talking (Biber & Vásquez, 2008; Harley, 2001; Treiman et al., 2003).

Writing and speaking also differ in other ways. When you speak, you are more likely to refer to yourself. When speaking, you also interact more with your listeners, and you have a better opportunity to establish common ground with them (Chafe & Danielewicz, 1987; Gibbs, 1998; Harley, 2008).

Writing consists of three phases: planning, sentence generation, and revising (Mayer, 2004). However—like the similar stages we discussed in connection with spoken language—these tasks often overlap in time (Kellogg, 1994, 1996; Ransdell & Levy, 1999). For example, you may be planning your overall writing strategy while you generate parts of several sentences.

All components of the writing task are complex, and they strain the limits of attention (Kellogg, 1994, 1998; Torrance & Jeffery, 1999). In fact, a classic article about writing emphasizes that a person working on a writing assignment is "a thinker on full-time cognitive overload" (Flower & Hayes, 1980, p. 33). However, college students can learn to write more skillfully if they have extensive practice in academic writing and if the assignments emphasize high-quality writing (Beauvais et al., 2011; Engle, 2011; Kellogg & Whiteford, 2009).

We begin by considering the cognitive aspects of writing. After that, we examine three phases of writing: planning, sentence generation, and revising. Then, we emphasize the importance of metacognition throughout the writing process. Finally, we discuss several examples of writing in real-world settings.

The Role of Working Memory in Writing

Several leading researchers have developed models of writing that emphasize the importance of cognitive processes (Chenoweth & Hayes, 2001; Hayes, 1996; Kellogg, 1994, 2001a, 2001b; McCutchen et al., 2008). Here, we focus on the role of working memory in the writing process.

In Chapter 4, we discussed Alan Baddeley's model of working memory (e.g., Baddeley, 2007). **Working memory** refers to the brief, immediate memory for material that you are currently processing; working memory also coordinates your ongoing mental activities. Working memory plays a central role in writing (Kellogg et al., 2007; Raulerson et al., 2010). Certainly, sometimes I think of good sentences or organizational plans while typing a current sentence, just to realize that I have forgotten them once I have finished typing. Perhaps many of you have had the same frustrating experience.

Ronald Kellogg and colleagues (2007) examined which components of working memory might be active during the writing process. These researchers asked college students to write definitions for words while they worked on a secondary task at the same time. There were three different kinds of secondary tasks, each focusing on a specific component of working memory. If the students responded more slowly on a particular secondary task, Kellogg and his coauthors reasoned that this particular skill would be an important component of writing.

One component of working memory, called the **phonological loop**, stores a limited number of sounds for a short period of time. To test whether the phonological loop is active during writing, Kellogg and his colleagues included a specific secondary task. This task required students to remember a spoken syllable. The results showed that—when the students were writing—they required significantly more time to remember the syllables. Presumably, the phonological processing required during the writing process created demands on the limited capacity of the phonological loop, thus making it more difficult to access and recall the syllables.

Another component of working memory, called the **visuospatial sketchpad**, processes both visual and spatial information. Let's first consider how Kellogg and his coauthors examined the "visual information" component. To test whether the *visual* part of the sketchpad is active during writing, another secondary task required students to remember the visual shape of the item. The results showed that, when students were writing about *concrete* nouns, they required significantly longer to remember the item's visual shape. However, when they wrote about *abstract* nouns, they showed no delay in remembering the item's visual shape. As we might expect, visual information is relevant when you are trying to define a concrete word, because you are likely to create a mental image. In contrast, visual activity is minimal when you are trying to define an abstract word.

To examine the *spatial* part of the sketchpad, Kellogg and his coauthors included a different secondary task. This task required the students to remember a particular location while they were writing definitions. In this case, the students' reaction times were not affected by the writing task. In general, then, writing does not require us to emphasize locations.

Planning a Formal Writing Assignment

So far, we have discussed how memory can influence a variety of writing tasks. However, most people begin a formal writing project by generating a list of ideas; this process is called **prewriting**. Prewriting is difficult and strategic—very different from many relatively automatic language tasks (Collins, 1998; Torrance et al., 1996). As you can imagine, students differ enormously in the quality of the ideas they generate during this phase (Bruning et al., 1999). According to the research, good writers are more likely than poor writers to spend high-quality time in planning during prewriting (Hayes, 1989).

Some people prefer to outline a paper before they begin to write (Kellogg, 1998; McCutchen et al., 2008). An outline may help you avoid overloaded attention. You've probably had the experience of beginning to write a paper, only to find that each of several interrelated ideas needs to be placed first! An outline can help you sort these ideas into an orderly, linear sequence, although not all writers find that an outline is helpful (Engle, 2011).

Sentence Generation during Writing

Before you read further, try Demonstration 10.5, which requires you to generate some sentences. During sentence generation, the writer must translate the general ideas developed during planning, thus creating the actual sentences of the text (Mayer, 2004).

During sentence generation, your fluent phases tend to alternate with your hesitant phases (Chenoweth & Hayes, 2001). Think about your own pattern when you were writing the sentences in Demonstration 10.5. Did you show a similar pattern of pauses alternating with fluent writing?

Demonstration 10.5   ‖ Producing Written Sentences

For this exercise, you should be alone in a room, with no one else present to inhibit your spontaneity. Take a piece of paper on which you will write two sentences as requested below. For this writing task, however, say out loud the thoughts you are considering while you write each sentence. Then, read the next section, on sentence generation.

1. Write one sentence to answer the question, "What are the most important characteristics that a good student should have?"

2. Write one sentence to answer the question, "What do you consider to be your strongest personality characteristics—the ones that you most admire in yourself?"

Students often believe that their writing will sound more sophisticated if they use lengthy words. However, according to research by Oppenheimer (2006), people actually judge writers to be more intelligent if their essay uses shorter words.

Earlier in this chapter, we discussed slips-of-the-tongue. People also make errors when they write, whether they use a keyboard or a pen. For example, I often type "form" instead of "from" while writing, a mistake that is especially annoying because spell-check won't catch that error. However, writing errors are usually confined to a spelling error within a single word, whereas speaking errors often reflect switches between words (Berg, 2002).

The Revision Phase of Writing

Remember that writing is a cognitively challenging task. When writing their first draft, writers have numerous opportunities to make mistakes (Kellogg, 1998). We cannot manage to generate new sentences and revise them at the same time (Silvia, 2007). During the revision phase of writing, you should therefore emphasize the importance of organization and coherence, so that the parts of your paper are interrelated (Britton, 1996). You'll also need to reconsider whether your paper accomplishes the goals of the assignment. In fact, the revision task should be time consuming.

The most effective writers use flexible revision strategies, and they make substantial changes if their paper doesn't accomplish its goal (Harley, 2001). However, college students typically devote little time to revising a paper (Mayer, 2004). For instance, college students in one study estimated that they had spent 30% of their writing time on revising their papers, but observation of their actual writing behavior showed that they consistently spent less than 10% of their time on revisions (Levy & Ransdell, 1995). One reason for the lack of revision could be that many students start to write a paper right before it's due. Think back to the discussion of study skills in Chapter 6. Many of those principles can apply equally well to the writing process.

As you can imagine, expert writers are especially skilled at making appropriate revisions. Hayes and colleagues (1987) compared how first-year college students and expert writers revised a poorly written two-page letter. Most first-year students revised the text one sentence at a time. They fixed relatively minor problems with spelling and grammar, but they ignored problems of organization, focus, and transition between ideas.

The college students in this study were also more likely to say that some defective sentences were appropriate. For example, several students found no fault with the sentence, "In sports like fencing for a long time many of our varsity team members had no previous experience anyway." Furthermore, the students were less likely than the expert writers to identify the source of a problem in a sentence. A student might say, "This sentence just doesn't sound right," whereas an expert might say, "The subject and the verb don't agree here."

One final caution about the revision process focuses on the proofreading stage. Daneman and Stainton (1993) confirmed what many people already suspected: You can proofread someone else's writing more accurately than your own. When you are very familiar with a paper that you've just written, you often overlook the errors in the text. Top-down processing (Theme 5) triumphs again!

Bilingualism

Between 6,000 and 7,000 languages exist in the world (Lupyan & Dale, 2010; Segalowitz, 2010), and many people throughout the world can speak at least two of those languages (Schwartz & Kroll, 2006). In fact, knowing multiple languages is more typical than knowing only one.

A **bilingual speaker** is someone who is fluent in two different languages (Harley, 2008; Schwartz & Kroll, 2006). The related term **multilingual speaker** refers to someone who speaks more than two languages.

Some bilinguals learn two languages simultaneously during childhood, an arrangement called **simultaneous bilingualism**. Other bilinguals experience **sequential bilingualism**; their native language is referred to as their **first language**, and the nonnative language that they acquire is their **second language** (De Groot, 2011).

In this section on bilingualism, we first discuss some background information, as well as the social context of bilingualism. Then, we note some advantages that people experience as a result of being bilingual.

Background on Bilingualism

More than half of the people in the world are at least somewhat bilingual (Luna, 2011; Schwartz & Kroll, 2006). Some people live in countries where at least two languages are commonly used. These countries include Canada, Belgium, Spain, and Switzerland.

Other people become bilingual because their home language is different from the language used for school and business. For example, in Italy, almost everyone speaks what is referred to as Standard Italian. This is the language used in national newspapers and on television, and is taught to children in school. In many cases, however, Italians also learn a dialect that is specific to the region where they grew up. Dialect learning typically happens in the home environment. For example, the dialect spoken by people from areas surrounding Brescia, a medium-sized city between Milan and Verona, is quite noticeably different than Standard Italian in terms of its phonology, vocabulary, and grammar. In fact, it has much in common with the French language. In many respects, these individuals are bilingual.

People may also become bilingual because colonization has imposed another language upon them. Still others become bilingual because they have studied another language in school, or because they grew up in homes where family members routinely used two languages. In addition, immigrants moving to a new country usually need to master the language of that culture (Bialystok, 2001; Fishman, 2006; Parry, 2006). Even in a relatively small region of one country, people often learn multiple languages. As with the Italian dialect example, people in these situations use both languages each day depending on the background of the person with whom they are speaking and on the communicative demands of a specific context.

English is the most common language in both Canada and the United States, but many other languages are also widely used in these countries. Table 10.1 shows the 10 languages most frequently "spoken at home" in the United States. Table 10.2 shows the 10 languages most frequently listed as a person's "mother tongue" in Canada. Bilingualism is important in the lives of many residents of Canada and the United States, and many people speak a language other than English in their homes.

In the last decade, bilingualism has become an increasingly popular topic in psychology and linguistics. For instance, this interdisciplinary area now has its own journal, *Bilingualism: Language & Cognition*. Several recent books also focus on bilingualism (Cook & Bassetti, 2011; De Groot, 2011; Flores Salgado, 2011; Gaskell, 2009a; Kaplan, 2010a; Kroll & De Groot, 2005; Segalowitz, 2010).

Table 10.1 Ten Languages Most Frequently Spoken at Home in the United States, Based on the U.S. Census Bureau (2012) for People Aged 5 and Older

Language	Estimated number of speakers[1]
English	228,700,000
Spanish	35,500,000
Chinese	2,600,000
Tagalog[2]	1,500,000
French	1,300,000
Vietnamese	1,300,000
German	1,100,000
Korean	1,000,000
Russian	900,000
Arabic	800,000

[1] The number of speakers is rounded to the nearest 100,000. In case of a tie, the language with the larger number of speakers is placed first.
[2] Tagalog is a language spoken in the Philippines.
Source: U.S. Census Bureau (2012). Table 53. Languages spoken at home: 2009.

Table 10.2   Ten Languages Most Frequently Identified as the "Mother Tongue" in Canada, Based on 2006 Census

Language	Estimated number of speakers[1]
English	17,900,000
French	6,800,000
Chinese	1,000,000
Italian	500,000
German	500,000
Punjabi[2]	400,000
Spanish	300,000
Arabic	300,000
Tagalog	200,000
Portuguese	200,000

[1] The number of speakers is rounded to the nearest 100,000. In case of a tie, the language with the larger number of speakers is placed first.
[2] Punjabi is a language spoken in India and Pakistan.
Source: Statistics Canada, 2006.

We begin our discussion by looking at the social context of bilingualism. Then, we consider the advantages of bilingualism, as well as the relationship between age of acquisition and language mastery.

The Social Context of Bilingualism

Many children in the United States and in Canada speak a language other than English in their homes. Unfortunately, the educational system frequently does not value this other language. For example, one of my students described an incident that she had observed in a kindergarten class at a school where many children speak both English and Spanish. Two boys were playing together, and they spoke several sentences to each other in Spanish. The teacher rushed toward them and shouted, "I don't want to hear another word from either of you in that language!" Language is a defining characteristic of every cultural group (Gardner, 2010). Don't you wonder how these two children—and their classmates—interpreted their teacher's response? Many schools do not appreciate the value of keeping a child fluent in a first language such as Korean, Arabic, or Spanish (Fishman, 2006; Pita & Utakis, 2006; Zentella, 2006). Research demonstrates, however, that if a school values a child's first language, he or she may actually become more fluent in English (Atkinson & Connor, 2008; De Groot, 2011). Caring teachers and administrators can provide a school-wide culture that supports children who are learning English as a second language (Goldenberg & Coleman, 2010).

As you can imagine, the topic of bilingualism has important political and social implications. This topic is especially important when educators and politicians make biased statements about various ethnic groups (Genesee & Gándara, 1999; Phillipson, 2000).

Social forces are also important when an individual wants to become bilingual. Two important predictors of success in acquiring a second language are a person's motivation and her or his attitude toward the people who speak that language (Harley, 2008; Segalowitz, 2010; Tokuhama-Espinosa, 2001).

In fact, researchers have tried to predict how well English Canadian high school students would learn French. The research shows that the students' *attitude* toward French Canadians was just as important as their cognitive, language-learning *aptitude* (Gardner & Lambert, 1959; Lambert, 1992). Other researchers have found the same relationship between attitudes and mastery of English, for people who come from Hungary, Japan, China, and Iran (Segalowitz, 2010; Taguchi et al., 2009).

As you might expect, the relationship between attitudes and language proficiency also works in the reverse direction. For example, when English Canadians learn French in elementary school, they are more likely to develop positive attitudes toward French Canadians, compared to children in a monolingual control group of English Canadian children (Genesee & Gándara, 1999; Lambert, 1987).

Here's further evidence that language can influence students' attitudes. Danziger and Ward (2010) studied Arab Israeli students who were enrolled at Ben-Gurian University. This university is located in Israel, and classes are taught in Hebrew. However, all of the participants were fluent in both Arabic and Hebrew.

Danziger and Ward used the Implicit Association Test, an instrument that assesses people's attitudes. As discussed in Chapter 8, the **Implicit Association Test (IAT)** is based on the principle that people can mentally pair related words together much more easily than they can pair unrelated words. Using the IAT, Danziger and Ward found that these Arab students were more positive about Jewish individuals when the fluently bilingual researcher was speaking Hebrew than when she was speaking Arabic.

Advantages (and Minor Disadvantages) of Bilingualism

During the early 1900s, theorists proposed that bilingualism produced cognitive deficits because the brain must store two linguistic systems (Erwin-Tripp, 2011; De Groot, 2011). However, in the 1960s, researchers found that after controlling for factors such as age and social class, bilingual children actually scored higher than monolinguals on a variety of tasks. In one of the best-known studies, for example, bilingual children were more advanced in school. They also scored better on tests of first-language skills, and they showed greater mental flexibility (Lambert, 1990; Peal & Lambert, 1962). Additionally, research shows that bilinguals do not have two different language systems, one per each language. Instead, both languages appear to be stored together in the same system (Marian & Spivey, 2003).

Recent research has demonstrated that being bilingual has many benefits. Here are some of them:

1. Bilinguals acquire more expertise in their native (first) language (De Groot, 2011; Rhodes et al., 2005; van Hell & Dijkstra, 2002). For example, English-speaking Canadian children whose classes are taught in French gain greater understanding of English-language structure (Diaz, 1985; Lambert et al., 1991). Bilingual children are also more likely to realize that a word such as *rainbow* can be divided into two morphemes, *rain* and *bow* (Campbell & Sais, 1995).

2. Bilinguals are more aware that the names assigned to concepts are arbitrary (Cromdal, 1999; De Groot, 2011; Hakuta, 1986). For example, many monolingual children cannot imagine that a cow could just as easily have been assigned the name *dog*. A number of studies have examined **metalinguistics**, or knowledge about the form and structure of language. On many measures of metalinguistic skill—but not all of them—bilinguals outperform monolinguals (Bialystok, 1988, 1992, 2001; Campbell & Sais, 1995; De Groot, 2011; Galambos & Goldin-Meadow, 1990).

3. Bilinguals perform better on concept-formation tasks and on tests of nonverbal intelligence that require reorganization of visual patterns (Peal & Lambert, 1962). Bilinguals also score higher on problem-solving tasks that require them to ignore irrelevant information (Bialystok, 2001; Bialystok & Codd, 1997; Bialystok & Majumder, 1998).

4. Bilingual children are better at following complicated instructions and performing tasks where the instructions change from one trial to the next (Bialystok, 2005, 2009; Bialystok & Martin, 2004). For example, Bialystok and Martin (2004) asked preschoolers to sort some cards that featured a blue circle, a red circle, a blue square, or a red square. The researchers first instructed them to sort the cards on one dimension (e.g., shape). Later, the researchers instructed them to sort the cards on the other dimension (e.g., color). Bilingual children were much faster than monolingual children in switching to the new dimension.

5. Bilinguals excel at paying selective attention to relatively subtle aspects of a language task, while ignoring more obvious linguistic characteristics (Bialystok, 2001, 2005, 2010; Bialystok & Feng, 2009; Bialystok & Viswanathan, 2009; De Groot, 2011).

   Bialystok (2009) also reported that bilingual individuals are more accurate and respond more quickly on the Stroop Test, a task that requires people to emphasize an item's color and ignore its meaning. Bialystok (2005) proposes that the increased experiences that bilinguals have with selective attention may facilitate the development of a portion of the frontal lobe, labeled "executive attention network." For example, a bilingual who knows two languages and wants to use the word for "window" must inhibit that word in one language in order to say it in the other. Thus, bilinguals have more practice with this type of inhibitory process, and the executive attention network contributes heavily to one's ability to inhibit. Extra practice with inhibition in bilinguals, relative to monolinguals, leads to better inhibitory control.

6. Bilingual children are more sensitive to some pragmatic aspects of language (Comeau & Genesee, 2001). For example, English-speaking children whose classes are taught in French are more aware than monolinguals that—when you speak to a blindfolded child—you may need to supply additional information (Genesee et al., 1975).

7. Bilingual adults who have dementia typically develop signs of dementia *later* than monolingual adults with dementia (Bialystok, 2009; Bialystok et al., 2007). As you may know, **dementia** is an acquired, persistent syndrome of cognitive deficits (Kolb & Whishaw, 2011). For example, Bialystok and her coauthors (2007) examined the medical history of 184 people at a memory clinic. All of them had a medical diagnosis of dementia. However, the bilinguals had received this diagnosis at the average age of 75.5, in contrast to an average age of 71.4 for the monolinguals. This difference is especially important because the monolingual individuals actually had an average of 1.6 *more* years of formal education than did the bilingual individuals.

There is recent controversy regarding some of the effects discussed above. Specifically, the attention-related benefits associated with bilingualism (points (4) and (5), above) do not reliably replicate (see Paap, Johnson, Sawi, 2015; Paap et al., 2017 for an overview of research regarding this observation). Note here that this observation does not refer specifically to the studies cited above, but more generally to the body of research on the bilingual advantage as it pertains to task-switching and executive functioning. Valian (2015) notes that one reason for the conflicted nature of the research on this topic stems from the fact that the life experiences of participants in these experiments are difficult to control. Nonlinguistic experiential factors may differ on any number of dimensions between monolinguals and bilinguals. These factors, and not language skill itself, may contribute to performance on attention-related cognitive tasks. Further, these relevant experiential components are unlikely to be controlled between monolinguals and bilinguals in most experiments on the topic. Thus, across-experiment differences in participant characteristics may provide some insight into why the bilingual advantage is so difficult to empirically nail down.

Another reason for the ephemeral nature of the bilingual advantage as identified on attention-related tasks may stem from a publication bias. Paap et al. (2017), for example, gathered research on the topic from conference abstracts published in the proceedings of relevant past conferences. It is often the case that research presented at conferences is unpublished. Indeed, conferences are one of the best places to stay up-to-date on the most recent findings in a field, as participants are very likely to present their newest (unpublished) research findings. Paap et al. then looked to see which of the preliminary research reports on the topic were subsequently published in respected, peer-reviewed journals.

They found that conference-presented studies reporting evidence in favor of the bilingual advantage on attention tasks were the most likely to have been subsequently published, followed by research reporting mixed results. Research studies that failed to identify a significant effect of bilingual status (mono- vs bilingual) were the least likely to be published. Journals may be biased to publish research in which a significant effect is reported. When one takes into account, however, the larger body of work on a topic—including unpublished experiments on a topic that failed to find a purported effect—it may be the case that the evidence in favor of a finding is actually less compelling. This observation is not specific to reported effects of the bilingual advantage on attention, but instead represents a general bias in how scientific research is reported (Rosenthal, 1979).

The disadvantages of being bilingual are relatively minor. People who use two languages extensively may subtly alter how they pronounce some speech sounds in both languages (Gollan et al., 2005). Bilingual individuals may also process language slightly more slowly, in comparison to monolinguals. Furthermore, bilingual children may have somewhat smaller vocabularies for words that are used in a home setting (Bialystok, 2009; Bialystok et al., 2010). However, these disadvantages are far outweighed by the advantages of being able to communicate effectively in two languages (Michael & Gollan, 2005).

Proficiency and Second Language Acquisition

We next consider the relationship between age of acquisition of a second language and proficiency in that second language. We then conclude this chapter with a focus on simultaneous interpreters. Simultaneous interpreters are people who have high levels of proficiency in two or more languages, allowing them the ability to translate across languages very quickly and accurately.

Second Language Proficiency

In research on bilingualism, the term **age of acquisition** refers to the age at which you learned a second language. Does your ability to learn a new language decrease as you grow older? Some theorists have proposed a critical period hypothesis (e.g., Johnson & Newport, 1989). According to the **critical period hypothesis**, your ability to acquire a second language is strictly limited to a specific period of your life. The critical period hypothesis proposes that individuals who have already reached a specified age—perhaps early puberty—will no longer be able to acquire a new language with native-like fluency. Fortunately, however, the current research evidence does not support a clear-cut, biologically based "deadline" for learning a second language (Bialystok 2001; Birdsong, 2006; De Groot, 2011; Leal et al., 2017).

Even if we reject the critical period hypothesis, we still need to explore a more general issue: Do older people have more difficulty than younger people in mastering a new language? Like so many psychological controversies, the answer varies as a function of the dependent variable. As you'll see, researchers draw different conclusions depending on whether the dependent variable is vocabulary, phonology, or grammar.

Vocabulary

When the measure of language proficiency is vocabulary, age of acquisition is *not* related to language skills (Bialystok, 2001). Several studies report that adults and children are equally skilled in learning words in their new language (Bialystok & Hakuta, 1994). This finding makes sense, because people continue to learn new terms in their own language throughout their lifetime. For example, you have already learned several hundred new terms in cognitive psychology since you began this course!

Phonology

The research suggests that age of acquisition *does* influence the mastery of **phonology**, or the sounds of a person's speech. Specifically, people who acquire a second language during childhood are more likely to pronounce words like a native speaker of that language. In contrast, those who acquire a second language during adulthood are more likely to have a foreign accent when they speak their new language (Bialystok, 2001; Flege et al., 1999; MacKay et al., 2006).

For example, Flege and his coauthors (1999) tested people who had immigrated to the United States from Korea when they were between the ages of 1 and 23 years. At the time of the study, all participants had lived in the United States for at least eight years.

To test phonology, Flege and his colleagues asked their participants to listen to an English sentence, and then repeat it. The phonology of each sentence was later judged by speakers whose native language was English.

As you can see, Figure 10.4 shows that Korean immigrants who had arrived in the United States during childhood typically had minimal accents when speaking English; you can see that most have scores of 7 or 8. Those who had arrived as adolescents or adults usually had stronger accents, with scores of 2 to 4. However, notice the fairly smooth decline with age of acquisition, rather than the abrupt drop predicted by the critical period hypothesis (Bialystok, 2001). In later research, MacKay and his coauthors (2006) found similar results in phonology, with people who had emigrated from Italy.

Grammar

Let's review the conclusions—so far—about age of acquisition and mastering a second language. As far as vocabulary, age doesn't matter. As far as phonology, age *does* matter; if people learn a new language when they are young, they will have a less noticeable accent.

The controversy about age of acquisition is strongest when we consider mastery of grammar (e.g., Bialystok, 2001; Johnson & Newport, 1989). Let's focus on another component of the study by Flege and his coauthors (1999) that we just discussed in connection with phonology. These researchers also examined how the native speakers of Korean had mastered English grammar. Specifically, the researchers asked the participants to judge whether a variety of English sentences were grammatical. Here are three representative examples of ungrammatical sentences:

1. Should have Timothy gone to the party?

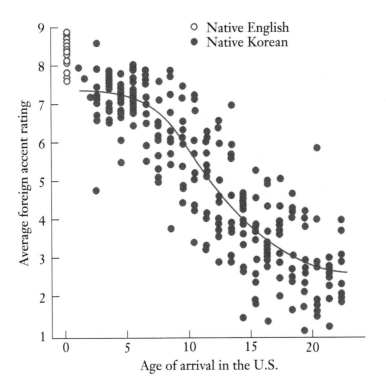

FIGURE 10.4 The average rating for foreign accent, as a function of the individual's age of arrival in the United States (9 = no accent; 1 = strong accent).

Note: For comparison, the study by Flege and his coauthors (1999) also provided an average rating of foreign accent, for 10 speakers whose native language was English. In the upper left corner of the graph, you can see that the judges rated them as having virtually no foreign accent. *Source:* Flege, J. E., Yeni-Komshiam, G. H., & Lui, S. (1999). Age constraints on second-language acquisition. *Journal of Memory and Language, 41,* 78–104.

2. Susan is making some cookies for we.

3. Todd has many coat in his closet.

The initial analysis of the data showed that those who had learned English during childhood had better mastery of English grammar. However, Flege and colleagues (1999) then discovered that the "early arrivers" had much more experience in U.S. schools and therefore more formal education in the English language. In other words, the "early arrivers" had an unfair advantage.

The researchers therefore conducted a second analysis, by carefully matching some of the early arrivers with some of the late arrivers. Each subgroup had an average of 10.5 years of U.S. education. In this second analysis, the early arrivers received an average score of 84% on the grammar test, virtually identical to the average score of 83% for the late arrivers. In other words, once we control for years of education in the United States, age of acquisition is not related to an individual's mastery of English grammar (Flege et al., 1999).

So far, we have emphasized the grammatical performance of people with an Asian first language, a language that is very different from English. What happens when researchers examine the grammatical competence of bilinguals whose first language is more similar to English? The research with Spanish and Dutch does not show any consistent relationship between age of arrival and mastery of English grammar (Bahrick et al., 1994; Birdsong & Molis, 2001; Jia et al., 2002).

In short, the studies show that English-speaking people can begin to learn a new language during adulthood. Specifically, the research shows the following:

1. Age of acquisition is not related to vocabulary in the new language.

2. Age of acquisition is related to phonology.

3. Age of acquisition is sometimes related to grammar for people whose first language is different from English, but there may be no relationship when the first language is similar to English.

As an exercise in helping you understand bilingualism, try Demonstration 10.6 at your next opportunity. Quite clearly, bilinguals and multilinguals provide the best illustration of how Theme 2 applies to language. These fortunate people often manage to achieve accurate and rapid communication in two or more languages.

Next, we focus on people who listen to speech in one language and simultaneously produce the translation in a different language. These individuals are highly skilled bilinguals.

Demonstration 10.6 || Exploring Bilingualism

If you are fortunate enough to be bilingual or multilingual, you can answer these questions yourself. If you are not, locate someone you know well enough to ask the following questions:

1. How old were you when you were first exposed to your second language?

2. Under what circumstances did you acquire this second language? For example, did you have formal lessons in this language?

3. When you began to learn this second language, did you find yourself becoming any less fluent in your native language? If so, can you provide any examples?

4. Do you think you have any special insights about the nature of language that a monolingual may not have?

5. Does the North American culture (including peer groups) discourage bilinguals from using their first language?

Simultaneous Interpreters

If you have studied another language, you've probably had the experience of looking at a written passage in that language and writing down the English equivalent of that passage. The technical term **translation** refers to this process of translating from a text written in one language into a second *written* language. In contrast, the technical term **interpreting** usually refers to the process of changing from a spoken message in one language into a second *spoken* language. (One exception is sign language, which refers to the process of changing between a spoken message in one language into a second language that is signed, or else from a signed message into a spoken form.)

Simultaneous interpreting is one of the most challenging linguistic tasks that humans can perform (Christoffels & De Groot, 2005). Imagine that you are a simultaneous interpreter, listening to a person speaking in Spanish and producing the English version of that message for a group of listeners who are fluent in English but are not familiar with Spanish. You would need to manage three working-memory tasks at exactly the same time:

1. Comprehend one Spanish segment (perhaps a sentence or two).

2. Mentally transform the previous Spanish segment into English.

3. Actually speak out loud—in English—an even earlier segment.

Furthermore, you must manage to perform these cognitive gymnastics at the rate of between 100 and 200 words per minute!

It's hard to think of any other occupation that would create such an ongoing challenge for a person's working memory. Let's look at research that compares simultaneous interpreters with other bilingual individuals, on two kinds of working-memory tasks.

Ingrid Christoffels, Annette De Groot, and Judith Kroll (2006) studied three groups of bilingual people whose native language was Dutch. In addition, all these individuals were also fluent in English. These groups included 39 Dutch undergraduate students at the University of Amsterdam, 15 Dutch teachers of English who had an average of 19 years of professional experience, and 13 Dutch simultaneous interpreters who had an average of 16 years of professional experience. Christoffels and her colleagues hypothesized that the professional interpreters would have higher scores than the other two groups on tests of working memory. Let's consider two of these working-memory tasks, which the researchers called the reading-span test and the speaking-span test.

For the *reading-span test*, the researchers created 42 sentences in both English and Dutch. The final word of each sentence was matched for the two languages, in terms of both word length and the frequency of the word in the appropriate language. The researchers showed several series of sentences, which were two, three, four, or five sentences in length. Each sentence was shown on a screen, for half a second. At the end of each series, the participants tried to recall the last word of each of the sentences in that specific series. Furthermore, the participants completed this reading-span test in both English and Dutch.

For the *speaking-span test*, the researchers selected 42 words in both English and Dutch, matching for both word length and the frequency of the word in the appropriate language. The researchers presented several series of words, which were two, three, four, or five words in length. Each word was shown on a screen, for only half a second. At the end of each series, the participants tried to produce—out loud—a grammatically correct sentence for each word in the series that they could recall. Again, the participants tried this speaking-span test in both English and Dutch.

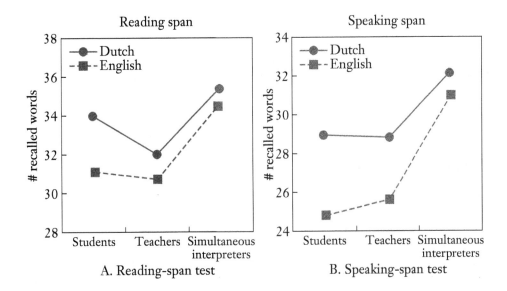

FIGURE 10.5
Average score on the reading-span test and the speaking-span test, as a function of the language (Dutch and English) and profession.

Source: Christoffels, I. K., De Groot, A. M. B., & Kroll, J. F. (2006). Memory and language skills in simultaneous interpreters: The role of expertise and language proficiency. *Journal of Memory and Language, 54,* 324–345.

Figure 10.5 shows that all three groups of bilinguals recalled more words in their native language of Dutch, as compared to their second language of English. The more interesting comparison focuses on the three groups of people. As you can see, the simultaneous interpreters remembered significantly more Dutch and English words than the other two groups, in terms of both their reading span and speaking span.

As you know, psychologists emphasize that it's sometimes difficult to explain significant differences between groups. In this case, we know that simultaneous interpreters perform better than either bilingual students or teachers. One possible explanation is that the experience of managing simultaneous tasks increased the working-memory skills for the simultaneous interpreters. However, another possibility is that only people with superb working-memory skills can manage to survive in a profession that requires an extremely high level of proficiency in working memory. In reality, both these explanations may be correct.

SECTION SUMMARY POINTS

Speaking I: Overview of Production Processes

1. Researchers conduct relatively little research on language production, compared to the research on language comprehension.

2. Word production is an impressive accomplishment; researchers disagree about whether grammatical, semantic, and phonological information about a word is accessed simultaneously or at different times.

3. According to Dell and other researchers, slip-of-the-tongue errors occur because a speech sound other than the intended one is highly activated; researchers explain these errors in terms of a parallel distributed processing model with spreading activation.

4. Four stages in producing a sentence include working out the gist, formulating the general structure of the sentence, making the word choice, and articulating the phonemes; these processes overlap in time.

5. A narrative is a kind of discourse that typically includes certain specified story components.

Speaking II: Language Production and Naturalistic Communication

1. Gestures can help a speaker to access information when retrieval becomes difficult during conversation.

2. Gestures can also help a listener better understand the speaker, and can convey information independent of speech.

3. Embodied cognition is a theoretical perspective that helps explain why gestures are useful to both speakers and listeners.

4. The social context of language production (pragmatics) includes the skilled use of common ground, directives, and framing.

Language Production and Writing

1. Writing is a frequent activity for most people, but research on this topic is limited.

2. The cognitive model of writing emphasizes the three major components of working memory.

3. Good writers spend high-quality time in planning; outlining can be helpful in relieving overloaded attention.

4. When people generate sentences during writing, their fluent phases alternate with hesitant phases.

5. During revision, writers should emphasize organization and coherence, making appropriate revisions and diagnosing defective sentences; students also overestimate the amount of time that they spend on revisions.

Bilingualism

1. More than half of the world's population is at least somewhat bilingual. Many residents of Canada and the United States speak a first language other than English; children's schools may not value fluency in another language.

2. Research shows that motivation and attitudes are important determinants of bilingual skills.

3. If people are fluent in a second language, they tend to be more positive toward people who speak that language.

4. Bilingual people tend to have more positive impressions of people whose language is currently being spoken (e.g., attitudes toward Jews when the message is spoken in Hebrew).

5. Bilinguals have an advantage over monolinguals in their ability to communicate in two languages, their understanding of first-language structure, their awareness of the arbitrary nature of concept names, and their ability to pay attention to subtle aspects of language.

6. Bilinguals also show superior ability in following complex instructions and forming concepts; they also tend to be more sensitive to pragmatics.

7. A comparison of bilingual adults with dementia and monolingual adults with dementia showed that the monolinguals developed this disorder about four years earlier.

Proficiency and Second Language Acquisition

1. People who acquire a second language during adulthood are similar to child learners with respect to acquiring vocabulary, but they are more likely to have an accent in this new language.

2. Age of acquisition is not consistently related to competency in grammar, and educational attainment may explain some of the discrepancies among different studies.

3. Simultaneous interpreters typically perform better than bilingual students and foreign-language teachers on two tasks that assess working memory.

CHAPTER REVIEW QUESTIONS

1. The cognitive tasks required for language production (Chapter 10) are somewhat similar to the cognitive tasks required for language comprehension (Chapter 9). Describe some of the more complex cognitive tasks that are specifically necessary for language production, but not language comprehension.

2. Think of a slip-of-the-tongue that you recently made or heard in a conversation. What kind of error is this, according to Dell's classification, and how would Dell's theory explain this particular error? What slips-of-the-tongue would you be *least* likely to make?

3. Recall several conversations you've had in the last day or two. Describe how these conversations reflected the pragmatic components of speech production, such as common ground, and directives.

4. What is "embodied cognition"? How is it relevant in language production in Chapter 10? How is it similar to the findings about mirror neurons in Chapter 9?

5. "Language is more than simply a sequence of words." Discuss this statement with respect to the social aspects of language production, including topics such as gestures, prosody, and bilingualism.

6. Based on the material in the section on writing, what hints could you adopt to produce a better paper, when you next begin to work on a formal writing assignment?

7. Think of another language that you would like to speak with some fluency. What factors could facilitate your mastery of that language? Describe several tasks in which bilinguals are likely to perform better than monolinguals. Which tasks would monolinguals probably perform better than bilinguals?

8. Language is perhaps the most social of our cognitive activities. Describe how social factors are relevant in our speaking and writing, as well as in bilingual interactions.

KEYWORDS

slips-of-the-tongue	prosody	frame	sequential bilingualism	critical
morphemes	discourse	working memory	first language	period hypothesis
gestures	narrative	phonological loop	second language	phonology
iconic gestures	pragmatics	visuospatial sketchpad	Implicit Association Test	translation
deictic gestures	common ground	prewriting	(IAT)	interpreting
beat gestures	directive	bilingual speaker	metalinguistics	
embodied cognition	direct request	multilingual speaker	dementia	
gist	indirect request	simultaneous bilingualism	age of acquisition	

RECOMMENDED READINGS

Bazerman, C. (Ed.). (2008). *Handbook of research on writing: History, society, school, individual, text*. Mahwah, NJ: Erlbaum. Many of the chapters in this book explore topics unrelated to psychology. However, the last 13 chapters focus on psychological aspects of writing.

De Groot, A. M. B. (2011). *Language and cognition in bilinguals and multilinguals: An introduction*. New York: Psychology Press. I strongly recommend Annette De Groot's book for anyone who would like an in-depth examination of the topic. It is current, well organized, and comprehensive.

Sedivy, J. (2014). *Language in the mind: An introduction to psycholinguistics*. Sunderland, MA: Sinauer Associates. This textbook provides a detailed yet accessible overview of the topics covered in both Chapters 9 and 10.

Segalowitz, N. (2010). *Cognitive bases of second language fluency*. New York: Routledge. Norman Segalowitz's book is briefer than De Groot's book, and it is written more from the perspective of cognitive psychology. It examines topics such as the pragmatics of second-language usage, as well as the important topic of fluency in a second language.

11

Problem Solving and Creativity

Chapter Introduction

You solve dozens of problems every day. Just think about the problems you worked on today. Perhaps you wanted to contact a student in your social psychology class, but you didn't know his last name or his e-mail address. You may have also tried to solve the problem of choosing a topic for your cognitive psychology paper. Then maybe you took a break by working on a Sudoku puzzle, which is yet another example of problem solving. In Chapter 1, we defined the term *cognition* as the acquisition, storage, transformation, and use of knowledge. So far in this textbook, we've paid the least attention to the component called "transformation of knowledge." However, in this chapter and in the next chapter on reasoning and decision making (Chapter 12), we focus on how people must gather the information that they acquired and then *transform* this information to reach an appropriate answer. Problem solving and decision making are both included within the general category called "thinking." **Thinking** requires you to go beyond the information you were given, so that you can reach a goal. The goal may be a solution, a belief, or a decision.

The initial step in problem solving is understanding the problem, so we consider this topic in the first section of this chapter. Once you understand a problem, the next step is to select a strategy for solving it; we examine several problem-solving approaches in the second section. Next we examine factors that influence effective problem solving. For example, expertise is clearly helpful, but a mental set is counterproductive. Our final topic in this chapter is creativity—an area that requires finding novel solutions to challenging problems.

Understanding the Problem

The term **problem solving** refers to the processes necessary to reach a goal, typically in situations where the solution is not immediately obvious. The solution may not be obvious for many reasons, although this situation tends to occur when you are missing important information and/or it is not clear how to reach the goal (Bassok & Novick, 2012; D'Zurilla & Maydeu-Olivares, 2004; Reif, 2008). These situations—or problems—vary widely. For example, a toddler could try to solve the problem of bringing pasta to her mouth without spilling it (Keen, 2011). An English-speaking student—studying in France—might try to solve the problem of asking for directions while possessing only a limited vocabulary in French (Segalowitz, 2010). A counseling psychologist may try to help a high school student solve a personal problem about his interactions with his peers (Heppner, 2008).

Although the nature of these problems may differ, every problem includes three components: (1) the initial state, (2) the goal state, and (3) the obstacles. For example, suppose that you need to reach Jim in your social psychology class. The **initial state** describes the situation at the beginning of the problem. In this case, your initial state might be, "I need to reach Jim tonight so that we can begin to work on our social psychology project. . .but I don't know his last name, his e-mail address, or his phone number." You reach the **goal state** when you solve the problem (Levy, 2010). Here, it could be, "I have Jim's last name and his e-mail address." The **obstacles** describe the restrictions that make it difficult to proceed from the initial state to the goal state (Thagard, 2005). The obstacles in this hypothetical problem might include the following: "Jim wasn't in class yesterday," "The professor said she was going to be away this afternoon," and "We need to turn in a draft of our project on Friday."

When some people try to solve a problem, they may take a trial-and-error approach, trying different options at random until they find a solution (Reif, 2008). However, effective problem solvers typically plan their attack. They often break a problem into its component parts and devise a strategy for solving each part. In addition, people use certain strategies that are likely to produce a solution relatively quickly. People also use metacognition to monitor whether their problem-solving strategies seem to be working effectively (Hinsz, 2004; Mayer, 2004; Reif, 2008). As this textbook emphasizes, humans do not passively absorb information from the environment. Instead, we plan our approach to problems, and we choose strategies that are likely to provide useful solutions.

Take a moment to recall a problem you solved recently. Determine the initial state, the goal state, and the obstacles, so that you are familiar with these three concepts. Then, try Demonstration 11.1.

In problem-solving research, the term **understanding** means that you have constructed a well-organized mental representation of the problem based on both the information provided in the problem and your own previous experience (Benjamin & Ross, 2011; Fiore & Schooler, 2004). Think about an occasion when you realized that your mental representation was inaccurate. I recall my mother giving her friend a recipe for homemade yogurt. The instructions included the sentence, "Then you put the yogurt in a warm blanket." The friend looked alarmed, and she asked, "But isn't it awfully messy to wash the blanket out?" Unfortunately, the friend's internal representation had omitted the fact that the yogurt was in a container.

During problem solving, you must decide which information is most relevant to the problem's solution and then attend to that information. Notice here that one cognitive task—problem solving—relies on other cognitive activities such as attention, memory, and decision making. Attention is

---

Demonstration 11.1 ‖ Attention and Problem Solving

Suppose you are a bus driver. On the first stop, you pick up four men and four women. At the second stop, three men, two women, and one child board the bus. Then at the third stop, two men leave and two women get on. At the fourth stop, three women get off. At the fifth stop, two men get off, three men get on, one woman gets off, and two women get on. What is the bus driver's name?

Source: Based on Halpern, 2003, p. 389.

important in understanding problems because competing thoughts can produce divided attention. For instance, Bransford and Stein (1984) presented algebra "story problems" to a group of college students. You'll remember these problems—a typical one might ask about a train traveling north, while a car is traveling south. In this particular study, the students were asked to record their thoughts and emotions as they inspected the problem. Many students had an immediate negative reaction to the algebra problem. A typical comment was, "Oh no, this is a math word problem—I hate those things." These negative thoughts occurred frequently throughout the five minutes allotted to the task. The thoughts clearly distracted the students' attention away from the central task of problem solving.

A second major challenge in understanding a problem is focusing on the appropriate part. Researchers have found that effective problem solvers read the description of a problem very carefully. They pay particular attention to inconsistencies (Mayer & Hegarty, 1996). Effective problem solvers also scan strategically, deciding which information is most important (Nievelstein et al., 2011). Incidentally, if you paid attention to the question about the bus driver above, you could solve it without needing to read it a second time. However, if you didn't pay attention, you can locate the answer in the first sentence of Demonstration 11.1. In summary, then, attention is a necessary initial component of understanding a problem.

In this first section of this chapter, we consider several topics related to understanding a problem: (1) methods of representing the problem, (2) *situated cognition*, which emphasizes how context helps you understand a problem, and (3) *embodied cognition*, which emphasizes how your own body helps you understand a problem.

Methods of Representing the Problem

As soon as the problem solver has decided which information is essential and which can be ignored, the next step is to find a good method for representing the problem. **Problem representation** refers to the way you translate the elements of the problem into a different format. If you choose an appropriate representation, you are more likely to reach an effective solution to the problem.

Chapter 1 introduced the gestalt psychologists, who emphasized that we actively organize our cognitive experiences. When they studied problem solving, they emphasized the importance of finding an effective method of representing the problem (Bassok & Novick, 2012; Schnotz et al., 2010). Working-memory capacity is correlated with a person's ability to solve algebra word problems (Lee et al., 2009), and with the ability to categorize geometric patterns (Lewandowsky, 2011). If you have a good working memory, you can keep the relevant parts of the problem in your mind simultaneously. The result of this ability is that you are more likely to create a helpful representation of the problem (Leighton & Sternberg, 2003; Ward & Morris, 2005).

Your representation of the problem must show the essential information that you need in order to solve it. Some of the most effective methods of representing problems include symbols, matrices, diagrams, and visual images.

Symbols

Sometimes the most effective way to represent an abstract problem is by using symbols, as you learned to do in high school algebra (Mayer, 2004; Nickerson, 2010). Consider Demonstration 11.2.

The usual way of solving this problem is to let a symbol such as m represent Mary's age and a symbol such as s represent Susan's age. We can then "translate" each sentence into a formula. The first sentence becomes $m = 2s - 10$ and the second sentence becomes $m + 5 = s + 5 + 8$. We can then substitute for m in the second sentence and perform the necessary arithmetic. We then learn that Susan must be 18 and Mary must be 26.

A major challenge is that problem solvers often make mistakes when they try to translate words into symbols (Mayer, 2004). One common error is that they reverse the roles of the two variables (Fisher et al., 2011).

Demonstration 11.2 ‖ Using Symbols in Problem Solving

Solve the following problem: Mary is 10 years younger than twice Susan's age. Five years from now, Mary will be eight years older than Susan's age at that time. How old are Mary and Susan? (The answer appears in text).

For example, suppose that college students read the sentence, "There are 8 times as many cats as dogs." Many students make a mistake by translating this sentence into the equation: $8 \times C = D$. Instead, the equation should be: $8 \times D = C$.

An additional error may occur when problem solvers try to translate sentences into symbols: They may oversimplify the sentence, so that they misrepresent the information (Mayer, 2004). For example, Mayer and Hegarty (1996) asked college students to read a series of algebra word problems and then to recall them later. The students often misremembered the problems that contained relational statements. Consider a sentence in an algebra problem about a boat traveling in water: "The engine's rate in still water is 12 miles per hour more than the rate of the current." Many students transformed this statement into a simpler, incorrect form, for example, "The engine's rate in still water is 12 miles per hour."

Matrices

You can solve some problems effectively by using a **matrix**, which is a grid consisting of rows and columns; it shows all possible combinations of items (Hurley & Novick, 2010). A matrix is an excellent way to keep track of items, particularly if the problem is complex and if the relevant information is categorical (Halpern, 2003). For example, you can solve Demonstration 11.3 most effectively by using a matrix like the one at the bottom of this demonstration.

Try Demonstration 11.3. It is based on research by Steven Schwartz and his colleagues (Schwartz, 1971; Schwartz & Fattaleh, 1972; Schwartz & Polish, 1974). Schwartz and his coworkers found that students who represented the problem by a matrix were likely to solve the problem correctly. In contrast, students who used alternative problem representations were less successful. Furthermore, you need to use the appropriate labels for a matrix, such as the one in Demonstration 11.3. Otherwise, you are less likely to solve the problem correctly (Hurley & Novick, 2010). The matrix method is especially suitable when the information is stable, as in Demonstration 11.3, rather than changing over time.

Diagrams

If you've ever assembled a new piece of equipment, you probably know that diagrams can be helpful. For example, Novick and Morse (2000) asked students to construct origami objects—such as a miniature piano—using folded paper. People who received both a verbal description and a step-by-step diagram were much more accurate than people who received only a verbal description. Diagrams allow you to represent abstract information in a concrete fashion. They also let you discard unnecessary details (Bassok & Novick, 2012; Reed, 2010; Reif, 2008; Schneider et al., 2010).

Diagrams can also be useful when you want to represent a large amount of information. For example, a **hierarchical tree diagram** is a figure that uses a tree-like structure to show various possible options in a problem. This kind of diagram is especially helpful in showing the relationship between categorized items (Hurley & Novick, 2010; Reed, 2010).

Demonstration 11.3 | Representing a Problem

Read the following information, and fill in the information in the matrix. Then answer the following question, "What disease does Ms. Anderson have, and what is her room number?" (The answer is at the end of the chapter.)

Five people are in a hospital. Each person has only one disease, and each has a different disease. Each person occupies a separate room; the room numbers are 101 through 105.

1. The person with asthma is in Room 101.
2. Ms. Lopez has heart disease.
3. Ms. Green is in Room 105.
4. Ms. Smith has influenza.
5. The woman with a liver problem is in Room 104.
6. Ms. Thomas is in Room 101.
7. Ms. Smith is in Room 102.
8. One of the patients, other than Ms. Anderson, has gallbladder disease.

| | \multicolumn{5}{c}{Room Number} |
	101	102	103	104	105
Anderson					
Lopez					
Green					
Smith					
Thomas					

Source: Based on Schwartz, 1971.

| The Buddhist Monk Problem

At sunrise one morning, a Buddhist monk began to climb a tall mountain. The path was narrow, and it wound around the mountain to a beautiful, gleaming temple at the very top of the mountain.

The monk sometimes climbed the path quickly, and he sometimes went more slowly. From time to time, he also stopped along the way to rest or to eat the fruit he had brought with him. Finally, he reached the temple, just a few minutes before sunset. At the temple, he meditated for several days. Then, he began his descent back along the same path. He left the temple at sunrise. As before, he walked slowly at times, but more quickly when the pathway was smooth. Again, he made many stops along the way. Of course, he walked down the hill more quickly than when he was walking up the hill.

Demonstrate that there must be a spot along the path that the monk will pass on both trips at exactly the same time of day. (The answer is found in Figure 11.1.)

Diagrams can also represent complicated information in a clear, concrete form. As a result, you have more "mental space" in your working memory for solving other parts of the problem (Halpern, 2003; Hurley & Novick, 2006). Students can master some kinds of diagrams with relatively little effort (Reed, 2010). For example, Novick and her colleagues (1999) provided students with a brief training session on matrices and hierarchical diagrams. After this training session, students were more skilled in choosing the most appropriate method for representing a variety of problems.

Diagrams also help people understand a problem. For instance, Grant and Spivey (2003) found that the participants' eye movements were drawn to the most relevant areas of a diagram that accompanied the verbal part of the problem. As a result, they solved problems more successfully. Try Demonstration 11.4 before continuing.

A graph is sometimes the most effective kind of diagram for representing visual information during problem solving. Consider, for example, the Buddhist monk problem you tried to solve in Demonstration 11.4. As Figure 11.1 illustrates, you could use one line to show the monk going up the mountain on the first day. You could then use a second line to show the monk coming down the mountain several days later. Notice where the lines cross in this figure. This crossing point tells us the spot where the monk will pass at the same time on each of the two days. I have arbitrarily drawn the lines so that they cross at a point 900 feet up the mountain at 12 noon. However, the two paths must always cross at some point, even if you vary the monk's rate of ascent and descent.

Visual Images

Other people prefer to solve problems like the one about the Buddhist monk by using visual imagery. One young woman reported that she suddenly saw a visual image of one monk walking up the hill. He was then joined by a second monk walking down. As she said, "I realized in a flash that the two figures must meet at some point, some time—regardless at what speed they walk and how often each of them stops" (Koestler,

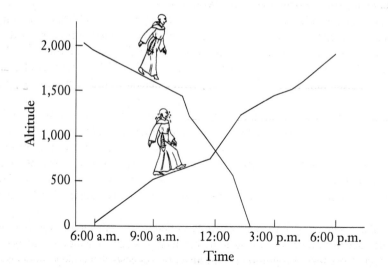

FIGURE 11.1

A graphic representation of the Buddhist monk problem in Demonstration 11.4.

1964, p. 184). Notice that a visual image allows us to escape from the boundaries of traditional, concrete representations. Good visual-imagery skills also provide an advantage when a problem requires you to construct a figure (Gorman, 2006; Pylyshyn, 2006).

Situated and Embodied Cognition Perspectives on Problem Solving

Our discussion of problem solving began by emphasizing that attention is an important component of understanding problems. We've also seen that problems can be represented according to several different formats, including symbols, matrices, diagrams, and visual images. Our final topic in this section moves into a new dimension because it emphasizes the rich external and internal context in which we understand the problems that we must solve.

When you think about your problem-solving skills, it's tempting to focus only on the information inside your head. In recent years, however, psychologists and cognitive scientists have begun to emphasize additional factors that help us think more quickly and more accurately.

For instance, Chapter 7 introduced the situated cognition approach, in connection with mental maps. According to the **situated cognition approach**, we often use helpful information in our immediate environment to create spatial representations. For instance, we make decisions about the up–down dimension more quickly than decisions about the left–right dimension (e.g., Tversky, 2009).

In Chapter 10, we discussed a related concept, the embodied cognition approach. According to the **embodied cognition approach**, we often use our own body and our own motor actions, in order to express our abstract thoughts and knowledge (Kirsh, 2009; Reed, 2010; Thomas & Lleras, 2009a). For example, suppose that you are trying to remember a word that is on the tip of your tongue, such as *metronome*. You are more likely to succeed if you are allowed to use gestures, such as waving your hand back and forth, using the same motion as a metronome (Hostetter, 2011; Hostetter & Alibali, 2008).

You often use both situated and embodied cognition when you try to solve problems. You do not need to rely only on the most obvious sources of information. These two terms may sound similar. However, situated cognition emphasizes the external *situation* that surrounds you. In contrast, embodied cognition emphasizes your own *body*.

Situated Cognition

One of the first examples of *situated cognition* comes from studies conducted in Brazil. On the streets of several large Brazilian cities, 10-year-old boys frequently sold candy to people passing by. Researchers studied these children. Although they had little formal education, they demonstrated a sophisticated understanding of mathematics. During that era, Brazil was using an inflated monetary system in which an entire box of candy bars could sell for 20,000 Brazilian cruzeiros. However, the children managed to figure out how to compare two ratios involving large numbers. For instance, a young boy might offer two candy bars for 500 cruzeiros, but five candy bars for 1,000 cruzeiros. In other words, this 10-year-old needed to understand that a buyer might be tempted to pay less for each candy bar by purchasing a greater number of candy bars (Carraher et al., 1985; Robertson, 2001; Woll, 2002).

How can children understand ratio comparisons, with such large numbers? This is a concept that 10-year-olds seldom learn in North American schools. The situated cognition approach argues that our ability to solve a problem is tied into the specific physical and social context in which we learned to solve that problem (Lave, 1997; Proctor & Vu, 2010; Robertson, 2001). These theorists also argue that an abstract intelligence test often fails to reveal how competent a person would be in solving problems in real-life settings (Kyllonen & Lee, 2005).

The traditional cognitive approach to thinking emphasizes the processes that take place inside an individual person's head. The situated cognition approach argues that the traditional cognitive approach is too simplistic. After all, in real life, our cognitive processes take advantage of an information-rich environment (Chrisley, 2004; Olson & Olson, 2003; Wilson, 2002). In real life, for example, we interact with other people who provide information and help us clarify our cognitive processes. All these factors help us become more competent in understanding and solving problems (Glaser, 2001; Kirsh, 2009; Seifert, 1999).

As you can imagine, the situated cognition perspective has important implications for education. It suggests that children should have experience in solving authentic math problems that they are likely to encounter outside a school setting. The situated cognition perspective also suggests that college students can learn especially effectively during internships and other practical settings (Hakel, 2001; Jitendra et al., 2007). We will return to this issue later in the chapter, when we examine how people often fail to appreciate an analogy between previous abstract problem-solving tasks and the problem they are currently trying to solve.

This situated cognition perspective is consistent with the idea that psychologists should emphasize ecological validity if they want to accurately understand cognitive processes. As we discussed earlier in this book, a study has **ecological validity** if the conditions in which the research is conducted are similar to the natural setting in which the results will be applied. For example, a study of children's mathematical skills in selling candy would have greater ecological validity than a study of children's mathematical skills on a paper-and-pencil, standardized examination.

Embodied Cognition

Many studies have shown that we solve certain kinds of problems more quickly or more accurately if we are allowed to move parts of our body. For example, Chapter 7 discussed mental rotation tasks—in which people must mentally rotate a geometric figure—to see if it matches another similar figure. This research also shows that people perform more accurately on these mental-rotation tasks if they are allowed to move their hands (Chu & Kita, 2011).

Another study about embodied cognition focused on a classic problem-solving task, which required the participants to tie together two ropes that were suspended from the ceiling. This problem could be solved if the participant managed to swing one of the ropes toward the other rope. The research on embodied cognition shows that people are more likely to solve this problem correctly if they had been instructed—during an "exercise break"—to move their arms in a swinging motion (Thomas & Lleras, 2009b). Similarly, participants are more likely to choose a hand-movement strategy to solve a mechanical problem about the movement of gears if they had previous experience with hand gestures (Alibali et al., 2011).

Problem-Solving Strategies

Once you have represented the problem, you try to solve it by using a strategy. Some strategies are very time consuming. For instance, an **algorithm** is a method that will always produce a solution to the problem, although the process can sometimes be inefficient (Sternberg & Ben-Zeev, 2001; Thagard, 2005). One example of an algorithm is a method called an **exhaustive search**, in which you try out all possible answers using a specified system.

Algorithms are often inefficient and unsophisticated. Other, more sophisticated methods reduce the possibilities that must be explored to find a solution. For example, suppose that you have been working on some anagrams, rearranging a random string of letters to create an English word. The next anagram is LSSTNEUIAMYOUL. You might begin to solve that lengthy anagram by trying to identify the first two letters of your target word. Specifically, you decide to pick out only pronounceable two-letter combinations that frequently appear at the beginning of an English word. Perhaps you would reject combinations such as LS, LT, and LY, but you consider LE, LU, and—ideally—SI. This strategy would probably lead you to a solution much faster than an exhaustive search of all the more than 87 billion possible arrangements of the 14 letters in SIMULTANEOUSLY.

The strategy of looking only for pronounceable letter combinations is an example of a heuristic. As you know from other chapters, a **heuristic** is a general rule that is usually correct (Nickerson, 2010). If you use a heuristic strategy to solve a problem, you would ignore some alternatives and explore only those alternatives that seem especially likely to produce a solution.

We noted that algorithms such as an exhaustive search will always produce a solution, although you may grow a few years older in the process. Heuristics, in contrast, do not guarantee a correct solution. For instance, suppose you were given the anagram IPMHYLOD. Suppose also that you use the heuristic of rejecting a combination of letters if it seldom appears at the beginning of a word. If you reject words beginning with LY, then you would fail to find the correct solution, LYMPHOID. When solving a problem, you'll need to weigh the benefits of a heuristic's speed against the costs of possibly missing the correct solution.

Psychologists have conducted more research on problem solvers' heuristics than on their algorithms. One reason is that we are more likely to successfully solve everyday problems with heuristics than algorithms. Three of the most widely used heuristics are the analogy, the means-ends heuristic, and the hill-climbing heuristic. We examine each of these three heuristics in the following sections.

The Analogy Approach

Every day, you use analogies to solve problems. When confronted with a problem in a statistics course, for example, you refer to previous examples in your textbook. When you write a paper for your cognitive psychology course, you use many of the same strategies that were helpful when you wrote a previous paper for social psychology. When you use the **analogy approach** in problem solving, you employ a solution to a similar, earlier problem to help you solve a new problem (Benjamin & Ross, 2011; Leighton & Sternberg, 2003; Schelhorn et al., 2007).

Analogies are widely used in problem solving (Bassok & Novick, 2012). For example, one study reported that engineers created an average of 102 analogies during nine hours spent on problem solving (Christensen & Schunn, 2007). In a cross-cultural study, students in Brazil, India, and the United States typically chose the analogy approach as their preferred strategy in solving problems (Güss & Wiley, 2007).

Analogies are also prominent when people make creative breakthroughs in areas such as art, politics, science, and engineering (Kyllonen & Lee, 2005; Schwering et al., 2009; Young, 2007). For example, Wilbur and Orville Wright designed some of the features of their airplanes by creating an analogy between the wings of a bird and the wings of an airplane. Specifically, they noticed that birds could control their flight patterns by making small adjustments in the orientation of their wing tips. They therefore designed airplane wing tips so that pilots could make subtle adjustments by using metal rods and gears (Weisberg, 2006).

We first consider the general structure of the analogy approach. Then we look at some of the factors that can encourage problem solvers to use the analogy approach most effectively.

The Structure of the Analogy Approach

The major challenge for people who use the analogy strategy is to determine the real problem—that is, the abstract puzzle underneath all the details. In the section on understanding the problem, we emphasized that problem solvers must peel away the irrelevant, superficial details in order to reach the core of the problem (Whitten & Graesser, 2003). Researchers use the term **problem isomorphs** to refer to a set of problems that have the same underlying structures and solutions, but different specific details.

Unfortunately, people tend to focus more on the superficial content of the problem than on its abstract, underlying meaning (Bassok, 2003; Whitten & Graesser, 2003). In other words, they pay attention to the obvious **surface features** such as the specific objects and terms used in the question. As a result, they fail to emphasize the **structural features**, the underlying core that they must understand in order to solve the problem correctly.

For example, Rutgers University wanted to design a system that would allow prospective students to keep track of the status of their college applications. At first, Rutgers staff members looked only at the systems used by other universities, which were similar to their own existing system in terms of surface features. This analogy was not effective. Fortunately, however, the Rutgers staff then shifted their attention to structural features, rather than superficial features. At this point, the staff realized that the *real* problem involved tracking the applicants. They then decided to examine Federal Express to see how this company solved the problem of tracking the location of its packages. Their system provided a highly effective solution to Rutgers' college-application problem (Ruben, 2001).

People often fail to see the analogy between a problem they have solved and a new problem isomorph that has similar structural features (e.g., Barnett & Ceci, 2002; Bassok & Novick, 2012; Leighton & Sternberg, 2003; Lovett, 2002). As we saw in the discussion of the situated cognition perspective, above, people often have trouble solving the same problem in a new setting; they fail to transfer their knowledge. Similarly, they have trouble solving the same problem when it is "dressed up" with a superficially different cover story (Bassok, 2003). People who have limited problem-solving skills and limited metacognitive ability are especially likely to have difficulty using analogies (Chen et al., 2004; Davidson & Sternberg, 1998).

Fortunately, people often overcome the influence of context, and can use the analogy method appropriately (Lovett, 2002). They are more likely to use the analogy strategy correctly when they try several structurally similar problems before they tackle the target problem (Bassok, 2003). Furthermore, students solve statistics problems more accurately if they have been trained to sort problems into categories on the basis of structural similarities (Quilici & Mayer, 2002).

The Means-Ends Heuristic

The means-ends heuristic has two important components: (1) First, you divide the problem into a number of **subproblems**, or smaller problems, and (2) then you try to reduce the difference between the initial state and the goal state for each of the subproblems (Bassok & Novick, 2012; Davies, 2005; Ormerod, 2005). The name **means-ends heuristic** is appropriate because it requires you to identify the "ends" (or final result) that you want and then figure out the "means" or methods that you will use to reach those ends (Ward & Morris, 2005). When problem solvers use the means-ends heuristic, they must focus their attention on the difference between the initial problem state and the goal state. Researchers emphasize that this heuristic is one of the most effective and flexible problem-solving strategies (Dunbar, 1998; Lovett, 2002).

On a daily basis, we solve problems by using means-ends analysis. For example, several years ago, a student I knew well came running into my office saying, "Can I use your stapler, Dr. Matlin?" When I handed her the stapler, she immediately inserted the bottom edge of her skirt and deftly tacked up the hem. As she explained in a more leisurely fashion later that day, she had been faced with a problem: At 11:50, she realized that the hem of her skirt had come loose, and she was scheduled to deliver a class presentation in 10 minutes. Using the means-ends heuristic, she divided the problem into two subproblems: (1) identifying an object that could fix the hem—even though this object was not a traditional "hem-fixer"—and (2) locating this object.

Try Demonstration 11.5 now before continuing.

Research on the Means-Ends Heuristic

People do organize problems in terms of subproblems. For example, Greeno (1974) examined how people solve the Elves-and-Goblins problem in Demonstration 11.5. His study showed that people pause at points in the problem when they begin to tackle a subproblem and need to organize a sequence of moves. Working memory is especially active when people are planning one of these movement sequences (Simon, 2001; Ward & Allport, 1997).

Sometimes the correct solution to a problem requires you to move backward, temporarily *increasing* the difference between the initial state and the goal state. For example, how did you solve the Elves-and-Goblins problem in Demonstration 11.5? Maybe you concentrated on *decreasing* the difference between

---

Demonstration 11.5 ‖ The Elves-and-Goblins Problem

Try solving this problem. (The answer is at the end of the chapter.)

As you may know, Elves and Goblins are mythical creatures. Imagine that three Elves and three Goblins all arrive at the right side of a riverbank, and they all want to cross to the left side. Fortunately, there is a boat. However, the boat is small, and it can hold only two creatures at one time. There is another problem. The three hostile-looking creatures at the bottom of this sketch are Goblins, and Goblins are vicious creatures. The three gentle-looking creatures are Elves. Here is the problem: Whenever there are more Goblins than Elves on one side of the river, the Goblins will immediately attack the Elves and gobble them up. Therefore, you must be absolutely certain that you never leave more Goblins than Elves on any riverbank. How would you solve this dilemma? (Please note that the Goblins, though vicious, can be trusted to bring the boat back!)

the initial state (all creatures on the right side) and the goal state (all creatures on the left side). You therefore moved them only from right to left. If you did, you would have ignored some steps that were crucial for solving the problem. For example, in Step 6 you needed to move two creatures backward across the river to the riverbank on the right. (See the steps in the answer at the end of this chapter).

Research confirms that people are reluctant to move away from the goal state—even if the correct solution requires you to make this temporary detour (Bassok & Novick, 2012). In real life, as in the Elves-and-Goblins problem, the most effective way to move forward is sometimes to move backward temporarily.

Computer Simulation

One of the best-known examples of computer simulation was devised to account for the way humans use means-ends analysis to solve well-defined problems. Specifically, Allen Newell and Herbert Simon developed a theory that featured subgoals and reducing the difference between the initial state and the goal state (Newell & Simon, 1972; Simon, 1995, 1999). We first consider some general characteristics of computer simulation when applied to problem solving. Then, we briefly discuss Newell and Simon's approach, as well as more recent developments in computer simulation.

When researchers use **computer simulation**, they write a computer program that will perform a task in the same way that a human would. For example, a researcher might try to write a computer program for the Elves-and-Goblins problem, which you tried in Demonstration 11.5. The program should make some false starts, just as a human would. The program should be no better at solving the problem than a human would be, and it also should be no worse. The researchers test the program by having it solve a problem and noting whether the steps it takes would match the steps that humans would take in solving the problem.

In 1972, Newell and Simon developed a now-classic computer simulation called General Problem Solver. **General Problem Solver (GPS)** is a program whose basic strategy is means-ends analysis. The goal of the GPS is to mimic the processes that normal humans use when they tackle these problems (Lovett, 2002; Simon, 1996). GPS has several different methods of operating, including the difference-reduction strategy.

Newell and Simon (1972) began by asking participants to talk out loud while working on a relevant problem. They used the narrative from the participants to create specific computer simulations to solve problems such as the Elves-and-Goblins transport problem. The GPS was the first program to simulate a variety of human symbolic behaviors (Sobel, 2001; Sternberg & Ben-Zeev, 2001). As a result, GPS has had an important impact on the history of cognitive psychology (Bassok & Novick, 2012). However, Newell and Simon eventually discarded the GPS because its generality was not as great as they had wished, especially because real-life problems are not so clear cut (Gardner, 1985; Sobel, 2001).

More recently, John Anderson and his colleagues have designed and tested many computer simulations for solving problems similar to the Elves-and-Goblins one, as well as problems in algebra, geometry, and computer science (e.g., Anderson et al., 1995; Anderson et al., 2008; Anderson & Gluck, 2001). These projects are related to Anderson's ACT-R theory, summarized in Chapter 8. These programs were originally developed to learn more about how people acquire skills in problem solving. However, these researchers have also developed "cognitive tutors" that can be used in high school mathematics classes (Anderson et al., 1995; Anderson et al., 2005). Notice, then, that a project initially designed to examine theoretical questions can be applied to real-life situations.

The Hill-Climbing Heuristic

One of the most straightforward problem-solving strategies is called the hill-climbing heuristic. To understand this heuristic, imagine that you are hiking along a path in an unfamiliar area. Your goal is to reach the top of a hill. Just ahead, you see a fork in this path. Unfortunately, you cannot see far into the distance on either of the two paths. Because your goal is to climb upward, you select the path that has the steepest incline. Similarly, if you are using the **hill-climbing heuristic**—and you reach a choice point—you consistently choose the alternative that seems to lead most directly toward your goal (Lovett, 2002; Ward & Morris, 2005).

The hill-climbing heuristic can be useful when you do not have enough information about your alternatives, because you can see only the immediate next step. However, like many heuristics, the hill-climbing heuristic can lead you astray. The biggest drawback to this heuristic is that problem solvers must consistently choose the alternative that appears to lead most directly toward the goal. In doing so, they may fail to choose an *indirect* alternative, which may have greater long-term benefits. For example, a hillside path that seems to lead upward may quickly come to an abrupt end. The hill-climbing heuristic does not guarantee that you'll end up on the top of the hill (Robertson, 2001).

Similarly, a student whose career goal is to earn a high salary may decide to take a job immediately after graduating from college, although a graduate degree would probably yield greater long-term benefits. Sometimes the best solution to a problem requires us to move temporarily backward—away from the goal (Lovett, 2002). The major point to remember about the hill-climbing heuristic is that it encourages short-term goals rather than long-term solutions.

Factors That Influence Problem Solving

Our cognitive processes rely on both bottom-up processing and top-down processing (Theme 5). **Bottom-up processing** emphasizes the information about the stimulus, as registered on our sensory receptors. In contrast, **top-down processing** emphasizes our concepts, expectations, and memory, which we have acquired from past experience.

In this section, we discuss the manner in which these two types of processing help us understand how several important factors can influence our ability to solve a problem. For example, people with expertise use top-down processing effectively when they solve problems—that is, they take advantage of factors such as their knowledge, memory, and strategies. In contrast, both mental set and functional fixedness can interfere when we try to solve a problem; both these factors rely too heavily on top-down processing. Stereotypes—such as stereotypes about gender—may also encourage people to rely on overactive top-down processing, leading to poor problem-solving performance. Finally, if the problem requires insight, we must also overcome overactive top-down processing in order to approach the problem from an unfamiliar perspective. We discuss each of these issues in the following sections.

Expertise

An individual with **expertise** demonstrates consistently exceptional skill and performance on representative tasks for a particular area (Ericsson, 2006; Ericsson & Towne, 2010; Ericsson et al., 2009). For many years, researchers also specified that an expert needed at least 10 years of experience in a particular area of expertise. Many researchers have, however, dropped that criterion. This change arose in large part as a result of research demonstrating that the number of years of experience was not strongly correlated with excellent performance in a variety of fields, such as being skilled as a psychotherapist.

Earlier in this book, we noted that experts in a particular discipline are likely to have superior long-term memory related to that discipline (Chapter 5), as well as the detailed structure of their concepts (Chapter 8). Now we explore how expertise facilitates performance in problem solving. Specifically, experts have developed top-down processes that allow them to perform well on many different components of problem solving in their particular area. However, people with expertise in one area typically do not excel in other areas (Feltovich et al., 2006; Robertson, 2001). Let's trace how experts differ from novices on a variety of dimensions that are crucial to problem solving.

Knowledge Base

Experts and novices differ substantially in their knowledge base and schemas (Bransford et al., 2000; Ericsson & Towne, 2010; Feltovich et al., 2006; Robertson, 2001). In a classic study on the effects of expertise, Chi (1981) demonstrated that novices asked to solve physics problems simply lacked important knowledge about the principles of physics. As we discussed in the previous chapters, you need the appropriate schemas in order to understand a topic properly. Experts may solve problems especially well if they have had training in a variety of relevant settings, and if the training includes immediate detailed feedback (Barnett & Koslowski, 2002; Ericsson & Towne, 2010).

Memory

Experts differ from novices with respect to their memory for information related to their area of expertise (Bransford et al., 2000; Chi, 2006; Robertson, 2001). The memory skills of experts tend to be very specific. For example, expert chess players have much better memory than novices for various chess positions.

According to one estimate, chess experts can remember about 50,000 "chunks," or familiar arrangements of chess pieces (Chi, 2006; Gobet & Simon, 1996a). Expert chess players can also rapidly retrieve information from long-term memory (Ericsson & Towne, 2010). Surprisingly, though, chess experts are only slightly better than novices at remembering random arrangements of the chess pieces (Gobet et al., 2004). Experts' memory is thus substantially better only if a chess arrangement fits into a particular schema (Feltovich et al., 2006; Lovett, 2002).

Problem-Solving Strategies

When experts encounter a novel problem in their area of expertise, they are more likely than novices to use the means-ends heuristic effectively (Sternberg & Ben-Zeev, 2001). That is, they divide a problem into several subproblems, which they solve in a specified order. They are also more likely to approach a problem systematically, whereas novices are more likely to have a haphazard approach (Reif, 2008). In addition, experts and novices differ in the way they use the analogy approach. When solving physics problems, experts are more likely to emphasize the structural similarity between problems. In contrast, novices are more likely to be distracted by surface similarities (Chi, 2006; Leighton & Sternberg, 2003).

Speed and Accuracy

Experts are much faster than novices at solving a problem in their area of expertise, and they solve problems very accurately (Chi, 2006; Ericsson, 2003b; Ericsson & Towne, 2010). Their operations become more automatic, and a particular stimulus situation also quickly triggers a response (Bransford et al., 2000; Glaser & Chi, 1988; Robertson, 2001).

On some tasks, experts may solve problems faster because they use parallel rather than serial processing. As we noted earlier in the book, **parallel processing** handles two or more items at the same time. In contrast, **serial processing** handles only one item at a time. Novick and Coté (1992) discovered that experts frequently solved anagrams in less than two seconds. In fact, they typically solved the anagrams so quickly that they must have been considering several possible solutions at the same time. In contrast, the novices solved the anagrams so slowly that they were probably using serial processing.

Metacognitive Skills

Experts are better than novices at monitoring their problem solving. As discussed in Chapter 6, self-monitoring is a component of metacognition. For example, experts seem to be better at judging the difficulty of a problem, and they are more skilled at allocating their time while solving problems (Bransford et al., 2000). According to a study of people who are inventors, the expert inventors skillfully monitor ideas to see that they are both useful and creative (Mieg, 2011). Experts can also recover relatively quickly when they realize that they have made an error (Feltovich et al., 2006).

Although expertise confers many advantages when solving a problem, experts do perform poorly on one task related to metacognition. Specifically, experts underestimate the amount of time that novices will require to solve a problem in the experts' area of specialization (Hinds, 1999). In contrast, the novices are more accurate in realizing that they will have trouble solving the problem!

Before you read further, be sure to try Demonstration 11.6.

Mental Set

When you have a **mental set**, you keep trying the same solution you used in previous problems, even though you could solve the problem by using a different, easier method. If you have a mental set, you close your mind prematurely, and you stop thinking about how to solve a problem effectively (Kruglanski, 2004; Zhao et al., 2011). Interestingly, recent research shows that people have a greater change in their event-related brain potentials (ERPs) on trials when they break a mental set, compared to trials when they keep trying their customary problem-solving strategy (Zhao et al., 2011).

The classic experiment on mental set is Abraham Luchins's (1942) water-jar problem, illustrated in Part A of Demonstration 11.6. The best way to solve Problem 1 in Part A is to fill up jar B and remove one jarful with jar A and two jarfuls with jar C. You can solve Problems 1 through 5 by using this strategy, so you develop a mental set. Most people will keep using this complex method when they reach Problem 6. Unfortunately, however, the previous learning will actually hinder your performance, because you can solve these last two problems by using easier, more direct methods. For example, you can solve Problem 6

Try these two examples to see the effects of mental set.

A. Luchins's Water-Jar Problem
Suppose that you have three jars, A, B, and C. Each of six problems (listed below) shows the capacity of the three jars. You must use these jars in order to obtain the amount of liquid specified in the Goal column. You may obtain the goal amount by adding or subtracting the quantities listed in A, B, and C. (The answers can be found later in the text, in the discussion of mental set.)

Problem	A	B	C	Goal
1	24	130	3	100
2	9	44	7	21
3	21	58	4	29
4	12	160	25	98
5	19	75	5	46
6	23	49	3	20

B. A Number Puzzle
You are no doubt familiar with the kind of number puzzles in which you try to figure out the pattern for the order of numbers. Why are these numbers arranged in this order?

8, 5, 4, 9, 1, 7, 6, 3, 2, 0

The answer appears at the end of the chapter.
Source: Part A of this demonstration is based on Luchins, 1942.

by subtracting C from A, and you can solve Problem 7 by adding C to A. Luchins also tested a group who began right away with problems such as Problem 6 in Demonstration 11.6. These people almost always solved these problems in the easier fashion.

Both mental set and functional fixedness (which we'll discuss in a moment) represent overactive top-down processing. In both these cases, problem solvers are so strongly guided by their previous experience that they fail to consider more effective solutions to their problems.

Mental sets are related to a concept that Carol Dweck (2006) calls a "fixed mindset." If you have a **fixed mindset**, you believe that you possess a certain amount of intelligence and other skills, and that no amount of effort can help you perform better. You give up on trying to discover new ways to improve your abilities. In contrast, if you have a **growth mindset**, you believe that you can cultivate your intelligence and other skills. You challenge yourself to perform better, whether you are trying to learn how to play tennis, how to adjust to a new roommate, or how to perform better on your next examination in your course in cognitive psychology.

Functional Fixedness

Like a mental set, functional fixedness occurs when our top-down processing is overactive. However, mental set refers to our problem-solving *strategies*, whereas functional fixedness refers to the way we think about *physical objects*. Specifically, **functional fixedness** means that we tend to assign stable (or "fixed") functions to an object. As a result, we fail to think about the features of this object that might be useful in helping us solve a problem (German & Barrett, 2005).

The classic study in functional fixedness is called *Duncker's candle problem* (Duncker, 1945). Imagine that a researcher has led you into a room that contains a table. On the table are three objects: a candle, a matchbox holding some matches, and a box of thumbtacks. Your task is to find a way to attach a candle to the wall of the room so that it burns properly, using only the objects on the table. The solution requires overcoming functional fixedness by thinking flexibly about other ways to use an object (Bassok & Novick, 2012). In this situation, you need to realize that the matchbox can also be used for a different purpose—holding a candle—rather than just holding some matches. In fact, you can use the tack to fasten the empty matchbox to the wall, so that it can serve as a candle-holder.

In our everyday life, most of us have access to a variety of tools and objects, so functional fixedness does not create a significant handicap. In contrast, consider the quandary of Dr. Angus Wallace and Dr. Tom Wong, who provided a heroic example of overcoming functional fixedness. These physicians had just left on a plane for Hong Kong when they learned that another passenger was experiencing a collapsed lung. The only surgical items they had brought onboard were a segment of rubber tubing and a scalpel. Still, they operated on the woman and saved her life, using only this modest equipment and objects in the airplane that normally have fixed functions—a coat hanger, a knife, a fork, and a bottle of Evian water (Adler & Hall, 1995).

Interestingly, functional fixedness can also be demonstrated in cultures with little experience using manufactured objects. For example, German and Barrett (2005) showed some simple kitchen objects to adolescents living near the Amazon River in Ecuador. If the adolescents saw a spoon being used to stir rice, they later had difficulty imagining that the spoon could also serve as a bridge between two other objects.

Mental set and functional fixedness are two examples of part of Theme 2: Mistakes in cognitive processing can often be traced to a strategy that is basically very rational. It is generally a wise strategy to use the knowledge you learned in solving earlier problems to solve a current dilemma. If an old idea happens to work well, keep using it!

In the case of a mental set, we are too rigid in applying a strategy that we learned from previous experience. We therefore fail to think about more efficient solutions. Similarly, objects in our world often have fixed functions, such that the strategy of using one object for one task and a second object for a different task is appropriate. Functional fixedness occurs, however, when we apply that strategy too rigidly.

Gender Stereotypes and Math Problem Solving

In certain cases, our top-down processes may be overactive because stereotypes can influence our beliefs about our own abilities (Walton & Dweck, 2009). As we noted in Chapter 8, **gender stereotypes** are the beliefs and opinions that we associate with females and males (Jackson, 2011; Matlin, 2012; Whitley & Kite, 2010). A typical gender stereotype is that men are more skilled than women in solving mathematics problems. Is there evidence in support of this gender stereotype? Janet Hyde and colleagues (2008) analyzed scores on standardized mathematics tests for 7,200,000 U.S. students (see also Hyde, 2016). They found consistent gender similarities for students of all ages, from second grade through 11th grade (see Scheiber et al., 2015, for a similar result in college students). The same pattern of gender similarities is found in studies conducted with international samples (Else-Quest et al., 2010; Halpern, 2012). Furthermore, females earn *higher* grades in math courses, beginning with elementary school and continuing up through college (Halpern, 2012; Kimball, 1989). Some evidence thus calls into question the validity of this gender stereotype.

Now, imagine two high school seniors, Jennifer and Matthew, who are about to begin the math portion of the Scholastic Assessment Test (SAT). Both are excellent students with A averages in their math courses. They know that this may be the most important test they will ever take because the results could determine which college they will attend. Both students are anxious, but Jennifer has an additional source of anxiety: She must struggle with the widespread stereotype that, because she is a female, she should score lower than male students (Quinn & Spencer, 2001). This additional anxiety may in fact lead her to solve math problems less effectively and to earn a relatively low score on the math portion of the SAT. In this example, Jennifer is experiencing **stereotype threat**: If you belong to a group that is hampered by a negative stereotype—and you think about your membership in that group—your performance may suffer (Smith et al., 2007; Steele, 1997; Whitley & Kite, 2010).

The contributions of this gender stereotype to stereotype threat in female participants have been demonstrated multiple times (see Doyle & Voyer, 2016, for a review of this literature; O'Brien & Crandall, 2003; Quinn & Spencer, 2001). For instance, O'Brien and Crandall (2003) studied a group of college women who were taking a difficult math test. Some women had been told that they would take a math test that was known to show higher scores for men than for women. These women performed significantly worse than women in a second group, who had been told that the math test had not shown gender differences. In a similar study, Thoman and colleagues (2008) told one group of female students that males tend to perform better than females on math tests because males have greater *ability*. A second group of female students heard the same instructions, except that the males' better performance occurred because males *try harder*. A third group served as the control group; they received no information about gender differences. Interestingly, the women in the "try harder" condition answered a significantly greater percentage of questions correctly, compared to the women in the other two conditions.

Research with Asian American Females

In North America, one stereotype is that Asian Americans are "good at math," compared to those from other ethnic groups. In contrast, as we just discussed, another stereotype is that women are "bad at math," compared to men. Let's examine a study conducted by Margaret Shih and her coauthors (1999), in which all the participants were Asian American female college students. Shih and her coworkers (1999) divided these Asian American women into three different conditions. Let's examine how these conditions influenced their scores on a challenging math test.

1. **Ethnicity-emphasis condition:** These participants were asked to indicate their ethnicity and then answer several questions about their ethnic identity. Then, they took a challenging math test. These women answered 54% of the questions correctly.

2. **Control-group condition:** A second group of participants did not answer any questions beforehand. They simply took the challenging math test. These women answered 49% of the questions correctly.

3. **Gender-emphasis condition:** A third group of participants were asked to indicate their gender and then answer several questions about their gender identity. Then, they took the challenging math test. These women answered only 43% of the questions correctly.

Apparently, when Asian American women are reminded of their ethnicity, they perform relatively well. However, when Asian American women are reminded of their gender, they may experience stereotype threat, and their problem-solving ability can decline. Nalini Ambady and her coauthors (2001) demonstrated this same pattern among Asian American girls enrolled in elementary and middle school.

Potential Explanations

Why should stereotype threat often lead to poorer performance? Two factors probably contribute to the problem. One factor is that stereotype threat can produce high arousal (Blascovich et al., 2001; O'Brien & Crandall, 2003). High arousal is likely to interfere with working memory, especially on difficult tasks. Research shows that people may "choke under pressure" on a challenging math test. This anxiety apparently reduces the capacity of working memory (Beilock & Carr, 2005). A second factor is that females who are taking a difficult math test may work hard to suppress the thought that they are supposed to perform poorly (Quinn & Spencer, 2001). As we pointed out in Chapter 3, thought suppression requires great effort, which reduces the capacity of working memory even further.

In what way do the increased arousal and reduced working memory actually decrease women's ability to solve math problems? Quinn and Spencer (2001) proposed that these factors decrease women's abilities to construct problem-solving strategies. They studied female and male undergraduates. Half of each group completed a test with word problems requiring strategies in order to convert the words into algebraic equations. The other half of each group completed a test with algebra problems that were presented as numerical equations. These items did not require any conversion strategies. Figure 11.2 shows that the

FIGURE 11.2
Average performance by men and women on word-problem test and numerical test.

Source: Quinn, D. M., & Spencer, S. J. (2001). The interference of stereotype threat with women's generation of mathematical problem-solving strategies. *Journal of Social Issues, 57,* 55–71.

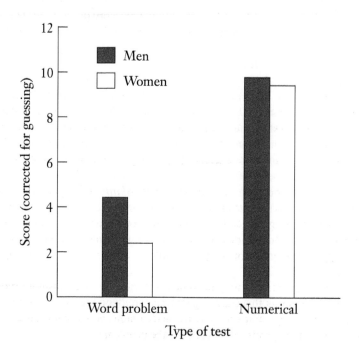

Demonstration 11.7 | Two Insight Problems

A. **The Sahara Problem** (based on Perkins, 2001). Suppose that you are driving through the Sahara Desert in Africa. Suddenly, you see someone lying facedown in the sand. When you explore further, you see that it's a dead man. You cannot see any tracks anywhere nearby, and there have been no recent winds to erase the tracks. You look in a pack on the man's back. What do you find?

B. **The Triangle Problem**. With six matches, construct four equilateral triangles. One intact match (not broken or bent) must make up one side of each triangle. The answers to these two problems are at the end of the chapter.

men performed significantly better than the women on the word-problem test, but there were no gender differences on the numerical test.

Insight versus Noninsight Problems

When you solve an **insight problem**, the problem initially seems impossible to solve, but then an alternative approach suddenly bursts into your consciousness. You immediately realize that your new solution is correct (Gibson et al., 2011; Johnson-Laird, 2005b; Reed, 2010). In general, people who have a large working-memory capacity solve insight problems relatively quickly (Chein et al., 2010).

In contrast, when you work on a **noninsight problem**, you solve the problem gradually, by using your memory, reasoning skills, and a routine set of strategies (Davidson, 1995; Schooler et al., 1995). For example, Demonstration 11.1 at the beginning of this chapter was a noninsight problem, because you gradually pursued the answer in a logical, step-by-step fashion. Before you read further, try Demonstration 11.7.

When cartoonists represent insight, they show a gleaming light bulb above a person's head. You can probably think of a time when you or someone you know suddenly experienced an "aha!" moment. For example, I recall a vivid "aha!" moment that our daughter Sally demonstrated in connection with the Tooth Fairy. As you may know, many North American families have an eccentric custom. When a child has lost a tooth, he or she places it in a sealed envelope, underneath a pillow at nighttime. Then, when the child is asleep, an adult quietly replaces that envelope with a different envelope that contains a modest amount of money, presumably brought by the small, surreptitious Tooth Fairy. After several visits from the Tooth Fairy, we noticed that our daughter wore a perplexed expression. She then described her puzzlement: "What I don't understand is how the Tooth Fairy can take out the tooth and put the money in the envelope without tearing the envelope. . .*unless* there are two different envelopes!!!" If you solved the problems successfully in Demonstration 11.7, you experienced a similar feeling of sudden success.

We examine several components of insight. Then, we consider people's metacognitions when working on insight and noninsight problems.

The Nature of Insight

The concept of insight was very important to gestalt psychologists (Fioratou & Cowley, 2011; Johnson-Laird, 2005b; Lovett, 2002). As noted in Chapters 1 and 2, gestalt psychologists emphasized organizational tendencies, especially in perception and in problem solving. They argued that the parts of a problem may initially seem unrelated to one another, but a sudden flash of insight could make the parts instantly fit together into a solution. In contrast to the gestalt psychologists, the behaviorists rejected the concept of insight.

According to the psychologists who favor this concept of insight, people who are working on an insight problem usually hold some incorrect assumptions when they begin to solve the problem (Chi, 2006; Ormerod et al., 2006; Reed, 2010). For example, when you began to solve Part B of Demonstration 11.7, at first you probably assumed that the six matches needed to be arranged on a flat surface. In other words, top-down processing inappropriately dominated your thinking, and you were considering the wrong set of alternatives (Ormerod et al., 2006).

We've noted that top-down processing may prevent you from solving an insight problem. In contrast, noninsight problems—such as straightforward algebra problems—typically do benefit from top-down processing (McCormick, 2003). The strategies you learned in high school math classes offer guidance as you work, step-by-step, toward the proper conclusion of the problem.

Metacognition during Problem Solving

When you are working on a problem, how confident are you that you are on the right track? Metcalfe (1986) emphasizes that the pattern of your metacognitions differs for noninsight and insight problems. Specifically, people's confidence builds gradually for problems that do not require insight, such as standard high-school algebra problems. In contrast, when people work on insight problems, they experience a sudden leap in confidence when they are close to a correct solution. In fact, this sudden rise in confidence can be used to distinguish insight from noninsight problems (Hélie & Sun, 2010; Herzog & Robinson, 2005; Metcalfe & Wiebe, 1987).

Metcalfe presented students with problems like this one:

> *A stranger approached a museum curator and offered him an ancient bronze coin. The coin had an authentic appearance and was marked with the date 544 B.C. The curator had happily made acquisitions from suspicious sources before, but this time he promptly called the police and had the stranger arrested. Why? (p. 624).*

As students worked on this kind of insight problem, they supplied ratings every 10 seconds on a "feeling-of-warmth" scale. A rating of 0 indicated that they were completely "cold" about the problem, with no glimmer of a solution. A score of 10 meant that they were certain they had a solution.

As you can see from the left-hand side of Figure 11.3, the participants' warmth ratings initially showed only gradual increases for the insight problems. However, their warmth ratings soared dramatically when they discovered the correct solution. If you figured out the answer to the coin question, did you experience this same sudden burst of certainty? (Incidentally, the answer to this problem is that someone who had actually lived in 544 B.C. could not possibly have used the designation "B.C." to indicate the birth of Christ half a millennium later.) Metcalfe's results have been replicated (Davidson, 1995), confirming that problem solvers typically report a dramatic increase in their confidence when they believe they have located the correct solution to an insight problem.

Advice about Problem Solving

The potential difference between noninsight problems and insight problems suggests some strategies. You might begin to solve a problem by contemplating whether you have had previous experience with similar problems. Top-down processing will be especially useful when you approach a noninsight problem. From time to time, however, you should also consider whether the problem might require

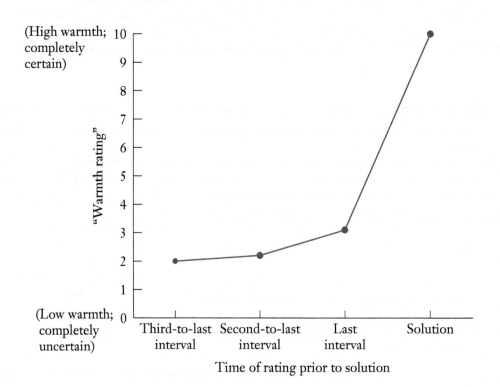

FIGURE 11.3
"Warmth ratings" for answers that were correct, as a function of time of rating prior to answering.

Source: Metcalfe, J. (1986). Premonitions of insight predict impending error. *Journal of Experimental Psychology: Learning, Memory, and Cognition, 12,* 623–634.

insight. You'll need a different approach to solve an insight problem, because there are no clear rules for these problems (Chi, 2006). You might try to represent the problem in a different way or think about a different meaning for an ambiguous word (Lovett, 2002; Perkins, 2001). In some cases, it's helpful to draw sketches, work with physical objects, or use gestures when you are trying to solve an insight problem (Fioratou & Cowley, 2011; Shapiro, 2011). An insight problem forces you to search for the answer "outside the box" by abandoning your customary top-down assumptions and looking for novel solutions.

Creativity

The topic of creativity is itself an area of problem solving—like the problem-solving tasks we have already considered, creativity requires moving from an initial state to a goal state. People who think creatively often experience moments of genius, and light bulbs flash continuously above their heads.

Creativity is definitely a popular topic, both within and beyond psychology. In fact, more than 10,000 papers about creativity were published between 1999 and 2009 (Kaufman & Sternberg, 2010b). It would be easy to write an entire chapter on the variety of definitions for creativity. Most theorists emphasize, however, that **creativity** requires solutions that are both novel and useful (Hennessey & Amabile, 2010; Kaufman & Sternberg, 2010b; Runco, 2007).

Although many theorists agree on the basic definition of creativity, their views differ on other characteristics. For instance, some psychologists argue that creativity is based on ordinary thinking, a process similar to our everyday problem solving (e.g., De Dreu et al., 2008; Halpern, 2003; Kozbelt et al., 2010). In contrast, other psychologists argue that ordinary people seldom produce creative products. Instead, certain exceptional people are extraordinarily creative in their specific area of expertise, such as music, literature, or science (e.g., Feldman et al., 1994; Kozbelt et al., 2010; Simonton, 2010).

The Nature of Creativity

For more than a century, researchers have devised a variety of theories about creativity. However, the initial scientific research is typically traced to J. P. Guilford (Runco, 2014). Guilford (1967) proposed that psychologists should measure creativity in terms of **divergent production**, or the number of different responses made to a test item. Incidentally, take a few minutes to complete Demonstration 11.8.

Many researchers agree that creativity requires divergent thinking, rather than one single best answer (Runco, 2007; Russ, 2001; Smith & Ward, 2012). Demonstration 11.8 shows several ways in which Guilford measured divergent production. To earn a high score, the problem solver must explore in many

---

Demonstration 11.8 ‖ Divergent Production Tests

Try the following items, which are similar to Guilford's divergent production tests.

1. Many words begin with an L and end with an N. In one minute, list as many words as possible that have the form L _____ N. (The words can have any number of letters between the L and the N.)

2. Suppose that people reached their final height at the age of 2, and so normal adult height would be less than three feet. In one minute, list as many consequences as possible that would result from this change.

3. Below is a list of names. They can be classified in many ways. For example, one classification would be in terms of the number of syllables: JACOB, MAYA, and HAROLD have two syllables, whereas BETH, GAIL, and JUAN have one syllable. Classify them in as many other ways as possible in one minute.

BETH HAROLD GAIL JACOB JUAN MAYA

4. Below are four shapes. In one minute, combine them to make each of the following objects: a face, a lamp, a piece of playground equipment, and a tree. Each shape may be used once, many times, or not at all in forming each object, and it may be expanded or shrunk to any size. Each shape may also be rotated.

different directions from the initial problem state. As you can see, some items require test takers to overcome functional fixedness. Indeed, moderate correlations have been reported between people's test scores and other judgments of their creativity (Guilford, 1967; Runco, 2014). However, the number of different ideas may not be the best measure of creativity. After all, this measure does not assess whether the solutions meet the two criteria for creativity: The solution must be both novel and useful.

With so much research on the topic of creativity, no one list of creativity-related characteristics can capture the rich variety of the research. Here are three general observations, however, which psychologists have discovered about the nature of creativity—in fact, these observations do not match the reports that you find in the popular media.

1. **Creativity includes convergent thinking, as well as divergent thinking**   (Dietrich & Kanso, 2010; Ward & Kolomyts, 2010). As previously discussed, divergent production is measured by the number of different responses that the test-taker makes. In contrast, **convergent production** asks the test-taker to supply a single, best response, and the researchers measure the quality of that response. Many situations require one especially creative solution, rather than several less-useful solutions.

2. **Creativity is associated with many regions within both the left and right hemispheres** Creativity is associated with many locations in both of the brain's hemispheres, as well as other regions and structures in the brain (Dietrich, 2007; Dietrich & Kanso, 2010; Feist, 2010).

3. **Creativity can occur when we use focused attention (conscious attention) as well as defocused attention (altered states of consciousness)**   People can be creative when they are consciously focusing on a task. If ideas occur to people when they are daydreaming, these ideas are not especially creative (Dietrich & Kanso, 2010).

Motivation and Creativity

Think about a recent time when you worked especially hard on a course assignment or some project at your job. Researchers propose two general types of motivation. One type is called **extrinsic motivation**, or the motivation to work on a task—not because you find it enjoyable—but in order to earn a promised reward or to win a competition.

The other type of motivation is called **intrinsic motivation**, or the motivation to work on tasks for their own sake, because you find them interesting, exciting, or personally challenging (Collins & Amabile, 1999; Eliott & Mapes, 2002; Runco, 2005).

Research on extrinsic motivation demonstrates that people often produce less-creative projects if they are working on these projects for external reasons (Amabile, 1997; Hennessey, 2000; Prabhu et al., 2008). When people believe that a particular task is just a means of earning a reward, a good grade, or a positive evaluation, their extrinsic motivation is high. Consequently, their creativity is also likely to decrease (Hennessey, 2000; Prabhu et al., 2008; Runco, 2007). In fact, for many years, researchers had adopted a simple perspective that extrinsic motivation is consistently harmful. You've probably studied psychology long enough to know that no conclusions in our discipline could be that straightforward. In fact, the research suggests that creativity can actually be enhanced if the extrinsic factors provide *useful feedback* (Collins & Amabile, 1999; Eisenberger & Rhoades, 2001).

We do know that people are more likely to be creative when they are working on a task that they truly enjoy (e.g., Amabile, 1997; Hennessey, 2000; Runco, 2005), and thus when intrinsic motivation is high. For example, Ruscio and his coauthors (1998) gave college students a standardized test of intrinsic motivation. The test asked them to rate their level of interest in three representative kinds of creative activities: writing, art, and problem solving. Several weeks later, the students were asked to perform tasks in these three areas. Demonstration 11.9 is similar to the writing task, for example. Take a few minutes to try this demonstration. A group of trained judges then rated the students' creative projects. The results showed that the students who had earned high intrinsic-motivation scores on the standardized test were also more likely to produce more creative projects.

Furthermore, Prabhu, Sutton, and Sauser (2008) proposed that certain personality traits might be related to creativity, but only if the person has high intrinsic motivation. Prabhu and her colleagues, therefore, gave several self-rating questionnaires to 124 undergraduate students who were enrolled in an introductory management course at Auburn University. These questionnaires assessed a variety of characteristics, such

Demonstration 11.9 | Writing a Creative Poem

For this demonstration, you will write an American haiku. These instructions are similar to those that Ruscio and his colleagues (1998) supplied to the participants in their study, as follows:

An American haiku is a five-line poem. As you can see from the sample poem below, the first line simply contains a noun, in this case the noun ocean. *The second line has two adjectives describing the noun. The third line features three verbs related to the noun. The fourth line is a phrase of any length, which is related to the noun. Notice that the last line simply repeats the first line.*

Ocean
Wavy, foamy
Roll, tumble, crash
All captured in this shell at my ear.
Ocean

Your task is to write a similar American haiku, featuring the noun *summer*. Take five minutes to write this poem.

Source: Based on Ruscio et al., 1998, p. 249.

---

as intrinsic and extrinsic motivation. They also assessed personality traits, such as **self-efficacy**, which is the belief that you have the ability to organize and carry out a specific task, and **perseverance**, which is the ability to keep working on a task, even when you encounter obstacles. Let's look at the results of this study:

1. Consistent with the previous research, the students with high scores on intrinsic motivation tended to earn high scores on creativity. If you are working on a project because you find it interesting, your work is likely to be *more* creative.

2. Also consistent with the previous research, the students with high scores on extrinsic motivation tended to earn low scores on creativity. As we discussed earlier, if you are working on a project because you want some kind of reward, your work is likely to be *less* creative.

3. Prabhu and her coauthors (2008) also found that self-efficacy was closely correlated with creativity. Furthermore, a more detailed statistical analysis showed that this correlation could be explained by the students' intrinsic motivation. That is, when students are high in self-efficacy, they tend to have high intrinsic motivation, and this high intrinsic motivation encourages their creativity.

4. Surprisingly, Prabhu and her colleagues discovered that perseverance was *not* consistently correlated with creativity.

Prabhu and her coauthors (2008) point out a potential problem that might have occurred to you: Can self-reports be trusted? The students' responses on the questionnaires were completely anonymous, so they would not be especially likely to answer the questions in a socially desirable fashion. Still, Prabhu and her coauthors (2008) suggest that future research should evaluate the participants' *actual* creative performance, rather than the participants' own evaluation of their creativity.

SECTION SUMMARY POINTS

Understanding the Problem

1. During problem solving, you begin with the initial state and try to overcome the obstacles in order to reach the goal state.

2. To understand a problem, you need to create an accurate mental representation of the problem.

3. Attention is relevant in problem solving because attention is limited, because competing thoughts can produce divided attention, and because problem solvers must focus their attention on the appropriate part of the problem.

4. You can represent a problem by using approaches such as symbols, matrices, diagrams, and visual images.

5. Environmental cues (situated cognition) and cues related to your own body (embodied cognition) can influence the way you represent a problem; as a result, you can solve the problem more accurately.

Problem-Solving Strategies

1. With algorithms, such as exhaustive search, the problem solver eventually reaches a solution. However, this method is often very time consuming. In contrast, heuristics are faster because they examine only a few of the alternatives; unfortunately, they do not guarantee an appropriate solution.

2. One important heuristic is the analogy approach, in which people solve a new problem by referring to an earlier problem. They may

be distracted by superficial similarity, but several precautions can encourage people to emphasize structural similarity.

3. The means-ends heuristic requires dividing a problem into subproblems and then trying to reduce the difference between the initial state and the goal state for each of the subproblems. The General Problem Solver (GPS) is a computer simulation that was designed to use means-ends analysis.

4. One of the simplest problem-solving strategies is the hill-climbing heuristic; at every choice point, you select the alternative that seems to lead most directly to the goal. However, this strategy may not produce the best long-term solution.

Factors That Influence Problem Solving

1. Experts differ from novices with respect to attributes such as their knowledge base, problem-solving strategies, accuracy, and metacognitive skills.

2. Mental set can influence your problem solving; you keep trying the same ineffective strategy, although another strategy would be more effective. Functional fixedness can also influence your problem solving; you assign a specific function to an object, although this object could be used for other tasks. In both cases, top-down processing is overactive. However, both strategies can be traced to a basically intelligent strategy.

3. Males and females typically earn similar scores on mathematics tasks. However, females may experience stereotype threat if they think about the stereotype that females are less skilled in math. As a result, their performance on a math test may suffer.

4. Insight problems are solved when the answer appears suddenly; noninsight problems are solved gradually, using top-down processing.

5. Research on metacognition shows that your confidence builds gradually for *noninsight* problems; in contrast, your confidence on *insight* problems is initially low, but it suddenly increases when you solve the problem.

Creativity

1. Many definitions have been proposed for creativity; one common definition is that creativity requires finding a solution that is both novel and useful.

2. Guilford's measure of divergent production is the classic approach to creativity.

3. The research demonstrates that extrinsic motivation can reduce creativity.

4. The research also demonstrates that intrinsic motivation promotes high levels of creativity. However, self-reported perseverance does not seem to be correlated with creativity.

CHAPTER REVIEW QUESTIONS

1. This chapter examined several different methods of representing a problem. Point out how each method could be used to solve a problem that you have recently faced, either in college classes or in your personal life. In addition, identify how the situated cognition and the embodied cognition perspectives can be applied to your understanding of this problem.

2. What barriers prevent people from successfully using the analogy approach to problem solving? Think of an area in which you are an expert, such as an academic subject, a hobby, or knowledge related to your work. When are you most likely to recognize the structural similarities shared by problem isomorphs?

3. In problem solving, how do algorithms differ from heuristics? When you solve problems, what situations encourage each of these two approaches? Describe a situation in where the means-ends heuristic was more useful than an algorithm. Identify a time when you used the hill-climbing heuristic, and note whether it helped you solve the problem.

4. Think of someone you know well, who is an expert in a particular area. Explain the cognitive areas in which he or she may have an advantage over a novice. When discussing this area of expertise, does this person fail to realize that other people might not understand this discussion?

5. How are mental set and functional fixedness related to each other, and how do they limit problem solving? How could insight help you to overcome these two barriers to effective problem solving?

6. On two occasions, this chapter discussed metacognition. Discuss these two topics, and point out how metacognitive measures can help us determine which problems require insight and which do not.

7. Imagine that you are teaching seventh grade, and your students are about to take a series of standardized tests in mathematics. Assume that your students hold the stereotype that boys are better at math than girls are. Just before the test, you hear the students discussing whether the boys or the girls will earn a higher score. How might stereotype threat influence their performance? Describe two specific ways in which stereotype threat could influence the students' cognitive processes.

8. Think of an example of an insight problem and a noninsight problem that you have solved recently. Based on the discussion of this topic, how would these two problems differ with respect to the way you made progress in solving the problem and the nature of your metacognitions about your progress in problem solving?

9. We discussed how the external environment can influence problem solving, in connection with (a) situated cognition, (b) the analogy approach, and (c) factors influencing creativity. Using this information, point out why environmental factors are important in problem solving.

10. Imagine that you are supervising 10 employees in a small company. Describe how you might use the material in this chapter to encourage more effective problem solving and greater creativity. Then, describe the activities you would want to *avoid* because they might hinder problem solving and creativity.

KEYWORDS

thinking
problem solving
initial state
goal state
obstacles
understanding
problem representation
matrix
hierarchical tree
  diagram

situated cognition
  approach
embodied cognition
  approach
ecological validity
algorithm
exhaustive search
heuristic
analogy approach
problem isomorphs

surface features
structural features
subproblems
means-ends heuristic
computer simulation
General Problem Solver
(GPS)
hill-climbing heuristic
bottom-up processing
top-down processing

expertise
parallel processing
serial processing
mental set
fixed mindset
growth mindset
functional fixedness
gender stereotypes
stereotype threat
insight problem

noninsight problem
creativity
divergent production
convergent production
extrinsic motivation
intrinsic motivation
self-efficacy
perseverance

RECOMMENDED READINGS

Ericsson, K. A., Charness, N., Feltovich, P. J., & Hoffman, R. R. (Eds.). (2006). *The Cambridge handbook of expertise and expert performance.* New York: Cambridge University Press. K. Anders Ericsson is the acknowledged "expert on expertise"; this handbook includes 42 chapters on theoretical, empirical, and applied aspects of expertise.

Hennessey, B. A., & Amabile, T. M. (2010). Creativity. *Annual Review of Psychology, 61,* 569–598. Beth Hennessey and Teresa Amabile are well-known researchers in the area of creativity, and this chapter provides an excellent summary of the research.

Kaufman, J. C., & Sternberg, R. J. (Eds.). (2010a). *The Cambridge handbook of creativity.* New York: Cambridge University Press. This handbook examines

topics such as theories of creativity, everyday creativity, and the relationship between creativity and mental illness.

Nickerson, R. S. (2010). *Mathematical reasoning: Patterns, problems, conjectures, and proofs.* New York: Psychology Press. Most books about mathematics are written by mathematicians, but Raymond Nickerson is a psychology professor. This book examines topics such as young children's understanding of numbers, representation in mathematics, and the concept of infinity.

Shapiro, L. (Ed.). (2014). *The Routledge handbook of embodied cognition.* Routledge. Readers will find an overview of theoretical views on embodied cognition as applied to multiple cognitive and social domains.

ANSWER TO DEMONSTRATION 11.3

In the hospital room problem, Ms. Anderson has a liver problem, and she is in Room 104.

ANSWER TO DEMONSTRATION 11.5

In the Elves-and-Goblins problem (with R representing the right bank and L representing the left bank), here are the steps in the solution:

1. Move 2 Goblins, R to L.
2. Move 1 Goblin, L to R.
3. Move 2 Goblins, R to L.
4. Move 1 Goblin, L to R.
5. Move 2 Elves, R to L.
6. Move 1 Goblin, 1 Elf, L to R.
7. Move 2 Elves, R to L.
8. Move 1 Goblin, L to R.
9. Move 2 Goblins, R to L.
10. Move 1 Goblin, L to R.
11. Move 2 Goblins, R to L.

ANSWER TO DEMONSTRATION 11.6B

The numbers are in alphabetical order; your mental set probably suggested that the numbers were in some mathematical sequence, not a language-based sequence.

ANSWER TO DEMONSTRATION 11.7A

The pack on the man's back contained an unopened parachute. (Other solutions would also be possible.)

ANSWER TO DEMONSTRATION 11.7B

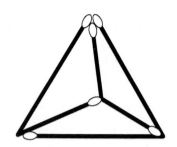

Deductive Reasoning and Decision Making

12

Chapter Introduction

The topics of problem solving, deductive reasoning, and decision making are all interrelated. All three topics are included in the general category called "thinking." Thinking requires you to go beyond the information you were given. Thinking typically involves a goal such as a solution, a belief, or a decision. In other words, you begin with several pieces of information, and you must mentally transform that information so that you can solve a problem or make a decision. We covered problem solving in Chapter 11. In this chapter, we discuss deductive reasoning and decision making.

Deductive Reasoning is a type of reasoning that begins with some specific premises, which are generally assumed to be true. Based on those premises, you judge whether they allow a particular conclusion to be drawn, as determined by the principles of logic. For example, suppose that a student named Jenna wants to enroll next semester in a course called "Biopsychology." The course description says, "To enroll in this course, students must have completed a course in research methods." However, Jenna has not completed this course; she plans to enroll in it next semester. Therefore, we draw the logical conclusion, "Jenna cannot enroll in Biopsychology next semester."

During decision making, you assess information and choose among two or more alternatives. Many decisions are trivial: Do you want mustard on your sandwich? Other decisions are momentous: Should you apply to graduate programs for next year, or should you try to find a job?

In this chapter, we first explore deductive reasoning, focusing heavily on a series of classic effects that have been studied, in order to unlock the general cognitive principles that govern our ability to deduce. In the following two sections, we cover the topic of decision making. We first consider a number of heuristics that guide the decision-making process. In our second section on decision making, we consider phenomena that have direct applications to decision making in our daily lives.

Deductive Reasoning

In **deductive reasoning**, you begin with some specific premises that are generally true, and you need to judge whether those premises allow you to draw a particular conclusion, based on the principles of logic (Halpern, 2003; Johnson-Laird, 2005a; Levy, 2010). A deductive-reasoning task provides you with all the information you need to draw a conclusion. Furthermore, the premises are either true or false, and you must use the rules of formal logic in order to draw conclusions (Levy, 2010; Roberts & Newton, 2005; Wilhelm, 2005).

One of the most common kinds of deductive reasoning tasks is called conditional reasoning. A **conditional reasoning task** (also called a **propositional reasoning task**) describes the relationship between conditions.

Here's a typical conditional reasoning task:

> *If a child is allergic to peanuts, then eating peanuts produces a breathing problem.*
> *A child has a breathing problem.*
> *Therefore, this child has eaten peanuts.*

Notice that this task tells us about the relationship between two conditions, such as the relationship between eating peanuts and a breathing problem. The kind of conditional reasoning we consider in this chapter explores reasoning tasks that have an "if. . .then. . ." kind of structure. When researchers study conditional reasoning, people judge whether the conclusion is valid or invalid. In the example above, the conclusion "Therefore, this child has eaten peanuts" is *not* valid, because some other substance or medical condition could have caused the problem.

Another common kind of deductive reasoning task is called a syllogism. A **syllogism** consists of two statements that we must assume to be true, plus a conclusion. Syllogisms refer to quantities, so they use the words *all, none, some,* and other similar terms. Here's a typical syllogism:

> *Some psychology majors are friendly people.*
> *Some friendly people are concerned about poverty.*
> *Therefore, some psychology majors are concerned about poverty.*

In a syllogism, you must judge whether the conclusion is valid, invalid, or indeterminate. In this example, the answer is indeterminate. In fact, those psychology majors who are friendly people and those friendly people who are concerned about poverty could really be two separate populations, with no overlap whatsoever.

Notice that your everyday experience tempts you to conclude, "Yes, the conclusion is valid." After all, you know many psychology majors who are concerned about poverty. Many people would automatically respond, "valid conclusion." In contrast, with a little more explicit thinking, you'll reexamine that syllogism and realize that the strict rules of deductive reasoning require you to respond, "The conclusion is indeterminate" (Stanovich, 2009, 2011; Tsujii & Watanabe, 2009).

In a college course in logic, you could spend an entire semester learning about the structure and solution of deductive reasoning tasks such as these. However, we emphasize the *cognitive* factors that influence deductive reasoning. Furthermore, we limit ourselves to conditional reasoning, a kind of deductive reasoning that students typically find more approachable than syllogisms (Schmidt & Thompson, 2008).

As it happens, researchers have found that conditional reasoning tasks and syllogisms are influenced by similar cognitive factors (Mercier & Sperber, 2011; Schmidt & Thompson, 2008; Stanovich, 2011). In addition, people's performance on conditional reasoning tasks is correlated with their performance on syllogism tasks (Stanovich & West, 2000).

In the remainder of this section, we first explore four basic kinds of conditional reasoning tasks before turning to a discussion of factors that cause difficulty in reasoning. We then conclude this section with a discussion of two cognitive errors that people often make when they solve these reasoning tasks.

Overview of Conditional Reasoning

Conditional reasoning situations occur frequently in our daily life. However, these reasoning tasks are surprisingly difficult to solve correctly (Evans, 2004; Johnson-Laird, 2011). Let's examine the formal principles that have been devised for solving these tasks correctly.

Table 12.1 illustrates **propositional calculus**, which is a system for categorizing the four kinds of reasoning used in analyzing **propositions** or statements.

Let's first introduce some basic terminology. The word **antecedent** refers to the first proposition or statement; the antecedent is contained in the "if. . ." part of the sentence. The word **consequent** refers to the proposition that comes second; it is the consequence. The consequent is contained in the "then. . ." part of the sentence.

When we work on a conditional reasoning task, we can perform two possible actions: (1) We can *affirm* part of the sentence, saying that it is true; or (2) we can *deny* part of the sentence, saying that it is false. By combining the two parts of the sentence with these two actions, we have four conditional reasoning situations. As you can see, two of them are valid, and two of them are invalid.

1. **Affirming the antecedent** means that you say that the "if. . ." part of the sentence is true. As shown in the upper-left corner of Table 12.1, this kind of reasoning leads to a valid, or correct, conclusion.

2. The fallacy (or error) of **affirming the consequent** means that you say that the "then. . ." part of the sentence is true. This kind of reasoning leads to an invalid conclusion. Notice the upper-right corner of Table 12.1; the conclusion "This is an apple" is incorrect. After all, the item could be a pear, or a mango, or numerous other kinds of nonapple fruit.

3. The fallacy of **denying the antecedent** means that you say that the "if. . ." part of the sentence is false. Denying the antecedent also leads to an invalid conclusion, as you can see from the lower-left corner of Table 12.1. Again, the item could be some fruit other than an apple.

4. **Denying the consequent** means that you say that the "then. . ." part of the sentence is false. In the lower-right corner of Table 12.1, notice that this kind of reasoning leads to a correct conclusion.[*]

Now test yourself on the four kinds of conditional reasoning tasks by trying Demonstration 12.1.

Let's now reconsider the "affirming the consequent" task in more detail, because this task causes the largest number of errors (Byrne & Johnson-Laird, 2009). It's easy to see why people are tempted to affirm the consequent. In real life, we are likely to be correct when we make this kind of conclusion (Evans, 2000). For example, consider the two propositions, "If a person is a talented singer, then he or she has musical abilities" and "Paula has musical abilities." In reality, it's often a good bet that Paula *is* a talented

Table 12.1 Propositional Calculus: The Four Kinds of Reasoning Tasks

	Portion of the statement	
Action taken	**Antecedent**	**Consequent**
Affirm	Affirming the antecedent (valid) *This is an apple; therefore this a fruit.*	Affirming the consequent (invalid) *This is a fruit; therefore this is an apple.*
Deny	Denying the antecedent (invalid) *This is not an apple; therefore it is not a fruit.*	Denying the consequent (valid) *This is not a fruit; therefore this is not an apple.*

Note: Each of these examples is based on the statement, "If this is an apple, then this is a fruit."

[*]If you have taken courses in research methods or statistics, you will recognize that scientific reasoning is based on the strategy of denying the consequent—that is, ruling out the null hypothesis.

Demonstration 12.1 | Propositional Calculus

Decide which of the following conclusions are valid and which are invalid. The answers are at the end of the chapter.

1. Affirming the antecedent

If today is Tuesday, then I have my bowling class.

Today is Tuesday.

Therefore, I have my bowling class.

2. Affirming the consequent

If Sarita is a psychology major, then she is a student.

Sarita is a student.

Therefore, Sarita is a psychology major.

3. Denying the antecedent

If I am a first-year student, then I must register for next semester's classes today.

I am not a first-year student.

Therefore, I must not register for next semester's classes today.

4. Denying the consequent

If the judge is fair, then Susan is the winner.

Susan is not the winner.

Therefore, the judge is not fair.

---

singer. However, in logical reasoning, we cannot rely on statements such as, "It's a good bet that.. . ." For example, I remember a student whose musical skills as a violinist were exceptional, yet she sang off-key.

As Theme 2 emphasizes, many cognitive errors can be traced to a **heuristic**, a general strategy that usually works well. In this example of logical reasoning, however, "it's a good bet" is not the same as "always" (Leighton & Sternberg, 2003). In the second part of this chapter, you'll see that decision-making tasks actually do allow us to use the concept, "it's a good bet." However, propositional reasoning tasks require us to use the word "always" before we conclude that the conclusion is valid.

Still, many people do manage to solve these reasoning tasks correctly. How do they succeed? When contemporary psychologists study reasoning and decision making, they may adopt a **dual-process theory**, which distinguishes between two types of cognitive processing (De Neys & Goel, 2011; Evans, 2006, 2012; Kahneman, 2011; Stanovich, 2009, 2011). In general, **Type 1 processing** is fast and automatic; it requires little conscious attention. For example, we use Type 1 processing during depth perception, recognition of facial expression, and automatic stereotyping.

In contrast, **Type 2 processing** is relatively slow and controlled. It requires focused attention, and it is typically more accurate. For example, we use Type 2 processing when we think of exceptions to a general rule, when we realize that we made a stereotyped response, and when we acknowledge that our Type 1 response may have been incorrect.

With respect to conditional reasoning, people may initially use Type 1 processing, which is quick and generally correct. However, they sometimes pause and then shift to Type 2 processing, which requires a more effortful analytic approach. This approach requires focused attention and working memory so that people can realize that their initial conclusion would not necessarily be correct (De Neys & Goel, 2011; Evans, 2004, 2006; Kahneman, 2011; Stanovich, 2009, 2011).

Our performance on reasoning tasks is a good example of Theme 4, which emphasizes that our cognitive processes are interrelated. For example, conditional reasoning relies upon working memory, especially the central-executive component of working memory that we discussed in Chapter 4 (Evans, 2006; Gilhooly, 2005; Reverberi et al., 2009). Reasoning also requires general knowledge and language skills (Rips, 2002; Schaeken et al., 2000; Wilhelm, 2005). In addition, it often uses mental imagery (Evans, 2002; Goodwin & Johnson-Laird, 2005).

Let's examine these two topics, and then consider two cognitive tendencies that people demonstrate on these conditional reasoning tasks.

Factors That Cause Difficulty in Reasoning

The cognitive burden of deductive reasoning is especially heavy when some of the propositions contain negative terms (rather than just positive terms), and when people try to solve abstract reasoning tasks (rather than concrete terms). In the text that follows, we discuss research that highlights the effects of these factors on reasoning.

Theme 3 of this book states that people can handle positive information better than negative information. As you may recall from Chapter 9, people have trouble processing sentences that contain words such as *no* or *not*. This same issue is also true for conditional reasoning tasks. For example, try the following reasoning task:

If today is not Friday, then we will not have a quiz today.

We will not have a quiz today.

Therefore, today is not Friday.

This item has four instances of the word *not*, and it is more challenging than a similar but linguistically positive item that begins, "If today is Friday.. . ."

Research shows that people take longer time to evaluate problems that contain linguistically negative information, and they are also more likely to make errors on these problems (Garnham & Oakhill, 1994; Halpern, 2003). A reasoning problem is especially likely to strain our working memory if the problem involves denying the antecedent or denying the consequent. Most of us squirm when we see a reasoning task that includes a statement like, "It is not true that today is not Friday." Furthermore, we often make errors when we translate either the initial statement or the conclusion into more accessible, linguistically positive forms.

People also tend to be more accurate when they solve reasoning problems that use concrete examples about everyday categories, rather than abstract, theoretical examples. For instance, you probably worked through the items in Demonstration 12.1 somewhat easily. In contrast, even short reasoning problems are difficult if they refer to abstract items with abstract characteristics (Evans, 2004, 2005; Manktelow, 1999). For example, try this problem about geometric objects, and decide whether the conclusion is valid or invalid:

> *If an object is red, then it is rectangular.*
> *This object is not rectangular.*
> *Therefore, it is not red.*

Now check the answer to this item, located at the bottom of Demonstration 12.2. Incidentally, the research shows that people's accuracy typically increases when they use diagrams to make the problem more concrete (Halpern, 2003). However, we often make errors on concrete reasoning tasks if our everyday knowledge overrides the principles of logic (Evans, 2011; Mercier & Sperber, 2011).

Belief-Bias Effect

In our lives outside the psychology laboratory, our background (or top-down) knowledge helps us function well. Inside the psychology laboratory—or in a course on logic—this background information sometimes encourages us to make mistakes. For example, try the following reasoning task (Markovits et al., 2009, p. 112):

If a feather is thrown at a window, the window will break.

A feather is thrown at a window.

Therefore, the window will break.

Demonstration 12.2 ‖ The Confirmation Bias

Imagine that each square below represents a card. Suppose that you are participating in a study in which the experimenter tells you that every card has a letter on one side and a number on the other side.

You are then given this rule about these four cards: "IF A CARD HAS A VOWEL ON ONE SIDE, THEN IT HAS AN EVEN NUMBER ON THE OTHER SIDE."

Your task is to decide which card (or cards) you would need to turn over, so that you can find out whether this rule is valid or invalid. What is your answer? The correct answer is discussed later in the chapter.

(Incidentally, the answer to the problem about the objects is "valid.")

Source: The confirmation-bias task in this demonstration is based on Wason, 1968.

In everyday life, it's a good bet that this conclusion is *incorrect*; how could a feather possibly break a window? However, in the world of logic, this feather–window task actually affirms the antecedent, so it must be correct. Similarly, your common sense may have encouraged you to decide that the conclusion was valid for the syllogism about the psychology majors who are concerned about poverty.

The **belief-bias effect** occurs in reasoning when people make judgments based on prior beliefs and general knowledge, rather than on the rules of logic. In general, people make errors when the logic of a reasoning problem conflicts with their background knowledge (Dube et al., 2010, 2011; Levy, 2010; Markovits et al., 2009; Stanovich, 2011).

The belief-bias effect is one more example of top-down processing (Theme 5). Our prior expectations help us to organize our experiences and understand the world. For example, when we see a conclusion in a reasoning task that looks correct in the "real world," we may not pay attention to the reasoning process that generated this conclusion (Stanovich, 2003). As a result, we may question a valid conclusion.

People vary widely in their susceptibility to the belief-bias effect. For example, people with low scores on an intelligence test are especially likely to demonstrate the belief-bias effect (Macpherson & Stanovich, 2007). People are also likely to demonstrate the belief-bias effect if they have low scores on a test of flexible thinking (Stanovich, 1999; Stanovich & West, 1997, 1998). An inflexible person is likely to agree with statements such as, "No one can talk me out of something I know is right."

In contrast, people who are flexible thinkers agree with statements such as, "People should always take into consideration any evidence that goes against their beliefs." These people are more likely to solve the reasoning problems correctly, without being distracted by the belief-bias effect. In fact, these people actively *block* their everyday knowledge, such as their knowledge that a feather could not break a window (Markovitz et al., 2009). In general, they also tend to carefully inspect a reasoning problem, trying to determine whether the logic is faulty (Macpherson & Stanovich, 2007; Markovits et al., 2009). Fortunately, when students have been taught about the belief-bias effect, they make fewer errors (Kruglanski & Gigerenzer, 2011).

Confirmation Bias

Be sure to try Demonstration 12.2 (above) before you read any further. Peter Wason's (1968) selection task has inspired more psychological research than any other deductive reasoning problem. It has also raised many questions about whether humans are basically rational (Mercier & Sperber, 2011; Lilienfeld et al., 2009; Oswald & Grosjean, 2004). Let's first examine the original version of the selection task and then see how people typically perform better on a more concrete variation of this task.

The Standard Wason Selection Task

Demonstration 12.2 shows the original version of the selection task. Peter Wason (1968) found that people show a **confirmation bias**; they would rather try to confirm or support a hypothesis than try to disprove it (Kida, 2006; Krizan & Windschitl, 2007; Levy, 2010). When people try this classical selection task, they typically choose to turn over the E card (Mercier & Sperber, 2011; Oaksford & Chater, 1994). This strategy allows the participants to confirm the hypothesis by the valid method of affirming the antecedent, because this card has a vowel on it. If this E card has an even number on the other side, then the rule is correct. If the number is odd, then the rule is incorrect.

As discussed above, the other valid method in deductive reasoning is to deny the consequent. To accomplish this goal, you must choose to turn over the 7 card. The information about the other side of the 7 card is very valuable. In fact, it is just as valuable as the information about the other side of the E card. Remember that the rule is: "If a card has a vowel on its letter side, then it has an even number on its number side."

To deny the consequent in this Wason Task, we need to check out a card that does *not* have an even number on its number side. In this case, then, we must check out the 7 card. We noted that many people are eager to affirm the antecedent. In contrast, they are reluctant to deny the consequent by searching for counterexamples. This approach would be a smart strategy for rejecting a hypothesis, but people seldom choose this appropriate strategy (Lilienfeld et al., 2009; Oaksford & Chater, 1994). Keep in mind that most participants in these selection-task studies are college students, so they should be able to master an abstract task (Evans, 2005).

You may wonder why we did not need to check on the J and the 6. Take a moment to read the rule again. Actually, the rule did not say anything about consonants, such as J. The other side of the J could show an odd number, an even number, or even a Vermeer painting, and we wouldn't care. A review of the literature showed that most people appropriately avoid the J card (Oaksford & Chater, 1994).

The rule also does not specify what must appear on the other side of the even numbers, such as 6. However, most people select the 6 card to turn over (Oaksford & Chater, 1994). People often assume that the two parts of the rule can be switched, so that it reads, "If a card has an even number on its number side, then it has a vowel on its letter side." Thus, they make an error by choosing the 6.

This preference for confirming a hypothesis—rather than disproving it—corresponds to Theme 3 of this book. On the Wason selection task, we see that people who are given a choice would rather know what something *is* than what it *is not*.

Concrete Versions of the Wason Selection Task

In most of the recent research on the Wason Task, psychologists focus on versions in which the numbers and letters on the cards are replaced by concrete situations that we encounter in our everyday lives. As you might guess, people perform much better when the task is concrete, familiar, and realistic (Evans, 2011; Mercier & Sperber, 2011).

For example, Griggs and Cox (1982) tested college students in Florida using a variation of the selection task. This task focused on the drinking age, which was then 19 in the state of Florida. Specifically, the students were asked to test this rule: "If a person is drinking beer, then the person must be over 19 years of age" (p. 415). Each participant was instructed to choose two cards to turn over—out of four—in order to test whether people were lying about their age.

Griggs and Cox (1982) found that 73% of the students who tried the drinking age problem made the correct selections, in contrast to 0% of the students who tried the standard, abstract form of the selection task. According to later research, people are especially likely to choose the correct answer when the wording of the selection task implies some kind of social contract designed to prevent people from cheating (Barrett & Kurzban, 2006; Cosmides & Tooby, 2006).

Applications in Medicine

Several studies point out that the confirmation bias can be applied in medical situations. For example, researchers have studied people who seek medical advice for insomnia (Harvey & Tang, 2012). As it happens, when people believe that they have insomnia, they overestimate how long it takes them to fall asleep. They also underestimate the amount of time they spend sleeping at night. One explanation for these data is that people seek confirming evidence that they are indeed "bad sleepers," and they provide estimates that are consistent with this diagnosis.

Another study focused on the diagnosis of psychological disorders (Mendel et al., 2011). Medical students and psychiatrists first read a case vignette about a 65-year-old man, and then they were instructed to provide a preliminary diagnosis of either Alzheimer's disease or severe depression. Each person then decided what kind of additional information they would like; six items were consistent with each of the two diagnoses. The results showed that 25% of the medical students and 13% of the psychiatrists selected only the information that was consistent with their original diagnosis. In other words, they did not investigate information that might be consistent with the other diagnosis.

Further Perspectives

How can we translate the confirmation bias into real-life experiences? Try noticing your own behavior when you are searching for evidence. Do you consistently look for information that will *confirm* that you are right, or do you valiantly pursue ways in which your conclusion can be wrong?

The confirmation bias might sound relatively harmless. However, thousands of people die each year because our political leaders fall victim to this confirmation bias (Kida, 2006). For example, suppose that Country A wants to start a war in Country B. The leaders in Country A will keep seeking support for their position. These leaders will also *avoid* seeking information that their position may not be correct. Here's a remedy for the confirmation bias: Try to explain why another person might hold the opposite view (Lilienfeld et al., 2009; Myers, 2002). In an ideal world, for example, the leaders of Country A should sincerely try to construct arguments *against* attacking Country B.

This overview of conditional reasoning does not provide much evidence for Theme 2 of this book. At least in the psychology laboratory, people are not especially accurate when they try to solve "if. . .then. . ." kinds of problems. However, the circumstances are usually more favorable in our daily lives, where problems are more concrete and situations are more consistent with our belief biases (Mercier & Sperber, 2011). Deductive reasoning is such a challenging task that we are not as efficient and accurate as we are in perception and memory—two areas in which humans are generally very competent.

Decision Making I: Overview of Heuristics

In **decision making**, you must assess the information and choose among two or more alternatives. Compared to deductive reasoning, the area of decision making is much more ambiguous. Some information may be missing or contradictory. In addition, we do not have clear-cut rules that tell us how to proceed from the information to the conclusions. Also, you may never know whether your decision was correct, the consequences of that decision won't be immediately apparent, and you may need to take additional factors into account (Johnson-Laird et al., 2004; Simon et al., 2001).

In real life, the uncertainty of decision making is more common than the certainty of deductive reasoning. However, people have difficulty with both kinds of tasks, and they do not always reach the appropriate conclusions (Goodwin & Johnson-Laird, 2005; Stanovich, 2009, 2011).

When you engage in reasoning, you use the established rules of propositional calculus to draw clear-cut conclusions. In contrast, when you make a decision, there is no comparable list of rules. Furthermore, you may never even know whether your decision is correct. Some critical information may be missing, and you may suspect that other information is not accurate. Should you apply to graduate school or get a job after college? Should you take social psychology in the morning or in the afternoon? In addition, emotional factors frequently influence our everyday decision making (Kahneman, 2011; Lehrer, 2009; Stanovich, 2009, 2011).

As you'll see, this section emphasizes several kinds of decision-making heuristics. Heuristics are general strategies that typically produce a correct solution. When we need to make a decision, we often use a heuristic that is simple, fast, and easy to access (Bazerman & Tenbrunsel, 2011; Kahneman, 2011; Kahneman & Frederick, 2005; Stanovich, 2009, 2011). These heuristics reduce the difficulty of making a decision (Shah & Oppenheimer, 2008). In many cases, however, humans fail to appreciate the limitations of these heuristics. When we use this fast, Type 1 processing, we can make inappropriate decisions. However, if we pause and shift to slow, Type 2 processing, we can correct that original error and end up with a good decision.

Throughout this section, you will often see the names of two researchers, Daniel Kahneman and Amos Tversky. Kahneman won the Nobel Prize in Economics in 2002 for his research in decision making. Kahneman and Tversky proposed that a small number of heuristics guide human decision making. As they emphasized, the same strategies that normally guide us toward the correct decision may sometimes lead us astray (Kahneman, 2011; Kahneman & Frederick, 2002, 2005; Kahneman & Tversky, 1996).

Notice that this heuristics approach is consistent with Theme 2 of this book: Our cognitive processes are usually efficient and accurate, and our mistakes can often be traced to a rational strategy. In this part of the chapter, we discuss many studies that illustrate errors in decision making. These errors should not lead us to conclude that humans are foolish creatures. Instead, people's decision-making heuristics are well adapted to handle a wide range of problems (Kahneman, 2011; Kahneman & Frederick, 2005; Kahneman & Tversky, 1996). However, these same heuristics become a liability when they are applied too broadly—for example, when we emphasize heuristics rather than other important information.

We now explore three classic decision-making heuristics: representativeness, availability, and anchoring and adjustment. We conclude this section by considering the current status of heuristics in decision-making research.

Representativeness Heuristic

Here's a remarkable coincidence: Three early U.S. presidents—Adams, Jefferson, and Monroe—all died on the Fourth of July, although in different years (Myers, 2002). This information doesn't seem correct, because the dates should be randomly scattered throughout the 365 days a year.

You've probably discovered some personal coincidences in your own life. For example, one afternoon, I was searching for some resources on political decision making, and I found two relevant books. While recording the citations, I noticed an amazing coincidence: One was published by Stanford University Press, and the other by the University of Michigan Press. As it happened, I had earned my bachelor's degree from Stanford and my PhD from the University of Michigan.

Now consider this example. Suppose that you have a regular penny with one head (H) and one tail (T), and you toss it six times. Which outcome seems most likely, T H H T H T or H H H T T T? Most people choose T H H T H T (Teigen, 2004). After all, you know that coin tossing should produce heads and tails in random order, and the order T H H T H T looks much more random.

A sample looks **representative** if it is similar in important characteristics to the population from which it was selected. For instance, if a sample was selected by a random process, then that sample must look random in order for people to say that it looks representative. Thus, T H H T H T is a sample that looks representative because it has an equal number of heads and tails (which would be the case in random coin tosses). Furthermore, T H H T H T looks more representative because the order of the Ts and Hs looks random rather than orderly.

The research shows that we often use the **representativeness heuristic**; we judge that a sample is likely if it is similar to the population from which this sample was selected (Kahneman, 2011; Kahneman & Tversky, 1972; Levy, 2010). According to the representativeness heuristic, we believe that random-looking outcomes are more likely than orderly outcomes. Suppose, for example, that a cashier adds up your grocery bill, and the total is $21.97. This very random-looking outcome is a representative kind of answer, and so it looks "normal."

However, suppose that the total bill is $22.22. This total does not look random, and you might even decide to check the arithmetic. After all, addition is a process that should yield a random-looking outcome. In reality, though, a random process occasionally produces an outcome that looks nonrandom. In fact, chance alone can produce an orderly sum like $22.22, just as chance alone can produce an orderly pattern like the three presidents dying on the Fourth of July.

The representativeness heuristic raises a major problem: This heuristic is so persuasive that people often ignore important statistical information that they should consider (Kahneman, 2011; Newell et al., 2007; Thaler & Sunstein, 2008). We see that two especially useful statistics are the sample size and the base rate. In addition, people have trouble thinking about the probability of two combined characteristics.

Sample Size and Representativeness

When we make a decision, representativeness is such a compelling heuristic that we often fail to pay attention to sample size. For example, Kahneman and Tversky (1972) asked college students to consider a hypothetical small hospital, where about 15 babies are born each day, and a hypothetical large hospital, where about 45 babies are born each day. Which hospital would be more likely to report that more than 60% of the babies on a given day would be boys, or would they both be equally likely to report more than 60% boys?

The results showed that 56% of the students responded, "About the same." In other words, the majority of students thought that a large hospital and a small hospital were equally likely to report having at least 60% baby boys born on a given day. Thus, they ignored sample size.

In reality, however, sample size is an important characteristic that you *should* consider whenever you make decisions. A large sample is statistically more likely to reflect the true proportions in a population. In contrast, a small sample will often reveal an extreme proportion (e.g., at least 60% baby boys). However, people are often unaware that deviations from a population proportion are more likely in these small samples (Newell et al., 2007; Teigen, 2004).

In one of their first publications, Tversky and Kahneman (1971) pointed out that people often commit the **small-sample fallacy** because they assume that a small sample will be representative of the population from which it is selected (Poulton, 1994). Unfortunately, the small-sample fallacy leads us to incorrect decisions.

We often commit the small-sample fallacy in social situations, as well as in relatively abstract statistics problems. For example, we may draw unwarranted stereotypes about a group of people on the basis of a small number of group members (Hamilton & Sherman, 1994). One effective way of combating inappropriate stereotypes is to become acquainted with a large number of people from the target group—for example, through exchange programs with groups of people from other countries.

Base Rate and Representativeness

Representativeness is such a compelling heuristic that people often ignore the **base rate**, or how often the item occurs in the population. Be sure you have tried Demonstration 12.3 before reading further.

Using problems such as the ones in Demonstration 12.3, Kahneman and Tversky (1973) demonstrated that people rely on representativeness when they are asked to judge category membership. In other words, we focus on whether a description is representative of members of each category. When we emphasize representativeness, we commit the **base-rate fallacy**, paying too little attention to important information about base rate (Kahneman, 2011; Levy, 2010; Swinkels, 2003).

If people pay appropriate attention to the base rate in this demonstration, they should select graduate programs that have a relatively high enrollment (base rate). These would include the two options "humanities and education" and "social science and social work." However, most students in this study used the representativeness heuristic, and they most frequently guessed that Tom W was a graduate student in either computer science or engineering (Kahneman, 2011; Kahneman & Tversky, 1973). The description of Tom W was highly similar to (i.e., representative of) the stereotype of a computer scientist or an engineer.

You might argue, however, that the Tom W study was unfair. After all, the base rates of the various graduate programs were not even mentioned in the problem. Maybe the students failed to consider that there are more graduate students in the "social sciences and social work" category than in the "computer science" category. However, when Kahneman and Tversky's (1973) study included this base-rate information, most people ignored it. Instead, they judged mostly on the basis of representativeness. In fact, this description for Tom W is highly representative of our stereotype for students in computer science. As a result, people tend to select this particular answer.

We should emphasize, however, that the representativeness heuristic—like all heuristics—frequently helps us make a correct decision (Levy, 2010; Newell et al., 2007; Shepperd & Koch, 2005). Heuristics are also relatively simple to use (Hogarth & Karelaia, 2007). In addition, some problems—and some alternative wording of problems—produce more accurate decisions (Gigerenzer, 1998; Shafir & LeBoeuf, 2002).

Incidentally, research on this kind of "base-rate" task provides support for the dual-process approach. Specifically, different parts of the brain are activated when people use automatic, Type 1 processing, rather than slow, Type 2 processing (De Neys & Goel, 2011). Furthermore, training sessions can encourage students to use base-rate information appropriately (Krynski & Tenenbaum, 2007; Shepperd & Koch, 2005). Training would make people more aware that they should pause and use Type 2 processing to examine the question more carefully.

You should also look out for other everyday examples of the base-rate fallacy. For instance, one study of pedestrians killed at intersections showed that 10% were killed when crossing at a signal that said "walk." In contrast, only 6% were killed when crossing at a signal that said "stop" (Poulton, 1994). So—for your own safety—should you cross the street only when the signal says "stop"? Now, compare the two base rates: Many more people cross the street when the signal says "walk."

Demonstration 12.3 | Base Rates and Representativeness

Imagine that a psychologist wrote the following description of Tom W, when Tom was a senior in high school. This description was based on some psychological tests that had uncertain validity.

Tom W is highly intelligent, but he is not genuinely creative. Tom needs everything to be orderly and clear, and he likes every detail to be in its appropriate place. His writing is quite dull and mechanical, although he loves corny puns. He sometimes makes up plots about science fiction. Tom has a strong drive for competence. He seems to have little feeling for other people, and he has little sympathy for their problems. He does not actually like interacting with others. Although he is self-centered, he does have a deep moral sense. (Based on a description by Kahneman, 2011, p. 147)

Now suppose that Tom W is a graduate student at a large university. Rank the following nine fields of specialization, in terms of the likelihood that Tom W is now a student in that program. Write 1 for "most likely," and 7 for "least likely."

_____ business administration

_____ computer science

_____ engineering

_____ humanities and education

_____ law

_____ medicine

_____ library science

_____ physical and life sciences

_____ social sciences and social work

The Conjunction Fallacy and Representativeness

Be sure to try Demonstration 12.4 before you read further.

Now inspect your answers, and compare which of these two choices you ranked more likely: (1) Linda is a bank teller or (2) Linda is a bank teller and is active in the feminist movement.

Tversky and Kahneman (1983) presented the "Linda" problem and another similar problem to three groups of people. One was a "statistically naïve" group of undergraduates. The "intermediate-knowledge" group consisted of first-year graduate students who had taken one or more courses in statistics. The "statistically sophisticated" group consisted of doctoral students in a decision science program who had taken several advanced courses in statistics. In each case, the participants were asked to rank all eight statements according to their probability, with the rank of 1 assigned to the most likely statement.

Figure 12.1 shows the average rank for each of the three groups for the two critical statements: (1) "Linda is a bank teller" and (2) "Linda is a bank teller and is active in the feminist movement." Notice that the people in all three groups believed—incorrectly—that the second statement would be more likely than the first.

Think for a moment about why this conclusion is mathematically impossible. According to the **conjunction rule**, the probability of the conjunction of two events cannot be larger than the probability

---

Demonstration 12.4 | The Conjunction Fallacy

Read the following paragraph:

> *Linda is 31 years old, single, outspoken, and very bright. She majored in philosophy. As a student, she was deeply concerned with issues of discrimination and social justice, and she also participated in antinuclear demonstrations.*

Now rank the following options in terms of the probability of their describing Linda. Give a ranking of 1 to the most likely option and a ranking of 8 to the least likely option:

_____ Linda is a teacher at an elementary school.

_____ Linda works in a bookstore and takes yoga classes.

_____ Linda is active in the feminist movement.

_____ Linda is a psychiatric social worker.

_____ Linda is a member of the League of Women Voters.

_____ Linda is a bank teller.

_____ Linda is an insurance salesperson.

_____ Linda is a bank teller and is active in the feminist movement.

Source: Tversky, A., & Kahneman, D. (1983). Extensional versus intuitive reasoning: The conjunction fallacy in probability judgment. *Psychological Review, 90,* 293–315.

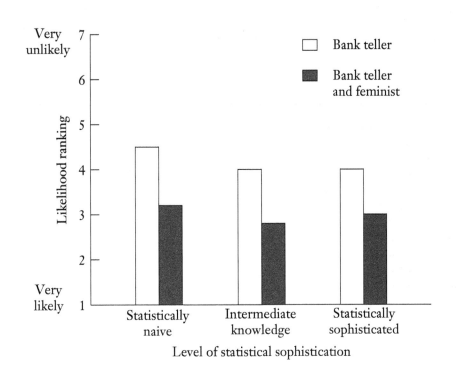

FIGURE 12.1
The influence of the type of statement and level of statistical sophistication on likelihood rankings.

Low numbers on the ranking indicate that people think the event is very likely. *Source:* Tversky, A., & Kahneman, D. (1983). Extensional versus intuitive reasoning: The conjunction fallacy in probability judgment. *Psychological Review, 90,* 293–315.

of either of its constituent events (Newell et al., 2007). In the Linda problem, the conjunction of the two events—bank teller and feminist—cannot occur more often than either event by itself. Consider another situation where the conjunction rule operates: The number of murders last year in Detroit cannot be greater than the number of murders last year in Michigan (Kahneman & Frederick, 2005).

As we saw earlier in this section, representativeness is such a powerful heuristic that people may ignore useful statistical information, such as sample size and base rate. Apparently, they also ignore the mathematical implications of the conjunction rule (Kahneman, 2011; Kahneman & Frederick, 2005). Specifically, when most people try the "Linda problem," they commit the conjunction fallacy. When people commit the **conjunction fallacy**, they judge the probability of the conjunction of two events to be greater than the probability of either constituent event.

Tversky and Kahneman (1983) traced the conjunction fallacy to the representativeness heuristic. They argued that people judge the conjunction of "bank teller" and "feminist" to be more likely than the simple event "bank teller." After all, "feminist" is a characteristic that is very representative of (i.e., similar to) someone who is single, outspoken, bright, a philosophy major, concerned about social justice, and an antinuclear activist. A person with these characteristics doesn't seem likely to become a bank teller, but seems instead highly likely to be a feminist. By adding the extra detail of "feminist" to "bank teller," the description seems more representative and also more plausible—even though this description is *statistically* less likely (Swoyer, 2002).

Psychologists are intrigued with the conjunction fallacy, especially because it demonstrates that people can ignore one of the most basic principles of probability theory. Furthermore, research by Keith Stanovich (2011) shows that college students with high SAT scores are actually *more* likely than other students to demonstrate this conjunction fallacy.

The results for the conjunction fallacy have been replicated many times, with generally consistent findings (Fisk, 2004; Kahneman & Frederick, 2005; Stanovich, 2009). For example, the probability of "spilling hot coffee" seems greater than the probability of "spilling coffee" (Moldoveanu & Langer, 2002). . .until you identify the conjunction fallacy.

Availability Heuristic

A second important heuristic that people use in making decisions is availability. You use the **availability heuristic** when you estimate frequency or probability in terms of how easy it is to think of relevant examples of something (Hertwig et al., 2005; Kahneman, 2011; Tversky & Kahneman, 1973). In other words, people judge frequency by assessing whether they can easily retrieve relevant examples from memory or whether this memory retrieval is difficult.

The availability heuristic is generally helpful in everyday life. For example, suppose that someone asked you whether your college had more students from Illinois or more from Idaho. You haven't memorized these geography statistics, so you would be likely to answer the question in terms of the relative availability of examples of Illinois students and Idaho students. Let's also say that your memory has stored the names of dozens of Illinois students, and so you can easily retrieve their names ("Jessica, Akiko, Bob. . ."). Let's also say that your memory has stored only one name of an Idaho student, so you cannot think of many examples of this category. Because examples of Illinois students were relatively easy to retrieve, you conclude that your college has more Illinois students. In general, then, this availability heuristic can be a relatively accurate method for making decisions about frequency (Kahneman, 2011).

A heuristic is a general strategy that is typically accurate. The availability heuristic is accurate as long as availability is correlated with true, objective frequency—and it usually is. However, the availability heuristic can lead to errors (Levy, 2010; Thaler & Sunstein, 2008). As we will see in a moment, several factors can influence memory retrieval, even though they are not correlated with true, objective frequency. These factors can bias availability, and so they may decrease the accuracy of our decisions. We will see that recency and familiarity—both factors that influence memory—can potentially distort availability. Figure 12.2 illustrates how these two factors can contaminate the relationship between true frequency and availability.

Before exploring the research about availability, let's briefly review how representativeness—the first decision-making heuristic—differs from availability. When we use the representativeness heuristic, we are given a specific example (such as T H H T H T or Linda the bank teller). We then make judgments about whether the specific example is *similar* to the general category that it is supposed to represent (such as

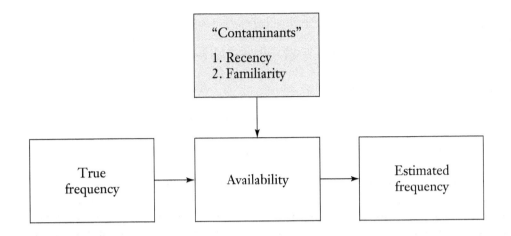

FIGURE 12.2
The relationship between true frequency and estimated frequency, with recency and familiarity as "contaminating" factors

coin tosses or philosophy majors concerned about social justice). In contrast, when we use the availability heuristic, we are given a general category, and we must recall the specific examples (such as examples of Illinois students). We then make decisions based on whether the specific examples come easily to mind. So here is a way to remember the two heuristics:

1. If the problem is based on a judgment about *similarity*, you are dealing with the representativeness heuristic.

2. If the problem requires you to *remember examples*, you are dealing with the availability heuristic.

Recency and Availability

As you know from Chapters 4–6, your memory is better for items that you've recently seen, compared to items you saw long ago. In other words, those more recent items are more *available*. As a result, we judge recent items to be more likely than they really are. For example, take yourself back to the fall of 2011. Several university coaches and administrators had been fired following the discovery that young boys had been sexually abused (e.g., Bartlett, 2011; Bazerman & Tenbrunsel, 2011). If you had been asked to estimate the frequency of these crimes—and the cover-ups—you probably would have provided a high estimate.

Research on the availability heuristic has important implications for clinical psychology. Consider a study by MacLeod and Campbell (1992), who encouraged one group of people to recall pleasant events from their past. These individuals later judged pleasant events to be more likely in their future. The researchers also encouraged another group to recall unpleasant events. These individuals later judged unpleasant events to be more likely in their future. Psychotherapists might encourage depressed clients to envision a more hopeful future by having them recall and focus on previous pleasant events.

Familiarity and Availability

The familiarity of the examples—as well as their recency—can also produce a distortion in frequency estimation (Kahneman, 2011). Norman Brown and his colleagues conducted research on this topic in Canada, the United States, and China (Brown, Cui, & Gordon, 2002; Brown & Siegler, 1992). They discovered that the media can distort people's estimates of a country's population.

Brown and Siegler (1992), for example, conducted a study during an era when El Salvador was frequently mentioned in the news because of U.S. intervention in Latin America. In contrast, Indonesia was seldom mentioned. Brown and Siegler found that the students' estimates for the population of these two countries were similar, even though the population of Indonesia was about 35 times as large as the population of El Salvador.

The media can also influence viewers' ideas about the prevalence of different points of view. For instance, the media often give equal coverage to several thousand protesters and to several dozen counterprotesters. Notice whether you can spot the same tendency in current news broadcasts. Does the media coverage create our cognitive realities?

How can we counteract Type 1 processing, which happens when we first encounter some information? Kahneman (2011) suggests that we can overcome that initial reaction by using critical thinking and shifting to Type 2 processing. For example, someone might analyze a friend's use of the availability heuristic and argue, "He underestimates the risks of indoor pollution because there are few media stories on them. That's an availability effect. He should look at the statistics." (p. 136).

The Recognition Heuristic

We have emphasized that the decision-making heuristics are generally helpful and accurate. However, most of the examples have emphasized that judgment accuracy is hindered by factors such as recency and familiarity. Let's discuss a special case of the availability heuristic, which often leads to an *accurate* decision (Goldstein & Gigerenzer, 2002; Kahneman, 2011; Volz et al., 2006).

Suppose that someone asks you which of two Italian cities has the larger population, Milan or Modena. Most U.S. students have heard of Milan, but they may not recognize the name of a nearby city called Modena. The **recognition heuristic** typically operates when you must compare the relative frequency of two categories; if you recognize one category, but not the other, you conclude that the recognized category has the higher frequency. In this case, you would correctly respond that Milan has the greater population (Volz et al., 2006). Keep this example of correct decision making in mind as you read the remainder of this chapter.

Illusory Correlation and Availability

We have seen that availability is typically a useful heuristic, although it can become "contaminated" by factors such as recency and familiarity, thus leading to inappropriate decisions about the true frequency of an event. Here, we examine how the availability heuristic can contribute to another cognitive error called an *illusory correlation*.

The word *illusory* means deceptive or unreal, and a correlation is a statistical relationship between two variables. Therefore, an **illusory correlation** occurs when people believe that two variables are statistically related, even though there is no actual evidence for this relationship. According to the research, we often believe that a certain group of people tends to have certain kinds of characteristics, even though an accurate tabulation would show that the relationship is not statistically significant (Fiedler & Walther, 2004; Hamilton et al., 1993; Risen et al., 2007).

Think of some stereotypes that arise from illusory correlations. These illusory correlations may either have no basis in fact or much less basis than is commonly believed. For example, consider the following illusory correlations: (1) Females have poor math skills, (2) people on welfare are cheaters. According to the **social cognition approach**, stereotypes can be traced to our normal cognitive processes. In the case of illusory correlations, an important cognitive factor is the availability heuristic (Reber, 2004; Risen et al., 2007).

Chapman and Chapman (1969) performed a classic investigation of the illusory correlation. Their data showed that students formed an illusory correlation between people's reported sexual orientation and their responses on an inkblot test. Let's see how the availability heuristic might help to explain illusory correlations.

When we try to figure out whether two variables are related to each other, we should consider the data about four categories in a 2 × 2 matrix. For example, suppose that we want to determine whether people who are lesbians or gay males are more likely than heterosexuals to have psychological problems.[*] Imagine, for example, that researchers gathered the data in Table 12.2. These data show that six out of 60 gay people (or 10%) have psychological problems, and eight out of 80 straight people (also 10%) have psychological problems. We should therefore conclude that sexual orientation is not related to psychological problems.

Unfortunately, however, people typically pay the most attention to only one cell in the matrix, especially if the two descriptive characteristics are statistically less frequent (Risen et al., 2007). In this example, some people notice only the six gay people who have psychological problems, ignoring the important information in the other three cells.

People with an established bias against gay people might be especially likely to pay attention to this cell. Furthermore, they may continue to look for information that confirms their hypothesis that gay people have problems. You'll recall from the earlier discussion of conditional reasoning that people would rather try to confirm a hypothesis than try to disprove it, consistent with Theme 3.

---

[*]Although some people believe in this illusory correlation, the research does not show a consistent relationship between sexual orientation and psychological problems (e.g., Garnets, 2008; Herek & Garnets, 2007; Rothblum & Factor, 2001).

Table 12.2   A Matrix Showing Hypothetical Information about Sexual Orientation and Psychological Problems

	Number in each category		
	Gay people	Straight people	Totals
People with psychological problems	6	8	14
People without psychological problems	54	72	126
Totals	60	80	140

Try applying the information about illusory correlations to some stereotype that you hold. Notice whether you tend to focus on only one cell in the matrix, ignoring the other three. Have you specifically tried to *disconfirm* the stereotypes? Also, notice how politicians and the media often base their arguments on illusory correlations (Myers, 2002). For example, they may focus on the number of welfare recipients with fraudulent claims. This number is meaningless unless we know additional information, such as the number of welfare recipients *without* fraudulent claims.

Anchoring and Adjustment Heuristic

You've probably had a number of incidents like this one. A friend asks you, "Can you meet me at the library in 15 minutes?" You know that it takes longer than 15 minutes to get there, so you make a modest adjustment and agree to meet in 20 minutes. However, you didn't count on needing to find your coat, or your cell phone ringing, or stopping to tie a shoelace, or several other trivial events. Basically, you could have arrived in 20 minutes (well, maybe 25), if everything had gone smoothly. In retrospect, you failed to make large enough adjustments to account for the inevitable delays. (Try Demonstration 12.5 when it's convenient, but complete Demonstration 12.6 before you read further.)

According to the **anchoring and adjustment heuristic**—also known as the **anchoring effect**—we begin with a first approximation, which serves as an **anchor**; then we make adjustments to that number based on additional information (Mussweiler et al., 2004; Thaler & Sunstein, 2008; Tversky & Kahneman, 1982). This heuristic often leads to a reasonable answer, just as the representativeness and availability heuristics often lead to reasonable answers. However, people typically rely too heavily on the anchor, such that their adjustments are too small (Kahneman, 2011).

The anchoring and adjustment heuristic illustrates once more that people tend to endorse their current hypotheses or beliefs, rather than trying to question them (Baron, 2000; Kida, 2006). That is, they emphasize top-down processing, consistent with Theme 5. We've seen several other examples of this tendency in the present chapter:

1. The *belief-bias effect*: We rely too heavily on our established beliefs.

2. The *confirmation bias*: We prefer to confirm a current hypothesis, rather than to reject it.

3. The *illusory correlation*: We rely too strongly on one well-known cell in a 2 × 2 data matrix, and we fail to seek information about the other three cells.

Demonstration 12.5 ║ The Anchoring and Adjustment Heuristic

Copy the two multiplication problems listed below on separate pieces of paper. Show Problem A to at least five friends, and show Problem B to at least five other friends. In each case, ask the participants to estimate the answer within five seconds.

A. $8 \times 7 \times 6 \times 5 \times 4 \times 3 \times 2 \times 1$

B. $1 \times 2 \times 3 \times 4 \times 5 \times 6 \times 7 \times 8$

Now, tally the answers separately for the two problems, listing the answers from smallest to largest. Calculate the median for each problem. (If you have an uneven number of participants, the median is the answer in the middle of the distribution—with half larger and half smaller. If you have an even number of participants, take the average between the two answers in the middle of the distribution.)

Demonstration 12.6 ‖ Estimating Confidence Intervals

For each of the following questions, answer in terms of a range, rather than a single number. Specifically, you should supply a 98% confidence interval. A confidence interval is the range within which you expect the correct answer to fall. For example, suppose you answer a question by supplying a 98% confidence interval that is 2,000 to 7,000. This means that you think there is only a 2% chance that the real answer is either less than 2,000 or more than 7,000. The correct answers can be found at the end of the chapter.

1. How many full-time students were enrolled in U.S. colleges and universities in 2011?

2. According to the official count, how many people died in the 2011 earthquake and tsunami in Japan?

3. In what year did Martin Van Buren begin his term as the president of the United States?

4. In 2009, what was the average life expectancy in Canada?

5. How many dollars did the United States spend for military expenditures in 2010?

6. In what year did New Zealand give women the right to vote?

7. What was the median salary of a U.S. male college graduate in 2009?

8. What is the total area of Canada (in either square kilometers or square miles)?

9. What was the estimated population of France in 2010?

10. Of the residents of Canada, what percentage report that they are Roman Catholics?

Source: All questions are based on information from "Countries of the World," 2012; "Student Demographics," 2011; and Statistics Canada, 2012b.

Let's begin by considering some research on the anchoring and adjustment heuristic. Then, we will see how this heuristic can be applied to estimating confidence intervals.

Research on the Anchoring and Adjustment Heuristic

Demonstration 12.5 illustrates the anchoring and adjustment heuristic. In a classic study, high school students were asked to estimate the answers to these two multiplication problems (Tversky & Kahneman, 1982). The students were allowed only five seconds to respond. The results showed that the two problems generated widely different answers. If the first number in this sequence was 8, a relatively large number, the median of their estimates was 2,250. (i.e., half the students estimated higher than 2,250, and half estimated lower.) In contrast, if the first number was 1, a small number, their median estimate was only 512.

Furthermore, both groups anchored too heavily on the initial impression that every number in the problem was only a single digit, because both estimates were far too low. The correct answer for both problems is 40,320. Did the anchoring and adjustment heuristic influence the people you tested?

The anchoring and adjustment heuristic is so powerful that it operates even when the anchor is obviously arbitrary or impossibly extreme, such as a person living to the age of 140. It also operates for both novices and experts (Herbert, 2010; Kahneman, 2011; Mussweiler et al., 2004; Tversky & Kahneman, 1974). Researchers have not developed precise explanations for the anchoring and adjustment heuristic. However, one likely mechanism is that the anchor restricts the search for relevant information in memory. Specifically, people concentrate their search on information relatively close to the anchor, even if this anchor is not a realistic number (Kahneman, 2011; Pohl et al., 2003).

The anchoring and adjustment heuristic has many applications in everyday life (Janiszewski, 2011; Mussweiler et al., 2004; Newell et al., 2007). For example, Englich and Mussweiler (2001) studied anchoring effects in courtroom sentencing. Trial judges with an average of 15 years of experience listened to a typical legal case. The role of the prosecutor was played by a person who was introduced as a computer science student. This student was obviously a novice in terms of legal experience, so the judges should not take him seriously. However, when the "prosecutor" demanded a sentence of 12 months, these experienced judges recommended 28 months. In contrast, when the "prosecutor" demanded a sentence of 34 months, these judges recommended a sentence of 36 months.

Estimating Confidence Intervals

We use anchoring and adjustment when we estimate a single number. We also use this heuristic when we estimate a confidence interval. A **confidence interval** is the range within which we expect a number to fall a certain percentage of the time. For example, you might guess that the 98% confidence interval for the number of students at a particular college is 3,000 to 5,000. This guess would mean that you think there is a 98% chance that the number is between 3,000 and 5,000, and only a 2% chance that the number is outside of this range.

Demonstration 12.6 tested the accuracy of your estimates for various kinds of numerical information. Turn to the end of this chapter to see how many of your confidence-interval estimates included the correct answer. Suppose that a large number of people were instructed to provide a confidence interval for each of these 10 questions. Then, we would expect their confidence intervals to include the correct answer about 98% of the time, assuming that their estimation techniques had been correct. Studies have shown, however, that people provide 98% confidence intervals that actually include the correct answer only about 60% of the time (Block & Harper, 1991; Hoffrage, 2004). In other words, our estimates for these confidence intervals are definitely too narrow.

The research by Tversky and Kahneman (1974) pointed out how the anchoring and adjustment heuristic is relevant when we make confidence-interval estimates. We first provide a best estimate, and we use this figure as an anchor. Next, we make adjustments upward and downward from this anchor to construct the confidence-interval estimate. However, our adjustments are typically too small. Consider, for example, Question 1 in Demonstration 12.6. Perhaps, you initially guessed that the United States currently has eight million full-time students in college. You might then say that your 98% confidence interval was between six million and 10 million. This interval would be too narrow, because you had made a large error in your original estimate. Check the correct answers at the end of this chapter. Again, we establish our anchor, and we do not wander far from it in the adjustment process (Kahneman, 2011; Kruglanski, 2004). When we shut our minds to new possibilities, we rely too heavily on top-down processing.

An additional problem is that most people don't really understand confidence intervals. For instance, when you estimated the confidence intervals in Demonstration 12.6, did you emphasize to yourself that each confidence interval should be so wide that there was only a 2% chance of the actual number being either larger or smaller than this interval? Teigen and Jørgensen (2005) found that college students tend to misinterpret these confidence intervals. In their study, the students' 90% confidence intervals were associated with an actual certainty of only about 50%.

You can overcome potential biases from the anchoring and adjustment heuristic. First, think carefully about your initial estimate. Then, ask yourself whether you are paying enough attention to the features of this specific situation that might require you to change your anchor, or else to make large adjustments away from your initial anchor.

Current Status of Heuristics and Decision Making

Some researchers have argued that the heuristic approach—developed by Kahneman and Tversky—may underestimate people's decision-making skills. For example, research by Adam Harris and his colleagues found that people make fairly realistic judgments about future events (Harris et al., 2009; Harris & Hahn, 2011). Gerd Gigerenzer and his colleagues agree that people are not perfectly rational decision makers, especially under time pressure. They emphasize that people can, however, do relatively well when they are given a fair chance on decision-making tasks. For instance, we saw that the recognition heuristic is reasonably accurate. Other research shows that people answer questions more accurately in naturalistic settings, especially if the questions focus on frequencies, rather than probabilities (e.g., Gigerenzer, 2006a, 2006b, 2008; Todd & Gigerenzer, 2007).

Peter Todd and Gerd Gigerenzer (2007) devised a term called **ecological rationality** to describe how people create a wide variety of heuristics to help themselves make useful, adaptive decisions in the real world. For example, only 28% of U.S. residents become potential organ donors, in contrast to 99.9% of French residents. Gigerenzer (2008) suggests that both groups are using a simple **default heuristic**; specifically, if there is a standard option—which happens if people do nothing—then people will choose it. In the United States, you typically need to sign up to become an organ donor. Therefore, the majority of U.S. residents—using the default heuristic—remain in the nondonor category. In France, you are an organ donor unless you specifically opt out of the donor program. Therefore, the majority of French residents—using the default heuristic—remain in the donor category.

Furthermore, people bring their world knowledge into the research laboratory, where researchers often design the tasks to specifically contradict their schemas. For example, do you really believe that Linda *wouldn't* be a feminist given her long-time commitment to social justice?

The two approaches—one proposed by Kahneman and one by Gigerenzer—may seem fairly different. However, both approaches suggest that decision-making heuristics generally serve us well in the real world. Furthermore, we can become more effective decision makers by realizing the limitations of these important strategies (Kahneman & Tversky, 2000).

Decision Making II: Applications of Decision Making Research

Decision making is an interdisciplinary field that includes research in all the social sciences, including psychology, economics, political science, and sociology (LeBoeuf & Shafir, 2012; Mosier & Fischer, 2011). It also includes other areas such as statistics, philosophy, medicine, education, and law (Reif, 2008; Mosier & Fischer, 2011; Schoenfeld, 2011). Within the discipline of psychology, decision making inspires numerous books and articles each year. For example, many books provide a general overview of decision making (e.g., Bazerman & Tenbrunsel, 2011; Bennett & Gibson, 2006; Hallinan, 2009; Herbert, 2010; Holyoak & Morrison, 2012; Kahneman, 2011; Kida, 2006; Lehrer, 2009; Schoenfeld, 2011; Stanovich, 2009, 2011). Other recent books consider decision-making approaches, such as critical thinking (Levy, 2010). And, many other books consider decision making in specific areas, such as business (Bazerman & Tenbrunsel, 2011; Belsky & Gilovich, 1999; 2010; Henderson & Hooper, 2006; Mosier & Fischer, 2011; Useem, 2006); politics (Thaler & Sunstein, 2008; Weinberg, 2012); the neurological correlates of decision making (Delgado et al., 2011; Vartanian & Mandel, 2011); healthcare (Groopman, 2007; Mosier & Fischer, 2011); and education (Reif, 2008; Schoenfeld, 2011). In general, the research on decision making examines concrete, realistic scenarios, rather than the kind of abstract situations used in research on deductive reasoning.

Research on decision making can be particularly useful with respect to helping us develop strategies to make better decisions in real-life situations. In this section, we focus more squarely on the applied nature of decision making research.

Framing Effect

As I was writing this chapter, I took a break to read the mail that had just arrived. I opened an envelope from an organization I support, called "The Feminist Majority." The letter pointed out that in a previous year, right-wing organizations had introduced legislation in 17 state governments that would eliminate affirmative action programs for women and people of color. This figure surprised and saddened me; apparently the antiaffirmative action supporters had more influence than I had imagined! And then I realized that the framing effect might be operating. Perhaps, at that very moment, other people throughout the United States were opening their mail from organizations that endorsed the other perspective. Perhaps, their letter pointed out that their organization—and others with a similar viewpoint—had failed to introduce legislation in 33 state governments. Yes, a fairly subtle change in the wording of a sentence can produce a very different emotional reaction! Are political organizations perhaps hiring cognitive psychologists?

The **framing effect** demonstrates that the outcome of your decision can be influenced by two factors: (1) the background context of the choice and (2) the way in which a question is worded—or, framed (LeBoeuf & Shafir, 2012; McGraw et al., 2010). However, before we discuss these two factors, be sure you have tried Demonstration 12.7, which appears below.

| *Demonstration 12.7* | The Framing Effect and Background Information |

Try the following two problems:

Problem 1

Imagine that you decided to see a concert, and you paid $20 for the admission price of one ticket. You are about to enter the theater, when you discover that you cannot find your ticket. The theater doesn't keep a record of ticket purchases, so you cannot simply get another ticket. You have $60 in your wallet. Would you pay $20 for another ticket for the concert?

Problem 2

Imagine that you decided to buy a ticket for a concert; the ticket will cost $20. You go to the theater box office. Then you open your wallet and discover that a $20 bill is missing. (Fortunately, you still have $40 left in your wallet.) Would you pay $20 for a ticket for the concert?

Source: Based on Tversky & Kahneman, 1981.

Take a moment to read Demonstration 12.7 once more. Notice that the amount of money is $20 in both cases. If decision makers were perfectly "rational," they would respond identically to both problems (Kahneman, 2011; LeBoef & Shafir, 2012; Moran & Ritov, 2011). However, the decision frame differs for these two situations, so they seem psychologically different from each other.

We frequently organize our mental expense accounts according to topics. Specifically, we view going to a concert as a transaction in which the cost of the ticket is exchanged for the experience of seeing a concert. If you buy another ticket, the cost of seeing that concert has increased to a level that many people find unacceptable. When Kahneman and Tversky (1984) asked people what they would do in the case of Problem 1, only 46% said that they would pay for another ticket.

In contrast, in Problem 2, people did not tally the lost $20 bill in the same account as the cost of a ticket. In this second case, people viewed the lost $20 as being generally irrelevant to the ticket. In Kahneman and Tversky's (1984) study, 88% of the participants said that they would purchase the ticket in Problem 2. In other words, the background information provides different frames for the two problems, and the specific frame strongly influences the decision.

The Wording of a Question and the Framing Effect

In Chapter 11, we saw that people often fail to realize that two problems may share the same deep structure, for instance in algebra problems. In other words, people are distracted by the differences in the surface structure of the problems. When people make decisions, they are also distracted by differences in surface structure. For example, people who conduct surveys have found that the exact wording of a question can have a major effect on the answers that respondents provide (Bruine de Bruin, 2011).

Tversky and Kahneman (1981) tested college students in both Canada and the United States, using Problem 1 in Demonstration 12.8. Notice that both choices emphasize the number of lives that would be *saved*. They found that 72% of their participants chose Program A, and only 28% chose Program B. Notice that the participants in this group were "risk averse." That is, they preferred the certainty of saving 200 lives, rather than the risky prospect of a one-in-three possibility of saving 600 lives. Notice, however, that the benefits of Programs A and B in Problem 1 are statistically identical.

Now inspect your answer to Problem 2, in which both choices emphasize the number of lives that would be *lost* (i.e., the number of deaths). Tversky and Kahneman (1981) presented this problem to a different group of students from the same colleges that they had tested with Problem 1. Only 22% favored Program C, but 78% favored Program D. Here the participants were "risk taking"; they preferred the two-in-three chance that 600 would die, rather than the guaranteed death of 400 people. Again, however, the benefits of the two programs are statistically equal. Furthermore, notice that Problem 1 and Problem 2 have identical deep structures. The only difference is that the outcomes are described in Problem 1 in terms of the lives saved, but in Problem 2 in terms of the lives lost.

The way that a question is framed—lives saved or lives lost—has an important effect on people's decisions (Hardman, 2009; Moran & Ritov, 2011; Stanovich, 2009). This framing changes people from

---

Demonstration 12.8 | The Framing Effect and the Wording of a Question

Try the following two problems:

Problem 1

Imagine that a country in Europe is preparing for the outbreak of an unusual disease, which is expected to kill 600 people. The public health officials have proposed two alternative programs to combat the disease. Assume that these officials have scientifically estimated the consequences of the programs, as follows:

If they adopt Program A, 200 people will be saved.

If they adopt Program B, there is a one-third probability that 600 people will be saved, and a two-thirds probability that zero people will be saved.

Which of these two programs would you choose?

Problem 2

Now imagine the same situation, but with these two alternatives:

If Program C is adopted, 400 people will die.

If Program D is adopted, there is a one-third probability that no one will die, and a two-thirds probability that 600 people will die.

Which of these two programs would you choose?

Source: Based on Tversky & Kahneman, 1981.

focusing on the possible gains (lives saved) to focusing on the possible losses (lives lost). In the case of Problem 1, we tend to prefer the certainty of having 200 lives saved, so we avoid the option where it's possible that no lives will be saved. In the case of Problem 2, however, we tend to prefer the risk that nobody will die (even though there is a good chance that 600 will die); we avoid the option where 400 face certain death. Tversky and Kahneman (1981) chose the name **prospect theory** to refer to people's tendencies to think that possible gains are different from possible losses. Specifically:

1. When dealing with possible *gains* (e.g., lives saved), people tend to avoid risks.

2. When dealing with possible *losses* (e.g., lives lost), people tend to seek risks.

Numerous studies have replicated the general framing effect, and the effect is typically strong (Kahneman, 2011; LeBoeuf & Shafir, 2012; Stanovich, 1999). Furthermore, the framing effect is common among statistically sophisticated people as well as statistically naive people, and the magnitude of the effect is relatively large. In addition, Mayhorn and his colleagues (2002) found framing effects with both students in their 20s and with older adults.

The research on framing suggests some practical advice: When you are making an important decision, try rewording the description of this decision. For example, suppose that you need to decide whether to accept a particular job offer. Ask yourself how you would feel about having this job, and then ask yourself how you would feel about *not* having this job. This kind of Type 2 processing can help you make wiser decisions (Kahneman, 2011).

Overconfidence about Decisions

In the previous section, we saw that decisions can be influenced by three decision-making heuristics: the representativeness heuristic, the availability heuristic, and the anchoring and adjustment heuristic. Furthermore, the framing effect—discussed in this section—demonstrates that both the background information and the wording of a statement can encourage us to make unwise decisions. Given these sources of error, people should realize that their decision-making skills are nothing to boast about. Unfortunately, however, the research shows that people are frequently overconfident (Kahneman, 2011; Krizan & Windschitl, 2007; Moore & Healy, 2008). **Overconfidence** means that your confidence judgments are higher than they should be based on your actual performance on the task.

We have already discussed two examples of overconfidence in decision making in this chapter. In an illusory correlation, people are confident that two variables are related, when in fact the relationship is either weak or nonexistent. In anchoring and adjustment, people are so confident in their estimation abilities that they supply very narrow confidence intervals for these estimates.

Let's now consider research on several aspects of overconfidence before considering several factors that help to create overconfidence.

General Studies on Overconfidence

A variety of studies show that humans are overconfident in many decision-making situations. For example, people are overconfident about how long a person with a fatal disease will live, which firms will go bankrupt, and whether the defendant is guilty in a court trial (Kahneman & Tversky, 1995). People typically have more confidence in their own decisions than in predictions that are based on statistically objective measurements. In addition, people tend to overestimate their own social skills, creativity, leadership abilities, and a wide range of academic skills (Kahneman & Renshon, 2007; Matlin, 2004; Matlin & Stang, 1978; Moore & Healy, 2008). In addition, physicists, economists, and other researchers are overconfident that their theories are correct (Trout, 2002).

We need to emphasize, however, that individuals differ widely with respect to overconfidence (Oreg & Bayazit, 2009; Steel, 2007). For example, a large-scale study showed that 77% of the student participants were overconfident about their accuracy in answering general-knowledge questions such as those in Demonstration 12.6. Still, these results tell us that 23% were either on target or underconfident (Stanovich, 1999). Furthermore, people from different countries may differ with respect to their confidence (Weber & Morris, 2010). For example, a cross-cultural study in three countries reported that Chinese residents showed greater overconfidence, and the U.S. residents were intermediate. However, the least-confident group was Japanese residents, who also took the longest to make their decisions (Yates, 2010).

Let's consider two research areas in which overconfidence has been extensively documented. As you'll see, students are usually overconfident that they will complete their academic projects on time, and politicians are often overconfident about the decisions they make.

Overconfidence about Completing Projects on Time

Are you surprised to learn that students are frequently overly optimistic about how quickly they can complete a project? In reality, this overconfidence applies to most people. Even Daniel Kahneman (2011) describes examples of his own failure in completing projects on time.

According to the **planning fallacy**, people typically underestimate the amount of time (or money) required to complete a project; they also estimate that the task will be relatively easy to complete (Buehler et al., 2002; Buehler et al., 2012; Kahneman, 2011; Peetz et al., 2010; Sanna et al., 2009). Notice why this fallacy is related to overconfidence. Suppose that you are overconfident when you make decisions. You will then estimate that your paper for cognitive psychology will take only 10 hours to complete, and you can easily finish it on time if you start next Tuesday.

Researchers certainly have not discovered a method for eliminating the planning fallacy. However, research suggests several strategies that can help you make more realistic estimates about the amount of time a large project will require.

1. Divide your project into several parts, and estimate how long each part will take. This process will provide a more realistic estimate of the time you will need to complete the project (Forsyth & Burt, 2008).

2. Envision each step in the process of completing your project, such as gathering the materials, organizing the project's basic structure, and so forth. Each day, rehearse these components (Taylor et al., 1998).

3. Try thinking about some person other than yourself, and visualize how long this person took to complete the project; be sure to visualize the potential obstacles in your imagery (Buehler et al., 2012).

The planning fallacy has been replicated in several studies in the United States, Canada, and Japan. How can we explain people's overconfidence that they will complete a task on time? One factor is that people create an optimistic scenario that represents the ideal way in which they will make progress on a project. This scenario fails to consider the large number of problems that can arise (Buehler et al., 2002).

People also recall that they completed similar tasks relatively quickly in the past (Roy & Christenfeld, 2007; Roy et al., 2005). In addition, they estimate that they will have more free time in the future, compared to the free time they have right now (Zauberman & Lynch, 2005). In other words, people use the anchoring and adjustment heuristic, and they do not make large enough adjustments to their original scenario, based on other useful information.

Overconfidence in Political Decision Making

Even powerful politicians can make unwise personal decisions, as we have recently seen with elected officials in the United States. Let's consider the decisions that politicians make about international policy—decisions that can affect thousands of people. Unfortunately, political leaders seldom think systematically about the risks involved in important decisions. For instance, they often fail to consider the risks involved when they (1) invade another country, (2) continue a war that they cannot win, and (3) leave the other country in a worse situation following the war. In an international conflict, each side tends to overestimate its own chances of success (Johnson, 2004; Kahneman & Renshon, 2007; Kahneman & Tversky, 1995).

When politicians need to make a decision, they are also overconfident that their data are accurate (Moore & Healy, 2008). For example, the United States went to war with Iraq because our political leaders were overconfident that Iraq had owned weapons of mass destruction. For instance, Vice President Dick Cheney had stated on August 26, 2002, "There is no doubt that Saddam Hussein now has weapons of mass destruction." President George W. Bush had declared on March 17, 2003, "Intelligence gathered by this and other governments leaves no doubt that the Iraq regime continues to possess and conceal some of the most lethal weapons ever devised." It then became progressively more clear, however, that crucial information had been a forgery, and that these weapons did not exist (Tavris & Aronson, 2007).

Researchers have created methods for reducing overconfidence about decisions. For example, the **crystal-ball technique** asks decision makers to imagine that a completely accurate crystal ball has determined that their favored hypothesis is actually incorrect; the decision makers must therefore search for alternative explanations for the outcome (Cannon-Bowers & Salas, 1998; Paris et al., 2000). They must also find reasonable evidence to support these alternative explanations. If the Bush administration had used the crystal-ball technique, for example, they would have been instructed to describe several reasons why Saddam Hussein could *not* have weapons of mass destruction.

Unfortunately, political leaders apparently do not use de-biasing techniques to make important political decisions. As Griffin and Tversky (2002) point out:

> *It can be argued that people's willingness to engage in military, legal, and other costly battles would be reduced if they had a more realistic assessment of their chances of success. We doubt that the benefits of over-confidence outweigh its costs. (p. 249)*

Reasons for Overconfidence

We have seen many examples demonstrating that people tend to be overconfident about the correctness of their decisions. This overconfidence arises from errors during many different stages in the decision-making process:

1. People are often unaware that their knowledge is based on very tenuous, uncertain assumptions and on information from unreliable or inappropriate sources (Bishop & Trout, 2002; Johnson, 2004).

2. Examples that *confirm* our hypotheses are readily available, but we resist searching for counterexamples (Hardman, 2009; Lilienfeld et al., 2009; Mercier & Sperber, 2011). You'll recall from the discussion of deductive reasoning that people also persist in confirming their current hypothesis, rather than looking for negative evidence.

3. People have difficulty recalling the other possible hypotheses, and decision making depends on memory (Theme 4). If you cannot recall the competing hypotheses, you will be overly confident about the hypothesis you have endorsed (Trout, 2002).

4. Even if people manage to recall the other possible hypotheses, they do not treat them seriously. The choice once seemed ambiguous, but the alternatives now seem trivial (Kida, 2006; Simon et al., 2001).

5. Researchers do not educate the public about the overconfidence problem (Lilienfeld et al., 2009). As a result, we typically do not pause—on the brink of making a decision—and ask ourselves, "Am I relying only on Type 1 thinking? I need to switch over to Type 2 thinking!"

When people are overconfident in a risky situation, the outcome can often produce disasters, deaths, and widespread destruction. The term **my-side bias** describes the overconfidence that your own view is correct in a confrontational situation (Stanovich, 2009; Toplak & Stanovich, 2002). Conflict often arises when individuals (or groups or national leaders) each fall victim to my-side bias. People are so confident that their position is correct that they cannot even consider the possibility that their opponent's position may be at least partially correct. If you find yourself in conflict with someone, try to overcome my-side bias. Could some part of the other people's position be worth considering?

More generally, try to reduce the overconfidence bias when you face an important decision. Emphasize Type 2 processing, and review the five points listed above. Are you perhaps overconfident that this decision will have a good outcome?

Hindsight Bias

People are overconfident about predicting events that will happen in the future. In contrast, **hindsight** refers to our judgments about events that already happened in the past. The **hindsight bias** occurs when an event has happened, and we say that the event had been inevitable; we had actually "known it all along" (Hastie & Dawes, 2010).

In other words, the hindsight bias reflects our overconfidence that we could have accurately predicted a particular outcome at some point in the past (Hardt et al., 2010; Pezzo & Beckstead, 2008; Pohl, 2004; Sanna & Schwarz, 2006). The hindsight bias demonstrates that we often reconstruct the past so that it matches our present knowledge (Schacter, 2001).

The hindsight bias can operate for the judgments we make about people. In a thought-provoking study, Linda Carli (1999) asked students to read a two-page story about a young woman named Barbara and her relationship with Jack, a man she had met in graduate school. The story, told from Barbara's viewpoint, provided background information about Barbara and her growing relationship with Jack. Half of the students read a version that had a tragic ending, in which Jack rapes Barbara. The other half read a version that was identical except that it had a happy ending, in which Jack proposes marriage to Barbara.

After reading the story, each student then completed a true/false memory test. This test examined recall for the facts of the story, but it also included questions about information that had not been mentioned in the story. Some of these questions were consistent with a stereotyped version of a rape scenario, such as, "Barbara met many men at parties." Other questions were consistent with a marriage-proposal scenario, such as, "Barbara wanted a family very much."

The results of Carli's (1999) study demonstrated the hindsight bias. People who read the version about the rape responded that they could have predicted Barbara would be raped. Furthermore, people who read the marriage-proposal version responded that they could have predicted Jack would propose to Barbara. (Remember that the two versions were actually identical, except for the final ending.) Furthermore, each group committed systematic errors on the memory test. Each group recalled items that were consistent with the ending they had read, even though this information had not appeared in the story.

Carli's (1999) study is especially important because it helps us understand why many people "blame the victim" following a tragic event such as a rape. In reality, this person's earlier actions may have been perfectly appropriate. However, people often search the past for reasons why a victim deserved that outcome. As we've seen in Carli's research, people may even "reconstruct" some reasons that did not actually occur.

The hindsight bias has been demonstrated in a number of different studies, though the effect is not always strong (e.g., Hardt et al., 2010; Harley et al., 2004; Kahneman, 2011; Koriat et al., 2006; Pohl, 2004), and has been documented in North America, Europe, Asia, and Australia (Pohl et al., 2002). Doctors show the hindsight bias when guessing a medical diagnosis (Kahneman, 2011), people demonstrate the hindsight bias for political events and for business decisions (Hardt et al., 2010; Kahneman, 2011), and the hindsight bias is stronger for individual who are experts in a particular domain (Knoll & Arkes, 2017). Furthermore, the hindsight bias varies as a function of psychological well-being. Groß, Blank, and Bayen (2017) found, for example, that depressed individuals viewed descriptions of events with negative outcomes as more foreseeable than events with positive outcomes.

Explanations for the Hindsight Bias

Despite all the research, the explanations for the hindsight bias are not clear (Hardt et al., 2010; Pohl, 2004). However, one likely cognitive explanation is that people might use anchoring and adjustment. After all, they have been told that a particular outcome actually did happen—that it was 100% certain. Therefore, they use this 100% value as the anchor in estimating the likelihood that they would have predicted the answer, and then they do not adjust their certainty downward as much as they should.

We also noted in discussing Carli's (1999) study that people may misremember past events, so that those events are consistent with current information. These events help to justify the outcome. Did the results of Carli's study about the tragic ending versus the upbeat story ending surprise anyone? Of course not. . .we knew it all along.

Decision-Making Style and Psychological Well-Being

Think back to the last time you needed to buy something in a fairly large store. Let's say that you needed to buy a shirt. Did you carefully inspect every shirt that seemed to be the right size, and then reconsider the top contenders before buying the shirt? **Maximizers** are people who have a **maximizing decision-making style**; they tend to examine as many options as possible. The task becomes even more challenging as the number of options increases, leading to "choice overload" (Schwartz, 2009).

In contrast, did you look through an assortment of shirts until you found one that was good enough to meet your standards, even if it wasn't the best possible shirt? **Satisficers** are people who have a **satisficing decision-making style**; they tend to settle for something that is satisfactory (Simon, 1955). Satisficers are not concerned about a potential shirt in another location that might be even better (Campitelli & Gobet, 2010; Schwartz, 2004, 2009). Now, before reading further, try Demonstration 12.9.

Now look at your answers to Demonstration 12.9, and add up the total number of points. If your total is 65 or higher, you would tend toward the "maximizer" region of the scale. If your total is 40 or lower,

Demonstration 12.9 | Decision-Making Style

1	2	3	4	5	6	7
Completely disagree						Completely agree

Using the scale above, answer each of the following questions:

1. Whenever I'm faced with a choice, I try to imagine what all the other possibilities are, even ones that aren't present at the moment.

2. Whenever I make a choice, I try to get information about how the other alternatives turned out.

3. When I am in the car listening to the radio, I often check other stations to see if something better is playing, even if I am relatively satisfied with what I'm listening to.

4. When I watch TV, I channel surf, often scanning through the available options even while attempting to watch one program.

5. I treat relationships like clothing: I expect to try a lot on before finding the perfect fit.

6. I often find it difficult to shop for a gift for a friend.

7. Renting videos or DVDs is really difficult. I'm always struggling to pick the best one.

8. When shopping, I have a hard time finding clothing that I really love.

9. I'm a big fan of lists that attempt to rank things (the best movies, the best singers, the best athletes, the best novels, etc.).

10. I find that writing is very difficult, even if it's just writing a letter to a friend, because it's so hard to word things just right. I often do several drafts of even simple things.

11. No matter what I do, I have the highest standards for myself.

12. I never settle for second best.

13. I often fantasize about living in ways that are quite different from my actual life.

Source: Schwartz, B., et al., (2002). Maximizing versus satisfaction: Happiness is a matter of choice. *Journal of Personality and Social Psychology, 83,* 1178–1197.

you would tend toward the "satisficer" region of the scale. (Scores between 41 and 64 would be in the intermediate region.)

Barry Schwartz and his coauthors (2002) administered the questionnaire in Demonstration 12.9 to a total of 1,747 individuals, including college students in the United States and Canada, as well as groups such as health-care professionals and people waiting at a train station. The researchers also administered several other measures. One of these assessed regret about past choices. It included such items as "When I think about how I'm doing in life, I often assess opportunities I have passed up" (p. 1182).

Schwartz and his colleagues found a significant correlation $r = +.52$ between people's scores on the maximizing–satisficing scale and their score on the regret scale. Those who were maximizers tended to experience more regret. They blame themselves for picking a less-than-ideal item (Schwartz, 2009).

The researchers also found a significant correlation $r = +.34$ between people's scores on the maximizing–satisficing scale and their score on a standard scale of depressive symptoms, the Beck Depression Inventory. The maximizers tended to experience more depression (Schwartz, 2004, 2009).

Keep in mind that these data are correlational, so they do not necessarily demonstrate that a maximizing decision-making style actually *causes* depression. However, people seem to pay a price for their extremely careful decision-making style. They keep thinking about how their choice might not have been ideal, and so they experience regret. The research by Schwartz and his coauthors (2002) suggests that this regret contributes to a person's more generalized depression.

An important conclusion from Schwartz's (2004) research is that having an abundance of choices certainly doesn't make the maximizers any happier. In fact, if they are relatively wealthy, they will need to make even more choices about their purchases, leading to even greater regret about the items that they did not buy. Schwartz (2009) chose a thought-provoking title for a recent chapter: "Be careful what you wish for: The dark side of freedom."

SECTION SUMMARY POINTS

Deductive Reasoning

1. Conditional reasoning focuses on "if. . .then. . ." relationships.

2. People's accuracy is higher for linguistically positive sentences, rather than linguistically negative statements. Accuracy is also higher for concrete problems, rather than abstract problems.

3. The belief-bias effect encourages people to trust their prior knowledge, rather than the rules of logic; overactive top-down processing therefore leads to errors.

4. Furthermore, people often fall victim to the confirmation bias; they keep trying to confirm a hypothesis, rather than rejecting it.

5. The Wason selection task provides strong evidence for the confirmation bias; however, people are more accurate when the task describes a concrete situation that is governed by societal rules.

6. Other examples of the confirmation bias can be found in medical diagnoses and in political situations.

Decision Making I: Overview of Heuristics

1. Decision-making heuristics are typically helpful in our daily lives; however, we can make errors in decision making when we overemphasize heuristics and underemphasize other important information.

2. According to the representativeness heuristic, we judge that a sample is likely if it resembles the population from which it was drawn. For example, the sample should look random if it was gathered by random selection.

3. We are so persuaded by the representativeness heuristic that we tend to ignore important statistical information such as the size of the sample and the base rates in the population; furthermore, the representativeness heuristic helps to create the conjunction fallacy.

4. According to the availability heuristic, we estimate frequency or probability in terms of how easily we think of relevant examples of something. The availability heuristic produces errors when availability is influenced by biasing factors such as recency and familiarity. However, a related phenomenon—called the recognition heuristic—helps us make accurate decisions about relative frequency.

5. The availability heuristic helps to explain the phenomenon of illusory correlation, which is related to stereotypes.

6. According to the anchoring and adjustment heuristic, we establish an anchor, and then we make adjustments, based on other information; the problem is that these adjustments are usually too small.

7. We also use the anchoring and adjustment heuristic when we estimate confidence intervals. We begin with a single best estimate, and then we make very small adjustments on either side of that estimate; however, this confidence interval is usually too narrow.

8. Gigerenzer and his colleagues emphasize that humans are reasonably skilled at making decisions in natural settings, using a wide variety of heuristics. This approach and the heuristics approach of Kahneman and his colleagues both emphasize that heuristics usually lead to appropriate decisions.

Decision Making II: Applications of Decision Making Research

1. The way in which a question is framed can influence our decisions; background information can influence our decisions inappropriately.

2. The framing effect also depends on wording. When the wording implies gains, we tend to avoid risks; when the wording implies losses, we tend to seek out risks.

3. People are frequently overconfident about their decisions. For instance, political decision makers may risk lives when they are overconfident. In addition, college students tend to be overconfident when they estimate the completion time for various projects.

4. In the hindsight bias, people already know the outcome of an event, and they are overly optimistic that they could have predicted that specific outcome before it actually happened.

5. Satisficers make decisions quickly; in contrast, maximizers agonize over their decisions, which may lead to regret and depressive symptoms.

CHAPTER REVIEW QUESTIONS

1. Describe the basic differences between deductive reasoning and decision making. Provide an example from your daily life that illustrates each of these cognitive processes. Why can both of them be categorized as "thinking"?

2. To make certain that you understand conditional reasoning, begin with this sentence: "If today is Monday, the art museum is closed." Apply the four conditional reasoning situations (propositional calculus) to this sentence, and point out which are valid and which are invalid.

3. Many of the errors that people make in reasoning can be traced to overreliance on previous knowledge or overactive top-down processes. Discuss this point, and then relate it to the anchoring and adjustment heuristic.

4. Throughout this chapter, you have seen many examples of a general cognitive tendency: We tend to accept the status quo (or the currently favored hypothesis), without sufficiently exploring other options. Describe how this statement applies to deductive reasoning and to several kinds of decision-making tasks.

5. Describe which heuristic is illustrated in each of the following everyday errors: (1) Someone asks you whether cardinals or robins are more common, and you make this decision based on the number of birds of each kind that you have seen this winter. (2) You are looking at a deck of cards that are in random order, and you see that there are three cards in a row that are Kings, which doesn't seem likely by chance alone. (3) You estimate the number of bottles of soda you will need for a picnic in July, based on the Christmas party consumption, taking into account the fact that the weather will be warmer in July.

6. In the case of the representativeness heuristic, people fail to take into account two important factors that should be emphasized. In the case of the availability heuristic, people take into account two important factors that should be ignored. Discuss these two statements, with reference to the information in this chapter. Give examples of each of these four kinds of errors.

7. Describe the variety of ways in which people tend to be overconfident in their decision making. Think of relevant examples from your own experience. Then point out methods for avoiding the planning fallacy when you face a deadline for a class assignment.

8. Think of a recent example from the news in which a politician made a decision for which he or she was criticized by news commentators. How could overconfidence have led to this unwise decision? Why might the hindsight bias be relevant here?

9. Suppose that you are planning to enroll in a course in social psychology next semester. Summarize at least five topics from this material on decision making that would have implications for that particular course.

10. Imagine that you have been hired by your local high school district to create a course in critical thinking. Review the chapter and make 15 to 20 suggestions (each only one sentence long) about precautions that should be included in such a program.

KEYWORDS

deductive reasoning
conditional reasoning task
propositional reasoning task
syllogism
propositional calculus
propositions
antecedent
consequent
affirming the antecedent

affirming the consequent
denying the antecedent
denying the consequent heuristic
dual-process theory
Type 1 processing
Type 2 processing
belief-bias effect
confirmation bias
decision making
representative

representativeness heuristic
small-sample fallacy
base rate
base-rate fallacy
conjunction rule
conjunction fallacy
availability heuristic
recognition heuristic
illusory correlation
social cognition approach

anchoring and adjustment heuristic
anchoring effect
anchor
confidence interval
framing effect
prospect theory
overconfidence
crystal-ball technique
planning fallacy
my-side bias

hindsight
hindsight bias
ecological rationality
default heuristic
maximizers
maximizing decision-making style
satisficers
satisficing decision-making style

RECOMMENDED READINGS

Gilovich, T., Griffin, D. W., & Kahneman, D. (2002). *The psychology of intuitive judgment: Heuristic and biases.* Cambridge: Cambridge University Press. This book provides a compelling overview of the role that heuristics play in judgment and decision making.

Kahneman, D. (2011). *Thinking, fast and slow.* New York: Farrar, Straus and Giroux. Daniel Kahneman's book is superb, because he clearly describes how he and Amos Tversky collaborated in developing their approach to decision making. He also provides examples of numerous heuristics. Each chapter ends with critical-thinking examples that readers can model if they want to improve their Type 2 processing.

Pohl, R. F. (Ed.). (2016). *Cognitive illusions: Intriguing phenomena in judgement, thinking and memory.* New York: Psychology Press. This edited volume provides an overview of modern research on many of the effects discussed in this chapter, such as the hindsight bias and overconfidence. It is accessible to undergraduate psychology students.

Manktelow, K. D., Over, D., & Elqayam, S. (Eds.). (2011). *The science of reason: A festschrift for Jonathan St B. T. Evans* (pp. 119–143). New York:

Psychology Press. This book was created to honor Dr. Evans, a British psychologist whose research has focused on logical reasoning. This book would be useful for students who are searching for an advanced-level examination of the discipline.

Schwartz, B. (2004). *The paradox of choice: Why more is less: How the culture of abundance robs us of satisfaction.* New York: HarperCollins. Schwartz's book explores the topic of maximizers and satisficers, discussed in this chapter's Individual Differences feature. The book goes beyond decision making to examine our cultural values. Although this book was published during the previous decade, it certainly has current relevance.

Smith, M. R., & Alpert, G. P. (2007). Explaining police bias: A theory of social conditioning and illusory correlation. *Criminal Justice and Behavior, 34,* 1262–1283. This journal article provides a clear, accessible overview of research that sheds light on the manner in which racial profiling by individual police officers may arise through social conditioning and illusory correlations (two topics discussed in this chapter).

ANSWER TO DEMONSTRATION 12.1

1. valid
2. invalid
3. invalid
4. valid

ANSWER TO DEMONSTRATION 12.6

1. 12,198,540 students were enrolled full-time in the United States.
2. 15,839 people died.
3. Martin Van Buren began his term in 1837.
4. The average life expectancy in Canada in 2009 was 81.3 years.
5. The United States paid $698,000,000,000 for military expenditures in 2010.
6. New Zealand gave women the right to vote in 1893. (They were the first country to do so.)
7. The median salary of a U.S. male college graduate in 2009 was $51,000.
8. The total area of Canada is 9,984,670 square kilometers or 3,855,102 square miles.
9. The population of France is 64,057.792.
10. Of the residents of Canada, 43% report that their religion is Roman Catholic.

Did most of your confidence intervals include the correct answers, or were your confidence intervals too narrow?

Cognitive Development throughout the Lifespan

13

Chapter Introduction

A friend described an interesting example of her granddaughter's cognitive sophistication. Five-year-old Isabelle had been on a family outing to go ice skating, a new experience for her. As they left the skating rink, Isabelle said, "That wasn't as much fun as I thought it was going to be." This chapter examines cognitive development in three areas, and Isabelle's remark reveals her expertise in all of these areas.

1. Memory: Isabelle remembers her original expectation that ice skating would be fun.

2. Metacognition: Isabelle had predicted that the skating experience would be fun.

3. Language: Isabelle's description successfully navigates among the three time periods, beginning with her anticipation of an enjoyable skating experience, and then the actual (not-so-enjoyable) skating experience, and finally her current acknowledgment of the discrepancy between the first and second time periods.

This interaction captures the considerable cognitive potential of young children. It also illustrates Theme 1 of this textbook, because children actively pursue information, and they try to make sense of their experiences (Gelman & Frazier, 2012).

Why should we study the cognitive processes of infants and children? One reason is theoretical: This research helps us understand the origins of cognitive skills, as well as the evolution of more complex skills (Gelman & Frazier, 2012; Rovee-Collier & Cuevas, 2009a). Another reason is practical: Many of you will have careers that require background knowledge about infancy and childhood.

It's important to note, however, that development isn't limited to infants, children, and young adults. In reality, we never stop developing—that is, we continue to change and adapt throughout our entire lives (Smith & Baltes, 1999; Whitbourne & Whitbourne, 2011). In today's world, humans are living longer than ever before, and the percentage of older adults has increased dramatically in recent years (U.S. Census

Bureau, 2012a). With this shift in population dynamics, cognitive psychologists have started to focus on how cognitive processing abilities change as people enter their older years (often defined in the field of cognitive aging as adults who are 65 or older). Some cognitive skills decline during the aging process, but many other capabilities remain stable. Understanding which cognitive processes change as adults age—along with the factors that drive those changes—can provide information that may directly inform many real-life issues facing aging adult populations.

This chapter focuses on cognitive development in three areas: memory, metamemory, and language. I organized this textbook so that the final chapter would encourage you to review many of the major concepts from these three important areas within cognitive psychology. As you'll also learn, infants and young children possess cognitive skills that you might not expect. In addition, you'll see that elderly people are much more cognitively competent than the popular stereotype suggests (Whitley & Kite, 2010).

The Lifespan Development of Memory

Theme 5 of this textbook highlights that many of our cognitive abilities depend upon both sensory-based bottom-up processes and knowledge-driven top-down processes. But, these processes aren't fully developed at birth. Instead, complex interactions between the properties of an organism's biological make-up and its environment drive the emergence of cognitive abilities over time. And, in many respects, we never really stop developing. Information newly acquired through the mechanisms that drive learning and development will influence how we perceive, interpret, and interact with our environments on subsequent occasions. Thus, in our final chapter on cognitive development, we take a **lifespan approach to development**. That is, we focus not only on development in infancy and young childhood, but instead on developmental issues that occur throughout one's lifetime, including adulthood and older adulthood.

When we study the cognitive abilities of infants, children, and elderly adults, the research problems are more complex than when we study young adults. For example, how can young infants convey their cognitive abilities, given their limited language and motor skills? With creative research techniques, however, researchers can partially overcome these limitations and discover that even young infants can understand information about the people and objects in their world (e.g., Gelman & Frazier, 2012; Mandler, 2004a; Rovee-Collier & Cuevas, 2009a, 2009b).

Research with elderly individuals presents a different set of methodological problems (Boker & Bisconti, 2006; Whitbourne & Whitbourne, 2011). Hundreds of studies have compared the cognitive performance of young, healthy college students with the performance of elderly people. And yet, across-group differences in health, self-confidence, formal education, and familiarity with technology may serve as confounding variables. For example, suppose that older adults perform less well on a cognitive processing task—such as a memory task—than college students. In such a case, it is often unclear whether the differences are due to cognitive decline as opposed to across-group differences in these potentially confounding variables. In general, researchers believe that confounding variables can explain a major proportion of the differences in cognitive performance between college students and older adults. That said, researchers have identified some age-related differences that persist, even when they eliminate confounding variables (Rabbitt, 2002; Salthouse, 2012; Whitbourne & Whitbourne, 2011).

Chapters 4–6 focused specifically on memory, and the remaining chapters frequently discussed how memory contributes to other cognitive processes. In this first section, we now focus on how memory develops during infancy (the first two years of life), childhood, and old age.

Memory in Infants

Try to picture an infant who is about four months old—not yet old enough to sit upright without support. Would you expect that this baby would recognize his or her mother or remember how to make a mobile move? Several decades ago, psychologists believed that infants as young as four months of age could not remember anything for more than a brief period (Gelman, 2002). Of course, we cannot expect young infants to demonstrate sophisticated memory feats, because regions of the cortex most relevant to working memory and long-term memory are not yet fully developed (Bauer, 2004; Kagan & Herschkowitz, 2005).

Furthermore, early researchers underestimated infants' memory capacities because of methodological problems. Fortunately, current developmental psychologists have devised several research methods to test infants' ability to remember people and objects (Gelman & Frazier, 2012; Reznick, 2009). This research shows that infants have greater memory capabilities than you might expect. For example, we now know that six-month-old infants can create an association between two objects, even if they have never previously seen the objects together at the same time and even if they were never reinforced for creating these associations (Cuevas et al., 2006; Giles & Rovee-Collier, 2011).

One way to assess infants' memory is to see whether they look longer at one stimulus than another (e.g., Kibbe & Leslie, 2011; Sangrigoli & de Schonen, 2004). Let's consider two other research techniques that demonstrate infants' memory skills: (1) recognizing mother and (2) conjugate reinforcement with a mobile. As you'll see, babies can demonstrate substantial memory ability, even during their first month of life.

Recognizing Mother

Research on visual recognition shows that three-day-old infants can distinguish their mother from a stranger (Rovee-Collier et al., 2001; Slater & Butterworth, 1997). Additionally, infants' ability to recognize their mother's voice is especially remarkable (Markowitsch & Welzer, 2010; Siegler et al., 2003). Kisilevsky and her coauthors (2003), for example, tested infants about one or two weeks *before* they were born. Specifically, these researchers approached pregnant women who were receiving prenatal care at a hospital in China. The researchers asked each woman about testing her infant's voice-recognition ability, while she was still pregnant. If the mother agreed, the researchers presented either the mother's voice reading a Chinese poem or a female stranger's voice reading the same poem. Impressively, the infants' heart rate changed more when they listened to their mother's voice, rather than the stranger's voice.

Conjugate Reinforcement

Obviously, young infants cannot verbally tell us that they remember something they saw earlier. Carolyn Rovee-Collier and her colleagues designed a nonverbal measure to assess infant memory. Many studies now use this conjugate reinforcement technique to examine infant memory (Markowitsch & Welzer, 2010; Ornstein & Haden, 2009; Rovee-Collier & Cuevas, 2009a, 2009b). In the **conjugate reinforcement technique**, a mobile hangs above a young infant's crib; a ribbon connects the infant's ankle and the mobile, so that the infant's kicks will make the mobile move (see Figure 13.1).

This game is especially appealing to two- to six-month-old infants. After several minutes, they begin to kick rapidly and pump up the mobile. Then, the infants lie quietly and watch parts of the mobile move.

In loving memory of Carolyn Rovee-Collier.

FIGURE 13.1
The conjugate reinforcement setup in Rovee-Collier's research.

As the movement dies down, they typically shriek and then kick vigorously, thereby pumping it up again. In operant conditioning terms, the response is a foot kick, and the reinforcement is the movement of the mobile (Barr et al., 2005; Rovee-Collier & Cuevas, 2009a, 2009b).

Let's see how the conjugate reinforcement technique can be used to assess infant memory. All the training and testing take place in the infant's crib at home, so that measurements are not distorted by the infant's reactions to the new surroundings. For a three-minute period at the beginning of the first session, the experimenter takes a baseline measure. During this time, the ribbon is connected from the infant's ankle to an "empty" mobile stand, rather than to the mobile. Thus, the experimenters can measure the amount of spontaneous kicking that occurs in the presence of the mobile, before the infant learns how to make the mobile move (Rovee-Collier & Barr, 2002; Rovee-Collier & Cuevas, 2009a).

Next, the experimenter moves the ribbon so that it runs from the baby's ankle to the stand from which the mobile is hung. The babies are allowed nine minutes to discover that their kicks can activate the mobile; this is the acquisition phase. The infants typically receive two training sessions like this, spaced 24 hours apart. At the end of the second training session, the ribbon is unhooked and returned to the empty stand for three minutes in order to measure what the infants remember. The number of kicks that the infant produces is a test of immediate retention.

Researchers then measure long-term memory after 1 to 42 days have elapsed. The mobile is once again hung above the infant's crib, with the ribbon hooked to the empty stand. Suppose that three-month-old Jason recognizes the mobile and recalls how his kicking had produced movement. Then, Jason will soon produce the foot-kick response.

Notice, then, that Rovee-Collier devised a clever way to "ask" infants if they remember how to activate the mobile. She also devised an objective method for assessing long-term memory, because she can compare two measures: (1) the number of kicks produced in the immediate retention test and (2) the number of kicks produced following the delay.

Rovee-Collier later devised a second operant conditioning task that is more appealing to infants between the ages of six and 18 months. In this second task, older infants learn to press a lever in order to make a miniature train move along a circular track. By combining information from the two tasks, researchers can trace infant memory from two months through 18 months of age (Barr et al., 2011; Hsu & Rovee-Collier, 2006; Rovee-Collier & Barr, 2002).

Figure 13.2 shows how much time can pass before infants no longer show significant recall for the relevant task. For example, six-month-olds can recall how to move the mobile and also how to move the

FIGURE 13.2

The maximum duration for which different groups of infants demonstrated significant retention.

In this study, two- to six-month-old infants kicked to activate a mobile, and six- to 18-month-old infants pressed a lever to activate a train.
Source: Rovee-Collier, C. K. (1999). The development of infant memory. *Current Directions in Psychological Science, 8,* 80–85.

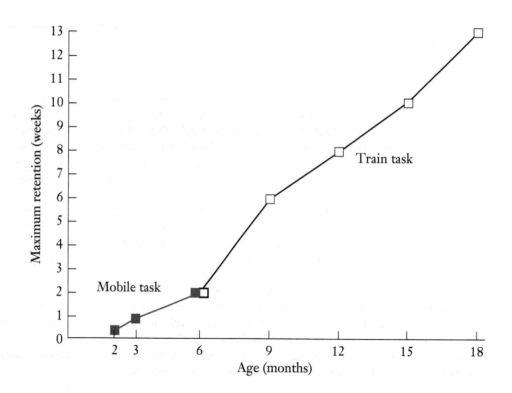

train, even after a two-week delay. This research demonstrates that long-term retention shows a steady, linear improvement during the first 18 months of life (Hsu & Rovee-Collier, 2006).

Several decades ago, researchers thought that infant memory was extremely limited. However, Rovee-Collier and her coworkers have demonstrated that infants can remember actions, even after a substantial delay. Furthermore, infant memory and adult memory are influenced by many of the same factors (Barr et al., 2011; Rovee-Collier & Barr, 2002; Rovee-Collier & Cuevas, 2009a, 2009b; Rovee-Collier et al., 2001).

For example, you saw in Chapter 5 that context sometimes influences adult memory. Context effects are even stronger for infants. Rovee-Collier and her colleagues (1985) used the conjugate reinforcement technique to test three-month-old infants whose cribs were lined with a fabric that had a distinctive, colorful pattern. The infants' delayed recall was significantly stronger when they were tested seven days later with the same, familiar crib liner, rather than an unfamiliar crib liner. Without the proper environmental context, infants' memories decline sharply (Markowitsch & Welzer, 2010; Rovee-Collier & Cuervas, 2009a; Rovee-Collier & Hayne, 2000).

In additional research, Rovee-Collier and her associates have discovered numerous other similarities between infant and adult memory. For example, in Chapter 6, we discussed the spacing effect: College students learn most effectively if their practice is distributed over time (**spaced learning**), rather than if they learn the material all at once (**massed learning**). A number of studies have demonstrated that infants can also remember better with distributed practice (Barr et al., 2005; Bearce & Rovee-Collier, 2006).

In summary, a number of tasks allow infants to demonstrate their memory skills. For example, babies can recognize their mother's voice, even prior to birth. Furthermore, six-month-olds can remember how to activate a mobile after a two-week delay, and some of the same factors that influence an adult's memory also influence an infant's memory.

Memory in Children

We have seen that researchers need to be extremely inventive when they study infant memory. By using the conjugate reinforcement technique and other creative methods, they have concluded that infants' memory is reasonably impressive.

Children can respond verbally, so it's much easier to assess their memory than infants' memory. However, the task is still challenging. Young children may have trouble understanding the task instructions, and they might not recognize letters of the alphabet or printed words. With these problems in mind, let's consider five topics: (1) children's working memory, (2) their long-term memory, (3) their memory strategies, (4) their eyewitness testimony, and (5) the relationship between children's intelligence and the accuracy of their eyewitness testimony.

Children's Working Memory

Working memory is often measured in terms of memory span, or the number of items that can be correctly recalled in order, immediately after presentation. Memory spans improve dramatically during childhood (Cowan & Alloway, 2009; Gathercole et al., 2006; Hitch, 2006). According to one estimate, for example, a two-year-old can recall an average of two numbers in a row, whereas a nine-year-old can recall six (Kail, 1992). By the age of 11 or 12, children's working memory is even more impressive. In fact, under ideal conditions, typically developing children almost match the performance of college students (Cowan et al., 2009).

As you saw in Chapter 4, Alan Baddeley (2006) and other theorists propose that adult working memory has three especially important components: the central executive, the phonological loop, and the visuospatial sketchpad. Susan Gathercole and her colleagues (2004) found that this same structural model also applies to the working memory of children as young as four, with older children, and with adolescents.

As you might expect, children's working-memory skills are correlated with their performance in school. For instance, children with high scores on *phonological* working memory are likely to excel in reading, writing, and listening (Alloway et al., 2005). Furthermore, children with high scores on *visuospatial* working memory are likely to excel in mathematics (Gathercole & Pickering, 2000; Hitch, 2006).

Now let's turn our attention to long-term memory in children. Later, we see how older children's use of memory strategies helps to explain the improvement in their memory performance.

Demonstration 13.1 ‖ Age Differences in Recall and Recognition

In this study, you will need to test a college-age person and a pre-school child. You should reassure the child's parents that you are simply testing memory as part of a class project.

You will be examining both recall and recognition in this demonstration. First, assemble 20 common objects, such as a pen, pencil, piece of paper, leaf, stick, rock, book, key, apple, and so forth. Place the objects in a box or cover them with a cloth.

You will use the same testing procedure for both people, although the preschool child will require a more extensive explanation. Remove 10 objects in all, one at a time. Show each object for about five seconds and then conceal it again. After you have shown all 10 objects, ask each person to recall as many of the objects as possible. Do not provide feedback about the correctness of the responses. After recall is complete, test for recognition. Show one object at a time, randomly presenting the old objects mixed in sequence with several new objects. For each item, ask whether the object is old or new.

Count the number of correct recalls and the number of correct recognitions for each person. You should find that both the child and the adult are quite accurate on the *recognition* measures, but the adult *recalls* more items than the child.

Children's Long-Term Memory

With respect to long-term memory, young children typically have excellent recognition memory but relatively poor recall memory (e.g., Flavell et al., 2002; Howe, 2000; Schwenk et al., 2009). In a classic study, Myers and Perlmutter (1978) administered research tasks similar to those in Demonstration 13.1, using two- and four-year-old children. To test *recognition*, the researchers began by showing children 18 objects. Then, they presented 36 items, including the 18 previous objects as well as 18 new objects. The two-year-olds recognized an impressive 80% of the items, and the 4-year-olds recognized about 90% of the items.

To examine *recall*, Myers and Perlmutter (1978) tested two additional groups of children. These researchers began by showing the children nine items. The two-year-olds recalled only about 20% of the items, and the four-year-olds recalled about 40% of the items. Recall memory seems to require the active use of memory strategies. As you see later in this section, children do not develop these strategies until middle childhood (Schneider & Bjorklund, 1998). Let's now consider two additional topics related to long-term memory: (1) autobiographical memory for events from childhood and (2) children's source monitoring.

1. *Autobiographical memory and early childhood.* As we discussed in Chapter 5, **autobiographical memory** refers to your memory for experiences and information that are related to yourself (Brewin, 2011). When researchers study autobiographical memory in children, they emphasize how children link their previous experiences together. Children therefore create a personal history or "life narrative" (Fivush, 2011). Most children's language skills grow rapidly as they approach the age of 2. These skills help them remember their personal experiences more accurately. Notice that this connection between language and memory is a good example of Theme 4 of your textbook.

   Children who are three years old can typically produce simple scripts to describe a recent experience (Howe et al., 2009; Hudson & Mayhew, 2009; Pipe & Salmon, 2009). As discussed in Chapter 8, a **script** is a simple, well-structured sequence of events—in a specified order—that are associated with a highly familiar activity (Baddeley et al., 2009). After the age of two, children are increasingly likely to reminisce about their previous experiences, especially with their parents (Fivush, 2011; Laible & Panfile, 2009). According to the research, when mothers encourage their children to provide detailed descriptions of events, these children are more likely to develop a narrative style that is detailed and coherent (Fivush, 2009, 2011).

   Now take a moment to answer this question: Can you clearly recall any events that happened when you were two or three years old? Are you sure that you're not actually recalling another person's description of this event? David Rubin (2000) located previous studies that had asked adolescents and adults to recall autobiographical memories from the first 10 years of their lives. As you can see in Figure 13.3, people seldom recalled events that happened when they were younger than 3. Recent studies confirm Rubin's results (e.g., Fitzgerald, 2010; Janssen & Rubin, 2011; Markowitsch & Welzer, 2010; Peterson et al., 2011).

   The reason for this phenomenon is not clear, especially because two-year-old children frequently describe an event that occurred several weeks or months ago. This observation suggests that they must be able to store verbal memories for several months (Gauvain, 2001; Ornstein & Haden, 2001).

   One possibility is that children younger than 2 do not have a well-organized sense of who they are (Fivush & Nelson, 2004; Goodman & Melinder, 2007; Markowitsch & Welzer, 2010).

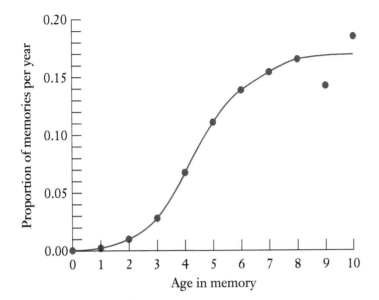

FIGURE 13.3
The proportion of memories supplied by adolescents and adults that occurred for each year, 1 to 10 years of age.
Source: Rubin, D. C. (2000). The distribution of early childhood memories. *Memory, 8,* 265–269.

As a result, they may have difficulty encoding and retrieving a series of events connected with themselves, when the interval is longer than several months (Newcombe et al., 2000). This explanation could be especially relevant, because the study by Rubin (2000) examined adolescents and adults. Apparently, they have trouble accessing their memories about early childhood.

2. *Children's source monitoring.*   Chapter 5 discussed **source monitoring**, which is the process of trying to identify the origin of a particular memory. In general, children younger than about seven years of age typically have more difficulty than adults in distinguishing between reality and pure fantasy (Foley, 2012; Ratner et al., 2001; Sluzenski et al., 2004). For example, I know an extremely bright child who had participated in an imaginary trip to the moon one day at school. Later that day, she insisted to her parents that she really *had* visited the moon. Children who are younger than seven years of age also have difficulty distinguishing between something they saw in real life, as opposed to something from a storybook or a video (Thierry et al., 2010).

Research by Mary Ann Foley, Hilary Horn Ratner, and their colleagues has systematically clarified the conditions in which young children are most likely to make these source-monitoring errors. For example, Foley and Ratner (1998) asked one group of six-year-olds to perform specific physical activities, such as making a motion like an airplane. A second group of six-year-olds was instructed, "Try to imagine what it would actually feel like to do that." A third group was instructed, "Try to picture what you look like. . . ."

According to the results, when children had actually performed an action, they seldom reported that they had simply imagined it. In contrast, when children had simply *imagined* an action, they often reported that they had actually performed it. The children who made the most source-monitoring errors were those who had imagined how it would feel to make airplane movements; they often convinced themselves that they had actually circled around the room.

Other research on source monitoring shows that children sometimes recall that they had performed a task, when someone else had actually performed it (Foley, 2012; Foley, Ratner, & House, 2002; Ratner et al., 2001). Apparently, children between the ages of 4 and 6 can watch another person at work, and they anticipate the steps in the project. Later, they become confused, and they remember actually completing the project themselves. As you might guess, children's source monitoring is especially poor if they are questioned a long time after the original event (Sluzenski et al., 2004).

In another investigation of children's source monitoring, Mary Ann Foley and her colleagues (2010) arranged to have pairs of four-year-old children work together on a task. These children took turns placing pieces of construction paper on a poster board to make a collage. Consistent with earlier research, children often claimed "I did it," when the other child had actually made the placement. Incidentally, you might wonder if the children's responses simply reflect an egocentric bias. However, the "I did it" bias seldom occurs when an adult and a child take turns (Foley, 2012).

In one of these studies, the researcher asked the child to think what the adult would feel like, raising her arms and moving them like an airplane (Foley et al., 2010). This procedure provided a framework for imagining the adult make other motor movements. Then, the researcher told the child to watch the adult placing each piece on the collage, and think what it would feel like to actually go through the motions of placing the piece. The results showed that these "feel like" instructions actually increased the likelihood that the child would claim, "I did it." Notice, then, that preschool children seem to have a significant problem with source monitoring.

Children's Memory Strategies

So far, our exploration of children's memory has demonstrated that young children are fairly similar to adults in recognizing items. However, children are much less accurate than adults in terms of recall and source monitoring. Adults have another advantage: When they want to remember something that must be recalled at a later time, they often use memory strategies. Here is one important reason that young children have relatively poor recall: They cannot use memory strategies effectively (Cowan & Alloway, 2009; Kail, 2010; Torbeyns et al., 2010). During elementary school, children become increasingly skilled in using these strategies (Bjorklund et al., 2009; Grammer et al., 2011).

Memory strategies are intentional, goal-oriented activities that we use to improve our memories. Young children may not realize that strategies can be helpful. Their working memory may not be developed enough to choose a strategy and actually use it on a memory task (Torbeyns et al., 2010). Furthermore, some young children may not actually *use* the strategies effectively; this problem is called **utilization deficiency** (Pressley & Hilden, 2006). As a result, the strategies may not improve their recall (Ornstein et al., 2006; Schneider, 2002).

In contrast, older children are more likely than younger children to realize that strategies are helpful. In addition, they choose their strategies more carefully and use them more consistently. Also, older children often use a variety of strategies when they need to learn several items, and they may monitor how they use these strategies (Bjorkland et al., 2009; Schneider, 1998). As a result, older children can recall items with reasonable accuracy. Let's survey three major kinds of memory strategies: rehearsal, organization, and imagery.

1. *Rehearsal,* or merely repeating items over and over, is not a particularly effective strategy, but it may be useful for maintaining items in working memory. Research suggests that four- and five-year-olds do not spontaneously rehearse material they want to remember. However, seven-year-olds do use rehearsal strategies, often silently rehearsing several words together (Bjorklund et al., 2009; Gathercole, 1998; Schneider & Bjorklund, 1998).

   Another important point is that younger children can benefit from learning to use rehearsal strategies, even though they may not use these strategies spontaneously (e.g., Flavell et al., 2002; Gathercole, 1998). Children with reading disorders also tend to recall more items when they have been taught about rehearsal (Swanson et al., 2010). As we will see in the section on metamemory, young children often fail to realize that they could improve their memory performance by using strategies.

2. *Organizational strategies,* such as categorizing and grouping, are helpful for adults, as we saw in Chapter 6. However, young children are typically less likely than older children to spontaneously group similar items together to aid memorization (Flavell et al., 2002; Ornstein et al., 2006; Pressley & Hilden, 2006; Schwenck et al., 2009). Try Demonstration 13.2; are the children in your sample reluctant to adopt an organizational strategy?

   Demonstration 13.2 is based on a classic study by Moely and her colleagues (1969), in which children studied pictures from four categories: animals, clothing, furniture, and vehicles. During the two-minute study period, they were told that they could rearrange the pictures in any order they wished. Younger children rarely moved the pictures next to other similar pictures, but older children frequently organized the pictures into categories. The researchers specifically urged other groups of children to organize the pictures. Even the younger children saw that the organizational strategy was useful, and this strategy increased their recall.

3. *Imagery*, a topic discussed in Chapters 6 and 7, is an extremely useful device for improving memory in adults. Research shows that even six-year-olds can be trained to use visual imagery effectively (Foley et al., 1993; Howe, 2006). However, young children usually do not use imagery spontaneously. In fact, the spontaneous use of imagery does not develop until adolescence. Even most college students do not use this helpful strategy often enough (Pressley & Hilden, 2006; Schneider & Bjorklund, 1998).

Demonstration 13.2 || Organizational Strategies in Children

Make a photocopy of the pictures on this page and use scissors to cut them apart. In this study you will test a child between the ages of 4 and 8; ideally, it would be interesting to test children of several different ages. Arrange these pictures in random order in a circle facing the child. Instruct him or her to study the pictures so that they can be remembered later. Mention that the pictures can be rearranged in any order they want. After a four-minute study period, remove the pictures and ask the child to list as many items as possible. Notice two things in this demonstration: (1) Does the child spontaneously rearrange the items at all during the study period? (2) Does the child show clustering during recall, with similar items appearing together?

In short, preschool children are unlikely to use memory strategies in a careful, consistent fashion. In fact, as we have suggested here—and will further discuss in connection with metamemory—young children seldom appreciate that they need to use memory strategies (Ornstein et al., 2006; Schneider, 1999). However, as children develop, they learn how to use memory strategies such as rehearsal, organization, and (eventually) imagery.

It's also worth mentioning that teachers can help children by showing them how to use age-appropriate memory strategies. Furthermore, teachers can use spaced rather than massed presentation in the classroom to improve their students' recall (Seabrook et al., 2005).

Children's Eyewitness Testimony

So far, we have examined children's working memory, long-term memory, and memory strategies. We've seen that young children's performance in those three areas is definitely inferior when compared with adults' performance. This information has implications for an applied area of cognition, the accuracy of their eyewitness testimony. As you might guess, older children typically provide much more accurate eyewitness testimony than younger children (Melnyk et al., 2007; Pipe & Salmon, 2009; Schwartz, 2011).

A real-life court case inspired Michelle Leichtman and Stephen Ceci (1995) to conduct an experiment. In the original court case, a nine-year-old girl had provided eyewitness testimony, and it seemed likely that both stereotypes and suggestions could have influenced her report. Leichtman and Ceci's classic study explored the impact of these two factors.

Leichtman and Ceci tested 176 preschoolers, assigning each child to one of four conditions. In the *control condition*, a stranger named Sam Stone visited the classroom, strolling around and making several bland comments for a period of about two minutes. In the *stereotype condition*, a research assistant presented one story each week to the children, for three weeks prior to Sam Stone's visit. Each story emphasized that Sam Stone was nice but very clumsy. In the *suggestion condition*, the research assistant told the children two incorrect suggestions after Sam Stone's visit—that Sam Stone had ripped a book and that he had spilled a chocolate drink on a white teddy bear. Finally, in the *stereotype-plus-suggestion condition*, children were exposed to both the stereotype before Sam Stone's visit and the incorrect suggestions afterward.

Ten weeks after Sam Stone's classroom visit, a new interviewer asked the children what Sam Stone had done during his visit. The children were specifically asked whether they had actually seen Sam Stone tear up the book and spill the chocolate drink on the teddy bear. Figure 13.4 shows the percentage of children in each condition who said that they had witnessed at least one of these two events.

Notice, first of all, that the children in the control group were highly accurate. In other words, children can provide valid eyewitness testimony if they do not receive misleading information, either before or after the target event (Bruck & Ceci, 1999; Schneider, 2002).

As Figure 13.4 also shows, however, a worrisome number of children claimed that they had actually witnessed these actions, in the condition where the researchers had established a previous stereotype. Even more of the younger children claimed that they had actually witnessed the actions if they had received inaccurate suggestions after the event. The most worrisome data came from the younger children who had received both the stereotype and the suggestions. Almost half of the younger children falsely reported that they had seen Sam Stone damage either the book or the teddy bear.

Other research confirms that the accuracy of children's eyewitness testimony is influenced by the child's age, stereotyping, and misleading suggestions (Melnyk et al., 2007; Memon et al., 2006; Roebers et al., 2005; Schwartz, 2011). As you might imagine, social factors can also have a major impact. For example, children make more errors when interviewers ask questions in a highly emotional tone or when the interviewer uses complex language (Bruck & Ceci, 1999; Imhoff & Baker-Ward, 1999; Melnyk et al., 2007).

FIGURE 13.4

The effects of stereotypes and suggestions on young children's eyewitness testimony.

Graph shows the percentage who reported actually seeing events that had not occurred.
Source: Leichtman, M. D., & Ceci, S. J. (1995). The effects of stereotypes and suggestions of preschoolers' reports. *Developmental Psychology, 31*, 568–578.

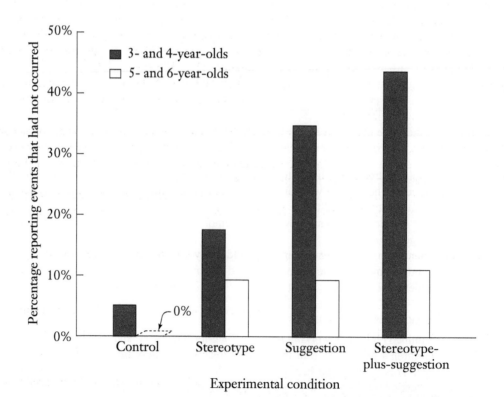

In addition, children are extremely reluctant to say, "I don't know" when an adult asks a question (Bruck & Ceci, 1999). Furthermore, children are likely to change their statements if someone cross-examines them, and this tendency is stronger among five- and six-year-olds than among nine- and 10-year-olds (Zajac & Hayne, 2006).

Children's Intellectual Abilities and Eyewitness Testimony

So far, this chapter has focused on typically developing children, and we have seen that the accuracy of children's eyewitness testimony increases as they grow older. What happens for children with intellectual disabilities? Lucy Henry and Gisli Gudjonsson (2007) studied children in England, who were either enrolled in special schools for children with intellectual disabilities or enrolled in mainstream schools. In each of these two groups, they tested children who were an average of either nine years two months old or 12 years 8 months old.

All the children saw a three-minute video clip that featured four people pulling up to a gas station in a car, filling up the car with gas, and driving off without paying for the gas. Each child then performed a short irrelevant task, and then the researcher asked the child to describe as much as possible about the video. The researchers scored the recall narrative in terms of the total number of correct items supplied by the child. As Table 13.1 shows, older children recalled more items than the younger children. Furthermore, this age difference was especially strong for the typically developing children.

In addition, Henry and Gudjonsson (2007) asked some specific misleading questions, for example, about the color of the police car, even though there was no police car. In this misleading-question situation, the older children made the same number of errors as the younger children. However, within each age group, the typically developing children provided a greater number of correct answers and a smaller number of errors in response to misleading questions. These results are consistent with the outcomes of other research (e.g., Pipe & Salmon, 2009).

However, Henry and Gudjonsson (2007) point out that there was only a short delay period between seeing the event and providing eyewitness testimony. Further research would need to include a longer delay, consistent with the real-life situations in which children are asked to supply eyewitness testimony.

Memory in Elderly People

The popular stereotype for elderly people is that they may be pleasant, but they are typically forgetful and cognitively incompetent (Cuddy & Fiske, 2002; Hess et al., 2003; Levy & Banaji, 2002). Here's an example of this stereotype (Hulicka, 1982). A 78-year-old woman served a meal to her guests, and the meal was excellent, except that she had used bleach instead of vinegar in the salad dressing. Her concerned relatives attributed the error to impaired memory and general intellectual decline, and they discussed placing her in a nursing home. As it turned out, someone else had placed the bottle of bleach in the cupboard where the vinegar was kept. Understandably, the woman had reached for the wrong bottle, which was similar in size, shape, and color to the vinegar bottle.

Some time later, the same people were guests in another home. A young woman in search of hair spray reached into a bathroom cabinet and found a can of the correct size and shape. She proceeded to drench her hair with Lysol. In this case, however, no one suggested that the younger woman should be institutionalized; they merely teased her about her absentmindedness.

In mainstream North American culture, people often believe that elderly people have substantial cognitive deficits. Unfortunately, this stereotype can lead elderly people to think that they actually *are* less

Table 13.1 The Number of Correct Items Supplied by Children in Free Recall

	Average age of child	
Category of children	**9 years 2 months**	**12 years 8 months**
Children with intellectual disability	7.2 items	13.6 items
Typically developing children	18.9 items	34.5 items

Source: Henry, L. A., & Gudjonsson, G. H. (2007). Individual and developmental differences in eyewitness recall and suggestibility in children with intellectual disabilities. *Applied Cognitive Psychology, 21,* 361–381.

competent. As a result, elderly people may remember less information (Moulin & Gathercole, 2008; Whitbourne & Whitbourne, 2011; Zacks & Hasher, 2006).

The research on age-related changes in memory has increased dramatically during the last 10 years, and we now have a wide variety of review articles and books (e.g., Bialystok & Craik, 2006; Erber, 2005; Park & Reuter-Lorenz, 2009; Whitbourne & Whitbourne, 2011). However, the research shows large individual differences and complex developmental trends in various components of memory. Let's first consider the research on working memory and long-term memory in elderly people. Then, we will examine some potential explanations for the memory changes during aging.

Working Memory in Elderly People

How well do elderly adults perform on tasks requiring working memory, when they need to retain information in memory for less than a minute? You've probably noticed that your psychology professors frequently use the phrase, "It all depends on. . .." In the case of working memory, factors such as the nature of the task determine whether we find age similarities or age differences (Whitbourne & Whitbourne, 2011).

In general, we find age similarities in working memory when the task is relatively straightforward and requires simple storage. In contrast, we typically find age differences when the task is complicated and requires manipulation of information (Park & Payer, 2006; Schwartz, 2011; Whitbourne & Whitbourne, 2011; Zacks & Hasher, 2006). For example, younger and older adults perform similarly on a standard digit-span test of working memory. On these tasks, people are instructed to recall a list of numbers in order (Bäckman et al., 2001; Dixon & Cohen, 2003; Fabiani & Wee, 2001).

In contrast, age differences are substantial on a working-memory task in which people must ignore irrelevant information, manipulate information, or perform two simultaneous tasks (Cansino et al., 2011; Carstensen, 2007; Kramer & Kray, 2006; Schwartz, 2011). For instance, in one study, people were given short lists of unrelated words, with the instructions to remember them, and report these words in correct alphabetical order (Craik, 1990). On this complex task, the average young participant reported 3.2 correct items on the alphabetical-order task, whereas the average elderly participant reported 1.7 correct items. Incidentally, an occupation that requires superb working memory is air traffic controller. U.S. regulations require controllers to retire at age 56, a policy that is clearly appropriate (Salthouse, 2012).

Long-Term Memory in Elderly People

Do elderly people differ from younger adults in their long-term memory? Once again, the answer depends on the characteristics of the task. In general, elderly people perform quite well on tests of semantic memory (Park & Reuter-Lorenz, 2009; Schwartz, 2011; Whitbourne & Whitbourne, 2011; Zacks & Hasher, 2006). In fact, a study by Salthouse (2012) showed that 50- to 80-year-olds actually perform *better* than 30- to 40-year-olds on crossword puzzles.

Elderly individuals also tend to perform well on tasks that they can do relatively automatically (Economou et al., 2006; Little et al., 2004). However, age differences emerge on more challenging tasks, such as source monitoring (Mitchell & Johnson, 2009; Whitbourne & Whitbourne, 2011).

In this discussion of long-term memory, we consider four topics: (1) prospective memory, (2) implicit memory, (3) explicit recognition memory, and (4) explicit recall memory.

1. *Prospective memory.* Chapter 6 discussed **prospective memory**, or remembering to do something in the future. In general, older adults have difficulty on many prospective-memory tasks (Scullin et al., 2011; Zimmermann & Meier, 2010). For example, one prospective-memory task—high in ecological validity—simulates a shopping task. Participants saw a list of items they were supposed to purchase. For example, when they saw an image of a fast-food restaurant, they were supposed to "buy" a hamburger. On these tasks, younger adults successfully completed a greater number of tasks than the older adults (Farrimond et al., 2006; McDermott & Knight, 2004).

   Why would older adults tend to make more errors on prospective-memory tasks? One important reason is that prospective memory relies heavily on working memory. People need to keep reminding themselves to do the relevant task, and—as we saw earlier—older adults often show a decline in working memory.

   In contrast, older adults perform relatively accurately when they have an environmental cue, such as a book placed near the door, reminding them to take it to the library (Einstein & McDaniel, 2004; Scullin et al., 2011). Occasionally, older adults even perform more accurately than younger adults, for example, when instructed to take a certain medicine on a daily basis (Park & Hedden, 2001; Park et al., 1999).

2. *Implicit Memory.*   Chapter 5 pointed out that an **explicit memory task** requires people to remember information that they have previously learned. In contrast, an **implicit memory task** requires people to perform a perceptual or cognitive task (e.g., to complete a series of word fragments); previous experience with the material facilitates their performance on the task.

In a representative study, Light and her colleagues (1995) measured implicit memory in terms of the amount of time that the participants needed to read a letter sequence that was either familiar or unfamiliar. People demonstrated implicit memory if they read a familiar sequence faster than an unfamiliar sequence. On this implicit memory task, adults between the ages of 64 and 78 performed just as well as the younger adults, who were between the ages of 18 and 24.

Other research on implicit memory shows either similar performance by younger adults, or else just a slight deficit for older adults (e.g., Economou et al., 2006; Park & Reuter-Lorenz, 2009; Whitbourne & Whitbourne, 2011; Zacks & Hasher, 2006). Thus, age differences are minimal when the memory task does not require effortful remembering.

3. *Recognition Memory.*   The research shows that long-term recognition memory declines either slowly or not at all, as people grow older (Burke, 2006; Erber, 2005; Moulin et al., 2007; Schwartz, 2011). For example, a classic study on recognition memory found that 20-year-olds correctly recognized 67% of words that had been presented earlier. On this same task, the 70-year-olds recalled a nearly identical 66% of the words (Intons-Peterson et al., 1999).

4. *Explicit Recall Memory.*   So far, our discussion of long-term memory has shown that elderly people often have difficulty with prospective memory, but they perform reasonably well on two kinds of long-term memory tasks: (1) implicit memory and (2) recognition memory. Let us now turn to performance on explicit recall tasks. Here, the differences between a young adult and an older adult are frequently more substantial (Brown, 2012; Schwartz, 2011; Zacks & Hasher, 2006).

Consider a study by Alaitz Aizpurua and her colleagues (2009). These researchers compared college students (age range = 19 to 25 years) with people who were enrolled in a college course designed for older adults (age range = 56 to 72 years). Notice that the researchers chose appropriate comparison groups for this study. In fact, the two groups were similar in the number of years of formal education and also similar in their self-rated health.

The participants in this study watched a short video of a robbery. After a short delay, they were given 10 minutes to recall the events from the video. The results showed that the older adults recalled less information than the younger adults. However, the two age groups were similar in (1) the number of events they described that did not occur in the video and (2) the nature of these errors.

Elderly individuals differ widely in their performance on long-term recall tasks. For example, people with low verbal ability and little education are more likely to show a decline in recall as they grow older. In contrast, age differences are minimal for people who have high verbal ability and are well educated (Manly et al., 2003; Rabbitt, 2002). Suppose that the two groups in the previous study had differed greatly in both education and health. The memory differences would have been substantially larger.

Lynn Hasher and her coauthors have explored another variable that can influence researchers' conclusions about age differences in memory. This variable is the time of day when people's memory is tested (Hasher et al., 2002; Zacks & Hasher, 2006). Specifically, older adults tend to function relatively well when they are tested in the morning. In contrast, older adults make substantially more memory errors than younger adults when both groups are tested in the afternoon. Interestingly, most research on memory is scheduled for afternoons, so the data underestimate the memory of older adults.

So, are older people more likely than younger people to have trouble with their long-term memory? As you can see, it's impossible to provide a simple answer. Instead, the research results are consistent with the "It all depends on. . .." principle. Elderly people are fairly similar to younger people on implicit memory tasks and on recognition tasks.

What happens when we examine an area in which age differences are more prominent, for example, on an explicit recall task? Here we cannot draw a simple conclusion. For instance, highly verbal, well-educated elderly people perform relatively well. Elderly people also perform relatively well when tested in the morning.

In other words, memory deficits are far from universal among elderly people. In fact, Zacks and Hasher (2006) end their chapter on aging and long-term memory with the following statement: "Taken together, these recent findings suggest that we may have seriously underestimated the memory abilities of older adults" (p. 174).

Explanations for Age Differences in Memory

We have examined a complex pattern of age-related memory effects. On some tasks, young people remember better than older people; in other cases, the age differences are minimal. As you might expect, this complex pattern of effects requires a complex explanation, rather than just one straightforward cause.

1. *Neurocognitive changes.*   Research in cognitive neuroscience demonstrates that some changes in brain structures occur during normal aging. Remember that explicit recall memory is especially likely to show a deficit. From a neuroscience perspective, this makes sense, because explicit recall relies on a complex network of different brain structures. Because parts of the brain must work together, explicit recall memory can be disrupted if one component of the network is not functioning appropriately. Furthermore, many of these brain structures are known to decrease in volume during normal aging (Moulin et al., 2007; Park & Reuter-Lorenz, 2009).

    Surprisingly, however, the research with elderly individuals shows *increased* activation in the frontal lobe, even though its actual size may decrease. This frontal-lobe activation helps to compensate for some of the age-related decreases in other parts of the brain (Park & Reuter-Lorenz, 2009).

    Let's now consider several psychological processes that help to explain the pattern of changes in memory performance during normal aging. To account for these changes, we would need to identify several mechanisms, because no single explanation would be sufficient (Moulin et al., 2007).

2. *Difficulty paying attention.*   In general, the research suggests that elderly adults are more likely than younger adults to have difficulty paying attention (Guerreiro & Van Gerven, 2011; Mueller-Johnson & Ceci, 2007; Whitbourne & Whitbourne, 2011). In fact, when elderly adults work on a standard memory task, they often perform about the same as when young adults work on a memory task that requires divided attention (Naveh-Benjamin et al., 2005; Naveh-Benjamin et al., 2007).

3. *Less effective use of memory strategies.*   Elderly people could have impaired memory because they use memory strategies and metamemory less effectively. Some research suggests that elderly adults construct fewer chunks in working memory, compared to younger adults (Naveh-Benjamin et al., 2007). As you may recall from Chapter 4, a **chunk** is a memory unit that consists of several components that are strongly associated with one another (Schwartz, 2011). If elderly people have trouble using working-memory strategies, they are likely to make errors on tasks such as prospective memory and explicit recall.

    In contrast, many studies conclude that elderly adults and young adults use similar memory strategies in *long-term memory* (Dunlosky & Hertzog, 1998; Light, 2000). Therefore, the strategy-deficit hypothesis cannot explain age differences in long-term memory.

4. *The contextual-cues hypothesis.*   As we saw earlier, elderly people perform relatively well on recognition tasks. Contextual cues are present on recognition tasks, because researchers display an item, and the participants report whether they had seen it previously. In other words, these contextual cues can encourage recognition for elderly individuals.

    In contrast, contextual cues are absent on explicit recall tasks; instead, these recall tasks require people to use effortful, deliberate processing. The research shows that young adults are relatively skilled in remembering contextual cues, such as where they were and what date it was when they heard a particular news item (Grady & Craik, 2000; Light, 2000). These contextual cues may therefore boost the accuracy of young adults' explicit recall. In contrast, we noted that elderly adults typically recall fewer contextual cues. Therefore, elderly adults must rely on effortful, deliberate processing in order to retrieve the information, and the explicit recall task is more challenging.

5. *Cognitive slowing.*   A final explanation is one that has been acknowledged for decades: Elderly people often experience **cognitive slowing**, or a slower rate of responding on cognitive tasks (e.g., Bunce & Macready, 2005; Einstein & McDaniel, 2004; Schwartz, 2011). The cognitive-slowing explanation can account for some of the age-related differences in memory, but it cannot fully explain why elderly people function relatively well on some other memory tasks.

In summary, several hypotheses can each explain some portion of the memory differences between older and younger adults. Perhaps researchers will develop a more refined version of several of these hypotheses, or they may propose additional hypotheses. At this point, we currently have a complex set of findings about memory in elderly individuals, but no comprehensive explanation for these results.

The Lifespan Development of Metamemory

As we discussed in Chapter 6, **metacognition** is a term that refers to your thoughts about thinking; it is your knowledge about your cognitive processes, as well as your control of these cognitive processes. One important kind of metacognition is **metamemory**, a term that refers to your knowledge, monitoring, and control of your memory.

Another kind of metacognition is called **theory of mind**, a term that refers to your ideas about how your mind works, as well as how other people's minds work. For example, you know that other people hold certain beliefs that are different from your own. However, young children have trouble with this concept (Dunlosky & Metcalfe, 2009; Schneider & Lockl, 2008; Schwartz, 2011).

A third kind of metacognition is **metacomprehension**, a term that refers to your thoughts about your comprehension, such as your understanding of written material or spoken language. Although there are a small number of exceptions (e.g., Baker et al., 2010; Hacker et al., 2009), researchers have not explored metacomprehension in children or elderly individuals. In this chapter, we therefore focus specifically on *metamemory* in children and elderly people.

Metamemory in Children

In this discussion of children's metamemory, we examine children's beliefs about how their memory works, their awareness that learning requires an effort, and their judgments about their own memory performance. Then, we discuss how metamemory is related to memory performance.

Children's Understanding of How Memory Works

An important component of metamemory is a person's knowledge about how memory works. Demonstration 13.3 includes some questions about this aspect of children's metamemory. Try this demonstration when you have an opportunity. You may need to simplify the questions for young children, because their responses might be influenced by their limited language skills (Fritz et al., 2010).

Demonstration 13.3 | Metamemory in Children

Locate a child who is at least five years old, and ask the following questions about his or her memory. Compare the accuracy and the completeness of the answers with your own responses. If the child is young, you may need to modify the wording.

Suppose that a child named Katie is supposed to bring her favorite book to school tomorrow. She is afraid that she might forget to bring it. What kind of things can she do to make sure that she brings the book to school?

Suppose that I decide to read you a list of 10 words. How many words do you think that you could remember, in the correct order? (Then, read the following list fairly slowly, and count how many words the child recalls correctly. If the child is young, substitute the number "5" for "10" and read only the first five words.)

dog chair flower sky ball bicycle apple pencil house car

Suppose that you memorize a friend's address. Will you remember the address better after *2 minutes* have passed or after *2 days* have passed?

Two children want to remember a list of words. One child has a list of 10 words, and the other has a list of five words. Which child will be more likely to remember all the words on the list correctly?

Suppose that a boy named Bob is telling you a story about a birthday party he went to. Later on, you tell this story to a friend. Would it be easier for you to tell the whole story word for word? Or would it be easier for you to tell the main idea about the story?

Children often have unsophisticated ideas about some aspects of their memory (Fritz et al., 2010; Larkin, 2010). For example, seven-year-olds are not yet aware that words are easier to remember when they are related to one another, rather than randomly selected (Schneider & Pressley, 1997). Furthermore, when young children are taught to use a memory strategy, they often fail to realize that the strategy actually improved their memory performance (Bjorklund, 2005). If children don't know how their memory works, they won't know how to plan effective study strategies (Bjorklund, 2005; Schneider, 2002).

Children's Awareness That Effort Is Necessary

Another important component of metamemory is the awareness that memory is not an automatic process. Instead, you need to make an effort, if you really want to remember something (Bjorklund, 2005; Schwartz, 2011). Unfortunately, young children do not appreciate this principle. Furthermore, they are not accurate in judging whether they have successfully committed some information to memory. They typically report to the experimenter that they have satisfactorily memorized a list, yet they recall little on a test (Pressley & Hilden, 2006).

In addition, children often fail to realize that they need to make an effort to use a memory strategy. However, they are more likely to successfully use a memory strategy if they have received instructions about why the strategy should help their memory (Pressley & Hilden, 2006).

Older children also have naive ideas about the effort required in memorization. I recall a visit from an 11-year-old in our neighborhood who had been memorizing some information about the U.S. Constitution. My husband asked her how she was doing and whether she would like him to quiz her on the material. She replied that she knew the material well, but he could quiz her if he wanted. Her recall turned out to be minimal for both factual and conceptual information. She had assumed that by allowing her eyes to wander over the text several times, the material had magically worked its way into her memory.

Children's Judgments about Their Memory Performance

In general, young children are extremely overconfident when they assess their memory performance. In contrast, older children are somewhat more accurate (Dunlosky & Metcalfe, 2009; Keast et al., 2007; Larkin, 2010; Schneider & Lockl, 2008).

For example, Claudia Roebers and her colleagues (2004) gathered measures of metamemory as part of their larger study on children's eyewitness testimony. Children between the ages of five and 10 years of age watched a live magic show, which lasted eight minutes.

One week later, an interviewer met with each child individually and asked a series of 56 questions about the show. In this study by Roebers and her colleagues, a typical question was, "Where did the magician get the bag from?" (p. 326). After answering each question, children rated how confident they were that their answer had been correct. Specifically, they used a rating scale consisting of five cartoon faces. The facial expressions varied from a very frowning face ("very unsure," corresponding to a rating of 1) to a very smiling face ("very sure," corresponding to a rating of 5).

Figure 13.5 shows the results. As you can see, when children answered a question correctly, all three age groups were very sure that their answer had been correct. In contrast, when they answered a question *incorrectly*, they should have circled either the very frowning face or the somewhat frowning face. Notice that even the older children were overconfident that their incorrect answer had been correct. However, this overly optimistic assessment may be adaptive: If children knew that their performance had been so dismal, they would not persist on a difficult task (Dunlosky & Metcalfe, 2009).

Children's Metamemory: The Relationship between Metamemory and Memory Performance

Let us summarize several observations from this chapter that are related to memory in young children:

1. Their metamemory is faulty; they do not realize that they need to make an effort to memorize, and they also do not realize how little they can remember.

2. They do not spontaneously use helpful memory strategies.

3. Relative to older children, their performance on a memory test is poor.

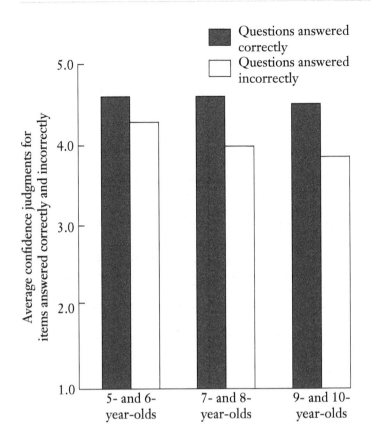

FIGURE 13.5
Average level of confidence for questions answered correctly and questions answered incorrectly. (1 = Very unsure; 5 = Very sure).

Source: Roebers, C. M., Gelhar, T., & Schneider, W. (2004). "It's magic!" The effects of presentation modality on children's event memory, suggestibility, and confidence judgments. *Journal of Experimental Child Psychology, 87,* 320–355.

Does a causal relationship link these three observations? Perhaps the three are related in this fashion:

Metamemory → Strategy use → Memory performance

According to this argument, when children have poor metamemory, they will not be aware that they must use strategies to commit material to memory. If they do not use strategies, then their memory performance will be poor.

We have some evidence that metamemory is related to strategy use. For example, children with sophisticated metamemory skills are more likely to report using memory strategies. They are also somewhat more likely to use these strategies effectively (e.g., Dunlosky & Metcalfe, 2009). In addition, we have extensive evidence to support the second link in the chain. As we've just seen, children's strategy use is related to memory performance.

So, metamemory is linked to strategy use, and strategy use is linked to memory performance. Is there a relationship between the two ends in that chain—that is, a relationship between metamemory and memory performance? Analysis of the research shows that the correlation between metamemory and memory performance is moderate (Ornstein et al., 2006; Schneider, 2002).

It makes sense that the correlations are not stronger. One reason is that it's difficult to test children's metamemory, because they haven't yet developed the sophisticated vocabulary necessary to describe their mental states (Joyner & Kurtz-Costes, 1997; Sodian, 2005). Furthermore, children may already know that memory strategies would be helpful, but they do not actually use them. After all, bright college students may have finely tuned metamemory skills; however, they may lack either the time or the motivation to actually use some potentially useful memory strategies.

To some extent, elementary-school teachers can take advantage of "teachable moments" in the classroom, and they can help children understand how to think about improving their memory (Duffy et al., 2009; Grammer et al., 2011; Ornstein et al., 2011). Parents can also provide guidance. Furthermore, when parents reminisce with their young children, they provide a model that helps children understand how to think about future events (Laible & Panfile, 2009).

In summary, we can conclude that metamemory is moderately related to memory performance (Dunlosky & Metcalfe, 2009; Schneider, 2002). Consequently, the proposed causal sequence (Metamemory → Strategy use → Memory performance) could account for a substantial portion of the improvement in memory performance as children grow older.

Metamemory in Elderly People

What do elderly adults believe about their memory? Let's begin by examining comparisons between older and younger adults in two areas: (1) their beliefs about how memory operates, and (2) their skill in monitoring their memory. Then, let's consider another topic: (3) whether elderly people are aware of their memory problems.

Beliefs about Memory

Older and younger adults share similar beliefs about the properties of memory tasks (Dunlosky & Metcalfe, 2009; Light, 1996). Both groups have the same fundamental knowledge about how memory works. They also have similar ideas about which strategies are most effective, and what kinds of material can be remembered most readily (Hertzog et al., 1999).

Memory Monitoring

On some tasks, older and younger adults are equally skilled in monitoring their memory performance (Bieman-Copland & Charness, 1994; Hertzog & Dixon, 1994). For example, the two groups are similar in their ability to predict—on an item-by-item basis—which items they can recall at a later time (Connor et al., 1997).

Older and younger adults are also similar with respect to selecting the most difficult items for further study, rather than studying the items that they have already mastered (Dunlosky & Hertzog, 1997). The two groups also perform equally well in judging their accuracy when answering general-knowledge questions and when deciding whether a particular item is old or new (Dodson et al., 2007).

However, older adults are more likely than younger adults to be overconfident on some memory tasks (e.g., Dunlosky & Metcalfe, 2009). For example, Chad Dodson and his colleagues (2007) studied adults whose average age was 67 and college students whose average age was 21. The older adults were more likely than the young adults to overestimate their overall performance on a test of memory for specific details about a recent event.

Furthermore, older adults are especially likely to overestimate their performance on a task where their working memory is "overworked" (Shake et al., 2009). In addition, older adults may be skilled in monitoring their memory, but then they may not use this information to decide how to remember some information (Krätzig & Arbuthnot, 2009).

Finally, some older adults have **dementia**, a medical disorder that includes memory problems and other cognitive impairments (American Psychiatric Association, 2000). These individuals typically have difficulty in estimating their memory abilities (Youn et al., 2009).

Awareness of Memory Problems

The research about memory-problem awareness does not compare older and younger adults. Instead, it focuses on surveys of elderly individuals. Elderly people are likely to report problems with their everyday memory, especially on explicit recall tasks such as remembering names and phone numbers (Dunlosky & Metcalfe, 2009; Kester et al., 2002; Rendell et al., 2005). They are also likely to say that their memory failures have increased over the years. Based on the research that we reviewed on explicit recall in elderly individuals, these reports may be accurate.

The problem is that the popular stereotype about elderly people's poor memory may encourage elderly individuals to think that memory decline is inevitable. As a result, many elderly people will not try to develop helpful memory strategies (Dunlosky & Metcalfe, 2009; Hess, 2005). In contrast, some elderly people are high in **memory self-efficacy**, which is a person's belief in his or her own potential to perform well on memory tasks. They think that it's important to keep developing their memory. As a result, they typically use effective memory strategies, and they perform relatively well (Dunlosky & Metcalfe, 2009; Zacks & Hasher, 2006).

In summary, our examination of metamemory has revealed that elderly adults and young adults are similar in some respects (Dodson et al., 2007; Light, 2000). We saw earlier in this section that young children's metamemory is less accurate than young adults' metamemory. In contrast, most elderly adults do not experience overwhelming metamemory impairments, and they remain quite competent on some metamemory tasks.

The Development of Language

"Mama!" (8 months old)

"Wash hair." (1 year, 4 months old)

"Don't tickle my tummy, Mommy!" (1 year, 11 months old)

"My grandma gave me this dolly, Cara. My grandma is my mommy's mommy. I have another grandma, too. She's my daddy's mommy. And Aunt Elli is my daddy's sister." (2 years, 9 months old)

These selections from the early language of my daughter Sally are typical of children's remarkable achievements during language acquisition. Individual children differ in the rate at which they master language (e.g., Fernald & Marchman, 2006; Hayne & Simcock, 2009; Tomasello, 2006). Still, within a period of 2–3 years, all typically developed children progress from one-word utterances to complex discourse. In fact, by the age of five, most children produce sentences that resemble adult speech (Kuhl, 2000).

Many linguists say that language acquisition is the most spectacular of human accomplishments (Thompson & Madigan, 2005; Tomasello, 2006). Therefore, as you might expect, children's linguistic skills clearly exemplify Theme 2. For instance, the average six-year-old can speak between about 10,000 and 14,000 words (MacWhinney, 2011). To acquire a vocabulary of this size, children must learn approximately seven new words each day, from the time they start speaking until their sixth birthday (Carroll, 2008; Wellman, 2000). If you are not impressed by a 14,000-word vocabulary, consider how much effort high school students must exert to learn 1,000 words in another language—and those six-year-old language learners are only waist-high!

However, language acquisition includes much more than the simple acquisition of new words. For example, children combine these words into phrases that they have never heard before, such as, "My dolly dreamed about toys" (2 years, 2 months).

Researchers have typically ignored developmental and learning-based changes in language during late adulthood, although some research is emerging (e.g., de Bot & Makoni, 2005; Fine et al., 2013; Kamide, 2012; Kemper, 2006; Stine-Morrow et al., 2006; Whitbourne & Whitbourne, 2011). Our discussion of language development is therefore limited to infancy and childhood.

Language in Infants

During the first 18 months of life—and even shortly before birth—human infants are preparing to use language (Curtin & Werker, 2009). Let's begin by considering how young infants perceive the basic sounds of speech. Then, we look at several early skills in language comprehension and language production. We also see that adults provide infants with a very helpful kind of language, which clearly helps them acquire language. Our last topic in this part of the chapter focuses on a question from applied psychology: Can infants learn language by watching a popular DVD?

Speech Perception during Infancy

To acquire language, infants must be able to distinguish between **phonemes**, which are the smallest sound units in a language. However, the ability to make distinctions is only half of the struggle. Infants must also be able to group together the sounds that are phonetically equivalent. For example, infants must be able to recognize that the sounds *b* and *p* are different from each other. In addition, they must recognize that the sound *b*, spoken by the deepest bass voice, is the same as the sound *b*, spoken by the highest soprano voice (Harley, 2008; Jusczyk & Luce, 2002; Saffran et al., 2006).

If you have recently observed a baby who is younger than six months old, you might have concluded that the baby's mastery of language was roughly equivalent to the linguistic skills of your elbow. Until the early 1970s, psychologists were not much more optimistic. However, more than 40 years of research have demonstrated that infants' speech perception is surprisingly advanced (Fennell, 2012). Infants can perceive almost all the speech-sound contrasts used in language, either at birth or within the first few weeks of life (Houston, 2005; Todd et al., 2006; Werker & Tees, 1984). They can also recognize similarities, an important early stage in language comprehension. Young infants' abilities clearly encourage them to learn languages (Curtin & Werker, 2009; Jusczyk & Aslin, 1995; Saffran et al., 2006; Traxler, 2012).

In some cases, young infants are even more skilled than older infants and adults in making phonemic distinctions (Curtin & Werker, 2009). For example, Hindi is a language spoken in India. In Hindi, the *t* sound is sometimes made by placing the tongue against the back of the teeth. However, the *t* sound can also be made by placing the tongue farther back along the roof of the mouth. Hindi speakers can easily distinguish between these two sounds in their language. As it happens, however, English-speaking adults *cannot* distinguish between these two *t* sounds. Do the children of English speakers tend to be more skilled? Werker and Tees (1984) tested infants who were being raised in an English-speaking environment. Impressively, infants could distinguish between these two Hindi phonemes with about 95% accuracy when they are 6–8 months old. Their accuracy drops to about 70% at 8–10 months of age, and to about 20% at 10 to 12 months of age. In contrast, consider 10- to 12-month-old infants who have been raised in a Hindi-speaking environment. These infants distinguish between these two phonemes with close to 100% accuracy (Werker &Tees, 1984).

Apparently, young infants can appreciate numerous phonetic distinctions in every language. Later, however, they reorganize their perceptual categories so that they focus on the important distinctions from their own language environment (Curtin & Werker, 2009; Lany & Saffran, 2010; MacWhinney, 2011; Todd et al., 2006).

According to other research on speech perception, newborns can discriminate between two languages that have different rhythms, such as English and Italian (Saffran et al., 2006). Furthermore, research by Bosch and Sebastián-Gallés (2001) focused on children being raised in bilingual homes where the parents spoke two rhythmically similar languages, Spanish and Catalan (Catalan is a language spoken in Barcelona, Spain, and the surrounding region). Impressively, 4-month-olds could discriminate between these two languages! These discrimination skills help infants to keep these two languages from being confused with each other (Curtin & Werker, 2009; Saffran et al., 2006).

Language Comprehension during Infancy

The research about speech perception in infancy has been active for several decades. In contrast, researchers have been slower to explore how infants master the more complex aspects of language *comprehension*, beyond the level of the phoneme. However, we now have information about young infants' comprehension skills in several areas: (1) recognizing important words, (2) understanding the correspondence between a speaker's facial expression and the emotional tone of the speaker's voice, and (3) appreciating semantic concepts.

1. *Recognizing important words.*   Interestingly, infants between the ages of four and five months can already recognize the sound patterns in their own name. Specifically, Mandel and her colleagues (1995) found that infants are likely to turn their heads to look at a location from which their own name is spoken. In contrast, they seldom turn their heads when a different name is spoken that is similar in length and accented syllable (e.g., *Megan* for an infant named *Rachel*).

   Young infants can also understand a few selected words (Curtin & Werker, 2009; Piotroski & Naigles, 2012; Saffran et al., 2006). For example, Tincoff and Jusczyk (1999) showed each 6-month-old two videos placed next to each other. One video showed the infant's mother, and the other showed the infant's father. Meanwhile, the infants heard either the word *mommy* or the word *daddy*. When *mommy* was presented, the infants preferred to look at the video of their mother. When *daddy* was presented, they preferred to look at the video of their father.

2. *Understanding the correspondence between sound and sight.*   Infants also appreciate another component of language comprehension: the emotional tone of spoken language (Flavell et al., 2002). For example, Walker-Andrews (1986) played recordings of either a happy voice or an angry voice to seven-month-old infants. Meanwhile, the infants saw a pair of films—one of a happy speaker and one of an angry speaker—projected side-by-side. The mouth region of each face was covered so that the infants could not rely on lip movements to match the voice with the film. Therefore, the infants had to look for emotional cues only in the speaker's cheeks and eyes, rather than in the most obvious location, the speaker's mouth.

   The results of Walker-Andrews's (1986) study showed that infants who heard a happy voice watched the happy face more often. In contrast, the infants who heard an angry voice watched the angry face more often. In other words, even young infants appreciate that facial expression must correspond with vocal intonation.

3. *Appreciating semantic concepts.*   So far, we've seen that infants respond when they hear their own names. They also link the words "mommy" and "daddy" with the visual image of the appropriate parent. In addition, they know that sight and sound must be linked together.

According to research by Jean Mandler and her colleagues, infants also show remarkable skills when we consider their concepts about objects. For example, by about nine months of age, infants can distinguish between animate objects, which move by themselves, and inanimate objects, which cannot move independently (Mandler, 2003, 2004a, 2007).

In another study, McDonough and Mandler (1998) showed nine-month-old infants a dog drinking from a cup and a car giving a doll a ride. The researchers then handed the infants some new objects from two categories—such as a cat and an anteater for the animal category and a truck and a forklift for the vehicle category. The infants showed the appropriate imitation patterns for the new objects, even for the relatively unfamiliar ones. For example, they showed the anteater drinking, whereas they showed the forklift giving the doll a ride. Infants therefore have the ability to generalize across a category such as "animal" or "vehicle" (Mandler, 2003, 2004a). In other words, children can understand concepts before they are 1-year old (Mandler, 2007).

As children mature, their categories become more refined. For example, 14-month-old children watched a researcher give a toy dog a drink from a cup. Then, the researcher handed the cup to a child, together with a different dog, a cat, an unfamiliar mammal, and a bird. Children typically gave the cup to all three mammals, but not to the bird (Mandler, 2004a, 2004b). By their actions, young children reveal their sophisticated knowledge about categories: "Land animals can drink from a cup, but birds cannot" (Mandler, 2007).

Chapter 8 emphasized that your conceptual ability allows you to categorize similar objects together and to make inferences based on these categories. As we've just seen, this skill begins to develop before a child's first birthday.

The word "infant" originally meant "not capable of speech" (Pan, 2012). In a moment, you will see that the language *production* of young infants is definitely limited. However, their speech perception and language comprehension are impressively sophisticated, even when they are only a few months old.

Language Production during Infancy

The early vocalizations of infants pass through a series of stages. By about two months of age, infants begin to make **cooing** noises, sounds that involve vowels such as *oo*. By about six months they have developed **babbling**, a vocalization that uses both consonants and vowels, often repeating sounds in a series such as *dadada* (Harley, 2010; Kail, 2010). By about 10 months of age, these vocalizations begin to sound like the infant's native language (DeHart et al., 2004; Thompson & Madigan, 2005). This observation coincides with infants' decreased ability to discriminate between phonemes that are irrelevant in their native language (MacWhinney, 2011; Werker & Tees, 1999).

At about eight to 10 months of age, babies begin to produce actions that are designed to capture the attention of other people. They may hand an object to an adult or point to an object. They may also repeat an action—such as clapping—that has attracted attention in the past (Herriot, 2004; Taylor, 2005). Let's now consider the nature of the language that adults provide to infants.

Adults' Language to Infants

Infants learn language relatively quickly because of their impressive auditory skills, their memory capacity, and their receptivity to language. In addition, most infants receive superb assistance from their parents and other adults. Adults tend to make language acquisition somewhat simpler by adjusting their language when speaking with the children. The term **child-directed speech** refers to the language spoken to children. Child-directed speech uses repetition, short sentences, simple vocabulary, basic syntax, a slow pace, a high pitch, exaggerated changes in pitch, and exaggerated facial expressions (Harley, 2008; Kuhl, 2006). Indeed, appropriately structured verbal input and social interactions are considered to be extremely important components of the language acquisition process (Goldstein et al., 2010; Gros-Louis et al., 2006). Demonstration 13.4 illustrates child-directed speech.

Incidentally, **motherese** is a term that linguists previously used for child-directed speech. Infants as young as four months old have been shown to prefer speech spoken in motherese (Fernald, 1985).

Demonstration 13.4 ‖ Producing Child-Directed Speech

Locate a doll that resembles an infant as closely as possible in features and size. Select a friend who has had experience with infants, and ask him or her to imagine that the doll is a niece or nephew who just arrived with parents for a first visit. Encourage your friend to interact with the "baby" in a normal fashion. Observe your friend's language for qualities such as pitch, variation in pitch, vocabulary, sentence length, repetition, and intonation. Also observe any non-verbal communication. What qualities are different from the language used with adults?

However, this gender-biased term neglects the fact that many fathers, other adults, and older children speak "motherese" to infants and young children (DeHart et al., 2004; Harley, 2008; Kail, 2010; Weisleder & Fernald, 2013).

Research in a variety of language communities throughout the world shows that adults typically use a different language style when speaking to infants and young children than when speaking to older people. In general, the features of child-directed language help young language learners understand the meaning and structure of language (Kail, 2010).

Can Infants Learn Language from a DVD?

Have you seen advertisements for DVDs that claim to increase an infant's vocabulary? Since the release of the first baby media—called "Baby Einstein"—people have spent hundreds of millions of dollars on these items (DeLoache et al., 2010). The ads claim that parents can boost their infants' vocabulary by playing a video that shows objects with their spoken names. For example, one ad featured a parent who reported that her 18-month-old child had shown a sudden increase in vocabulary after watching one of these videos.

However, you have probably completed many psychology courses that emphasize research methods. As a result, you should ask, "Are there any factors—other than the DVD—that could explain these results?" or "Where's the control group?" As Judy DeLoache and her coauthors (2010) point out, young children normally show a rapid increase in their vocabulary at about 18 months of age. Without a control group, we cannot trust the advertisements' claims.

DeLoache and her colleagues therefore decided to conduct a well-controlled study to determine whether a best-selling language DVD actually does lead to an increase in infants' language. The researchers located 72 infants between the ages of 12 and 18 months. (None of these infants had any previous experience with any "baby media.") The infants were randomly assigned to one of four groups:

1. *The parent-teaching condition* did not use any DVD; instead, the parents were given a list of the 25 words from the DVD, and they were instructed to try to teach their infant as many words as possible for a 4-week period.

2. In the *DVD-with-interaction condition*, the child and the parent watched the DVD together at least five times each week for a four-week period.

3. In the *DVD-with-no-interaction condition*, the children watched the DVD by themselves, at least five times each week for a four-week period.

4. In the *control condition*, there was no DVD and the parents did not try to teach specific words to their children.

After 4 weeks, each child was shown a pair of objects: one object represented in the DVD (perhaps a clock) and one control object (perhaps a plate), which had not been shown in the DVD. The child was asked, for example, "Can you show me the clock?" Figure 13.6 shows the results of this experiment. A statistical analysis showed that the children in the parent-teaching condition were more likely to point to the correct answer, compared to the children in all the other three groups. The bottom line? If you've considered buying a language DVD for an infant you know, you will want to consider a more useful gift.

Language in Children

Sometime around their first birthday, most infants throughout the world speak their first word. Let's look at the characteristics of these initial words, as well as the words spoken by older children. Then, we consider

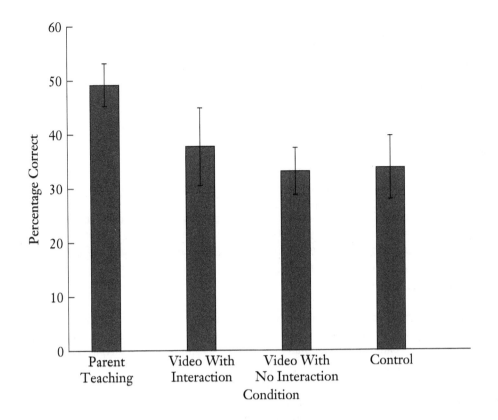

FIGURE 13.6
Infants' average performance on the word-recognition test, as a function of group.
Note: The vertical bars are a measure of variability.
Source: DeLoache, J. S., et al. (2010). Do babies learn from baby media? *Psychological Science, 21*, 1570–1574.

two components of children's grammar, morphology and syntax. Finally, we examine how children master pragmatics, or the social rules of language.

Words

Children typically produce their first word when they are about one year of age. However, the vocabulary size for normal one-year-old children ranges from 0 to about 50 words (MacWhinney, 2011; Thompson & Madigan, 2005). A child's first words usually refer to people, objects, and their own activities (Bloom, 2001; Waxman, 2002). However, these first concepts may be quite different from the standard adult version. For example, a baby's concept of "animal" may simply refer to any object that moves by itself (Mandler, 2006).

Word production increases rapidly. By the time children are 20 months old, they produce an average of about 150 to 180 words. By 28 months, the average is about 380 words (MacWhinney, 2011; Woodward & Markman, 1998).

Children's vocabulary growth is especially rapid if caregivers frequently read to them and if caregivers frequently talk about activities they are doing with the child (Fernald et al., 2013; Hoff, 2013; Patterson, 2002; Rollins, 2003). In developing countries, parents are more likely to tell stories to their children, rather than reading to them. Storytelling is equally helpful in developing children's language skills (Bornstein & Putnick, 2012).

Children's comprehension of words also increases rapidly (Rollins, 2003). For example, when they hear a particular word, they quickly direct their attention to the appropriate object (Fernald et al., 1998). Children can also learn the meaning of some words by overhearing them in other people's conversations (Akhtar et al., 2001). Children typically understand about twice as many words as they can produce (MacWhinney, 2011).

Children's memory skills also improve rapidly during this period, which boosts both their language production and their language comprehension (MacWhinney, 2011). This interrelationship between memory and language is an example of Theme 4 of this textbook. As you might expect, five-year-olds are more likely than three-year-olds to provide a detailed account about their previous experiences (Hayne et al., 2011).

Another factor that helps children learn new words is called **fast mapping**, or using context to make a reasonable guess about a word's meaning after just one or two exposures (Harley, 2008; Mandler, 2004b).

Chapter 9 emphasized that adults are guided by the context in which a word appears. Fast mapping demonstrates that context is also critically important for young children.

Young children may apply a newly learned label to a category that is either too broad or too narrow. An **overextension** is the use of a word to refer to other objects in addition to objects that adults would consider appropriate (Donaldson, 2004; Harley, 2010). For example, when my daughter Beth was one year old, she used the word *baish* to refer initially to her blanket. Then, she later applied the term to a diaper, a diaper pin, and a vitamin pill. Often an object's shape or function is important in determining overextensions. However, sometimes—as in the case of the vitamin pill—word usage can wander away from the original meaning.

Around the age of two, children often produce overextensions for words such as *dog* and *ball*. For example, one child produced the name *dog* for nine species of dog and one toy dog—all correct answers. However, he also used the word *dog* for two bears, a wolf, a fox, a doe, a rhinoceros, a hippopotamus, and a fish—all overextensions. Some overextensions occur when a child does not yet know the correct word for an unfamiliar item (Harley, 2010; Taylor, 2005). Few two-year-olds have ever seen a rhinoceros or a hippopotamus. However, in many cases, a child may be confused about the exact differences between two similar concepts, such as a tulip versus a daffodil.

Morphology

Children initially use the simple form of a word in every context—for example, "girl run," rather than "girl runs." However, they soon begin to master how to add on morphemes. **Morphemes** are the basic units of meaning, which include endings such as -*s* and -*ed*, as well as simple words such as *run*. **Morphology** is the study of these basic units of meaning.

After children have learned many words with regular plurals and past tenses—such as *girls* and *kicked*—they progress to a more advanced understanding of morphology. At this point, they sometimes create their own regular forms, such as *mouses* and *runned*, although children are typically accurate (Bates et al., 2001; Harley, 2008). These errors show that language acquisition is not simply a matter of imitating the words produced by parents, because parents seldom produce mistakes such as *mouses* and *runned* (Stromswold, 1999).

This tendency to add the most customary grammatical morphemes to create new forms of irregular words is called **overregularization**. Keep in mind, then, that *overextension* refers to the tendency to extend a word's meaning inappropriately. In contrast, *overregularization* refers to the tendency to add regular morphemes inappropriately. Later still, children learn that many words have regular plurals and past tenses, but some words have irregular forms, such as *mice* and *ran* (Kail, 2010).

Theorists have developed several different explanations of children's overregularizations. For example, Gary Marcus (1996) has proposed an explanation for overregularization. According to Marcus's **rule-and-memory theory**, children learn a general rule for past-tense verbs, which specifies that they must add -*ed*; however, they also store in memory the past tenses for many irregular verbs. English has about 200 verbs with irregular past tenses, so young children would store only the most common of these irregular verbs (Kagan & Herschkowitz, 2005; Marcus, 1996).

Marcus's theory also proposes that children who remember an irregular form will consistently use it, rather than applying the default "add -*ed*" rule. As children gather more expertise about language, they gradually replace the overregularized words with the appropriate past-tense verbs. Marcus (1996) applied his theory to a sample of more than 11,000 past-tense verbs that children had generated. He found that specific components of the theory predicted the patterns of overregularization. He also observed a linear decrease in the number of overregularizations, from 4% among preschoolers to 1% among fourth graders.

Syntax

At about 18 to 24 months of age, the average child begins to combine two words—usually after acquiring between 50 and 100 words (de Boysson-Bardies, 1999; Flavell et al., 2002; Tomasello, 2006). An important issue that arises at this point is syntax. **Syntax** refers to the grammatical rules that govern how words can be combined into sentences. An important factor that contributes to this rapid increase in word combinations is the growing capacity of children's working memory.

Children's two-word utterances express many different kinds of relationships, such as possessor–possession ("Mama dress"), action–object ("Eat cookie"), and agent–action ("Teddy fall"). Furthermore, a two-word phrase can have different meanings in different contexts. "Daddy sock" may signify that the father is putting the child's sock on her or his foot, or that a particular sock belongs to the father (de Villiers

& de Villiers, 1999). Many of these utterances, such as "me going" may not be grammatically correct, but they obviously convey the message (Tomasello, 2006).

After children have reached the two-word stage, they begin to fill in the missing words and word endings, and they also improve their word order. "Baby cry" becomes "The baby is crying," for example. By 3.5 years of age, most children are reasonably accurate with respect to both morphology and syntax (Kail, 2010).

Language learning is definitely an active process, consistent with Theme 1 of this book. Children learn language by actively constructing their own speech. They produce phrases that adults would never say, such as "Allgone sticky," "Bye-bye hot," and "More page." These phrases show us that children's speech is far richer than a simple imitation of adult language.

As children grow increasingly skilled in producing sophisticated language, they also grow increasingly skilled in understanding it. Consider, for example, how a child manages to understand the sentence, "Pat hit Chris." How does the child know who is the actor in that sentence and who is the recipient of the action? In English, the word order of the sentence is the most important cue, and children use this information appropriately (Hirsh-Pasek & Golinkoff, 1996). We might be tempted to assume that word order is similarly helpful in all languages. However, young children learning Turkish or Polish use the endings of words—rather than word-order information—to decode the meaning of sentences (Weist, 1985).

Children seem to be clever strategists who quickly learn to use whatever syntactic and other linguistic cues available in the language they hear to build knowledge of grammar (Bates & MacWhinney, 1987; Monaghan et al., 2005; Snedeker & Trueswell, 2004; Snedeker & Yuan, 2008; Trueswell, 1999). Furthermore, children usually realize that the purpose of language is to communicate with others. Therefore, it's no surprise that they try to produce language that adults can comprehend (Baldwin & Meyer, 2007).

Pragmatics

As we discussed in Chapter 10, **pragmatics** focuses on the social rules and world knowledge that allow speakers to successfully communicate messages to other people (De Groot, 2011). Research on pragmatics focuses on how speakers successfully communicate messages to their listeners.

Children need to learn what should be said (and what should *not* be said) in certain circumstances. They must also understand that they should use different language styles when speaking to their parents, their teachers, their peers, and younger children (Bjorklund, 2005; MacWhinney, 2011). In addition, they have to learn that two speakers need to coordinate a conversation by taking turns and by being a responsive listener.

Every family has stories about children's wildly inappropriate remarks to elderly relatives, friendly neighbors, and complete strangers. A student in my child development class described an example of a pragmatic violation. Her family was attending a church service, and her four-year-old brother noticed that their father was starting to fall asleep during the sermon. So the little boy stood up on the church pew and announced in a loud voice, "Be quiet everyone! My daddy is trying to sleep!" As you can imagine, everyone reacted more strongly to the fact that the child had broken a pragmatic rule than to the fact that he had tried to help his dozing daddy.

Another pragmatic skill that children learn is to adapt their language to the listener. For instance, they must determine whether their listener has the appropriate background information about a topic (MacWhinney, 2011; Pan & Snow, 1999). Until the early 1970s, psychologists believed that children's language ignored the listener's level of understanding.

However, an influential study by Shatz and Gelman (1973) showed that children often make appropriate adjustments. In this study, four-year-olds modified their speech substantially when the listener was a two-year-old, rather than a peer or an adult. For example, the four-year-olds described a toy to their two-year-old listeners using short, simple utterances. However, when describing the toy to another four-year-old or an adult, their descriptions were much longer and more complex.

Even two-year-olds tend to simplify their language when speaking to their infant siblings (Dunn & Kendrick, 1982). If you know any young preschoolers, you may wish to repeat Demonstration 13.3 with them. Children clearly understand some of the social aspects of language before they enter kindergarten.

Children also learn to take turns in a conversation. Sophisticated turn-taking requires each speaker to anticipate when the conversational partner will complete his or her remark. This requirement demands an impressive knowledge of language structure (Siegal, 1996; Snow, 1999).

The next time you observe two adults conversing, notice how the listener responds to the speaker by smiling, gazing, and other gestures of interest. In one study, researchers recorded these kinds of listener responses in young children who were talking with an adult about topics such as toys, a popular film, and siblings (Miller et al., 1985). All these listener responses were more abundant in the older children. For example, 8% of three-year-olds said "uh-hum" at some point while the adult was speaking, in contrast to 50% of five-year-olds. Furthermore, only 67% of three-year-old listeners nodded their heads, in contrast to an impressive 100% of five-year-olds. Thus, children learn how to be pragmatically skilled listeners, as well as speakers (MacWhinney, 2011; Snow, 1999).

Infants and children seem to be specially prepared to notice and interact socially (Wellman & Gelman, 1992). Children are eager to master language and to become active participants in ongoing conversations. This enthusiasm about learning language encourages children to master the words, morphemes, syntax, and pragmatics of speech.

Throughout this chapter, we have seen examples of the early competence of infants and children. For instance, young infants are remarkably skilled at remembering faces and distinguishing speech sounds. These early skills foreshadow the impressive cognitive skills that adults exhibit (Theme 2). Furthermore, children's active, inquiring interactions with the people, objects, and concepts in their world (Theme 1) help them develop memory, metamemory, and language. Finally, the research on the cognitive skills of elderly people reveals some specific deficits. However, many cognitive abilities remain both accurate and active throughout the life span.

SECTION SUMMARY POINTS

The Lifespan Development of Memory

1. The lifespan approach to development emphasizes that changes and adaptations continue throughout the lifespan, from infancy through old age.

2. Psychologists interested in the development of cognition encounter methodological problems in their research, particularly when they study infants and elderly people.

3. Research demonstrates that three-day-olds can recognize their mothers' face and voice. Older infants can recall how to move a mobile—following a delay of several days—when they are tested with the conjugate reinforcement technique.

4. Infant memory is influenced by many factors—such as context effects and the spacing effect—that are also important in adulthood.

5. Compared to adults, children have reduced working memory, reasonably strong recognition memory, and poor memory on long-term recall tasks.

6. Studies of autobiographical memory show that most people cannot recall events that occurred prior to the age of two or three. In general, children have poor source monitoring.

7. In general, children have difficulty with source monitoring. For example, they sometimes recall that they had performed a task that someone else had actually performed.

8. As children grow older, they increasingly use memory strategies such as rehearsal and organization. By adolescence, they can also use imagery appropriately.

9. Under ideal circumstances, children's eyewitness reports can be trustworthy, but young children's reports may be unreliable when they have been supplied with stereotypes and suggestive questions.

10. Compared to others in their age group, children with intellectual disabilities tend to recall fewer items on an eyewitness-testimony task; they also make more errors following misleading information.

11. As adults grow older, their working memory remains intact for some tasks, but it is limited if the task is complicated or if it requires manipulation of information.

12. With respect to long-term memory in adulthood, age differences are relatively large for prospective memory tasks; in contrast, age differences are relatively small for implicit memory tasks and for recognition tasks.

13. Age differences on explicit recall tasks are typically more substantial, but the deficits depend on a variety of factors. For instance, elderly individuals perform relatively well if they have high verbal ability, if they are well educated, or if they are tested early in the day.

14. Cognitive neuroscience research shows changes in the brain structure during normal aging. Potential psychological explanations for age-related memory changes during adulthood include (1) neurocognitive changes, (2) difficulty paying attention, (3) less effective use of memory strategies, (4) the contextual-cues hypothesis, and (5) cognitive slowing.

The Lifespan Development of Metamemory

1. Young children have some knowledge of the factors that influence memory, and their knowledge increases as they mature.

2. Young children are not aware that they need to make an effort to learn a list of items, and they also cannot accurately judge when they have mastered the material.

3. Older children and adults are much more accurate than younger children in judging their accuracy on a memory task that they had performed; younger children tend to be extremely overconfident.

4. To some extent, children's deficits in metamemory partly explain their poor performance on memory tasks.

5. As children grow older, their metamemory improves, leading to increased strategy use, which helps to produce better memory performance.

6. Elementary-school teachers and parents can help children think about how to think about improving their memory.

7. Elderly adults and young adults have similar beliefs about memory tasks. They also have a similar ability to monitor their memory on an item-by-item basis. However, on some tasks, elderly adults are more likely to overestimate their overall performance.

8. Elderly adults report an increase in the frequency of some memory problems; this assessment is probably correct.

9. When elderly adults believe that a memory decline is inevitable, they may not try to develop useful memory strategies.

The Development of Language

1. Research with infants reveals their impressive speech perception abilities. For example, infants can perceive the difference between two similar phonemes and discriminate between two similar languages,

2. Infants can also recognize their name, understand that a happy voice should be accompanied by a smiling face, and appreciate some important semantic concepts.

3. During late infancy, babbling begins to resemble the language that is spoken to the infant, and the infant attempts intentional communication.

4. The child-friendly language that parents use with infants helps to encourage their language development.

5. Infants cannot learn vocabulary by merely watching a DVD in which spoken words are linked with appropriate objects.

6. Young children rapidly acquire new words from context (fast mapping), but their word usage frequently includes overextensions.

7. During language acquisition, children show overregularization, adding regular morphemes to words that have irregular plurals and past tenses.

8. Between the ages of 18 and 24 months, children begin active efforts to master syntax by combining words into simple phrases.

9. Young children sometimes violate pragmatic rules. As children mature, however, they adapt their language to the listener, and they develop turn-taking strategies. They also learn how they are supposed to respond to someone who is speaking with them.

CHAPTER REVIEW QUESTIONS

1. Prior to the 1970s, most psychologists were pessimistic about the cognitive skills of infants and young children. However, psychologists have become more optimistic. If you wanted to impress someone with infants' and children's cognitive skills, what information would you provide about their memory and their language abilities?

2. Part of the challenge in studying infants is designing experiments that reveal an infant's true abilities. Describe several procedures that researchers have developed so that they can discover infants' skills in memory and language.

3. Compare children, young adults, and elderly adults with respect to their skills in the following areas: working memory, recognition memory, and recall memory. Be sure to list factors that might influence your conclusions.

4. Suppose that the outcome of an important court case in your community depends on the eyewitness testimony of a young child. What factors would encourage you to trust the child's report? What factors would make you think that the child's memory might not be accurate?

5. Describe the proposed explanation for children's memory performance, which focuses on memory strategies and metamemory. Discuss the evidence for this explanation, including information about the correlation between metamemory and memory performance.

6. In general, what kinds of memory tasks are especially difficult for elderly people? What explanations can best account for memory deficits in elderly individuals? How might overconfidence and stereotypes about older adults help to explain these difficulties?

7. This chapter describes children's metamemory and strategy use. What could a third-grade teacher do to encourage students' memory skills? What should this teacher know about children's metacognitive ability?

8. In 1985, Branthwaite and Rogers commented that being a child is like being a spy who is trying to break a code to discover how the world works. Apply this idea to a child's understanding of word meaning, morphology, word order, and pragmatic rules.

9. Describe some of the pragmatic rules of language that are important in our culture. How does the mastery of these rules change as children develop?

10. Consider the information about cognitive processes in this chapter. Are infants as different from children as you had originally thought? Do any of the findings on elderly people surprise you, or do they match your original impressions?

KEYWORDS

lifespan approach to development	script	chunk	memory self-efficacy	overextension
conjugate reinforcement technique	source monitoring	cognitive slowing	phonemes	morphemes
spaced learning	memory strategies	metacognition	cooing	morphology
massed learning	utilization deficiency	metamemory	babbling	overregularization
autobiographical memory	prospective memory	theory of mind	child-directed speech	rule-and-memory theory
	explicit memory task	metacomprehension	motherese	syntax
	implicit memory task	dementia	fast mapping	pragmatics

RECOMMENDED READINGS

Courage, M. L., & Cowan, N. (Eds.). (2009). *The development of memory in infancy and childhood*. New York: Psychology Press. This excellent book includes chapters about memory development in both infants and toddlers, as well as the development of processes such as working memory, memory strategies, and autobiographical memory.

Dunlosky, J., & Metcalfe, J. (2009). *Metacognition*. Los Angeles: Sage. The two final chapters in this book focus on metacognition during childhood development and older adulthood. These authors provide an excellent summary of the research in these two areas, and their writing style is superb.

Hacker, D. J., Dunlosky, J., & Graesser, A. C. (Eds.). (2009). *Handbook of metacognition in education*. New York: Routledge. Here's a perfect book for someone interested in cognitive development and education. In addition to the topics discussed in your textbook, this handbook examines how metacognition is relevant in reading, mathematics, and judgment.

Hoff, E. (2013). *Language development*. Cengage Learning. A comprehensive and accessible overview of research on language development.

Whitbourne, S. K., & Whitbourne, S. B. (2011). *Adult development and aging: Biopsychosocial perspectives* (4th ed.). Hoboken, NJ: Wiley. Susan K. Whitbourne and her daughter Stacey B. Whitbourne are both experts in development during adulthood and old age. Their book provides a clear overview of the research about memory and related areas in older adults; they also explore related topics such as perception, health, and social interactions.

GLOSSARY

abstraction A memory process that stores the meaning of a message, rather than the exact words.

acoustic confusions In memory research, the observation that people are likely to confuse similar-sounding stimuli.

ACT-R An acronym for "Adaptive Control of Thought-Rational"; this approach uses a series of network models in an attempt to account for a wide variety of tasks including memory, learning, spatial cognition, language, reasoning, problem solving, and decision making.

ADHD *See* Attention-Deficit/Hyperactivity Disorder (ADHD)

affirming the antecedent In conditional reasoning tasks, claiming that the "if . . ." part of the statement is true. This kind of reasoning leads to a valid or correct conclusion.

affirming the consequent In conditional reasoning tasks, the fallacy (or error) of claiming that the "then . . ." part of the sentence is true. This kind of reasoning leads to an invalid conclusion.

age of acquisition In psycholinguistics, the age at which a person begins to learn a second language.

AI *See* artificial intelligence

algorithm A method that will always produce a solution to the problem, although the process can sometimes be inefficient.

alignment heuristic In cognitive maps, the finding that people tend to remember a series of separate geographic structures as being more lined up than they really are.

ambiguous figure-ground relationship A perceptual phenomenon studied by gestalt psychologists, in which the figure and the ground of a visual stimulus reverse from time to time, so that the figure becomes the ground and then becomes the figure again.

ambiguous sentences Two sentences that have identical surface structures but very different deep structures.

amnesia Severe deficits in episodic memory.

analog code In the imagery debate, a mental representation that closely resembles the physical object.

analogy approach In problem solving, the use of a solution to a similar, earlier problem to help solve a new problem.

anchor In decision making, the first approximation used in the anchoring and adjustment heuristic.

anchoring and adjustment heuristic In decision making, beginning with a first approximation, which serves as an anchor, and then making adjustments to that anchor, based on additional information. Typically, people rely too heavily on the anchor and their adjustments are too small. This heuristic is also known as the *anchoring effect*.

anchoring effect *See* anchoring and adjustment heuristic.

antecedent In conditional reasoning tasks, the first proposition or statement; the antecedent is contained in the "if . . ." part of the sentence.

anterograde amnesia The inability to form memories for events that occur after brain damage.

anxiety disorders A broad category of psychological disorders that includes problems such as generalized anxiety disorder, posttraumatic stress disorder, and social phobia.

aphasia Difficulty communicating, caused by damage to the speech areas of the brain. This damage is typically caused by a stroke or a tumor.

artificial intelligence (AI) A branch of computer science that explores human cognitive processes by creating computer models that demonstrate "intelligent behavior" and also accomplish the same tasks that humans do.

Atkinson–Shiffrin model The proposal that memory involves a sequence of separate steps; in each step, information is transferred from one storage area to another.

attention A concentration of mental activity.

Attention-Deficit/Hyperactivity Disorder (ADHD) A psychological disorder characterized by difficulty paying attention at school, at work, and in other activities, as well as hyperactivity and impulsivity. People with ADHD often have more difficulty than others on central-executive tasks, especially when they must inhibit a response, plan a project, or work on two tasks at the same time.

auditory imagery The mental representation of auditory stimuli (sounds) when the sounds are not physically present.

autobiographical memory Memory for experiences and information related to oneself. Autobiographical memory usually includes a verbal narrative. Research in this area typically examines recall for events that happen outside the laboratory.

availability heuristic Estimating frequency or probability in terms of how easy it is to think of relevant examples of something.

babbling A vocalization that uses both consonants and vowels, often repeating sounds in a series such as *dadada*. Infants develop these vocalizations by about 6 months of age.

base rate In decision making, how often an item occurs in the population. People often ignore this useful information.

base-rate fallacy In decision making, paying too little attention to important information about how often an item occurs in the population (its base rate).

basic-level categories In the prototype approach to semantic memory, categories that are moderately specific; "chair," "dog," and "screwdriver" are examples of basic-level categories.

beat gesture Gestures that occur in a rhythm that matches speech rate and prosodic content of speech.

behaviorism An approach to psychology that focuses on objective, observable reactions to stimuli in the environment.

belief-bias effect When people make reasoning judgments based on prior beliefs and general knowledge, rather than on the rules of logic. In general, people make errors when the logic of a reasoning problem conflicts with their background knowledge.

betrayal trauma An explanation of recovered memory that emphasizes the adaptive nature of memory; actively inhibiting memories of abuse may be necessary in order to maintain an attachment to a parent or caretaker.

bilingual speaker Someone who is fluent in two different languages.

binding problem A characteristic of the visual system, in which characteristics such as color and shape are registered separately; as a result, the visual system does not represent these important features of an object as a unified whole.

blindsight A condition in which an individual with a damaged visual cortex claims not to see an object; however, he or she can accurately report some characteristics of this object, such as its location.

border bias In cognitive maps, the finding that people tend to estimate the distance between two locations on different sides of a geographic border as larger than two locations the same distance apart but on the same side of a geographic border.

bottleneck theories In attention, the proposal that a narrow passageway in human information processing limits the quantity of information to which one can pay attention.

bottom-up processing The kind of cognitive processing that emphasizes stimulus characteristics in object recognition and other cognitive tasks. For example, the physical stimuli from the environment are registered on the sensory receptors. This information is then passed on to higher, more sophisticated levels in the perceptual system.

boundary extension The tendency to remember having viewed a greater portion of a scene than was actually shown.

brain lesion Specific brain damage caused by strokes, tumors, blows to the head, accidents, or other traumas.

Broca's aphasia An expressive-language deficit—trouble producing speech—characterized by hesitant speech using isolated words and short phrases. This deficit is caused by damage to Broca's area.

Broca's area A region toward the front of the brain that is important in speech production.

Brown/Peterson & Peterson Technique A technique designed by John Brown, Lloyd Peterson, and Margaret Peterson. Researchers present several items to a participant, who is instructed to remember these items. Next the participant performs a distracting task and then attempts to recall the original items.

categorical perception A phenomenon in which people report hearing a clear-cut phoneme (e.g., a clear-cut *b* or a clear-cut *p*) even though they actually heard an ambiguous sound, between the two phonemes (e.g., a sound partway between a *b* and a *p*).

category A set of objects that belong together and are considered by the cognitive system to be at least partly equivalent. Categories provide useful information about their members.

central executive The component of working memory that integrates information from the phonological loop, visuospatial working memory, the episodic buffer, and long-term memory. The central executive also plays a role in attention, planning, and coordinating other cognitive activities.

cerebral cortex The outer layer of the brain that is essential for cognitive processes.

change blindness The failure to detect a change in an object or a scene due to overuse of top-down processing.

child-directed speech The kind of language spoken to children. Child-directed speech typically includes characteristics such as repetition, short sentences, simple vocabulary, basic syntax, a slow pace, a high pitch, exaggerated changes in pitch, and exaggerated facial expressions.

chunk A memory unit that consists of several components that are strongly associated with one another.

chunking A memory strategy in which the learner combines several small units to create larger units.

coarticulation One of the causes of phoneme variation, in this case created by surrounding phonemes. Specifically, when pronouncing a particular phoneme, the mouth remains in somewhat the same shape as when it pronounced the previous phoneme; in addition, the mouth is preparing to pronounce the next phoneme.

cocktail party effect The phenomenon of noticing one's own name, when it is mentioned in a nearby conversation, even when paying close attention to another conversation.

cognition Mental activity, including the acquisition, storage, transformation, and use of knowledge.

cognitive approach A theoretical orientation that emphasizes people's thought processes and their knowledge.

cognitive map The mental representation of geographic information, including a person's surrounding environment.

cognitive neuroscience An approach to studying mental activity that uses the research techniques of cognitive psychology, along with various neuroscience techniques for assessing the structure and function of the brain.

cognitive psychology (1) A synonym for cognition. (2) The theoretical approach to psychology that focuses on studying people's thought processes and knowledge.

cognitive science An interdisciplinary field that tries to answer questions about the mind. Cognitive science includes cognitive psychology, neuroscience, artificial intelligence, philosophy, linguistics, anthropology, sociology, and economics.

cognitive slowing A reduced rate of responding on cognitive tasks; often observed in elderly individuals.

cognitive-behavioral approach The theory that psychological problems arise from inappropriate thinking (cognitive factors) and inappropriate learning (behavioral factors).

cognitive-functional approach The idea that the function of human language in everyday life is to communicate meaning to other individuals.

common ground A situation where the people in a conversation share similar background knowledge, schemas, and perspectives. These elements of common ground are necessary for mutual understanding.

computer metaphor A way of describing cognition as a complex, multipurpose machine that processes information quickly and accurately.

computer modeling *See* computer simulation.

computer simulation Programming a computer to perform a specific cognitive task in the same way that humans actually perform this task. Also called *computer modeling*.

concept The mental representation of a category.

conditional reasoning task A deductive reasoning task that describes the relationship between conditions. Conditional reasoning tasks are often presented in an "if . . . then . . ." format. Also called a *propositional reasoning task.*

confidence interval In decision making, the range within which a number is expected to fall a certain percentage of the time.

confirmation bias The tendency to try to confirm or support a hypothesis rather than try to disprove it.

conjugate reinforcement technique A method for investigating cognition in infants, using a mobile hanging above a young infant's crib. A ribbon connects the infant's ankle and the mobile, so that the infant's kicks will make the mobile move.

conjunction fallacy A decision-making error that occurs when people judge the probability of the conjunction of two events to be greater than the probability of either constituent event.

conjunction rule A rule stating that the probability of the conjunction of two events cannot be larger than the probability of either of its constituent events.

connection weights In parallel distributed processing, characteristic of neural networks that determines how much activation one unit can pass on to another unit.

connectionism *See* parallel-distributed processing approach (PDP).

connectionist approach *See* parallel-distributed processing approach (PDP).

consciousness A person's awareness of the external world and of her or his own perceptions, images, thoughts, memories, and feelings.

consequent In conditional reasoning tasks, the proposition that comes second; it is the consequence. The consequent is contained in the "then . . ." part of the sentence.

consistency bias In autobiographical memory, the tendency to exaggerate the consistency between past feelings or beliefs and one's current viewpoint.

constructionist view of inferences In long-term memory, the observation that readers usually draw inferences about the causes of events and the relationships between events.

constructive model of memory In long-term memory, the proposal that people integrate information from individual sentences in order to construct larger ideas.

constructivist approach In long-term memory, the proposal that people construct knowledge by integrating the information they know. As a result, their understanding of an event or a topic is coherent, and it makes sense.

control processes Intentional strategies—such as rehearsal—that people may use to improve their memory.

convergent production A measure of creativity requiring the test-taker to supply a single, best response; the researchers measure the quality of that response.

cooing Sounds involving vowels such as *oo* that infants begin to make by about 2 months of age.

creativity In problem solving, finding solutions that are both novel and useful.

critical period hypothesis The proposal that the ability to acquire a new language is strictly limited to a specific period of life. The critical period hypothesis proposes that individuals who have already reached a specified age—perhaps early puberty—will no longer be able to acquire a new language with native-like fluency. In general, the research does not support this hypothesis.

cross-ethnicity effect *See* own-ethnicity bias.

crystal-ball technique In decision making, imagining that a completely accurate crystal ball has determined that a favored hypothesis is actually incorrect. Therefore, the decision makers must search for alternative explanations for the outcome.

decision making Assessing information and choosing among two or more alternatives. Compared to deductive reasoning, decision making is much more ambiguous.

declarative knowledge In semantic memory, knowledge about facts and things.

deductive reasoning The type of reasoning that begins with some specific premises that are assumed to be true. Next one judges whether those premises allow a particular conclusion to be drawn, based on the principles of logic.

deep structure In psycholinguistics, the underlying, more abstract meaning of a sentence, in contrast to *surface structure.*

default assignment In parallel distributed processing, a method used to fill in missing information about a particular person or object based on information from other similar people or objects.

default heuristic In decision making, the tendency to choose a default option, when one is presented.

deictic gesture Gestures that involve pointing to an object or location.

demand characteristics Cues that might convey the experimenter's hypothesis to a participant in a research study.

dementia A disorder that includes memory problems and other cognitive deficits. Individuals with dementia typically have difficulty estimating their memory abilities.

denying the antecedent In conditional reasoning tasks, the fallacy (or error) of claiming that the "if . . ." part of the sentence is false. Denying the antecedent leads to an invalid conclusion.

denying the consequent In conditional reasoning tasks, claiming that the "then . . ." part of the sentence is false. This kind of reasoning leads to a correct conclusion.

depth-of-processing approach *See* levels-of-processing approach.

desirable difficulties A learning situation that is somewhat challenging, but not too difficult; this situation is helpful for increasing long-term recall.

dichotic listening A laboratory technique in which one message is presented to the left ear and a different message is presented to the right ear.

direct request In language, resolving an interpersonal situation or problem by using a very obvious statement or question.

direct-access route During reading, when a word is recognized directly through vision, without "sounding out" the word.

directive In language, a sentence that asks someone to do something.

discourse Interrelated units of language that are longer than a sentence.

dissociation In cognitive neuroscience, an outcome that occurs (a) when a variable has large effects on Test A, but little or no effects on Test B; or (b) when a variable has one kind of effect if measured by Test A, and the opposite effect if measured by Test B. A dissociation is similar to the concept of a statistical interaction.

distal stimulus In perception, the actual object that is "out there" in the environment, for example, a pen on a desk.

distinctive feature In visual perception, an important characteristic of the visual stimulus.

distinctiveness In the levels-of-processing approach to memory, the situation in which one memory trace is different from all other memory traces. People tend to forget information if it is not distinctly different from the other memory traces in their long-term memory.

distributed attention In feature-integration theory, a relatively fast, low-level kind of processing, in which the viewer registers the features of the stimulus automatically and simultaneously, using parallel processing,

distributed-practice effect The observation that memory is better when the learning trials are spread over time (spaced learning), as compared with trying to learn the material all at once (massed learning). The studies generally support this effect for both recall tasks and recognition tasks.

divergent production A measure of creativity that emphasizes the number of different responses made to a test item.

divided-attention task A situation in which people try to pay attention to two or more simultaneous messages, responding appropriately to each message. Both speed and accuracy frequently suffer during this task.

dual-process theory In reasoning and decision making, the approach that distinguishes between two types of cognitive processing: *Type 1 processing* is fast and automatic, requiring little conscious attention. In contrast, *Type 2 processing* is relatively slow and controlled, requiring focused attention, and is typically more accurate.

dual-route approach to reading The proposal that skilled readers use both (1) a direct-access route and (2) an indirect-access route to recognize words during reading.

ecological rationality In decision making, a description of how people create a wide variety of heuristics to help make useful, adaptive choices in the real world.

ecological validity A principle of research design in which the research uses conditions that are similar to the natural setting where the results will be applied.

elaboration In the levels-of-processing approach to memory, rich processing emphasizing the meaning of a particular concept and relating the concept to prior knowledge and interconnected concepts already mastered.

embodied cognition approach The proposal that people often use their own bodies and motor actions in order to express their abstract thoughts and knowledge.

emotion A psychological reaction to a specific stimulus, in contrast to a mood, which is a more general, long-lasting experience.

emotional Stroop task When people are instructed to name the ink color of words that could have strong emotional significance to them, they often require more time to name the color of the stimuli, presumably because they have trouble ignoring their emotional reactions to the words.

empirical evidence Scientific evidence obtained by careful observation and experimentation.

encoding The initial acquisition of information. During encoding, we process and represent this information in memory.

encoding-specificity principle The observation that recall is often better if the context at the time of encoding matches the context at the time of retrieval.

episodic buffer In working memory, a temporary storehouse that can hold and combine information from the phonological loop, visuospatial working memory, and long-term memory.

episodic memory People's memories for events that happened to them personally, in contrast with semantic memory.

ERP *See* event-related potential (ERP) technique.

event-related potential (ERP) technique A procedure for recording the very brief, small fluctuations in the brain's electrical activity in response to a stimulus such as an auditory tone.

executive attention network A cognitive system that is responsible for the kind of attention one uses when a task focuses on conflict.

exemplar In concept representation, the examples of a concept stored in memory. A new stimulus is classified by comparing it with these exemplars.

exemplar approach In concept representation, the proposal that people first learn information about some specific examples of a concept; then classify each new stimulus by deciding how closely it resembles all of those specific examples.

exhaustive search In problem solving, an example of an algorithm in which a person tests all the possible answers, using a specified system.

experimenter expectancy In research, when researchers' biases and expectations influence the outcomes of an experiment.

expertise A person's impressive memory abilities or this person's consistently exceptional performance on representative tasks in a particular area.

explicit memory task A memory task in which participants are instructed to remember some information. Later, a recall or recognition test requires them to intentionally retrieve that previously learned information.

external memory aid Any device, external to one's self, that facilitates memory in some way; this memory aid is especially helpful on prospective-memory tasks.

extrinsic motivation The motivation to work on a task—not because it is enjoyable—but in order to earn a promised reward or to win a competition.

face-inversion effect The observation that people are much more accurate in identifying upright faces, compared to upside-down faces.

false alarm In memory research, when people "remember" an item that was not originally presented.

false-memory perspective The proposal that most recovered memories are actually incorrect memories; in other words, these recovered memories are constructed stories about events that never occurred. This perspective is contrasted with the recovered-memory perspective.

family resemblance In the prototype approach to semantic memory, the observation that for some concepts no single attribute is shared by all examples of the concept. Each example has at least one attribute in common with some other example of the concept.

fast mapping In language learning, using context to make a reasonable guess about a word's meaning after just one or two exposures.

feature-analysis theories In perception, the proposal that we recognize visual objects, based on a small number of characteristics or components known as distinctive features.

feature-integration theory This theory of attention, developed by Anne Triesman, proposes two elements: (1) distributed attention, processing all parts of the scene at the same time, and (2) focused attention, processing each item in the scene, one at a time.

feature-present/feature-absent effect In visual search research, the finding that people can typically locate a feature that is present more quickly than a feature that is absent.

feeling-of-knowing effect In memory, the subjective experience of knowing some information, but not being able to recall it right now.

figure In gestalt psychology, when two areas share a common boundary, the figure is the area that has a distinct shape with clearly defined edges. This area seems closer and more dominant. In contrast, the ground is the area that forms the background.

first language In linguistics, the initial language that a person learned; this term is typically applied to someone who later learned a different language. *See* sequential bilingualism.

first-letter technique A memory strategy in which a person is learning a list of items; he or she composes a word or a sentence from the first letters of each word on the list to be remembered.

fixations Brief pauses occurring between saccadic eye movements, in which the visual system acquires information that is useful for reading and other visual tasks.

fixed mindset The belief that a person possesses a certain amount of intelligence and other skills, and no amount of effort can improve performance, in contrast to the *growth mindset.*

flashbulb memory Memory for the circumstances in which one first learned about a very surprising and emotionally arousing event.

fMRI *See* functional magnetic resonance imaging (fMRI).

focused attention In feature-integration theory, slower serial processing, in which a person identifies objects, one at a time. This kind of processing is necessary when objects are more complex.

foresight bias The tendency, when studying for a future exam, to be overconfident about performance on that exam.

fovea A very small region in the center of the retina that has better acuity than other retinal regions.

frame In linguistics, mental structures that simplify reality. Frames tend to structure what "counts" as facts. George Lakoff uses this term in discussing how language can structure thinking.

framing effect In decision making, when decisions are influenced by (1) the background context of the choice or (2) the way in which a question is worded (or framed).

functional fixedness The tendency to assign stable (or "fixed") functions to an object. As a result, people do not think about the features of this object that might be useful in helping solve a problem.

functional magnetic resonance imaging (fMRI) A method of measuring brain activity based on the principle that oxygen-rich blood is an index of brain activity. A magnetic field produces changes in the oxygen atoms in the brain while a person performs a cognitive task. A scanning device takes a "photo" of the changes.

gender stereotypes The beliefs and opinions that people associate with females and males.

general mechanism approach The idea that speech perception can be explained without proposing any specialized phonetic module. In other words, humans use the same neural mechanisms to process both speech sounds and nonspeech sounds.

General Problem Solver (GPS) In problem solving, a computer program whose basic strategy is means-ends analysis. The goal of the GPS is to mimic the processes that normal humans use when they tackle these problems.

generalized anxiety disorder A psychological disorder characterized by at least 6 months of intense, long-lasting anxiety and worry.

geons In recognition-by-components theory, the simple 3D shapes that people use in order to recognize visual objects.

gestalt (pronounced "geh-*shtahlt*") In perception and problem-solving, an overall quality that transcends the individual elements in the stimulus.

gestalt psychology (pronounced "geh-*shtahlt*") The theoretical approach which emphasizes that: (1) humans actively organize what they see, (2) they see patterns, and (3) the whole is greater than the sum of its parts.

gestures Communication using visible movements of any part of the body.

gist In psycholinguistics, the overall meaning of a message.

goal state In problem solving, the situation when the problem is solved.

GPS *See* General Problem Solver (GPS).

graceful degradation In parallel distributed processing, the brain's ability to provide partial memory. Graceful degradation explains why the brain continues to work somewhat accurately, even when an accident, stroke, or dementia has destroyed portions of the cortex.

graded structure In the prototype approach to category representation, a description of the variation between the category's most representative or prototypical members, less prototypical members, and nonprototypical members.

grammar In psycholinguistics, a term encompassing both morphology and syntax. The psycholinguistic study of grammar examines both word structure and sentence structure.

ground In gestalt psychology, when two areas share a common boundary, the area that is seen as being behind the figure, forming the background.

growth mindset The belief that people can cultivate intelligence and other skills by challenging themselves to perform better.

heuristic (pronounced "hyoo-*riss*-tick") A general rule or problem-solving strategy that usually produces a correct solution; however, it can sometimes lead to cognitive errors.

hierarchical tree diagram A figure that uses a tree-like structure to show various possible options in a problem. This kind of diagram is especially helpful in showing the relationship between categorized items.

hierarchy A memory strategy in which the learner arranges items in a series of classes, from the most general classes to the most specific.

hill-climbing heuristic In problem solving, consistently choosing—at each choice point—the alternative that seems to lead most directly toward the goal.

hindsight In decision making, people's judgments about events that already happened in the past.

hindsight bias In decision making, the belief, after an event has already happened, that the event had been inevitable and was predicted all along.

hippocampus A structure located underneath the cortex that is important in many learning and memory tasks.

holistic A term describing the recognition of faces and other selected stimuli, based on their overall shape and structure, or gestalt.

IAT *See* Implicit Association Test (IAT).

iconic gesture Gestures with a form that represents the concept being described.

iconic memory Sensory memory for visual information. Iconic memory preserves an image of a visual stimulus for a brief period after the stimulus has disappeared.

illusory conjunction An inappropriate combination of features (e.g., combining one object's shape with a nearby object's color). An illusory conjunction is formed when the visual system is overwhelmed by too many simultaneous tasks.

illusory contours The perception of edges in a visual stimulus even though edges are not physically present. Also known as *subjective contours*.

illusory correlation In decision making, a person's belief that two variables are statistically related, even though there is no actual evidence for this relationship.

imagery *See* mental imagery.

imagery debate An important controversy: Do mental images resemble perception (using an analog code), or do they resemble language (using a propositional code)?

Implicit Association Test (IAT) A research tool based on the principle that people can mentally pair related words together much more easily than they can pair unrelated words. The IAT is useful in assessing stereotypes, such as stereotypes about gender.

implicit memory task An indirect measure of memory. Participants see the material (usually a series of words or pictures). Later, during the test phase, they are instructed to complete a cognitive task that does not directly ask for either recall or recognition. Previous experience with the material facilitates performance on the later task.

inattentional blindness The failure to notice an unexpected but completely visible object that suddenly appears while attention is focused on some other events in a scene. Inattentional blindness results from the overuse of top-down processing.

indirect request In language, using subtle suggestions to resolve an interpersonal problem, rather than stating the request in a straightforward manner.

indirect-access route During reading, when—as soon as a word is seen—the letters on the page are translated into some form of sound, before the word and its meaning can be accessed.

individual differences Systematic variation in the way that groups of people perform on the same cognitive task.

inference In connection with schemas (Chapter 8), an *inference* refers to the logical interpretations or conclusions that go beyond the original material. In connection with reading (Chapter 9), an *inference* refers to the use of world knowledge in order to create information that is not explicitly stated in a written passage.

information-processing approach A theory of cognition proposing that (1) mental processes are similar to the operations of a computer and (2) information progresses through the cognitive system in a series of stages, one step at a time.

initial state In problem solving, the situation at the beginning of a problem.

insight problem The problem-solving situation in which a problem initially seems impossible to solve, but then an alternative approach suddenly bursts into consciousness. The problem solver immediately realizes that the new solution is correct.

interpreting The process of converting a spoken message in one language into a second spoken (or signed) language. In contrast, *translation* refers to the process of converting a text written in one language into a second written language.

Interspeaker variability Different speakers of the same language produce the same sound differently, and these differences can be traced to individual difference factors associated with different speakers.

intrinsic motivation The motivation to work on a task for its own sake, because it is interesting, exciting, or personally challenging.

introspection An early approach to studying mental activity, in which carefully trained observers systematically analyzed their own sensations and reported them as objectively as possible, under standardized conditions.

ironic effects of mental control The observation that people's efforts often backfire when they attempt to control the contents of consciousness; as a result, people are even more likely to think about the topic that they are trying to avoid.

isolated-feature/combined feature effect In visual-search studies, the finding that people can typically locate an isolated feature more quickly than a combined feature.

keyword method A memory technique for learning vocabulary words or people's names. The learner identifies an actual word (the keyword) that sounds similar to the new word. Then, she or he creates an image that links the keyword with the meaning of this new word.

landmark effect In cognitive maps, people tend to provide shorter distance estimates when traveling to a landmark—an important geographical location—rather than a nonlandmark.

language-localizer task A relatively new neuroscience technique that compensates for the problem of individual differences in the anatomical structure of the language-related regions of the brain. Researchers gather fMRI data while a person performs several relatively complex language tasks, and then use this information to create a "linguistic map" that applies only to this specific person.

latent semantic analysis (LSA) A computer program that can perform many fairly sophisticated language tasks, such as evaluating creative writing or analyzing a person's self-descriptions.

lateralization The proposal that each hemisphere of the brain has somewhat different functions.

levels of processing The observation that recall is generally more accurate when people process information at a deep, meaningful level, rather than a shallow sensory kind of processing.

levels-of-processing approach A theory of memory proposing that deep, meaningful processing of information leads to more accurate recall than shallow, sensory kinds of processing.

life script A list of events that a person believes would be most important throughout his or her lifetime.

lifespan approach to development The view that developmental changes continue beyond young adulthood. People continue to change and adapt throughout their entire lives.

long-term memory The large-capacity memory for experiences and information accumulated throughout one's lifetime. Atkinson and Shiffrin proposed that information stored in long-term memory is relatively permanent and not likely to be lost.

LSA *See* latent semantic analysis (LSA).

magnetoencephalography (MEG) technique A procedure for recording fluctuations in the magnetic fields produced by neural activity while simultaneously providing course-grained information about the neural sources of observed effects.

major depression A psychological disorder characterized by feeling sad, discouraged, and hopeless; fatigue and lack of interest in leisure activities are also common. This disorder can interfere with the ability to perform daily cognitive and physical tasks.

massed learning When learning new material, the situation in which the learner practices the material all at the same time, by "cramming"; this learning strategy is less effective than *spaced learning*.

matrix In problem solving, a grid consisting of rows and columns that shows all possible combinations of the items in the problem.

maximizers In decision making, people who tend to examine as many options as possible, rather than settling for something that is satisfactory.

maximizing decision-making style The tendency to examine as many options as possible when making a decision, rather than settling for something that is satisfactory, instead of the best possible choice.

McGurk effect The observation that visual information influences speech perception; listeners integrate both visual and auditory information when perceiving speech.

means-ends heuristic An approach to problem solving that consists of two important components: (1) dividing the problem into a number of subproblems, and (2) reducing the difference between the initial state and the goal state for each of the subproblems. The name *means-ends heuristic* is appropriate because it requires identifying the "ends" desired and then figuring out the "means" or methods to reach those ends.

memory The process of maintaining information over time.

memory integration Using background knowledge to incorporate new information into memory in a schema-consistent manner.

memory self-efficacy A person's belief in his or her own potential to perform well on memory tasks.

memory strategy Intentional, goal-oriented mental activities that a person performs, in order to improve encoding and retrieval of information in memory.

mental imagery The mental representation of stimuli when those stimuli are not physically present. Sensory receptors do not receive any input when a mental image is created.

mental set In problem solving, applying the same solution used in previous problems, even though there is a different, easier way to solve the problem.

meta-analysis A statistical method for combining numerous studies on a single topic. A meta-analysis computes a statistical index (known as effect size, or d) that tells us whether a particular variable has a statistically significant effect, when combining all the studies.

metacognition Knowledge and control of cognitive processes; metacognition helps to supervise the way one selects and uses memory strategies. The general term, metacognition, includes metamemory, metacomprehension, and metalinguistics. It is also related to both the tip-of-the-tongue phenomenon and the feeling of knowing.

metacomprehension A kind of metacognition, referring to a person's thoughts that specifically focus on language comprehension. Most research about metacomprehension focuses on reading comprehension, rather than on the comprehension of spoken speech or on other kinds of knowledge about language.

metalinguistics Knowledge about the form and structure of language, as opposed to knowledge about language comprehension. On many measures of metalinguistic skill—but not all of them—bilinguals outperform monolinguals.

metamemory A kind of metacognition that refers to one's knowledge, monitoring, and control of memory.

mind wandering A situation that occurs when a person's thoughts shift away from the external environment, and the person begins thinking about another topic.

mindless reading A situation that occurs when a person's eyes may move forward, but they do not process the meaning of the material being read.

mirror system A network of neurons in the brain's motor cortex. These neurons are activated when a person watches someone else perform an action.

mnemonics Mental strategies designed to improve memory.

modular In theories of language, the proposal that people have a set of specific linguistic abilities that are separate from other cognitive processes, such as memory and decision making.

mood A general, long-lasting experience, in contrast to an emotion, which is a reaction to a specific stimulus.

mood congruence The observation that material is recalled more accurately if it is congruent with a person's current mood.

morpheme (pronounced "*more*-feem") The basic unit of meaning in language. For example, the word *reactivated* actually contains four morphemes: *re-*, *active*, *-ate*, and *-ed*. Each of those segments conveys meaning.

morphology The study of morphemes; morphology examines how words are created by combining morphemes.

motherese A term that linguists previously used for *child-directed speech*.

multilingual speaker Someone who uses more than two languages; psycholinguists often use the term *bilingual* to include multilinguals as well.

multitask An attempt to accomplish two or more tasks at the same time. However, the research shows that people frequently work more slowly or make more mistakes when they try to multitask.

my-side bias In decision making, people are overconfident that their own view is correct in a confrontational situation.

narrative In language, a category of discourse in which someone describes a series of actual or fictional events.

narrative technique In memory, making up stories that link a series of words together, in order to enhance memory.

nested structure In language, when one phrase is embedded within another phrase. Readers often experience a memory overload when they try to read a sentence that has a nested structure.

network models Proposals that semantic memory consists of a netlike organization of concepts in memory, with numerous interconnections.

neural-network approach A theory describing cognitive processing in terms of networks that link together neuron-like units. These networks perform operations simultaneously and in parallel, rather than one step at a time. Also known as the *parallel distributed processing approach* (abbreviated *PDP*) and the *connectionist approach*.

neurolinguistics The discipline that examines how the brain processes language.

90-degree-angle heuristic In cognitive maps, when angles in a mental map are represented as being closer to 90 degrees than they really are.

node In network models, the representation of each concept, or one unit located within the network. When people see or hear the name of a concept, the node representing that concept is activated. The activation expands or spreads from that node to other connected nodes, a process called *spreading activation*.

noninsight problem A problem that a person solves gradually, by using memory, reasoning skills, and a routine set of strategies.

object recognition The process of identifying a complex arrangement of sensory stimuli and perceiving that this pattern is separate from its background.

obstacles In problem solving, the restrictions that make it difficult to proceed from the initial state to the goal state.

operational definition In psychology research, a precise definition that specifies exactly how researchers will measure a concept.

organization A mnemonic strategy in which a person applies a systematic order to the material that must be learned.

orienting attention network A system responsible for the kind of attention required for visual search, in which a person must shift attention around to various spatial locations.

other-ethnicity effect *See* own-ethnicity bias.

overconfidence When one's confidence judgments are higher than they should be, based on actual performance on the task.

overextension In the study of children's language, the use of a word to refer to other objects, in addition to objects that adults would consider appropriate.

overregularization In language learning, the tendency to add the most customary grammatical morphemes to create new forms of irregular words.

own-ethnicity bias The observation that people are generally more accurate in identifying members of their own ethnic group than members of another ethnic group; also known as *own-race bias*, the *other-ethnicity effect,* or the *cross-ethnicity effect.*

parafoveal preview In reading, the information that readers can access about upcoming text while that are currently fixated on a word appearing before that information in text.

parallel-distributed processing approach (PDP) A theory describing cognitive processing in terms of networks that link together neuron-like units. These networks perform operations simultaneously and in parallel, rather than one step at a time. Also known as the *connectionist approach* and the *neural-network approach.*

parallel processing A type of cognitive processing in which a person performs many operations simultaneously, in contrast to *serial processing.*

pattern recognition The process of identifying a complex arrangement of sensory stimuli and perceiving that this pattern is separate from its background.

PDP *See* parallel-distributed processing approach (PDP).

perception The use of previous knowledge to gather and interpret stimuli registered by the senses. Perception requires both bottom-up and top-down processing.

perceptual span In reading, the number of letters and spaces perceived during a fixation.

perseverance The ability to keep working on a task, even when obstacles are encountered.

PET scan *See* positron emission tomography (PET scan).

phobic disorder An anxiety disorder characterized by excessive fear of a specific object.

phoneme (pronounced "*foe*-neem") The basic unit of spoken language, such as the sounds *a, k,* and *th.* The English language has about 40 phonemes.

phonemic restoration In speech perception, filling in a missing phoneme based on contextual meaning.

phonetic module A special-purpose neural mechanism that specifically handles all aspects of speech perception, but not other kinds of auditory perception. Also known as the *speech module.*

phonics approach The proposal that readers recognize words by trying to pronounce ("sounding out") the individual letters in the word.

phonological loop The part of working memory that processes a limited number of sounds for a short period of time. The phonological loop processes language and other sounds that a person hears, as well as the sounds that they make. It is also active when he or she silently sounds out a word during reading.

phonology The sounds of a person's speech. People who acquire a second language during childhood are more likely to pronounce words like a native speaker of that language, compared to people who attempt to learn that language later in life.

pitch A characteristic of a sound stimulus that can be arranged on a scale from low to high.

planning fallacy The tendency (1) to underestimate the amount of time (or money) required to complete a project and (2) to estimate that the task will be relatively easy to complete.

Pollyanna principle In memory and other cognitive processes, the principle that people usually process pleasant items more efficiently and more accurately than less pleasant items.

positivity effect A phenomenon showing that people tend to rate previous negative events more positively with the passage of time.

positron emission tomography (PET scan) A procedure for measuring blood flow in the brain by injecting the participant with a radioactive chemical, just before this person performs a cognitive task. A special camera makes an image of this accumulated radioactive chemical in the regions of the brain active during the task.

postevent misinformation effect In eyewitness testimony, when people first view an event and then are given misleading information about the event. Later on, they mistakenly recall the misleading information, rather than the event they actually saw.

posttraumatic stress disorder An anxiety disorder characterized by repeated re-experiencing of an extremely traumatic event.

pragmatic view of memory The proposal (developed by Murphy and Shapiro) that people pay attention to the aspect of a message that is most relevant to their current goals. For example, knowing when only the gist of a sentence is important and when to pay attention to the specific wording.

pragmatics In language, the social rules and world knowledge that allow speakers to successfully communicate messages to other people.

prewriting Beginning a formal writing project by generating a list of ideas. Prewriting is difficult and strategic—much different from many relatively automatic language tasks.

primacy effect A tendency for items at the beginning of a list to be recalled better than items in the middle of a list, at least partly because people rehearse these early items more frequently.

primary visual cortex The portion of the cerebral cortex located in the occipital lobe of the brain, which is concerned with basic processing of visual stimuli. It is also the first place where information from the two eyes is combined.

proactive interference Difficulty learning or recalling new material because some previously learned material continues to interfere with the formation of new memories.

problem isomorphs A set of problems that have the same underlying structures and solutions but different specific details.

problem representation In problem solving, the process of translating the elements of a problem into a different format. Choosing an appropriate representation makes an effective solution to the problem more likely.

problem solving The processes used to reach a specified goal for which the solution is not immediately obvious. Either important information is missing and/or it is unclear how to reach the goal.

procedural memory A person's knowledge about how to do something.

proposition In John Anderson's ACT-R model, a *proposition* is the smallest unit of knowledge that people can judge to be either true or false.

proposition In deductive reasoning, propositions are the statements that are made up of antecedents and consequents.

propositional calculus In deductive reasoning, a system for categorizing the four kinds of reasoning used in analyzing statements that are made up of antecedents and consequents. When working on a conditional reasoning task, a person can perform two possible actions: (1) affirm part of the sentence, saying that it is true; or (2) deny part of the sentence, saying that it is false.

propositional code In the imagery debate (Chapter 7), an abstract, language-like representation. This form of storage is neither visual nor spatial, and it does not physically resemble the original stimulus.

propositional network According to Anderson's ACT-R model, the pattern of interconnected propositions representing a sentence.

propositional reasoning task *See* conditional reasoning task.

propositions In deductive reasoning, propositions are the statements that are made up of antecedents and consequents.

prosody In language, the "melody" of an utterance; its intonation, rhythm, and emphasis.

prosopagnosia (pronounced "pros-o-pag-*no*-zhe-ah") The inability to recognize human faces visually, though other objects may be perceived relatively normally. People with prosopagnosia also have comparable problems in creating visual imagery for faces.

prospect theory In decision making, people's tendencies to think that possible gains are different from possible losses. When dealing with possible gains (e.g., *lives saved*), people tend to avoid risks. When dealing with possible losses (e.g., *lives lost*), people tend to seek risks.

prospective memory Remembering that one needs to do something in the future, such as buying an item on the way home from classes. In contrast, retrospective memory refers to remembering things that happened in the past.

prototype The item that is the best, most typical example of a category; the ideal representative of a category.

prototype approach In semantic memory, the proposal that people decide whether a particular item belongs to a category, based on a comparison between this item and a prototype. If the item is similar to the prototype, then it will be included within this category.

prototypicality According to the prototype theory of semantic memory, the degree to which a member of a category is representative of its category.

proximal stimulus In perception, the information registered on the sensory receptors—for example, the image on the retina created by a pen on a desk.

psycholinguistics An interdisciplinary field that examines how people use language to communicate ideas.

pure AI *See* pure artificial intelligence.

pure artificial intelligence (pure AI) An approach that designs a computer program to accomplish a cognitive task as efficiently as possible, even if the computer's processes are completely different from the processes used by humans.

reality monitoring The attempt to identify whether an event really occurred, or whether the event was imagined.

recall task In memory research, a task requiring the participants to reproduce items learned earlier.

recency effect A tendency for items at the end of a list to be recalled better than items in the middle of a list.

recognition heuristic A situation in decision making that occurs when someone is trying to decide which of two categories occurs more frequently. If this person recognizes one category, but not the other, then she or he concludes that the recognized category has the higher frequency.

recognition task An explicit memory task that requires participants to identify which items on a list had been presented at an earlier time.

recognition-by-components theory In visual perception, a theory proposing that people can recognize three-dimensional shapes, in terms of an arrangement of simple 3D shapes called geons. Geons can be combined to form meaningful objects.

recovered-memory perspective The proposal that some individuals who experienced sexual abuse during childhood managed to forget that memory for many years. At a later time, this presumably forgotten memory may come flooding back into consciousness. This perspective is contrasted with the false-memory perspective.

regressions In reading, moving one's eyes backward to words that appear earlier in a sentence.

rehearsal Silently repeating the information to be learned. Rehearsal is not considered to be an effective memory strategy.

release from proactive interference A memory phenomenon in which proactive interference is reduced when a person switches from one category of stimuli, to a new category. (e.g., a person may initially see the names of fruits, but then he or she sees the names of occupations.) This release from proactive interference leads to increased recall for the new category.

repetition priming task A memory task in which recent exposure to a word increases the likelihood that a person will think of that particular word, when given a cue that could evoke many different words.

representative In decision making, when a sample looks similar in important characteristics to the population from which it was selected.

representativeness heuristic A general rule in decision making that people use when trying to decide which outcome would be more likely. People who use this heuristic make judgments in terms of the similarity between the sample and the population from which the sample was selected. For instance, people believe that a coin toss of HTTHTH is more likely than a coin toss of HHHTTT.

retina The part of the visual system covering the inside back portion of the eye. The retina contains millions of neurons that register and transmit visual information from the outside world.

retrieval Locating information in memory storage and accessing that information.

retrieval practice Preparing for an exam by trying to recall important concepts from memory. If retrieval is difficult, but successful, learning is enhanced and test performance is improved.

retroactive interference In memory, people often experience difficulty in learning or recalling old material, because some recently learned material interferes with these older memories.

retrograde amnesia Loss of memory for events that occurred prior to brain damage. This deficit is especially severe for events that occurred during the years just before the damage.

retrospective memory Remembering information that was acquired in the past. In contrast, prospective memory applies to remembering a task that needs to be done in the future.

rotation heuristic In cognitive maps, people tend to remember a figure that is slightly tilted as being either more vertical or more horizontal than it really is.

rule-and-memory theory In children's language learning, the proposal that children learn a general rule for past-tense verbs, which specifies that they must add -ed; however, they also store in memory the past tenses for many irregular verbs.

ruminative style Worrying continuously about the problems that are wrong in one's life.

saccadic eye movement Small changes in eye position during reading, in order to bring the center of the retina into position over the words currently being read.

satisficers In decision making, people who tend to settle for something that is satisfactory rather than examining numerous options.

satisficing decision-making style The tendency to settle for something that is satisfactory, rather than examining numerous options.

schema Generalized, well-integrated knowledge about a situation, an event, or a person. Schemas allow people to predict what will happen in a new situation. These predictions are generally correct.

schema therapy When a clinician and client work together in order to explore the client's core beliefs, and they also create appropriate new, more helpful strategies.

schizophrenia A serious psychological disorder characterized by lack of emotional expression, hallucinations, disordered thinking, and poor performance on many cognitive tasks.

script A simple, well-structured sequence of events in a specified order. Scripts are usually associated with a highly familiar activity.

second language In linguistics, the second language that a person learned; this term is typically applied to someone who first learned a different language. *See* sequential bilingualism.

selective-attention task A situation in which people are instructed to pay attention to certain kinds of information, while ignoring other ongoing information.

self-efficacy The belief that one has the ability to organize and carry out a specific task.

self-instruction Subvocal reminders about something that needs to be done. This process involves the phonological loop.

self-knowledge The information that people believe about themselves, including factual information, as well as knowledge of one's own social behavior, personality, and attitudes.

self-reference effect The enhancement of long-term memory by relating the material to oneself.

semantic memory A person's organized knowledge about the world, including knowledge about words and other factual information.

semantic priming effect The observation that people respond faster to an item if it was preceded by an item with similar meaning.

semantics The area of psycholinguistics that examines the meanings of words and sentences.

sensory memory The large-capacity storage system that records information from each of the senses with reasonable accuracy.

sequential bilingualism In linguistics, a term referring to people who speak two or more languages, but did not learn them at the same time. Their native language is referred to as their *first language*, and the non-native language that they acquire is their *second language*.

serial processing A type of cognitive processing in which a person performs operations one item at a time, rather than simultaneously, in contrast to *parallel processing*.

serial-position effect The U-shaped relationship between a word's position in a list and its probability of recall. Recall is especially accurate for the initial words and the final words in a list, and recall is least accurate for the words in the middle of the list.

shadow In attention research, a task in which participants can hear two messages; however, they are instructed to listen to only one message and then repeat it after the speaker.

short-term memory The part of memory that holds only the small amount of information that a person is actively using. The more current term for this type of memory is *working memory*.

short-term visual memory *See* visuospatial working memory.

simultaneous bilingualism In linguistics, a term referring to people who learned two languages at the same time during childhood.

situated cognition approach The proposal that a person makes use of information in the immediate environment or situation; thus knowledge typically depends on the context surrounding the person.

slips-of-the-tongue Errors during speaking, in which sounds or entire words are rearranged between two or more different words. Slips of the tongue are informative because they reveal people's extensive knowledge about the sounds, structure, and meaning of the language that they are speaking.

small-sample fallacy In decision making, the assumption that a small sample will be representative of the population from which it is selected. This assumption often leads to incorrect decisions.

social cognition approach The view that stereotypes and many other components of social psychology can be traced to normal cognitive processes.

social cognitive neuroscience A new discipline that uses neuroscience techniques to explore the kind of cognitive processes used in interactions with other people.

social phobia An anxiety disorder characterized by extreme anxiety in social situations.

source monitoring The process of trying to identify the origin of a particular memory.

spaced learning When learning new material, the situation in which the learner distributes her or his practice over time; this learning strategy is more effective than *massed learning*.

spatial cognition The mental processes involved in (1) thoughts about cognitive maps, (2) memory for the world that we navigate, and (3) keeping track of objects in a spatial array.

spatial framework model The proposal that the above–below spatial dimension is especially important in spatial imagery, the front–back dimension is moderately important, and the right–left dimension is least important.

special mechanism approach In psycholinguistics, the theory that humans are born with a specialized device that allows them to decode speech stimuli. As a result, speech sounds are processed more quickly and more accurately than other auditory stimuli, such as instrumental music.

speech module A hypothetical, special-purpose neural mechanism that specifically handles all aspects of speech perception, but not other kinds of auditory perception. Also known as the *phonetic module*.

speech perception The process by which the auditory system records sound vibrations that are generated by someone talking. The auditory system then translates these vibrations into a sequence of sounds that are perceived as speech.

speech-is-special approach *See* special mechanism approach.

spontaneous generalization In the parallel distributed processing approach, when information is missing, people use individual cases to draw inferences about general information.

spreading activation In network models of semantic memory, the process by which nodes excite nearby or related nodes.

STEM disciplines The fields of Science, Technology, Engineering, and Mathematics; spatial ability is especially important in these disciplines.

stereotype threat In social cognitive theory, people may be hampered by a negative stereotype about belonging to a group that is perceived as being less competent in a specific area. This theory proposes that, when these individuals are reminded of their membership in this group, their performance may suffer.

Stroop effect The observation that people take a long time to name an ink color that has been used in printing an incongruent word, even though they can quickly name that same ink color when it appears as a solid patch.

structural features The underlying core of a problem that must be understood in order to solve the problem correctly. Often contrasted with the *surface features* of a problem.

subjective contours The perception of edges in a visual stimulus, even though edges are not physically present. Also known as *illusory contours*.

subordinate-level categories In the prototype approach to semantic memory, lower-level or more specific categories; "Desk chair," "collie," and "Phillips screwdriver" are examples of subordinate-level categories.

subproblems In problem solving, a complex problem may be difficult to solve. One strategy is to divide that problem into two or more smaller problems and solve each of these subproblems separately.

subvocalization Silently pronouncing words during reading.

superordinate-level categories In the prototype approach to semantic memory, higher-level or more general categories; "Furniture," "animal," and "tool" are all examples of superordinate-level categories.

surface features In problem solving, the specific objects and terms used in the question. These elements are often not relevant to the underlying core of the problem, known as the *structural features*.

surface structure In psycholinguistics, the representation of a sentence based on the words that are actually spoken or written, in contrast to *deep structure*.

syllogism A common deductive reasoning task that consists of two statements that one must assume to be true, plus a conclusion. Syllogisms refer to quantities, so they use the words *all, none, some*, and other similar terms.

symmetry heuristic In cognitive maps, people tend to remember figures as being more symmetrical and regular than they truly are.

syntax The grammatical rules that govern how words can be combined into sentences.

templates According to an early theory of visual object recognition, the specific perceptual patterns stored in memory.

testing effect The observation that the act of taking a test is actually an excellent way to boost long-term recall for academic material.

the good-enough approach In language comprehension, the observation that people frequently process only part of a sentence.

Theme 1: *The cognitive processes are active, rather than passive.*

Theme 2: *The cognitive processes are remarkably efficient and accurate.*

Theme 3: *The cognitive processes handle positive information better than negative information.*

Theme 4: *The cognitive processes are interrelated with one another; they do not operate in isolation.*

Theme 5: *Many cognitive processes rely on both bottom-up and top-down processing.*

theory of mind A specific kind of metacognition, which refers to your ideas about how your own mind works, as well as how other people's minds work.

thinking In problem solving and decision making, going beyond the information given to reach a goal such as a solution, a decision, or a belief.

thought suppression The attempt, usually unsuccessful, to push an undesirable idea out of consciousness.

timbre (pronounced "*tam*-ber") The sound quality of a tone. Different musical instruments playing the same note differ in their timbre.

tip-of-the-finger effect In the deaf community, the subjective experience of knowing a target sign, but not being able to produce that sign because it is temporarily inaccessible.

tip-of-the-tongue effect The subjective experience of knowing which word is being sought, but not being able to retrieve the actual word. A person may know the word's first letter and the general sound of the word—even though the word itself refuses to leap into memory. Also known as the *tip-of-the-tongue phenomenon*.

tip-of-the-tongue phenomenon *See* tip-of-the-tongue effect.

TMS *See* Transcranial Magnetic Stimulation.

top-down processing The kind of cognitive processing that emphasizes the importance of concepts, expectations, and memory in object recognition and other cognitive tasks.

total-time hypothesis The concept that the amount of information you learn depends on the total time devoted to learning. This hypothesis is generally true, although the quality of study strategies used during the time is also important.

Transcranial Magnetic Stimulation (TMS) A nonsurgical neuroscience technique that uses a magnetic field to briefly stimulate a specific location on the cortex. This stimulation interferes—very briefly—with information processing, but it does not harm the brain.

transformational rules According to Noam Chomsky, the processes used to convert deep structure (the basic idea in a sentence) into a surface structure (a spoken or written sentence).

translation The process of converting a text written in one language into a second written language. In contrast, *interpreting* refers to the process of converting a spoken message in one language into a second spoken (or signed) language.

Type 1 processing According to dual-process theory in reasoning and decision making, Type 1 processing is relatively fast and automatic. It also requires little conscious attention.

Type 2 processing According to dual-process theory in reasoning and decision making, Type 2 processing is relatively slow and controlled. It also requires focused attention, and performance is typically more accurate than if a person used Type 1 processing on that same task.

typicality effect In the prototype theory of semantic memory, the observation that people judge typical items (prototypes) faster than items that are not typical (nonprototypes).

understanding In problem solving, having a well-organized mental representation of the problem, based on both the information provided in the problem and one's own previous experience.

unilateral spatial neglect A perceptual condition, resulting from brain damage to the parietal region, in which a person ignores part of his or her visual field.

utilization deficiency The problem of not using memory strategies effectively; common in young children.

validity A test's ability to predict a person's performance in another situation.

verbatim memory Word-for-word recall of material presented at an earlier time; the research shows that people usually have poor verbatim memory.

viewer-centered approach A modification of the recognition-by-components theory of object recognition. However, the viewer-centered approach proposes that people store a small number of views of a three-dimensional object, rather than just one view.

visual imagery The mental representation of visual stimuli.

visual search A task requiring the observer to find a target in a visual display that has numerous distractors.

visual sensory memory *See* iconic memory.

visuospatial sketchpad *See* visuospatial working memory.

visuospatial working memory The component of working memory that processes both visual and spatial information. Visuospatial working memory has also been known as *visuospatial sketchpad,* and *short-term visual memory.*

Wernicke's aphasia (pronounced either "*Ver*-nih-kees" or "*Wer*-nih-kees") Severe problems with language comprehension (e.g., understanding instructions), caused by damage to Wernicke's area. Many people with Wernicke's aphasia also have problems with language production.

Wernicke's area (pronounced either "*Ver*-nih-kees" or "*Wer*-nih-kees") An area toward the back of the brain that is important in language comprehension.

whole-language approach The idea that, in order to increase children's enthusiasm about learning to read, reading instruction should emphasize meaning, and it should also be enjoyable.

whole-word approach The proposal that readers can directly connect the written word—as an entire unit—with the meaning that this word represents.

word superiority effect The observation that a single letter is more accurately and rapidly recognized when it appears in a meaningful word, rather than when it appears alone or in a meaningless string of unrelated letters.

working memory The brief, immediate memory for the limited amount of material that a person is currently processing. Part of working memory also actively coordinates ongoing mental activities. In the current research, the term *working memory* is more popular than a similar but older term, *short-term memory.*

working-memory approach Baddeley's model of immediate memory, which proposed a multipart system that temporarily holds and manipulates information while cognitive tasks are performed.

REFERENCES

Abelson, R. P. (1981). Psychological status of the script concept. *American Psychologist, 36*, 715–729.

Acheson, D. J., & M. C. MacDonald (2009). Verbal working memory and language production: Common approaches to the serial ordering of verbal information. *Psychological Bulletin, 135*, 50–68.

Adler, J., & Hall, C. (1995, June 5). Surgery at 33,000 feet. *Newsweek*, p. 36.

Adler, T. (1991, July). Memory researcher wins Troland award. *APA Monitor*, pp. 12–13.

Ainsworth, W., & Greenberg, S. (2006). Auditory processing of speech. In S. Greenberg & W. A. Ainsworth (Eds.), *Listening to speech: An auditory perspective* (pp. 3–17). Mahwah, NJ: Erlbaum.

Aizpurua, A., Garcia-Bajos, E., & Migueles, M. (2009). False memories for a robbery in young and older adults. *Applied Cognitive Psychology, 23*, 341–363.

Akhtar, N., Jipson, J., & Callanan, M. A. (2001). Learning words through overhearing. *Child Development, 72*, 416–430.

Alibali, M. W., Spencer, R. C., Knox, L., & Kita, S. (2011). Spontaneous gestures influence strategy choices in problem solving. *Psychological Science, 22*, 1138–1144.

Allen, G. L. (2004). Preface: Routes of human spatial memory research. In G. L. Allen (Ed.), *Human spatial memory: Remembering where* (pp. xiii–xx). Mahwah, NJ: Erlbaum.

Alloway, T. P. (2011). *Improving working memory: Supporting students' learning.* Los Angeles: Sage.

Alloway, T. P., Gathercole, S. C., Adams, A-M., Willis, C., Eaglen, R., & Lamont, E. (2005). Working memory and phonological awareness as predictors of progress towards early learning goals at school entry. *British Journal of Developmental Psychology, 23*, 417–426.

Almeida, J., Mahon, B. Z., & Caramazza, A. (2010). The role of the dorsal visual processing stream in tool identification. *Psychological Science, 21*, 772–778.

Altmann, G. T. (1997). The ascent of Babel: An exploration of language, mind, and understanding. Oxford University Press.

Alter, J. (2000, July 3). A reckoning on death row. *Newsweek*, p. 31.

Altarriba, J., Kroll, J. F., Sholl, A., & Rayner, K. (1996). The influence of lexical and conceptual constraints on reading mixed-language sentences: Evidence from eye fixations and naming times. *Memory & Cognition, 24*, 477–492.

Alvarez, G. A., & Cavanaugh, P. (2004). The capacity of visual short-term memory is set both by visual information load and by number of objects. *Psychological Science, 15*, 106–111.

Amabile, T. M. (1997). Motivating creativity in organizations: On doing what you love and loving what you do. *California Management Review, 40*, 39–58.

Ambady, N., & Weisbuch, M. (2010). Nonverbal behavior. In S. T. Fiske, D. T. Gilbert, & G. Lindzey (Eds.), *Handbook of social psychology* (5th ed., Vol. 1, pp. 464–497). Hoboken, NJ: Wiley.

Ambady, N., Shih, M., Kim, A., & Pittinsky, T. L. (2001). Stereotype susceptibility in children: Effects of identity activation on quantitative performance. *Psychological Science, 12*, 385–390.

American Psychiatric Association. (2000). *Diagnostic and statistical manual of mental disorders* (4th ed., text revision). Washington, DC: Author.

American Psychological Association. (2010). *Publication manual of the American Psychological Association* (6th ed.). Washington, DC: Author.

Amir, N., & Selvig, A. (2005). Implicit memory tasks in clinical research. In A. Wenzel & D. C. Rubin (Eds.), *Cognitive methods and their application to clinical research* (pp. 153–171). Washington, DC: American Psychological Association.

Anastasi, J. S., & Rhodes, M. G. (2003). Evidence for an own-age bias in face recognition. *North American Journal of Psychology, 8*, 237–252.

Anderson, J. R. (1990). *The adaptive character of thought.* Hillsdale, NJ: Erlbaum.

Anderson, J. R. (2000). *Learning and memory: An integrated approach* (2nd ed.). New York: Wiley.

Anderson, J. R. (2009). *Cognitive psychology and its implications* (7th ed.). New York: Worth.

Anderson, J. R., & Gluck, K. A. (2001). What role do cognitive architectures play in intelligent tutoring systems? In S. M. Carver & D. Klahr (Eds.), *Cognition and instruction: Twenty-five years of progress* (pp. 227–261). Mahwah, NJ: Erlbaum.

Anderson, J. R., & Schooler, L. J. (2000). The adaptive nature of memory. In E. Tulving & F. I. M. Craik (Eds.), *The Oxford handbook of memory* (pp. 557–581). New York: Oxford University Press.

Anderson, J. R., & Schunn, C. D. (2000). Implications of the ACT-R learning theory: No magic bullets. In R. Glaser (Ed.), *Advances in instructional psychology* (Vol. **5**, pp. 1–33). Mahwah, NJ: Erlbaum.

Anderson, J. R., Corbett, A. T., Koedinger, K. R., & Pelletier, R. (1995). Cognitive tutors: Lessons learned. *The Journal of Learning Science, 4*, 167–207.

Anderson, J. R., Douglass, S., & Qin, Y. (2005). How should a theory of learning and cognition inform instruction? In A. F. Healy (Ed.), *Experimental cognitive psychology and its applications* (pp. 47–59). Washington, DC: American Psychological Association.

Anderson, J. R., Bothell, D., Byrne, M. D., Douglass, S., Lebiere, C., & Qin, Y. (2004). An integrated theory of mind. *Psychological Review, 111*, 1036–1060.

Anderson, J. R., Fincham, J. M., Qin, Y., & Stocco, A. (2008). A central circuit of the mind. *Trends in Cognitive Science, 12*, 136–143.

Anderson, R. E. (1998). Imagery and spatial representation. In W. Bechtel & G. Graham (Eds.), *A companion to cognitive science* (pp. 204–211). Malden, MA: Blackwell.

Ariel, R., & Dunlosky, J. (2011). The sensitivity of judgment-of-learning resolution to past test performance, new learning, and forgetting. *Memory & Cognition, 39*, 171–184.

Ashby, F. G., Prinzmetal, W., Ivry, R., & Maddox, W. T. (1996). A formal theory of feature binding in object perception. *Psychological Review, 103*, 165–192.

Ashby, J., & Rayner, K. (2004). Representing syllable information during silent reading: Evidence from eye movements. *Language and Cognitive Processes, 19*, 391–426.

Ashby, J., Rayner, K., & Clifton, C. (2005). Eye movements of highly skilled and average readers: Differential effects of frequency and predictability. *The Quarterly Journal of Experimental Psychology Section A, 58*, 1065–1086.

Association for Psychological Science. (n.d.). Retrieved from http://www.psychologicalscience.org/index.php/publications/observer/2012/may-june-12/remembering-the-father-of-cognitive-psychology.html

Atkinson, D., & Connor, U. (2008). Multilingual writing development. In C. Bazerman (Ed.), *Handbook of research on writing: History, society, school, individual, text* (pp. 515–532). Mahwah, NJ: Erlbaum.

Atkinson, R. C., & Shiffrin, R. M. (1968). Human memory: A proposed system and its control processes. In K. W. Spence & J. T. Spence (Eds.), *The psychology of learning and motivation: Advances in research and theory* (Vol. **2**, pp. 89–105). New York: Academic Press.

Awh, E., Jonides, J., Smith, E. E., Buxton, R. B., Frank, L. R., Love, T., . . . Gmeindl, l. (1999). Rehearsal in spatial working memory: Evidence from neuroimaging. *Psychological Science, 10*, 433–437.

Babb, K. A., & Ross, C. (2009). The timing of online lecture slide availability and its effect on attendance, participation, and exam performance. *Computers & Education, 52*, 868–881.

Bäckman, L., Small, B. J., & Wahlin, A. (2001). Aging and memory: Cognitive and biological perspectives. In J. E. Birren & K. W. Schaie (Eds.), *Handbook of the psychology of aging* (5th ed., pp. 349–377). San Diego: Academic Press.

Bacon, E. (2010). Further insight into cognitive and metacognitive processes of the tip-of-the-tongue state with an amnesic drug as cognitive tool. In A. Efklides & Misailidi (Eds.), *Trends and prospects in metacognition research* (pp. 81–104). New York: Springer.

Baddeley, A. D. (1986). *Working memory.* Oxford, UK: Clarendon.

Baddeley, A. D. (1994). The magical number seven: Still magic after all these years? *Psychological Review, 101*, 353–356.

Baddeley, A. D. (1997). *Human memory: Theory and practice* (Rev. ed.). East Sussex, UK: Psychology Press.

Baddeley, A. D. (1999). *Essentials of human memory.* East Sussex, UK: Psychology Press.

Baddeley, A. D. (2000a). Short-term and working memory. In E. Tulving & F. I. M. Craik (Eds.), *The Oxford handbook of memory* (pp. 77–92). New York: Oxford University Press.

Baddeley, A. D. (2000b). The episodic buffer: A new component of working memory? *Trends in Cognitive Sciences, 4*, 417–423.

Baddeley, A. D. (2001). Is working memory still working? *American Psychologist, 56*, 849–864.

Baddeley, A. D. (2003). Working memory and language: An overview. *Journal of Communication Disorders, 36*, 189–208.

Baddeley, A. D. (2004). Memory and context. In R. L. Gregory (Ed.), *The Oxford companion to the mind* (2nd ed., pp. 571–572). New York: Oxford University Press.

Baddeley, A. D. (2006). Working memory: An overview. In S. J. Pickering (Ed.), *Working memory and education* (pp. 3–31). Burlington, MA: Elsevier.

Baddeley, A. D. (2007). *Working memory, thought, and action*. Oxford, UK: Oxford University Press.

Baddeley, A. D. (2012). Working memory: Theories, models, and controversies. *Annual Review of Psychology, 63*, 1–29.

Baddeley, A. D., & Andrade, J. (1998). Working memory and consciousness: An empirical approach. In M. A. Conway, S. E. Gathercole, & C. Cornoldi (Eds.), *Theories of memory II* (pp. 1–24). Hove, UK: Psychology Press.

Baddeley, A. D., & Hitch, G. J. (1974). Working memory. In G. Bower (Ed.), *Recent advances in learning and memory* (Vol. **8**, pp. 47–90). New York: Academic Press.

Baddeley, A. D., Allen, R., & Hitch, G. J. (2011). Binding in visual working memory: The role of the episodic buffer. *Neuropsychologia, 49*, 1393–1400.

Baddeley, A. D., Allen, R., & Vargha-Khadem, F. (2010). Is the hippocampus necessary for visual and verbal binding in working memory? *Neuropsychologia, 48*, 1089–1095.

Baddeley, A. D., Grant, S., Wight, E., & Thomson, N. (1973). Imagery and visual working memory. In P. M. A. Rabbitt & S. Dornic (Eds.), *Attention and performance V* (pp. 205–217). London: Academic Press.

Baddeley, A., Eysenck, M. W., & Anderson, M. C. (2009). *Memory*. New York: Psychology Press.

Bahrick, H. P. (2005). The long-term neglect of long-term memory: Reasons and remedies. In A. F. Healy (Ed.), *Experimental cognitive psychology and its applications* (pp. 89–100). Washington, DC: American Psychological Association.

Bahrick, H. P., Bahrick, P. O., & Wittlinger, R. P. (1975). Fifty years of memory for names and faces: A cross-sectional approach. *Journal of Experimental Psychology: General, 104*(1), 54–75.

Bahrick, H. P., & Hall, L. K. (2005). The importance of retrieval failures to long-term retention: A metacognitive explanation of the spacing effect. *Journal of Memory and Language, 52*, 566–577.

Bahrick, H. P., Hall, L. K., Goggin, J. P., Bahrick, L. E., & Berger, S. A. (1994). Fifty years of language maintenance and language dominance in bilingual Hispanic immigrants. *Journal of Experimental Psychology: General, 123*, 264–283.

Bahrick, H. P., & Phelphs, E. (1987). Retention of Spanish vocabulary over 8 years. *Journal of Experimental Psychology: Learning, Memory, and Cognition, 13*, 344.

Baker, J. M. C., & Dunlosky, J. (2006). Does momentary accessibility influence metacomprehension judgments? The influence of study-judgment lags on accessibility effects. *Psychonomic Bulletin & Review, 13*, 60–65.

Baker, J. M. C., Dunlosky, J., & Hertzog, C. (2010). How accurately can older adults evaluate the quality of their text recall? The effect of providing standards on judgment accuracy. *Applied Cognitive Psychology, 24*, 134–147.

Baker, K. D. (1999). Personal Communication.

Baker, L. (2005). Developmental differences in metacognition: Implications for metacognitively oriented reading instruction. In S. E. Israel, C. C. Block, K. L. Bauserman, & K. Kinnucan-Welsch (Eds.), *Metacognition in literacy learning: Theory, assessment, instruction, and professional development* (pp. 61–79). Mahwah, NJ: Erlbaum.

Balch, W. R. (2006). Introducing psychology students to research methodology: A word-pleasantness experiment. *Teaching of Psychology, 33*, 132–134.

Baldwin, D., & Meyer, M. (2007). How inherently social is language? In E. Hoff & M. Shatz (Eds.), *Blackwell handbook of language development* (pp. 87–106). Malden, MA: Blackwell.

Baldwin, M. W., & Dandeneau, S. D. (2005). Understanding and modifying the relational schemas underlying insecurity. In M. W. Baldwin (Ed.), *Interpersonal cognition* (pp. 33–61). New York: Guilford.

Balota, D. A., Pollatsek, A., & Rayner, K. (1985). The interaction of contextual constraints and parafoveal visual information in reading. *Cognitive Psychology, 17*, 364–390.

Balota, D. A., Law, M. B., & Zevin, J. D. (2000). The attentional control of lexical processing pathways: Reversing the word frequency effect. *Memory & Cognition, 28*, 1081–1089.

Bar, M., Kassam, K. S., Ghuman, A. S., Boshyan, J., Schmid, A. M., Dale, A. M., . . . Halgren, E. (2006). Top-down facilitation of visual recognition. *Proceedings of the National Academy of Sciences of the United States of America, 103*, 449–454.

Barash, D. P. (2006, July 14). I am, therefore I think. *Chronicle of Higher Education*, pp. B9–B10.

Bardovi-Harlig, K. (2010). Pragmatics and second language acquisition. In R. B. Kaplan (Ed.), *The Oxford handbook of applied linguistics* (2nd ed., pp. 233–243). New York: Oxford University Press.

Bargh, J., & Ferguson, M. J. (2000). Beyond behaviorism: On the automaticity of higher mental processes. *Psychological Bulletin, 126*, 925–945.

Barkley, R. A. (2006). *Attention deficit hyperactivity disorder: A handbook for diagnosis and treatment* (3rd ed.). New York: Guilford.

Barkley, R. A. (2010). *Taking charge of adult ADHD*. New York: Guilford.

Barnes, J. B. (2004). Aristotle. In R. L. Gregory (Ed.), *The Oxford companion to the mind* (2nd ed., pp. 45–46). New York: Oxford University Press.

Barnett, S. M., & Ceci, S. J. (2002). When and where do we apply what we learn? A taxonomy for far transfer. *Psychological Bulletin, 128*, 612–637.

Barnett, S. M., & Koslowski, B. (2002). Adaptive expertise: Effects of type of experience and the level of theoretical understanding it generates. *Thinking and Reasoning, 8,* 237–267.

Barnhart, A. S., & Goldinger, S. D. (2010). Interpreting chicken-scratch: Lexical access for handwritten words. *Journal of Experimental Psychology: Human Perception and Performance, 36,* 906–923.

Baron, J. (2000). *Thinking and deciding* (3rd ed.). New York: Cambridge University Press.

Barr, D. J., & Keysar, B. (2006). Perspective taking and the coordination of meaning in language use. In M. J. Traxler & M. A. Gernsbacher (Eds.), *Handbook of psycholinguistics* (2nd ed., pp. 901–938). Amsterdam: Elsevier.

Barr, R., Rovee-Collier, C., & Campanella, J. (2005). Retrieval protracts deferred imitation by 6-month-olds. *Infancy, 7,* 263–283.

Barr, R., Rovee-Collier, C., & Learmonth, A. (2011). Potentiation in young infants: The origin of the prior knowledge effect? *Memory & Cognition, 39,* 625–636.

Barrett, H. C., & Kurzban, R. (2006). Modularity in cognition: Framing the debate. *Psychological Review, 113,* 628–647.

Barrett, L. F. (2009). The future of psychology: Connecting mind to brain. *Perspectives on Psychological Science, 4,* 326–339.

Barron, E., Roby, L. M., Greer, J., & Smallwood, J. (2011). Absorbed in thought: The effect of mind wandering on the processing of relevant and irrelevant events. *Psychological Science, 22,* 596–601.

Barsalou, L. W. (1990). On the indistinguishability of exemplar memory and abstraction in category representation. In T. K. Srull & R. S. Wyer (Eds.), *Advances in social cognition* (Vol. 3, pp. 61–88). Hillsdale, NJ: Erlbaum.

Barsalou, L. W. (1992). Frames, concepts, and conceptual fields. In A. Lehrer & E. F. Kittay (Eds.), *Frames, fields, and contrasts* (pp. 21–74). Hillsdale, NJ: Erlbaum.

Barsalou, L. W. (2003). Situated simulation in the human conceptual system. *Language and Cognitive Processes, 18,* 513–562.

Barsalou, L. W. (2009). Situating concepts. In P. Robbins & M. Aydede (Eds.), *The Cambridge handbook of situated cognition* (pp. 236–263). New York: Cambridge University Press.

Barshi, I., & Healy, A. F. (2011). The effects of spatial representation on memory for verbal navigation instructions. *Memory & Cognition, 39,* 47–62.

Bartlett, F. C. (1932). *Remembering: An experimental and social study.* Cambridge, UK: Cambridge University Press.

Bartlett, T. (2011, November 25). "Motivated blindness": One take on what went wrong at Penn State. *Chronicle of Higher Education,* p. A9.

Baruss, I. (2003). *Alterations of consciousness: An empirical analysis for social scientists.* Washington, DC: American Psychological Association.

Bassok, M. (2003). Analogical transfer in problem solving. In J. E. Davidson & R. J. Sternberg (Eds.), *The psychology of problem solving* (pp. 343–369). New York: Cambridge University Press.

Bassok, M., & Novick, L. R. (2012). Problem solving. In K. J. Holyoak & R. G. Morrison (Eds.), *Oxford handbook of thinking and reasoning* (pp. 413–432). Oxford University Press.

Bate, S., Bennetts, R., Mole, J. A., Ainge, J. A., Gregory, N. J., Bobak, A. K., . . . Bussunt, A. (2015). Rehabilitation of face-processing skills in an adolescent with prosopagnosia: Evaluation of an online perceptual training programme. *Neuropsychological Rehabilitation, 25*(5), 733–762.

Bates, E., Devescovi, A., & Wulfeck, B. (2001). Psycholinguistics: A cross-language perspective. *Annual Review of Psychology, 52,* 369–396.

Bates, E., & MacWhinney, B. (1987). A functionalist approach to the acquisition of grammar. *Functionalism in linguistics, 20,* 209.

Bauer, B., & Jolicoeur, P. (1996). Stimulus dimensionality effects in mental rotation. *Journal of Experimental Psychology: Human Perception and Performance, 22,* 82–94.

Bauer, P. J. (2004). Getting explicit memory off the ground: Steps toward construction of a neuro-developmental account of changes in the first two years of life. *Developmental Review, 24,* 347–373.

Baumeister, R. F., Masicampo, E. J., & Vohs, K. D. (2011). Do conscious thoughts cause behavior? *Annual Review of Psychology, 62,* 331–361.

Bayliss, D. M., Jarrold, C., Baddeley, A. D., & Leigh, E. (2005). Differential constraints on the working memory and reading abilities of individuals with learning difficulties and typically developing children. *Journal of Experimental Child Psychology, 92,* 76–99.

Bazerman, M. H., &Tenbrunsel, A. E. (2011). *Blind spots: Why we fail to do what's right and what to do about it.* Princeton: Princeton University Press.

Bearce, K. H., & Rovee-Collier, C. (2006). Repeated priming increases memory accessibility in infants. *Journal of Experimental Child Psychology, 93,* 357–376.

Beauchamp, M. S., Nath, A. R., & Passler, S. (2010). FMRI-guided transcranial magnetic stimulation reveals that the superior temporal sulcus is a cortical locus of the McGurk effect. *Journal of Neuroscience, 30,* 2414–2417.

Beauvais, C., Olive, T., & Passerault, J.-M. (2011). Why are some texts good and others not? Relationship between text quality and management of the writing process. *Journal of Educational Psychology*, *103*, 415–428.

Bechtel, W., Abrahamsen, A., & Graham, G. (1998). The life of cognitive science. In W. Bechtel & G. Graham (Eds.), *A companion to cognitive science* (pp. 2–104). Malden, MA: Blackwell.

Beck, J. S. (2011). *Cognitive behavior therapy: Basics and beyond* (2nd ed.). New York: Guilford.

Bediou, B., Franck, N., Saoud, M., Baudouin, J. Y., Tiberghien, G., Daléry, J., . . . d'Amato, T. (2005). Effects of emotion and identity on facial affect processing in schizophrenia. *Psychiatric Research*, *133*, 149–157.

Beeman, M., Bowden, E. M., & Gernsbacher, M. A. (2000). Right and left hemisphere cooperation for drawing predictive and coherence inferences during normal story comprehension. *Brain and Language*, *71*, 310–336.

Beilock, S. I., & Carr, T. H. (2005). When high-powered people fail: Working memory and "choking under pressure" in math. *Psychological Science*, *16*, 101–105.

Belsky, G., & Gilovich, T. (1999). *Why smart people make big money mistakes—and how to correct them: Lessons from the new science of behavioral economics*. New York: Simon and Schuster. (2nd ed., 2010).

Bellezza, F. S. (1984). The self as a mnemonic device: The role of internal cues. *Journal of Personality and Social Psychology*, *47*, 506–516.

Bellezza, F. S., & Hoyt, S. K. (1992). The self-reference effect and mental cueing. *Social Cognition*, *10*, 51–78.

Beni, R. D., Pazzaglia, F., & Gardini, S. (2006). The role of mental rotation and age in spatial perspective-taking tasks: When age does not impair perspective-taking performance. *Applied Cognitive Psychology*, *20*, 807–821.

Benjamin, A. S., & Ross, B. H. (2011). The causes and consequences of reminding. In A. S. Benjamin (Ed.), *Successful remembering and successful forgetting: A festschrift in honor of Robert A. Bjork* (pp. 71–87). New York: Psychology Press.

Benjamin, L. T., Jr. (2009). *A history of psychology* (3rd ed.). Malden, MA: Blackwell.

Bennett, M. D., & Gibson, J. M. (2006). *A field guide to good decisions*. Westport, CT: Praeger.

Bent, T., & Holt, R. F. (2017). Representation of speech variability. *Wiley Interdisciplinary Reviews: Cognitive Science*, *8*(4).

Ben-Zeev, T. (2002). If "ignorance makes us smart," then does reading books make us less smart? [Review of Simple heuristics that make us smart]. *Contemporary Psychology*, *47*, 653–656.

Berg, T. (2002). Slips of the typewriter key. *Applied Psycholinguistics*, *23*, 185–207.

Berger, C. R. (1997). Producing messages under uncertainty. In J. O. Greene (Ed.), *Message production* (pp. 221–224). Mahwah, NJ: Erlbaum.

Bermúdez, J. L. (2010). *Cognitive science: An introduction to the science of the mind*. New York: Cambridge University Press.

Bernstein, D. M., & Loftus, E. F. (2009). The consequences of false memories for food preferences and choices. *Perspectives on Psychological Science*, *4*, 135–139.

Bernstein, D. M., Laney, C., Morris, E. K., & Loftus, E. F. (2005). False memories about food can lead to food avoidance. *Social Cognition*, *23*, 11–34.

Bernstein, S. E., & Carr, T. H. (1996). Dual-route theories of pronouncing printed words: What can be learned from concurrent task performance? *Journal of Experimental Psychology: Learning, Memory, and Cognition*, *22*, 86–116.

Bharucha, J. J. (1987). Music cognition and perceptual facilitation: A connectionist framework. *Music Perception*, 1–30.

Bialystok, E. (1988). Levels of bilingualism and levels of linguistic awareness. *Developmental Psychology*, *24*, 560–567.

Bialystok, E. (1992). Selective attention in cognitive processing: The bilingual edge. In R. J. Harris (Ed.), *Language processing in bilingual children* (pp. 501–513). Amsterdam: Elsevier.

Bialystok, E. (2001). *Bilingualism in development: Language, literacy, & cognition*. New York: Cambridge University Press.

Bialystok, E. (2005). Consequences of bilingualism for cognitive development. In J. F. Kroll, & A. M. de Groot (Eds.), *Handbook of bilingualism: Psycholinguistic approaches* (pp. 417–432). New York: Oxford University Press.

Bialystok, E. (2009). Bilingualism: The good, the bad, and the indifferent. *Bilingualism: Language and Cognition*, *12*, 3–11.

Bialystok, E. (2010). Bilingualism. *Wiley Interdisciplinary Reviews: Cognitive Science*, *1*, 559–572.

Bialystok, E., & Codd, J. (1997). Cardinal limits: Evidence from language awareness and bilingualism for developing concepts of number. *Cognitive Development*, *12*, 85–106.

Bialystok, E., & Craik, F. I. M. (Eds.). (2006). *Lifespan cognition: Mechanisms of change*. New York: Oxford University Press.

Bialystok, E., & Feng, X. (2009). Language proficiency and executive control in proactive interference: Evidence from monolingual and bilingual children and adults. *Brain & Language*, *109*, 93–100.

Bialystok, E., & Hakuta, K. (1994). *In other words: The science and psychology of second-language acquisition*. New York: Basic Books.

Bialystok, E., & Majumder, S. (1998). The relationship between bilingualism and the development of cognitive processes in problem solving. *Applied Psycholinguistics, 19,* 69–85.

Bialystok, E., & Martin, M. (2004). Attention and inhibition in bilingual children: Evidence from the dimensional change card sort task. *Developmental Science, 7,* 325–339.

Bialystok, E., & Viswanathan, M. (2009). Components of executive control with advantages for bilingual children in two cultures. *Cognition, 112,* 494–500.

Bialystok, E., Craik, F. I. M., & Freedman, M. (2007). Bilingualism as a protection against the onset of symptoms of dementia. *Neuropsychologia, 45,* 459–464.

Biber, D., & Vásquez, C. (2008). Writing and speaking. In C. Bazerman (Ed.), *Handbook of research on writing: History, society, school, individual, text* (pp. 535–548). Mahwah, NJ: Erlbaum.

Bicknell, K., Elman, J. L., Hare, M., McRae, K., & Kutas, M. (2010). Effects of event knowledge in processing verbal arguments. *Journal of Memory and Language, 63,* 489–505.

Biederman, I. (1990). Higher-level vision. In E. N. Osherson, S. M. Kosslyn, & J. M. Hollerbach (Eds.), *An invitation to cognitive science* (Vol. **2**, pp. 41–72). Cambridge, MA: MIT Press.

Biederman, I. (1995). Visual object recognition. In S. F. Kosslyn & D. N. Osherson (Eds.), *An invitation to cognitive science* (2nd ed., pp. 121–165). Cambridge, MA: MIT Press.

Bieman-Copland, S., & Charness, N. (1994). Memory knowledge and memory monitoring in adulthood. *Psychology and Aging, 9,* 287–302.

Binkofski, F., Amunts, K., Stephan, K. M., Posse, S., Schormann, T., Freund, H. J., . . . & Seitz, R. J. (2000). Broca's region subserves imagery of motion: A combined cytoarchitectonic and fMRI study. *Human Brain Mapping, 11,* 273–285.

Birdsong, D. (2006). Age and second language acquisition and processing: A selective overview. *Language Learning, 56,* 9–48.

Birdsong, D., & Molis, M. (2001). On the evidence for maturational constraints in second-language acquisition. *Journal of Memory and Language, 44,* 235–249.

Bisby, J. A., King J. A., Brewin, C. R., Burgess, N., & Curran, H. V. (2010). Acute effects of alcohol on intrusive memory development and viewpoint dependence in spatial memory support a dual representation model. *Biological Psychiatry, 68,* 280–286.

Bishop, M. A., & Trout, J. D. (2002). 50 years of successful predictive modeling should be enough. *Lessons for Philosophy of Science, 69,* S197–S208.

Bjork, E. L., & Bjork, R. A. (1988). On the adaptive aspects of retrieval failure in autobiographical memory. In M. M. Gruneberg, P. E. Morris, & R. N. Sykes (Eds.), *Practical aspects of memory* (Vol. **2**). London: Academic Press.

Bjork, E. L., Bjork, R. A., & MacLeod, M. D. (2005). Types and consequences of forgetting: Intended and unintended. In L.-G. Nilsson & Nobuo Ohta (Eds.), *Memory and society: Psychological perspectives* (pp. 134–158). New York: Psychology Press.

Bjork, E. L., Storm, B. C., & deWinstanley, P. A. (2011). Learning from the consequences of retrieval: Another test effect. In A. S. Benjamin (Ed.), *Successful remembering and successful forgetting: A festschrift in honor of Robert A. Bjork* (pp. 347–364). New York: Psychology Press.

Bjorklund, D. F. (2005). *Children's thinking: Cognitive development and individual differences* (4th ed.). Belmont, CA: Thomson Wadsworth.

Bjorklund, D. F., Dukes, C., & Brown, R. D. (2009). The development of memory strategies. In M. Courage & N. Cowan (Eds.), *The development of memory in childhood* (pp. 145–175). Hove, UK: Psychology Press.

Blascovich, J., Spencer, S. J., Quinn, D., & Steele, C. (2001). African Americans and high blood pressure: The role of stereotype threat. *Psychological Science, 12,* 225–229.

Bleckley, M. K., Durso, F. T., Crutchfield, J. M., Engle, R. W., & Khanna, M. M. (2003). Individual differences in working memory capacity predict visual attention allocation. *Psychonomic Bulletin & Review, 10*(4), 884–889.

Block, R. A., & Harper, D. R. (1991). Overconfidence in estimation: Testing the anchoring-and-adjustment hypothesis. *Organizational Behavior and Human Decision Processes, 49,* 188–207.

Bloom, F. E., & Lazerson, A. (1988). *Brain, mind, and behavior* (2nd ed.). New York: Freeman.

Bloom, L. C., & Mudd, S. A. (1991). Depth of processing approach to face recognition: A test of two theories. *Journal of Experimental Psychology: Learning, Memory, and Cognition, 17,* 556–565.

Bloom, P. (2001). Précis of How children learn the meaning of words. *Behavioral and Brain Sciences, 24,* 1095–1103.

Blumenfeld, H. K., & Marian, V. (2014). Cognitive control in bilinguals: Advantages in stimulus–stimulus inhibition. *Bilingualism: Language and Cognition, 17,* 610–629.

Blumenthal, A. L. (2009). A reappraisal of Wilhelm Wundt. In L. T. Benjamin, Jr. (Ed.), (2009). *A history of psychology* (3rd ed., pp. 64–72). Malden, MA: Blackwell.

Bock, K., & Griffin, Z. M. (2000). Producing words: How mind meets mouth. In L. Wheeldon (Ed.), *Aspects of language production* (pp. 7–47). Philadelphia: Psychology Press.

Bock, K., Loebell, H., & Morey, R. (1992). From conceptual roles to structural relations: Bridging the syntactic cleft. *Psychological Review, 99*, 150–171.

Boden, M. (2004). Artificial intelligence (AI). In R. L. Gregory (Ed.), *The Oxford companion to the mind* (2nd ed., pp. 59–61). New York: Oxford University Press.

Bodenhausen, G. V., Macrae, C. N., & Hugenberg, K. (2003). Social cognition. In I. B. Weiner (Ed.), *Handbook of psychology* (Vol. 5, pp. 257–282). Hoboken, NJ: Wiley.

Bohanek, J. G., Fivush, R., & Walker, E. (2005). Memories of positive and negative emotional events. *Applied Cognitive Psychology, 19*, 51–66.

Bohn, A. (2010). Generational differences in cultural life scripts and life story memories of younger and older adults. *Applied Cognitive Psychology, 24*, 1324–1345.

Bohn-Gettler, C. M., Rapp, D. N., van den Broek, P., Kendeou, P., & Jane White, M. (2011). Adults' and children's monitoring of story events in the service of comprehension. *Memory & Cognition, 39*, 992–1011.

Boker, S. M., & Bisconti, T. L. (2006). Dynamical systems modeling for aging research. In C. S. Bergeman & S. M. Boker (Eds.), *Methodological issues in aging research* (pp. 185–229). Mahwah, NJ: Erlbaum.

Boot, W. E., Brockmole, J. R., & Simons, D. J. (2005). Attention capture is modulated in dual-task situations. *Psychonomic Bulletin & Review, 12*, 662–668.

Bornkessel, I., & Schlesewsky, M. (2006). The extended argument dependency model: A neurocognitive approach to sentence comprehension across languages. *Psychological Review, 113*, 787–821.

Bornstein, M. H., & Putnick, D. L. (2012). Cognitive and socioemotional caregiving in developing countries. *Child Development, 83*, 46–61.

Borst, G., & Kosslyn, S. M. (2008). Visual mental imagery and visual perception: Structural equivalence revealed by scanning processes. *Memory & Cognition*, 849–862.

Borst, G., & Kosslyn, S. M. (2010). Individual differences in spatial mental imagery. *Quarterly Journal of Experimental Psychology, 63*, 2031–2050.

Borst, G., Thompson, W. L., & Kosslyn, S. M. (2011). Understanding the dorsal and ventral systems of the human cerebral cortex. *American Psychologist, 66*, 624–632.

Bosch, L., & Sebastián-Gallés, N. (2001). Early language differentiation in bilingual infants. In J. Cenoz & F. Genesee (Eds.), *Trends in bilingual acquisition* (pp. 71–93). Amsterdam: Benjamins.

Botella, J., Privado, J., Gil-Gómez de Liaño, B., & Suero, M. (2011). Illusory conjunctions reflect the time course of the attentional blink. *Attention, Perception, & Psychophysics, 73*, 1361–1373.

Bouvier, S., & Treisman, A. (2010). Visual feature binding requires reentry. *Psychological Science, 21*, 202–204.

Bower, G. H. (2000). A brief history of memory research. In E. Tulving & F. I. M. Craik (Eds.), *The Oxford handbook of memory* (pp. 3–32). New York: Oxford University Press.

Bower, G. H. (2008). The evolution of a cognitive psychologist: A journey from simple behavior to complex mental acts. *Annual Review of Psychology, 59*, 1–27.

Bower, G. H., & Clark, M. C. (1969). Narrative stories as mediators for serial learning. *Psychonomic Science, 14*, 181–182.

Bower, G. H., & Forgas, J. P. (2000). Affect, memory, and social cognition. In E. Eich, et al. (Eds.), *Cognition and emotion* (pp. 87–168). New York: Oxford University Press.

Bower, G. H., & Springston, F. (1970). Pauses as recoding points in letter series. *Journal of Experimental Psychology, 83*, 421–430.

Bower, G. H., & Winzenz, D. (1970). Comparison of associative learning strategies. *Psychonomic Science, 20*, 119–120.

Bowman, L. L., Levine, L. E., Waite, B. M., & Gendron, M. (2010). Can students really multitask? An experimental study of instant messaging while reading. *Computers & Education, 54*, 927–931.

Bradshaw, J. L., & Nettleton, N. C. (1974). Articulatory inference and the MOWN-DOWN heterophone effect. *Journal of Experimental Psychology, 102*, 88–94.

Brainerd, C. J., & Reyna, V. F. (2005). *The science of false memory*. New York: Oxford University Press.

Brandimonte, M. A., Einstein, G. O., & McDaniel, M. A. (Eds.). (2014). *Prospective memory: Theory and applications*. Psychology Press.

Brandimonte, M. A., & Gerbino, W. (1996). When imagery fails: Effects of verbal recoding on accessibility of visual memories. In C. Cornoldi, et al. (Eds.), *Stretching the imagination: Representation and transformation in mental imagery* (pp. 31–76). New York: Oxford University Press.

Brandimonte, M. A., Hitch, G. J., & Bishop, D. V. M. (1992). Influence of short-term memory codes on visual image processing: Evidence from image transformation tasks. *Journal of Experimental Psychology: Learning, Memory, and Cognition, 18,* 157–165.

Brann, E. T. H. (1991). *The World of the Imagination: Sum and Substance.* Savage, MD: Rowman & Littlefield.

Bransford, J. D., & Franks, J. J. (1971). Abstraction of linguistic ideas. *Cognitive Psychology, 2,* 331–350.

Bransford, J. D., & Stein, B. S. (1984). *The IDEAL problem solver.* New York: Freeman.

Bransford, J. D., Brown, A. L., & Cocking, R. R. (2000). *How people learn: Brain, mind, experience, and school* (expanded edition). Washington, DC: National Academy Press.

Bransford, J. D., Franks, J. J., Morris, C. D., & Stein, B. S. (1979). Some general constraints on learning and memory research. In L. S. Cermak & F. I. M. Craik (Eds.), *Levels of processing in human memory* (pp. 331–354). Hillsdale, NJ: Erlbaum.

Branthwaite, A., & Rogers, D. (1985). Introduction. In A. Branthwaite & D. Rogers (Eds.), *Children growing up* (pp. 1–2). Milton Keynes, UK: Open University Press.

Brewer, N., Weber, N., & Semmler, C. (2005). Eyewitness identification. In N. Brewer & K. D. Williams (Eds.), *Psychology and law: An empirical perspective* (pp. 177–221). New York: Guilford.

Brewer, W. F. (2000). Bartlett's concept of the schema and its impact on theories of knowledge representation in contemporary cognitive psychology. In A. Saito (Ed.), *Bartlett, culture and cognition* (pp. 69–89). East Sussex, UK: Psychology Press.

Brewer, W. F., & Treyens, J. C. (1981). Role of schemata in memory for places. *Cognitive Psychology, 13,* 207–230.

Brewin, C. R. (2011). The nature and significance of memory disturbance in posttraumatic stress disorder. *Annual Review of Clinical Psychology, 7,* 203–227.

Brewin, C. R., Gregory, J. D., Lipton, M., & Burgess, N. (2010). Intrusive images in psychological disorders: Characteristics, neural mechanisms, and treatment implications. *Psychological Review, 117,* 210–232.

Briggs, F., & Usrey, W. M. (2010). Visual system structure. In E. B. Goldstein (Ed.) *Encyclopedia of perception* (Vol. **2.**, pp. 1130–1134). Thousand Oaks, CA: Sage.

Brigham, J. C., Bennett, L. B., Meissner, C. A., & Mitchell, T. L. (2007). The influence of race on eyewitness memory. In R. C. L. Lindsay, D. F. Ross, J. D. Read, & M. P. Toglia (Eds.), *Handbook of eyewitness psychology* (Vol. **2,** pp. 257–281). Mahwah, NJ: Erlbaum.

Britton, B. K. (1996). Rewriting: The arts and sciences of improving expository instructional text. In C. Michael Levy & S. Ransdell (Eds.), *The science of writing: Theories, methods, individual differences, and applications* (pp. 323–345). Mahwah, NJ: Erlbaum.

Broadbent, D. E. (1958). *Perception and communication.* New York: Pergamon.

Bromme, R., Jucks, R., & Wagner, T. (2005). How to refer to 'diabetes'? Language in online health advice. *Applied Cognitive Psychology, 19,* 569–586.

Brown, A. S. (2012). *The tip of the tongue state.* New York: Psychology Press.

Brown, C. H., & Sinnott, J. M. (2006). Cross-species comparisons of vocal perception. In S. Greenberg & W. A. Ainsworth (Eds.), *Listening to speech: An auditory perspective* (pp. 183–201). Mahwah, NJ: Erlbaum.

Brown, J. (1958). Some tests of the decay theory of immediate memory. *Quarterly Journal of Experimental Psychology, 10,* 12–21.

Brown, J. (2004). Memory: Biological basis. In R. L. Gregory (Ed.), *The Oxford companion to the mind* (2nd ed., pp. 564–568). New York: Oxford University Press.

Brown, M., Salverda, A. P., Dilley, L. C., & Tanenhaus, M. K. (2011). Expectations from preceding prosody influence segmentation in online sentence processing. *Psychonomic Bulletin and Review, 18,* 1189–1196.

Brown, N. R., & Siegler, R. S. (1992). The role of availability in the estimation of national populations. *Memory & Cognition, 20,* 406–412.

Brown, N. R., Cui, X., & Gordon, R. D. (2002). Estimating national populations: Cross-cultural differences and availability effects. *Applied Cognitive Psychology, 16,* 811–827.

Brown, R., & Kulik, J. (1977). Flashbulb memories. *Cognition, 5,* 73–99.

Brown, R., & McNeill, D. (1966). The "tip of the tongue" phenomenon. *Journal of Verbal Learning and Verbal Behavior, 5,* 325–377.

Brown-Schmidt, S., Gunlogson, C., & Tanenhaus, M. K. (2008). Addressees distinguish shared from private information when interpreting questions during interactive conversation. *Cognition, 107,* 1122–1134.

Bruce, V., Green, P. R., & Georgeson, M. A. (2003). *Visual perception* (4th ed.). Hove, UK: Psychology Press.

Bruce, V., Henderson, A., Newman, C., & Burton, A. M. (2001). Matching identities of familiar and unfamiliar faces caught on CCTV images. *Journal of Experimental Psychology: Applied, 7,* 207–218.

Bruck, M., & Ceci, S. J. (1999). The suggestibility of children's memory. *Annual Review of Psychology, 50,* 419–439.

Bruine de Bruin, W., (2011). Framing effects in surveys: How respondents make sense of the questions we ask. In G. Keren (Ed.), *Perspectives on framing* (pp. 303–324). New York: Psychology Press.

Bruner, J. (1997). Will cognitive revolutions ever stop? In D. M. Johnson & C. E. Erneling (Eds.), *The future of the cognitive revolution* (pp. 279–292). New York: Oxford University Press.

Bruning, R. H., Schraw, G. J., & Ronning, R. R. (1999). *Cognitive psychology and instruction* (3rd ed.). Upper Saddle River, NJ: Prentice Hall.

Bruno, L., Zarrinpar, A., & Kosslyn, S. M., (2003). Do separate processes identify objects as exemplars versus members of basic-level categories? Evidence from hemispheric specialization. *Brain and Cognition, 53*, 15–27.

Bryant, D. J., & Tversky, B. (1999). Mental representations of perspective and spatial relations from diagrams and models. *Journal of Experimental Psychology: Learning, Memory, and Cognition, 25*, 137–156.

Buckner, R. L. (2010). The role of the hippocampus in prediction and imagination. *Annual Review of Psychology, 61*, 27–48.

Buehler, R., Griffin, D., & Ross, M. (2002). Inside the planning fallacy: The causes and consequences of optimistic time predictions. In T. Gilovich, D. Griffin, & D. Kahneman (Eds.), *Heuristics and biases: The psychology of intuitive judgment* (pp. 250–270). New York: Cambridge University Press.

Buehler, R., Griffin, D., Lama, C. H., & Deslaurier, J. (2012). Perspectives on prediction: Does third-person imagery improve task completion estimates? *Organizational Behavior and Human Decision Processes, 117*, 138–149.

Bull, R., & Espy, K. A. (2006). Working memory, executive functioning, and children's mathematics. In S. J. Pickering (Ed.), *Working memory and education* (pp. 93–123). Burlington, MA: Elsevier.

Bunce, D., & Macready, A. (2005). Processing speed, executive function, and age differences in remembering and knowing. *Quarterly Journal of Experimental Psychology, 58A*, 155–168.

Bundesen, C., & Habekost, T. (2005). Attention. In K. Lamberts & R. L. Goldstone (Eds.), *Handbook of cognition.* Thousand Oaks, CA: Sage.

Burke, D. M. (2006). Representation and aging. In E. Bialystok & F. I. M. Craik (Eds.), *Lifespan cognition: Mechanisms of change* (pp. 193–206). New York: Oxford University Press.

Burns, D. J. (2006). Assessing distinctiveness: Measures of item-specific and relational processing. In R. R. Hunt & J. B. Worthen (Eds.), *Distinctiveness and memory* (pp. 109–130). New York: Oxford University Press.

Burton, A. M., Wilson, S., Cowan, M., & Bruce, V. (1999). Face recognition in poor-quality video: Evidence from security surveillance. *Psychological Science, 10*, 243–248.

Bus, A. G., & van IJzendoorn, M. H. (1999). Phonological awareness and early reading: A meta-analysis of experimental training studies. *Journal of Educational Psychology, 91*, 403–414.

Bushman, B. J. (1998). Effects of television violence on memory for commercial messages. *Journal of Experimental Psychology: Applied, 4*, 291–307.

Bushman, B. J. (2005). Violence and sex in television programs do not sell products in advertisements. *Psychological Science, 16*, 702–708.

Bushman, B. J., & Gibson, B. (2011). Violent video games cause an increase in aggression long after the game has been turned off. *Social Psychological and Personality Science, 2*, 29–32.

Bushman, B. J., & Huesmann, L. R. (2010). Aggression. In S. K. Fiske, D. T. Gilbert, & G. Lindzey (Eds.), *Handbook of social psychology* (5th ed., pp. 833–863). Hoboken, NJ: Wiley.

Butcher, K. R., & Kintsch, W. (2003). Text comprehension and discourse processing. In A. F. Healy & R. W. Proctor (Eds.), *Handbook of psychology* (Vol. **4**, pp. 575–595). Hoboken, NJ: Wiley.

Byrne, R. M. J. & Johnson-Laird, P. N. (2009). "If" and the problems of conditional reasoning. *Trends in Cognitive Sciences, 13*, 282–287.

Cacioppo, J. T. (2007), December. *The structure of psychology. Association for Psychological Science, 3*, 50–51.

Cacioppo, J. T., & Berntson, G. G. (2005b). Volume overview: Analyses of the social brain through the lens of human brain imaging. In J. T. Cacioppo & G. G. Berntson (Eds.), *Social neuroscience: Key readings* (pp. 1–17). New York: Psychology Press.

Cacioppo, J. T., & Berntson, G. G. (Eds.). (2005a). *Social neuroscience: Key readings.* New York: Psychology Press.

Cain, K. (2006). Children's reading comprehension: The role of working memory in normal and impaired development. In S. J. Pickering (Ed.), *Working memory and education* (pp. 61–91). Burlington, MA: Elsevier.

Calbris, G. (2011). *Elements of meaning in gesture.* Philadelphia: John Benjamins.

Calkins, M. W. (1910). The teaching of elementary psychology in colleges supposed to have no laboratory. *Psychological Monographs, 124*(51), 41–53.

Calvo-Merino, B., Glaser, D. E., Grèzes, J., Passingham, R. E., & Haggard, P. (2005). Action observation and acquired motor skills: An fMRI study with expert dancers. *Cerebral Cortex, 15*, 1243–1249.

Cameron, C. D., Payne, B. K., & Doris, J. M. (2013). Morality in high definition: Emotion differentiation calibrates the influence of incidental disgust on moral judgments. *Journal of Experimental Social Psychology, 49*, 719–725.

Campbell, J., & Mayer, R. E. (2009). Questioning as an instructional method: Does it affect learning from lectures? *Applied Cognitive Psychology, 23*, 747–759.

Campbell, R., & Sais, E. (1995). Accelerated metalinguistic (phonological) awareness in bilingual children. *British Journal of Developmental Psychology, 13*, 61–68.

Campitelli, G., & Gobet, F. (2010). Herbert Simon's decision-making approach: Investigations of cognitive processes in experts. *Review of General Psychology, 14*, 354–364.

Cannon-Bowers, J. A., & Salas, E. (Eds.). (1998). *Making decisions under stress: Implications for individuals and team training.* Washington, DC: American Psychological Association.

Cansino, S., Guzzon, D., Martinelli, M., Barollo, M., & Casco, C. (2011). Effects of aging on interference control in selective attention and working memory. *Memory & Cognition, 39*, 1409–1422.

Caplan, P. J., & Caplan, J. B. (2009). *Thinking critically about research on sex and gender* (3rd ed.). Boston, MA: Pearson.

Caplan, D., & Waters, G. S. (1999). Verbal working memory and sentence comprehension. *Behavioral and brain Sciences, 22*, 77–94.

Caramazza, A., & Miozzo, M. (1997). The relation between syntactic and phonological knowledge in lexical access: Evidence from the "tip-of-the-tongue" phenomenon. *Cognition, 69*, 309–343.

Carli, L. L. (1999). Cognitive reconstruction, hindsight, and reactions to victims and perpetrators. *Personality and Social Psychology Bulletin, 25*, 966–979.

Carlson, L. A. (2010) Top-down and bottom-up processing. In E. B. Goldstein (Ed.), *Encyclopedia of perception* (Vol. **2**, pp. 1011–1013). Thousand Oaks, CA: Sage.

Carlson, S. M. (2005). Developmentally sensitive measures of executive function in preschool children. *Developmental Neuropsychology, 28*, 595–616.

Carney, R. N., & Levin, J. R. (2001). Remembering the names of unfamiliar animals: Keywords as keys to their kingdom. *Applied Cognitive Psychology, 15*, 133–143.

Carney, R. N., & Levin, J. R. (2011). Delayed mnemonic benefits for a combined pegword-keyword strategy, time after time, rhyme after rhyme. *Applied Cognitive Psychology, 25*, 204–2011.

Carpenter, P. A., & Just, M. A. (1999). Computational modeling of high-level cognition versus hypothesis testing. In R. J. Sternberg (Ed.), *The nature of cognition* (pp. 245–293). Cambridge, MA: MIT Press.

Carpenter, P. A., Miyake, A., & Just, M. A. (1995). Language comprehension: Sentence and discourse processing. *Annual Review of Psychology, 46*, 91–120.

Carpenter, S. K., Pashler, H., & Cepeda, N. J. (2009). Using tests to enhance 8th grade students' retention of US history facts. *Applied Cognitive Psychology, 23*, 760–771.

Carpenter, S. K., Pashler, H., & Vul, E. (2006). What types of learning are enhanced by a cued recall test?. *Psychonomic Bulletin & Review, 13*, 826–830.

Carpenter, S. K., Pashler, H., Wixted, J. T., & Vul, E. (2008). The effects of tests on learning and forgetting. *Memory & Cognition, 36*, 438–448.

Carpenter, S. K., & DeLosh, E. L. (2005). Application of the testing and spacing effects to name learning. *Applied Cognitive Psychology, 19*, 619–636.

Carr, W., & Roskos-Ewoldsen, B. (1999). Spatial orientation by mental transformation. *Psychological Research/Psychologische Forschung, 62*, 36–47.

Carraher, T. N., Carraher, D. W., & Schliemann, A. D. (1985). Mathematics in the streets and in schools. *British Journal of Developmental Psychology, 3*, 21–29.

Carreiras, M., Armstrong, B. C., Perea, M., & Frost, R. (2013). The what, when, where, and how of visual word recognition. *Trends in Cognitive Sciences, 18*, 90–98.

Carroll, D. W. (2004). *Psychology of language* (4th ed.). Belmont, CA: Thomson Wadsworth.

Carroll, D. W. (2008). *Psychology of language* (5th ed.). Belmont, CA: Thomson Wadsworth.

Carstensen, L. L. (2007, Winter). Growing old or living long: Take your pick. *Issues in Science and Technology*, pp. 41–50.

Cassady, J. (2004). The impact of cognitive test anxiety on text comprehension and recall in the absence of external evaluative pressure. *Applied Cognitive Psychology, 18*, 311–325.

Castelhano, M. S., & Rayner, K. (2008). Eye movements during reading, visual search and scene perception: An overview. In K. Rayner, D. Shen, X. Bai, & G. Yan (Eds.), *Cognitive and cultural influences on eye movements* (pp. 3–33). Tianjin, China: Tianjin People's Publishing House.

Castelli, P., Goodman, G. S., Edelstein, R. S., Mitchell, E. B., Alonso, P. M. P., Lyons, K. E., & Newton, J. W. (2006). Evaluating eyewitness testimony in adults and children. In I. B. Weiner & A. K. Hess (Eds.), *The handbook of forensic psychology* (3rd ed., pp. 243–304). Hoboken, NJ: Wiley.

Ceballo, R. (1999). Negotiating the life narrative: A dialogue with an African American social worker. *Psychology of Women Quarterly, 23,* 309–321.

Ceci, S. J., & Liker, J. K. (1986). A day at the races: A study of IQ, expertise, and cognitive complexity. *Journal of Experimental Psychology: General, 115,* 255–266.

Cepeda, N. J., Pashler, H., Vul, E., Wixted, J. T., & Rohrer, D. (2006). Distributed practice in verbal recall tasks: A review and quantitative synthesis. *Psychological Bulletin, 132,* 354–380.

Cha, C. B., Pashler, H., Vul, E., Wixted, J. T., & Rohrer, D. (2010). Attentional bias toward suicide-related stimuli predicts suicidal behavior. *Journal of Abnormal Psychology, 119,* 616–622.

Chabris, C. F., & Simons, D. J. (2010). *The invisible gorilla and other ways our intuitions deceive us.* New York: Crown.

Chafe, W., & Danielewicz, J. (1987). Properties of spoken and written language. In R. Horowitz & S. J. Samuels (Eds.), *Comprehending oral and written language* (pp. 83–113). San Diego: Academic Press.

Chalmers, D. (2007). The hard problem of consciousness. In M. Velmans & S. Schneider (Eds.), *The Blackwell companion to consciousness* (pp. 225–235). Malden, MA: Blackwell.

Chambers, D., & Reisberg, D. (1985). Can mental images be ambiguous? *Journal of Experimental Psychology: Human Perception and Performance, 11,* 317–328.

Chan, J. C. K., & McDermott, K. B. (2006). Remembering pragmatic inferences. *Applied Cognitive Psychology, 20,* 633–639.

Chang, F., Dell, G. S., & Bock, K. (2006). Becoming syntactic. *Psychological review, 113,* 234.

Chapman, L. J., & Chapman, J. P. (1969). Illusory correlations as an obstacle to the use of valid psycho-diagnostic signs. *Journal of Abnormal Psychology, 74,* 271–280.

Chapman, P., & Underwood, G. (2000). Forgetting near-accidents: The roles of severity, culpability and experience in the poor recall of dangerous driving situations. *Applied Cognitive Psychology, 14,* 31–44.

Chein, J. M., Weisberg, R. W., Streeter, N. L., & Kwok, S. (2010). Working memory and insight in the nine-dot problem. *Memory & Cognition, 38,* 883–892.

Chen, Z., Mo, L., & Honomichl, R. (2004). Having the memory of an elephant: Long-term retrieval and the use of analogues in problem solving. *Journal of Experimental Psycholgoy: General, 133,* 415–433.

Chenoweth, N. A., & Hayes, J. R. (2001). Fluency in writing. *Written Communication, 18,* 80–98.

Cherry, C. (1953). Some experiments on the recognition of speech with one and with two ears. *Journal of the Acoustical Society of America, 25,* 975–979.

Chi, M. T. H. (1981). Knowledge development and memory performance. In M. Friedman, J. P. Das, & N. O'Connor (Eds.), *Intelligence and learning* (pp. 221–230). New York: Plenum.

Chi, M. T. H. (2006). Two approaches to the study of experts' characteristics. In K. A. Ericsson, N. Charness, P. J. Feltovich, & R. R. Hoffman (Eds.), *The Cambridge handbook of expertise and expert performance* (pp. 21–30). New York: Cambridge University Press.

Chi, M. T. H., & Ohlsson, S. (2005). Complex declarative learning. In K. J. Holyoak & R. G. Morrison (Eds.), *The Cambridge handbook of thinking and reasoning* (pp. 371–399). New York: Cambridge University Press.

Chiang, E. S., Therriault, D. J., & Franks, B. A. (2010). Individual differences in relative metacomprehension accuracy: Variation within and across task manipulations. *Metacognition and Learning, 5,* 121–135.

Chin-Parker, S., & Ross, B. H. (2004). Diagnosticity and prototypicality in category learning: A comparison of inference learning and classification learning. *Journal of Experimental Psyhcology: Learning, Memory, and Cognition, 30,* 216–236.

Chipman, S. F. (2004). Research on the women and mathematics issue: A personal case history. In A. M. Gallagher & J. C. Kaufman (Eds.), *Gender differences in mathematics: An integrative psychological approach* (pp. 1–24). New York: Cambridge University Press.

Chiroro, P. M., Tredoux, C. G., Radaelli, S., & Meissner, C. A. (2008). Recognizing faces across continents: The effect of within-race variations on the own-race bias in face recognition. *Psychonomic Bulletin & Review, 15,* 1089–1092.

Chomsky, N. (1957). *Syntactic structures.* The Hague: Mouton.

Chomsky, N. (1965). *Aspects of the theory of syntax.* Cambridge, MA: MIT Press.

Chomsky, N. (1975). *Reflections on language.* New York: Pantheon

Chomsky, N. (1981). *Lectures on government and binding.* Dordrecht, Netherlands: Foris.

Chomsky, N. (2000). *New horizons in the study of language and mind.* Cambridge, UK: Cambridge University Press.

Chomsky, N. (2002). *On nature and language.* Cambridge, UK: Cambridge University Press.

Chomsky, N. (2004). Language: Chomsky's theory. In R. L. Gregory (Ed.), *The Oxford companion to the mind* (2nd ed., pp. 511–513). New York: Oxford University Press.

Chomsky, N. (2006). *Language and mind* (3rd ed.). New York: Cambridge University Press.

Chong, S. C., Joo, S. J., Emmanouil, T.-A., & Treisman, A. (2008). Statistical processing: Not so implausible after all. *Perception & Psychophysics*, *70*, 1327–1334.

Chrisley, R. (2004). Artificial intelligence (AI). In R. L. Gregory (Ed.), *The Oxford companion to the mind* (2nd ed., pp. 61–63). New York: Oxford University Press.

Christensen, B. T., & Schunn, C. D. (2007). The relationship of analogical distance to analogical function and pre-inventive structure: The case of engineering design. *Memory & Cognition*, *35*, 29–38.

Christiansen, M. H. & Chater, N. (2016). *Creating language: Integrating evolution, acquisition, and processing*. Cambridge, MA: MIT Press.

Christiansen, M. H. & Chater, N. (2008). Language as shaped by the brain. *Behavioral & Brain Sciences*, *31*, 489–558.

Christiansen, M. H. & Chater, N. (1999). Toward a connectionist model of recursion in human linguistic performance. *Cognitive Science*, *23*, 157–205.

Christiansen, M. H., & Chater, N. (Eds.). (2001). *Connectionist psycholinguistics*. Greenwood Publishing Group.

Christianson, K., Luke, S. G., & Ferreira, F. (2010). Effects of plausibility on structural priming. *Journal of Experimental Psychology: Learning, Memory, and Cognition*, *36*, 538–544.

Christoffels, I. K., & De Groot, A. M. B. (2005). Simultaneous interpreting: A cognitive perspective. In J. F. Kroll & A. M. B. De Groot (Eds.), *Handbook of bilingualism: Psycholinguistic approaches* (pp. 454–479). New York: Oxford University Press.

Christoffels, I. K., De Groot, A. M. B., & Kroll, J. F. (2006). Memory and language skills in simultaneous interpreters: The role of expertise and language proficiency. *Journal of Memory and Language*, *54*, 324–345.

Christopher, G., & MacDonald, J. (2005). The impact of clinical depression on working memory. *Cognitive Neuropsychiatry*, *10*, 379–399.

Chu, M., & Kita, S. (2011). The nature of gestures' beneficial role in spatial problem solving. *Journal of Experimental Psychology: General*, *140*, 102–116.

Chun, M. M., & Wolfe, J. M. (2001). Visual attention. In E. B. Goldstein (Ed.), *Blackwell handbook of perception* (pp. 272–310). Malden, MA: Blackwell.

Chun, M. M., Golumb, J. D., & Turk-Browne, N. B. (2011). A taxonomy of external and internal attention. *Annual Review of Psychology*, *62*, 73–101.

Clark, A. (2013a). Whatever next? Predictive brains, situated agents, and the future of cognitive science. *Behavioral and Brain Sciences*, *36*, 181–204.

Clark, A. (2013b). *Mindware: An introduction to the philosophy of cognitive science*. Oxford University Press, Inc.

Clark, D. A. (2005). *Intrusive thoughts in clinical disorders: Theory, research, and treatment*. New York: Guilford Press.

Clark, H. H. (1985). Language use and language users. In G. Lindzey & E. Aronson (Eds.), *Handbook of social psychology* (2nd ed., Vol. **2**, pp. 179–231). New York: Random House.

Clark, H. H. (1994). Discourse in production. In M. A. Gernsbacher (Ed.), *Handbook of psycholinguistics* (pp. 985–1021). San Diego: Academic Press.

Clark, H. H., & Chase, W. G. (1972). On the process of comparing sentences against pictures. *Cognitive Psychology*, *3*, 472–517.

Clark, H. H., & Van Der Wege, M. M. (2002). Psycholinguistics. In D. Medin (Ed.), *Stevens' handbook of experimental psychology* (3rd ed., Vol. **2**, pp. 209–259). New York: Wiley.

Clark, H. H., & Wilkes-Gibbs, D. (1986). Referring as a collaborative process. *Cognition*, *22*, 1–39.

Cleary, M., & Pisoni, D. B. (2001). Speech perception and spoken word recognition: Research and theory. In E. B. Goldstein (Ed.), *Blackwell handbook of perception* (pp. 499–534). Malden, MA: Blackwell.

Clifton, C., Jr, & Staub, A. (2011). Syntactic influences on eye movements during reading. In S. P. Liversedge, I. D. Gilchrist, & S. Everling (Eds.), *The Oxford Handbook of Eye Movements* (pp. 895–909). Oxford, England: OUP.

Clifton, C., Staub, A., & Rayner, K. (2007). Eye movements in reading words and sentences. In R. van Gompel, M. H. Fischer, W. S. Murray, & R. L. Hill (Eds.), *Eye movements: A window on mind and brain* (pp. 341–372). Oxford, UK: Elsevier.

Close, J., Hahn, U., Hodgetts, C. J., & Pothos, E. M. (2010). Rules and similarity in adult concept learning. In D. Mareschal, P. C. Quinn, & S. E. G. Lea (Eds.), *The making of human concepts* (pp. 29–51). New York: Oxford University Press.

Clump, M. A. (2006). An active learning classroom activity for the "Cocktail Party Phenomenon." *Teaching of Psychology*, *33*, 51–53.

Cohen, A. L., Jaudas, A., Hirschhorn, E., Sobin, Y., & Gollwitzer, P. M. (2012). The specificity of prospective memory costs. *Memory*, *20*(8), 848–864.

Cohen, D. J., White, S., & Cohen, S. B. (2011). A time use diary: Study of adult everyday writing behavior. *Written Communication*, *28*, 3–33.

Collet, C., Clarion, A., Morel, M., Chapon, A., & Petit, C. (2009). Physiological and behavioural changes associated to the management of secondary tasks while driving. *Applied Ergonomics, 40*, 1041–1046.

Collins, A. M., & Loftus, E. F. (1975). A spreading-activation theory of semantic memory. *Psychological Review, 82*, 407–428.

Collins, J. L. (1998). *Strategies for struggling writers.* New York: Guilford.

Collins, M. A., & Amabile, T. M. (1999). Motivation and creativity. In R. J. Sternberg (Ed.), *Handbook of creativity* (pp. 297–312). New York: Cambridge University Press.

Coltheart, M. (2005). Modeling reading: The dual-route approach. In J. Snowling & C. Hulme (Eds.), *The science of reading: A handbook* (pp. 6–23). Malden, MA: Blackwell.

Coluccia, E. (2008). Learning from maps: The role of visuo-spatial working memory. *Applied Cognitive Psychology, 22*, 217–233.

Coluccia, E., Bianco, C., & Brandimonte, M. A. (2010). Autobiographical and event memories for surprising and unsurprising events. *Applied Cognitive Psychology, 24*, 177–199.

Comeau, L., & Genesee, F. (2001). Bilingual children's repair strategies during dyadic communication. In J. Cenoz & F. Genesee (Eds.), *Trends in bilingual acquisition* (pp. 231–256). New York: John Benjamins.

Connor, L. T., Dunlosky, J., & Hertzog, C. (1997). Age-related differences in absolute but not relative metamemory accuracy. *Psychology and Aging, 12*, 50–71.

Connor-Greene, P. A. (2000). Making connections: Evaluating the effectiveness of journal writing in enhancing student learning. *Teaching of Psychology, 27*, 44–46.

Conrad, R., & Hull, A. J. (1964). Information, acoustic confusion, and, memory span. *British Journal of Psychology, 55*, 432–439.

Conway, A. R. A., Cowan, N., & Bunting, M. F. (2001). The cocktail party phenomenon revisited: The importance of working memory capacity. *Psychonomic Bulletin & Review, 8*, 331–335.

Conway, A. R. A., Jarrold, C., Kane, M., Miyake, A., & Towse, J. (Eds.). (2007). *Variation in working memory.* New York: Oxford University Press.

Conway, A. R. A., Skitka, L. J., Hemmerich, J. A., & Kershaw, T. C. (2009). Flashbulb for 11 September 2001. *Applied Cognitive Psychology, 23*, 605–623.

Conway, C. M., Loebach, J. L., & Pisoni, D. B. (2010). Speech perception. In E. B. Goldstein (Ed.), *Encyclopedia of perception* (Vol. **2**, pp. 918–923). Thousand Oaks, CA: Sage.

Conway, M. A., & Fthenaki, A. (2000). Disruption and loss of autobiographical memory. In F. Boller & J. Grafman (Eds.), *Handbook of neuropsychology* (2nd ed., Vol. **2**, pp. 281–312). Amsterdam: Elsevier.

Cook, V., & Bassetti, B. (Eds.). (2011). *Language and bilingual cognition.* New York: Psychology Press.

Cook, S. W., Duggan, K. A., Friedman, H. S., Cui+, J., & Popescu, V. (2017). Hand gesture and mathematics learning: Lessons from an avatar. *Cognitive Science, 41*, 518–535.

Cook, G. I., Marsh, R. L., & Hicks, J. L. (2005). Associating a time-based prospective memory task with an expected context can improve or impair intention completion. *Applied Cognitive Psychology, 19*, 345–360.

Cook, S. W., & Tanenhaus, M. K. (2009). Embodied communication: Speakers' gestures affect listeners' actions. *Cognition, 113*, 98–104.

Cooper, R. M. (1974). The control of eye fixation by the meaning of spoken language: A new methodology for the real-time investigation of speech perception, memory, and language processing. *Cognitive Psychology, 6*, 84–107.

Cooper, L. A., & Lang, J. M. (1996). Imagery and visual-spatial representations. In E. L. Bjork & R. A. Bjork (Eds.), *Memory* (pp. 129–164). San Diego: Academic Press.

Corballis, M. C. (2006). Language. In K. Pawlik & G. d'Ydewalle (Eds.), *Psychological concepts: An international historical perspective* (pp. 197–221). New York: Psychology Press.

Corballis, M. C., & Suddendorf, T. (2010). The evolution of concepts: A timely look. In D. Mareschal, P. C. Quinn, & S. E. G. Lea (Eds.), *The making of human concepts* (pp. 365–384). New York: Oxford University Press.

Coren, S., Ward, L. M., & Enns, J. T. (2004). *Sensation and perception* (6th ed.). Hoboken, NJ: Wiley.

Cosmides, L., & Tooby, J. (2006). Evolutionary psychology, moral heuristics, and the law. In G. Gigerenzer & C. Engel (Eds.), *Heuristics and the law* (pp. 175–205). Cambridge, MA: MIT Press.

Costa, A., Alario, F.-X., & Sebastián-Gallés, N. (2009). Cross-linguistic research on language production. In M. G. Gaskell (Ed.), *The Oxford handbook of psycholinguistics* (pp. 531–546). New York: Oxford University Press.

Countries of the World. (2012). *Information about France, Canada, and Japan.* Retrieved March 14, 2012, from www.infoplease.com/countries.html

Courage, M. L., & Cowan, N. (Eds.). (2009). *The development of memory in infancy and childhood.* New York: Psychology Press.

Cowan, N. (2005). *Working memory capacity.* New York: Psychology Press.

Cowan, N. (2010). The magical mystery four: How is working memory capacity limited, and why? *Current Directions in Psychological Science, 19,* 51–57.

Cowan, N., & Alloway, T. (2009). Development of working memory in childhood. In M. Courage & N. Cowan (Eds.), *The development of memory in childhood* (pp. 303–342). Hove, UK: Psychology Press.

Cowan, N., Morey, C. C., Chen, Z., & Bunting, M. F. (2007). What do estimates of working memory capacity tell us? In N. Osaka & R. Logie (Eds.), *Working memory: Behavioural & neural correlates.* New York: Oxford University Press.

Coward, L. A., & Sun, R. (2004). Criteria for an effective theory of consciousness and some preliminary attempts. *Consciousness and Cognition, 13,* 268–301.

Cowley, S. J. (2011). Distributed language. In S. J. Cowley (Ed.), *Distributed language* (pp. 1–14). Philadelphia: John Benjamins.

Cox, W. M., Fadardi, J. S., & Pothos, E. M. (2006). The addiction-Stroop test: Theoretical considerations and procedural recommendations. *Psychological Bulletin, 132,* 443–476.

Craik, F. I. M. (1990). Changes in memory with normal aging: A functional view. In R. J. Wurtman (Ed.), *Advances in neurology: Vol. 51. Alzheimer's disease* (pp. 201–205). New York: Raven.

Craik, F. I. M. (1999). Levels of encoding and retrieval. In B. H. Challis & B. M. Velichkovsky (Eds.), *Stratification in cognition and consciousness* (pp. 97–104). Philadelphia: John Benjamins.

Craik, F. I. M., & Lockhart, R. S. (1972). Levels of processing: A framework for memory research. *Journal of Verbal Learning and Verbal Behavior, 11,* 671–684.

Craik, F. I. M., & Tulving, E. (1975). Depth of processing and the retention of words in episodic memory. *Journal of Experimental Psychology: General, 104,* 268–294.

Craske, M. G. (2010). *Cognitive-behavioral therapy.* Washington, DC: American Psychological Association.

Craver-Lemley, C., & Reeves, A. (1992). How visual imagery interferes with vision. *Psychological Review, 99,* 633–649.

Critcher, C. R., Inbar, Y., & Pizarro, D. A. (2013). How quick decisions illuminate moral character. *Social Psychological and Personality Science, 4,* 308–315.

Cromdal, J. (1999). Childhood bilingualism and metalinguistic skills: Analysis and control in young Swedish-English bilinguals. *Applied Psycholinguistics, 20,* 1–20.

Cromer, L. D., & Freyd, J. J. (2007). What influences believing child sexual abuse disclosures? The roles of depicted memory persistence, participant gender, trauma history, and sexism. *Psychology of Women, 31,* 13–22.

Cuddy, A. J. C., & Fiske, S. T. (2002). Doddering but dear: Process, content, and function in stereotyping of older persons. In T. D. Nelson (Ed.), *Ageism: Stereotyping and prejudice against older persons* (pp. 3–26). Cambridge, MA: MIT Press.

Cuevas, K., Rovee-Collier, C., & Learmonth, A. E. (2006). Infants form associations between memory representations of stimuli that are absent. *Psychological Science, 17,* 543–549.

Curci, A., & Luminet, O. (2009). Flashbulb memories for expected events: A test of the emotional-integrative model. *Applied Cognitive Psychology, 23,* 98–114.

Curtin, S., & Werker, J. E. (2009). The perceptual foundations of phonological development. In M. G. Gaskell (Ed.), *The Oxford handbook of psycholinguistics* (pp. 579–599). New York: Oxford University Press.

Dąbrowska, E. (2012) "Different speakers, different grammars: Individual differences in native language attainment". *Linguistic Approaches to Bilingualism, 2,* 219–253.

Dahan, D. (2010). Word recognition. In E. B. Goldstein (Ed.), *Encyclopedia of perception* (Vol. **2**, pp. 1141–1145). Thousand Oaks, CA: Sage.

Dahan, D., & Magnuson, J. S. (2006). Spoken word recognition. In M. J. Traxler & M. A. Gernsbacher (Eds.), *Handbook of psycholinguistics* (2nd ed., pp. 249–283). Amsterdam: Elsevier.

Dahan, D. & Tanenhaus, M. K. (2004). Continuous mapping from sound to meaning in spoken-language comprehension: Evidence from immediate effects of verb-based constraints. *Journal of Experimental Psychology: Learning, Memory & Cognition, 30,* 498–513.

Dahlstrom-Hakki, I., Pollatsek, A., Fisher, D. L., & Miller, B. (2008). Eye movements and individual differences in mental rotation. In K. Rayner, D. Shen, X. Bai, & G. Yan (Eds.), *Cognitive and cultural influences on eye movements* (pp. 210–232). Tianjin, China: Tianjin People's Publishing House.

Dale, R., Kehoe, C., & Spivey, M. J. (2007). Graded motor responses in the time course of categorizing atypical exemplars. *Memory & Cognition, 35,* 15–28.

Damian, M. F., & Martin, R. C. (1999). Semantic and phonological codes interact in a single word production. *Journal of Experimental Psychology: Learning, Memory, and Cognition, 25,* 345–361.

Daneman, M., & Carpenter, P. A. (1980). Individual differences in working memory and reading. *Journal of verbal learning and verbal behavior, 19,* 450–466.

Daneman, M. F., & Stainton, M. (1993). The generation effect in reading and proofreading. *Reading and Writing: An Interdisciplinary Journal, 5*, 297–313.

Danziger, S., & Ward, R. (2010). Language changes implicit associations between ethnic groups and evaluation in bilinguals. *Psychological Science, 21*, 799–800.

Dargan, P., Reid, G., & Hodge, S. (2015). Exploring the role of mental imagery in the experience of self-injury: An interpretative phenomenological analysis. *Behavioural and Cognitive Psychotherapy*, 1–12. https://doi.org/10.1017/S1352465814000666

Darwin, C. J., Turvey, M. T., & Crowder, R. G. (1972). An auditory analogue of the Sperling partial report procedure: Evidence for brief auditory storage. *Cognitive Psychology, 3*, 255–267.

Davelaar, E. J., Goshen-Gottstein, Y., Ashkenazi, A., Haarmann, H. J., & Usher, M. (2005). The demise of short-term memory revisited: Empirical and computational investigations of recency effects. *Psychological Review, 112*, 3–42.

Davelaar, E. J., Haarmann, H. J., Goshen-Gottstein, Y., & Usher, M. (2006). Semantic similarity dissociates short- from long-term effects: Testing a neurocomputational model of list memory. *Memory & Cognition, 34*, 323–334.

Davenport, T., & Coulson, S. (2011). Predictability and novelty in literal language comprehension: An ERP study. *Brain Research, 1418*, 70–82.

Davidson, D. (1994). Recognition and recall of irrelevant and interruptive atypical actions in script-based stories. *Journal of Memory and Language, 33*, 757–775.

Davidson, D. (2006). Memory for bizarre and other unusual events: Evidence from script research. In R. R. Hunt & J. B. Worthen (Eds.), *Distinctiveness and memory* (pp. 157–179). New York: Oxford University Press.

Davidson, J. E. (1995). The suddenness of insight. In R. J. Sternberg & J. E. Davidson (Eds.), *The nature of insight* (pp. 125–155). Cambridge, MA: MIT Press.

Davidson, J. E., & Sternberg, R. J. (1998). Smart problem solving: How metacognition helps. In D. J. Hacker, J. Dunlosky, & A. C. Graesser (Eds.), *Meta-cognition in educational theory and practice* (pp. 47–65). Mahwah, NJ: Erlbaum.

Davies, G. M., & Wright, D. B. (2010b). Introduction. In G. M. Davies & D. B. Wright (Eds.), *Current issues in applied memory research* (pp. 1–7). New York: Psychology Press.

Davies, G. M., & Wright, D. B. (Eds.). (2010a). *Current issues in applied memory research* (pp. 1–7). New York: Psychology Press.

Davies, S. P. (2005). Planning and problem solving in well-defined domains. In R. Morris & G. Ward (Eds.), *The cognitive psychology of planning* (pp. 35–51). Hove, UK: Psychology Press.

Davis, D., & Friedman, R. D. (2007). Memory for conversation: The orphan child of witness memory researchers. In M. P. Toglia, J. D. Read, D. F. Ross, & R. C. L. Lindsay (Eds.), *Handbook of eyewitness psychology* (Vol. 1, pp. 3–52). Mahwah, NJ: Erlbaum.

Davis, D., & Loftus, E. F. (2007). Internal and external sources of misinformation in adult witness memory. In M. P. Toglia, J. D. Read, D. F. Ross, & R. C. L. Lindsay (Eds.), *Handbook of eyewitness psychology* (Vol. 1, pp. 195–237). Mahwah, NJ: Erlbaum.

Davis, M. H., Marslen-Wilson, W. D., & Gaskell, M. G. (2002). Leading up the lexical garden path: Segmentation and ambiguity in spoken word recognition. *Journal of Experimental Psychology: Human Perception and Performance, 28*, 218–244.

Davis, T., & Love, B. C. (2010). Memory for category information is idealized through contrast with competing options. *Psychological Science, 21*, 234–242.

de Bot, K., & Makoni, S. (2005). *Language and aging in multilingual contexts.* Clevedon, UK: Multilingual Matters.

de Boysson-Bardies, B. (1999). *How language comes to children: From birth to two years.* Cambridge, MA: MIT Press.

De Dreu, C., Baas, M., & Nijstad, B. A. (2008). Hedonic tone and activation level in the mood-creativity link: Toward a dual pathway to creativity model. *Journal of Personality and Social Psychology, 94*, 739–756.

De Groot, A. M. B. (2011). *Language and cognition in bilinguals and multilinguals: An introduction.* New York: Psychology Press.

De Haan, E. H. F., Young, A. W., & Newcombe, F. (1991). Covert and overt recognition in prosopagnosia. *Brain, 114*, 2575–2591.

De Houwer, J., Teige-Mocigemba, S., Spruyt, A., & Moors, A. (2009). Implicit measures: A normative analysis and review. *Psychological Bulletin, 135*, 347–368.

de Jong, P. F. (2006). Understanding normal and impaired reading development: A working memory perspective. In S. J. Pickering (Ed.), *Working memory and education* (pp. 33–60). Burlington, MA: Elsevier.

De Koning, B. B., Tabbers, H. K., Rikers, R. M. J. P., & Paas, F. (2011). Improved effectiveness of cueing by self-explanations when learning from a complex animation. *Applied Cognitive Psychology, 25*, 183–194.

De Lissnyder, E., Koster, E. H. W., Derakshan, N., & De Raedt, R. (2010). The association between depressive symptoms and executive control impairments in response to emotional and non-emotional information. In N. Derakshan & M. Eysenck (Eds.), *Emotional states, attention, and working memory* (pp. 264–280). New York: Psychology Press.

De Neys, W., & Goel, V. (2011). Heuristics and biases in the brain: Dual neural pathways for decision making. In O. Vartanian & D. R. Mandel (Eds.), *Neuroscience of decision making* (pp. 125–141). New York: Psychology Press.

De Smedt, B., Janssen, R., Bouwens, K., Verschaffel, L., Boets, B., & Ghesquière, P. (2009). Working memory and individual differences in mathematics achievement: A longitudinal study from first grade to second grade. *Journal of Experimental Child Psychology, 103*(2), 186–201.

de Villiers, J. G., & de Villiers, P. A. (1999). Language development. In M. H. Bornstein & M. E. Lamb (Eds.), *Developmental psychology: An advanced textbook* (4th ed., pp. 313–373). Mahwah, NJ: Erlbaum.

Defeldre, A.-C. (2005). Inadvertent plagiarism in everyday life. *Applied Cognitive Psychology, 19*, 1033–1040.

Degen, J., & Tanenhaus, M. K. (2014). Processing scalar implicature: A constraint-based approach. *Cognitive Science, 39*, 667–710.

Dehaene, S., & Naccache, L. (2001). Towards a cognitive neuroscience of consciousness: Basic evidence and a workspace framework. In S. Dehaene (Ed.), *The cognitive neuroscience of consciousness* (pp. 1–37). Cambridge, MA: MIT Press.

Dehaene, S., Le Clec'H, G., Poline, J. B., Le Bihan, D., & Cohen, L. (2002). The visual word form area: A prelexical representation of visual words in the fusiform gyrus. *Neuroreport, 13*, 321–325.

Dehaene, S., Changeux, J. P., Naccache, L., Sackur, J., & Sergent, C. (2006). Conscious, preconscious, and subliminal processing: A testable taxonomy. *Trends in Cognitive Sciences, 10*, 204–211.

DeHart, G. B., Sroufe, L. A., & Cooper, R. G. (2004). *Child development: Its nature and course* (5th ed.). New York: McGraw Hill.

Delgado, M. R., Phelps, E. A., & Robbins, T. W. (Eds.). (2011). *Decision making, affect, and learning.* New York: Oxford University Press.

DeLong, K. A., Urbach, T. P., & Kutas, M. (2005). Probabilistic word pre-activation during language comprehension inferred from electrical brain activity. *Nature neuroscience, 8*, 1117–1121.

Dell, G. S. (1986). A spreading-activation theory of retrieval in sentence production. *Psychological Review, 93*, 283–321.

Dell, G. S. (1995). Speaking and misspeaking. In L. R. Gleitman & M. Liberman (Eds.), *Language* (pp. 183–208). Cambridge, MA: MIT Press.

Dell, G. S. (2005). Language production, lexical access, and aphasia. In G. Houghton (Ed.), *Connectionist models in cognitive psychology* (pp. 373–401). New York: Psychology Press.

Dell, G. S., & Chang, F. (2014). The P-chain: Relating sentence production and its disorders to comprehension and acquisition. *Philosophical Transactions of the Royal Society B: Biological Sciences, 369*, 20120394.

Dell, G. S., Burger, L. K., & Svec, W. R. (1997). Language production and serial order: A functional analysis and a model. *Psychological Review, 104*, 123–147.

Dell, G. S., Chang, F., & Griffin, Z. M. (1999). Connectionist models of language production: Lexical access and grammatical encoding. *Cognitive Science, 23*, 517–542.

Dell, G. S., Reed, K. D., Adams, D. R., & Meyer, A. S. (2000). Speech errors, phonotactic constraints, and implicit learning: A study of the role of experience in language production. *Journal of Experimental Psychology: Learning, Memory, and Cognition, 26*, 1355–1367.

Dell, G. S., Warker, J. A., & Whalen, C. A. (2008). Speech errors and the implicit learning of phonological sequences. In E. Morsella, J. A. Bargh, & P. M. Gollwitzer (Eds.), *The psychology of action.* New York: Oxford University Press.

DeLoache, J. S., Chiong, C., Sherman, K., Islam, N., Vanderborght, M., Troseth, GL, . . . O'Doherty K. (2010). Do babies learn from baby media? *Psychological Science, 21*, 1570–1574.

Denis, M., & Kosslyn, S. M. (1999). Scanning visual mental images: A window on the mind. *Cahiers de Psychologie Cognitive, 18*, 409–465.

Denis, M., Mellet, E., & Kosslyn, S. M. (2004). Neuroimaging of mental imagery: An introduction. *European Journal of Cognitive Psychology, 16*, 625–630.

Department of Veterans Affairs. (2010). *Mild traumatic brain injury-concussion.* Retrieved April 28, 2012, from http://www.publichealth.va.gov/docs/exposures/TBI-pocketcard.pdf

DePrince, A. P., & Freyd, J. J. (2004). Forgetting trauma stimuli. *Psychological Science, 15*, 488–492.

Derakshan, N., & Eysenck, M. (2010b). Introduction to the special issue: Emotional states, attention, and working memory. In N. Derakshan, & M. Eysenck (Eds.), *Emotional states, attention, and working memory* (pp. 189–199). New York: Psychology Press.

D'Esposito, M., Zarahn, E., & Aguirre, G. K. (1999). Event-related functional MRI: Implications for cognitive psychology. *Psychological Bulletin, 125*, 155–164.

Devlin, A. S. (2001). *Mind and maze: Spatial cognition and environmental behavior.* Westport, CT: Praeger.

deWinstanley, P. A., & Bjork, R. A. (2002). Successful lecturing: Presenting information in ways that engage effective processing. In D. F. Halpern & M. D. Hakel (Eds.), *Applying the science of learning to university teaching and beyond* (pp. 19–31). San Francisco: Jossey-Bass.

Diamond, A. (2006). The early development of executive functions. In E. Bialystok & F. Craik (Eds.), *Lifespan cognition: Mechanisms of change* (pp. 70–95). New York, NY: Oxford University Press.

Diamond, A., & Amso, D. (2008). Contributions of neuroscience to our understanding of cognitive development. *Current Directions in Psychological Science, 17*, 136–141.

Diana, R. A., & Reder, L. M. (2004). Visual and verbal metacognition: Are they really different? In D. T. Levin (Ed.), *Thinking and seeing: Visual metacognition in adults and children* (pp. 187–201). Cambridge, MA: MIT Press.

Diaz, M., & Benjamin, A. S. (2011). The effects of proactive interference (PI) and release from PI on judgments of learning. *Memory & Cognition, 39*, 196–203.

Diaz, R. M. (1985). Bilingual cognitive development: Addressing three gaps in current research. *Child Development, 56*, 1376–1388.

Dick, F., Bates, E., Wulfeck, B., Utman, J. A., Dronkers, N., & Gernsbacher, M. A. (2001). Language deficits, localization, and grammar: Evidence for a distributive model of language breakdown in aphasic patients and neurologically intact individuals. *Psychological Review, 108*, 759–788.

Diehl, R. L., Lotto, A. J., & Holt, L. L. (2004). Speech perception. *Annual Review of Psychology, 55*, 149–179.

Dietrich, A. (2007). Who's afraid of a cognitive neuroscience of creativity? *Methods, 42*, 22–27.

Dietrich, A., & Kanso, R. (2010). A review of EEG, ERP, and neuroimaging studies of creativity and insight. *Psychological Bulletin, 136*, 822–848.

Dijkerman, C. H., Ietswaart, M., & Johnston, M. (2010). Motor imagery and the rehabilitation of movement disorders: An overview. In A. Guillot & C. Collet (Eds.), *The neurophysiological foundations of mental and motor imagery* (pp. 127–142). New York: Oxford University Press.

Dijksterhuis, A., & Aarts, H. (2010). Goals, attention and (un)consciousness. *Annual Review of Psychology, 61*, 467–490.

Dikker, S., Rabagliati, H., Farmer, T. A., & Pylkkanen, L. (2010). Early occipital sensitivity to syntactic category is based on form typicality. *Psychological Science, 21*, 629–634.

Dikker, S., Rabagliati, H., & Pylkkänen, L. (2009). Sensitivity to syntax in visual cortex. *Cognition, 110*, 293–321.

Dismukes, R. K., & Nowinski, J. L. (2007). Prospective memory, concurrent task management, and pilot error. In A. Kramer, D. Wiegmann, & A. Kirlik (Eds.), *Attention: From theory to practice*. New York: Oxford University Press.

Dixon, R. A., & Cohen, A. L. (2003). Cognitive development in adulthood. In R. M. Lerner, M. A. Easterbrooks, & J. Mistry (Eds.), *Handbook of psychology* (Vol. **6**, pp. 443–461). Hoboken, NJ: Wiley.

Dodson, C. S., Bawa, S., & Krueger, L. F. (2007). Aging, metamemory, and high-confidence errors: A misrecollection account. *Psychology and Aging, 22*, 122–133.

Dominowski, R. L. (2002). *Teaching undergraduates*. Mahwah, NJ: Erlbaum.

Donaldson, M. (2004). Language: Learning word meanings. In R. L. Gregory (Ed.), *The Oxford companion to the mind* (2nd ed., pp. 513–515). New York: Oxford University Press.

Donderi, D. C. (2006). Visual complexity: A review. *Psychological Bulletin, 132*, 73–97.

Douglass, A. B., & Steblay, N. (2006). Memory distortion in eyewitnesses: A meta-analysis of the post-identification feedback effect. *Applied Cognitive Psychology, 20*, 859–869.

Doumas, L. A. A., & Hummel, J. E. (2012). Computation models of higher cognition. In K. J. Holyoak & R. G. Morrison (Eds.), *The Oxford handbook of thinking and reasoning* (pp. 52–66). New York: Oxford University Press.

Doumas, L. A. A., & Hummel, J. F. (2010). A computational account of the development of the generalization of shape information. *Cognitive Science, 34*, 698–712.

Doyle, R. A., & Voyer, D. (2016). Stereotype manipulation effects on math and spatial test performance: A meta-analysis. *Learning and Individual Differences, 47*, 103–116.

Drieghe, D., Brysbaert, M., Desmet, T., & DeBaecke, C. (2004). Word skipping in reading: On the interplay of linguistic and visual factors. In R. Radach, A. Kennedy, & K. Rayner (Eds.), *Eye movements and information processing during reading* (pp. 79–103). Hove, UK: Psychology Press.

Dror, I. E., & Kosslyn, S. M. (1994). Mental imagery and aging. *Psychology and Aging, 9*, 90–102.

Dube, C., Rotello, C. M., & Heit, E. (2010). Assessing the belief bias effect with ROCs: It's a response bias effect. *Psychological Review, 117*, 831–863.

Dube, C., Rotello, C. M., & Heit, E. (2011). The belief bias effect is aptly named: A reply to Klauer and Kellen (2011). *Psychological Review, 118*, 155–163.

Duchaine, B. C., & Nakayama, K. (2006). Developmental prosopagnosia: A window to content-specific face processing. *Current Opinion in Neurobiology, 16*, 166–173.

Duckworth, A. L., Kirby, T. A., Tsukayama, E., Berstein, H., & Anders Ericsson, K. (2011). Deliberate practice spells success: Why grittier competitors triumph at the National Spelling Bee. *Social Psychological and Personality Science, 2*, 174–181.

Dudukovic, N. M., Marsh, E. J., & Tversky, B. (2004). Telling a story or telling it straight: The effects of entertaining versus accurate retellings on memory. *Applied Cognitive Psychology, 18*, 125–143.

Duffy, G. G., Miller, S., Parsons, S., & Meloth, M. (2009). Teachers as metacognitive professionals. In D. J. Hacker, J. Dunlosky, & A. C. Graesser (Eds.), *Handbook of metacognition in education* (pp. 240–256). New York: Routledge.

Dunbar, K. (1998). Problem solving. In W. Bechtel & G. Graham (Eds.), *A companion to cognitive science* (pp. 289–298). Malden, MA: Blackwell.

Duncan, J. (1999). Attention. In R. A. Wilson & F. C. Keil (Eds.), *The MIT encyclopedia of the cognitive sciences* (pp. 39–41). Cambridge, MA: MIT Press.

Duncan, J. (2000). A neural basis for general intelligence. *Science, 289*, 457–460.

Duncker, K. (1945). On problem solving. *Psychological Monographs, 58* (Whole No. 270).

Dunlosky, J., & Bjork, R. A. (2008a). *Handbook of metamemory and memory*. New York: Psychology Press.

Dunlosky, J., & Bjork, R. A. (2008b). The integrated nature of metamemory and memory. In J. Dunlosky & R. A. Bjork (Eds.), *Handbook of metamemory and memory* (pp. 11–28). New York: Psychology Press.

Dunlosky, J., & Hertzog, C. (1998). Aging and deficits in associative memory: What is the role of strategy production? *Psychology and Aging, 13*, 597–607.

Dunlosky, J., & Lipko, A. R. (2007). Metacomprehension: A brief history and how to improve its accuracy. *Current Directions in Psychological Science, 16*, 228–232.

Dunlosky, J., & Metcalfe, J. (2009). *Metacognition*. Thousand Oaks, CA: Sage.

Dunlosky, J., Rawson, K. A., & Middleton, E. L. (2005). What constrains the accuracy of metacomprehension judgments? Testing the transfer-appropriate-monitoring and accessibility hypotheses. *Journal of Memory and Language, 52*, 551–565.

Dunn, J., & Kendrick, C. (1982). The speech of two- and three-year-olds to infant siblings: "Baby talk" and the context of communication. *Journal of Child Language, 9*, 579–595.

Dunning, D., & Sherman, D. A. (1997). Stereotypes and tacit inference. *Journal of Personality and Social Psychology, 73*, 459–471.

Dunning, D., Johnson, K., Ehrlinger, J., & Kruger, J. (2003). Why people fail to recognize their own incompetence. *Current Directions in Psychological Science, 12*, 83–87.

Dweck, C. S. (2006). *Mindset: The new psychology of success*. New York: Random House.

Dysart, J. E., & Lindsay, R. C. L. (2007). The effects of delay on eyewitness identification accuracy: Should we be concerned? In R. C. L. Lindsay, D. F. Ross, J. D. Read, & M. P. Toglia (Eds.), *Handbook of eyewitness psychology* (Vol. 2, pp. 361–376). Mahwah, NJ: Erlbaum.

D'Zurilla, T. J., & Maydeu-Olivares, A. (2004). Social problem solving: Theory and assessment. In E. C. Chang, T. J. D'Zurilla, & L. J. Sanna (Eds.), *Social problem solving: Theory, research, and training* (pp. 11–27). Washington, DC: American Psychological Association.

Eagly, A. H., & Carli, L. L. (2007). *Through the labyrinth: The truth about how women become leaders*. Boston: Harvard Business School Press.

Easton, A., & Emery, N. J. (Eds.). (2005). *The cognitive neuroscience of social behaviour* (pp. 1–16). New York: Psychology Press.

Economou, A., Simos, P. G., & Papanicolaou, A. C. (2006). Age-related memory decline. In A. C. Papanicolaou (Ed.), *The amnesias: A clinical textbook of memory disorders* (pp. 57–74). New York: Oxford University Press.

Edelman, G. M. (2005). *Wider than the sky: The phenomenal gift of consciousness*. New Haven: Yale University Press.

Edwards, D. (1997). *Discourse and cognition*. London: Sage.

Ehrlich, M. (1998). Metacognitive monitoring in the processing of anaphoric devices in skilled and less skilled comprehenders. In C. Cornoldi & J. Oakhill (Eds.), *Reading comprehension difficulties: Processes and interventions* (pp. 221–249). Mahwah, NJ: Erlbaum.

Ehrlich, S. F., & Rayner, K. (1981). Contextual effects on word perception and eye movements during reading. *Journal of Verbal Learning and Verbal Behavior, 20*, 641–655.

Eich, E. (1995). Mood as a mediator of place dependent memory. *Journal of Experimental Psychology: General, 124*, 293–308.

Einstein, G. O., & McDaniel, M. A. (2004). *Memory fitness: A guide for successful aging*. New Haven, CT: Yale University Press.

Eisenberger, R., & Rhoades, L. (2001). Incremental effects of rewards on creativity. *Journal of Personality and Social Psychology, 81*, 728–741.

Eliott, A. J., & Mapes, R. R. (2002). Enhancing the yield. [Review of the book *Intrinsic and extrinsic motivation: The search for optimal motivation and performance*]. *Contemporary Psychology, 47*, 200–202.

Ellis, H. D., & Young, A. W. (1988). Training in face-processing skills for a child with acquired prosopagnosia. *Developmental Neuropsychology, 4*, 283–294.

Elman, J. L. (Ed.). (1996). *Rethinking innateness: A connectionist perspective on development* (Vol. 10). *MIT Press*.

Elman, J. L. (1990). Finding structure in time. *Cognitive Science, 14*, 179–211.

Else-Quest, N., Hyde, J. S., & Linn, M. C. (2010). Cross-national patterns of gender differences in mathematics: A meta-analysis. *Psychological Bulletin, 136*, 103–127.

Emberson, L. J., Lupyan, G., Goldstein, M. H., & Spivey, M. J. (2010). Overheard cell-phone conversations: When less speech is more distracting. *Psychological Science, 21*, 1383–1388.

Emery, N. J., & Easton, A. (2005). Introduction: What is social cognitive neuroscience (SCN)? In A. Easton & N. J. Emery (Eds.), *The cognitive neuroscience of social behaviour* (pp. 1–16). New York: Psychology Press.

Emmorey, K., Klima, E., & Hickok, G. (1998). Mental rotation within linguistic and non-linguistic domains in users of American Sign Language. *Cognition, 68*, 221–246.

Endsley, M. R. (2006). Expertise and situation awareness. In K. A. Ericsson, N. Charness, P. J. Feltovich, & R. R. Hoffman (Eds.), *The Cambridge handbook of expertise and expert performance* (pp. 633–651). New York: Cambridge University Press.

Engbert, R., & Krügel, A. (2010). Readers use Bayesian estimation for eye movement control. *Psychological Science, 21*, 366–371.

Engbert, R., Nuthman, A., Richter, E. M., & Kliegl, R. (2005). SWIFT: A dynamic model of saccade generation during reading. *Psychological Review, 112*, 777–813.

Engelkamp, J. (1998). *Memory for actions.* Hove, UK: Psychology Press.

Engle, R. W. (2011, May). *Perspectives on scientific writing. Presented at the annual meeting of the Association for Psychological Science*, Washington, DC.

Englich, B., & Mussweiler, T. (2001). Sentencing under uncertainty: Anchoring effects in the courtroom. *Journal of Applied Social Psychology, 31*, 1535–1551.

Epstein, R., & Kanwisher, N. (1998). A cortical representation of the local visual environment. *Nature, 392*, 598–601.

Epstein, R. (2004). Watson, John Broadus. In R. L. Gregory (Ed.), *The Oxford companion to the mind* (2nd ed., pp. 942–943). New York: Oxford University Press.

Erber, J. T. (2005). *Aging and older adulthood.* Belmont, CA: Thomson Wadsworth.

Erdelyi, M. H., & Goldberg, B. (2014). Let's not sweep repression under the rug: Toward a cognitive psychology of repression. In J. F. Kihl- slrom & F. J. Evans (Eds.), *Functional disorders of memory* (pp. 355–402). Hillsdale, NJ: Erlbaum.

Erdoğan, A., Baran, B., Avlar, B., Çağlar Taş, A., & Tekcan, A. I. (2008). On the persistence of positive events in life scripts. *Applied Cognitive Psychology, 22*, 95–111.

Erickson, M. A., & Kruschke, J. K. (1998). Rules and exemplars in category learning. *Journal of Experimental Psychology: General, 127*, 107–140.

Erickson, M. A., & Kruschke, J. K. (2002). Rule-based extrapolation in perceptual categorization. *Psychonomic Bulletin & Review, 9*, 160–168.

Ericsson, K. A. (2003a). Exceptional memorizers: Made, not born. *Trends in Cognitive Psychology, 7*, 233–235.

Ericsson, K. A. (2003b). The search for general abilities and basic capacities: Theoretical implications from the modifiability and complexity of mechanisms mediating expert performance. In R. J. Sternberg & E. L. Grigorenko (Eds.), *The psychology of abilities, competencies, and expertise* (pp. 93–125). New York: Cambridge University Press.

Ericsson, K. A. (2006). An introduction to Cambridge handbook of expertise and expert performance: Its development, organization and content. In K. A. Ericsson, N. Charness, P. J. Feltovich, & R. R. Hoffman (Eds.), *The Cambridge handbook of expertise and performance* (pp. 3–19). New York: Cambridge University Press.

Ericsson, K. A., & Fox, M. C. (2011). Thinking aloud is not a form of introspection but a qualitatively different methodology: Reply to schooler (2011). *Psychological Bulletin, 137*, 351–354.

Ericsson, K. A., & Kintsch, W. (1995). Long-term working memory. *Psychological Review, 102*, 211–245.

Ericsson, K. A., & Lehmann, A. C. (1996). Expert and exceptional performance: Evidence of maximal adaptation to task constraints. *Annual Review of Psychology, 47*, 273–305.

Ericsson, K. A., & Towne, T. J. (2010). Expertise. *Wiley Interdisciplinary Reviews: Cognitive Science, 1*, 404–416.

Ericsson, K. A., Charness, N., Feltovich, P. J., & Hoffman, R. R. (Eds.). (2006). *The Cambridge handbook of expertise and expert performance.* New York: Cambridge University Press.

Ericsson, K. A., Delaney, P. F., Weaver, G., & Mahadevan, R. (2004). Uncovering the structure of a memorist's "basic" memory capacity." *Cognitive Psychology, 49*, 191–237.

Ericsson, K. A., Nandagopal, K., & Roring, R. W. (2009). Toward a science of exceptional achievement: Attaining superior performance through deliberate practice. *Longevity, Regeneration, and Optimal Health: Annals of the New York Academy of Sciences*, 199–217.

Erskine, J. A. K., Georgiou, G. J., & Kvavilashvili, L. (2010). I suppress, therefore I smoke: Effects of thought suppression on smoking behavior. *Psychological Science, 21*, 1225–1230.

Erwin-Tripp, S. (2011). Advances in the study of bilingualism: A personal view. In V. Cook & B. Bassetti (Eds.), *Language and bilingual cognition* (pp. 219–228). New York: Psychology Press.

Esgate, A., & Groome, D. (2005). *An introduction to applied cognitive psychology.* Hove, UK: Psychology Press.

Ester, E. F., Fukuda, K., May, L. M., Vogel, E. K., & Awh, E. (2014). Evidence for a fixed capacity limit in attending multiple locations. *Cognitive, Affective, & Behavioral Neuroscience, 14,* 62–77.

Evans, J. St. B. T. (2000). What could and could not be a strategy in reasoning. In W. Schaeken, G. DeVooght, A. Vandierendonck, & G. d'Ydewalle (Eds.), *Deductive reasoning and strategies* (pp. 1–22). Mahwah, NJ: Erlbaum.

Evans, J. St. B. T. (2002). Logic and human reasoning: An assessment of the deduction paradigm. *Psychological Bulletin, 128,* 978–996.

Evans, J. St. B. T. (2004). Biases in deductive reasoning. In R. F. Pohl (Eds.), *Cognitive illusions: A handbook on fallacies and biases in thinking, judgement, and memory* (pp. 127–144). Hove, UK: Psychology Press.

Evans, J. St. B. T. (2005). Insight and self-insight in reasoning and decision making. In V. Girotto & P. N. Johnson-Laird (Eds.), *The shape of reason: Essays in honour of Paolo Legrenzi* (pp. 27–47). Hove, UK: Psychology Press.

Evans, J. St. B. T. (2006). The heuristic-analytic theory of reasoning: Extension and evaluation. *Psychonomic Bulletin & Review, 13,* 378–395

Evans, J. St. B. T. (2011). Reasoning is for thinking, not just for arguing. *Behavioral and Brain Sciences, 34,* 57–111.

Evans, J. St. B. T. (2012). Dual-process theories of deductive reasoning: Facts and fallacies. In K. J. Holyoak & R. G. Morrison (Eds.), *The Oxford handbook of thinking and reasoning* (pp. 115–133). New York: Oxford University Press.

Evans, V., & Green, M. (2006). *Cognitive linguistics: An introduction.* Mahwah, NJ: Erlbaum.

Everett, D. L. (2005). Cultural constraints on grammar and cognition in Pirahã: Another look at the design features of human language. *Current Anthropology, 76,* 621–646.

Everett, D. L. (2007). Challenging Chomskyan Linguistics: The case of Pirahã. *Human Development, 50,* 297–299.

Eysenck, M. W., & Keane, M. T. (2010). *Cognitive psychology: A student's handbook* (6th ed.). Hove, UK: Psychology Press.

Fabiani, M., & Wee, E. (2001). Age-related changes in working memory and frontal lobe function: A review. In C. A. Nelson & M. Luciana (Eds.), *Handbook of developmental cognitive neuroscience* (pp. 473–488). Cambridge, MA: MIT Press.

Falsetti, S. A., Monnier, J., & Resnick, H. S. (2005). Intrusive thoughts in postraumatic stress disorder. In D. A. Clark (Ed.), *Intrusive thoughts in clinical disorders: Theory, research, and treatment* (pp. 30–53). New York: Guilford Press.

Fan, J., McCandliss, B. D., Sommer, T., Raz, A., & Posner, M. I. (2002). Testing the efficiency and independence of attentional networks. *Journal of Cognitive Neuroscience, 14,* 340–347.

Farah, M. J. (2000). *The cognitive neuroscience of vision.* Malden, MA: Blackwell.

Farah, M. J. (2001). Consciousness. In B. Rapp (Ed.), *The handbook of cognitive neuropsychology* (pp. 159–182). Philadelphia: Psychology Press.

Farah, M. J. (2004). *Visual agnosia* (2nd ed.). Cambridge, MA: MIT Press.

Farmer, T. A., Yan, S., Bicknell, K., Tanenhaus, M. K. (2015). Form-to-expectation matching effects on first-pass eye-movement measures during reading. *Journal of Experimental Psychology: Human Perception and Performance, 70,* 413–433.

Farmer, T. A., Christiansen, M. H., & Monaghan, P. (2006). Phonological typicality influences on-line sentence comprehension. *Proceedings of the National Academy of Sciences of the USA, 103,* 12203–12208.

Farrimond, S., Knight, R. G., & Titov, N. (2006). The effects of aging on remembering intentions: Performance on a simulated shopping task. *Applied Cognitive Psychology, 20,* 533–555.

Fay, N., Page, A. C., Serfaty, C., Tai, V., & Winkler, C. (2008). Speaker overestimation of communication effectiveness and fear of negative evaluation: Being realistic is unrealistic. *Psychonomic Bulletin & Review, 15,* 1160–1165.

Federmeier, K. D. (2007). Thinking ahead: The role and roots of prediction in language comprehension. *Psychophysiology, 44,* 491–505.

Federmeier, K. D., & Kutas, M. (2001). Meaning and modality: influences of context, semantic memory organization, and perceptual predictability on picture processing. *Journal of Experimental Psychology: Learning, Memory, and Cognition, 27,* 202–224.

Fedorenko, E., & Thompson-Schill, S. L. (2014). Reworking the language network. *Trends in cognitive sciences, 18,* 120–126.

Fedorenko, E., Nieto Castañón, A., & Kanwisher, N. (2011). Syntactic processing in the human brain: What we know, what we don't know, and a suggestion for how to proceed. *Brain & Language,* doi: 10.1016/j.bandl.2011.01.001.

Fehr, B. (2005). The role of prototypes in interpersonal cognition. In M. W. Baldwin (Ed.), *Interpersonal cognition* (pp. 180–205). New York: Guilford.

Fehr, B., & Sprecher, S. (2009). Prototype analysis of the concept of compassionate love. *Personal Relationships, 16,* 343–364.

Feist, G. J. (2006). Why the studies of science need a psychology of science. *Review of General Psychology, 10,* 183–187.

Feist, G. J. (2010). The function of personality in creativity: The nature and nurture of the creative personality. In J. C. Kaufman & R. J. Sternberg (Eds.), *The Cambridge handbook of creativity* (pp. 113–130). New York: Cambridge University Press.

Feldman, D. H., Csikszentmihalyi, M., & Gardner, H. (1994). *Changing the world: A framework for the study of creativity*. Westport, CT: Praeger.

Felleman, D. J., & Van Essen, D. C. (1991). Distributed hierarchical processing in the primate cerebral cortex. *Cerebral cortex, 1*, 1–47.

Fenn, K. M., Shintel, H., Atkins, A. S., Skipper, J. I., Bond, V. C., & Nusbaum, H. C. (2011). When less is heard than meets the ear: Change deafness in a telephone conversation. *The Quarterly Journal of Experimental Psychology, 64*, 1442–1456.

Fennell, C. T. (2012). Habituation procedures. *Research methods in child language: A practical guide* (pp. 3–16). Malden, MA: Blackwell.

Fernald, A. (1985). Four-month-old infants prefer to listen to motherese. *Infant behavior and development, 8*, 181–195.

Fernald, A., & Marchman, V. A. (2006). Language learning in infancy. In M. J. Traxler & M. A. Gernsbacher (Eds.), *Handbook of psycholinguistics* (2nd ed., pp. 1027–1071). Amsterdam: Elsevier.

Fernald, A., Marchman, V. A., & Weisleder, A. (2013). SES differences in language processing skill and vocabulary are evident at 18 months. *Developmental Science, 16*, 234–248.

Fernald, A., Pinto, J. P., Swingley, D., Weinbergy, A., & McRoberts, G. W. (1998). Rapid gains in speed of verbal processing by infants in the 2nd year. *Psychological Science, 9*, 228–231.

Ferreira, F., & Patson, N. D. (2007). The "good enough" approach to language comprehension. *Language and Linguistics Compass, 1*, 71–83.

Ferreira, F., Bailey, K. G. D., & Ferraro, V. (2002). Good-enough representations in language comprehension. *Current Directions in Psychological Science, 11*, 11–15.

Ferreira, V. S., & Slevc, L. R. (2009). Grammatical encoding. In M. G. Gaskell (Ed.), *The Oxford handbook of psycholinguistics* (pp. 453–487). New York: Oxford University Press.

Fetzer, A., & Oishi, E. (Eds.). (2011). *Context and contexts*. Amsterdam: John Benjamins Publishing Company.

Fiedler, K., & Walther, E. (2004). *Stereotyping as inductive hypothesis testing*. Hove, UK: Psychology Press.

Fiedler, K., Friese, M., & Wänke, M. (2011). Psycholinguistic methods in social psychology. In K. C. Klauer, A. Voss, & C. Stahl (Eds.), *Cognitive methods in social psychology* (206–235). New York: Guilford.

Fiedler, K., Nickel, S., Asbeck, J., & Pagel, U. (2003). Mood and the generation effect. *Cognition and Emotion, 17*, 585–608.

Field, J. (2004). *Psycholinguistics: The key concepts*. New York: Routledge.

Fields, A. W., & Shelton, A. L. (2006). Individual skill differences and large-scale environmental learning. *Journal of Experimental Psychology: Learning, Memory, and Cognition, 32*, 506–515.

Findlay, J. M., & Gilchrist, I. D. (2001). Visual attention: The active vision perspective. In M. Jenkin & L. Harris (Eds.), *Vision and attention* (pp. 83–103). New York: Springer-Verlag.

Fine, A. B., Jaeger, T. F., Farmer, T. A., & Qian, T. (2013). Rapid expectation adaptation during syntactic comprehension. *PLoS ONE, 8*(10): e77661.

Finke, R. A., Pinker, S., & Farah, M. J. (1989). Reinterpreting visual patterns in mental imagery. *Cognitive Science, 13*, 51–78.

Finstad, K., Bink, M., McDaniel, M., & Einstein, G. O. (2006). Breaks and task switches in prospective memory. *Applied Cognitive Psychology, 20*, 705–712.

Fioratou, E., & Cowley, S. J. (2011). Insightful thinking: Cognitive dynamics and material artifacts. In S. J. Cowley (Ed.), *Distributed language* (pp. 57–80). Amsterdam: John Benjamins.

Fiore, S., & Schooler, J. W. (2004). Process mapping and shared cognition: Teamwork and the development of shared problem models. In E. Salas & S. M. Fiore (Eds.), *Team cognition: Understanding the factors that drive process and performance* (pp. 133–152). Washington, DC: American Psychological Association.

Fisher, D. L., & Pollatsek, A. (2007). Novice driver crashes: Failure to divide attention or failure to recognize risks. In A. F. Kramer, D. A. Wiegmann, & A. Kirlik (Eds.), *Attention: From theory to practice* (pp. 134–153). New York: Oxford University Press.

Fisher, K. J., Borchert, K., & Bassok, M. (2011). Following the standard form: Effects of equation format on algebraic modeling. *Memory & Cognition, 39*, 502–515.

Fishman, J. A. (2006). The new linguistic order. In H. Luria, D. M. Seymour, & T. Smoke (Eds.), *Language and linguistics in context: Readings and applications for teachers* (pp. 175–189). Mahwah, NJ: Erlbaum.

Fisk, J. E. (2004). Conjunction fallacy. In R. Pohl (Ed.), *Cognitive illusions: Handbook on fallacies and biases in thinking, judgment, and memory* (pp. 23–42) Hove, UK: Psychology Press.

Fitzgerald, J. M. (2010). Culture, gender, and the first memories of black and white American students. *Memory & Cognition, 38*, 785–796.

Fivush, R. (2009). Co-constructing memories and meaning over time. In J. A. Quas & R. Fivush (Eds.), *Emotion and memory in development: Biological, cognitive, and social considerations* (pp. 343–354). New York: Oxford University Press.

Fivush, R. (2011). The development of autobiographical memory. *Annual Review of Psychology, 62*, 559–582.

Fivush, R., & Nelson, K. (2004). Culture and language in the emergence of autobiographical memory. *Psychological Science, 15*, 573–577.

Flavell, J. H., Miller, P. H., & Miller, S. A. (2002). *Cognitive development* (4th ed.). Upper Saddle River, NJ: Prentice-Hall.

Flege, J. E., Yeni-Komshiam, G. H., & Liu, S. (1999). Age constraints on second-language acquisition. *Journal of Memory and Language, 41*, 78–104.

Flores Salgado, E. F. (2011). *The pragmatics of requests and apologies*. Philadelphia: John Benjamins.

Flower, L. S., & Hayes, J. R. (1980). The dynamics of composing: Making plans and juggling constraints. In L. W. Gregg & E. R. Steinberg (Eds.), *Cognitive processes in writing* (pp. 31–50). Hillsdale, NJ: Erlbaum.

Fodor, Jerry A. (1983). *Modularity of Mind: An Essay on Faculty Psychology*. Cambridge, Mass.: MIT Press.

Foley, H. J., & Matlin, M. W. (2010). *Sensation and perception* (5th ed.). Boston, MA: Allyn & Bacon.

Foley, M. A. (2012). Remember *imagining that?* Children's source monitoring of memories for imagination. In M. Taylor (Ed.), *Development of imagination*. New York: Oxford University Press.

Foley, M. A., & Foley, H. J. (1998). A study of face identification: Are people looking beyond disguises? In M. J. Intons-Peterson & D. L. Best (Eds.), *Memory distortions and their prevention* (pp. 29–47). Mahwah, NJ: Erlbaum.

Foley, M. A., & Ratner, H. H. (1998). Distinguishing between memories for thoughts and deeds: The role of prospective processing in children's source monitoring. *British Journal of Developmental Psychology, 16*, 465–484.

Foley, M. A., Belch, C., Mann, R., & McLean, M. (1999). Self-referencing: How incessant the stream? *American Journal of Psychology, 112*, 73–96.

Foley, M. A., Foley, H. J., & Korenman, L. M. (2002). Adapting a memory framework (source monitoring) to the study of closure processes. *Memory & Cognition, 30*, 412–422.

Foley, M. A., Ratner, H. H., & Gentes, E. (2010). Helping children enter into another's experiences: The look and feel of it. *Journal of Cognition and Development, 11*, 217–239.

Foley, M. A., Ratner, H. H., & House, A. T. (2002). Anticipation and source-monitoring errors: Children's memory for collaborative activities. *Journal of Cognition and Development, 3*, 385–414.

Foley, M. A., Wilder, A., McCall, R., & Van Vorst, R. (1993). The consequences for recall of children's ability to generate interactive imagery in the absence of external supports. *Journal of Experimental Child Psychology, 56*, 173–200.

Folk, C. L. (2010). Attention: Divided. In E. B. Goldstein (Ed.), *Encyclopedia of perception* (Vol. **1**., pp. 84–87). Thousand Oaks, CA: Sage.

Forgas, J. P. (2001). The Affect Infusion Model (AIM): An integrative theory of mood effects on cognition and judgment. In L. L. Martin & G. L. Clore (Eds.), *Theories of mood and cognition* (pp. 99–134). Mahwah, NJ: Erlbaum.

Forster, K. I. (1981). Priming and the effects of sentence and lexical contexts on naming time: Evidence for autonomous lexical processing. *Quarterly Journal of Experimental Psychology, 33A*, 465–495.

Forsyth, D. K., & Burt, C. D. B. (2008). Allocating time to future tasks: The effect of task segmentation on planning fallacy bias. *Memory & Cognition, 36*, 791–798.

Fowler, C. A. (2003). Speech production and perception. In A. F. Healy & R. W. Proctor (Eds.), *Handbook of psychology* (Vol. **4**, pp. 237–266). Hoboken, NJ: Wiley.

Fowler, C. A., & Galantucci, B. (2005). The relation of speech perception and speech production. In D. B. Pisoni & R. E. Remez (Eds.), *The handbook of speech perception* (pp. 633–652). Malden, MA: Blackwell.

Fox, E. (Ed.). (2005). *Visual social cognition*. Hove, UK: Psychology Press.

Franconeri, S. I., Hollingworth, A., & Simons, D. J. (2005). Do new objects capture attention? *Psychological Science, 16*, 275–281.

Franklin, N., & Tversky, B. (1990). Searching imagined environments. *Journal of Experimental Psychology: General, 119*, 63–76.

Franklin, S. (1995). *Artificial minds*. Cambridge, MA: MIT Press.

Freeman, J. B. & Ambady, N. (2010). MouseTracker: Software for studying real-time mental processing using a computer mouse-tracking method. *Behavior Research Methods, 42*, 226–241.

Freyd, J. J., & Quina, K. (2000). Feminist ethics in the practice of science: The contested memory controversy as an example. In M. M. Brabeck (Ed.), *Practicing feminist ethics in psychology* (pp. 101–123). Washington, DC: American Psychological Association.

Freyd, J. J. (2005). The science of child sexual abuse. *Science, 308*, 501–503.

Freyd, J. J., Klest, B., & DePrince, A. P. (2010). Avoiding awareness of betrayal: Comment on Lindblom and Gray (2009). *Applied Cognitive Psychology, 24*, 20–26.

Frick-Horbury, D., & Guttentag, R. E. (1998). The effects of restricting hand gesture production on lexical retrieval and free recall. *American Journal of Psychology, 111*, 43–62.

Fried, C. B. (2008). In-class laptop use and its effects on student learning. *Computers & Education, 50*, 906–914.

Friederici, A. D. (2002). Towards a neural basis of auditory sentence processing. *Trends in Cognitive Sciences, 6*, 78–84.

Friedman, A., & Montello, D. R. (2006). Global-scale location and distance estimates: Common representations and strategies in absolute and relative judgments. *Journal of Experimental Psychology: Learning, Memory, and Cognition, 32*, 333–346.

Friedman, A., Brown, N. R., & McGaffey, A. P. (2002). A basis for bias in geographical judgments. *Psychonomic Bulletin & Review, 9*, 151–159.

Friedman, A., Spetch, M. L., & Ferrey, A. (2005). Recognition by humans and pigeons of novel views of 3–D objects and their photographs. *Journal of Experimental Psychology: General, 134*, 149–162.

Frishman, L. J. (2001). Basic visual processes. In E. B. Goldstein (Ed.), *Blackwell handbook of perception* (pp. 53–91). Malden, MA: Blackwell.

Frith, C., & Rees, G. (2004). Brain imaging: The methods. In R. L. Gregory (Ed.), *The Oxford companion to the mind* (2nd ed., pp. 131–133). New York: Oxford University Press.

Fritz, K., Howie, P., & Kleitman, S. (2010). "How do I remember when I got my dog?" The structure and development of children's metamemory. *Metacognition, 5*, 207–228.

Fuchs, A. H., & Milar, K. J. (2003). Psychology as a science. In D. F. Freedheim (Ed.), *Handbook of psychology (Vol. 1: The history of psychology*, pp. 1–26). Hoboken, NJ: Wiley.

Fuster, J. M. (2003). *Cortex and mind: Unifying cognition.* New York: Oxford University Press.

Galambos, S. J., & Goldin-Meadow, S. (1990). The effects of learning two languages on levels of metalinguistic awareness. *Cognition, 34*, 1–56.

Gallese, V., Gernsbacher, M. A., Heyes, C., Hickok, G., Iacoboni, M. (2011). Mirror neuron forum. *Perspectives on Psychological Science, 6*, 369–407.

Gallistel, C. R., & King, A. P. (2009). *Memory and the computational brain: Why cognitive science will transform neuroscience.* Hoboken, NJ: Wiley-Blackwell.

Gallo, D. A. (2006). *Associative illusions of memory.* New York: Psychology Press.

Gallo, D. A. (2010). False memories and fantastic beliefs: 15 years of the DRM illusion. *Memory & Cognition, 38*, 833–848.

Ganellen, R. J., & Carver, C. S. (1985). Why does self-reference promote incidental encoding? *Journal of Experimental Social Psychology, 21*, 284–300.

Ganis, G., Thompson, W. L., & Kosslyn, S. M. (2009). Visual mental imagery: More than "seeing with the mind's eye." In J. R. Brockmole (Ed.), *The visual world in memory* (pp. 211–249). New York: Routledge.

Gardner, H. (1985). *The mind's new science: A history of the cognitive revolution.* New York: Basic Books.

Gardner, R. C. (2010). Second language acquisition: A social psychological perspective. In R. B. Kaplan (Ed.), *The Oxford handbook of applied linguistics* (2nd ed., pp. 204–216). New York: Oxford University Press.

Gardner, R. C., & Lambert, W. E. (1959). Motivational variables in second-language acquisition. *Canadian Journal of Psychology, 13*, 266–272.

Garnets, L. D. (2008). Life as a lesbian: What does gender have to do with it? In J. C. Chrisler, C. Golden, & P. D. Rozee (Eds.), *Lectures on the psychology of women* (4th ed., pp. 232–267). New York: Boston.

Garnham, A. (2005). Language comprehension. In K. Lamberts & R. L. Goldstone (Eds.), *Handbook of cognition* (pp. 241–254). Thousand Oaks, CA: Sage.

Garnham, A., & Oakhill, J. (1994). *Thinking and reasoning.* Oxford, UK: Blackwell.

Garrett, M. (2009). Thinking across boundaries: Psycholinguistics perspectives. In M. G. Gaskell (Ed.), *The Oxford handbook of psycholinguistics* (pp. 805–820). New York: Oxford University Press.

Gaskell, M. G. (2009b). Statistical and connectionist models of speech perception and word recognition. In M. G. Gaskell (Ed.), *The Oxford handbook of psycholinguistics* (pp. 55–69). New York: Oxford University Press.

Gaskell, M. G. (Ed.). (2009a). *The Oxford handbook of psycholinguistics.* New York: Oxford University Press.

Gathercole, S. E. (1998). The development of memory. *Journal of Child Psychology and Psychiatry, 39*, 3–27.

Gathercole, S. E., & Baddeley, A. D. (1993). *Working memory and language.* Hove, UK: Erlbaum.

Gathercole, S. E., & Pickering, S. J. (2000). Working memory deficits in children with low achievement in the national curriculum at 7 years of age. *British Journal of Educational Psychology, 70*, 177–194.

Gathercole, S. E., Lamont, E., & Alloway, T. P. (2006). Working memory in the classroom. In S. J. Pickering (Ed.), *Working memory and education* (pp. 219–240). Burlington, MA: Elsevier.

Gathercole, S. E., Pickering, S. J., Ambridge, B., & Wearing, H. (2004). The structure of working memory from 4 to 15 years of age. *Developmental Psychology, 40,* 177–190.

Gauthier, I., Skudlarski, P., Gore, J. C., & Anderson, A. W. (2000). Expertise for cars and birds recruits brain areas involved in face recognition. *Nature Neuroscience, 3,* 191–197.

Gauvain, M. (2001). *The social context of cognitive development.* New York: Guilford.

Gazzaniga, M. S., Ivry, R. B., & Mangun, G. R. (2009). *Cognitive neuroscience: The biology of the mind.* New York: Norton.

Geisler, W. S. (2008). Visual perception and statistical properties of natural scenes. *Annual Review of Psychology, 59,* 167–192.

Geisler, W. S., & Super, B. J. (2000). Perceptual organization of two-dimensional patterns. *Psychological Review, 107,* 677–708.

Gelman, R. (2002). Cognitive development. In H. Pashler (Ed.), *Stevens' handbook of experimental psychology* (Vol. **2,** pp. 533–550). New York: Wiley.

Gelman, S. A., & Frazier, B. N. (2012). Development of thinking in children. In K. J. Holyoak & R. G. Morrison (Eds.), *The Cambridge handbook of thinking and reasoning* (pp. 513–528). New York: Cambridge University Press.

Genesee, F., & Gándara, P. (1999). Bilingual education programs: A cross-national perspective. *Journal of Social Issues, 55,* 665–685.

Genesee, F., Tucker, R., & Lambert, W. E. (1975). Communication skills of bilingual children. *Child Development, 46,* 1010–1014.

Geraerts, E., Raymaekers, & Merkelbach, H. (2010). Mechanisms underlying recovered memories. In G. M. Davies & D. B. Wright (Eds.), *Current issues in applied memory research* (pp. 101–118). New York: Psychology Press.

German, T. P., & Barrett, H. C. (2005). Functional fixedness in a technologically sparse culture. *Psychological Science, 16,* 1–5.

Gernsbacher, M. A., & Kaschak, M. P. (2003). Neuroimaging studies of language production and comprehension. *Annual Review of Psychology, 54,* 91–114.

Gernsbacher, M. A., & Robertson, D. A. (2005). Watching the brain comprehend discourse. In A. F. Healy (Ed.), *Experimental cognitive psychology and its applications* (pp. 157–167). Washington, DC: American Psychological Association.

Gerrie, M. P., Garry, M., & Loftus, E. F. (2005). False memories. In N. Brewer & K. D. Williams (Eds.), *Psychology and law: An empirical perspective* (pp. 222–253). New York: Guilford.

Gerrig, R. J. (1998). *Experiencing narrative words.* Boulder, CO: Westview Press.

Gerrig, R. J., & McKoon, G. (2001). Memory processes and experiential continuity. *Psychological Science, 12,* 81–85.

Gibbs, R. W., Jr. (1998). The varieties of intentions in interpersonal communication. In S. R. Fussell & R. J. Kreuz (Eds.), *Social and cognitive approaches to interpersonal communications* (pp. 19–37). Mahwah, NJ: Erlbaum.

Gibson, E. (1998). Linguistic complexity: Locality of syntactic dependencies. *Cognition, 68,* 1–76.

Gibson, E. J. (1969). *Principles of perceptual learning and development.* New York: Prentice Hall.

Gibson, J. M., Dhuse, S., Hrachovec, L., & Grimm, L. R. (2011). Priming insight in groups: Facilitating and inhibiting solving an ambiguously worded insight problem. *Memory & Cognition, 39,* 128–146.

Gigerenzer, G. (1998). Ecological intelligence: An adaptation for frequencies. In D. D. Cummins & C. Allen (Eds.), *The evolution of mind* (pp. 9–29). New York: Oxford University Press.

Gigerenzer, G. (2006a). Bounded and rational. In R. J. Stainton (Ed.), *Contemporary debates in cognitive science* (pp. 115–133). Oxford, UK: Blackwell.

Gigerenzer, G. (2006b). Heuristics. In G. Gigerenzer & C. Engel (Eds.), *Heuristics and the law* (pp. 17–44). Cambridge, MA: MIT Press.

Gigerenzer, G. (2008). Why heuristics work. *Perspectives in Psychological Science, 3,* 20–29.

Giles, A., & Rovee-Collier, C. (2011). Infant long-term memory for associations formed during mere exposure. *Infant Behavior and Development, 34,* 327–338.

Gilhooly, K. J. (2005). Working memory and strategies in reasoning. In M. J. Roberts & E. J. Newton (Eds.), *Methods of thought: Individual differences in reasoning strategies* (pp. 57–80). Hove, UK: Psychology Press.

Gilovich, T., Griffin, D. W., & Kahneman, D. (2002). *The psychology of intuitive judgment: Heuristic and biases.* Cambridge: Cambridge University Press.

Gillam, B., Sedgwick, H. A., & Peterson, M. A. (2007). Introduction. In M. A. Peterson, B. Gillam, & H. A. Sedgwick (Eds.), *In the mind's eye: Julian Hochberg on the perception of pictures, films, and the world.* New York: Oxford University Press.

Gillihan, S. J., & Farah, M. J. (2005). Is self special? A critical review of evidence from experimental psychology and cognitive neuroscience. *Psychological Bulletin, 131,* 76–97.

Glaser, R. (2001). Progress then and now. In S. M. Carver & D. Klahr (Eds.), *Cognition and instruction: Twenty-five years of progress* (pp. 493–507). Mahwah, NJ: Erlbaum.

Glaser, R., & Chi, M. T. H. (1988). Overview. In M. T. H. Chi, R. Glaser, & M. J. Farr (Eds.), *The nature of expertise* (pp. xv–xxxvi). Hillsdale, NJ: Erlbaum.

Glenberg, A. M. (2011a). Introduction to the mirror neuron forum. *Perspectives on Psychological Science, 6*, 363–368.

Glenberg, A. M. (2011b). Positions in the mirror are closer than they appear. *Perspectives on Psychological Science, 6*, 408–410.

Glenberg, A. M., Goldberg, A., Zhu, X. (2011). Improving early reading comprehension using embodied CAI. *Instructional Science, 39*, 27–39. DOI 10.1007/s11251-009-9096-7.

Glenberg, A. M., & Kaschak, M. P. (2002). Grounding language in action. *Psychonomic Bulletin & Review, 9*, 558–565.

Glicksohn, J. (1994). Rotation, orientation, and cognitive mapping. *American Journal of Psychology, 107*, 39–51.

Gluck, M. A., & Myers, C. E. (2001). *Gateway to memory: An introduction to neural network modeling of the hippocampus and learning.* Cambridge, MA: MIT Press.

Gobet, F., & Simon, H. A. (1996a). Recall of random and distorted chess positions: Implications for the theory of expertise. *Memory & Cognition, 24*, 493–503.

Gobet, F., de Voogt, A., & Retschitzki, J. (2004). *Moves in mind: The psychology of board games.* Hove, UK: Psychology Press.

Goldenberg, C., & Coleman, R. (2010). *Promoting academic achievement among English learners: A guide to the research.* Thousand Oaks, CA: Corwin.

Goldin-Meadow, S. (2003). *Hearing gesture: How our hands help us think.* Cambridge, MA: Harvard University Press.

Goldin-Meadow, S., & Beilock, S. L. (2010). Action's influence on thought: The case of gesture. *Perspectives on Psychological Science, 5*, 664–674.

Goldsmith, M., Koriat, A., & Pansky, A. (2005). Strategic regulation of grain size in memory reporting over time. *Journal of Memory and Language, 52*, 505–525.

Goldstein, D. G., & Gigerenzer, G. (2002). Models of ecological rationality: The recognition heuristic. *Psychological Review, 109*, 75–90.

Goldstein, E. B. (2010b). *Sensation and perception* (8th ed.). Belmont, CA: Wadsworth.

Goldstein, E. B. (Ed.). (2010a). *Encyclopedia of perception.* Thousand Oaks, CA: Sage.

Goldstein, M. H., Schwade, J. A., Briesch, J., & Syal, S. (2010). Learning while babbling: Prelinguistic object-directed vocalizations signal a readiness to learn. *Infancy, 15*, 362–391.

Goldstone, R. L., & Kersten, A. (2003). Concepts and categorization. In I. B. Weiner (Ed.), *Handbook of psychology* (Vol. **4**). Hoboken, NJ: Wiley.

Gollan, T. H., & Acenas, L.-A. R. (2004). What is a TOT? Cognate and translation effects on tip-of-the-tongue states in Spanish-English and Tagalog-English bilinguals. *Journal of Experimental Psychology: Learning, Memory, and Cognition, 29*, 1095–1105.

Gollan, T. H., Bonanni, M. P., & Montoya, R. I. (2005). Proper names get stuck on bilingual and monolingual speakers' tip of the tongue equally often. *Neuropsychology, 19*, 278–287.

Goodman, G. S., & Melinder, A. (2007). The development of autobiographical memory: A new model. In S. Magnussen & T. Helstrup (Eds.), *Everyday memory* (pp. 111–135). New York: Psychology Press.

Goodman, G. S., & Paz-Alonso, P. M. (2006). Trauma and memory: Normal versus special memory mechanisms. In B. Uttl, N. Ohta, & A. L. Siegenthaler (Eds.), *Memory and emotion: Interdisciplinary perspectives* (pp. 234–257). Malden, MA: Blackwell.

Goodman, G. S., Ghetti, S., Quas, J. A., Edelstein, R. S., Alexander, K. W., Redlich, A. D., . . . Jones, D. P. H. (2003). A prospective study of memory for child sexual abuse: New findings relevant to the repressed-memory controversy. *Psychological Science, 14*, 113–118.

Goodwin, G. P., & Johnson-Laird, P. N. (2005). Reasoning about relations. *Psychological Review, 112*, 468–493.

Gordon, I. E. (2004). *Theories of visual perception* (3rd ed.). Hove, UK: Psychology Press.

Gordon, P. C., Hendrick, R., & Johnson, M. (2004). Effects of noun phrase type on sentence complexity. *Journal of Memory and Language, 51*, 97–114.

Gordon, R., Franklin, N., & Beck, J. (2005). Wishful thinking and source monitoring. *Memory & Cognition, 33*, 418–438.

Gorman, M. E. (2006). Scientific and technological thinking. *Review of General Psychology, 10*, 113–129.

Gorrell, P. (1999). Sentence processing. In R. A. Wilson & F. C. Keil (Eds.), *The MIT encyclopedia of the cognitive sciences* (pp. 748–751). Cambridge, MA: MIT Press.

Grady, C. L., & Craik, F. I. M. (2000). Changes in memory processing with age. *Current Opinion in Neurobiology, 10*, 224–231.

Graesser, A. C., Gernsbacher, M. A., & Goldman, S. R. (2003). Introduction to the handbook of discourse processes. In A. C. Graesser, M. A. Gernsbacher, & S. R. Goldman (Eds.), *Handbook of discourse processes* (pp. 1–23). Mahwah, NJ: Erlbaum.

Graf, M., Kaping, D., & Bülthoff, H. H. (2005). Orientation congruency effects for familiar objects: Coordinate transformations in object recognition. *Psychological Science, 16*, 214–221.

Grainger, J., & Jacobs, A. M. (2005). Pseudoword context effects on letter perception: The role of word misperception. *European Journal of Cognitive Psychology, 17*, 289–318.

Grammer, J. K., Purtell, K. M., Coffman, J. L., & Ornstein, P. A. (2011). Relations between children's metamemory and strategic performance: Time-varying covariates in early elementary school. *Journal of Experimental Child Psychology, 108*, 139–155.

Grant, E. R., & Spivey, M. J. (2003). Eye movements and problem solving: Guiding attention guides thought. *Psychological Science, 14*, 462–466.

Gratton, G., & Fabiani, M. (2010). Fast optical imaging of human brain function. *Frontiers in Human Neuroscience, 4*, 52.

Greeno, J. G. (1974). Hobbits and Orcs: Acquisition of a sequential concept. *Cognitive Psychology, 6*, 270–292.

Greenwald, A. G., & Nosek, B. A. (2001). Health of the Implicit Association Test at age 3. *Zeitschrift für Experimentelle Psychologie, 48*, 85–93.

Greenwald, A. G., McGee, D. E., & Schwartz, J. L. K. (1998). Measuring individual differences in implicit cognition: The Implicit Association Test. *Journal of Personality and Social Psychology, 74*, 1464–1480.

Gregory, E., McCloskey, M., & Landau, B. (2014). Profound loss of general knowledge in retrograde amnesia: evidence from an amnesic artist. *Frontiers in Human Neuroscience, 8*, 287.

Gregory, R. L. (2004a). Perception. In R. L. Gregory (Ed.), *The Oxford companion to the mind* (2nd ed., pp. 707–710). New York: Oxford University Press.

Gregory, R. L. (2004b). Piaget and education. In R. L. Gregory (Ed.), *The Oxford companion to the mind* (2nd ed., pp. 732–733). New York: Oxford University Press.

Grice, H. P. (1989). *Studies in the way of words*. Cambridge, MA: Harvard University Press.

Griffin, D., & Tversky, A. (2002). The weighing of evidence and the determinants of confidence. In T. Gilovich, D. Griffin, & D. Kahneman (Eds.), *Heuristics and biases: The psychology of intuitive judgment* (pp. 230–249). New York: Cambridge University Press.

Griffin, T. D., Wiley, J., & Thiede, K. W. (2008). Individual differences, rereading, and self-explanation: Concurrent processing and cue validity as constraints on metacomprehension accuracy. *Memory & Cognition, 36*, 93–103.

Griffin, Z. M. (2004). Why look? Reasons for eye movements related to language production. In J. M. Henderson & F. Ferreira (Eds.), *The interface of language, vision, and action: Eye movements and the visual world* (pp. 213–247). New York: Psychology Press.

Griffin, Z. M., & Ferreira, V. S. (2006). Properties of spoken language production. In M. J. Traxler & M. A. Gernsbacher (Eds.), *Handbook of psycholinguistics* (2nd ed., pp. 505–527). Amsterdam: Elsevier.

Griffith, P. L., & Ruan, J. (2005). What is metacognition and what should be its role in literacy instruction? In S. E. Israel, C. C. Block, K. L. Bauserman, & K. Kinnucan-Welsch (Eds.), *Metacognition in literacy learning: Theory, assessment, instruction, and professional development* (pp. 3–18). Mahwah, NJ: Erlbaum.

Griggs, R. A., & Cox, J. R. (1982). The elusive thematic-materials effect in Wason's selection task. *British Journal of Psychology, 73*, 407–420.

Grill-Spector, K., & Kanwisher, N. (2005). Visual recognition: As soon as you know it is there, you know what it is. *Psychological Science, 16*, 152–160.

Groß, J., Blank, H., & Bayen, U. J. (2017). Hindsight bias in depression. *Clinical Psychological Science, 5*(5), 771–788.

Grodzinsky, Y. (2006). A blueprint for a brain map of syntax. In Y. Grodzinsky & K. Amunts (Eds.), *Broca's region* (pp. 83–107). New York: Oxford University Press.

Groninger, L. D. (1971). Mnemonic imagery and forgetting. *Psychonomic Science, 23*, 161–163.

Groome, D. (1999). *An introduction to cognitive psychology: Processes and disorders*. Hove, UK: Psychology Press.

Groopman, J. (2007). *How doctors think*. Boston: Houghton Mifflin.

Gros-Louis, J. G., West, M. J., Goldstein, M. H., & King, A. P. (2006). Mothers provide differential feedback to infants' prelinguistic sounds. *International Journal of Behavioral Development, 30*, 509–516.

Gross, T. F. (2009). Own-race/ethnicity bias in the recognition of Hispanic-Mestiso, African, Asian, and Caucasian children and adult faces. *Basic and Applied Social Psychology, 31*, 128–135.

Grossberg, S. (2000). The complementary brain: Unifying brain dynamics and modularity. *Trends in Cognitive Sciences, 4*, 233–245.

Grossberg, S., Govindarajan, K. K., Wyse, L. L., & Cohen, M. A. (2004). ARTSTREAM: A neural network model of auditory scene analysis and source segregation. *Neural Networks, 17*, 511–536.

Gu, J., Strauss, C., Bond, R., & Cavanagh, K. (2015). How do mindfulness-based cognitive therapy and mindfulness-based stress reduction improve mental health and wellbeing? A systematic review and meta-analysis of mediation studies. *Clinical Psychology Review, 37*, 1–12.

Guerin, B. (2003). Language use as social strategy: A review and an analytic framework for the social sciences. *Review of General Psychology, 7*, 251–298.

Guerreiro, M. J. S., & Van Gerven, P. W. M. (2011). Now you see it, now you don't: Evidence for age-dependent and age-independent cross-modal distraction. *Psychology and Aging, 26*, 415–426.

Guilford, J. P. (1967). *The nature of human intelligence.* New York: McGraw-Hill.

Gunter, B., Furman, A., & Pappa, E. (2005). Effects of television violence on memory for violent and nonviolent advertising. *Journal of Applied Social Psychology, 35,* 1680–1697.

Gupta, P. & MacWhinney, B. (1997). Vocabulary acquisition and verbal short-term memory: Computational and neural bases. *Brain and Language, 59,* 267–333.

Gurung, R. A. R. (2003). Pedagogical aids and student performance. *Teaching of Psychology, 30,* 92–95.

Gurung, R. A. R. (2004). Pedagogical aids: Learning enhancers or dangerous detours? *Teaching of Psychology, 31,* 164–166.

Gurung, R. A. R., & McCann, L. I. (2011, April). How should students study? Tips, advice, and pitfalls. *Association for Psychological Sciences Observer, pp.* 33–35.

Güss, C. D., & Wiley, B. (2007). Metacognition of problem-solving strategies in Brazil, India, and the United States. *Journal of Cognition and Culture, 7,* 1–25.

Guynn, M. J., McDaniel, M. A., & Einstein, G. O. (1998). Prospective memory: When reminders fail. *Memory & Cognition, 26,* 287–298.

Gyselinck, V., & Meneghetti, C. (2011). The role of spatial working memory in understanding descriptions. In A. Vandierendonck & A. Szmalec (Eds.), *Spatial working memory* (pp. 159–180). New York: Psychology Press.

Haberlandt, K. (1999). *Human memory: Exploration and application.* Boston: Allyn and Bacon.

Hacker, D. J., Bol, L., & Keener, M. C. (2008). Metacognition in education: A focus on calibration. In J. Dunlosky & R. A. Bjork (Eds.), *Handbook of metamemory and memory* (pp. 429–455). New York: Psychology Press.

Hacker, D. J., Dunlosky, J., & Graesser, A. C. (Eds.). (2009). *Handbook of metacognition in education.* New York: Routledge.

Hakel, M. D. (2001). Learning that lasts. *Psychological Science, 12,* 433–434.

Hakuta, K. (1986). *Mirror of language: The debate on bilingualism.* New York: Basic Books.

Hall, J., Harris, J. M., Sprengelmeyer, R., Sprengelmeyer, A., Young, A. W., Santos, I. W., . . . Lawrie, S. M.. (2004). Social cognition and face processing and schizophrenia. *British Journal of Psychiatry, 185,* 169–170.

Hallinan, J. T. (2009). *Why we make mistakes.* New York: Broadway Books.

Halpern, A. R., Zatorre, R. J., Bouffard, M., & Johnson, J. A. (2004). Behavioral and neural correlates of perceived and imagined musical timbre. *Neuropsychologia, 42,* 1281–1292.

Halpern, D. F. (2003). *Thought and knowledge: An introduction to critical thinking* (4th ed.). Mahwah, NJ: Erlbaum.

Halpern, D. F. (2012). *Sex differences in cognitive abilities* (4th ed.). New York: Psychology Press.

Hämäläinen, M., Hari, R., Ilmoniemi, R. J., Knuutila, J., & Lounasmaa, O. V. (1993). Magnetoencephalography—theory, instrumentation, and applications to noninvasive studies of the working human brain. *Reviews of Modern Physics, 65*(2), 413–497.

Hamilton, D. L. (2005). Social cognition: An introductory overview. In D. L. Hamilton (Ed.), *Social cognition: Key readings* (pp. 1–36). New York: Psychology Press.

Hamilton, D. L., & Sherman, J. W. (1994). Stereotypes. In R. S. Wyer, Jr., & T. K. Srull (Eds.), *Handbook of social cognition* (2nd ed., Vol. 2, pp. 1–68). Hillsdale, NJ: Erlbaum.

Hamilton, D. L., Stroessner, S. J., & Mackie, D. M. (1993). The influence of affect on stereotyping: The case of illusory correlations. In D. M. Mackie & D. L. Hamilton (Eds.), *Affect, cognition, and stereotyping: Interactive processes in group perception* (pp. 39–61). San Diego: Academic Press.

Hampton, J. A. (1997a). Conceptual combination. In K. Lamberts & D. Shanks (Eds.), *Knowledge, concepts, and categories* (pp. 133–159). Cambridge, MA: MIT Press.

Hampton, J. A. (1997b). Psychological representation of concepts. In M. A. Conway (Ed.), *Cognitive models of memory* (pp. 81–110). Cambridge, MA: MIT Press.

Hannon, B., Lozano, G., Frias, S., Picallo-Hernandez, S., & Fuhrman, R. (2010). Differential-associative processing: A new strategy for learning highly-similar concepts. *Applied Cognitive Psychology, 24,* 1222–1244.

Hardman, D. (2009). *Judgment and decision making: Psychology perspectives.* Chichester, Sussex, UK: Blackwell.

Hardt, O., Einarsson, E. Ö., & Nader, K. (2010). A bridge over troubled water: Reconsolidation as a link between cognitive and neuroscientific memory research traditions. *Annual Review of Psychology, 61,* 141–167.

Harley, E. M., Carlsen, K. A., & Loftus, G. R. (2004). The "saw-it-all-along" effect: Demonstrations of visual hindsight bias. *Journal of Experimental Psychology: Learning, Memory, and Cognition, 30,* 960–968.

Harley, T. A. (2001). *The psychology of language: From data to theory* (2nd ed.). East Sussex, UK: Psychology Press.

Harley, T. A. (2008). *The psychology of language: From data to theory* (3rd ed.). New York: Psychology Press.

Harley, T. A. (2010). *Talking the talk: Language, psychology and science.* New York: Psychology Press.

Harm, M. W., & Seidenberg, M. S. (1999). Phonology, reading acquisition, and dyslexia: insights from connectionist models. *Psychological Review, 106,* 491–528.

Harm, M. W., McCandliss, B. D., & Seidenberg, M. S. (2003). Modeling the successes and failures of interventions for disabled readers. *Scientific Studies of Reading, 7,* 155–182.

Harris, A. J. L., & Hahn, U. (2011). Unrealistic optimism about future life events: A cautionary note. *Psychological Review, 118,* 135–154.

Harris, A. J. L., Corner, A., & Hahn, U. (2009). Estimating the probability of negative events. *Cognition, 110,* 51–64.

Harris, C. R., & Pashler, H. (2004). Attention and the processing of emotional words and names: Not so special after all. *Psychological Science, 15,* 171–178.

Harris, R. J., Sardarpoor-Bascom, F., & Meyer, T. (1989). The role of cultural knowledge in distorting recall for stories. *Bulletin of the Psychonomic Society, 27,* 9–10.

Hartwig, M. K., & Dunlosky, J. (2012). Study strategies of college students: Are self-testing and scheduling related to achievement? *Psychonomic Bulletin & Review, 19,* 126–134.

Harvey, A. G. (2005). Unwanted intrusive thoughts in insomnia. In D. A. Clark (Ed.), *Intrusive thoughts in clinical disorders: Theory, research, and treatment* (pp. 86–118). New York: Guilford Press.

Harvey, A. G., & Tang, N. K. Y. (2012). (Mis)perception of sleep in insomnia: A puzzle and a resolution. *Psychological Bulletin, 138,* 77–101.

Hasher, L., Chung, C., May, C. P., & Foong, N. (2002). Age, time of testing, and proactive interference. *Canadian Journal of Experimental Psychology, 56,* 200–207.

Hasher, L., Lustig, C., & Zacks, R. (2007). Inhibitory mechanisms and the control of attention. In A. R. A. Conway, C. Jarrold, M. J. Kane, A. Miyake, & J. N. Towse (Eds.), *Variations in working memory* (pp. 227–249). New York: Oxford University Press.

Hassin, R. R. (2005). Nonconscious control and implicit working memory. In R. R. Hassin, J. E. Uleman, & J. A. Bargh (Eds.), *The new unconscious* (pp. 196–222). New York: Oxford University Press.

Hastie, R., & Dawes, R. M. (2010). *Rational choice in an uncertain world: The psychology of judgment and decision making* (2nd ed.). Los Angeles: Sage.

Hayes, J. R. (1989). Writing research: The analysis of a very complex task. In D. Klahr & K. Kotovsky (Eds.), *Complex information processing: The impact of Herbert A. Simon* (pp. 209–234). Hillsdale, NJ: Erlbaum

Hayes, J. R. (1996). A new framework for understanding cognition and affect in writing. In C. M. Levy & S. Randsell (Eds.), *The science of writing: Theories, methods, individual differences, and applications* (pp. 1–27). Mahwah, NJ: Erlbaum.

Hayes, S., Hirsch, C., & Mathews, A. (2008). Restriction of working memory capacity during worry. *Journal of Abnormal Psychology, 117*(3), 712.

Hayes, J. R., Schriver, K., Flower, L., & Carey. L. (1987). Cognitive processes in revision. In S. Rosenberg (Ed.), *Advances in psycholinguistics: Vol. 2. Reading, writing, and languages processing.* Cambridge, UK: Cambridge University Press.

Hayne, H., & Simcock, G. (2009). Memory development in toddlers. In M. Courage & N. Cowan (Eds.), *The development of memory in childhood* (pp. 43–68). Hove, UK: Psychology Press.

Hayne, H., Gross, J., McNamee, S., Fitzgibbon, O., & Tustin, K. (2011). Episodic memory and episodic foresight in 3- and 5-year-old children. *Cognitive Development, 26,* 343–355.

Haywood, S. J., Pickering, M. J., & Branigan, H. P. (2005). Do speakers avoid ambiguities during dialogue? *Psychological Science, 16,* 362–366.

Hayworth, K. J., & Biederman, I. (2006). Neural evidence for intermediate representations in object recognition. *Vision Research, 46,* 4024–4031.

Hazeltine, R. E., Prinzmetal, W., & Elliott, K. (1997). If it's not there, where is it? Locating illusory conjunctions. *Journal of Experimental Psychology: Human Perception and Performance, 23,* 263–277.

Hearst, E. (1991). Psychology and nothing. *American Scientist, 79,* 432–443.

Hein, G., & Knight, R. T. (2008). Superior temporal sulcus—it's my area: Or is it? *Journal of Cognitive Neuroscience, 20,* 2125–2136.

Heine, S. J. (2010). Cultural psychology. In S. T. Fiske, D. T. Gilbert, & G. Lindzey (Eds.), *Handbook of social psychology* (6th ed., pp. 1423–1464). Hoboken, NJ: Wiley.

Heit, E., & Barsalou, L. W. (1996). The instantiation principle in natural categories. *Memory, 4,* 413–451.

Hélie, S., & Sun, R. (2010). Incubation, insight, and creative problem solving: A united theory and a connectionist model. *Psychological Review, 117,* 994–1024.

Henderson, D. R., & Hooper, C. L. (2006). *Making great decisions in business and life.* Chicago Park, CA: Chicago Park Press.

Henderson, J. M. (Ed.). (2005). *Real-world scene perception.* Hove, UK: Psychology Press.

Henderson, J. M., & Ferreira, F. (2004b). Scene perception for psycholinguists. In J. M. Henderson & F. Ferreira (Eds.), *The interface of language, vision, and action: Eye movements and the visual world* (pp. 1–58). New York: Psychology Press.

Henkel, L. A. (2011). Photograph-induced memory errors: When photographs make people claim they have done things they have not. *Applied Cognitive Psychology, 25*, 78–86.

Hennessey, B. A. (2000). Rewards and creativity. In C. Sansone & J. M. Harackiewicz (Eds.), *Intrinsic and extrinsic motivation: The search for optimal motivation and perormance* (pp. 55–78). San Diego, CA: Academic Press.

Hennessey, B. A., & Amabile, T. M. (2010). Creativity. *Annual Review of Psychology, 61*, 569–598.

Henry, L. A., & Gudjonsson, G. H. (2007). Individual and developmental differences in eyewitness recall and suggestibility in children with intellectual disabilities. *Applied Cognitive Psychology, 21*, 361–381.

Heppner, P. P. (2008). Expanding the conceptualization and measurement of applied problem solving and coping: From stages to dimensions to the almost forgotten cultural context. *American Psychologist, 63*, 805–816.

Herbert, W. (2010). *On second thought*. New York: Crown.

Herek, G. M., & Garnets, L. D. (2007). Sexual orientation and mental health. *Annual Review of Clinical Psychology, 3*, 353–375.

Hernandez-García, L., Wager, T., & Jonides, J. (2002). Functional brain imaging. In H. Pashler & J. Wixted (Eds.), *Stevens' handbook of experimental psychology* (3rd ed., Vol. **4**, pp. 175–221). New York: Wiley.

Herriot, P. (2004). Language development in children. In R. L. Gregory (Ed.), *The Oxford companion to the mind* (2nd ed., pp. 519–521). New York: Oxford University Press.

Herrmann, D. J., & Gruneberg, M. (2006). Memory failures and their causes in everyday life. In L.-G. Nilsson & Nobuo Ohta (Eds.), *Memory and society: Psychological perspectives* (pp. 251–268). New York: Psychology Press.

Herrmann, D. J., Raybeck, D., & Gruneberg, M. (2002). *Improving memory and study skills*. Kirkland, WA: Hogrefe & Huber.

Herrmann, D. J., Yoder, C. Y., Gruneberg, M., & Payne, D. G. (2006). *Applied cognitive psychology: A textbook*. Mahwah, NJ: Erlbaum.

Hertwig, R., Pachur, T., & Kurzenhäuser, S. (2005). Judgments of risk frequencies: Tests of possible cognitive mechanisms. *Journal of Experimental Psychology: Learning, Memory, and Cognition, 31*, 621–642.

Hertzog, C., & Dixon, R. A. (1994). Metacognitive development in adulthood and old age. In J. Metcalfe & A. P. Shimamura (Eds.), *Metacognition: Knowing about knowing* (pp. 227–251). Cambridge, MA: MIT Press.

Hertzog, C., Dunlosky, J., & Sinclair, S. M. (2010). Episodic feeling-of-knowing resolution derives from the quality of original encoding. Memory & Cognition, *38*(6), 771–784.

Hertzog, C., Lineweaver, T. T., & McGuire, C. L. (1999). Beliefs about memory and aging. In F. Blanchard-Fields & T. M. Hess (Eds.), *Social cognition and aging* (pp. 43–68). New York: Academic Press.

Herzog, C., & Robinson, A. E. (2005). Metacognition and intelligence. In O. Wilhelm & R. W. Engle (Eds.), *Handbook of understanding and measuring intelligence* (pp. 101–123). Thousand Oaks: Sage.

Hess, T. M. (2005). Memory and aging in context. *Psychological Bulletin, 131*, 383–406.

Hess, T. M., Auman, C., Colcombe, S. J., & Rahhal, T. A. (2003). The impact of stereotype threat on age differences in memory performance. *Journal of Gerontology Psychological Sciences, 58B*, P3–P11.

Heth, C. D., Cornell, E. H., & Flood, T. L. (2002). Self-ratings of sense of direction and route reversal performance. *Applied Cognitive Psychology, 16*, 309–324.

Higham, P., Luna, K., & Bloomfield, J. (2011). Trace strength and source-monitoring accounts of accuracy and metacognitive resolution in the misinformation paradigm. *Applied Cognitive Psychology, 25*, 324–335.

Hinds, P. J. (1999). The curse of expertise: The effects of expertise and debiasing methods on predictions of novice performance. *Journal of Experimental Psychology: Applied, 5*, 205–211.

Hinsz, V. B. (2004). Metacognition and mental models in groups: An illustration with metamemory of group recognition memory. In E. Salas & S. M. Fiore (Eds.), *Team cognition: Understanding the factors that drive process and performance* (pp. 33–58). Washington, DC: American Psychological Association.

Hintzman, D. L. (2011). Research strategies in the study of memory: Fads, falacies, and the search for the "coordinates of truth." *Perspectives on Psychological Science, 6*, 253–271.

Hirsh-Pasek, K., & Golinkoff, R. M. (1996). *The origins of grammar: Evidence from early language comprehension*. Cambridge, MA: MIT Press.

Hirt, E. R., McDonald, H. E., & Markman, K. D. (1998). Expectancy effects in reconstructive memory: When the past is just what we expected. In S. J. Lynn & K. M. McConkey (Eds.), *Truth in memory* (pp. 62–89). New York: Guilford.

Hirtle, S. C., & Mascolo, M. F. (1986). Effect of semantic clustering on the memory of spatial locations. *Journal of Experimental Psychology: Learning, Memory, and Cognition, 12*, 182–189.

Hitch, G. J. (2006). Working memory in children: A cognitive approach. In E. Bialystok & F. I. M. Craik (Eds.), *Lifespan cognition: Mechanisms of change* (pp. 112–127). New York: Oxford University Press.

Hoff, E. (2013). *Language development*. Cengage Learning.

Hoffman, D. D. (2010). Consciousness. In E. B. Goldstein (Ed.), *Encyclopedia of perception* (Vol. **1**, pp. 300–304). Thousand Oaks, CA: Sage.

Hoffrage, U. (2004). Overconfidence. In R. Pohl (Ed.), *Cognitive illusions: Handbook on fallacies and biases in thinking, judgment, and memory*. Hove, UK: Psychology Press.

Hogarth, R. M., & Karelaia, N. (2007). Heuristic and linear models of judgment: Matching rules and environments. *Psychological Review, 114*, 733–758.

Holcombe, A. O. (2010). Binding problem. In E. B. Goldstein (Ed.), *Encyclopedia of perception* (Vol. **1**, pp. 205–208). Thousand Oaks, CA: Sage.

Hollingworth, A. (2004). Constructing visual representations of natural scenes. *The roles of short- and long-term visual memory. Journal of Experimental Psychology: Human Perception and Performance, 30*, 519–537.

Hollingworth, A. (2006a). Scene and position specificity in visual memory for objects. *Journal of Experimental Psychology: Learning, Memory, and Cognition, 32*, 58–69.

Hollingworth, A. (2006b). Visual memory for natural scenes: Evidence from change detection and visual search. *Visual Cognition, 14*, 781–807.

Hollingworth, A., & Henderson, J. M. (2004). Sustained change blindness to incremental scene rotation: A dissociation between explicit change detection and visual memory. *Perception and Psychophysics, 66*, 800–807.

Hollingworth, H. (1910). The oblivescence of the disagreeable. *Journal of Philosophy, Psychology and Scientific Methods, 7*, 709–714.

Holmes, J. B., Waters, H. S., & Rajaram, S. (1998). The phenomenology of false memories: Episodic content and confidence. *Journal of Experimental Psychology: Learning, Memory, and Cognition, 24*, 1026–1040.

Holmes, J., Gathercole, S. E., Place, M., Dunning, D. L., Hilton, K. A., & Elliott, J. G. (2010). Working memory deficits can be overcome: Impacts of training and medication on working memory in Children with ADHD. *Applied Cognitive Psychology, 24*, 827–836.

Holt, L. L., & Lotto, A. J. (2008). Speech perception within an auditory cognitive science framework. *Current Directions in Psychological Science, 17*, 42–46.

Holtgraves, T. (2010). Social psychology and language: Words, utterances, and conversations. In S. T. Fiske, D. T. Gilbert, & G. Lindzey (Eds.), *Handbook of social psychology* (5th ed., Vol. **2**, pp. 13–86). Hoboken, NJ: Wiley.

Holyoak, K. J., & Morrison, R. G. (Eds.). (2012). *The Oxford handbook of thinking and reasoning*. New York: Oxford University Press.

Hong, Y., Morris, M. W., Chiu, C., & Benet-Martínez, V. (2000). Multicultural minds: A dynamic constructivist approach to culture and cognition. *American Psychologist, 55*, 709–720.

Honig, E. (1997). Striking lives: Oral history and the politics of memory. *Journal of Women's History, 9*, 139–157.

Hopkins, J. R. (2011, December). The enduring influence of Jean Piaget. *APS Observer, pp.* 35–36.

Hostetter, A. B. (2011). When do gestures communicate? A meta-analysis. *Psychological Bulletin, 137*, 297–315.

Hostetter, A. B., & Alibali, M. W. (2008). Visible embodiment: Gestures as simulated action. *Psychonomic Bulletin & Review, 15*, 495–514.

Hostetter, A. B., & Alibali, M. W. (2010). Language, gesture, action! A test of the gesture as simulated action framework. *Journal of Memory and Language, 63*, 245–257.

Houston, D. M. (2005). Speech perception in infants. In D. B. Pisoni & R. E. Remez (Eds.), *The handbook of speech perception* (pp. 417–448). Malden, MA: Blackwell.

Howard, D. J., & Kerin, R. A. (2011). The effects of name similarity on message processing and persuasion. *Journal of Experimental Social Psychology, 47*, 63–71.

Howe, M. L. (2000). *The fate of early memories*. Washington, DC: American Psychological Association.

Howe, M. L. (2006). Distinctiveness effects in children's memory. In R. R. Hunt & J. B. Worthen (Eds.), *Distinctiveness and memory*. New York: Oxford University Press.

Howe, M. L., Courage, M. L., & Rooksby, M. (2009). The genesis and development of autobiographical memory. In M. Courage & N. Cowan (Eds.), *The development of memory in childhood* (pp. 177–196). Hove, UK: Psychology Press.

Howes, M. B. (2007). *Human memory: Structures and images*. Thousand Oaks, CA: Sage.

Hruska, P., Krigolson, O., Coderre, S., McLaughlin, K., Cortese, F., Doig, C., . . . & Hecker, K. G. (2016). Working memory, reasoning, and expertise in medicine—insights into their relationship using functional neuroimaging. *Advances in Health Sciences Education, 21*(5), 935–952.

Hsu, V. C., & Rovee-Collier, C. (2006). Memory reactivation in the second year of life. *Infant Behavior & Development, 29*, 91–107.

Hu, Y., Ericsson, K. A., Yang, D., & Lu, C. (2009). Superior self-paced memorization of digits in spite of a normal digit span: The structure of a memorist's skill. *Journal of Experimental Psychology: Learning, Memory, and Cognition, 35*, 1426–1442.

Hubbard, T. L. (2010). Auditory imagery: Empirical findings. *Psychological Bulletin, 136*, 302–329.

Hubel, D. H. (1982). Explorations of the primary visual cortex, 1955–1978. *Nature, 299*, 515–524.

Hubel, D. H., & Wiesel, T. N. (1965). Receptive fields of single neurons in two nonstriate visual areas (18 and 19) of the cat. *Journal of Neurophysiology, 28*, 229–289.

Hubel, D. H., & Wiesel, T. N. (1979). Brain mechanisms and vision. *Scientific American, 241* (3), 150–162.

Hubel, D. H., & Wiesel, T. N. (2005). *Brain and visual perception: The story of a 25-year collaboration.* New York: Oxford University Press.

Hudson, J. A., & Mayhew, E. M. Y. (2009). The development of memory for recurring events. In M. Courage & N. Cowan (Eds.), *The development of memory in childhood* (pp. 69–91). Hove, UK: Psychology Press.

Huettel, S. A., Song, A. W., & McCarthy, G. (2004). *Functional magnetic resonance imaging.* Sunderland, MA: Sinauer.

Hugenberg, K., Young, S. G., Bernstein, M. J., & Sacco, D. F. (2010). The categorization-individuation model: An integrative account of the other-race recognition deficit. *Psychological Review, 117*, 1168–1187.

Huitema, J. S., Dopkins, S., Klin, C. M., & Myers, J. L. (1993). Connecting goals and actions during reading. *Journal of Experimental Psychology: Learning, Memory, and Cognition, 19*, 1053–1060.

Hulicka, I. M. (1982). Memory functioning in late adulthood. In F. I. M. Craik & S. Trehub (Eds.), *Advances in the study of communication and affect* (Vol. **8**, pp. 331–351). New York: Plenum.

Hulme, C., & Snowling, M. J. (2011). Children's reading comprehension difficulties: Nature, causes, and treatments. *Current Directions in Psychological Science, 20*, 139–142.

Humphreys, G. W., & Riddoch, M. J. (2001). The neuropsychology of visual object and space perception. In E. B. Goldstein (Ed.), *Blackwell handbook of perception* (pp. 204–236). Malden, MA: Blackwell.

Hunter, I. M. L. (2004a). James, William. In R. L. Gregory (Ed.), *The Oxford companion to the mind* (2nd ed., pp. 492–494). New York: Oxford University Press.

Hunter, I. M. L. (2004b). Mnemonics. In R. L. Gregory (Ed.), *The Oxford companion to the mind* (2nd ed., 610–612). New York: Oxford University Press.

Hurley, M. M. (2011). *Inside jokes: Using humor to reverse-engineer the mind.* Cambridge, MA: MIT Press.

Hurley, S. M., & Novick, L. R. (2006). Context and structure: The nature of students' knowledge about three spatial diagram representations. *Thinking & Reasoning, 12*, 281–308.

Hurley, S. M., & Novick, L. R. (2010). Solving problems using matrix, network, and hierarchy diagrams: The consequences of violating construction conventions. *The Quarterly Journal of Experimental Psychology, 63*, 275–290.

Hyde, J. S. (2005). The gender similarities hypothesis. *American Psychologist, 60*, 581–592.

Hyde, J. S., Lindberg, S. M., Linn, M. C., Ellis, A. B., & Williams, C. C. (2008). Gender similarities characterize math performance. *Science, 321*, 494–495.

Hyde, J. S. (2016). Sex and cognition: gender and cognitive functions. *Current Opinion in Neurobiology, 38*, 53–56.

Hyman, I. E., Jr. (2010). Did you see the unicycling clown? Inattentional blindness while walking and talking on a cell phone. *Applied Cognitive Psychology, 24*, 597–607.

Hyman, I. E., Jr., & Kleinknecht, E. E. (1999). False childhood memories: Research, theory, and applications. In L. M. Williams & V. L. Banyard (Eds.), *Trauma & memory* (pp. 175–188). Thousand Oaks, CA: Sage.

Hyman, I. E., Jr., & Loftus, E. F. (2002). False childhood memories and eyewitness memory errors. In M. L. Eisen, J. A. Quas, & G. S. Goodman (Eds.), *Memory and suggestibility in the forensic interview* (pp. 63–84). Mahwah, NJ: Erlbaum.

Hyman, I. E., Jr., Husband, T. H., & Billings, F. J. (1995). False memories of childhood experiences. *Applied Cognitive Psychology, 9*, 181–197.

Imhoff, M. C., & Baker-Ward, L. (1999). Preschoolers' suggestibility: Effects of developmentally appropriate language and interviewer supportiveness. *Journal of Applied Developmental Psychology, 20*, 407–429.

Intons-Peterson, M. J., Rocchi, P., West, T., McLellan, K., & Hackney, A. (1999). Age, testing at preferred or nonpreferred times (testing optimality) and false memory. *Journal of Experimental Psychology: Learning, Memory, and Cognition, 25*, 23–40.

Intons-Peterson, M. J., Russell, W., & Dressel, S. (1992). The role of pitch in auditory imagery. *Journal of Experimental Psychology: Learning, Memory, and Cognition, 13*, 490–500.

Intraub, H. (1997). The representation of visual scenes. *Trends in Cognitive Sciences, 1*, 217–222.

Intraub, H., & Berkowits, D. (1996). Beyond the edges of a picture. *American Journal of Psychology, 109*, 581–598.

Intraub, H., Gottesman, C. V., & Bills, A. J. (1998). Effects of perceiving and imagining scenes on memory for pictures. *Journal of Experimental Psychology: Learning, Memory, and Cognition, 24*, 186–201.

Irwin, D. E. (2003). Eye movements and visual cognitive suppression. *The Psychology of Learning and Motivation, 42*, 265–293.

Irwin, D. E. (2004). Fixation location and fixation duration as indices of cognitive processing. In J. M. Henderson & F. Ferreira (Eds.), *The interface of language, vision, and action: Eye movements and the visual world* (pp. 105–133). New York: Psychology Press

Irwin, D. E., & Zelinsky, G. J. (2002). Eye movements and scene perception: Memory for things observed. *Perception & Psychophysics, 64,* 882–895.

Ishai, A., & Sagi, D. (1995). Common mechanisms of visual imagery and perception. *Science, 268,* 1772–1774.

Isikoff, M. & Lipper, T. (2003, July 21). A spy takes the bullet. *Newsweek,* pp.24–25.

Israel, S. E., & Massey, D. (2005). Metacognitive think-aloud: Using a gradual release model with middle school students. In S. E. Israel, C. C. Block, K. L. Bauserman, & K. Kinnucan-Welsch (Eds.), *Metacognition in literacy learning: Theory, assessment, instruction, and professional development* (pp. 183–198). Mahwah, NJ: Erlbaum.

Ito, T. A., Urland, G. R., Willadsen-Jensen, E., & Correll, J. (2006). The social neuroscience of stereotyping and prejudice: Using event-related brain potentials to study social perception. In J. T. Cacioppo, P. S. Visser, & C. L. Pickett (Eds.), *Social neuroscience: People thinking about thinking people* (pp. 189–208). Cambridge, MA: MIT Press.

Jackendoff, R. (1994). *Patterns in the mind.* New York: Basic Books.

Jackendoff, R. (1997). *The architecture of the language faculty.* Cambridge, MA: MIT Press.

Jackson, L. M. (2011). *The psychology of prejudice: From attitudes to social action.* Washington, DC: American Psychological Association.

Jacobs, N., & Garnham, A. (2007). The role of conversational hand gestures in a narrative task. *Journal of Memory and Language, 56,* 291–303.

Jahn, G. (2004). Three turtles in danger: Spontaneous construction of causally relevant spatial situation models. *Journal of Experimental Psychology: Learning, Memory, and Cognition, 30,* 969–987.

Jain, A. K., & Duin, R. P. W. (2004). Pattern recognition. In R. L. Gregory (Ed.), *The Oxford companion to the mind* (2nd ed., p. 698–703). New York: Oxford University Press.

Jäkel, F., Schölkopf, B., & Wickmann, F. A. (2008). Generalization and similarity in exemplar models of categorization: Insights from machine learning. *Psychonomic Bulletin & Review, 15,* 256–271.

James, L. E., & MacKay, D. G. (2001). H.M., word knowledge, and aging: Support for a new theory of long-term retrograde amnesia. *Psychological Science, 12,* 485–492.

James, W. (1890). *The principles of psychology.* New York: Henry Holt.

Janiszewski, C. (2011). Too many views to capture: Reference sets in human judgment. In G. Keren (Ed.), *Perspectives on framing* (pp. 93–115). New York: Psychology Press.

Janssen, S. M. J., & Rubin, D. C. (2011). Age effects in cultural life scripts. *Applied Cognitive Psychology, 25,* 291–298.

January, D., Trueswell, J. C., & Thompson-Schill, S. L. (2009). Co-localization of stroop and syntactic ambiguity resolution in Broca's area: Implications for the neural bsis of sentence processing. *Journal of Cognitive Neuroscience, 21,* 2434–2444.

Jared, D., Levy, B. A., & Rayner, K. (1999). The role of phonology in the activation of word meanings during reading: Evidence from proofreading and eye movements. *Journal of Experimental Psychology: General, 128,* 219–264.

Jarrold, C., & Bayliss, D. M. (2007). Variation in working memory due to typical and atypical development. In A. R. A. Conway, M. J. Kane, A. Miyake, & J. N. Towse (Eds.), *Variations in working memory* (pp. 134–161). New York: Oxford University Press.

Jaschinski, U., & Wentura, D. (2002). Misleading postevent information and working memory capacity: An individual differences approach to eyewitness memory. *Applied Cognitive Psychology, 16*(2), 223–231.

Jenkins, J. J. (1974). Remember that old theory of memory? Well, forget it. *American Psychologist, 29,* 785–795.

Jia, G., Aaronson, D., & Wu, Y. (2002). Long-term language attainment of bilingual immigrants: Predictive variables and language group differences. *Applied Psycholinguistics, 23,* 599–621.

Jitendra, A. K., Griffin, C. C., Haria, P., Leh, J., Adams, A., & Kaduvettoor, A. (2007). A comparison of single and multiple strategy instruction on third-grade students' mathematical problem solving. *Journal of Educational Psychology, 99,* 115–127.

Jobard, G., Crivello, F., & Tzourio-Mazoyer, N. (2003). Evaluation of the dual route theory of reading: A meta-analysis of 35 neuroimaging studies. *Neuroimage, 20,* 693–712.

Johansson, P., Hall, L., Sikström, S., Tärning, B., & Lind, A. (2006). How something can be said about telling more than we can know: On choice blindness and introspection. *Consciousness and Cognition, 15,* 673–692.

Johnson, J. S., & Newport, E. L. (1989). Critical effects in second language learning: The influence of maturational state on the acquisition of English as a second language. *Cognitive Psychology, 21,* 60–99.

Johnson, M. H., & Bolhuis, J. J. (2000). Predispositions in perceptual and cognitive development. In J. J. Bolhuis (Ed.), *Brain, perception, memory* (pp. 68–84). New York: Oxford University Press.

Johnson, M. K. (1996). Fact, fantasy, and public policy. In D. J. Herrmann et al. (Eds.), *Basic and applied memory research theory in context* (Vol. **1**, pp. 83–103). Mahwah, NJ: Erlbaum.

Johnson, M. K. (1997). Identifying the origin of mental experience. In M. S. Myslobodsky (Ed.), *The mythomanias: The nature of deception and self-deception* (pp. 133–180). Mahwah, NJ: Erlbaum.

Johnson, M. K. (1998). Individual and cultural reality monitoring. *Annals of the American Academy of Political and Social Science*, *560*, 179–193.

Johnson, M. K. (2002, October). Reality monitoring: Varying levels of analysis. *APS Observer, pp. 8*, 28–29.

Johnson-Laird, P. N. (2005a). Mental models and thought. In K. J. Holyoak & R. G. Morrison (Eds.), *The Cambridge handbook of thinking and reasoning* (pp. 185–208). New York: Cambridge University Press.

Johnson-Laird, P. N. (2005b). The shape of problems. In V. Girotto & P. N. Johnson-Laird (Eds.), *The shape of reason: Essays in honour of Paolo Legrenzi* (pp. 3–26). Hove, UK: Psychology Press.

Johnson-Laird, P. N. (2011). The truth about conditionals. In K. Manktelow, D. Over, & S. Elqayam (Eds.), *The science of reason: A festschrift for Jonathan St B. T. Evans* (pp. 119–143). New York: Psychology Press.

Johnson-Laird, P. N., Girotto, V., & Legrenzi, P. (2004). Reasoning from inconsistency to consistency. *Psychological Review, 111*, 640–661

Jones, D. M., Macken, W. J., & Nicholls, A. P. (2004). The phonological store of working memory: Is it phonological and is it a store? *Journal of Experimental Psychology, Learning, Memory, and Cognition, 30*, 656–674.

Jones, E. L., & Ross, B. H. (2011). Classification versus inference learning contrasted with real-world categories. *Memory and Cognition, 39*, 764–777.

Jones, J. (1999). *The psychotherapist's guide to human memory*. New York: Basic Books.

Jonides, J., Lewis, R. L., Nee, D. E., Lustig, Berman, M. G., & Moore, K. S. (2008). The mind and brain of short-term memory. *Annual Review of Psychology, 59*, 193–224.

Joorman, J., & Siemer, M. (2004). Memory accessibility, mood regulation, and dysphoria: Difficulties in repairing sad mood with happy memories? *Journal of Abnormal Psychology, 113*, 179–188.

Joyner, M. H., & Kurtz-Costes, B. (1997). Metamemory development. In N. Cowan & C. Hulme (Eds.), *The development of memory in childhood* (pp. 275–300). East Sussex, UK: Psychology Press.

Juffs, A. (2010). Perspectives from formal linguistics on second language acquisition. In R. B. Kaplan (Ed.), *The Oxford handbook of applied linguistics* (2nd ed., pp. 143–162). New York: Oxford University Press.

Juhasz, B. J., & Rayner, K. (2003). Investigating the effects of a set of intercorrelated variables on eye fixation durations in reading. *Journal of Experimental Psychology: Learning, Memory, and Cognition, 29*, 1312–1318.

Jusczyk, P. W., & Aslin, R. N. (1995). Infants' detection of the sound patterns of words in fluent speech. *Cognitive Psychology, 29*, 1–23.

Jusczyk, P. W., & Luce, P. A. (2002). Speech perception. In H. Pashler (Ed.), *Stevens' handbook of experimental psychology* (3rd ed., Vol. 1, pp. 493–536). New York: Wiley.

Just, M. A., Carpenter, P. A., & Woolley, J. D. (1982). Paradigms and processes in reading comprehension. *Journal of Experimental Psychology: General, 111*, 228–238.

Just, M. A., & Carpenter, P. A. (1992). A capacity theory of comprehension: individual differences in working memory. *Psychological Review, 99*, 122–149.

Just, M. A., Newman, S. D., Keller, T. A., McEleney, A., & Carpenter, P. A. (2004). Imagery in sentence comprehension: An fMRI study. *NeuroImage, 21*, 112–124.

Kagan, J., & Herschkowitz, N. (2005). *A young mind in a growing brain*. Mahwah, NJ: Erlbaum.

Kahneman, D. (2011). *Thinking, fast and slow*. New York: Farrar, Straus and Giroux.

Kahneman, D., & Frederick, S. (2002). Representativeness revisited: Attribute substitution in intuitive judgment. In T. Gilovich, D. Griffin, & D. Kahneman (Eds.), *Heuristics and biases: The psychology of intuitive judgment* (pp. 49–81). New York: Cambridge University Press.

Kahneman, D., & Frederick, S. (2005). A model of heuristic judgment. In K. J. Holyoak. & R. G. Morrison (Eds.), *The Cambridge handbook of thinking and reasoning* (pp. 267–293). New York: Cambridge University Press.

Kahneman, D., & Renshon, J. (2007, January/February). Why hawks win. *Foreign Policy*, pp. 34–38.

Kahneman, D., & Tversky, A. (1972). Subjective probability: A judgment of representativeness. *Cognitive Psychology, 3*, 430–454.

Kahneman, D., & Tversky, A. (1973). On the psychology of prediction. *Psychological Review, 80*, 237–251.

Kahneman, D., & Tversky, A. (1984). Choices, values, and frames. *American Psychologist, 39*, 341–350.

Kahneman, D., & Tversky, A. (1995). Conflict resolution: A cognitive perspective. In K. Arrow, R. H. Mnookin, L. Ross, A. Tversky, & R. B. Wilson (Eds.), *Barriers to conflict resolution* (pp. 44–60). New York: Norton.

Kahneman, D., & Tversky, A. (1996). On the reality of cognitive illusions. *Psychological Review, 103*, 582–591.

Kahneman, D., & Tversky, A. (2000). *Choice, values, and frames*. New York: Cambridge University Press.

Kail, R. V. (1992). Development of memory in children. In L. R. Squire (Ed.), *Encyclopedia of learning and memory* (pp. 99–102). New York: Macmillan.

Kail, R. V. (2010). *Children and their development* (5th ed.). Upper Saddle River: Prentice Hall.

Kalat, J. W. (2009). *Biological psychology* (10th ed.). Belmont, CA: Wadsworth.

Kamide, Y 2012, Learning individual talkers' structural preferences. *Cognition, 124*, 66–71.

Kanwisher, N. (2010). Functional specificity in the human brain: A window into the functional architecture of the mind. *PNAS Proceedings of the National Academy of Sciences of the United States of America, 107*, 11163–11170.

Kanwisher, N., Downing, P., Epstein, R., & Kourtzi, Z. (2001). Functional neuroimaging of visual recognition. In R. Cabeza & A. Kingstone (Eds.), *Handbook of functional neuroimaging of cognition* (pp. 110–151). Cambridge, MA: MIT Press.

Kanwisher, N., McDermott, J., Chun, M. M. (1997). The fusiform face area: a module in human extrastriate cortex specialized for face perception. *Journal of Neuroscience, 17*, 4302–4311.

Kaplan, R. B. (Ed.). (2010a). *The Oxford handbook of applied linguistics* (2nd ed.). New York: Oxford University Press.

Kaschak, M. P., Kutta, T. & Schachneider, C. (2011). Long-term cumulative structural priming persists for (at least) one week. *Memory & Cognition, 39*, 381–388.

Kaufman, J. C., & Sternberg, R. J. (2010b). Preface. In J. C. Kaufman & R. J. Sternberg (Eds.), *The Cambridge handbook of creativity* (pp. xiii–xv). New York: Cambridge University Press.

Kaufman, N. J., Randlett, A. L., & Price, J. (1985). Awareness of the use of comprehension strategies in good and poor college readers. *Reading Psychology, 6*, 1–11.

Kayaert, G., Biederman, I., & Vogels, R. (2003). Shape tuning in macaque inferior temporal cortex. *Journal of Neuroscience, 23*, 3016–3027.

Keast, A., Brewer, N., & Wells, G. L. (2007). Children's metacognitive judgments in an eyewitness identification task. *Journal of Experimental Child Psychology, 97*, 286–314.

Keating, P. A. (2006). Phonetic encoding of prosodic structure. In J. Harrington & M. Tabain (Eds.), *Speech production: Models, phonetic processes, and techniques* (pp. 167–186). New York: Psychology Press.

Keen, R. (2011). The development of problem solving in young children: A critical cognitive skill. *Annual Review of Psychology, 62*, 1–21.

Keller, T. A., Carpenter, P. A., & Just, M. A. (2003). Brain imaging of tongue-twister sentence comprehension: Twisting the tongue and the brain. *Brain and Language, 84*, 189–203.

Kellogg, R. T. (1994). *The psychology of writing.* New York: Oxford University Press.

Kellogg, R. T. (1996). A model of working memory in writing. In C. M. Levy & S. Ransdell (Eds.), *The science of writing: Theories, methods, individual differences, and applications* (pp. 57–71). Mahwah, NJ: Erlbaum.

Kellogg, R. T. (1998). Components of working memory in text production. In M. Torrance & G. C. Jeffery (Eds.), *The cognitive demands of writing: Processing capacity and working memory effects in text production.* Amsterdam: Amsterdam University Press.

Kellogg, R. T. (2001a). Competition for working memory among writing processes. *American Journal of Psychology, 114*, 175–191.

Kellogg, R. T. (2001b). Long-term working memory in text production. *Memory & Cognition, 29*, 43–52.

Kellogg, R. T., & Whiteford, A. P. (2009). Training advanced writing skills: The case for deliberate practice. *Educational Psychologist, 44*, 250–266.

Kellogg, R. T., Olive, T., & Piolat, A. (2007). Verbal, visual, and spatial working memory in written language production. *Acta Psychologica, 124*, 382–397.

Kelly, F., & Grossberg, S. (2000). Neural dynamics of 3-D surface perception: Figure-ground separation and lightness perception. *Perception & Psychophysics, 62*, 1596–1618.

Kemp, R., Towell, N., & Pike, G. (1997). When seeing should not be believing: Photographs, credit cards, and fraud. *Journal of Applied Psychology, 11*, 211–222.

Kemper, S. (2006). Language and adulthood. Aging and attention. In E. Bialystok & F. I. M. Craik (Eds.), *Lifespan cognition: Mechanisms of change* (pp. 223–238). New York: Oxford University Press.

Kersten, D., Mamassian, P., & Yuille, A. (2004). Object perception as Bayesian inference. *Annual Review of Psychology, 55*, 271–304.

Kesibir, S., & Oishi, S. (2010). Spontaneous self-reference effect in memory: Why some birthdays are harder to remember than others. *Psychological Science, 21*, 1525–1531.

Kester, J. D., Benjamin, A. S., Castel, A. D., & Craik, F. I. M. (2002). Memory in elderly people. In A. D. Baddeley, M. D. Kopelman, & B. A. Wilson (Eds.), *The handbook of memory disorders* (2nd ed., pp. 543–567). New York: Wiley.

Ketelsen, K., & Welsh, M. (2010). Working memory and mental arithmetic: A case for dual central executive resources. *Brain and Cognition, 74*, 203–209.

Khanna, M. M., Badura-Brack, A. S., McDermott, T. J., Embury, C. M., Wiesman, A. I., Shepherd, A., . . . & Wilson, T. W. (2017). Veterans with post-traumatic stress disorder exhibit altered emotional processing and attentional control during an emotional Stroop task. *Psychological Medicine, 47*(11), 2017–2027.

Kibbe, M. M., & Leslie, A. M. (2011). What do infants remember when they forget? Location and identity in 6-month-olds' memory for objects. *Psychological Science*, *22*, 1500–1505.

Kida, T. (2006). *Don't believe everything you think: The 6 basic mistakes we make in thinking*. Amherst, NY: Prometheus Books.

Kiesel, A., Steinhauser, M., Wendt, M., Falkenstein, M., Jost, K., Philipp, A. M., . . . Koch, I. (2010). Control and interference in task switching—a review. *Psychological Bulletin*, 849–874.

Kifner, J. (1994, May 20). Pollster finds error on Holocaust doubts. *New York Times* (Late New York Edition), p. A12.

Kihlstrom, J. F. (2009). 'So that we might have roses in December': The function of autobiographical memory. *Applied Cognitive Psychology*, 1179–1192.

Kihlstrom, J. F., Dorfman, J., & Park, L. (2007). Implicit and explicit memory and learning. In M. Velmans & S. Schneider (Eds.), *The Blackwell companion to consciousness*(pp. 526–539). Malden, MA: Blackwell.

Kimball, D. R., & Holyoak, K. K. (2000). Transfer and expertise. In E. Tulving & F. I. M. Craik (Eds.), *The Oxford handbook of memory* (pp. 109–122). New York: Oxford University Press.

Kimball, M. M. (1989). A new perspective on women's math achievement. *Psychological Bulletin*, *105*, 198–214.

Kinsbourne, M. (1998). The right hemisphere and recovery from aphasia. In B. Stemmer & H. A. Whitaker (Eds.), *Handbook of neurolinguistics* (pp. 385–392). San Diego: Academic Press.

Kintsch, W. (1998). *Comprehension: A paradigm for cognition*. New York: Cambridge University Press.

Kintsch, W., & Buschke, H. (1969). Homophones and synonyms in short-term memory. *Journal of Experimental Psychology*, *80*, 403–407.

Kintsch, W., et al. (1999). Models of working memory. In A. Miyake & P. Shah (Eds.), *Models of working memory: Mechanisms of active maintenance and executive control* (pp. 412–441). New York: Cambridge University Press.

Kirsh, D. (2009). Problem solving and situated cognition. In P. Robbins & M. Aydede (Eds.), *The Cambridge handbook of situated cognition* (pp. 264–306). New York: Cambridge University Press.

Kirsh, S. J. (2011). *Children, adolescents, and media violence: A critical look at the research* (2nd ed.). Los Angeles: Sage.

Kisilevsky, B. S., Hains, S. M. J., Lee, K., Xie, X., Huang, H., Hui Ye, . . . Wang, Z. (2003). Effects of experience on fetal voice recognition. *Psychological Science*, *14*, 220–224.

Kitchin, R., & Blades, M. (2002). *The cognition of geographic space*. London: Tauris.

Klein, S. B., & Kihlstrom, J. F. (1986). Elaboration, organization, and the self-reference effect in memory. *Journal of Experimental Psychology: General*, *115*, 26–38.

Kleinschmidt, D., & Jaeger, T. F. (2015). Robust speech perception: Recognize the familiar, generalize to the similar, and adapt to the novel. *Psychological Review*, *122*, 148–203.

Kliegl, R., Grabner, E., Rolfe, M., & Engbert, R. (2004). Length, frequency, and predictability effects of words on eye movements in reading. In R. Radach, A. Kennedy, & K. Rayner (Eds.), *Eye movements and information processing during reading* (pp. 262–284). Hove, UK: Psychology Press.

Klin, C. M., Guzmán, A. E., & Levine, W. H. (1999). Prevalence and persistence of predictive inferences. *Journal of Memory and Learning*, *40*, 593–604.

Knoll, M. A., & Arkes, H. R. (2017). The Effects of Expertise on the Hindsight Bias. *Journal of Behavioral Decision Making*, *30*(2), 389–399.

Knott, R., & Marslen-Wilson, W. (2001). Does the medial temporal lobe bind phonological memories? *Journal of Cognitive Neuroscience*, *13*, 593–609.

Knouse, L. E., Paradise, M. J., & Dunlosky, J. (2006). Does ADHD in adults affect the relative accuracy of metamemory judgments? *Journal of Attention Disorders*, *10*, 160–170.

Knowlton, B. (1997). Declarative and nondeclarative knowledge: Insights from cognitive neuroscience. In K. Lamberts & D. Shanks (Eds.), *Knowledge, concepts and categories* (pp. 215–246). Cambridge, MA: MIT Press.

Koestler, A. (1964). *The act of creation*. London: Hutchin.

Kolb, B., & Whishaw, I. Q. (2009). *Fundamentals of human neuropsychology* (6th ed.). New York: Worth.

Kolb, B., & Whishaw, I. Q. (2011). *An introduction to brain and behavior* (3rd ed.). New York: Worth.

Koelsch, S., Maess, B., & Friederici, A. D. (2000). Musical syntax is processed in the area of Broca: an MEG study. *Neuroimage*, *11*, S56.

Koriat, A. (2000). Control processes in remembering. In E. Tulving & F. I. M. Craik (Eds.), *The Oxford handbook of memory* (pp. 333–346). New York: Oxford University Press.

Koriat, A. (2007). Metacognition and consciousness. In P. D. Zelazo, M. Moscovitch, & E. Thompson (Eds.), *The Cambridge handbook of consciousness* (pp. 289–325). Cambridge, UK: Cambridge University Press.

Koriat, A., & Bjork, R. A. (2006a). Illusions of competence during study can be remedied by manipulations that enhance learners' sensitivity to retrieval conditions at test. *Memory & Cognition*, *34*, 959–972.

Koriat, A., & Bjork, R. A. (2006b). Mending metacognitive illusions: A comparison of mnemonic-based and theory-based procedures. *Journal of Experimental Psychology: Learning, Memory, and Cognition, 32*, 1133–1145.

Koriat, A., & Helstrup, T. (2007). Metacognitive aspects of memory. In S. Magnussen & T. Helstrup (Eds.), *Everyday memories* (pp. 251–274). New York: Psychology Press.

Koriat, A., Fiedler, K., & Bjork, R. A. (2006). Inflation of conditional predictions. *Journal of Experimental Psychology: General, 135*, 429–447.

Koriat, A., Nussinson, R., Bless, H., & Shaked, N. (2008). Information-based and experience-based metacognitive judgments: Evidence from subjective confidence. In J. Dunlosky & R. A. Bjork (Eds.), *Handbook of metamemory and memory* (pp. 117–135). New York: Psychology Press.

Kornell, N. (2009). Optimising learning using flashcards: Spacing is more effective than cramming. *Applied Cognitive Psychology, 23*, 1297–1317.

Kornell, N., & Metcalfe, J. (2006). Study efficacy and the region of proximal learning framework. *Journal of Experimental Psychology: Learning, Memory, and Cognition, 37*, 609–622.

Kornell, N., Rhodes, M. G., Castel, A. D., & Tauber, S. K. (2011). The ease-of-processing heuristic and the stability bias: Dissociating memory, memory beliefs, and memory judgments. *Psychological Science, 22*, 787–794.

Kosslyn, S. M. (1983). *Ghosts in the mind's machine: Creating and using images in the brain.* New York: Norton.

Kosslyn, S. M. (2001). Visual consciousness. *Advances in Consciousness Research, 8*, 79–103.

Kosslyn, S. M., & Thompson, W. L. (2000). Shared mechanisms in visual imagery and visual perception: Insights from cognitive neurosciences. In M. S. Gazzaniga (Ed.), *The new cognitive neurosciences* (2nd ed., pp. 975–985). Cambridge, MA: MIT Press.

Kosslyn, S. M., Alpert, N. M., & Thompson, W. L. (1995). Identifying objects at different levels of hierarchy: A positron emission tomography study. *Human Brain Mapping, 3*, 107–132.

Kosslyn, S. M., Ganis, G., & Thompson, W. L. (2001). Neural foundations of imagery. *Nature Reviews/Neuroscience, 2*, 635–642.

Kosslyn, S. M., Ganis, G., & Thompson, W. L. (2010). Multimodal images in the brain. In A. Guillot & C. Collet (Eds.), *The neurophysiological foundations of mental and motor imagery* (pp. 3–16). New York: Oxford University Press.

Kosslyn, S. M., Seger, C., Pani, J. R., & Hillger, L. A. (1990). When is imagery used in everyday life? A diary study. *Journal of Mental Imagery, 14*, 131–152.

Kosslyn, S. M., Thompson, W. L., & Ganis, G. (2006). *The case for mental imagery.* New York: Oxford University Press.

Kovera, K. B., & Borgida, E. (2010). Social psychology and law. In S. T. Fiske, D. T. Gilbert, & G. Lindzey (Eds.), *The handbook of social psychology* (5th ed., Vol. **2**, pp. 1343–1385). Hoboken, NJ: Wiley.

Kozbelt, A., Beghetto, R. A., & Runco, M. A. (2010). Theories of creativity. In J. C. Kaufman & R. J. Sternberg (Eds.), *The Cambridge handbook of creativity* (pp. 20–47). New York: Cambridge University Press.

Kramer, A. F., & Kray, J. (2006). Aging and attention. In E. Bialystok & F. I. M. Craik (Eds.), *Lifespan cognition: Mechanisms of change* (pp. 57–69). New York: Oxford University Press.

Krätzig, G. P., & Arbuthnot, K. D. (2009). Metacognitive learning: The effect of item-specific experience and age on metamemory calibration and planning. *Metacognition and Learning, 4*, 125–144.

Krizan, Z., & Windschitl, P. D. (2007). The influence of outcome desirability on optimism. *Psychological Bulletin, 133*, 95–121.

Kroll, J. F., & De Groot, A. M. (Eds.). (2005). *Handbook of bilingualism: Psycholinguistic approaches.* New York: Oxford University Press.

Krueger, L. E. (1992). The word-superiority effect and phonological recoding. *Memory & Cognition, 20*, 685–694.

Kruglanski, A. W. (2004). *The psychology of closed mindedness.* New York: Psychology Press.

Kruglanski, A. W., & Gigerenzer, G. (2011). Intuitive and deliberate judgments are based on common principles. *Psychological Review, 118*, 97–109.

Krynski, R. R., & Tenenbaum, J. B. (2007). The role of causality in judgments under uncertainty. *Journal of Experimental Psychology: General, 136*, 430–450.

Kubose, T. T., Bock, K., Dell, G. S., Garnsey, S. M., Kramer, A. F., & Mayhugh, J. (2006). The effects of speech production and speech comprehension on simulated driving performance. *Applied Cognitive Psychology, 20*, 43–64.

Kuhl, P. K. (1994). Learning and representation in speech and language. *Current Opinion in Neurobiology, 4*, 812–822.

Kuhl, P. K. (2000). Language, mind, and brain: Experience alters perception. In M. Gazzaniga (Ed.), *The new cognitive neurosciences* (pp. 99–115). Cambridge, MA: MIT Press.

Kuhl, P. K. (2006). A new view of language acquisition. In H. Luria, D. M. Seymour, & T. Smoke (Eds.), *Language and linguistics in context: Readings and applications for teachers* (pp. 29–41). Mahwah, NJ: Erlbaum.

Kutas, M., & Federmeier, K. D. (2011). Thirty years and counting: Finding meaning in the N400 component of the event-related brain potential (ERP). *Annual Review of Psychology, 62*, 621–647.

Kvavilashvili, L., Mirani, J., Schlagman, S., & Kornbrot, D. E. (2003). Comparing flashbulb memories of September 11 and the death of Princess Diana: Effects of time delays and nationalities. *Applied Cognitive Psychology, 17,* 1017–1031.

Kwon, H., & Linderholm, T. (2014). Effects of self-perception of reading skill on absolute accuracy of metacomprehension judgements. *Current Psychology, 33,* 73–88.

Kyllonen, P. C., & Lee, S. (2005). Assessing problem solving in context. In O. Wilhelm & R. W. Engle (Eds.), *Handbook of understanding and measuring intelligence* (pp. 11–25). Thousand Oaks, CA: Sage.

LaBerge, D. (1995). *Attentional processing: The brain's art of mindfulness.* Cambridge, MA: Harvard University Press.

Laeng, B., Zarrinpar, A., & Kosslyn, S. M. (2003). Do separate processes identify objects as exemplars versus members of basic-level categories? Evidence from hemispheric specialization. *Brain and Cognition, 53,* 15–27.

Laible, D., & Panfile, T. (2009). Mother-child reminiscing in the context of secure attachment relationships: Lessons in understanding and coping with negative emotions. In J. A. Quas & R. Fivus (Eds.), *Emotion and memory in development: Biological, cognitive, and social considerations* (pp. 166–195). New York: Oxford University Press.

Lakoff, G. (1987). *Women, fire and dangerous things: What categories reveal about the mind.* Chicago: University of Chicago Press.

Lakoff, G. (2007). *Whose freedom? The battle over America's most important idea.* New York: Picador.

Lakoff, G. (2009). *The political mind: A cognitive scientist's guide to your brain and its politics.* New York: Penguin.

Lakoff, G. (2011, October 19). Framing Occupy Wall Street. Retrieved January 23, 2012, from www.truth-out.org/how-frame-yourself-framing/131>9031142

Lambert, W. E. (1987). The effects of bilingual and bicultural experiences on children's attitudes and social perspectives. In P. Homel, M. Palij, & D. Aaronson (Eds.), *Childhood bilingualism: Aspects of linguistic, cognitive, and social development* (pp. 197–228). Hillsdale, NJ: Erlbaum.

Lambert, W. E. (1990). Persistent issues in bilingualism. In B. Harley, P. Allen, J. Cummins, & M. Swain (Eds.), *The development of second language proficiency* (pp. 201–218). Cambridge, UK: Cambridge University Press.

Lambert, W. E. (1992). Challenging established views on social issues. *American Psychologist, 47,* 533–542.

Lambert, W. E., Genesee, F., Holobow, N., & Chartrand, L. (1991). *Bilingual education for majority English-speaking children.* Montreal: McGill University, Psychology Department.

Lampinen, J. M., Beike, D. R., & Behrend, D. A. (2004). The self and memory: It's about time. In D. R. Beike, & J. M. Behrend (Eds.), *The self and memory* (pp. 255–262). New York: Psychology Press.

Lampinen, J. M., Copeland, S. M., & Neuschatz, J. S. (2001). Recollection of things schematic: Room schemas revisited. *Journal of Experimental Psychology: Learning, Memory, & Cognition, 27,* 1211–1222.

Lampinen, J. M., Faries, J. M., Neuschatz, J. S., & Toglia, M. P. (2000). Recollections of things schematic: The influence of scripts on recollective experience. *Applied Cognitive Psychology, 14,* 543–554.

Landau, M. J., Meier, B. P., & Keefer, L. A. (2010). A metaphor-enriched social cognition. *Psychological Bulletin, 136,* 1045–1067.

Landauer, T. K. (2011). Distributed learning and the size of memory: A 50-year spacing odyssey. In A. S. Benjamin (Ed.), *Successful remembering and successful forgetting: A festschrift in honor of Robert A. Bjork* (pp. 49–69). New York: Psychology Press.

Landauer, T. K., & Dumais, S. T. (1997). A solution to Plato's problem: The latent semantic analysis theory of acquisition, induction, and representation of knowledge. *Psychological Review, 104,* 211–240.

Lane, K. A., Banaji, M. R., & Greenwald, A. G. (2007). Understanding and using the Implicit Association Test: IV. What we know (so far) about the method). In B. Wittenbrink & N. Schwarz (Eds.), *Implicit measures of attitudes.* New York: Guilford.

Lany, J., & Saffran, J. B. (2010). From statistics to meaning: Infants' acquisition of lexical categories. *Psychological Science, 21,* 284–291.

Lappin, J. S., & Craft, W. D. (2000). Foundations of spatial vision: From retinal images to perceived shapes. *Psychological Review, 107,* 6–38.

Larkin, S. (2010). *Metacognition in young children.* London: Routledge.

Larsen, A., & Bundesen, C. (1996). A template-matching pandemonium recognizes unconstrained handwritten characters with high accuracy. *Memory & Cognition, 24,* 136–143.

Lave, J. (1997). What's special about experiments as contexts for thinking. In M. Cole, Y. Engeström, & O. Vasquez (Eds.), *Mind, culture, and activity* (pp. 56–69). New York: Cambridge University Press.

Lavie, N. (2007). Attention and consciousness. In M. Velmans & S. Schneider (Eds.), *The Blackwell companion to consciousness* (pp. 489–503). Malden, MA: Blackwell.

Lea, R. B., Mulligan, E. J., & Walton, J. L. (2005). Accessing distant premise information: How memory feeds reasoning. *Journal of Experimental Psychology: Learning, Memory, and Cognition, 31,* 387–395.

Leahey, T. H. (2003). Cognition and learning. In D. F. Freedheim (Ed.), *Handbook of psychology* (Vol. **1**: *The history of psychology,* pp. 109–133). Hoboken, NJ: Wiley.

Leal, T., Slabakova, R., & Farmer, T. A. (2017). The fine-tuning of linguistic expectations over the course of L2 learning. *Studies in Second Language Acquisition*, *39*, 493–525.

Leary, D. E. (2009). William James and the art of human understanding. In L. T. Benjamin, Jr. (Ed.), *A history of psychology* (3rd ed., pp. 88–100). Malden, MA: Blackwell.

Leavitt, J. D., & Christenfeld, N. J. S. (2011). Story spoilers don't spoil stories. *Psychological Science*, *22*, 1152–1154.

LeBoeuf, R. A., & Shafir, E. B. (2012). Decision making. In K. J. Holyoak & R. G. Morrison (Eds.), *The Cambridge handbook of thinking and reasoning* (pp. 301–321). New York: Cambridge University Press.

Lee, J. J., & Pinker, S. (2010). Rationales for indirect speech: The theory of the strategic speaker. *Psychological Review*, *117*, 785–807.

Lee, K., Ng, E. L., & Ng, S. F. (2009). The contributions of working memory and executive functioning to problem representation and solution generation in algebraic word problems. *Journal of Educational Psychology*, *101*, 373–387.

Lehrer, J. (2009). *How we decide*. Boston: Houghton Mifflin Harcourt.

Leichtman, M. D., & Ceci, S. J. (1995). The effects of stereotypes and suggestions on preschoolers' reports. *Developmental Psychology*, *31*, 568–578.

Leighton, J. P., & Sternberg, R. J. (2003). Reasoning and problem solving. In A. F. Healy & R. W. Proctor (Eds.), *Handbook of psychology* (Vol. **4**, pp. 623–648). Hoboken, NJ: Wiley.

Leippe, M., & Eisenstadt, D. (2007). Eyewitness confidence and the confidence-accuracy relationship in memory for people. In R. C. L. Lindsay, D. F. Ross, J. D. Read, & M. P. Toglia (Eds.), *Handbook of eyewitness psychology* (Vol. **2**, pp. 377–425). Mahwah, NJ: Erlbaum.

LeMoult, J., Hertel, P. T., & Joormann, J. (2010). Training the forgetting of negative words: The role of direct suppression and the relation to stress reactivity. *Applied Cognitive Psychology*, *24*, 365–375.

Lenzner, T., Kaczmirek, L., & Lenzner, A. (2010). Cognitive burden of survey questions and response times: A psycholinguistic experiment. *Applied Cognitive Psychology*, *24*, 1003–1020.

Levelt, W. J. (1993). *Speaking: From intention to articulation* (Vol. **1**). MIT press.

Levelt, W. J. (1992). Accessing words in speech production: Stages, processes and representations. *Cognition*, *42*, 1–22.

Levelt, W. J. M. (1998). The genetic perspective in psycholinguistics or where do spoken words come from? *Journal of Psycholinguistic Research*, *27*, 167–180.

Levin, D. S., Thurman, S. K., & Kiepert, M. H. (2010). More than just a memory: The nature and validity of working memory in educational settings. In G. M. Davies & D. B. Wright (Eds.), *Current issues in applied memory research* (pp. 72–95). New York: Psychology Press.

Levin, D. T. (2004). Introduction. In D. T. Levin (Ed.), *Thinking and seeing: Visual metacognition in adults and children* (pp. 1–11). Cambridge, MA: MIT Press.

Levine, D. S. (2002). Neural network modeling. In H. Pashler (Ed.), *Stevens' handbook of experimental psychology* (3rd ed., Vol. **4**, pp. 223–269). New York: Wiley.

Levy, B., & Banaji, M. R. (2002). Implicit ageism. In T. D. Nelson (Ed.), *Ageism: Stereotyping and prejudice against older persons* (pp. 49–75). Cambridge, MA: MIT Press.

Levy, C. M., & Ransdell, S. (1995). Is writing as difficult as it seems? *Memory & Cognition*, *23*, 767–779.

Levy, D. A. (2010). *Tools of critical thinking: Metathoughts for psychology* (2nd ed.). Long Grove, IL: Waveland Press.

Lewandowsky, S. (2011). Working memory capacity and categorization: Individual differences and modeling. *Journal of Experimental Psychology: Learning, Memory, and Cognition*, *37*, 720–738.

Lewis, R. L. (1996). Interference in short-term memory: The magical number two (or three) in sentence processing. *Journal of Psycholinguistic Research*, *25*, 93–115.

Lewis, R. L., Vasishth, S., & Van Dyke, J. A. (2006). Computational principles of working memory in sentence processing. *Trends in Cognitive Sciences*, *10*, 447–454.

Liberman, A. M. (1996). *Speech: A special code*. Cambridge, MA: MIT Press.

Liberman, A. M., & Mattingly, I. G. (1989). A specialization for speech perception. *Science*, *243*, 489–494.

Lieberman, M. D. (2007). Social cognitive neuroscience: A review of core processes. *Annual Review of Psychology*, *58*, 259–259.

Liederman, J., Gilbert, K., Fisher, J. M., Mathews, G., Frye, R. E., & Joshi, P. (2011). Are women more influenced than men by top-down semantic information when listening to disrupted speech? *Language and Speech*, *54*, 33–48.

Light, L. L. (1996). Memory and aging. In E. L. Bjork & R. A. Bjork (Eds.), *Memory* (2nd ed., pp. 443–490). San Diego: Academic Press.

Light, L. L. (2000). Memory changes in adulthood. In S. H. Qualls & N. Abeles (Eds.), *Psychology and the aging revolution* (pp. 73–97). Washington, DC: American Psychological Association.

Light, L. L., La Voie, D., & Kennison, R. (1995). Repetition priming of nonwords in young and older adults. *Journal of Experimental Psychology: Learning, Memory, and Cognition, 21*, 327–346.

Lilienfeld, S. O., Ammirati, R., & Landfield, K. (2009). Giving debiasing away: Can psychological research on correcting cognitive errors promote human welfare? *Perspectives on Psychological Science, 4*, 390–398.

Little, D. M., Prentice, K. J., & Wingfield, A. (2004). Adult age differences in judgments of semantic fit. *Applied Psycholinguistics, 25*, 135–142.

Liu, K. P., & Chan, C. C. (2015). Metacognitive strategies for training of daily living skills in people with brain damage: The self-regulation and mental imagery program. In *International handbook of occupational therapy interventions* (pp. 475–485). Springer International Publishing.

Lockhart, R. S. (2001). Commentary: Levels of processing and memory theory. In M. Naveh-Benjamin, M. Moscovitch, & H. L. Roediger, III (Eds.), *Perspectives on human memory and cognitive aging: Essays in honour of Fergus Craik* (pp. 99–102). New York: Psychology Press.

Loftus, E. F., Miller, D. G., & Burns, H. J. (1978). Semantic integration of verbal information into visual memory. *Journal of Experimental Psychology: Human Learning and Memory, 4*, 19–31.

Logie, R. H. (1995). *Visuo-spatial working memory.* Hove, UK: Erlbaum.

Logie, R. H. (2003). Spatial and visual working memory: A mental workspace. *The Psychology of Learning and Motivation, 42*, 37–78.

Logie, R. H. (2011). The visual and the spatial of a multicomponent working memory. In A. Vandierendonck & A. Szmalec (Eds.), *Spatial working memory* (pp. 19–45). New York: Psychology Press.

Logie, R. H., & Della Sala, S. (2005). Disorders of visuospatial working memory. In P. Shah & A. Miyaki (Eds.), *The Cambridge handbook of visuospatial thinking* (pp. 81–120). New York: Cambridge University Press.

Logie, R. H., & van der Meulen, M. (2009). Fragmenting and integrating visuospatial working memory. In J. R. Brockmole (Ed.), *The visual world in memory* (pp. 1–32). New York: Psychology Press.

Long, D. L., Johns, C. L., & Morris, P. E. (2006). Comprehension ability in mature readers. In M. J. Traxler & M. A. Gernsbacher (Eds.), *Handbook of psycholinguistics* (2nd ed., pp. 801–833). Amsterdam: Elsevier.

Long, G. M., & Toppino, T. C. (2004). Enduring interest in perceptual ambiguity: Alternating views of reversible figures. *Psychological Bulletin, 130*, 748–768.

Lovatt, P., Avons, S. E., & Masterson, J. (2002). Output decay in immediate serial recall: Speech time revisited. *Journal of Memory and Language, 46*, 227–243.

Love, B. C., & Tomlinson, M. (2010). Mechanistic models of associative and rule-based category learning. In D. Mareschal, P. C. Quinn, & S. E. G. Lea (Eds.), *The making of human concepts* (pp. 53–74). New York: Oxford University Press.

Lovelace, E. A. (1984). Metamemory: Monitoring future recallability during study. *Journal of Experimental Psychology: Learning, Memory, and Cognition, 10*, 756–766.

Lovett, M. C. (2002). Problem solving. In D. Medin (Ed.), *Stevens' handbook of experimental psychology* (pp. 317–362). New York: Wiley.

Luchins, A. S. (1942). Mechanization in problem solving. *Psychological Monographs, 54* (Whole No. 248).

Luck, S. J. (2014). *An introduction to the event-related potential technique.* MIT press.

Luck, S. J., & Vecera, S. P. (2002). Attention. In H. Pashler (Ed.), *Stevens' handbook of experimental psychology* (3rd ed., Vol. **1**, pp. 235–286). New York: Wiley.

Luck, S. J., & Vogel, E. K. (2013). Visual working memory capacity: From psychophysics and neurobiology to individual differences. *Trends in Cognitive Sciences, 17*(8), 391–400.

Luo, C. R., Johnson, R. A., & Gallo, D. A. (1998). Automatic activation of phonological information in reading: Evidence from the semantic relatedness decision task. *Memory & Cognition, 26*, 833–843.

Lupyan, G. (2012). *Linguistically modulated perception and cognition: the label-feedback hypothesis. Frontiers in psychology, 3*.

Lupyan, G., & Dale, R. (2010). Language structure is partly determined by social structure. *PloS ONE, 5*(1), e8559.

Lupyan, G., Thompson-Schill, S. L., & Swingley, D. (2010). Conceptual penetration of visual processing. *Psychological Science, 21*, 682–691.

Luria, H. (2006). Introduction to Unit III: Literacy and education in a globalized world. In H. Luria, D. M. Seymour, & T. Smoke (Eds.), *Language and linguistics in context: Readings and applications for teachers* (pp. 233–242). Mahwah, NJ: Erlbaum.

Lynch, T. (2010). Listening: Sources, skills, and strategies. In R. B. Kaplan (Ed.), *The Oxford handbook of applied linguistics* (2nd ed., pp. 74–87). New York: Oxford University Press.

MacDonald, M. C. (1999). Distributional information in language comprehension, production, and acquisition: Three puzzles and a moral. In B. MacWhinney (Ed.), *The emergence of language* (pp. 177–196). Mahwah, NJ: Erlbaum.

MacDonald, M. C. (2013). How language production shapes language form and comprehension. *Frontiers in psychology*, *4*.

MacDonald, M. C., & Christiansen, M. H. (2002). Reassessing working memory: comment on Just and Carpenter (1992) and Waters and Caplan (1996). *Psychological Review*, *109*, 35–54.

MacKay, D. (2004). Information theory. In R. L. Gregory (Ed.), *The Oxford companion to the mind* (2nd ed., pp. 456–467). New York: Oxford University Press.

MacKay, I. R. A., Flege, J. E., & Imai, S. (2006). Evaluating the effects of chronological age and sentence duration on degree of perceived foreign accent. *Applied Psycholinguistics*, *27*, 153–183.

MacLeod, C., & Campbell, L. (1992). Memory accessibility and probability judgments: An experimental evaluation of the availability heuristic. *Journal of Personality and Social Psychology*, *63*, 890–902.

MacLin, O. H., & Malpass, R. S. (2001). Racial categorization of faces: The ambiguous race face effect. *Psychology, Public Policy, and Law*, *7*, 98–118.

Macpherson, R., & Stanovich, K. E. (2007). Cognitive ability, thinking dispositions, and instructional set as predictors of critical thinking. *Learning and Individual Differences*, *17*, 115–127.

Macrae, C. N., & Quadflieg, S. (2010). Perceiving people. In S. T. Fiske, D. T. Gilbert & G. Lindzey (Eds.), *Handbook on social psychology* (5th ed., Vol. **2**, pp. 428–463). Hoboken, NJ: Wiley.

MacWhinney, B. (2011). Language development. In M. H. Bornstein & M. E. Lamb (Eds.), *Developmental science: An advanced textbook* (pp. 389–423). Mahwah, NJ: Erlbaum.

Magloughlin, L. (2016). Accounting for variability in North American English /ɹ/: Evidence from children's articulation. *Journal of Phonetics*, *54*, 51–67.

Magnuson, J. S., Tanenhaus, M. K., Aslin, R. N. (2008). Immediate effects of form-class constraints on spoken word recognition. *Cognition*, *108*, 866–873.

Magnussen, S., Andersson, J., Cornoldi, C., De Beni, R., Endestad, T., Goodman, G. S., . . . Zimmer, H. (2006). What people believe about memory. *Memory*, *14*, 595–613.

Maki, R. H., & McGuire, M. J. (2002). Metacognition for text: Findings and implications for education. In T. J. Perfect & B. L. Schwartz (Eds.), *Applied metacognition* (pp. 39–67). Cambridge, UK: Cambridge University Press.

Maki, R. H., & Serra, M. (1992). The basis of test prediction for text material. *Journal of Experimental Psychology: Learning, Memory, and Cognition*, *18*, 116–126.

Maki, R. H., Jonas, D., & Kallod, M. (1994). The relationship between comprehension and metacomprehension ability. *Psychonomic Bulletin & Review*, *1*, 126–129.

Maki, R. H., Shields, M., Wheeler, A. E., & Zacchilli, T. L. (2005). Individual differences in absolute and relative metacomprehension accuracy. *Journal of Educational Psychology*, *97*, 723–731.

Maki, W. S., & Maki, R. H. (2000). Evaluation of a web-based introductory psychology course: II. Contingency management to increase use of on-line study aids. *Behavior Research Methods, Instruments & Computers*, *32*, 240–245.

Mandel, D. R., Jusczyk, P. W., & Pisoni, D. B. (1995). Infants' recognition of the sound patterns of their own names. *Psychological Science*, *6*, 314–317.

Mandler, G. (2002). Origins of the cognitive (R)evolution. *Journal of the Behavioral Sciences*, *38*, 339–353.

Mandler, J. M. (2003). Conceptual categorization. In D. Rakison & L. M. Oakes (Eds.), *Early category and concept development*. New York: Oxford University Press.

Mandler, J. M. (2004a). *The foundations of mind: Origins of conceptual thought*. New York: Oxford University Press.

Mandler, J. M. (2004b). Thought before language. *Trends in Cognitive Science*, *8*, 508–524.

Mandler, J. M. (2006). Actions organize the infant's world. In K. Hirsh-Pasek & R. M. Golinkoff (Eds.), *Action meets word: How children learn verbs* (pp. 111–133). New York: Oxford University Press.

Mandler, J. M. (2007). On the origins of the conceptual system. *American Psychologist*, *62*, 741–751.

Manktelow, K. D. (1999). *Reasoning and thinking*. East Sussex, UK: Psychology Press.

Manly, J. J., Touradji, P., Tang, M., & Stern, Y. (2003). Literacy and memory decline among ethnically diverse elders. *Journal of Clinical and Experimental Neuropsychology*, *25*, 680–690.

Mäntylä, T. (1997). Recollections of faces: Remembering differences and knowing similarities. *Journal of Experimental Psychology: Learning, Memory, and Cognition*, *23*, 1203–1216.

Mar, R. A. (2011). The neural bases of social cognition and story comprehension. *Annual Review of Psychology*, *62*, 103–134.

Mar, R. A., Tackett, J. L., & Moore, C. (2010). Exposure to media and theory-of-mind development in preschoolers. *Cognitive Development*, *25*, 69–78.

Marcus, G. F. (1996). Why do children say "breaked"? *Current Directions in Psychological Science*, *5*, 81–85.

Marian, V., & Fausey, C. M. (2006). Language-dependent memory in bilingual learning. *Applied Cognitive Psychology, 20,* 1025–1047.

Marian, V., & Spivey, M. (2003). Competing activation in bilingual language processing: Within-and between-language competition. *Bilingualism: Language and Cognition, 6,* 97–115.

Maril, A., Simons, J. S., Weaver, J. J., & Schacter, D. L. (2005). Graded recall success: An event-related fMRI comparison of tip of the tongue and feeling of knowing. *NeuroImage, 24,* 1130–1138.

Markman, A. B. (1999). *Knowledge representation.* Mahwah, NJ: Erlbaum.

Markman, A. B. (2002). Knowledge representation. In D. Medin (Ed.), *Stevens' handbook of experimental psychology* (3rd ed., Vol. **2,** pp. 165–208). New York: Wiley.

Markman, A. B., & Ross, B. H. (2003). Category use and category learning. *Psychological Bulletin, 129,* 592–613.

Markovits, H., Saelen, C., & Forgues, H. L. (2009). An inverse belief-bias effect: More evidence for the role of inhibitory processes in logical reasoning. *Experimental Psychology, 56,* 112–120.

Markowitsch, H. J., & Welzer, H. (2010). *The development of autobiographical memory.* New York: Psychology Press.

Marr, D. (1982). *Vision.* W. H. Freeman and Co.

Marsh, E. J., & Sink, H. E. (2010). Access to handouts of presentation slides during lecture: Consequences for learning. *Applied Cognitive Psychology, 24,* 691–706.

Marsh, R. L., Cook, G. I., Thadeus Meeks, J., Clark-Foos, A., & Hicks, J. L. (2007). Memory for intention-related material presented in a to-be-ignored channel. *Memory & Cognition, 35,* 1197–1204.

Marsh, R. L., Hicks, J. L., & Hancock, T. W. (2000). On the interaction of ongoing cognitive activity and the nature of an event-based intention. *Applied Cognitive Psychology, 14,* S29–S41.

Marsh, R. L., Landau, J. D., & Hicks, J. L. (1997). Contributions of inadequate source monitoring to unconscious plagiarism during idea generation. *Journal of Experimental Psychology: Learning, Memory, and Cognition, 23,* 886–897.

Marshall, P. J. (2009). Relating psychology and neuroscience: Taking up the challenges. *Perspectives on Psychological Science, 4,* 113–125.

Marslen-Wilson, W. D., Tyler, L. K., & Koster, C. (1993). Integrative processes in utterance resolution. *Journal of Memory and Language, 32,* 647–666.

Martin, E. (1967). Personal communication.

Martin, F., Baudouin, J., Tiberghien, G., & Franck, N. (2005). Processing emotional expression and facial identity in schizophrenia. *Psychiatry Research, 134,* 43–53.

Martin, R. C., & Wu, D. H. (2005). The cognitive neuropsychology of language. In K. Lamberts & R. L. Goldstone (Eds.), *Handbook of cognition* (pp. 382–404). Thousand Oaks, CA: Sage.

Martins, M., Silva, C., & Pereira, M. (2010). The impact of the articulatory properties of phonemes on the evolution of preschool children's writing. *Applied Psycholinguistics, 31,* 693–709.

Martinussen, R., Hayden, J., Hogg-Johnson, S., & Tannock, R. (2005). A meta-analysis of working memory impairments in children with attention-deficit/hyperactivity disorder. *Journal of the American Academy of Child and Adolescent Psychology, 44,* 377–384.

Mason, R. A., & Just, M. A. (2006). Neuroimaging contributions to the understanding of discourse processes. In M. J. Traxler & M. A. Gernsbacher (Eds.), *Handbook of psycholinguistics* (2nd ed., pp. 765–799). New York: Academic Press.

Masoura, E., & Gathercole, S. E. (2005). Contrasting contributions of phonological short-term memory and long-term knowledge to vocabulary learning in a foreign language. *Memory, 13,* 422–429.

Massaro, D. W. (1998). *Perceiving talking faces.* Cambridge, MA: MIT Press.

Massaro, D. W., & Stork, D. G. (1998). Speech recognition and sensory integration. *American Scientist, 86,* 236–244.

Massaro, D. W., Cohen, M. M., & Smeele, P. M. T. (1995). Cross-linguistic comparisons in the integration of visual and auditory speech. *Memory & Cognition, 23,* 113–131.

Mast, F., Kosslyn, S. M., & Berthoz, A. (1999). Visual mental imagery interferes with allocentric orientation judgements. *NeuroReport, 10,* 3549–3553.

Mather, G. (2006). *Foundations of perception.* Hove, UK: Psychology Press.

Matlin, M. W. (2004). Pollyanna Principle. In R. Pohl (Ed.), *Cognitive illusions: Handbook on fallacies and biases in thinking, judgment, and memory* (pp. 255–272). Hove, UK: Psychology Press.

Matlin, M. W. (2012). *The psychology of women* (7th ed.). Belmont, CA: Wadsworth Cengage.

Matlin, M. W., & Stang, D. J. (1978). *The Pollyanna Principle: Selectivity in language, memory, and thought.* Cambridge, MA: Schenkman.

Matsumoto, E. (2010). Bias in attending to emotional facial expressions: Anxiety and visual search efficiency. *Applied Cognitive Psychology, 24*, 414–424.

Mattys, S. L., & Liss, J. M. (2008). On building models of spoken-word recognition: When there is as much to learn from natural "oddities" as artificial normality. *Perception & Psychophysics, 70*, 1235–1242.

Mayer, R. E. (2003). Memory and information processing. In W. M. Reynolds & G. E. Miller (Eds.), *Handbook of psychology* (Vol. **7**, pp. 47–57). Hoboken, NJ: Wiley.

Mayer, R. E. (2004). Teaching of subject matter. *Annual Review of Psychology, 55*, 715–744.

Mayer, R. E., & Hegarty, M. (1996). The process of understanding mathematical problems. In R. J. Sternberg & T. Ben-Zeev (Eds.), *The nature of mathematical thinking* (pp. 29–53). Mahwah, NJ: Erlbaum.

Mazhari, S., Tabrizi, Y. M., & Nejad, A. G. (2015). Neural Evidence for Compromised Mental Imagery in Individuals With Chronic Schizophrenia. *The Journal of neuropsychiatry and clinical neurosciences, 27*, 127–132.

Mayhorn, C. B., Fisk, A. B., & Whittle, J. D. (2002). Decisions, decisions: Analysis of age, cohort, and time of testing on framing of risky decision options. *Human Factors, 44*, 515–521.

Maynard, A. M. (2006). Personal communication.

Maynard, A. M., Maynard, D. C., & Rowe, K. A. (2004). Exposure to the fields of psychology: Evaluation of an introductory psychology project. *Teaching of Psychology, 31*, 37–40.

Mazzoni, G. A. L., & Memon, A. (2003). Imagination can create false autobiographical memories. *Psychological Science, 14*, 186–188.

McAdams, D. P. (2004). The redemptive self: Narrative identity in America today. In D. R. Beike, & J. M. Behrend (Eds.), *The self and memory* (pp. 95–115). New York: Psychology Press.

McAdams, S., & Drake, C. (2002). Auditory perception and cognition. In S. Yantis (Ed.), *Stevens' handbook of experimental psychology* (3rd ed., Vol. **1**, pp. 397–452). New York: Wiley.

McCabe, J. (2011). Metacognitive awareness of learning strategies in undergraduates. *Memory & Cognition, 39*, 462–476.

McCandliss, B. D., Cohen, L., & Dehaene, S. (2003). The visual word form area: expertise for reading in the fusiform gyrus. *Trends in Cognitive Sciences, 7*, 293–299.

McClelland, J. L. (1981). Retrieving general and specific knowledge from stored knowledge of specifics. *Proceedings of the Third Annual Conference of the Cognitive Science Society*, pp. 170–172.

McClelland, J. L. (1995). Constructive memory and memory distortions: A parallel-distributed processing approach. In D. L. Schacter (Ed.), *Memory distortion: How minds, brains, and societies reconstruct the past* (pp. 71–89). Cambridge, MA: Harvard University Press.

McClelland, J. L. (1999). Cognitive modeling, connectionist. In R. A. Wilson & F. C. Keil (Eds.), *The MIT encyclopedia of the cognitive sciences* (pp. 137–139). Cambridge, MA: MIT Press.

McClelland, J. L. (2000). Connectionist models of memory. In E. Tulving & F. I. M. Craik (Eds.), *The Oxford handbook of memory* (pp. 583–597). New York: Oxford University Press.

McClelland, J. L., & Elman, J. L. (1986). The TRACE model of speech perception. *Cognitive psychology, 18*, 1–86.

McClelland, J. L., & Rumelhart, D. E. (Eds.). (1986). *Parallel distributed processing: Explorations in the microstructure of cognition* (Vol. **2**). Cambridge, MA: MIT Press.

McCormick, A. C. (2011). It's about time: What to make of reported declines in how much college students study. *Liberal Education, 97*, 30–39.

McCormick, C. B. (2003). Metacognition and learning. In W. M. Reynolds & G. E. Miller (Eds.), *Handbook of psychology* (Vol. **7**, pp. 79–102). Hoboken, NJ: Wiley.

McCutchen, D., Teske, P., & Bangston, C. (2008). In C. Bazerman (Ed.), *Handbook of research on writing: History, society, school, individual, text* (pp. 451–470). Mahwah, NJ: Erlbaum.

McDaniel, M. A., & Butler, A. C. (2011). A contextual framework for understanding when difficulties are desirable. In A. S. Benjamin (Ed.), *Successful remembering and successful forgetting: A festschrift in honor of Robert A. Bjork* (pp. 175–198). New York: Psychology Press.

McDaniel, M. A., & Einstein, G. O. (2005). Material appropriate difficulty: A framework for determining when difficulty is desirable for improving learning. In A. F. Healy (Ed.), *Experimental cognitive psychology and its applications* (pp. 73–85). Washington, DC: American Psychological Association.

McDaniel, M. A., & Einstein, G. O. (2007). *Prospective memory: An overview and synthesis of an emerging field.* Thousand Oaks, CA: Sage.

McDaniel, M. A., Waddill, P. J., & Shakesby, P. S. (1996). Study strategies, interest, and learning from text: The application of material appropriate processing. In D. J. Herrmann, Cathy McEvoy, C., Hertzog, C., Hertel, P., & Johnson, M. K. (Eds.), *Basic and applied memory research: Practical applications* (Vol. **1**, pp. 385–397). Mahwah, NJ: Erlbaum.

McDermott, K., & Knight, R. G. (2004). The effects of aging on a measure of prospective remembering using naturalistic stimuli. *Applied Cognitive Psychology*, *18*, 349–362.

McDonald, S. A., & Shillcock, R. C. (2003). Eye movements reveal the on-line computation of lexical probabilities during reading. *Psychological Science*, *14*, 648–652.

McDonough, L., & Mandler, J. M. (1998). Inductive generalization in 9- and 11-month-olds. *Developmental Science*, *1*, 227–232.

McDougall, S., & Gruneberg, M. (2002). What memory strategy is best for examinations in psychology? *Applied Cognitive Psychology*, *16*, 451–458.

McGovern, T. V., & Brewer, C. L. (2003). Undergraduate education. In D. F. Freedheim (Ed.), *Handbook of psychology* (Vol. **1**: *The history of psychology*, pp. 465–481). Hoboken, NJ: Wiley.

McGraw, A. P., Larsen, J. T., Kahneman, D., & Schkade, D. (2010). Comparing gains and losses. *Psychological Science*, *21*, 1438–1435.

McGuinness, D. (2004). *Early reading instruction: What science really tells us about how to teach reading*. Cambridge, MA: Bradford.

McGurk, H., & MacDonald, J. (1976). Hearing lips and seeing voices. *Nature*, *264*, 746–748.

McKelvie, S. J., Sano, E. K., & Stout, D. (1994). Effects of colored separate and interactive pictures on cued recall. *Journal of General Psychology*, *12*, 241–251.

McKone, E. (2004). Isolating the special component of face recognition: Peripheral identification and a Mooney face. *Journal of Experimental Psychology: Learning, Memory, and Cognition*, *30*, 181–197.

McKoon, G., & Ratcliff, R. (1998). Memory-based language processing: Psycholinguistic research in the 1990s. *Annual Review of Psychology*, *49*, 25–42.

McNamara, D. S. (2011). Measuring deep, reflective comprehension and learning strategies: Challenges and successes. *Metacognition and Learning*, *6*, 195–203.

McNamara, T. P. (2005). *Semantic priming: Perspectives from memory and word recognition*. New York: Psychology Press.

McNamara, T. P., & Diwadkar, V. A. (1997). Symmetry and asymmetry of human spatial memory. *Cognitive Psychology*, *34*, 160–190.

McNamara, T. P., & Holbrook, J. B. (2003). The native mind: Biological categorization and reasoning in development across cultures. *Psychological Review*, *111*, 960–983.

McNeill, D. (2005). *Gesture and thought*. Chicago: University of Chicago Press.

McQueen, J. M. (2005). Speech perception. In K. Lamberts & R. L. Goldstone (Eds.), *Handbook of cognition* (pp. 255–275). London, UK: Sage.

McVay, J. C., & Kane, M. C. (2010). Does mind wandering reflect executive function or executive failure? Comment on Smallwood and Schooler (2006) and Watkins (2008). *Psychological Bulletin*, *136*, 188–197.

Medin, D. L., & Rips, L. J. (2005). Concepts and categories: Memory, meaning and metaphysics. In K. J. Holyoak & R. G. Morrison (Eds.), *The Cambridge handbook of thinking and reasoning* (pp. 37–72). New York: Cambridge University Press.

Medin, D. L., Lynch, E. B., & Solomon, K. O. (2000). Are there kinds of concepts? *Annual Review of Psychology*, *51*, 121–147.

Meeter, M., & Murre, J. M. J. (2004). Consolidation of long-term memory: Evidence and alternatives. *Psychological Bulletin*, *130*, 843–857.

Meeter, M., Eijsackers, E. V., & Mulder, J. L. (2006). Retrograde amnesia for autobiographical memories and public events in mild and moderate Alzheimer's disease. *Journal of Clinical and Experimental Neuropsychology*, *28*, 914–927.

Mehl, M. R., Vazire, S., Ramírez-Esparza, N., Slatcher, R. B., & Pennebaker, J. W. (2007). Are women really more talkative than men?. *Science*, *317*, 82–82.

Meissner, C. A., & Brigham, J. C. (2001). Thirty years of investigating the own-race bias in memory for faces: A meta-analytic review. *Psychology, Public Policy, & Law*, *7*, 3–35.

Meissner, C. A., Brigham, J. C., & Butz, D. A. (2005). Memory for own- and other-race faces: A dual-process approach. *Applied Cognitive Psychology*, *19*, 545–567.

Melnyk, L., Crossman, A. M., & Scullin, M. H. (2007). The suggestibility of children's memory. In M. Toglia, J. D. Read, D. F. Ross, & R. C. L. Lindsay (Eds.), *Handbook of eyewitness psychology* (Vol. **1**, pp. 401–451). Mahwah, NJ: Erlbaum.

Memon, A., Holliday, R., & Hill, C. (2006). Pre-event stereotypes and misinformation effects in young children. *Memory*, *14*, 104–114.

Mendel, R., Traut-Mattausch, E., Jonas, E., Leucht, S., Kane, J. M., Maino, K., Kissling, W., . . . & Hamann, J. (2011). Confirmation bias: Why psychiatrists stick to wrong preliminary diagnoses. *Psychological Medicine*, *41*, 2651–2659.

Mendola, J. (2003). Contextual shape processing in human visual cortex: Beginning to fill-in the blanks. In L. Pessoa & P. De Weerd (Eds.), *Filling-in: From perceptual completion to cortical reorganization* (pp. 38–58). New York: Oxford University Press.

Mercier, H., & Sperber, D. (2011). Why do humans reason? Arguments for an argumentative theory. *Behavioral and Brain Sciences*, *34*, 57–111.

Mervis, C. B., Catlin, J., & Rosch, E. (1976). Relationships among goodness-of-example, category norms, and word frequency. *Bulletin of the Psychonomic Society*, 7, 283–284.

Metcalfe, J. (1986). Premonitions of insight predict impending error. *Journal of Experimental Psychology: Learning, Memory, and Cognition*, *12*, 623–634.

Metcalfe, J. (2000). Metamemory. In E. Tulving & F. I. M. Craik (Eds.), *The Oxford handbook of memory* (pp. 197–211). New York: Oxford University Press.

Metcalfe, J. (2002). Is study time allocated selectively to a region of proximal learning? *Journal of Experimental Psychology: General*, *131*, 349–363.

Metcalfe, J. (2011). Desirable difficulties and studying in the region of proximal learning. In A. S. Benjamin (Ed.), *Successful remembering and successful forgetting: A festschrift in honor of Robert A. Bjork* (pp. 259–276). New York: Psychology Press.

Metcalfe, J., & Wiebe, D. (1987). Intuition in insight and noninsight problem solving. *Memory & Cognition*, *15*, 238–246.

Meyer, A. S. (2004). The use of eye tracking in studies of sentence generation. In J. M. Henderson & F. Ferreira (Eds.), *The interface of language, vision, and action: Eye movements and the visual world* (p. 191–211). New York: Psychology Press.

Meyer, A. S., & Belke, E. (2009). Word form retrieval in language production. In M. G. Gaskell (Ed.), *The Oxford handbook of psycholinguistics* (pp. 471–487). New York: Oxford University Press.

Michael, E. B., & Gollan, T. H. (2005). Being and becoming bilingual: Individual differences and consequences for language production. In J. F. Kroll & A. M. B. de Groot (Eds.), *Handbook of bilingualism: Psycholinguistic approaches* (pp. 389–407). New York: Oxford University Press.

Michie, D. (2004). Computer chess. In R. L. Gregory (Ed.), *The Oxford companion to the mind* (2nd ed., pp. 196–199). New York: Oxford University Press.

Mieg, H. A. (2011). Focused cognition: Information integration and complex problem solving by top inventors. In K. L. Mosier & U. M. Fisher (Eds.), *Informed by knowledge: Expert performance in complex situations* (pp. 41–54). New York: Psychology Press.

Miller, E. K., & Cohen, J. D. (2001). An integrative theory of prefrontal cortex function. *Annual review of neuroscience*, *24*, 167–202.

Miller, G. A. (1956). The magical number seven, plus or minus two: Some limits on our capacity for processing information. *Psychological Review*, *63*, 81–97.

Miller, G. A. (1967). The psycholinguists. In G. A. Miller (Ed.), *The psychology of communication* (pp. 70–92). London, UK: Penguin.

Miller, L. C., Lechner, R. E., & Rugs, D. (1985). Development of conversational responsiveness: Preschoolers' use of responsive listener cues and relevant comments. *Developmental Psychology*, *21*, 473–480.

Millis, K. K., & Graesser, A. C. (1994). The time-course of constructing knowledge-based inferences for scientific texts. *Journal of Memory and Language*, *33*, 583–599.

Milner, B. (1966). Amnesia. In C. W. M. Whitty & O. L. Zangwill (Eds.), *Amnesia following operation on the temporal lobes* (pp. 109–133). London, UK: Butterworth.

Milton, F., & Wills, A. J. (2004). The influence of stimulus properties on category construction. *Journal of Experimental Psychology: Learning, Memory, and Cognition*, *30*, 407–415.

Minda, J. P., & Smith, J. D. (2011). Prototype models of categorization: Basic formulation, predictions, and limitations. In D. M. Pothos & A. J. Wills (Eds.), *Formal approaches in categorization* (pp. 40–64). New York: Cambridge University Press.

Miozzo, M., & Caramazza, A. (1997). Retrieval of lexical-syntactic features in tip-of-the-tongue states. *Journal of Experimental Psychology: Learning, Memory, and Cognition*, *23*, 1410–1423.

Mishra, A., & Mishra, H. (2010). Border bias: The belief that state borders can protect against disasters. *Psychological Science*, *21*, 1582–1586.

Mitchell, K. J., & Johnson, M. K. (2009). Source monitoring 15 years later: What have we learned from fMRI about the neural mechanisms of source memory? *Psychological Bulletin*, *135*, 638–677.

Mitte, K. (2008). Memory bias for threatening information in anxiety and anxiety disorders: A meta-analytic review. *Psychological Bulletin*, *134*, 886–911.

Miyake, A., & Shah, P. (1999). Toward unified theories of working memory. In A. Miyake & P. Shah (Eds.), *Models of working memory: Mechanisms of active maintenance and executive control* (pp. 442–481). New York: Cambridge University Press.

Moar, I., & Bower, G. H. (1983). Inconsistency in spatial knowledge. *Memory & Cognition*, *11*, 107–113.

Moely, B. E., Olson, F. A., Halwes, T. G., & Flavell, J. H. (1969). Production deficiency in young children's clustered recall. *Developmental Psychology*, *1*, 26–34.

Mol, S. E., & Bus, A. G. (2011). To read or not to read: A meta-analysis of print exposure from infancy to early adulthood. *Psychology Bulletin, 137,* 267–296.

Moldoveanu, M., & Langer, E. (2002). When "stupid" is smarter than we are. In R. J. Sternberg (Ed.), *Why smart people can be so stupid* (pp. 212–231). New Haven, CT: Yale University Press.

Molinaro, N., Barraza, P., & Carreiras, M. (2013). Long-range neural synchronization supports fast and efficient reading: EEG correlates of processing expected words in sentences. *NeuroImage, 72,* 120–132.

Monaghan, P., Chater, N., & Christiansen, M. H. (2005). The differential role of phonological and distributional cues in grammatical categorisation. *Cognition, 96,* 143–182.

Montag, J. L., & MacDonald, M. C. (2015). Text exposure predicts spoken production of complex sentences in 8-and 12-year-old children and adults. *Journal of Experimental Psychology: General, 144,* 447.

Montello, D. R. (2005). Navigation. In P. Shah & A. Miyake (Eds.), *The Cambridge handbook of visuospatial thinking* (pp. 257–294). New York: Cambridge University Press.

Montello, D. R., Waller, D., Hegarty, M., & Richardson, A. E. (2004). Spatial memory of real environments, virtual environments, and maps. In G. L. Allen (Ed.), *Human spatial memory: Remembering where* (pp. 251–285). Mahwah, NJ: Erlbaum.

Moore, D. A., & Healy, P. J. (2008). The trouble with overconfidence. *Psychological Review, 115,* 502–517.

Moran, A., Bramham, J., Collet, C., Guillot, A., & MacIntyre, T. E. (2015). Motor imagery in clinical disorders: importance and implications. *Frontiers in psychiatry, 6.*

Moran, S. & Ritov, I., (2011). Valence framings in negotiations. In G. Keren (Ed.), *Perspectives on framing* (pp. 239–254). New York: Psychology Press.

Morey, C. C., & Cowan, N. (2004). When visual and verbal memories compete: Evidence of cross-domain limits in working memory. *Psychonomic Bulletin & Review, 11,* 296–301.

Morey, C. C., & Cowan, N. (2005). When do visual and verbal memories conflict? The importance of working-memory load and retrieval. *Journal of Experimental Psychology: Learning, Memory, and Cognition, 31,* 703–713.

Morris, R. K., & Binder, K. S. (2001). What happens to the unselected meaning of an ambiguous word in skilled reading? In D. S. Gorfein (Ed.), *On the consequences of meaning selection: Perspectives on resolving lexical ambiguity* (pp. 139–153). Washington, DC: American Psychological Association.

Morrison, A. P. (2005). Psychosis and the phenomenon of unwanted intrusive thoughts. In D. A. Clark (Ed.), *Intrusive thoughts in clinical disorders: Theory, research, and treatment* (pp. 175–198). New York: Guilford.

Morrison, R. G., & Knowlton, B. J. (2012). Neurocognitive methods in higher cognition. In K. J. Holyoak & R. G. Morrison (Eds.), *The Oxford handbook of thinking and reasoning* (pp. 67–89). New York: Oxford University Press.

Moscovitch, M., & Craik, F. I. M. (1976). Depth of processing, retrieval cues, and uniqueness of encoding as factors in recall. *Journal of Verbal Learning and Verbal Behavior, 15,* 447–458.

Mosier, K. L., & Fischer, U. M. (Eds.). (2011). *Informed by knowledge: Expert performance in complex situations.* New York: Psychology Press.

Most, S. B. (2010). Attention and emotion. In E. B. Goldstein (Ed.), *Encyclopedia of perception* (Vol. 1, pp. 116–119). Thousand Oaks, CA: Sage.

Most, S. B., Simons, D. J., Scholl, B. J., Jimenez, R., Clifford, E., & Chabris, C. F. (2001). How not to be seen: The contribution of similarity and selective ignoring to sustained inattentional blindness. *Psychological Science, 12,* 9–17.

Most, S. B., Scholl, B. J., Clifford, E. R., & Simons, D. J. (2005). What you see is what you set: Sustained inattentional blindness and the capture of awareness. *Psychological Review, 112,* 217–242.

Moulin, C. J. A., & Gathercole, S. E. (2008). Memory changes across the lifespan. In G. Cohen & M. A. Conway (Eds.), *Memory in the real world* (pp. 305–326). New York: Psychology Press.

Moulin, C. J. A., Thompson, R. G., Wright, D. B., & Conway, M. A. (2007). Eyewitness memory in older adults. In M. P. Toglia, J. D. Read, D. F. Ross, & R. C. L. Lindsay (Eds.), *Handbook of eyewitness psychology* (Vol. 1, pp. 627–646). Mahwah, NJ: Erlbaum.

Mueller, T. (2005, December 12). Your move: How computer chess programs are changing the game. *New Yorker, pp.* 62–69.

Mueller-Johnson, K., & Ceci, S. J. (2007). The elderly eyewitness: A review and prospectus. In M. P. Toglia, J. D. Read, D. F. Ross, & R. C. L. Lindsay (Eds.), *Handbook of eyewitness psychology* (Vol. 1, pp. 577–605). Mahwah, NJ: Erlbaum.

Müller, H. J., & Krummenacher, J. (2006). Visual search and selective attention. *Visual Cognition, 14,* 389–410.

Munger, M. P., Owens, T. R., & Conway, J. E. (2005). Are boundary extension and representational momentum related? *Visual Cognition, 12,* 1041–1056.

Murphy, G. L. (2002). *The big book of concepts.* Cambridge, MA: MIT Press.

Murphy, G. L. (2010). What are categories and concepts? In D. Mareschal, P. C. Quinn, & S. E. G. Lea (Eds.), *The making of human concepts* (pp. 11–28). New York: Oxford University Press.

Murphy, G. L., & Shapiro, A. M. (1994). Forgetting of verbatim information in discourse. *Memory & Cognition, 22*, 85–94.

Murray, L. A., Whitehouse, W. G., & Alloy, L. B. (1999). Mood congruence and depressive deficits in memory: A forced-recall analysis. *Memory, 7*, 175–196.

Musso, M., Moro, A., Glauche, V., Rijntjes, M., Reichenbach, J., Büchel, C., & Weiller, C. (2003). Broca's area and the language instinct. *Nature Neuroscience, 6*, 774–781.

Mussweiler, T., Englich, B., & Strack, F. (2004). Anchoring effects. In R. Pohl (Ed.), *Cognitive illusions: Handbook on fallacies and biases in thinking, judgment, and memory* (pp. 183–200). Hove, UK: Psychology Press.

Myers, D. G. (2002). *Intuition: Its powers and perils.* New Haven, CT: Yale University Press.

Myers, N. A., & Perlmutter, M. (1978). Memory in the years from two to five. In P. A. Ornstein (Ed.), *Memory development in children* (pp. 191–218). Hillsdale, NJ: Erlbaum.

Nairne, J. S. (2005). The functionalist agenda in memory. In A. F. Healy (Ed.), *Experimental cognitive psychology and its applications* (pp. 115–126). Washington, DC: American Psychological Association.

Narens, L., Nelson, T. O., & Scheck, P. (2008). Memory monitoring and the delayed JOL effect. In J. Dunlosky & R. A. Bjork (Eds.), *Handbook of metamemory and memory* (pp. 137–153). New York: Psychology Press.

National Center for Education Statistics. (2004). *Highlights from the Trends in International Mathematics and Science Study (TIMSS) 2003.* Washington, DC: U.S. Department of Education.

Naveh-Benjamin, M., Cowan, N., Kilb, A., & Chen, Z. (2007). Age-related differences in immediate serial recall: Dissociating chunk formation and capacity. *Memory & Cognition, 35*, 724–737.

Naveh-Benjamin, M., Craik, F. I. M., Guez, J., & Kreuger, S. (2005). Divided attention in younger and older adults: Effects of strategy and relatedness on memory performance and secondary task costs. *Journal of Experimental Psychology: Learning, Memory, and Cognition, 31*, 520–537.

Neel, R., Neufeld, S. L., & Neuberg, S. L. (2013). Would an obese person whistle Vivaldi? Targets of prejudice self-present to minimize appearance of specific threats. *Psychological Science, 24*, 678–687.

Neisser, U. (1967). *Cognitive psychology.* New York: Appleton.

Neisser, U. (2003). New directions for flashbulb memories: Comments on the ACP special issue. *Applied Cognitive Psychology, 17*, 1149–1155.

Neisser, U., & Libby, L. K. (2000). Remembering life experiences. In E. Tulving & F. I. M. Craik (Eds.), *The Oxford handbook of memory* (pp. 315–332). New York: Oxford University Press.

Nelson, J. R., Balass, M., & Perfetti, C. A. (2005). Differences between written and spoken input in learning new words. *Written Language and Literacy, 8*, 101–120.

Nelson, T. O., & Leonesio, R. J. (1988). Allocation of self-paced study time and the "labor-in-vain effect." *Journal of Experimental Psychology: Learning, Memory, and Cognition, 14*, 676–686.

Nelson, T. O., Dunlosky, J., Graf, A., & Narens, L. (1994). Utilization of metacognitive judgments in the allocation of study during multitrial learning. *Psychological Science, 5*, 207–213.

Neuschatz, J. S., Neuschatz, J. S., Lampinen, J. M., Preston, E. L., Hawkins, E. R., & Toglia, M. P. (2002). The effect of memory schemata on memory and the phenomenological experience of naturalistic situations. *Applied Cognitive Psychology, 16*, 687–708.

Neuschatz, J. S., et al. (2007). False memory research: History, theory, and applied implications. In M. P. Toglia, J. D. Read, D. F. Ross, & R. C. L. Lindsay (Eds.), *Handbook of eyewitness psychology* (Vol. **1**, pp. 239–260). Mahwah, NJ: Erlbaum.

Newcombe, N. S. (2002). Spatial cognition. In D. Medin (Ed.), *Stevens' handbook of experimental psychology* (3rd ed., Vol. **2**, pp. 113–163). New York: Wiley.

Newcombe, N. S. (2006, March 3). A plea for spatial literacy. *Chronicle of Higher Education*, p. B20.

Newcombe, N. S. (2010, Summer). Picture this: Increasing math and science learning by improving spatial thinking. *American Educator, 43*, 29–34.

Newcombe, N. S., & Huttenlocher, J. (2000). *Making space: The development of spatial representation and reasoning.* Cambridge, MA: MIT Press.

Newell, A., & Simon, H. A. (1972). *Human problem solving.* Englewood Cliffs, NJ: Prentice-Hall.

Newell, B. R., Lagnado, D. A., & Shanks, D. R. (2007). *Straight choices: The psychology of decision making.* New York: Psychology Press.

Newmeyer, F. J. (1998). *Language form and language function.* Cambridge, MA: MIT Press.

Ng, W.-K., & Lindsay, R. C. L. (1994). Cross-race facial recognition: Failure of the contact hypothesis. *Journal of Cross-Cultural Psychology, 25*, 217–232.

Nickerson, R. S. (2010). *Mathematical reasoning: Patterns, problems, conjectures, and proofs.* New York: Psychology Press.

Nievelstein, F., Van Gog, T., Van Dijck, G., & Boshuizen, H. P. (2011). Instructional support for novice law students: Reducing search processes and explaining concepts in cases. *Applied Cognitive Psychology, 25*, 408–413.

Nigg, J. T. (2006). *What causes ADHD?: Understanding what goes wrong and why.* Guilford Press.

Nikolas, M. A., & Nigg, J. T. (2013). Neuropsychological performance and attention-deficit hyperactivity disorder subtypes and symptom dimensions. *Neuropsychology, 27*, 107.

Nisbett, R. E., & Wilson, T. D. (1977). Telling more than we can know: Verbal reports on mental processes. *Psychological Review, 84*, 231–259.

Nishimura, K., Aoki, T., Inagawa, M., Tobinaga, Y., & Iwaki, S. (2016). Individual differences in mental imagery tasks: a study of visual thinkers and verbal thinkers. *Neuroscience Communications, 2*, e1126.

Noë, A. (2004). *Action in perception.* MIT press.

Noice, T., & Noice, H. (1997). *The nature of expertise in professional acting: A cognitive view.* Mahwah, NJ: Erlbaum.

Nolen-Hoeksema, S. (2006). The etiology of gender differences in depression. In C. M. Mazure & G. P. Keita (Eds.), *Understanding depression* (pp. 9–43). Washington, DC: American Psychological Association.

Norman, E., Price, M. C., & Duff, S. C. (2010). Fringe consciousness: A useful framework for clarifying the nature of experience-based metacognitive feelings. In A. Efklides & Misailidi (Eds.), *Trends and prospects in metacognition research* (pp. 63–80). New York: Springer.

Nosek, B. A., Banaji, M. R., & Greenwald, A. G. (2002). Math = male, me = female, therefore math ≠ me. *Journal of Personality and Social Psychology, 83*, 44–59.

Nosek, B. A., Smyth, F. L., Sriram, N., Lindner, N. M., Devos, T., Ayala, A., . . . Greenwald, A. G. (2009). National differences in gender-science stereotypes predict national sex differences in science and math achievement. *Proceedings of the National Academy of Sciences, 106*, 10593–10597.

Nosek, B. A., Greenwald, A. G., & Banaji, M. R. (2007). The Implicit Association Test at age 7: A methodological and conceptual review. In J. A. Bargh (Ed.), *Social psychology and the unconscious: The automaticity of higher mental processes* (pp. 265–292). New York: Psychology Press.

Nosofsky, R. M., & Palmeri, T. J. (1998). A rule-plus-exception model for classifying objects in continuous-dimension spaces. *Psychonomic Bulletin & Review, 5*, 345–369.

Novick, J. M., Trueswell, J. C. & Thompson-Schill, S. L. (2005). Cognitive control and parsing: Reexamining the role of Broca's area in sentence comprehension. *Cognitive, Affective, & Behavioral Neuroscience, 5*, 263–281. PMID: 16396089.

Novick, J. M., Trueswell, J. C., & Thomspon-Schill, S. L. (2010). Broca's area and language processing: Evidence for the cognitive control connection*Language and Linguistics Compass, 4*, 906–924.

Novick, L. R. (2003). At the forefront of thought: The effect of media exposure on airplane typicality. *Psychonomic Bulletin & Review, 10*, 971–974.

Novick, L. R., & Coté, N. (1992). The nature of expertise in anagram solution. *Proceedings of the Fourteenth Annual Conference of the Cognitive Science Society* (pp. 450–455). Hillsdale, NJ: Erlbaum.

Novick, L. R., & Morse, D. L. (2000). Folding a fish, making a mushroom: The role of diagrams in executing assembly procedures. *Memory & Cognition, 28*, 1242–1256.

Novick, L. R., Hurley, S. M., & Francis, M. (1999). Evidence for abstract, schematic knowledge of three spatial diagram representations. *Memory & Cognition, 27*, 288–308.

Nowak, L. G., Munk, M. H. J., Girard, P., & Bullier, J. (1995). Visual latencies in areas V1 and V2 of the macaque monkey. *Visual Neuroscience, 12*, 371–384.

Nusbaum, H. C., & Small, S. L. (2006). In J. T. Caciaoppi, P. S. Visser, & C. L. Pickett (Eds.), *Social neuroscience: People thinking about thinking people* (pp. 131–165). Cambridge, MA: MIT Press.

Oakhill, J., Garnham, A., & Reynolds, D. (2005). Immediate activation of stereotypical gender information. *Memory & Cognition, 33*, 972–983.

Oakie, S. (2005). Traumatic brain injury in the war zone. *New England Journal of Medicine, 352*, 2043–2047.

Oaksford, M., & Chater, N. (1994). A rational analysis of the selection task as optimal data selection. *Psychological Review, 101*, 608–631.

Oberauer, K., Süss, H.-M., Wilhelm, O., & Sander, N. (2007). Individual differences in working memory capacity and reasoning ability. In A. R. A. Conway et al. (Eds.), *Variations in working memory* (pp. 49–75). New York: Oxford University Press.

O'Boyle, C. G. (2006). *History of psychology: A cultural perspective.* Mahwah, NJ: Erlbaum.

O'Brien, L. T., & Crandall, C. S. (2003). Stereotype threat and arousal: Effects on women's math performance. *Personality and Social Psychology Bulletin, 29*, 782–789.

O'Donnell, A. M., & King, A. (Eds.). (2014). *Cognitive perspectives on peer learning.* Routledge.

Olesen, P. J., Westerberg, H., & Klingberg, T. (2004). Increased prefrontal and parietal activity after training of working memory. *Nature Neuroscience, 7,* 75–79.

Olson, G. M., & Olson, J. S. (2003). Human-computer interaction: Psychological aspects of the human use of computing. *Annual Review of Psychology, 54,* 491–516.

Oppenheimer, D. M. (2006). Consequences of erudite vernacular utilized irrespective of necessity: Problems with using long words needlessly. *Applied Cognitive Psychology, 20,* 139–156.

Oreg, S., & Bayazit, M. (2009). Prone to bias: Development of a bias taxonomy from an individual differences perspective. *Review of General Psychology, 13,* 175–193.

Ormerod, T. C. (2005). Planning and ill-defined problems. In R. Morris & G. Ward (Eds.), *The cognitive psychology of planning* (pp. 53–70). Hove, UK: Psychology Press.

Ormerod, T. C., Chronicle, E. P., & MacGregor, J. V. (2006). *The remnants of insight.* Proceedings of the Annual Cognitive Science Society Conference, Vancouver, CA.

Ornstein, P. A., & Haden, C. A. (2001). Memory development or the development of memory? *Current Directions in Psychological Science, 10,* 202–205.

Ornstein, P. A., & Haden, C. A. (2009). Developments in the study of the development of memory. In M. Courage & N. Cowan (Eds.), *The development of memory in childhood* (pp. 367–385). Hove, UK: Psychology Press.

Ornstein, P. A., Haden, C. A., & Elischberger, H. B. (2006). Children's memory development: Remembering the past and preparing for the future. In E. Bialystok & F. I. M. Craik (Eds.), *Lifespan cognition: Mechanisms of change* (pp. 143–161). New York: Oxford University Press.

Osterhout, L., Bersick, M., & McLaughlin, J. (1997). Brain potentials reflect violations of gender stereotypes. *Memory & Cognition, 25,* 273–285.

Oswald, M. E., & Grosjean, S. (2004). Confirmation bias. In R. Pohl (Ed.), *Cognitive illusions: Handbook on fallacies and biases in thinking, judgment, and memory* (pp. 77–96). Hove, UK: Psychology Press.

Owens, R. E., Jr. (2001). *Language development: An introduction.* Boston: Allyn and Bacon.

Öztekin, I., Davachi, L., & McElree, B. (2010). Are representations in working memory distinct from representations in long-term memory? Neural evidence in support of a single store. *Psychological Science, 21,* 1123–1133.

Paap, K. R., Johnson, H. A., & Sawi, O. (2015). Bilingual advantages in executive functioning either do not exist or are restricted to very specific and undetermined circumstances. *Cortex, 69,* 265–278.

Paap, K. R., Myuz, H. A., Anders, R. T., Bockelman, M. F., Mikulinsky, R., & Sawi, O. M. (2017). No compelling evidence for a bilingual advantage in switching or that frequent language switching reduces switch cost. *Journal of Cognitive Psychology, 29*(2), 89–112.

Paas, F., & Kester, L. (2006). Learner and information characteristics in the design of powerful learning environments. *Applied Cognitive Psychology, 20,* 281–285.

Paivio, A. (1978). Comparison of mental clocks. *Journal of Experimental Psychology: Human Perception and Performance, 4,* 61–71.

Paivio, A. (1995). Imagery and memory. In M. S. Gazzaniga (Ed.), *The cognitive neurosciences* (pp. 977–986). Cambridge, MA: MIT Press.

Paivio, A. & Harshman, R. (1983). Factor analysis of a questionnaire on imagery and verbal habits and skills. *Canadian Journal of Psychology, 33*(1), 17–28.

Palmer, S. E. (1999). *Vision science: Photons to phenomenology.* Cambridge, MA: MIT Press.

Palmer, S. E. (2002). Perceptual organization in vision. In S. Yantis (Ed.), *Stevens' handbook of experimental psychology* (3rd ed., Vol. **1**, pp. 177–234). New York: Wiley.

Palmer, S. E. (2003). Visual perception of objects. In A. F. Healy & R. W. Proctor (Eds.), *Handbook of psychology* (Vol. **4**, pp. 179–211). Hoboken, NJ: Wiley.

Pan, B. A. (2012). Assessing vocabulary skills. In E. Hoff (Ed.), *Research methods in child language: A practical guide* (pp. 100–112). Malden, MA: Wiley Blackwell.

Pan, B. A., & Snow, C. E. (1999). The development of conversational and discourse skills. In M. Barrett (Ed.), *The development of language* (pp. 229–249). Hove, UK: Psychology Press.

Pansky, A. & Koriat, A. (2004). The basic-level convergence effect on memory distortions. *Psychological Science, 15,* 52–59.

Papadopoulos, C., Hayes, B. K., & Newell, B. R. (2011). Noncategorical approaches to feature prediction with uncertain categories. *Memory & Cognition, 39,* 304–318.

Parasuraman, R., & Greenwood, P. (2007). Individual differences in attention and working memory: A molecular genetic approach. In A. F. Kramer, D. A. Wiegmann, & A. Kirlik (Eds.), *Attention: From theory to practice* (pp. 59–72). New York: Oxford University Press.

Paris, C. R., Salas, E., & Cannon-Bowers, J. A. (2000). Teamwork in multi-person systems: A review and analysis. *Ergonomics*, *43*, 1052–1075.

Park, D. C., & Hedden, T. (2001). Working memory and aging. In M. Naveh-Benjamin, M. Moscovitch, & H. L. Roediger, III (Eds.), *Perspectives on human memory and cognitive aging: Essays in honour of Fergus Craik* (pp. 148–169). New York: Psychology Press.

Park, D. C., & Payer, D. (2006). Working memory across the adult lifespan. In E. Bialystok & F. I. M. Craik (Eds.), *Lifespan cognition: Mechanisms of change* (pp. 128–142). New York: Oxford University Press.

Park, D. C., & Reuter-Lorenz, P. (2009). The adaptive brain: Aging and neurocognitive scaffolding. *Annual Review of Psychology*, *60*, 173–196.

Park, D. C., Hertzog, C., Leventhal, H., Morrell, R. W., Leventhal, E., Birchmore, D., . . . Bennett, J. (1999). Medication adherence in rheumatoid arthritis patients: Older is wiser. *Journal of the American Geriatric Society*, *47*, 172–183.

Parks, T. (2004). Iconic image. In R. L. Gregory (Ed.), *The Oxford companion to the mind* (2nd ed., p. 425). New York: Oxford University Press.

Parry, K. (2006). People and language. In H. Luria, D. M. Seymour, & T. Smoke (Eds.), *Language and linguistics in context: Readings and applications for teachers* (pp. 153–168). Mahwah, NJ: Erlbaum.

Pashler, H., Rohrer, D., Cepeda, N. J., & Carpenter, S. K. (2007). Enhancing learning and retarding forgetting: Choice and consequences. *Psychonomic Bulletin and Review*,*14*, 187–193.

Pasternak, T., Bisley, J. W., & Calkins, D. (2003). Visual processing in the primate brain. In M. Gallagher & R. J. Nelson (Eds.), *Handbook of psychology* (Vol. **3**, pp. 139–185). Hoboken, NJ: Wiley.

Patel, A. D., Gibson, E., Ratner, J., Besson, M., & Holcomb, P. J. (1998). Processing syntactic relations in language and music: An event-related potential study. *Journal of Cognitive Neuroscience*, *10*, 717–733.

Patterson, J. L. (2002). Relationships of expressive vocabulary to frequency of reading and television experience among bilingual toddlers. *Applied Psycholinguistics*, *23*, 493–508.

Pauker, K., Rule, N. O., & Ambady, N. (2010). Ambiguity and social perception. In E. Balcetis & G. D. Lassiter (Eds.), *Social psychology of visual perception* (pp. 7–26). New York: Psychology Press.

Peal, E., & Lambert, W. E. (1962). The relation of bilingualism to intelligence. *Psychological Monographs*, *546*.

Peetz, J., Buehler, R., & Wilson, A. (2010). Planning for the near and distant future: How does temporal distance affect task completion predictions? *Journal of Experimental Social Psychology*, *46*, 709–720.

Penolazzi, B., Hauk, O., & Pulvermüller, F. (2007). Early semantic context integration and lexical access as revealed by event-related brain potentials. *Biological Psychology*, *74*, 374–388.

Perfetti, C. (2003). The universal grammar of reading. *Scientific Studies of Reading*, *7*, 3–24.

Perfetti, C. (2011). Phonology is critical in reading but a phonological deficit is not the only source of low reading skill. In S. A. Brady, D. Braze, & C. A. Fowler (Eds.), *Explaining individual differences in reading: Theory and evidence* (pp. 153–171). New York: Psychology Press.

Perkins, D. (2001). *The Eureka Effect: The art and logic of breakthrough thinking*. New York: Norton.

Perry, L. K., Samuelson, L. K., & Burdinie, J. B. (2014). Highchair philosophers: the impact of seating context-dependent exploration on children's naming biases. *Developmental Science*, *17*, 757–765. doi:10.1111/desc.12147

Peterson, C., Warren, K. L., & Short, M. M. (2011). Infantile amnesia across the years: A 2-year follow-up of children's earliest memories. *Child Development*, *82*, 1092–1105.

Peterson, L. R., & Peterson, M. (1959). Short-term retention of individual verbal items. *Journal of Experimental Psychology*, *58*, 193–198.

Pezdek, K. (Ed.). (2003). Memory and cognition for the events of September 11, 2001 [Special issue]. *Applied Cognitive Psychology*, *17* (9).

Pezdek, K., & Freyd, J. J. (2009). The fallacy of generalizing from egg salad in false-belief research. *Analysis of Social Issues and Public Policy*, *9*, 177–183.

Pezdek, K., & Taylor, J. (2002). Memory for traumatic events in children and adults. In M. L. Eisen, J. A. Quas, & G. S. Goodman (Eds.), *Memory and suggestibility in the forensic interview* (pp. 165–183). Mahwah, NJ: Erlbaum.

Pezdek, K., Finger, K., & Hodge, D. (1997). Planting false childhood memories: The role of event plausibility. *Psychological Science*, *8*, 437–441

Pezzo, M. V., & Beckstead, J. W. (2008). The effects of disappointment on hindsight bias for real-world outcomes. *Applied Cognitive Psychology*, *22*, 491–506.

Phillips, W. D. (1995). Personal communication.

Phillipson, R. (Ed.). (2000). *Rights to language: Equity, power, and education*. Mahwah, NJ: Erlbaum.

Pickering, M. J., & Clark, A. (2014). Getting ahead: Forward models and their place in cognitive science. *Trends in Cognitive Sciences*, *18*, 451–456.

Pickering, M. J., & Garrod, S. (2004). Toward a mechanistic psychology of dialogue. *Behavioral and Brain Sciences*, *27*, 169–190.

Pickering, M. J., & Garrod, S. (2013). An integrated theory of language production and comprehension. *Behavioral and Brain Sciences*, *36*, 329–347.

Pickering, M. J., & Ferreira, V. S. (2008). Structural priming: A critical review. *Psychological Bulletin*, *134*, 427–459.

Pickering, S. J. (2006a). Assessment of working memory in children, In S. J. Pickering (Ed.), *Working memory and education* (pp. 241–271). Burlington, MA: Elsevier.

Pickering, S. J. (2006b). Introduction. In S. J. Pickering (Ed.), *Working memory and education* (pp. xv–xxii). Burlington, MA: Elsevier.

Pickrell, J. E., Bernstein, D. M., & Loftus, E. E. (2004). Misinformation effect. In R. Pohl (Ed.), *Cognitive illusions: Handbook on fallacies and biases in thinking, judgment, and memory* (pp. 345–361) Hove, UK: Psychology Press.

Pickren, W. E., & Rutherford, A. (2010). *A history of modern psychology in context*. Hoboken, NJ: Wiley.

Pinker, S. (1993). The central problem for the psycholinguist. In G. Harman (Ed.), *Conceptions of the human mind* (pp. 59–84). Hillsdale, NJ: Erlbaum.

Pinker, S. (2002). *The blank slate: The modern denial of human nature*. New York: Viking.

Pinker, S., Nowak, M. A., & Lee, J. J. (2008). The logic of indirect speech. *PNAS*, *105*, 833–838.

Piotroski, J., & Naigles, L. R. (2012). Intermodal preferential looking. In E. Hoff (Ed.), *Research methods in child language: A practical guide* (pp. 17–28). Malden, MA: Blackwell.

Pipe, M.-E., & Salmon, K. (2009). Memory development and forensic context. In M. Courage & N. Cowan (Eds.), *The development of memory in childhood* (pp. 241–282). Hove, UK: Psychology Press.

Pita, M. D., & Utakis, S. (2006). Educational polity for the transnational Dominican community. In H. Luria, D. M. Seymour, & T. Smoke (Eds.), *Language and linguistics in context: Readings and applications for teachers* (pp. 333–341). Mahwah, NJ: Erlbaum.

Pitt, M. A. (2009). The strength and time course of lexical activation of pronunciation variants. *Journal of Experimental Psychology: Human Perception and Performance*, *35*, 896–910.

Plack, C. J. (2005). *The sense of hearing*. Mahwah, NJ: Erlbaum.

Plack, C. J., & Oxenham, A. J. (2005). Overview: The present and future of pitch. In C. J. Plack, A. J. Oxenham, R. R. Fay, & A. N. Popper (Eds.), *Pitch: Neural coding and perception* (pp. 1–6). New York: Springer.

Plant, E. A., Ericsson, K. A., Hill, L., & Asberg, K. (2005). Why study time does not predict grade point average across college students: Implications of deliberate practice for academic performance. *Contemporary Educational Psychology*, *30*, 96–116.

Pohl, R. F. (Ed.). (2016). *Cognitive illusions: Intriguing phenomena in dudgement, thinking and memory*. Psychology Press.

Pohl, R. F. (2004). Hindsight bias. In R. Pohl (Ed.), *Cognitive illusions: Handbook on fallacies and biases in thinking, judgment, and memory* (pp. 363–378). Hove, UK: Psychology Press.

Pohl, R. F., Bender, M., & Lachmann, G. (2002). Hindsight bias around the world. *Experimental Psychology*, *49*, 270–282.

Pohl, R. F., Schwarz, S., Sczesny, S., & Stahlberg, D. (2003). Hindsight bias in gustatory judgments. *Experimental Psychology*, *50*, 107–115.

Poirel, N., Zago, L., Petit, L., & Mellet, E. (2010). Neural bases of topographical representation in humans: Contribution of neuro-imaging studies. In A. Guillot & C. Collet (Eds.), *The neurophysiological foundations of mental and motor imagery* (pp. 17–30). New York: Oxford University Press.

Polk, T. A., Stallcup, M., Aguirre, G. K., Alsop, D. C., D'Esposito, M., Detre, J. A., . . . Farah, M. J. (2002). Neural specialization for letter recognition. *Journal of Cognitive Neuroscience*, *14*, 145–159.

Pomarol-Clotet, E., Hynes, F., Ashwin, C., Bullmore, E. T., McKenna, P.J., & Laws, K. R. (2010). Facial emotion processing in schizophrenia: A non-specific neuropsychological deficit? *Psychological Medicine*, *40*, 911–919.

Poole, D., & Samraj, B. (2010). Discourse analysis and applied linguistics. In R. B. Kaplan (Ed.), *The Oxford handbook of applied linguistics* (2nd ed., pp. 128–140). New York: Oxford University Press.

Posner, M. I. (2004). Progress in attention research. In M. I. Posner (Ed.), *Cognitive neuroscience of attention* (pp. 3–9). New York: Guilford.

Posner, M. I., & Rothbart, M. K. (2007a). *Educating the human brain*. Washington, DC: American Psychological Association.

Posner, M. I., & Rothbart, M. K. (2007b). Research on attention networks as a model for the integration of psychological science. *Annual Review of Psychology*, *58*, 1–23.

Potter, M. C. (1999). Understanding sentences and scenes: The role of conceptual short-term memory. In V. Coltheart (Ed.), *Fleeting memories: Cognition of brief visual stimuli* (pp. 13–46). Cambridge, MA: MIT Press.

Poulton, E. C. (1994). *Behavioral decision theory: A new approach*. Cambridge, UK: Cambridge University Press.

Powell, J., Letson, S., Davidoff, J., Valentine, T., & Greenwood, R. (2008). Enhancement of face recognition learning in patients with brain injury using three cognitive training procedures. *Neuropsychological Rehabilitation*, *18*, 182–203.

Prabhu, V., Sutton, C., & Sauser, W. (2008). Creativity and certain personality traits: Understanding the mediating effects of intrinsic motivation. *Creativity Research Journal*, *20*, 53–66.

Pressley, M. (1996). Personal reflections on the study of practical memory in the mid-1990s: The complete cognitive researcher. In D. J. Herrmann et al. (Eds.), *Basic and applied memory research: Practical applications* (Vol. **2**, pp. 19–33). Mahwah, NJ: Erlbaum.

Pressley, M., & Ghatala, E. S. (1988). Delusions about performance on multiple-choice comprehension tests. *Reading Research Quarterly*, *23*, 454–464.

Pressley, M., & Hilden, K. (2006). Cognitive strategies. In D. Kuhn & R. Siegler (Eds.), *Handbook of child psychology* (6th ed., Vol. **2**, pp. 511–556). Hoboken, NJ: Wiley.

Pressley, M., Levin, J. R., & Ghatala, E. S. (1984). Memory strategy monitoring in adults and children. *Journal of Verbal Learning and Verbal Behavior*, *23*, 270–288.

Pringle, A., Harmer, C. J., & Cooper, M. J. (2010). Investigating vulnerability to eating disorders: Biases in emotional processing. *Psychological Medicine*, *40*, 645–655.

Proctor, R. W., & Vu, K.-P. L. (2010). Cumulative knowledge and progress in human factors. *Annual Review of Psychology*, **2010**, 623–651.

Puce, A., & Perrett, D. (2005). Electrophysiology and brain imaging of biological motion. In J. T. Cacioppo & G. G. Berntson (Eds.), *Social neuroscience: Key readings* (pp. 115–129). New York: Psychology Press.

Purdon, C., Rowa, K., & Antony, M. M. (2005). Thought suppression and its effects on thought frequency, appraisal and mood state in individuals with obsessive-compulsive disorder. *Behavior Research and Therapy*, *43*, 93–108.

Purves, D., & Lotto, R. B. (2003). *Why we see what we do*. Sunderland, MA: Sinauer.

Pylyshyn, Z. W. (2003). Return of the mental image: Are there pictures in the brain? *TRENDS in Cognitive Sciences*, *7*, 113–118.

Pylyshyn, Z. W. (2004). Mental imagery. In R. L. Gregory (Ed.), *The Oxford companion to the mind* (pp. 582–585). New York: Oxford University Press.

Pylyshyn, Z. W. (2006). *Seeing and visualizing: It's not what you think*. Cambridge, MA: MIT Press.

Pynte, J., Kennedy, A., & Ducrot, S. (2004). The influence of parafoveal typographical errors on eye movements in reading. In R. Radach, A. Kennedy, & K. Rayner (Eds.), *Eye movements and information processing during reading* (pp. 178–202). Hove, UK: Psychology Press.

Qu, Q., Damian, M. F., Zhang, Q., & Zhu, X. (2011). Phonology contributes to writing: Evidence from written word production in a nonalphabetic script. *Psychological Science*, *22*, 1107–1112.

Quilici, J. L., & Mayer, R. E. (2002). Teaching students to recognize structural similarities between statistics word problems. *Applied Cognitive Psychology*, *16*, 325–342.

Quinlan, P. (2010). Feature integration theory. In E. B. Goldstein (Ed.), *Encyclopedia of perception* (Vol. **1**, pp. 452–456). Thousand Oaks, CA: Sage.

Quinn, D. M., & Spencer, S. J. (2001). The interference of stereotype threat with women's generation of mathematical problem-solving strategies. *Journal of Social Issues*, *57*, 55–71.

Quinn, P. C., Bhatt, R. S., Brush, D., Grimes, A., & Sharpnack, H. (2002). Development of form similarity as a Gestalt grouping principle in infancy. *Psychological Science*, *13*, 320–328.

Raaijmakers, J. G. W., & Shiffrin, R. M. (2002). Models of memory. In D. Medin (Ed.), *Stevens' handbook of experimental psychology* (3rd ed., pp. 43–76). New York: Wiley.

Rabbitt, P. (2002). Aging and cognition. In H. Pashler (Ed.), *Stevens' handbook of experimental psychology* (3rd ed., Vol. **4**, pp. 793–860). New York: Wiley.

Rachlinski, J. J. (2004). Misunderstanding ability, misallocating responsibility. In D. T. Levin (Ed.), *Thinking and seeing: Visual metacognition in adults and children* (pp. 251–276). Cambridge, MA: MIT Press.

Radach, R., & Kennedy, A. (2004). Theoretical perspectives on eye movements in reading: Past controversies, current issues, and an agenda for future research. In R. Radach, A. Kennedy, & K. Rayner (Eds.), *Eye movements and information processing during reading* (pp. 3–26). Hove, UK: Psychology Press.

Radach, R., Kennedy, A., & Rayner, K. (2004b). Preface. In R. Radach, A. Kennedy, & K. Rayner (Eds.), *Eye movements and information processing during reading* (pp. 1–2). Hove, UK: Psychology Press.

Radvansky, G. A. (2008). Situation models in memory: Texts and stories. In G. Cohen & M. Conway (Eds.), *Memory in the real world* (3rd ed., pp. 230–247). New York: Psychology Press.

Rahman, R. A., & Sommer, W. (2008). Seeing what we know and understand: How knowledge shapes perception. *Psychonomic Bulletin & Review*, *15*, 1055–1063.

Randi, J., Grigorenko, E. L., & Sternberg, R. J. (2005). Revisiting definitions of reading comprehension: Just what is reading comprehension anyway? In S. E. Israel, C. C. Block, K. L. Bauserman, & K. Kinnucan-Welsch (Eds.), *Metacognition in literacy learning: Theory, assessment, instruction, and professional development* (pp. 19–39). Mahwah, NJ: Erlbaum.

Ransdell, S., & Levy, C. M. (1999). Writing, reading, and speaking memory spans and the importance of resource flexibility. In M. Torrance & G. C. Jeffery (Eds.), *The cognitive demands of writing: Processing capacity and working memory in text production* (pp. 99–113). Amsterdam: Amsterdam University Press.

Rapp, B., & Goldrick, M. (2000). Discreteness and interactivity in spoken word production. *Psychological Review, 107,* 460–499.

Rapp, D. N., & Gerrig, R. J. (2006). Predilections for narrative outcomes: The impact of story contexts and reader preferences. *Journal of Memory and Language, 54,* 54–67.

Raskin, S. A., Maye, J., Rogers, A., Correll, D., Zamroziewicz, M., & Kurtz, M. (2014). Prospective memory in schizophrenia: Relationship to medication management skills, neurocognition, and symptoms in individuals with schizophrenia. *Neuropsychology, 28,* 359.

Rasmussen, E. B. (2006). Expanding your coverage of neuroscience: An interview with Michael Gazzaniga. *Teaching of Psychology, 33,* 212–215.

Rathbone, C. K., & Moulin, C. J. A. (2010). When's your birthday? The self-reference effect in retrieval of dates. *Applied Cognitive Psychology, 24,* 737–743.

Ratner, H. H., Foley, M. A., & McCaskill, P. (2001). Understanding children's activity memory: The role of outcomes. *Journal of Experimental Child Psychology, 79,* 162–191.

Ratner, N. B., & Gleason, J. B. (1993). An introduction to psycholinguistics: What do language users know? In J. B. Gleason & N. B. Ratner (Eds.), *Psycholinguistics.* Fort Worth: Harcourt Brace Jovanovich.

Raulerson, B. A., III, Donovan, M. J., Whitford, A. B., & Kellogg, R. T. (2010). Differential verbal, visual, and spatial working memory in written language production. *Perceptual and Motor Skills, 110,* 229–244.

Rayner, K. (1975). The perceptual span and peripheral cues in reading. *Cognitive Psychology, 7,* 65–81.

Rayner, K. (1998). Eye movements in reading and information processing: 20 years of research. *Psychological Bulletin, 124,* 372–422.

Rayner, K. (2009). The 35th Sir Frederick Bartlett Lecture: Eye movements and attention in reading, scene perception, and visual search. *Quarterly Journal of Experimental Psychology, 62,* 1457–1506.

Rayner, K., & Clifton, C., Jr. (2002). Language processing. In D. Medin (Ed.), *Stevens' handbook of experimental psychology* (3rd ed., Vol. **2,** pp. 261–316). New York: Wiley.

Rayner, K., & Liversedge, S. P. (2004). Visual and linguistic processing during eye fixations in reading. In J. M. Henderson & F. Ferreira (Eds.), *The interface of language, vision, and action: Eye movements and the visual world* (pp. 59–104). New York: Psychology Press.

Rayner, K., Foorman, B. R., Perfetti, C. A., Pesetsky, D., & Seidenberg, M. S. (2001). How psychological science informs the teaching of reading. *Psychological Science in the Public Interest, 2,* 31–74.

Rayner, K., Juhasz, B. J., & Pollatsek, A. (2005). Eye movements during reading. In J. Snowling & C. Hulme (Eds.), *The science of reading: A handbook* (pp. 61–78). Malden, MA: Blackwell.

Rayner, K., Liversedge, S. P., & White, S. J. (2006). Eye movements when reading disappearing text: The importance of the word to the right of fixation. *Vision Research, 46,* 310–323.

Rayner, K., Pollatsek, A., & Starr, M. S. (2003). Reading. In I. B. Weiner (Ed.), *Handbook of psychology* (Vol. **4,** pp. 549–574). Hoboken, NJ: Wiley.

Rayner, K., Shen, D., Bai, X., & Yan, G. (Eds.). (2008). *Cognitive and cultural influences on eye movements.* Tianjin, China: Tianjin People's Publishing House.

Rayner, K., Slattery, T. J., Drieghe, D., & Liversedge, S. P. (2011). Eye movements and word skipping during reading: effects of word length and predictability. *Journal of Experimental Psychology: Human Perception and Performance, 37,* 514–528.

Read, J. D., & Connolly, D. A. (2007). The effects of delay on long-term memory for witnessed events. In M. P. Toglia, J. D. Read, D. F. Ross, & R. C. L. Lindsay (Eds.), *Handbook of eyewitness psychology* (Vol. **1,** pp. 117–155). Mahwah, NJ: Erlbaum.

Reber, R. (2004). Availability. In R. Pohl (Ed.), *Cognitive illusions: Handbook on fallacies and biases in thinking, judgment, and memory.* Hove, UK: Psychology Press.

Reddy, L., Tsuchiya, N., & Serre, T. (2010). Reading the mind's eye: Decoding category information during mental imagery. *NeuroImage, 50,* 818–835.

Reder, L. M., Park, H., & Keiffaber, P. D. (2009). Memory systems do not divide on consciousness: Reinterpreting memory in terms of activation and binding. *Psychological Bulletin, 135,* 23–49.

Reed, S. K. (1974). Structural descriptions and the limitations of visual images. *Memory & Cognition, 2,* 329–336.

Reed, S. K. (2010). *Thinking visually.* New York: Psychology Press.

Rehder, B., & Hoffman, A. B. (2005). Thirty-something categorization results explained: Selective attention, eyetracking, and models of category learning. *Journal of Experimental Psychology: Learning Memory, and Cognition, 31*, 811–929.

Reichenberg, A., & Harvey, P. D. (2007). Neuropsychological impairments in schizophrenia: Integration of performance-based and brain imaging findings. *Psychological Bulletin, 133*, 833–858.

Reicher, G. M. (1969). Perceptual recognition as a function of meaningfulness of stimuli material. *Journal of Experimental Psychology, 81*, 275–280.

Reichle, E. D., & Laurent, P. A. (2006). Using reinforcement learning to understand the emergence of "intelligent" eye-movement behavior during reading. *Psychological Review, 113*, 390–408.

Reichle, E. D., Pollatsek, A., Fisher, D. L., & Rayner, K. (1998). Toward a model of eye movement control in reading. *Psychological Review, 105*, 125–157.

Reichle, E. D., Reineberg, A. E., & Schooler, J. W. (2010). Eye movements during mindless reading. *Psychological Science, 21*, 1300–1310.

Reif, F. (2008). *Applying cognitive science to education: Thinking and learning in scientific and other complex domains.* Cambridge, MA: MIT Press.

Reisberg, D., & Heuer, F. (2005). Visuospatial images. In P. Shah & A. Miyake (Eds.), *The Cambridge handbook of visuospatial thinking* (pp. 35–80). New York: Cambridge University Press.

Reisberg, D., Pearson, D. G., & Kosslyn, S. M. (2003). Intuitions and introspections about imagery: The role of imagery experience in shaping an investigator's theoretical views. *Applied Cognitive Psychology, 17*, 147–160.

Rendell, P. G., Castel, A. D., & Craik, F. I. M. (2005). Memory for proper names in old age: A disproportionate impairment? *Quarterly Journal of Experimental Psychology, 58A*, 54–71.

Rendell, P. G., Phillips, L. H., Henry, J. D., Brumby-Rendell, T., de la Piedad Garcia, X., Altgassen, M., . . . Kliegel, M. (2011). Prospective memory, emotional valence and ageing. *Cognition & emotion, 25*, 916–925.

Rensink, R. A. (2010). Change detection. In E. B. Goldstein (Ed.), *Encyclopedia of perception* (Vol.1, pp. 241–244). Thousand Oaks, CA: Sage.

Rensink, R. A., O'Regan, J. K., & Clark, J. J. (1997). To see or not to see: The need for attention to perceive changes in scenes. *Psychological Science, 8*, 368–373.

Reuter-Lorenz, P. A., & Jonides, J. (2007). The executive is central to working memory: Insights from age, performance, and task variations. In A. R. A. Conway, M. J. Kane, A. Miyake, & J. N. Towse (Eds.), *Variations in working memory* (pp. 250–271). New York: Oxford University Press.

Reverberi, C., Shallice, T., D'Agostini, S., Skrap, M., & Bonatti, L. L. (2009). Cortical bases of elementary deductive reasoning: Inference, memory, and metadeduction. *Neuropsychologia, 47*, 1107–1116.

Revonsuo, A. (2010). *Consciousness: The science of subjectivity.* New York: Psychology Press.

Reyna, V. F., Mills, B., Estreada, S., & Brainerd, C. J. (2007). False memory in children: Data, theory, and legal implications. In M. P. Toglia, J. D. Read, D. F. Ross, & R. C. L. Lindsay (Eds.), *Handbook of eyewitness psychology* (Vol. 1, pp. 479–507). Mahwah, NJ: Erlbaum.

Reynolds, D. J., Garnham, A., & Oakhill, J. (2006). Evidence of immediate activation of gender information from a social role name. *Quarterly Journal of Experimental Psychology, 59*, 886–903.

Reznick, J. S. (2009). Working memory in infants and toddlers. In M. Courage & N. Cowan (Eds.), *The development of memory in childhood* (pp. 343–365). Hove, UK: Psychology Press.

Rhodes, M. G., & Tauber, S. K. (2011). The influence of delaying judgments of learning on metacognitive accuracy: A meta-analytic review. Psychological bulletin, *137*, 131–148.

Rhodes, M. G. (2009). Age estimation of faces: A review. *Applied Cognitive Psychology, 23*, 1–12.

Rhodes, M. G., & Castel, A. D. (2009). Metacognitive illusions for auditory information: Effects on monitoring and control. *Psychonomic Bulletin & Review, 16*, 550–554.

Rhodes, R. L., Ochoa, S. H., & Ortiz, S. O. (2005). *Assessing culturally and linguistically diverse students: A practical guide.* New York: Guilford.

Riccio, D. C., Millin, P. M., & Gisquet-Verrier, P. (2003). Retrograde amnesia: Forgetting back. *Current Directions in Psychological Science, 12*, 41–44.

Richardson, J. T. E. (1999). *Imagery.* East Sussex, UK: Psychology Press.

Richardson, D. C., Spivey, M. J., Barsalou, L. W., & McRae, K. (2003). Spatial representations activated during real-time comprehension of verbs. *Cognitive Science, 27*, 767–780.

Richardson-Klavehn, A., & Gardiner, J. M. (1998). Depth-of-processing effects on priming in stem completion: Tests of the voluntary-contamination, conceptual-processing, and lexical-processing hypotheses. *Journal of Experimental Psychology: Learning, Memory, and Cognition, 24*, 593–609.

Richler, J. J., Cheung, O. S., & Gauthier, I. (2011). Holistic processing predicts face recognition. *Psychological Science*, *22*, 464–471.

Riddoch, M. J., & Humphreys, G. W. (2001). Object recognition. In B. Rapp (Ed.), *The handbook of cognitive neuropsychology* (pp. 45–74). Philadelphia: Psychology Press.

Riding, R. J., Glass, A., & Douglas, G. (1993). Individual differences in thinking: Cognitive and neurophysiological perspectives. *Educational Psychology*, *13*(3–4), 267–279.

Rips, L. J. (2002). Reasoning. In D. Medin (Ed.), *Stevens' handbook of experimental psychology* (3rd ed., Vol. **2**, pp. 363–411). New York: Wiley.

Rips, L. J., Smith, E. E., & Medin, D. L. (2012). Concepts and categories: Memory, meaning, and metaphysics. In K. J. Holyoak & R. G. Morrison (Eds.), *The Oxford handbook of thinking and reasoning* (pp. 177–209). New York: Oxford University Press.

Risen, J. L., Gilovich, T., & Dunning, D. (2007). One-shot illusory correlations and stereotype formation. *Personality and Social Psychology Bulletin*, *33*, 1492–1502.

Rizzolatti, G., & Craighero, L. (2009). Language and mirror neurons. In M. G. Gaskell (Ed.), *The Oxford handbook of psycholinguistics* (pp. 771–785). New York: Oxford University Press.

Rizzolatti, G., Fadiga, L., Fogassi, L., & Gallese, V. (1996). Premotor cortex and the recognition of motor actions. *Cognitive Brain Research*, *3*, 131–141.

Robbins, P., & Aydede, M. (2009). A short primer on situated cognition. In P. Robbins & M. Aydede (Eds.), *The Cambridge handbook of situated cognition* (pp. 3–10). New York: Cambridge University Press.

Roberts, M. J., & Newton, E. J. (2005). Introduction: Individual differences in reasoning strategies. In M. J. Roberts & E. J. Newton (Eds.), *Methods of thought: Individual differences in reasoning strategies* (pp. 1–9). Hove, UK: Psychology Press.

Robertson, L. C., & Treisman, A. (2010). Consciousness: Disorders. In E. B. Goldstein (Ed.), *Encyclopedia of perception* (Vol. **1**, pp. 304–309). Thousand Oaks, CA: Sage.

Robertson, S. I. (2001). *Problem solving*. East Sussex, UK: Psychology Press.

Robins, R. W., Gosling, S. D., & Craik, K. H. (1999). An empirical analysis of trends in psychology. *American Psychologist*, *54*, 117–128.

Robins, S., & Treiman, R. (2009). Talking about writing: What we can learn from conversations between parents and their young children. *Applied Psycholinguistics*, *30*, 463–484.

Rodd, J., Gaskell, G., & Marslen-Wilson, W. (2002). Making sense of semantic ambiguity: Semantic competition in lexical access. *Journal of Memory and Language*, *46*, 245–266.

Roebers, C. M., & Schneider, W. (2000). The impact of misleading questions on eyewitness memory in children and adults. *Applied Cognitive Psychology*, *14*, 509–526.

Roebers, C. M., Gelhar, T., & Schneider, W. (2004). "It's magic!" The effects of presentation modality on children's event memory, suggestibility, and confidence judgments. *Journal of Experimental Child Psychology*, *87*, 320–335.

Roebers, C. M., Schwarz, S., & Neumann, R. (2005). Social influence and children's event recall and suggestibility. *European Journal of Developmental Psychology*, *2*, 47–69.

Roediger, H. L. III, Agarwal, P. K., Kang S. H. K., & Marsh, E. J. (2010). Benefits of testing memory: Best practices and boundary conditions. In G. M. Davies & D. B. Wright (Eds.), *Current issues in applied memory research* (pp. 13–49). New York: Psychology Press.

Roediger, H. L., III, & Amir, N. (2005). Implicit memory tasks: Retention without conscious recollection. In A. Wenzel & D. C. Rubin (Eds.), *Cognitive methods and their application to clinical research* (pp. 121–127). Washington, DC: American Psychological Association.

Roediger, H. L., III, & Gallo, D. A. (2001). Levels of processing: Some unanswered questions. In M. Naveh-Benjamin, M. Moscovitch, & H. L. Roediger, III (Eds.), *Perspectives on human memory and cognitive aging: Essays in honour of Fergus Craik* (pp. 28–47). New York: Psychology Press.

Roediger, H. L., III, & Guynn, M. J. (1996). Retrieval processes. In E. L. Bjork & R. A. Bjork (Eds.), *Memory* (pp. 197–236). San Diego: Academic Press.

Roediger, H. L., III, & Karpicke, J. D. (2006a). The power of testing memory: Basic research and implications for educational practice. *Perspectives on Psychological Science*, *1*, 181–210.

Roediger, H. L., III, & Karpicke, J. D. (2006b). Test-enhanced learning: Taking memory tests improves long-term retention. *Psychological Science*, *17*, 249–255.

Roediger, H. L., III, & McDermott, K. B. (1995). Creating false memories: Remembering words not presented in lists. *Journal of Experimental Psychology: Learning, Memory, and Cognition*, *21*, 803–814.

Roediger, H. L., III, & McDermott, K. B. (2000). Distortions of memory. In E. Tulving & F. I. M. Craik (Eds.), *The Oxford handbook of memory* (pp. 149–162). New York: Oxford University Press.

Roediger, H. L., III, Gallo, D. A., & Geraci, L. (2002). Processing approaches to cognition: The impetus from the levels-of-processing framework. *Memory*, *10*, 319–332.

Roediger, H. L., III, Marsh, E. J., & Lee, S. C. (2002). Kinds of memory. In D. Medin (Ed.), *Stevens' handbook of experimental psychology* (3rd ed., pp. 1–41). New York: Wiley.

Roediger, H. L., III. (2000). Why retrieval is the key process in understanding human memory. In E. Tulving (Ed.), *Memory, consciousness, and the brain* (pp. 52–75). Philadelphia: Psychology Press.

Roediger, H. L., III. (2008). Relativity of remembering: Why the laws of memory vanished. *Annual Review of Psychology, 59,* 225–254.

Roelofs, A., & Baayen, H. (2002). Morphology by itself in planning the production of spoken words. *Psychonomic Bulletin & Review, 9,* 132–138.

Rogers, T. B., Kuiper, N. A., & Kirker, W. S. (1977). Self-reference and the encoding of personal information. *Journal of Personality and Social Psychology, 35,* 677–688.

Rogers, T. T. & McClelland, J. L. (2004). *Semantic cognition: A parallel distributed processing approach.* Cambridge, MA: MIT Press.

Rogers, T. T., & McClelland, J. L. (2011). Semantics without categorization. In E. M. Pothos & A. J. Wills (Eds.), *Formal approaches in categorization* (pp. 88–119). New York: Cambridge University Press.

Rohrer, D., & Taylor, K. (2006). The effects of overlearning and distributed practice on the retention of mathematics knowledge. *Applied Cognitive Psychology, 20,* 1209–1224.

Rollins, P. R. (2003). Caregivers' contingent comments to 9-month-old infants: Relationships with later language. *Applied Psycholinguistics, 24,* 221–234.

Rolls, E. T. (2004). Neural networks in the brain. In R. L. Gregory (Ed.), *The Oxford companion to the mind* (2nd ed., pp. 639–641). New York: Oxford University Press.

Rolls, E. T., & Tovee, M. J. (1995). Sparseness of the neuronal representation of stimuli in the primate temporal visual cortex. *Journal of Neurophysiology, 73,* 713–726.

Romero Lauro, L. J., Reis, J., Cohen, L. G., Cecchetto, C., & Papagno, C. (2010). A case for the involvement of phonological loop in sentence comprehension. *Neuropsychologia, 48,* 4003–4011.

Rosch, E. H. (1973). Natural categories. *Cognitive Psychology, 4,* 328–350.

Rosch, E. H. (1975). The nature of mental codes for color categories. *Journal of Experimental Psychology: Human Perception and Performance, 1,* 303–322.

Rosch, E. H., & Mervis, C. B. (1975). Family resemblances: Studies in the internal structure of categories. *Cognitive Psychology, 7,* 573–605.

Rosch, E. H., Mervis, C. B., Gray, W. D., Johnson, D. M., & Boyes-Braem, P. (1976). Basic objects in natural categories. *Cognitive Psychology, 8,* 382–439.

Rose, S. P. R. (2004). Memory: Biological basis. In R. L. Gregory (Ed.), *The Oxford companion to the mind* (2nd ed., pp. 564–568). New York: Oxford University Press.

Rosenblum, L. D. (2005). Primacy of multimodal speech perception. In D. B. Pisoni & R. E. Remez (Eds.), *The handbook of speech perception* (pp. 51–78). Malden, MA: Blackwell.

Rosenthal, R. (1979). The file drawer problem and tolerance for null results. *Psychological Bulletin, 86*(3), 638–641.

Roskos-Ewoldsen, B., McNamara, T. P., Shelton, A. L., & Carr, W. (1998). Mental representations of large and small spatial layouts are orientation dependent. *Journal of Experimental Psychology: Learning, Memory, and Cognition, 24,* 215–226.

Ross, M., & Wang, Q. (2010). Why we remember and what we remember: Culture and autobiographical memory. *Perspectives on Psychological Science, 5,* 401–409.

Ross, N., & Tidwell, M. (2010). Concepts and culture. In D. Mareschal, P. C. Quinn, & S. E. G. Lea (Eds.), *The making of human concepts* (pp. 131–148). New York: Oxford University Press.

Rothbart, M. K., Sheese, B. F., Rueda, M. R., & Posner, M. J. (2011). Developing mechanisms of self-regulation in early life. *Emotion Review, 3,* 207–213.

Rothblum, E. D., & Factor, R. (2001). Lesbians and their sisters as a control group. *Psychological Science, 12,* 63–69.

Rouw, R., Kosslyn, S. M., & Hamel, R. (1997). Detecting high-level and low-level properties in visual images and visual precepts. *Cognition, 63,* 209–226.

Rovee-Collier, C. K. & Cuevas, K. (2009a). The development of infant memory. In M. Courage & N. Cowan (Eds.), *The development of memory in childhood* (pp. 11–41). Hove, UK: Psychology Press.

Rovee-Collier, C. K., & Barr, R. (2002). Infant cognition. In H. Pashler (Ed.), *Stevens' handbook of experimental psychology* (Vol. **4,** pp. 693–791). New York: Wiley.

Rovee-Collier, C. K., Griesler, P. C., & Earley, L. A. (1985). Contextual determinants of retrieval in three-month-old infants. *Learning and Motivation, 16,* 139–157.

Rovee-Collier, C., & Cuevas, K. (2009b). Multiple memory systems are unnecessary to account for infant memory development: An ecological model. *Developmental Psychology, 43,* 160–174.

Rovee-Collier, C., & Hayne, H. (2000). Memory in infancy and early childhood. In E. Tulving & F. I. M. Craik (Eds.), *The Oxford handbook of memory* (pp. 267–282). New York: Oxford University Press.

Rovee-Collier, C., Hayne, H., & Colombo, M. (2001). *The development of implicit and explicit memory.* Philadelphia: John Benjamins Publishing Company.

Roy, M. M., & Christenfeld, N. J. S. (2007). Bias in memory predicts bias in estimation of future task duration. *Memory & Cognition, 35,* 557–564.

Roy, M. M., Christenfeld, N. J. S., & McKenzie, C. R. M. (2005). Underestimating the duration of future events: Memory incorrectly used or memory bias? *Psychological Review, 131,* 738–756.

Royden, C. S., Wolfe, J. M., & Klempen, N. (2001). Visual search asymmetries in motion and optic flow fields. *Perception & Psychophysics, 63,* 436–444.

Ruben, B. D. (2001, July 13). We need excellence beyond the classroom. *Chronicle of Higher Education,* pp. B15–B16.

Rubin, D. C. (2000). The distribution of early childhood memories. *Memory, 8,* 265–269.

Rubin, D. C., & Berentsen, D. (2009). The frequency of voluntary and involuntary autobiographical memories across the life span. *Memory & Cogniton, 37,* 679–688.

Rubin, D. C., Berntsen, D., & Bohni, M. K. (2008). A memory-based model of posttraumatic stress disorder: Evaluating basic assumptions underlying the PTSD diagnosis. *Psychological Review, 115,* 985–1011.

Rucker, D. D., Briñol, P., & Petty, R. E. (2011). Metacognition: Methods to assess primary versus secondary cognition. In K. C. Klauer, A. Voss, & C. Stahl (Eds.), *Cognitive methods in social psychology* (pp. 236–264). New York: Guilford.

Ruddle, R. A., Volkova, E., Mohler, B., & Bülthoff, H. H. (2011). The effect of landmark and body-based sensory information on route knowledge. *Memory & Cognition, 39,* 686–699.

Rudman, L. A. (2005). Rejection of women? Beyond prejudice as antipathy. In J. F. Dovidio, P. Glick, & L. A. Rudman (Eds.), *On the nature of prejudice: Fifty years after Allport* (pp. 106–120). Malden, MA: Blackwell.

Rueckl, J. G. (1995). Ambiguity and connectionist networks: Still settling into a solution—comment on Joordens and Besner (1994). *Journal of Experimental Psychology: Learning, Memory, and Cognition, 21,* 501–508

Rueckl, J. G., & Oden, G. C. (1986). The integration of contextual and featural information during word identification. *Journal of Memory and Language, 25,* 445–460.

Rumelhart, D. E., J. L. McClelland and the PDP Research Group (1986a). *Parallel Distributed Processing: Explorations in the Microstructure of Cognition. Volume 1: Foundations,* Cambridge, MA: MIT Press.

Runco, M. A. (2005). Motivation, competence, and creativity. In A. J. Elliot & C. S. Dweck (Eds.), *Handbook of competence and motivation* (pp. 609–623). New York: Guilford.

Runco, M. A. (2007). *Creativity: Theories and themes: Research, development, and practice.* London: Elsevier Academic Press.

Rundus, D. (1971). Analysis of rehearsal processes in free recall. *Journal of Experimental Psychology, 89,* 63–77.

Ruscio, J., Whitney, D. M., & Amabile, T. M. (1998). Looking inside the fishbowl of creativity: Verbal and behavioral predictors of creative performance. *Creativity Research Journal, 11,* 243–263.

Russ, S. W. (2001). Writing creatively: How to do it. [Review of the book *Writing in flow: Keys to enhanced creativity*]. *Contemporary Psychology, 46,* 181–182.

Rutherford, A. (2009). *Beyond the box: B.F. Skinner's technology of behavior from laboratory to life, 1950s–1970s.* Toronto: University of Toronto Press.

Sachs, J. (1967). Recognition memory for syntactic and semantic aspects of a connected discourse. *Perception & Psychophysics, 2,* 437–442.

Saffran, E. M., & Schwartz, M. F. (2003). Language. In I. B. Weiner (Ed.), *Handbook of psychology* (Vol. **4,** pp. 595–636). Hoboken, NJ: Wiley.

Saffran, J. B., Werker, J. F., & Werner, L. A. (2006). The infant's auditory world: Hearing, speech, and the beginnings of language. In D. Kuhn & R. Siegler (Eds.), *Handbook of child psychology* (6th ed., Vol. **2,** pp. 58–108). Hoboken, NJ: Wiley.

Salthouse, T. (2012). Consequences of age-related cognitive declines. *Annual Review of Psychology, 63,* 201–226.

Salvucci, D. D., & Taatgen, N. A. (2008). Threaded cognition: An integrated theory of concurrent multitasking. *Psychological Review, 115,* 101–130.

Samelson, F. (2009). Struggle for scientific authority. In L. T. Benjamin, Jr. (Ed.), *A brief history of psychology: Original sources and contemporary research* (pp. 265–280). Malden, MA: Blackwell.

Samuel, A. G. (2011). Speech perception. *Annual Review of Psychology, 62,* 49–72.

Sangrigoli, S., & de Schonen, S. (2004). Recognition of own-face and other-race faces by three-month-old infants. *Journal of Child Psychology and Psychiatry, 45*, 1219–1227.

Sanna, L. J., & Schwarz, N. (2006). Metacognitive experiences and human judgment: The case of hindsight bias and its debiasing. *Current Directions in Psychological Science, 15*, 172–176.

Sanna, L. J., Schwarz, N., & Kennedy, L. A. (2009). It's hard to imagine: Mental simulation, metacognitive experiences, and the success of debiasing. In K. D. Markman, W. M. P. Klein, & Suhr, J. A. (Eds.), *Handbook of imagination and mental simulation* (pp. 197–210). New York: Psychology Press.

Saylor, M. M., & Baldwin, D. A. (2004). Action analysis and change blindness: Possible links. In D. T. Levin (Ed.), *Thinking and seeing: Visual metacognition in adults and children* (pp. 37–56). Cambridge, MA: MIT Press.

Schacter, D. L. (1999). The seven sins of memory: Insights from psychology and cognitive neuroscience. *American Psychologist, 54*, 182–203.

Schacter, D. L. (2001). *The seven sins of memory*. Boston: Houghton Mifflin.

Schacter, D. L., & Wiseman, A. L. (2006). Reducing memory errors: The distinctiveness heuristic. In R. R. Hunt & J. B. Worthen (Eds.), *Distinctiveness and memory* (pp. 89–107). New York: Oxford University Press.

Schacter, D. L., Church, B., & Treadwell, J. (1994). Implicit memory in amnesic patients: Evidence for spared auditory priming. *Psychological Science, 5*, 20–25.

Schacter, D. L., Norman, K. A., & Koustaal, W. (1998). The cognitive neuroscience of constructive memory. *Annual Review of Psychology, 49*, 289–318.

Schaeken, W., DeVooght, G., Vandierendonck, A., & d'Ydewalle, G. (2000). Strategies and tactics in deductive reasoning. In W. Schaeken, G. DeVooght, A. Vandierendonck, & G. d'Ydewalle (Eds.), *Deductive reasoning and strategies* (pp. 301–309). Mahwah, NJ: Erlbaum.

Schank, R. C., & Abelson, R. P. (1977). *Scripts, plans, goals, and understanding*. Hillsdale, NJ: Erlbaum.

Schank, R. C., & Abelson, R. P. (1995). Knowledge and memory: The real story. In R. S. Wyer, Jr. (Ed.), *Knowledge and memory: The real story* (pp. 1–85). Hillsdale, NJ: Erlbaum.

Scheiber, C., Reynolds, M. R., Hajovsky, D. B., & Kaufman, A. S. (2015). Gender differences in achievement in a large, nationally representative sample of children and adolescents. *Psychology in the Schools, 52*(4), 335–348.

Schelhorn, S.-E., Griego, J., & Schmid, U. (2007). Transformational and derivational strategies in analogical problem solving. *Cognitive Processes, 8*, 45–55.

Schirillo, J. A. (2010). Gestalt approach. In E. B. Goldstein (Ed.), *Encyclopedia of perception* (Vol.1., pp. 469–472). Thousand Oaks, CA: Sage.

Schmalzl, L., Palermo, R., Green, M., Brunsdon, R., & Coltheart, M. (2008). Training of familiar face recognition and visual scan paths for faces in a child with congenital prosopagnosia. *Cognitive Neuropsychology, 25*, 704–729.

Schmeichel, B. J., & Hoffman, W. (2011). Working memory capacity in social psychology. In K. C. Klauer, A. Voss, & C. Stahl, *Cognitive methods in social psychology* (pp. 184–205). New York: Guilford.

Schmeichel, B. J., Volokhov, R. N., & Demaree, H. A. (2008). Working memory capacity and the self-regulation of emotional expression and experience. *Journal of Personality and Social Psychology, 95*(6), 1526.

Schmidt, J. R., & Thompson, V. A. (2008). "At least one" problem with "some" formal reasoning paradigms. *Memory & Cognition, 36*, 217–229.

Schmitt, N. (2014). Size and depth of vocabulary knowledge: What the research shows. *Language Learning, 64*, 913–951.

Schmidt, S. R. (2006). Emotion, significance, distinctiveness, and memory. In R. R. Hunt & J. B. Worthen (Eds.), *Distinctiveness and memory* (pp. 47–64). New York: Oxford University Press.

Schneider, M., Rode, C., & Stern, E. (2010). Secondary school students' availability and activation of diagrammatic strategies for learning from texts. In L. Verschaffel, E. De Corte, T. de Jong, & J. Elen (Eds.), *Use of representations in reasoning and problem solving: Analysis and improvement* (pp. 112–130). London: Routledge.

Schneider, V. I., Healy, A. F., Barshi, I., & Kole, J. A. (2011). Following navigation instructions presented verbally or spatially: Effects on training, retention and transfer. *Applied Cognitive Psychology, 25*, 53–67.

Schneider, W. (1998). The development of procedural metamemory in childhood and adolescence. In G. Mazzoni & T. O. Nelson (Eds.), *Metacognition and cognitive neuropsychology* (pp. 1–21). Mahwah, NJ: Erlbaum.

Schneider, W. (1999). The development of metamemory in children. In D. Gopher & A. Koriat (Eds.), *Attention and performance XVII* (pp. 487–514). Cambridge, MA: MIT Press.

Schneider, W. (2002). Memory development in childhood. In U. Goswami (Ed.), *Blackwell handbook of childhood cognitive development* (pp. 236–256). Malden, MA: Blackwell.

Schneider, W., & Bjorklund, D. F. (1998). Memory. In D. Kuhn & R. S. Siegler (Eds.), *Handbook of child psychology* (5th ed., Vol. **2**, pp. 467–521). New York: Wiley.

Schneider, W., & Lockl, K. (2008). Procedural metacognition in children: Evidence for developmental trends. In J. Dunlosky & R. A. Bjork (Eds.), *Handbook of metamemory and memory* (pp. 391–409). New York: Psychology Press.

Schneider, W., & Pressley, M. (1997). *Memory development: Between two and twenty* (2nd ed.). Mahwah, NJ: Erlbaum.

Schnotz, W., Baadtem C., Müller, A., & Rasch, R. (2010). Creative thinking and problem solving with depictive and descriptive representations. In L. Verschaffel, E. De Corte, T. de Jong, & J. Elen (Eds.), *Use of representations in reasoning and problem solving: Analysis and improvement* (pp. 11–35). London: Routledge.

Schober, M. F., & Brennan, S. E. (2003). Processes of interactive spoken discourse: The role of the partner. In A. C. Graesser, M. A. Gernsbacher, & S. R. Goldman (Eds.), *Handbook of discourse processes* (pp. 123–164). Mahwah, NJ: Erlbaum.

Schoenfeld, A. H. (2011). *How we think: A theory of goal-oriented decision making and its educational applications.* New York: Routledge.

Scholl, B. J., Simons, D. J., & Levin, D. T. (2004). "Change blindness" blindness: An implicit measure of a metacognitive error. In D. T. Levin (Ed.), *Thinking and seeing: Visual metacognition in adults and children* (pp. 145–165). Cambridge, MA: MIT Press.

Schonert-Reichl, K. A., Oberle, E., Lawlor, M. S., Abbott, D., Thomson, K., Oberlander, T. F., . . . Diamond, A. (2015). Enhancing cognitive and social–emotional development through a simple-to-administer mindfulness-based school program for elementary school children: A randomized controlled trial. *Developmental Psychology, 51*(1), 52–66.

Schönpflug, U. (2008). The influence of instruction on verbatim and content text recall. *Educational Psychology, 28*, 97–108.

Schooler, J. W., Reichle, E. D., & Halpern, D. V. (2005). Zoning-out during reading: Evidence for dissociations between experience and meta-consciousness. In D. T. Levin (Ed.), *Thinking and seeing: Visual metacognition in adults and children* (pp. 204–226). Cambridge, MA: MIT Press.

Schooler, J. W., & Eich, E. (2000). Memory for emotional events. In E. Tulving & F. I. M. Craik (Eds.), *The Oxford handbook of memory* (pp. 379–392). New York: Oxford University Press.

Schooler, J. W., Fallshore, M., & Fiore, S. M. (1995). Epilogue: Putting insight into perspective. In R. J. Sternberg & J. E. Davidson (Eds.), *The nature of insight* (pp. 559–587). Cambridge, MA: MIT Press.

Schotter, E. R., Angele, B., & Rayner, K. (2012). Parafoveal processing in reading. *Attention, Perception, & Psychophysics, 74*, 5–35.

Schraw, G. (2005). An interview with K. *Anders Ericsson. Educational Psychology Review, 17*, 389–412.

Schreiber, F. J. (2005). Metacognition and self-regulation in literacy. In S. E. Israel, C. C. Block, K. L. Bauserman, & K. Kinnucan-Welsch (Eds.), *Metacognition in literacy learning: Theory, assessment, instruction, and professional development* (pp. 215–239). Mahwah, NJ: Erlbaum.

Schumann, J. H. (2010). Applied linguistics and the neurobiology of language. In R. B. Kaplan (Ed.), *The Oxford handbook of applied linguistics* (2nd ed., pp. 244–259). New York: Oxford University Press.

Schwartz, A. L., & Kroll, J. F. (2006). Language processing in bilingual speakers. In M. J. Traxler & M. A. Gernsbacher (Eds.), *Handbook of psycholinguistics* (2nd ed., pp. 967–999). Amsterdam: Elsevier.

Schwartz, B. (2004). *The paradox of choice: Why more is less: How the culture of abundance robs us of satisfaction.* New York: HarperCollins.

Schwartz, B. (2009). Be careful what you wish for: The dark side of freedom. In R. M. Arkin, K. C. Oleson, & P. J. Carroll (Eds.), *Handbook of the uncertain self.* New York: Psychology Press.

Schwartz, B. L. (1999). Sparkling at the end of the tongue: The etiology of tip-of-the-tongue phenomenology. *Psychonomic Bulletin & Review, 6*, 379–393.

Schwartz, B. L. (2011). *Memory: Foundations and applications.* Thousand Oaks, CA: Sage.

Schwartz, B. L., & Metcalfe, J. (2011). Tip-of-the-tongue (TOT) states: Retrieval, behavior, and experience. *Memory & Cognition, 39*, 737–749.

Schwartz, B. L., & Smith, S. M. (1997). The retrieval of related information influences tip-of-the-tongue states. *Journal of Memory and Language, 36*, 68–86.

Schwartz, B. L., Benjamin, A. S., & Bjork, R. A. (1997). The inferential and experiential bases of metamemory. *Current Directions in Psychological Science, 6*, 132–137.

Schwartz, B., Ward, A., Monterosso, J., Lyubomirsky, S., White, K., & Lehman, D. R. (2002). Maximizing versus satisficing: Happiness is a matter of choice. *Journal of Personality and Social Psychology, 83*, 1178–1197.

Schwartz, S. H. (1971). Modes of representation and problem solving: Well evolved is half solved. *Journal of Experimental Psychology, 91*, 347–350.

Schwartz, S. H., & Fattaleh, D. (1972). Representation in deductive problem solving: The matrix. *Journal of Experimental Psychology, 95*, 343–348.

Schwartz, S. H., & Polish, J. (1974). The effect of problem size on representation in deductive problem solving. *Memory & Cognition, 2*, 683–686.

Schwarz, N. (2001). Feelings as information: Implications for affective influences on information processing. In L. L. Martin & G. L. Clore (Eds.), *Theories of mood and cognition* (pp. 159–176). Mahwah, NJ: Erlbaum.

Schwenck, C., Bjorklund, D. F., & Schneider, W. (2009). Developmental and individual differences in young children's use and maintenance of a selective memory strategy. *Developmental Psychology, 45*, 1034–1050.

Schwering, A., Kühnberger, K.-U., & Kokinov, B. (2009). Analogies—Intergrating cognitive abilities. *Cognitive Systems Research, 10*, 175–177.

Scott, S. K. (2005). The neurobiology of speech perception. In A. Cutler (Ed.), *Twenty-first century psycholinguistics: Four cornerstones* (pp. 141–156). Mahwah, NJ: Erlbaum.

Scullin, M. K., Bugg, J. M., McDaniel, M. A., & Einstein, G. O. (2011). Prospective memory and aging: Preserved spontaneous retrieval, but impaired deactivation in older adults. *Memory & Cognition, 39*, 1232–1240.

Seabrook, R., Brown, G. D. A., & Solity, J. E. (2005). Distributed and massed practice: From laboratory to classroom. *Applied Cognitive Psychology, 19*, 107–122.

Sedivy, J. (2014). *Language in the mind: An introduction to psycholinguistics.* Sunderland, MA: Sinauer Associates.

Segal, S. J., & Fusella, V. (1970). Influence of imagined pictures and sounds on detection of visual and auditory signals. *Journal of Experimental Psychology, 83*, 458–464.

Segalowitz, N. (2010). *Cognitive bases of second language fluency.* New York: Routledge.

Seidenberg, M. S., & Zevin, J. D. (2006). Connectionist models in developmental cognitive neuroscience: Critical periods and the paradox of success. Attention & Performance XXI:*Processes of change in brain and cognitive development*, 585–612.

Seifert, C. M. (1999). Situated cognition and learning. In R. A. Wilson & F. C. Keil (Eds.), *The MIT encyclopedia of the cognitive sciences* (pp. 767–769). Cambridge, MA: MIT Press.

Sell, A. J., & Kaschak, M. P. (2009). Does visual speech information affect word segmentation? *Memory & Cognition, 37*, 889–894.

Semmler, C., & Brewer, N. (2006). Postidentification feedback effects on face recognition confidence: Evidence for metacognitive influences. *Applied Cognitive Psychology, 20*, 895–916.

Serences, J. T., Shomstein, S., Leber, A. B., Golay, X., Egeth, H. W., & Yantis, S. (2005). Coordination of voluntary and stimulus-driven control in human cortex. *Psychological Science, 16*, 114–122.

Sereno, S. C., Brewer, C. C., & O'Donnell, P. J. (2003). Context effects in word recognition: Evidence for early interactive processing. *Psychological Science, 14*, 328–333.

Sergent, J., Ohta, S., & MacDonald, B. (1992). Functional neuroanatomy of face and object processing: A positron emission tomography study. *Brain, 115*, 15–36.

Serra, M. J., & Dunlosky, J. (2010). Metacomprehension judgements reflect the belief that diagrams improve learning from text. Memory, *18*(7), 698–711.

Seyfarth, R. M., & Cheney, D. L. (2015). Social cognition. *Animal Behaviour, 103*, 191–202.

Seymour, P. H. K., Aro, M., & Erskine, J. M. (2003). Foundation literacy acquisition in European orthographies. *British Journal of Psychology*, 143–174.

Shafir, E. B., & LeBoeuf, R. A. (2002). Rationality. *Annual Review of Psychology, 53*, 491–517.

Shah, A. J., & Oppenheimer, D. M. (2008). Heuristics made easy: An effort-reduction framework. *Psychological Bulletin, 134*, 207–222.

Shake, M. C., Noh, W. R., & Stine-Morrow, E. A. L. (2009). Age differences in learning from text: Evidence for functionally distinct text processing systems. *Applied Cognitive Psychology, 23*, 561–578.

Shapiro, L. (2011). *Embodied cognition.* New York: Routledge.

Shapiro, L. (Ed.). (2014). *The Routledge handbook of embodied cognition.* New York: Routledge.

Share, D. L. (2008). On the Anglocentricities of current reading research and practice: The perils of overreliance on an "outlier" orthography. *Psychological Bulletin, 134*, 584–615.

Sharps, M. J., & Wertheimer, M. (2000). Gestalt perspectives on cognitive science and on experimental psychology. *Review of General Psychology, 4*, 315–336.

Shatz, M., & Gelman, R. (1973). The development of communication skills: Modifications in the speech of young children as a function of listener. *Monographs of the Society for Research in Child Development, 38* (2, Serial No. 152).

Shelton, A. L. (2004). Putting spatial memories into perspective: Brain and behavioral evidence for representational differences. In G. L. Allen (Ed.), *Human spatial memory: Remembering where* (pp. 309–327). Mahwah, NJ: Erlbaum.

Shelton, A. L., & Gabrieli, J. D. E. (2004). Neural correlates of individual differences in spatial learning strategies. *Neuropsychology, 18*, 442–449.

Shelton, A. L., & McNamara, T. P. (2004). Orientation and perspective dependence in route and survey learning. *Journal of Experimental Psychology: Learning, Memory, and Cognition, 30*, 158–170.

Shelton, A. L., & Yamamoto, N. (2009), Visual memory, spatial representation, and navigation. In J. B. Brockmole (Ed.), *The visual world in memory* (pp. 140–177). New York: Routledge.

Shepard, R. N., & Chipman, S. (1970). Second-order isomorphism of internal representation: Shapes of states. *Cognitive Psychology*, *1*, 1–17.

Shepard, R. N., & Metzler, J. (1971). Mental rotation of three-dimensional objects. *Science*, *171*, 701–703.

Shepperd, J. A., & Koch, E. J. (2005). Pitfalls in teaching judgment heuristics. *Teaching of Psychology*, *32*, 43–46.

Sherman, J. W., & Bessenoff, G. R. (1999). Stereotypes as source-monitoring cues: On the interaction between episodic and semantic memory. *Psychological Science*, *10*, 106–110.

Sherman, M. A. (1976). Adjectival negation and the comprehension of multiply negated sentences. *Journal of Verbal Learning and Verbal Behavior*, *15*, 143–157.

Shih, M., Pittinsky, T. L., & Ambady, N. (1999). Stereotype susceptibility: Identity salience and shifts inquantitative performance. *Psychological Science*, *10*, 80–83.

Shiraev, E. (2011). *A history of psychology: A global perspective*. Thousand Oaks, CA: Sage.

Sholl, M. J., Kenny, R. J., & Della Porta, K. A. (2006). Allocentric-heading recall and its relation to self-reported sense-of-direction. *Journal of Experimental Psychology: Learning, Memory, and Cognition*, *32*, 516–533.

Shomstein, S. (2010). Attention: Effect of breakdown. In E. B. Goldstein (Ed.), *Encyclopedia of perception* (Vol. **1**., pp. 87–90). Thousand Oaks, CA: Sage.

Siegal, M. (1996). Conversation and cognition. In R. Gelman & T. K. Au (Eds.), *Perceptual and cognitive development* (pp. 243–282). San Diego: Academic Press.

Siegler, R. S., DeLoache, J., & Eisenberg, N. (2003). *How children develop*. New York: Worth.

Sillito, A. M. (2004). Visual system: Organization. In R. L. Gregory (Ed.), *The Oxford companion to the mind* (2nd ed., pp. 931–936). New York: Oxford University Press.

Silvia, P. J. (2007). *How to write a lot*. Washington, DC: American Psychological Association.

Simon, D., Pham, L. B., Le, Q. A., & Holyoak, K. J. (2001). The emergence of coherence over the course of decision making. *Journal of Experimental Psychology: Learning, Memory, and Cognition*, *27*, 1250–1260.

Simon, H. A. (1955). A behavioral model of rational choice. *Quarterly Journal of Economics*, *69*, 99–118.

Simon, H. A. (1995). Technology is not the problem. In P. Baumgartner & S. Payr (Eds.), *Speaking minds: Interviews with twenty eminent cognitive scientists* (pp. 231–248). Princeton, NJ: Princeton University Press.

Simon, H. A. (1996). *The sciences of the artificial* (3rd ed.). Cambridge, MA: MIT Press.

Simon, H. A. (1999). Problem solving. In R. A. Wilson & F. C. Keil (Eds.), *The MIT encyclopedia of the cognitive sciences* (pp. 674–676). Cambridge, MA: MIT Press.

Simon, H. A., & Gobet, F. (2000). Expertise effects in memory recall: Comment on Vicente and Wang (1998). *Psychological Review*, *107*, 593–600.

Simons, D. J., & Chabris, C. F. (1999). Gorillas in our midst: Sustained inattentional blindness for dynamic events. *Perception*, *28*, 1059–1074.

Simons, D. J., & Jensen, M. S. (2009). The effects of individual differences and task difficulty on inattentional blindness. *Psychonomic Bulletin & Review*, *16*, 398–403.

Simons, D. J., & Levin, D. T. (1997a). Change blindness. *TRENDS in Cognitive Sciences*, *1*, 261–267.

Simons, D. J., & Levin, D. T. (1997b). Failure to detect changes to unattended objects. *Investigative Ophthalmology and Visual Science*, *38*, S707.

Simons, D. J., & Levin, D. T. (1998). Failure to detect changes to people during a real-world interaction. *Psychonomic Bulletin & Review*, *5*, 644–649.

Simons, D. J., Chabris, C. F., Schnur, T., & Levin, D. T. (2002). Evidence for preserved representations in change blindness. *Consciousness and Cognition*, *11*, 78–97.

Simonton, D. K. (2010). Creativity in highly eminent individuals. In J. C. Kaufman & R. J. Sternberg (Eds.), *The Cambridge handbook of creativity* (pp. 174–188). New York: Cambridge University Press.

Sinha, P., Ostrovsky, Y., & Russell, R. (2010). Face perception. In E. B. Goldstein (Ed.) *Encyclopedia of perception* (Vol.**1**., pp. 445–448). Thousand Oaks, CA: Sage.

Skinner, B. F. (2004). Behaviorism, B. F. Skinner on. In R. L. Gregory (Ed.), *The Oxford companion to the mind* (2nd ed., pp. 90–92). New York: Oxford University Press.

Skipper, J. I., Goldin-Meadow, S., Nusbaum, H. C., & Small, S. L. (2007). Speech-associated gestures, Broca's area, and the human mirror system. *Brain and language*, *101*, 260–277.

Slater, A., & Butterworth, G. (1997). Perception of social stimuli: Face perception and imitation. In G. Brenner, A. Slater, & G. Butterworth (Eds.), *Infant development: Recent advances* (pp. 223–245). Hove, UK: Psychology Press.

Sluzenski, J., Newcombe, N., & Ottinger, W. (2004). Changes in reality monitoring and episodic memory in early childhood. *Developmental Science, 7*, 225–245.

Smallwood, J., & Schooler, J. W. (2006). The restless mind. *Psychological Bulletin, 132*, 946–958.

Smeding, A., Quinton, J. C., Lauer, K., Barca, L., & Pezzulo, G. (2016). Tracking and simulating dynamics of implicit stereotypes: A situated social cognition perspective. *Journal of Personality and Social Psychology, 111*(6), 817–834.

Smilek, D., Carriere, J. S. A., & Cheyne, J. A. (2010). Out of mind, out of sight: Eye blinking as indicator and embodiment of mind-wandering. *Psychological Science, 21*, 786–789.

Smith, M. R., & Alpert, G. P. (2007). Explaining police bias: A theory of social conditioning and illusory correlation. *Criminal justice and behavior, 34*(10), 1262–1283.

Smith, A. D., & Cohen, G. (2008). Memory for places: Routes, maps, and object locations. In G. Cohen & M. Conway (Eds.), *Memory in the real world* (3rd ed., pp. 173–206). New York: Psychology Press.

Smith, E. E. (2000). Neural bases of human working memory. *Current Directions in Psychological Science, 9*, 45–49.

Smith, J. L., Samsone, C., & White, P. H. (2007). The stereotyped task engagement process: The role of interest and achievement motivation. *Journal of Educational Psychology, 99*, 99–114.

Smith, J., & Baltes, P. B. (1999). Life-span perspectives on development. In M. H. Bornstein & M. E. Lamb (Eds.), *Developmental psychology: An advanced textbook* (4th ed., pp. 47–72). Mahwah, NJ: Erlbaum.

Smith, R. E. (2006). Adult age differences in episodic memory: Item-specific, relational, and distinctive processing. In R. R. Hunt & J. B. Worthen (Eds.), *Distinctiveness and memory* (pp. 259–289). New York: Oxford University Press.

Smith, S. M., & Gleaves, D. H. (2007). Recovered memories. In M. P. Toglia, J. D. Read, D. F. Ross, & R. C. L. Lindsay (Eds.), *Handbook of eyewitness psychology* (Vol. **1**, pp. 299–320). Mahwah, NJ: Erlbaum.

Smith, S. M., Gleaves, D. H., Pierce, B. H., Williams, T. L., Gilliland, T. R., & Gerkens, D. R. (2003). Eliciting and comparing false and recovered memories: An experimental approach. *Applied Cognitive Psychology, 17*, 251–279.

Smith, S. M., & Ward, T. B. (2012). Cognition and the creation of ideas. In K. J. Holyoak & R. G. Morrison (Eds), *The Oxford handbook of thinking and reasoning* (pp. 456–474). New York: Oxford University Press.

Smyth, M. M., Collins, A. F., Morris, P. E., & Levy, P. (1994). *Cognition in action* (2nd ed.). Hove, UK: Erlbaum.

Smyth, M. M., Morris, P. E., Levy, P., & Ellis, A. W. (1987). *Cognition in action*. Hillsdale, NJ: Erlbaum.

Snedeker, J., & Trueswell, J. C. (2004). The developing constraints on parsing decisions: The role of lexical-biases and referential scenes in child and adult sentence processing. *Cognitive Psychology, 49*, 238–299.

Snedeker, J., & Yuan, S. (2008). Effects of prosodic and lexical constraints on parsing in young children (and adults). *Journal of Memory and Language, 58*, 574–608.

Snow, C. E., & Juel, C. (2005). Teaching children to read: What do we know about how to do it? In M. J. Snowling & C. Hulme (Eds.), *The science of reading: A handbook* (pp. 501–520). Malden, MA: Blackwell.

Snyder, H. R., Miyake, A., & Hankin, B. L. (2015). Advancing understanding of executive function impairments and psychopathology: Bridging the gap between clinical and cognitive approaches. *Frontiers in Psychology, 6*: 328.

Sobel, C. P. (2001). *The cognitive sciences: An interdisciplinary approach*. Mountain View, CA: Mayfield.

Sobel, K. V., Gerrie, M. P., Poole, B. J., & Kane, M. J. (2007). Individual differences in working memory capacity and visual search: The roles of top-down and bottom-up processing. *Psychonomic Bulletin & Review, 14*(5), 840–845.

Sodian, B. (2005). Theory of mind—the case for conceptual development. In W. Schneider, R. Schumann-Hengsteler, & B. Sodian (Eds.), *Young children's cognitive development* (pp. 95–130). Mahwah, NJ: Erlbaum.

Son, L. K., & Kornell, N. (2008). Research on the allocation of study time: Key studies from 1890 to the present (and beyond). In J. Dunlosky & R. A. Bjork (Eds.), *Handbook of metamemory and memory* (pp. 333–351). New York: Psychology Press.

Son, L. K., & Metcalfe, J. (2000). Metacognitive and control strategies in study-time allocation. Journal of Experimental Psychology: Learning, Memory, and Cognition, *26*, 204–221.

Son, L. K., & Schwartz, B. L. (2002). The relation between metacognitive monitoring and control. In T. J. Perfect & B. L. Schwartz (Eds.), *Applied metacognition* (pp. 15–38). Cambridge, UK: Cambridge University Press.

Speer, S., & Blodgett, A. (2006). Prosody. In M. J. Traxler & M. A. Gernsbacher (Eds.), *Handbook of psycholinguistics* (2nd ed., pp. 505–527). Amsterdam: Elsevier.

Spence, I., & Feng, J. (2010). Video games and spatial cognition. *Review of General Psychology, 14*, 92–104.

Sperling, G. (1960). The information available in brief visual presentations. *Psychological Monographs, 74*, 1–29.

Spivey, M. (2007). *The continuity of mind*. Oxford University Press.

Spivey, M. J., Grosjean, M., & Knoblich, G. (2005). Continuous attraction toward phonological competitors. *Proceedings of the National Academy of Sciences of the United States of America, 102*(29), 10393–10398.

Sporer, S. L. (1991). Deep—deeper—deepest? Encoding strategies and the recognition of human faces. *Journal of Experimental Psychology: Learning, Memory, and Cognition, 17*, 323–333.

Sporer, S. L., & Horry, R. (2011). Recognizing faces from ethnic in-groups and out-groups: Importance of outer face features and effects of retention interval. *Applied Cognitive Psychology*, *25*, 424–431.

Srull, T. K., & Wyer Jr, R. S. (eds.). (2015). *The mental representation of trait and autobiographical knowledge about the self: Advances in social cognition* (Vol. **5**). *Psychology Press*.

Stanovich, K. E. (1986). Matthew effects in reading: Some consequences of individual differences in the acquisition of literacy. *Reading Research Quarterly*, *21*, 360–406.

Stanovich, K. E. (1988). The right and wrong places to look for the cognitive locus of reading disability. *Annals of Dyslexia*, *38*, 154–157.

Stanovich, K. E. (1999). *Who is rational? Studies of individual differences in reasoning*. Mahwah, NJ: Erlbaum.

Stanovich, K. E. (2003). The fundamental computational biases of human cognition: Heuristics that (sometimes) impair decision making and problem solving. In J. E. Davidson & R. J. Sternberg (Eds.), *The psychology of problem solving* (pp. 291–342). New York: Cambridge University Press.

Stanovich, K. E. (2009). *What intelligence tests miss: The psychology of rational thought*. New Haven, CT: Yale University Press.

Stanovich, K. E. (2011). *Rationality and the reflective mind*. New York: Oxford University Press.

Stanovich, K. E., & West, R. F. (1981). The effect of sentence processing on ongoing word recognition: Tests of a two-process theory. *Journal of Experimental Psychology: Human Perception and Performance*, *7*, 658–672.

Stanovich, K. E., & West, R. F. (1983). On priming by a sentence context. *Journal of Experimental Psychology: General*, *112*, 1–36.

Stanovich, K. E., & West, R. F. (1997). Reasoning independently of prior belief and individual differences in actively open-minded thinking. *Journal of Educational Psychology*, *89*, 342–357.

Stanovich, K. E., & West, R. F. (1998). Individual differences in rational thought. *Journal of Experimental Psychology: General*, *127*, 161–188.

Stanovich, K. E., & West, R. F. (2000). Individual differences in reasoning: Implications for the rationality debate? *Behavioral and Brain Sciences*, *23*, 645–726.

Statistics Canada. (2006). *Population by mother tongue, by province and territory (2006 Census)*. Retrieved June 21, 2012, from http://www.statcan.gc.ca/tables-tableaux/sum-som/l01/cst01/demo11a-eng.htm

Statistics Canada. (2012a). Canadians in context-aging population. Retrieved March 14, 2012, from http://www4.hrsdc.gc.ca/.3ndic.1 t.4r@-eng.jsp?iid=33

Statistics Canada. (2012b). *Information about life expectancy and religious services*. Retrieved March 15, 2012, from www.statcan. gc.ca/start-debut-eng.html

Steel, P. (2007). The nature of procrastination: A meta-analytic and theoretical review of quintessential self-regulatory failure. *Psychological Bulletin*, *133*, 65–94.

Steele, C. M. (1997). A threat in the air: How stereotypes shape intellectual identity and performance. *American Psychologist*, *52*, 613–629.

Steffensen, S. V. (2011). Beyond mind: An extended ecology of languaging. In S. J. Cowley (Ed.), *Distributed language* (pp. 185–210). Amsterdam: John Benjamins Publishing Company.

Sternberg, R. J. (1999). A dialectical basis for understanding the study of cognition. In R. J. Sternberg (Ed.), *The nature of cognition* (pp. 51–78). Cambridge, MA: MIT Press.

Sternberg, R. J., & Ben-Zeev, T. (2001). *Complex cognition: The psychology of human thought*. New York: Oxford University Press.

Stevens, A., & Coupe, P. (1978). Distortions in judged spatial relations. *Cognitive Psychology*, *10*, 422–437.

Stine-Morrow, E. A. L., Miller, L. M. S., & Hertzog, C. (2006). Aging and self-regulated language processing. *Psychological Bulletin*, *132*, 582–606.

Stone, M. (2005). Communicative intentions and conversational processes in human-human and human-computer dialogue. In J. C. Trueswell & M. K. Tanenhaus (Eds.), *Approaches to studying world-situated language use* (pp. 39–69). Cambridge, MA: Bradford.

Strayer, D. L., & Drews, F. A. (2007). Multitasking in the automobile. In A. F. Kramer, D. A. Wiegmann, & A. Kirlik (Eds.), *Attention: From theory to practice* (pp. 121–133). New York: Oxford University Press.

Strayer, D. L., Drews, F. A., & Johnston, W. A. (2003). Cell phone-induced failures of visual attention during simulated driving. *Journal of Experimental Psychology: Applied*, *9*, 23–32.

Street, J., & Dąbrowska, E. (2010) "More individual differences in Language Attainment: How much do adult native speakers of English know about passives and quantifiers?". *Lingua*, *120*, 2080–2094.

Strömqvist, S., & Verhoeven, L. (2004). Typological and contextual perspectives on narrative development. In S. Strömqvist, & L. Verhoven, *Relating events in narrative* (Vol. **2**, pp. 1–4). Mahwah, NJ: Erlbaum.

Stromswold, K. (1999). Cognitive and neural aspects of language acquisition. In E. Lepore & Z. Pylyshyn (Eds.), *What is cognitive science?* (pp. 356–400). Malden, MA: Blackwell.

Stroop, J. R. (1935). Studies of interference in serial verbal reactions. *Journal of Experimental Psychology, 18*, 643–662.

Student Demographics. (2011, August 26). *Chronicle of Higher Education* (Almanac Issue, 2011–2012), pp. 30–40.

Stuss, D. T., Binns, M. A., Murphy, K. J., & Alexander, M. P. (2002). Dissociations within the anterior attentional system: Effects of task complexity and irrelevant information on reaction time speed and accuracy. *Neuropsychology, 16*, 500–513.

Styles, E. A. (2005). *Attention, perception, and memory: An integrated introduction.* Hove, UK: Psychology Press.

Styles, E. A. (2006). *The psychology of attention* (2nd ed.). New York: Psychology Press.

Suh, S., & Trabasso, T. (1993). Inferences during reading: Converging evidence from discourse analysis, talk-aloud protocols, and recognition priming. *Journal of Memory and Language, 32*, 279–300.

Surprenant, A. M., & Neath, I. (2009). *Principles of memory.* New York: Psychology Press.

Suzuki-Slakter, N. S. (1988). Elaboration and metamemory during adolescence. *Contemporary Educational Psychology, 13*, 206–220.

Swanson, H. L. (2005). Working memory, intelligence, and learning disabilities. In O. Wilhelm & R. W. Engle (Eds.), *Handbook of understanding and measuring intelligence* (pp. 409–429). Thousand Oaks, CA: Sage.

Swanson, H. L., & Berninger, V. W. (1996). Individual differences in children's working memory and writing skill. *Journal of Experimental Child Psychology, 63*(2), 358–385.

Swanson, H. L., Kehler, P., & Jerman, O. (2010). Working memory, strategy knowledge, and strategy instruction in children with reading disabilities. *Journal of Learning Disabilities, 43*, 24–47.

Swets, B., Desmet, T., Clifton, C., Jr., & Ferreira, F. (2008). Underspecification of syntactic ambiguities: Evidence from self-paced reading. *Memory & Cognition, 36*, 201–216.

Swinkels, A. (2003). An effective exercise for teaching cognitive heuristics. *Teaching of Psychology, 30*, 120–122.

Swoyer, C. (2002). Judgment and decision making: Extrapolations and applications. In R. Gowda & J. C. Fox (Eds.), *Judgments, decisions, and public policy* (pp. 9–45). New York: Cambridge University Press.

Symons, C. S., & Johnson, B. T. (1997). The self-reference effect in memory: A meta-analysis. *Psychological Bulletin, 121*, 371–394.

Szokolsky, A. (2013). Interview with Ulric Neisser. *Ecological Psychology, 25*, 182–199.

Szpunar, K. K. (2010). Episodic future thought: An emerging concept. *Perspectives on Psychological Science, 5*, 142–162.

Tabor, W., & Hutchins, S. (2004). Evidence for self-organized sentence processing: Digging-in effects. *Journal of Experimental Psychology: Learning, Memory, and Cognition, 30*, 431–450.

Taguchi, T., Magid, M., & Papi, M. (2009). The L2 motivational self system among Japanese, Chinese and Iranian learners of English: A comparative study. In Z. Dörnyei & E. Ushiodi (Eds.), *Motivation, language identity, and the L2 self* (pp. 66–97). Bristol, UK: Multilingual Matters.

Takeda, K., Shimoda, N., Sato, Y., Ogano, M., & Kato, H. (2010). Reaction time differences between left- and right-handers during mental rotation of hand pictures. *Laterality, 15*, 415–425.

Talarico, J. M., & Rubin, D. C. (2003). Confidence, not consistency, characterizes flashbulb memories. *Psychological Science, 14*, 455–461.

Talarico, J. M., LaBar, K. S., & Rubin, D. C. (2004). Emotional intensity predicts autobiographical memory experience. *Memory & Cognition, 32*, 1118–1132.

Tanaka, J. W., & Farah, M. J. (1993). Parts and wholes in face recognition. *Quarterly Journal of Experimental Psychology, 46A*, 225–245.

Tanenhaus, M. K. (2004). On-line sentence processing: Past, present, and future. In M. Carreiras & C. Clifton, Jr. (Eds.), *The on-line study of sentence comprehension: Eyetracking, ERPs and beyond* (pp. 371–393). New York: Psychology Press.

Tanenhaus, M. K. (2007). Spoken language comprehension: Insights from eye movements. In G. Gaskell (Ed.), *Oxford handbook of psycholinguistics* (pp. 309–326). Oxford: Oxford University Press.

Tanenhaus, M. K., Spivey-Knowlton, M., Eberhard, K., & Sedivy, J. (1995). Integration of visual and linguistic information in spoken language comprehension. *Science, 268*, 1632–1634.

Tang, Y.-Y., & Posner, M. I. (2009). Attention training and attention state training. *Trends in Cognitive Science, 13*, 222–227.

Tarr, M. J., & Vuong, Q. C. (2002). Visual object recognition. In S. Yantis (Ed.), *Stevens' handbook of experimental psychology* (3rd ed., Vol. 1, pp. 287–314). New York: Wiley.

Tavris, C., & Aronson, E. (2007). *Mistakes were made (but not by me): Why we justify foolish beliefs, bad decisions, and hurtful acts.* Orlando, FL: Harcourt.

Taylor, H. A. (2005). Mapping the understanding of understanding maps. In P. Shah & A. Miyake (Eds.), *The Cambridge handbook of visuospatial thinking* (pp. 295–333). New York: Cambridge University Press.

Taylor, S. E., Phan, L. B., Rivkin, I. D., & Armor, D. A. (1998). Harnessing the imagination: Mental simulation, self-regulation, and coping. *American Psychologist, 53*, 429–439.

Teasdale, J. D., Dritschel, B. H., Taylor, M. J., Proctor, L., Lloyd, C. A., Nimmo-Smith, I., . . . Baddeley, A. D. (1995). Stimulus-independent thought depends on central executive resources. *Memory & Cognition, 23,* 551–559.

Teigen, K. H. (2004). Judgment by representativeness. In R. Pohl (Ed.), *Cognitive illusions: Handbook on fallacies and biases in thinking, judgment, and memory* (pp. 165–182). Hove, UK: Psychology Press.

Teigen, K. H., & Jørgensen, M. (2005). When 90% confidence intervals are 50% certainty. *Applied Cognitive Psychology, 19,* 455–475.

Terlecki, M. S., Newcombe, N. S., & Little, M. (2008). Durable and generalized effects of spatial experience on mental rotation: Gender differences in growth patterns. *Applied Cognitive Psychology, 22,* 996–1013.

Terrett, G., McLennan, S. N., Henry, J. D., Biernacki, K., Mercuri, K., Curran, H. V., . . . Rendell, P. G. (2014). Prospective memory impairment in long-term opiate users. *Psychopharmacology, 231,* 2623–2632.

Thagard, P. (2005). *Mind: Introduction to cognitive science* (2nd ed.). Cambridge, MA: MIT Press.

Thaler, R. H., & Sunstein, C. R. (2008). *Nudge: Improving decisions about health, wealth, and happiness.* New Haven: Yale University Press.

Thiede, K. W., Dunlosky, J., Griffin, T. D., & Wiley, J. (2005). Understanding the delayed-keyword effect on metacomprehension accuracy. *Journal of Experimental Psychology: Learning, Memory, and Cognition, 31,* 1267–1280.

Thierry, K. L., Lamb, M. E., Pipe, M.-E., & Spence, M. J. (2010). The flexibility of source-monitoring training: Reducing young children's source confusions. *Applied Cognitive Psychology, 24,* 626–644.

Thoman, D. B., White, P. H., Yamawaki, N., & Koishi, H. (2008). Variations of gender-math stereotype content affect women's vulnerability to stereotype threat. *Sex Roles, 58,* 702–712.

Thomas, L. E., & Lleras, A. (2009a). Covert shifts of attention function as an implicit aid to insight. *Cognition, 111,* 168–174.

Thomas, L. E., & Lleras, A. (2009b). Swinging into thought: Directed movement guides insight in problem solving. *Psychonomic Bulletin & Review, 16,* 719–723.

Thomas, N. J. T. (1999b). Are theories of imagery theories of imagination? An active perception approach to conscious mental content. *Cognitive Science, 23,* 207–245.

Thomas, R. D. (1998). Learning correlations in categorization tasks using large, ill-defined categories. *Journal of Experimental Psychology: Learning, Memory, and Cognition, 24,* 119–143.

Thompson, C. P., Skowronski, J. J., Larsen, S. F., & Betz, A. (1996). *Autobiographical memory: Remembering what and remembering when.* Mahwah, NJ: Erlbaum.

Thompson, R. F., & Madigan, S. A. (2005). *Memory: The key to consciousness.* Washington, DC: Joseph Henry Press.

Thorndyke, P. W. (1981). Distance estimation from cognitive maps. *Cognitive Psychology, 13,* 526–550.

Tincoff, R., & Jusczyk, P. W. (1999). Some beginnings of word comprehension in 6-month-olds. *Psychological Science, 10,* 172–175.

Tobias, R. (2009). Changing behavior by memory aids: A social psychological model of prospective memory and habit development tested with dynamic field data. *Psychological Review, 116,* 408–438.

Todd, A. R., & Burgmer, P. (2013). Perspective taking and automatic intergroup evaluation change: Testing an associative self-anchoring account. *Journal of Personality and Social Psychology, 104,* 786–802.

Todd, A. R., Thiem, K. C., & Neel, R. (2016). Does seeing faces of young Black boys facilitate the identification of threatening stimuli? *Psychological Science, 27,* 384–393.

Todd, N. P. M., Lee, C. S., & O'Boyle, D. J. (2006). A sensorimotor theory of speech perception: Implications for learning, organization, and recognition. In S. Greenberg & W. A. Ainsworth (Eds.), *Listening to speech: An auditory perspective* (pp. 351–373). Mahwah, NJ: Erlbaum.

Todd, P. M., & Gigerenzer, G. (2007). Environments that make us smart: Ecological rationality. *Current Directions in Psychological Science, 126,* 167–171.

Tokuhama-Espinosa, T. (2001). *Raising multilingual children: Foreign language acquisition and children.* Westport, CT: Bergin & Garvey.

Tolin, D. A., Abramowitz, J. S., Przeworski, A., & Foa, E. B. (2002). Thought suppression in obsessive-compulsive disorder. *Behaviour Research and Therapy, 40,* 1255–1274.

Tomasello, M. (1998a). Cognitive linguistics. In W. Bechtel & G. Graham (Eds.), *A companion to cognitive science* (pp. 477–487). Malden, MA: Blackwell.

Tomasello, M. (1998b). Introduction: A cognitive-functional perspective on language structure. In M. Tomasello (Ed.), *The new psychology of language: Cognitive and functional approaches to language structure* (pp. vii–xxiii). Mahwah, NJ: Erlbaum.

Tomasello, M. (2003). *Constructing a language: A usage-based theory of language acquisition.* Cambridge, MA: Harvard University Press.

Tomasello, M. (2006). Acquiring linguistic constructions. In D. Kuhn & R. Siegler (Eds.), *Handbook of child psychology* (6th ed., Vol. **2**, pp. 255–298). Hoboken, NJ: Wiley.

Tomasello, M. (2008). *Origins of human communication*. Cambridge, MA: Guilford.

Toplak, M. E., & Stanovich, K. E. (2002). The domain specificity and generality of disjunctive reasoning: Searching for a generalizable critical thinking skill. *Journal of Educational Psychology*, *94*, 197–209.

Toppino, T. C., & Long, G. M. (2005). Top-down and bottom-up processes in the perception of reversible figures: Toward a hybrid model. In N. Ohta, C. M. MacLeod, & B. Uttl (Eds.), *Dynamic cognitive processes* (pp. 37–58). Tokyo: Springer-Verlag.

Torbeyns, J., Arnaud, L., Lemaire, P., & Verschaffel, L. (2010). Cognitive change as strategy change. In A. Demetriou & A. Raftopoulos (Eds.), *Cognitive developmental change: Theories, models and measurement* (pp. 186–216). New York: Cambridge University Press.

Torcasio, S., & Sweller, J. (2010). The use of illustrations when learning to read: A cognitive load theory approach. *Applied Cognitive Psychology*, *24*, 659–672.

Torrance, M., & Jeffery, G. (1999). Writing processes and cognitive demands. In M. Torrance & G. C. Jeffery (Eds.), *The cognitive demands of writing: Processing capacity and working memory in text production* (pp. 1–11). Amsterdam: Amsterdam University Press.

Torrance, M., Thomas, G. V., & Robinson, E. J. (1996). Finding something to write about: Strategic and automatic processes in idea generation. In C. M. Levy & S. Ransdell (Eds.), *The science of writing: Theories, methods, individual differences, and applications* (pp. 189–205). Mahwah, NJ: Erlbaum.

Toscano, J. C., McMurray, B., Dennhardt, J., & Luck, S. J. (2010). Continuous perception and graded categorization electrophysiological evidence for a linear relationship between the acoustic signal and perceptual encoding of speech. *Psychological Science*, *21*, 1532–1540.

Townsend, C. L., & Heit, E. (2011). Judgments of learning and improvement. *Memory & Cognition*, *39*, 204–216.

Trabasso, T., & Suh, S. (1993). Understanding text: Achieving explanatory coherence through on-line inferences and mental operations in working memory. *Discourse Processes*, *16*, 3–34.

Trabasso, T., Suh, S., Payton, P., & Jain, R. (1995). Explanatory inferences and other strategies during comprehension and their effect on recall. In R. F. Lorch & E. J. O'Brien (Eds.), *Sources of coherence in reading* (pp. 219–239). Hillsdale, NJ: Erlbaum.

Trafimow, D., & Wyer, R. S., Jr. (1993). Cognitive representation of mundane social events. *Journal of Personality and Social Psychology*, *64*, 365–376.

Traxler, M. J. (2012). *Introduction to psycholinguistics: Understanding language science*. Malden, MA: Wiley-Blackwell.

Traxler, M. J. (2014). Trends in syntactic parsing: Anticipation, Bayesian estimation, and good-enough parsing. *Trends in Cognitive Sciences*, *18*, 605–611.

Treiman, R., & Kessler, B. (2009). Learning to read. In M. G. Gaskell (Ed.), *The Oxford handbook of psycholinguistics* (pp. 771–785). New York: Oxford University Press.

Treiman, R., Clifton, C., Jr., Meyer, A. S., & Wurm, L. H. (2003). Language comprehension and production. In A. F. Healy & R. W. Proctor (Eds.), *Handbook of psychology* (Vol. **4**, pp. 527–547). Hoboken, NJ: Wiley

Treisman, A. (1964). Monitoring and storage of irrelevant messages and selective attention. *Journal of Verbal Learning and Verbal Behavior*, *3*, 449–459.

Treisman, A. (1990). Visual coding of features and objects: Some evidence from behavioral studies. In National Research Council (Ed.), *Advances in the modularity of vision: Selections from a symposium on frontiers of visual science* (pp. 39–61). Washington, DC: National Academy Press.

Treisman, A. (1993). The perception of features and objects. In A. Baddeley & L. Weiskrantz (Eds.), *Attention: Selection, awareness, and control* (pp. 5–35). Oxford, UK: Clarendon.

Treisman, A. (2006). How the deployment of attention determines what we see. *Visual Cognition*, *14*, 411–443.

Treisman, A., & Gelade, G. (1980). A feature-integration theory of attention. *Cognitive Psychology*, *12*, 97–136.

Treisman, A., & Schmidt, H. (1982). Illusory conjunction in the perception of objects. *Cognitive Psychology*, *14*, 107–141.

Treisman, A., & Souther, J. (1985). Search asymmetry: A diagnostic for preattentive processing of separable features. *Journal of Experimental Psychology: General*, *114*, 285–310.

Treisman, A., & Souther, J. (1986). Illusory words: The roles of attention and of top-down constraints in conjoining letters to form words. *Journal of Experimental Psychology: Human Perception and Performance*, *12*, 3–17.

Trout, J. D. (2001). The biological basis of speech: What to infer from talking to the animals. *Psychological Review*, *108*, 523–549.

Trueswell, J. C., Sekerina, I., Hill, N. M., & Logrip, M. L. (1999). The kindergarten-path effect: Studying on-line sentence processing in young children. *Cognition*, *73*, 89–134.

Trueswell, J. C. & Tanenhaus, M. K. (Eds.) (2005). *Processing world-situated language: Bridging the language-as-action and language-as-product traditions*. Cambridge, Mass: MIT Press.

Tsang, P. S. (2007). The dynamics of attention and aging. In A. F. Kramer, D. A. Wiegmann, & A. Kirlik (Eds.), *Attention: From theory to practice* (pp. 170–184). New York: Oxford University Press.

Tsang, Y.-K., & Chen, H.-C. (2008). Eye movements in reading Chinese. In K. Rayner, D. Shen, X. Bai, & G. Yan (Eds.), *Cognitive and cultural influences on eye movements* (pp. 235–254). Tianjin, China: Tianjin People's Publishing House.

Tse, C. Y., Lee, C. L., Sullivan, J., Garnsey, S. M., Dell, G. S., Fabiani, M., . . . Gratton, G. (2007). Imaging cortical dynamics of language processing with the event-related optical signal. *Proceedings of the National Academy of Sciences, 104*(43), 17157–17162.

Tsujii, T., & Watanabe, S. (2009). Neural correlates of dual-task effect on belief-bias syllogistic reasoning: A near-infrared spectroscopy study. *Brain Research, 1287*, 118–125.

Tuckey, M. R., & Brewer, N. (2003). How schemas affect eyewitness memory over repeated retrieval attempts. *Applied Cognitive Psychology, 17*, 855–880.

Tulving, E., & Rosenbaum, S. (2006). What do explanations of the distinctiveness effect need to explain? In R. R. Hunt & J. B. Worthen (Eds.), *Distinctiveness and memory* (pp. 407–423). New York: Oxford University Press.

Turan, B., & Horowitz, L. M. (2007). Can I count on you to be there for me? Individual differences in a knowledge structure. *Journal of Personality and Social Psychology, 93*, 447–465.

Tversky, A., & Kahneman, D. (1971). Belief in the law of small numbers. *Psychological Bulletin, 76*, 105–110.

Tversky, A., & Kahneman, D. (1973). Availability: A heuristic for judging frequency and probability. *Cognitive Psychology, 5*, 207–232.

Tversky, A., & Kahneman, D. (1974). Judgments under uncertainty: Heuristics and biases. *Science, 185*, 1124–1131.

Tversky, A., & Kahneman, D. (1981). The framing of decisions and the psychology of choice. *Science, 211*, 453–458.

Tversky, A., & Kahneman, D. (1982). Judgment under uncertainty: Heuristics and biases. In D. Kahneman, P. Slovic, & A. Tversky (Eds.), *Judgment under uncertainty: Heuristics and biases* (pp. 3–20). New York: Cambridge University Press.

Tversky, A., & Kahneman, D. (1983). Extensional versus intuitive reasoning: The conjunction fallacy in probability judgment. *Psychological Review, 90*, 293–315.

Tversky, B. (1991). Spatial mental models. *The Psychology of Learning and Motivation, 27*, 109–145.

Tversky, B. (1997). Spatial constructions. In N. L. Stein, P. A. Ornstein, B. Tversky, & C. Brainerd (Eds.), *Memory for everyday and emotional events* (pp. 181–208). Mahwah, NJ: Erlbaum.

Tversky, B. (1998). Three dimensions of spatial cognition. In M. A. Conway, S. E. Gathercole, & C. Cornoldi (Eds.), *Theories of memory* (Vol. **2**, pp. 259–275). East Sussex, UK: Psychology Press.

Tversky, B. (2000a). Levels and structure of spatial knowledge. In S. M. Freundschuh & R. Kitchin (Eds.), *Cognitive mapping: Past, present, and future* (pp. 24–43). New York: Routledge.

Tversky, B. (2000b). Remembering spaces. In E. Tulving & F. I. M. Craik (Eds.), *The Oxford handbook of memory* (pp. 363–378). New York: Oxford University Press.

Tversky, B. (2005a). Functional significance of visuospatial representations. In P. Shah & A. Miyake (Eds.), *The Cambridge handbook of visuospatial thinking* (pp. 1–34). New York: Cambridge University Press.

Tversky, B. (2005b). Visuospatial reasoning. In K. J. Holyoak & R. G. Morrison (Eds.), *The Cambridge handbook of thinking and reasoning* (pp. 209–240). New York: Cambridge University Press.

Tversky, B. (2009). Spatial cognition: Embodied and situated. In P. Robbins & M. Aydede (Eds.), *The Cambridge handbook of situated cognition* (pp. 201–216). New York: Cambridge University Press.

Twyman, A. D., & Newcombe, N. S. (2010). Five reasons to doubt the existence of a geometric module. *Cognitive Science*, 1315–1356.

U. S. Census Bureau. (2012b). Statistical abstract of the United States, Table 6. Resident population by sex, race, and Hispanic-origin status: 2000 to 2009. Retrieved June 12, 2012, from http://www.census.gov/compendia/statab/2012/tables/12s0006.pdf

U.S. Census Bureau. (2012a). *State and County Quick Facts*. Retrieved March 14, 2012, from http://quickfacts.census.gov/qfd/states/00000.html

U.S. Census Bureau. (2012c). Statistical abstract of the United States, Table 53. Languages spoken at home. Retrieved May 17, 2012, from http://www.census.gov/compendia/statab/2012/tables/12 s0053.pdf

U. S. Department of Veteran Affairs (2016). *PTSD: National center for PTSD*. Retrieved May 30, 2018, from https://www.ptsd.va.gov/public/ptsd-overview/basics/how-common-is-ptsd.asp

Uchanski, R. M. (2005). Clear speech. In D. B. Pisoni & R. E. Remez (Eds.), *The handbook of speech perception* (pp. 207–235). Malden, MA: Blackwell.

Underwood, G., & Batt, V. (1996). *Reading and understanding: An introduction to the psychology of reading*. Cambridge, MA: Blackwell.

Useem, M. (2006). *The go point: When it's time to decide—knowing what to do and when to do it*. New York: Crown Publishing Group.

Uttal, D. H., Friedman, A., Hand, L. L., & Warren, C. (2010). Learning fine-grained and category information in navigable real-world space. *Memory & Cognition, 38*, 1026–1040.

Valentin, D., Abdi, H., O'Toole, A. J., & Cottrell, G. W. (1994). Connectionist models of face processing: A survey. *Pattern Recognition*, *27*, 1209–1230.

Valian, V. (2015). Bilingualism and cognition. *Bilingualism: Language and Cognition*, *18*(1), 3–24

Van Berkum, J. J., Brown, C. M., Zwitserlood, P., Kooijman, V., & Hagoort, P. (2005). Anticipating upcoming words in discourse: evidence from ERPs and reading times. *Journal of Experimental Psychology: Learning, Memory, and Cognition*, *31*, 443.

Van Dyke, J. A. (2007). Interference effects from grammatically unavailable constituents during sentence processing. *Journal of Experimental Psychology: Learning, Memory, and Cognition*, *33*, 407.

Van Dyke, J. A., & Johns, C. L. Kukona, A. (2014). Low working memory capacity is only spuriously related to poor reading comprehension. *Cognition*, *131*, 373–403.

van Hell, J. G., & Dijkstra, T. (2002). Foreign language knowledge can influence native language performance in exclusively native contexts. *Psychonomic Bulletin & Review*, *9*, 780–789.

Van Orden, G. C., & Kloos, H. (2005). The question of phonology and reading. In M. J. Snowling & C. Hulme (Eds.), *The science of reading: A handbook* (pp. 61–78). Malden, MA: Blackwell.

Van Overschelde, J. P., Rawson, K. A., Dunlosky, & Hunt, R. R. (2005). Distinctive processing underlies skilled memory. *Psychological Science*, *16*, 358–361.

van Turennout, M., Hagoort, P., & Brown, C. M. (1998). Brain activity during speaking: From syntax to phonology in 40 milliseconds. *Science*, *280*, 572–574.

Van Wallendael, L. R., & Kuhn, J. C. (1997). Distinctiveness is in the eye of the beholder: Cross-racial differences in perceptions of faces. *Psychological Reports*, *80*, 35–39.

Vandierendonck, A., & Szmalec, A. (2011a). Preface. In A. Vandierendonck & A. Szmalec (Eds.), *Spatial working memory* (pp. vii–xi). New York: Psychology Press.

Vandierendonck, A., & Szmalec, A. (2011b). Progress in spatial working memory research. In A. Vandierendonck & A. Szmalec (Eds.), *Spatial working memory* (pp. 1–18). New York: Psychology Press.

Vandierendonck, A., Liefooghe, B., & Verbruggen, F. (2010). Task switching: Interplay of reconfiguration and interference control. *Psychological Bulletin*, *136*, 601–626.

Vartanian, O., & Mandel, D. R. (2011). Introduction. In O. Vartanian & D. R. Mandel (Eds.), *Neuroscience of decision making* (pp. 1–7). New York: Psychology Press.

Vecera, S. P. (1998). Visual object representation: An introduction. *Psychobiology*, *26*, 281–308.

Vecera, S. P., & Lee, H. (2010). Vision: Cognitive influences. In E. B. Goldstein (Ed.), *Encyclopedia of perception* (Vol.**2**, pp. 1048–1053). Thousand Oaks, CA: Sage.

Velmans, M. (2009). *Understanding consciousness* (2nd ed.). New York: Routledge.

Velmans, M., & Schneider, S. (Eds.). (2007). *The Blackwell companion to consciousness*. Malden, MA: Blackwell.

Vigliocco, G., & Hartsuiker, R. J. (2002). The interplay of meaning, sound, and syntax in sentence production. *Psychological Bulletin*, *128*, 442–472.

Viney, W., & King, D. B. (2003). *A history of psychology: Ideas and context* (3rd ed.). Boston: Allyn & Bacon.

Vingerhoets, G., Berckmoes, C., & Stroobant, N. (2003). Cerebral hemodynamics during discrimination of prosodic and semantic emotion in speech studied by transcranial Doppler ultrasonography. *Neuropsychology*, *17*, 93–99.

Vojdanoska, M., Cranney, J., & Newell, B. R. (2010). The testing effect: The role of feedback and collaboration in a tertiary classroom setting. *Applied Cognitive Psychology*, *24*, 1183–1195.

Volz, K. G., Schooler, L. J., Schubotz, R. I., Raab, M., Gigerenzer, G., & von Cramon, D. Y. (2006). Why you think Milan is larger than Modena: Neural correlates of the recognition heuristic. *Journal of Cognitive Neuroscience*, *18*, 1924–1936.

Voyer, D., Nolan, C., & Voyer, S. (2000). The relation between experience and spatial performance in men and women. *Sex Roles*, *43*, 891–915.

Vu, E., & Rich, A. N. (2010). Independent sampling of features enables conscious perception of bound objects. *Psychological Science*, *21*, 1168–1175.

Vuong, Q. C. (2010). Object perception. In E. B. Goldstein (Ed.), *Encyclopedia of perception* (Vol. **2**, pp. 643–648). Thousand Oaks, CA: Sage.

Vuvan, D. T., & Schmuckler, M. A. (2011). Tonal hierarchy representations in auditory imagery. *Memory & Cognition*, *39*, 477–490.

Wade, K. A., Garry, M., Read, J. D., & Lindsay, D. S. (2002). A picture is worth a thousand lies: Using false photographs to create false childhood memories. *Psychonomic Bulletin and Review*, *9*, 597–603.

Wagner, M. (2006). *The geometries of visual space*. Mahwah, NJ: Erlbaum.

Wagner, R. K., & Stanovich, K. E. (1996). Expertise in reading. In K. A. Ericsson (Ed.), *The road to excellence: The acquisition of expert performance in the arts and sciences, sports, and games* (pp. 189–225). Mahwah, NJ: Erlbaum.

Walker, I., & Hulme, C. (1999). Concrete words are easier to recall than abstract: Evidence for a semantic contribution to short-term serial recall. *Journal of Experimental Psychology: Learning, Memory, & Cognition, 25*, 1256–1271.

Walker, P. M., & Hewstone, M. (2006). A perceptual discrimination investigation of the own-race effect and intergroup experience. *Applied Cognitive Psychology, 20*, 461–475.

Walker, W. R., Skowronski, J., Gibbons, J., Vogl, R., & Thompson, C. (2003). On the emotions that accompany autobiographical memories: Dysphoria disrupts the fading affect bias. *Cognition and Emotion, 17*, 703–724.

Walker, W. R., Vogl, R. J., & Thompson, C. P. (1997). Autobiographical memory: Unpleasantness fades faster than pleasantness over time. *Applied Cognitive Psychology, 11*, 399–413.

Walker-Andrews, A. S. (1986). Intermodal perception of expressive behaviors: Relation of eye and voice? *Developmental Psychology, 22*, 373–377.

Walton, G. M., & Dweck, C. S. (2009). Solving social problems like a psychologist. *Perspectives on Psychological Science, 4*, 101–102.

Wang, G., Tanaka, K., & Tanifuji, M. (1996). Optical imaging of functional organization in the monkey inferotemporal cortex. *Science, 272*, 1665–1668.

Ward, G., & Allport, A. (1997). Planning and problem-solving using the five-disc tower of London task. *Quarterly Journal of Experimental Psychology, 50A*, 49–78.

Ward, G., & Kolomyts, Y. (2010). Cognition and creativity. In J. C. Kaufman & R. J. Sternberg (Eds.), *The Cambridge handbook of creativity* (pp. 93–112). New York: Cambridge University Press.

Ward, G., & Morris, R. (2005). Introduction to the psychology of planning. In R. Morris & G. Ward (Eds.), *The cognitive psychology of planning* (pp. 1–34). Hove, UK: Psychology Press.

Waring, J. D., & Kensinger, E. A. (2011). How emotion leads to selective memory: Neuroimaging evidence. *Neuropsychologia, 40*, 1831–1842.

Warren, R. M. (2006). The relation of speech perception to the perception of nonverbal auditory patterns. In S. Greenberg & W. A. Ainsworth (Eds.), *Listening to speech: An auditory perspective* (pp. 333–349). Mahwah, NJ: Erlbaum.

Warren, R. M., & Warren, R. P. (1970, December). Auditory illusions and confusions. *Scientific American, 223* (6), 30–36.

Warrington, E. K., & Weiskrantz, L. (1970). Amnesic syndrome: Consolidation or retrieval? *Nature, 228*, 629–630.

Wason, P. C. (1968). Reasoning about a rule. *Quarterly Journal of Experimental Psychology, 20*, 273–281.

Watson, J. B. (1913). Psychology as the behaviorist views it. *Psychological Review, 20*, 158–177.

Watson, D., & Gibson, E. (2004). The relationship between intonational phrasing and syntactic structure in language production. *Language and Cognitive Processes, 19*, 713–755.

Waxman, S. R. (2002). Early word-learning and conceptual development: Everything had a name and each name gave birth to a new thought. In U. Goswami (Ed.), *Blackwell handbook of child cognitive development* (pp. 102–126). Malden, MA: Blackwell.

Weaver, C. A., III, Terrell, J. T., Krug, K. S., & Kelemen, W. L. (2008). The delayed JOL effect with very long delays: Evidence from flashbulb memories. In J. Dunlosky & R. A. Bjork (Eds.), *Handbook of metamemory and memory* (pp. 155–172). New York: Psychology Press.

Weber, E. U., & Morris, M. W. (2010). Culture and judgment and decision making: The constructivist turn. *Perspectives on Psychological Science, 5*, 410–419.

Wegner, D. M. (1994). Ironic processes of mental control. *Psychological Review, 101*, 34–52.

Wegner, D. M. (1996). Personal communication.

Wegner, D. M. (1997a). When the antidote is the poison: Ironic mental control processes. *Psychological Science, 8*, 148–153.

Wegner, D. M. (1997b). Why the mind wanders. In J. D. Cohen & J. W. Schooler (Eds.), *Scientific approaches to consciousness* (pp. 295–315). Mahwah, NJ: Erlbaum.

Wegner, D. M. (2002). *The illusion of conscious will.* Cambridge, MA: MIT Press.

Wegner, D. M., Schneider, D. J., Carter, S. R., III, & White, T. L. (1987). Paradoxical effects of thought suppression. *Journal of Personality and Social Psychology, 53*, 5–13.

Weisleder, A., & Fernald, A. (2013). Talking to children matters: Early language experience strengthens processing and builds vocabulary. *Psychological Science, 24*, 2143–2152.

Weierich, M., & Barrett, L. F. (2010). Affect as a source of visual attention. In E. Balcetis & G. D. Lassiter (Eds.), *Social psychology of visual perception.* New York: Psychology Press.

Weinberg, A. (Ed.). (2012). *The psychology of politicians.* New York: Cambridge.

Weisberg, R. W. (2006). Modes of expertise in creative thinking: Evidence from case studies. In K. A. Ericsson, N. Charness, P. J. Feltovich, & R. R. Hoffman (Eds.), *The Cambridge handbook on expertise and expert performance* (pp. 761–787). New York: Cambridge University Press.

Weiskrantz, L. (1997). *Consciousness lost and found: A neuropsychological explanation.* New York: Oxford University Press.

Weiskrantz, L. (2007). The case of blindsight. In M. Velmans & S. Schneider (Eds.), *The Blackwell companion to consciousness* (pp. 175–180). Malden, MA: Blackwell.

Weist, R. M. (1985). Cross-linguistic perspective on cognitive development. In T. M. Schlechter & M. P. Toglia (Eds.), *New directions in cognitive science* (pp. 191–216). Norwood, NJ: Ablex.

Wellman, H. M. (2000). Early childhood: Cognitive and mental development. In A. E. Kazdin (Ed.), *The encyclopedia of psychology.* New York: Oxford University Press.

Wellman, H. M., & Gelman, S. A. (1992). Cognitive development: Foundational theories of core domains. *Annual Review of Psychology, 43,* 337–375.

Wells, A. (2005). Worry, intrusive thoughts, and generalized anxiety disorder: The metacognitive theory and treatment. In D. A. Clark (Ed.), *Intrusive thoughts in clinical disorders: Theory, research, and treatment* (pp. 119–144). New York: Guilford Press.

Wells, G. L., & Olson, E. A. (2003). Eyewitness testimony. *Annual Review of Psychology, 54,* 277–295.

Wells, G. L., Malpass, R. S., Lindsay, R. C., Fisher, R. P., Turtle, J. W., & Fulero, S. M. (2000). From the lab to the police station: A successful application of eyewitness research. *American Psychologist, 55,* 581–598.

Wells, J. B., Christiansen, M. H., Race, D. S., Acheson, D. J., & MacDonald, M. C. (2009). Experience and sentence processing: Statistical learning and relative clause comprehension. *Cognitive Psychology, 58,* 250–271.

Wenzel, A. (2005). Autobiographical memory tasks in clinical research. In A. Wenzel & D. C. Rubin (Eds.), *Cognitive methods and their application to clinical research* (pp. 243–264). Washington, DC: American Psychological Association.

Wenzlaff, R. M (2005). Seeking solace but finding despair: The persistence of intrusive thoughts in depression. In D. A. Clark (Ed.), *Intrusive thoughts in clinical disorders: Theory, research, and treatment* (pp. 55–85). New York: Guilford Press.

Werker, J. F., & Tees, R. C. (1984). Cross-language speech perception: Evidence for perceptual reorganization during the first year of life. *Infant Behavior and Development, 7,* 49–63.

Werker, J. F., & Tees, R. C. (1999). Influences on infant speech processing: Toward a new synthesis. *Annual Review of Psychology, 50,* 509–535.

Wheeler, M. A. (2000). Episodic memory and autonoetic awareness. In E. Tulving & F. I. M. Craik (Eds.), *The Oxford handbook of memory* (pp. 597–608). New York: Oxford University Press.

Wheeler, M. E., & Treisman, A. M. (2002). Binding in short-term visual memory. *Journal of Experimental Psychology: General, 113,* 48–64.

Whitbourne, S. K., & Whitbourne, S. B. (2011). *Adult development and aging: Biopsychosocial perspectives* (4th ed.). Hoboken, NJ: Wiley.

White, J. (2003). Personal communication.

White, K. R., Crites, S. L., Jr., Taylor, J. H., & Coral, G. (2009). Wait, what? Assessing stereotype incongruities using the N400 ERP component. *Social Cognitive and Affective Neuroscience, 4,* 191–198.

White, S. J., & Liversedge, S. P. (2004). Orthographic familiarity influences initial eye fixation positions in reading. In R. Radach, A. Kennedy, & K. Rayner (Eds.), *Eye movements and information processing during reading* (pp. 52–78). Hove, UK: Psychology Press.

Whitley, B. E., Jr., & Kite, M. E. (2010). *The psychology of prejudice and discrimination* (2nd ed.). Belmont, CA: Wadsworth Cengage.

Whitten, S., & Graesser, A. C. (2003). Comprehension of text in problem solving. In J. E. Davidson & R. J. Sternberg (Eds.), *The psychology of problem solving* (pp. 207–229). New York: Cambridge University Press.

Whitten, W. B., II. (2011). Learning from and for tests. In A. S. Benjamin (Ed.), *Successful remembering and successful forgetting: A festschrift in honor of Robert A. Bjork* (pp. 217–234). New York: Psychology Press.

Wickelgren, W. A. (1965). Acoustic similarity and intrusion errors in short-term memory. *Journal of Experimental Psychology, 70,* 102–108.

Wickens, D. D., Dalezman, R. E., & Eggemeier, F. T. (1976). Multiple encoding of word attributes in memory. *Memory & Cognition, 4,* 307–310.

Wiers, R. W., & Stacy, A. W. (Eds.). (2006). *Handbook of implicit cognition and addiction.* Thousand Oaks, CA: Sage.

Wilding, J., & Valentine, E. (1997). *Superior memory.* Hove, UK: Psychology Press.

Wilford, M. M., & Wells, G. L. (2010). Does facial processing prioritize change detection? Change blindness illustrates costs and benefits of holistic processing. *Psychological Science, 21,* 1611–1615.

Wilhelm, O. (2005). Measuring reasoning ability. In O. Wilhelm & R. W. Engle (Eds.), *Handbook of understanding and measuring intelligence* (pp. 373–392). Thousand Oaks, CA: Sage.

Willcutt, E. G., Doyle, A. E., Nigg, J. T., Faraone, S. V., & Pennington, B. F. (2005). Validity of the executive function theory of attention-deficit/hyperactivity disorder: A meta-analytic review. *Biological Psychiatry, 57,* 1336–1346.

Williams, C. C., Perea, M., Pollatsek, A., & Rayner, K. (2006). Previewing the neighborhood: The role of orthographic neighbors as parafoveal previews in reading. *Journal of Experimental Psychology: Human Perception and Performance, 32*, 1072–1082.

Williams, J. D. (2005). *The teacher's grammar book* (2nd ed.). Mahwah, NJ: Erlbaum.

Williams, J. M. G., Mathews, A., & MacLeod, C. (1996). The emotional Stroop task and psychopathology. *Psychological Bulletin, 120*, 3–24.

Willingham, D. T. (2010, Summer). Have technology and multitasking rewired how students learn? *American Educator, 42*, 23–28.

Wilson, B. A. (1995). Management and remediation of memory problems in brain-injured adults. In A. D. Baddeley, B. A. Wilson, & F. N. Watts (Eds.), *Handbook of memory disorders* (pp. 451–479). Chichester, UK: Wiley.

Wilson, M. (2002). Six views of embodied cognition. *Psychonomic Bulletin & Review, 9*, 625–636

Wilson, T. D. (1997). The psychology of metapsychology. In J. D. Cohen & J. W. Schooler (Eds.), *Scientific approaches to consciousness* (pp. 317–332). Mahwah, NJ: Erlbaum.

Wilson, T. D. (2009). Know thyself. *Perspectives on Psychological Science, 4*, 384–389.

Wingfield, A. (1993). Sentence processing. In J. B. Gleason & N. Bernstein Ratner (Eds.), *Psycholinguistics* (pp. 199–235). Fort Worth: Harcourt Brace.

Winston, J. S., Strange, B. A., O'Doherty, J., & Dolan, R. J. (2005). Automatic and intentional brain responses during evaluation of trustworthiness of faces. In J. T. Cacioppo & G. G. Berntson (Eds.), *Social neuroscience: Key readings* (pp. 199–210). New York: Psychology Press.

Wise, R. A., Safer, M. A., & Maro, C. M. (2011). What U.S. Law enforcement officers know and believe about eyewitness factors, eyewitness interviews and identification procedures. *Applied Cognitive Psychology, 25*, 488–500.

Wisniewski, E. J. (2002). Concepts and categorization. In D. Medin (Ed.), *Stevens' handbook of experimental psychology* (3rd ed., Vol. **2**, pp. 467–531). New York: Wiley.

Wolfe, J. M. (2000). Visual attention. In K. K. De Valois (Ed.), *Seeing* (2nd ed., pp. 335–386). San Diego: Academic Press.

Wolfe, J. M., Kluender, K. R., Levi, D. M., Bartoshuk, L. M., Herz, R. S., Klatzky, R., . . . Merfeld, D. M. (2009). *Sensation & perception* (2nd ed.). Sunderland, MA: Sinauer.

Wolfe, J. M., Horowitz, T. S., & Kenner, N. M. (2005). Rare items often missed in visual searches. *Nature, 435*, 439–440.

Wolfe, M. B. W., & Goldman, S. R. (2005). Relations between adolescents' text processing and reasoning. *Cognition and Instruction, 23*, 467–502.

Woll, S. (2002). *Everyday thinking: Memory, reasoning, and judgment in the real world.* Mahwah, NJ: Erlbaum.

Wong, C. K., & Read, J. D. (2011). Positive and negative effects of physical context reinstatement on eyewitness recall and identification. *Applied Cognitive Psychology, 25*, 2–11.

Wood, J. N. (2011). A core knowledge architecture of visual working memory. *Journal of Experimental Psychology: Human Perception and Performance, 37*, 357–381.

Wood, N., & Cowan, N. (1995). The cocktail party phenomenon revisited: How frequent are attention shifts to one's name in an irrelevant auditory channel? *Journal of Experimental Psychology: Learning, Memory, and Cognition, 21*, 255–260.

Woodward, A. L., & Markman, E. M. (1998). Early word learning. In W. Damon (Ed.), *Handbook of child psychology: Cognition, perception, and language* (5th ed., Vol. **2**, 371–420). New York: Wiley.

Worthen, J. B. (2006). Resolution of discrepant memory strengths: An explanation of the effects of bizarreness on memory. In R. R. Hunt & J. B. Worthen (Eds.), *Distinctiveness and memory* (pp. 133–156). New York: Oxford University Press.

Worthen, J. B., & Hunt, R. R. (2011). *Mnemonology: Mnemonics for the 21st century.* New York: Psychology Press.

Wraga, M., Shephard, J. M., Church, J. A., Inati, S., & Kosslyn, S. M. (2005). Imagined rotations of self versus objects: An fMRI study. *Neuropsychologia, 43*, 1351–1361.

Wright, D. B., Boyd, C. E., & Tredoux, C. G. (2003). Inter-racial contact and the own-race bias for face recognition in South Africa and England. *Applied Cognitive Psychology, 17*, 365–373.

Wright, R. D., & Ward, L. M. (2008). *Orienting of attention.* New York: Oxford University Press.

Wu, J., Mai, X., Chan, C. C. H., Zheng, Y., & Luo, Y. (2006). Event-related potentials during mental imagery of animal sounds. *Psychophysiology, 43*, 592–597.

Yamauchi, T. (2005). Labeling bias and categorical induction: Generative aspects of category information. *Journal of Experimental Psychology: Learning, Memory, and Cognition, 31*, 538–553.

Yang, L.-X., & Lewandowsky, S. (2004). Knowledge partitioning in categorization: Constraints on exemplar models. *Journal of Experimental Psychology: Learning, Memory and Cognition, 30*, 1045–1064.

Yang, S.-N., & McConkie, G. W. (2004). Saccade generation during reading: Are words necessary? In R. Radach, A. Kennedy, & K. Rayner (Eds.), *Eye movements and information processing during reading* (pp. 226–261). Hove, UK: Psychology Press.

Yardley, L., McDermott, L., Pisarski, S., Duchaine, B., & Nakayama, K. (2008) Psychosocial consequences of developmental prosopagnosia: A problem of recognition. *Journal of Psychosomatic Research, 65*, 445–451.

Yates, J. F. (2010). Culture and probability judgment. *Social and Personality Psychology Compass, 4*, 174–188.

Yoder, J. D. (2007). *Women and gender: Making a difference.* (4th ed.). Cornwall-on-Hudson, NY: Sloan.

Youn, J. C., Kim, K. W., Lee, D. Y, Jhoo, J. H., Lee, S. B., Park, J. H., . . . Choi, E. A. (2009). Development of the subjective memory complaints questionnaire. *Dementia and Geriatric Disorders*, 310–317.

Young, C. A. (2007, July 21). Scientists endeavor to make humanoid robots more graceful. Retrieved July 25, 2007, from http://news-service.stanford.edu/news/2007/July11/robots-071107.html

Zacks, J. M., Tversky, B., & Iyer, G. (2001). Perceiving, remembering, and communicating structure in events. *Journal of Experimental Psychology: General, 130*, 29–58.

Zacks, J. M., Vettel, J. M., & Michelon, P. (2003). Imagined viewer and object rotations dissociated with event-related fMRI. *Journal of Cognitive Neuroscience, 15*, 1002–1018.

Zacks, R. T., & Hasher, L. (2006). Aging and long-term memory: Deficits are not inevitable. In E. Bialystok & F. I. M. Craik (Eds.), *Lifespan cognition: Mechanisms of change* (pp. 162–177). New York: Oxford University Press.

Zajac, R., & Hayne, H. (2006). The negative effect of cross-examination style questioning on children's accuracy: Older children are not immune. *Applied Cognitive Psychology, 20*, 3–16.

Zangwill, O. L. (2004a). Ebbinghaus, H. In R. L. Gregory (Ed.), *The Oxford companion to the mind* (2nd ed., p. 276). New York: Oxford University Press.

Zangwill, O. L. (2004b). Wundt, Wilhelm Max. In R. L. Gregory (Ed.), *The Oxford companion to the mind* (2nd ed., pp. 951–952). New York: Oxford University Press.

Zaromb, F. M., & Roediger, H. L., III. (2010). The testing effect in free recall is associated with enhanced organizational processes. *Memory & Cognition, 38*, 995–1008.

Zauberman, G., & Lynch, J. G., Jr. (2005). Resource slack and propensity to discount delayed investments of time versus money. *Journal of Experimental Psychology: General, 134*, 23–37.

Zeman, A. (2004). *Consciousness: A user's guide.* New Haven: Yale University.

Zentella, A. C. (2006). Hablamos Spanish and English. In H. Luria, D. M. Seymour, & T. Smoke (Eds.), *Language and linguistics in context: Readings and applications for teachers* (pp. 85–89). Mahwah, NJ: Erlbaum.

Zhao, Y., Tu, S., Lei, M., Qiu, J., Ybarra, O., & Zhang, Q. (2011). The neural basis of breaking mental set: An event-related potential study. *Experimental Brain Research, 208*, 181–187.

Zhu, B., Chen, C., Loftus, E. F., Lin, C., & Dong, Q. (2010). Treat and trick: A new way to increase false memory. *Applied Cognitive Psychology, 24*, 1199–1208.

Ziegler, J. C., Bertrand, D., Tóth, D., Csépe, V., Reis, A., Faísca, L., . . . Blomert, L. (2010). Orthographic depth and its impact on universal predictors of reading: A cross-language investigation. *Psychological Science, 21*, 551–559.

Zimmermann, T. D., & Meier, B. (2010). The effect of implementation intentions on prospective memory performance across the lifespan. *Applied Cognitive Psychology, 24*, 645–658.

Zwaan, R. A., & Rapp, D. N. (2006). Discourse comprehension. In M. J. Traxler & M. A. Gernsbacher (Eds.), *Handbook of psycholinguistics* (2nd ed., pp. 249–283). Amsterdam: Elsevier.

Zwaan, R. A., & Singer, M. (2003). Text comprehension. In A. C. Graesser, M. A. Gernsbacher, & S. R. Goldman (Eds.), *Handbook of discourse processes* (pp. 83–121).

Zwaan, R. A., Stanfield, R. A., & Yaxley, R. H. (2002). Language comprehenders mentally represent the shapes of objects. *Psychological Science, 13*, 168–171.

INDEX

PDP. *See* Parallel distributed processing (PDP) approach
People of Color. *See and specific groups, such as* Blacks; Stereotypes
Perception, 24, 26–27, 134
Perceptual processes
    attention, 54
    consciousness, 59
    definition of perception, 24
    face perception, 36–39, 103, 140
    imagery compared with perception, 135
    infancy and speech perception, 305–306
    object recognition, 23–30
    speech perception, 306, 307
    speech perception and, 39–43
    top-down processing and visual object recognition, 30–36
Perceptual span, 54
Perkins, D., 253
Perlmutter, M., 292
Perseverance, 257
Peterson, L. R., 67
Peterson, M., 67
Peterson & Peterson technique, 67
PET scan. *See* Positron emission tomography (PET) scan
Phelps, E., 116
Phobic disorder, 50
Phoneme, 40
Phonemes, 188–189, 204, 207, 305–307. *See also* Speech perception
Phonemic restoration, 41
Phonetic module, 42–43
Phonics approach, 207
Phonological loop, 74–75, 78, 226
Phonology, 228, 232
PI. *See* Proactive interference (PI)
Piaget, Jean, 7
Piaget's research on thought processes of, 7
Pitch, 147
Planning fallacy, 281
Poetry. *See* Haiku poetry
Political decision making, 281–282
Pollyanna Principle, 105
Pomarol-Clotet, E., 39
Positive information. *See* Theme 3 (positive information)
Positivity effect, 106
Positron emission tomography (PET) scan, 13, 56, 139, 164
Posner, M. I., 55, 56
Post-event misinformation effect, 99–101
Post-traumatic stress disorder (PTSD), 6, 50, 61, 94
Potter, Harry, 211
Prabhu, V., 257
Practice, 116–118. *See also* Rehearsal
Pragmatics in language, 189, 222, 311–312
Pragmatic view of memory, 179
Pressley, M., 130
Prewriting, 226
Primacy effect, 69
Primary visual cortex, 25, 62, 140
Priming effect. *See* Semantic priming effect
Principles of Psychology (James), 5
Pringle, A., 50
Proactive interference (PI), 69–70, 100
Problem isomorphs, 245
Problem representation, 240–243
Problem solving. *See also* Creativity; Decision making
    analogy approach to, 245
    attention and, 239
    bilingual students and, 230–231
    Buddhist monk problem, 242
    computer simulation for, 247
    definition of, 239
    diagrams and, 241–242
    Duncker's candle problem, 250

Elves-and-Goblins problem, 246, 247
    embodied cognition approach to, 243
    expertise and, 248–249
    factors influencing, 248–255
    functional fixedness and, 250–251
    gender stereotypes and math problem solving, 251–253
    General Problem Solver (GPS), 247
    goal state of, 239
    hill-climbing heuristic, 247
    initial state of, 239, 246
    insight *versus* noninsight problems, 253–255
    introduction to, 239–240
    matrix and, 241
    means-ends heuristic, 246–247
    mental set and, 249–250
    metacognition and, 249, 254
    methods of representing the problem, 240–243
    number puzzle, 250
    numbers involved in, 244
    obstacles in, 239
    Sahara problem, 253
    situated cognition approach to, 243
    strategies of, 244–247
    symbols in, 240–241
    triangle problem, 253
    understanding the problem, 239–244
    visual imagery and, 243
Procedural memory, 86
Pronunciation of letters of alphabet, 203
    of phonemes, 40–41
    pronunciation, 207
    of words, 205
Proposition (in ACT-R approach), 167
Propositional calculus, 263, 264
Propositional code, 139
Propositional network, 167
Propositional reasoning tasks, 262, 264
Propositions, in conditional reasoning, 263, 264
Prosody, 219
Prosopagnosia, 36, 37, 140
Prospective memory, 121–123, 298. *See also* Retrospective memory
Prospect theory, 280
Prototype, 160–164
Prototype approach, to semantic memory, 161–164
Prototypicality, 161
Proximal stimulus, 24
Psycholinguistics, 190–192. *See also headings beginning with* Language
Psychological well-being, 283–284
Pure artificial intelligence, 9–10
Pylyshyn, Z. W., 140

Q
Quinn, D. M., 252

R
Race. *See and specific countries, such as* China; *and specific groups, such as* Blacks; Stereotypes
Random-number generation tasks, 78
Ratner, H. H., 293
Rayner, K., 32
Reading
    artificial intelligence (AI) and, 10
    basic processes of, 203
    central-executive tasks and, 78
    comparison of written and spoken language, 204–205
    definition of discourse, 208
    direct-access route to, 205
    drawing inferences during, 209–211
    dual-route approach to, 205
    English as an "outlier" language, 206–207
    expertise and, 208
    forming integrated representation of text, 208

indirect-access route to, 205
    metacomprehension and, 130, 211
    phonics approach to, 207
    phonological loop, 74–75
    rate of, 203
    recognition of letters of alphabet, 32
    saccadic eye movement, 53–54
    SAT's reading ability test, 130
    selective attention in, 54–55
    statistics on literacy, 207
    Stroop effect and, 49–50
    teaching of, to children, 206–207
    theoretical approaches to, 205–206
    tongue twisters, 206
    top-down processing and, 32–33
    whole-language approach to, 207
    whole-word approach to, 207
    word superiority effect, 32
    working memory and, 208, 210, 211
Reading-span test, 234–235
Reality monitoring, 96–97
Reasoning. *See* Decision making; Deductive reasoning; Problem solving
Recall, 89–92, 106, 108–109, 114–120, 174, 292, 297, 299
Recall task, 90
Recency and availability, 273
Recency effect, 5, 68
Recognition, 289, 299
Recognition-by-components theory, 29–30
Recognition heuristic, 274
Recognition task, 91
Recovered-memory perspective, 107
Reed, S. K., 141, 142
Regressions, 55
Rehearsal, 67, 68, 70, 114, 294
Reisberg, D., 141, 142
Relative position and cognitive maps, 152–153
Release from proactive interference, 69
Rensink, R. A., 35
Repetition priming task, 93
Representation of problems, 240–243
Representativeness heuristic, 457–463
    base rate and representativeness, 270
    conjunction fallacy and representativeness, 271–272
    sample size and representativeness, 269
Retina, 25, 26, 28, 31, 62. *See also* Perceptual processes
Retrieval
    amnesia and, 94
    definition of, 86
    expertise, 102
    explicit *versus* implicit memory tasks, 92–94, 181, 300
    in long-term memory, 92–95
Retroactive interference, 100
Retrograde amnesia, 94
Retrospective memory, 121
Revision phase of writing, 227
Rhodes, M. G., 38, 104
Richardson, M., 176
Rizzolatti, G., 203
Robertson, D. A., 202
Roebers, C. M., 302
Roediger, Henry, 116
Roediger, H. L., 108, 117
Rogers, T. B., 88, 170
Rosch, E. H., 161, 162–164
Rosenbaum, S., 90
Roskos-Ewoldsen, B., 149
Rotation and imagery, 136–139, 146
Rotation heuristic, 152
Rothbart, M. K., 55, 56
Rovee-Collier, C. K., 289–291
Royden, C. S., 53
Rubin, D. C., 98, 99, 174, 292, 293
Rueckl, J. G., 32, 33